G000124295

A notable quartet

Janowitz · Ludwig · Gedda Fischer-Dieskau

Discographies compiled
by John Hunt

ISBN O 9525827 1 6
1995

ACKNOWLEDGEMENT

This publication has been made possible
by generous support from the following:

Richard Ames, New Barnet

Yoshihiro Asada, Osaka

Andrew Barker, Rochester

Edward Chibas, Caracas

F. De Vilder, Bussum

John Derry, Newcastle-upon-Tyne

Robert Donaldson, Edinburgh

Henry Fogel, Chicago

J.-P. Goossens, Luxembourg

Michael Harris, London

Tadashi Hasegawa, Nagoya

Martin Holland, Sale

John Hughes, Brisbane

Eugene Kaskey, New York

John Larsen, Mariager

James Pearson, Vienna

Donald Priddon, London

Vivienne Rendall, Great Ayton

Peter Russell, Calstock

Robin Scott, Bradford

Robert Simmons, Brentford

Göran Söderwall, Stockholm

Roger Smithson, London

Neville Sumpter, Northolt

Giovanna Visconti, Jackson Heights

David Woodhead, Ravenglass

CONTENTS

Published 1995 by John Hunt

Designed by Richard Chlupaty, London

Drawings of Dietrich Fischer-Dieskau by Brian Pinder

Printed by Short Run Press, London

ISBN 0 9525827 1 6

A notable quartet

This discography is devoted to four
exceptionally important concert singers
of the second half of the twentieth
century. They are artists who have also
made important contributions to the
world of opera - both on stage and in
recording studio - without ever assuming
the vanities of prima donna or primo
uomo. On publishing her recollections
at the time of her retirement from
singing, Christa Ludwig entitles the
book, tongue-in-cheek, "I wish I had
been a prima donna" („...und ich wäre so
gern Primadonna gewesen", Henschel
Verlag 1994).

These are voices whose progress has been
systematically documented by the
gramophone in a way that would have
been unthinkable to artists of earlier
generations. What would we give to
have such a thorough record of the
voices of Erna Berger, Elisabeth Höngen,
Anton Dermota and Heinrich Schlusnus,
to name just four representatives of
similar voice types from a previous era.

When I first envisaged this particular
grouping of singers' discographies,
all four of them were still active, on
the concert platform at least: now, only
Gundula Janowitz and Nicolai Gedda are
still singing occasionally, although
Dietrich Fischer-Dieskau continues to
recite - apart from conducting and
writing, that is ! Nevertheless, we
are dealing with a group of artists who
until very recently were first choices
when an international opera house or
recording company needed to assign
prestigious roles. In the thirty or
more years when the long-playing record
flourished, one can cite many a classic
performance which featured one, two or
even three of these artists together,
guaranteeing the particular recording a

PHILHARMONIA CONCERT SOCIETY

Artistic Director: WALTER LEGGE

BACH
ST MATTHEW PASSION

PHILHARMONIA ORCHESTRA

Leader: HUGH BEAN

PETER PEARS (Evangelist)   FRANZ CRASS (Christus)
ELISABETH SCHWARZKOPF   CHRISTA LUDWIG
NICOLAI GEDDA   WALTER BERRY
ROGER STALMAN

PHILHARMONIA CHOIR
Choir Master: WILHELM PITZ

OTTO KLEMPERER.

Sunday, February 25, 1962, at 5 p.m.

catalogue life far longer than the original producers can have envisaged. One of those producers, the omnipotent Walter Legge, probably did foresee that the quality of these singers would serve as an example to subsequent generations of performers and listeners - just think of his Columbia recordings of Beethoven's Missa Solemnis, Mozart's Zauberflöte or Bach's Saint Matthew Passion.

Having worked so closely with Walter Legge, the singers were able to repeat many recording assignments in other studios. Conductors like Herbert von Karajan accepted that Legge-trained artists would be a guarantee of quality for his own record productions, and he repeatedly selected the duo of Gundula Janowitz and Christa Ludwig (Missa Solemnis, Saint Matthew Passion and B Minor Mass). Nicolai Gedda and Dietrich Fischer-Dieskau, first heard together in the recording of Strauss' Capriccio, are later heard in partnership in Mendelssohn's Elijah and Pfitzner's Palestrina; and the Lieder singers Ludwig and Fischer-Dieskau came together in a DG version of Wolf's Italienisches Liederbuch.

1995 sees the 70th birthday of Fischer-Dieskau, occasion indeed to honour the most significant and prolific of all Lieder singers. If, as we are often told, there is little enthusiasm among the music-loving public for the art of the German Lied, it can only be encouraging that such a large amount of Fischer-Dieskau's song output is currently available in our CD catalogues. He is also the performer who has done most to encourage living composers to write song material for him, which he has then performed and recorded.

Similar services have been performed by Nicolai Gedda in his exploration of Scandinavian composers, particularly those of his native Sweden. His missionary zeal in that area recalls the work, a generation earlier, of his fellow Scandinavian Kirsten Flagstad.

Our female members of the quartet seem, by contrast, to have built their careers within the standard framework of music from Bach to Richard Strauss. In the best traditions of German lyric soprano and dramatic mezzo respectively, they have excelled both in Mozart and Italian opera, also committing themselves no

Mittwoch, 22. März, 20 Uhr
Samstag, 25. März, 17 Uhr

Ludwig van Beethoven

MISSA SOLEMNIS

in D-Dur, op. 123
für Soli, Chor, Orchester und Orgel

I. Kyrie
II. Gloria
III. Credo
IV. Sanctus
V. Agnus Dei

Ausführende: Das Berliner Philharmonische Orchester
Der Singverein der
Gesellschaft der Musikfreunde, Wien

Gundula Janowitz (Sopran)
Christa Ludwig (Alt)
Werner Krenn (Tenor)
Walter Berry (Baß)

Michel Schwalbé (Violine)
Josef Nebois (Orgel)

Dirigent: Herbert von Karajan

less fervently than their male
counterparts to work on the Lieder
platform. Between them, for example,
Janowitz and Ludwig have recorded most of
Schubert's songs for female voice, that
is the material not covered by Fischer-
Dieskau in his mammoth Schubert
undertaking.

As we are dealing with recitalists of
great significance in the history of
Lied interpretation, I now list almost
all songs separately as opposed to in
groups. Exception is made for works
like Schubert cycles Die schöne
Müllerin and Winterreise and the various
Schumann Liederkreise, almost always
performed, and recorded, as entities.
Groups of more esoteric material ,
probably recorded at a single session
and published only in that way, are
not separated. Song titles, given in
the language of the original and then
followed, if necessary, by an indication
of the larger cycle or group from which
the song is taken and finally, within
brackets, the words of the first line
of the poem if that differs from the
song's title. For Slav languages,
mainly Russian, I have decided to put
all song titles in English, with an
indication of the language being sung
only if it differs from the original.

The central column of the discography
layout contains the details of
accompaniment, either instrumentalists or
other singers, orchestra and conductor.
If only one single name appears there
(for example, Moore, Parsons or Werba),
then it is plainly a piano accompaniment.

In the case of operas, indication is
also given in the second column of the
role taken by the singer in question,
and it can be assumed that this applies
for subsequent entries under that
opera unless another role is indicated.
I have retained the German term
Querschnitt to indicate those LP potted
selections, particularly popular on
the German market: they were recorded
as such, and were not normally excerpts
taken from an existing complete
recording. On the other hand, excerpts
from complete recordings, or indeed
from these Querschnitte, are only
indicated where they involve the artist
being dealt with.

ROYAL FESTIVAL HALL

General Manager: T. E. Bean, C.B.E.

PHILHARMONIA CONCERT SOCIETY

ARTISTIC DIRECTOR:
WALTER LEGGE

DIETRICH
FISCHER-DIESKAU

GERALD MOORE

SCHUBERT

Monday, March 11, 1963
at 8 p.m.

Regular subscribers will realise that
these discographies do not contain all
catalogue numbers for all countries
but only main issues and re-issues in
varying formats. As far as EMI is
concerned, many Electrola numbers are
given in addition to the domestic HMV
ones, simply because the recordings
had a much longer catalogue life in
the other territory. And in the case
of Nicolai Gedda, whose recordings
formed such an important part of the
American Angel catalogue, as many Angel
LP numbers as possible have been
included. As complete a picture of the
recording's catalogue life is aimed at.

In order to round out the picture of the
particular artist in repertoire perhaps
not covered by his or her commercial
recordings, or in order to afford extra
comparisons in works frequently recorded,
I have sometimes added details of
unpublished audio and video recordings
known to be in circulation amongst
collectors. Both Christa Ludwig and
Nicolai Gedda performed regularly at
New York's Metropolitan Opera, and
their performances are therefore
preserved in countless Saturday Met
broadcasts.

Amongst the list of friends and
enthusiasts credited at the end of this
book for their assistance with my work,
I must single out Clifford Elkin: if
his extensive collection were not there
for me to refer to, then very many gaps
would sadly remain open. I am also
specially indebted to Mathias Erhard,
who has brought to my attention much
interesting written and background
material on the singers, mainly in
German books and periodicals.

John Hunt

Gundula Janowitz
born 1937

with valuable assistance from
Vivienne Rendall and Clifford Elkin

Discography compiled by John Hunt

Christmas Oratorio

Munich February, March and June 1965	C.Ludwig, Wunderlich, Crass Munich Bach Orchestra & Chorus K.Richter	LP: DG APM 14 353-14 355/ SAPM 198 353-198 355 LP: DG 2710 004/2723 063/2722 018 CD: DG 413 6252/427 2362 Excerpts LP: DG 136 498 Rehearsal extracts issued as a promotional LP

Mass in B minor

1972	Töpper, Laubenthal, Prey Munich Bach Orchestra & Chorus K.Richter	Unpublished video recording	X ✓
Berlin September and November 1973 and January 1974	C.Ludwig, Schreier, Kerns, Ridderbusch Vienna Singverein BPO Karajan	LP: DG 2740 112/415 0221 CD: DG 415 6222/439 6962	

Saint Matthew Passion

Berlin January 1972	C.Ludwig, Schreier, Laubenthal, Berry, Fischer-Dieskau, Diakov Vienna Singverein BPO Karajan	LP: DG 2720 070 CD: DG 419 7892 Excerpts LP: DG 2530 631

BEETHOVEN

Symphony No 9 "Choral"

Berlin October and November 1962	Rössel-Majdan, Kmennt, Berry Vienna Singverein BPO Karajan	LP: DG KL 1-8/SKL 101-108 LP: DG LPM 18 807-18 808/ SLPM 138 807-138 808 LP: DG 2720 007/2720 104/2720 111 LP: DG 2720 261/2721 055/2721 101 LP: DG 2726 503/2543 030 CD: DG 423 2042/423 5552/429 0362 CD: DG 447 4012/447 3982 Last movement and rehearsal sequences issued on various promotional LPs and CDs
Bayreuth July 1963	Bumbry, Thomas, London Bayreuth Festival Orchestra & Chorus Böhm	LP: Melodram MEL 650 CD: Melodram MEL 18005 CD: Classical Collection CD3-CLC 4015 CD: Rodolophe RP 12467-12468 Classical Collection omits third movement
✗ Berlin January 1968	C.Ludwig, Thomas, Berry Deutsche Oper Chorus BPO Karajan	CD: Claque GM 1003 CD: Curcio-Hunt CONB 1 Also unpublished video recording
Vienna June 1970	Reynolds, Hollweg, Ridderbusch Vienna Singverein BPO Karajan	CD: Natise HVK 112 CD: Nuova Era NE 2399-2404

Missa Solemnis

Berlin February 1966	C.Ludwig, Wunderlich, Berry Vienna Singverein BPO Karajan	LP: DG KL 95-96/SKL 195-196 LP: DG 2707 030/2720 013/2721 135 LP: DG 2726 048/410 5351 CD: DG 423 9132
Berlin February 1966	C.Ludwig, Wunderlich, Berry Vienna Singverein BPO Karajan	CD: Hunt CDKAR 214
Berlin September 1974	Baltsa, Schreier, Van Dam Vienna Singverein BPO Karajan	LP: EMI SLS 979/CFP 41 44203 CD: EMI CMS 769 2462

Mass in C

Munich August 1969	Hamari, Laubenthal, Schramm Munich Bach Orchestra & Chorus K.Richter	LP: DG 139 446/2720 013 CD: DG 429 5102

Elegischer Gesang

Munich August 1969	Hamari, Laubenthal, Schramm Munich Bach Orchestra & Chorus K.Richter	LP: DG 2720 017

Egmont: Excerpts (Freudvoll und leidvoll; Die Trommel grühret)

Berlin January 1969	BPO Karajan	LP: DG 2720 011/2721 137/2530 301 CD: DG 419 6242

Fidelio

Vienna May 1962	Role of Marzelline C.Ludwig, Vickers, Kmennt, Kreppel, Berry, Wächter Vienna Opera Chorus VPO Karajan	LP: Movimento musica 03.014
Vienna January 1978	Role of Leonore Popp, Kollo, Sotin, Jungwirth, Helm, Dallapozza Vienna Opera Chorus VPO Bernstein	VHS Video: Great Performance Series (USA) 7
Vienna January, February and April 1978	Popp, Kollo, Jungwirth, Sotin, Fischer-Dieskau, Dallapozza Vienna Opera Chorus VPO Bernstein	LP: DG 2709 082/2740 191/413 2881 CD: DG 419 4362 Excerpts LP: DG 2537 048 CD: DG 445 4612
Orange Date not confirmed	Vickers, Adam, Wildermann, Soumagnas New Philharmonia Chorus Israel PO Mehta	VHS Video: Lyric (USA) 1004 Laserdisc: Dreamlife (Japan) TE-S 166

BRAHMS

Ein deutsches Requiem

Vienna May 1964	Wächter Vienna Singverein BPO Karajan	LP: DG KL 33-39/SKL 133-139 LP: DG 2707 018/2726 078/2726 505 CD: DG 427 2522
Cleveland April 1969 .	Krause Cleveland Orchestra & Chorus Szell	CD: Melodram CDM 17503
Salzburg March 1978 VIDGo	Van Dam Vienna Singverein BPO Karajan	VHS Video: DG 072 1353 Laserdisc: DG 072 1351
Vienna April 1980	Krause Vienna Opera Chorus VPO Haitink	LP: Philips 6769 055 CD: Philips 411 4362/426 7432

GLUCK

Orfeo ed Euridice

Munich August 1967	Role of Euridice Moser, Fischer-Dieskau Munich Bach Orchestra & Chorus K.Richter	LP: DG 2707 033/2726 043 Excerpts LP: DG SLPEM 136 556

HANDEL

Giulio Cesare: Excerpt (Da tempeste)

Munich	Munich RO	CD: Originals SH 832
1968	Eichhorn	

Judas Maccabaeus

Berlin	Töpper, Haefliger,	LP: DG LPM 19 248-19 250/
November and	Schreier, Adam	SLPM 139 248-139 250
December 1966	Berlin Radio	LP: DG 2709 024
	Orchestra & Chorus	Excerpts
	Koch	LP: DG SLPEM 136 557

Messiah

Munich	Höffgen, Haefliger,	LP: DG 2709 015/2721 076/413 9671
June 1964	Crass	CD: DG 413 9672/439 7022
	Munich Bach	Excerpts
	Orchestra & Chorus	LP: DG SLPEM 136 476
	K.Richter	
	Sung in German	

HAYDN

Die Jahreszeiten

Vienna	Schreier, Talvela	LP: DG 2709 026
April and	Vienna Singverein	CD: DG 423 9222/439 9402
June 1967	VSO	Excerpts
	Böhm	LP: DG SLPEM 136 436/2535 480

Berlin	Hollweg, Berry	LP: EMI SLS 969
November 1972	Deutsche Oper Chorus	CD: EMI CMS 769 2242
	BPO	Excerpts
	Karajan	LP: EMI EG 29 05671
		CD: EMI CDM 769 0102

Die Schöpfung

Salzburg	Wunderlich, Borg,	CD: Hunt CDKAR 203
August 1965	Prey	
	Vienna Singverein	
	VPO	
	Karajan	

Berlin	C.Ludwig,	LP: DG 643 515-643 516
February 1966,	Wunderlich, Krenn,	LP: DG 2707 044/410 9511
September and	Fischer-Dieskau,	CD: DG 435 0772
November 1968	Berry	Excerpts
and April 1969	Vienna Singverein	LP: DG SLPEM 136 439
	BPO	CD: DG 439 4542
	Karajan	

HINDEMITH

Das Marienleben, song cycle

1982	Gage	LP: Jecklin 574-575
		CD: Jecklin 5742

KALMAN

Gräfin Maritza

Mörbisch	Dallapozza,	VHS Video: Lyric (USA) 8350
1987	Nadelmann, Dönch	
	Orchestra & Chorus	
	Theimer	

KORNGOLD

Die Kathrin: Excerpt (Ich bin ein Liedsänger)

Vienna	Christ	CD: Cambria CD 1032
1962	Austrian RO	Incorrectly dated 1949
	Loibner	

Der Ring des Polykrates: Excerpt (Tagesbuch der Laura)

Vienna	Austrian RO	CD: Cambria CD 1032
1962	Loibner	Incorrectly dated 1949

LORTZING

Der Waffenschmied, Querschnitt

Berlin	Wagner, Vantin,	LP: DG LPEM19 417/SLPEM 136 417
1963	Greindl, Stewart	LP: DG 2535 299
	RIAS Choir	CD: DG awaiting publication
	Berlin RO	Excerpt
	Stepp	LP: DG LPEM 19 456

MENDELSSOHN

Paulus

Leipzig	Lang, Blochwitz,	LP: Philips 420 2121
December 1986	Adam	CD: Philips 420 2122
	Leipzig Radio	
	Chorus	
	Leipzig Gewandhaus	
	Orchestra	
	Masur	

MONTEVERDI

L'Incoronazione di Poppea

Vienna	Roles of Drusilla	Unpublished radio broadcast
April 1963	and Pallas Athene	
	Jurinac, Lilowa,	
	Rössel-Majdan,	
	Stolze, Cava	
	Vienna Opera Chorus	
	VPO	
	Karajan	

MOZART

Requiem

Vienna 1972	C.Ludwig, Schreier, Berry Vienna Opera Chorus VSO Böhm	Unpublished video recording
London December 1989	Bernheimer, Hill, Thomas Hanover Band and Chorus Goodman	CD: Nimbus NI 5241/NI 1791

Missa solemnis "Waisenhausmesse"

Vienna October 1975	Von Stade, Ochman, Moll Vienna Opera Chorus VPO Abbado	LP: DG 2530 777 CD: DG 423 8862/427 2552

A questo seno deh vieni, concert aria

Vienna June 1966	VSO Boettcher	LP: DG SLPM 139 198/2548 216 CD: DG 437 9162/447 3522

Ah lo previdi!, concert aria

Vienna June 1966	VSO Boettcher	LP: DG SLPM 139 198/2548 216 CD: DG 437 9162/447 3522

Alma grande e nobil core, concert aria

Vienna June 1966	VSO Boettcher	LP: DG SLPM 139 198/2548 216 CD: DG 437 9162/447 3522

Bella mia fiamma, concert aria

| Vienna | VSO | LP: DG SLPM 139 198/2548 216 |
| June 1966 | Boettcher | CD: DG 437 9162/447 3522 |

Betracht dies Herz und fragt mich (Grabmusik K42)

| Vienna | VSO | DG unpublished |
| June 1966 | Boettcher | |

Misera, dove son?, concert aria

Vienna	VSO	LP: DG SLPM 139 198/2548 216
June 1966	Boettcher	LP: Philips 6866 015
		CD: DG 437 9162/447 3522

Vado, ma dove?, concert aria

| Vienna | VSO | LP: DG SLPM 139 198/2548 216 |
| June 1966 | Boettcher | CD: DG 437 9162/447 3522 |

Così fan tutte

Vienna	Role of Fiordiligi	Unpublished video recording
1970	Miljakovic,	
	C.Ludwig, Alva,	
	Prey, Berry	
	Chorus	
	VPO	
	Böhm	

Salzburg	Grist, Fassbaender,	CD: Foyer 2CF-2066
July 1972	Schreier, Prey,	
	Fischer-Dieskau	
	Vienna Opera Chorus	
	VPO	
	Böhm	

Salzburg	Grist, Fassbaender,	LP: DG 2709 059/2740 118
August 1974	Schreier, Prey,	LP: DG 2740 206/2740 222
	Panerai	CD: DG 429 8742/435 3942
	Vienna Opera Chorus	Excerpts
	VPO	LP: DG 2537 037
	Böhm	CD: DG 427 7122/427 8002/429 8242

Don Giovanni

Salzburg July 1968	Role of Donna Anna Zylis-Gara, Freni, Kraus, Ghiaurov, Evans, Talvela Vienna Opera Chorus VPO Karajan	LP: GOP Records GOP 53 CD: Paragon PCD 84009-84011
Salzburg August 1969	Zylis-Gara, Freni, Kraus, Ghiaurov, Evans, Halem Vienna Opera Chorus VPO Karajan	CD: Memories HR 4362-4364 CD: Hunt CDKAR 202
Rome May 1970	Jurinac, Miljakovic, Kraus, Ghiaurov, Bruscantini, Petkov RAI Rome Orchestra & Chorus Giulini	CD: Hunt CDLSMH 34050/CDMP 450 CD: Frequenz 043.019 CD: Rodolphe PRV 32675-32677 CD: Melodram CDM 37080 CD: Cetra CDAR 2049
Salzburg August 1970	Zylis-Gara, Miljakovic, Burrows, Ghiaurov, Evans, Halem Vienna Opera Chorus VPO Karajan	CD: Hunt CDKAR 231

Idomeneo

Glyndebourne July 1964	Role of Ilia Tarres, Lewis, Pavarotti, Hughes, Wicks Glyndebourne Festival Chorus LPO Pritchard	CD: Butterfly BMCD 010 Excerpt CD: Opera CD 54039
London August 1964	Tarres, Lewis, Pavarotti, Hughes, Wicks Glyndebourne Festival Chorus LPO Pritchard	LP: HRE Records HRE 364 CD: Melodram MEL 27003 CD: Verona 27038-27039 CD: NotaBlu 920.715 Excerpt CD: NotaBlu 920.711

Le Nozze di Figaro

Berlin March 1968	Role of Contessa Mathis, Troyanos, Prey, Fischer-Dieskau Deutsche Oper Orchestra & Chorus Böhm	LP: DG 2711 007/2740 108/2740 139 LP: DG 2740 202/2740 204 LP: DG 2740 222/415 5201 CD: DG 415 5202/429 8692/435 3942 Excerpts LP: DG 2537 023 CD: DG 423 1152/427 7122 CD: DG 429 8002/429 8222
Paris 1980	Popp, Von Stade, Van Dam, Bacquier Paris Opéra Orchestra & Chorus Solti	VHS Video: Sony (Japan) 002M 7015-7016 VHS Video: Lyric (USA) 1096 Laserdisc: Dreamlife (USA) DMLB 29 ✗
Tokyo September 1980	Popp, Baltsa, Prey, Weikl Vienna Opera Chorus VPO Böhm	VHS Video: Lyric (USA) 1097 ✗

Le Nozze di Figaro: Excerpt (Dove sono)

Munich 1968	Munich RO Eichhorn	CD: Originals SH 832

Die Zauberflöte

Aix-en-Provence July 1963	Role of Pamina D'Angelo, McAlpine, Mars, Tadeo Paris Conservatoire Orchestra & Chorus Pritchard	Unpublished video recording ✗
London March and April 1964	Popp, Gedda, Berry, Frick, Crass Philharmonia Orchestra & Chorus Klemperer	LP: EMI AN 137-139/SAN 137-139 LP: EMI SLS 912 CD: EMI CMS 769 9712 Excerpts LP: EMI ALP 2314/ASD 2314 LP: EMI ESD 100 3261 CD: EMI CDM 763 4512
Aix-en-Provence July 1965	Eda-Pierre, Kmennt, Van Dam, Tadeo Brasseur Choir Paris Conservatoire Orchestra Bellugi	Unpublished radio broadcast

Die Zauberflöte: Excerpt (Der, welcher wandert diese Strassen)

Vienna 1970	Dermota, Beirer, Pernerstorfer VPO Krips	CD: Melodram CDM 26522

ORFF

Carmina burana

Berlin October 1967	Stolze, Fischer-Dieskau Deutsche Oper Orchestra & Chorus Jochum	LP: DG SLPM 139 362/2726 510 CD: DG 423 8862/427 8782

PERGOLESI

Stabat mater

Salzburg August 1968	Forrester BPO Abbado	CD: Myto MCD 90525

PFITZNER

Palestrina

Vienna December 1964	Role of an Angelic Voice Jurinac, C.Ludwig, Wunderlich, Wiener, Kreppel, Welter Vienna Opera Chorus VPO Heger	CD: Myto MCD 92259

SCHOENBERG

Gurrelieder

Vienna June 1969	Role of Tove C.Ludwig, Sergi, Dickie, Lackner Vienna Singakademie VSO Krips	CD: Hunt CDHP 585

SCHUBERT

Die abgeblühte Linde (Wirst du halten, was du schwurst?)

Milan   Spencer   CD: Nuova Era NE 6860
October 1989

Abschied der Fürstin (Der Abend rötet nun das Tal)

Berlin   Gage   LP: DG 2713 012/2740 196
September 1976-   CD: DG (Japan) POCG 9022-9029
December 1977   CD: DG 445 4952

Am Grabe Anselmos (Dass ich dich verloren habe)

Milan   Spencer   CD: Nuova Era NE 6860
October 1989

An den Mond (Füllest wieder Busch und Tal)

Milan   Spencer   CD: Nuova Era NE 6860
October 1989

An die Musik (Du holde Kunst, in wieviel grauen Stunden)

Milan   Spencer   CD: Nuova Era NE 6860
October 1989

An die Nachtigall (Er liegt und schläft an meinem Herzen)

Berlin   Gage   LP: DG 2713 012/2740 196
September 1976-   CD: DG (Japan) POCG 9022-9029
December 1977   CD: DG 445 4952

An die Sonne (Sinke, liebe Sonne, sinke!)

Berlin   Gage   LP: DG 2713 012/2740 196
September 1976-   CD: DG (Japan) POCG 9022-9029
December 1977   CD: DG 437 9432/445 4952

An die untergehende Sonne (Sonne du sinkst, sink' in Frieden, o Sonne!)

Milan   Spencer   CD: Nuova Era NE 6860
October 1989

Schubert Lieder/continued

Auf dem See (Und frische Nahrung, neues Blut)

| Milan | Spencer | CD: Nuova Era NE 6860 |
| October 1989 | | |

Augenlied (Süsse Augen, klare Bronnen!)

| Milan | Spencer | CD: Nuova Era NE 6860 |
| October 1989 | | |

Bei dir allein

| Milan | Spencer | CD: Nuova Era NE 6860 |
| October 1989 | | |

Bertas Lied in der Nacht (Nacht umhüllt mit wehendem Flügel)

Berlin	Gage	LP: DG 2713 012/2740 196
September 1976-		CD: DG (Japan) POCG 9022-9029
December 1977		CD: DG 437 9432/445 4952

Blanka (Wenn mich einsam Lüfte fächeln)

Berlin	Gage	LP: DG 2713 012/2740 196
September 1976-		CD: DG (Japan) POCG 9022-9029
December 1977		CD: DG 445 4952

Der blinde Knabe (O sagt, ihr Lieben, mir einmal)

| Milan | Spencer | CD: Nuova Era NE 6860 |
| October 1989 | | |

Du bist die Ruh'

Berlin	Gage	LP: DG 2713 012/2740 196/2530 858
September 1976-		CD: DG (Japan) POCG 9022-9029
December 1977		CD: DG 437 9432/445 4952

Schubert Lieder/continued

Ellens Gesang I-III: Raste, Krieger, Krieg ist aus!;   Jäger, ruhe von der Jagd!)
Ave Maria, Jungfrau mild!

Berlin   Gage   LP: DG 2713 012/2740 196/2530 858
September 1976-   CD: DG (Japan) POCG 9022-9029
December 1977   CD: DG 437 9432/445 4952/447 3522

Fischerweise (Den Fischer fechten Sorgen)

Berlin   Gage   LP: DG 2713 012/2740 196
September 1976-   CD: DG (Japan) POCG 9022-9029
December 1977   CD: DG 437 9432/445 4952

Milan   Spencer   CD: Nuova Era NE 6860
October 1989

Der Fluss (Wie rein Gesang sich windet)

Berlin   Gage   LP: DG 2713 012/2740 196
September 1976-   CD: DG (Japan) POCG 9022-9029
December 1977   CD: DG 445 4952

Die Forelle (In einem Bächlein helle)

Berlin   Gage   LP: DG 2713 012/2740 196
September 1976-   LP: DG 2530 858/2535 656
December 1977   CD: DG (Japan) POCG 9022-9029
                                              CD: DG 437 9432/445 4952/447 3522

Geheimnis an Franz Schubert (Sag' an, wer lehrt dich Lieder?)

Milan   Spencer   CD: Nuova Era NE 6860
October 1989

Gesang der Norna (Mich führt mein Weg wohl meilenlang)

Berlin   Gage   LP: DG 2713 012/2740 196
September 1976-   CD: DG (Japan) POCG 9022-9029
December 1977   CD: DG 437 9432/445 4952

Gretchen am Spinnrade (Meine Ruh' ist hin, mein Herz ist schwer)

Berlin   Gage   LP: DG 2713 012/2740 196
September 1976-   CD: DG (Japan) POCG 9022-9029
December 1977   CD: DG 437 9432/445 4952

Schubert Lieder/continued

Gretchens Bitte (Ach neige, du Schmerzensreiche!)

Berlin   Gage   LP: DG 2713 012/2740 196
September 1976-   CD: DG (Japan) POCG 9022-9029
December 1977   CD: DG 445 4952

Hagars Klage (Hier am Hügel heissen Sandes)

Berlin   Gage   LP: DG 2713 012/2740 196
September 1976-   CD: DG (Japan) POCG 9022-9029
December 1977   CD: DG 445 4952

Heimliches Lieben (O du, wenn deine Lippen mich berühren)

Berlin   Gage   LP: DG 2713 012/2740 196
September 1976-   CD: DG (Japan) POCG 9022-9029
December 1977   CD: DG 445 4952

Der Hirt auf dem Felsen (Wenn auf dem höchsten Fels ich steh')

Berlin   Rodenhauser, clarinet LP: DG 2713 012/2740 196
September 1976-   Gage   CD: DG (Japan) POCG 9022-9029
December 1977   CD: DG 437 9432/445 4952

Im Freien (Draussen in der weiten Nacht)

Berlin   Gage   LP: DG 2713 012/2740 196/2530 858
September 1976-   CD: DG (Japan) POCG 9022-9029
December 1977   CD: DG 437 9432/445 4952

Im Frühling (Still sitz' ich an des Hügels Hang)

Berlin   Gage   LP: DG 2713 012/2740 196
September 1976-   CD: DG (Japan) POCG 9022-9029
December 1977   CD: DG 437 9432/445 4952

Iphigenia (Blüht denn hier an Tauris Strande)

Berlin   Gage   LP: DG 2713 012/2740 196
September 1976-   CD: DG (Japan) POCG 9022-9029
December 1977   CD: DG 445 4952

Schubert Lieder/continued

Die junge Nonne (Wie braust durch die Wipfel der heulende Sturm)

Berlin   Gage   LP: DG 2713 012/2740 196
September 1976-   CD: DG (Japan) POCG 9022-9029
December 1977   CD: DG 437 9432/445 4952

Klage der Ceres (Ist der holde Lenz erschienen?)

Berlin   Gage   LP: DG 2713 012/2740 196
September 1976-   CD: DG (Japan) POCG 9022-9029
December 1977   CD: DG 445 4952

Klagelied (Meine Ruh' ist dahin!)

Berlin   Gage   LP: DG 2713 012/2740 196
September 1976-   CD: DG (Japan) POCG 9022-9029
December 1977   CD: DG 445 4952

Kolmas Klage (Rund um mich Nacht)

Berlin   Gage   LP: DG 2713 012/2740 196
September 1976-   CD: DG (Japan) POCG 9022-9029
December 1977   CD: DG 445 4952

Der König in Thule (Es war ein König in Thule)

Berlin   Gage   LP: DG 2713 012/2740 196
September 1976-   CD: DG (Japan) POCG 9022-9029
December 1977   CD: DG 437 9432/445 4952

Lambertine (O Liebe, die mein Herz erfüllet)

Berlin   Gage   LP: DG 2713 012/2740 196
September 1976-   CD: DG (Japan) POCG 9022-9029
December 1977   CD: DG 445 4952

Liebe schwärmt auf allen Wegen/Ariette der Claudine

Berlin   Gage   LP: DG 2713 012/2740 196
September 1976-   CD: DG (Japan) POCG 9022-9029
December 1977   CD: DG 445 4952

Die Liebende schreibt (Ein Blick von deinen Augen in die meinen)

Berlin   Gage   LP: DG 2713 012/2740 196
September 1976-   CD: DG (Japan) POCG 9022-9029
December 1977   CD: DG 445 4952

Schubert Lieder/continued

Der liebliche Stern (Ihr Sternlein, still in der Höhe)

Milan	Spencer	CD: Nuova Era NE 6860
October 1989		

Lied der Anne Lyle (Wärst du bei mir im Lebenstal)

Berlin	Gage	LP: DG 2713 012/2740 196
September 1976-		CD: DG (Japan) POCG 9022-9029
December 1977		CD: DG 437 9432/445 4952

Das Lied im Grünen (Ins Grüne, ins Grüne, da lockt uns der Frühling)

Milan	Spencer	CD: Nuova Era NE 6860
October 1989		

Lilla an die Morgenröte (Wie schön bist du, du güld'ne Morgenröte)

Berlin	Gage	LP: DG 2713 012/2740 196
September 1976-		CD: DG (Japan) POCG 9022-9029
December 1977		CD: DG 445 4952

Das Mädchen (Wie so innig, möcht' ich sagen)

Berlin	Gage	LP: DG 2713 012/2740 196
September 1976-		CD: DG (Japan) POCG 9022-9029
December 1977		CD: DG 445 4952

Des Mädchens Klage (Der Eichwald brauset, die Wolken zieh'n), 1st, 2nd and 3rd settings

Berlin	Gage	LP: DG 2713 012/2740 196
September 1976-		CD: DG (Japan) POCG 9022-9029
December 1977		CD: DG 445 4952

Die Männer sind mechant (Du sagtest mir es, Mutter!)

Berlin	Gage	LP: DG 2713 012/2740 196
September 1976-		CD: DG (Japan) POCG 9022-9029
December 1977		CD: DG 437 9432/445 4952

Schubert Lieder/continued

Mignon (Heiss' mich nicht reden)

Berlin	Gage	LP: DG 2713 012/2740 196
September 1976-		CD: DG (Japan) POCG 9022-9029
December 1977		CD: DG 437 9432/445 4952

Mignon (Nur wer die Sehnsucht kennt)

Berlin	Gage	LP: DG 2713 012/2740 196
September 1976-		CD: DG (Japan) POCG 9022-9029
December 1977		CD: DG 437 9432/445 4952

Mignon (So lasst mich scheinen, bis ich werde)

Berlin	Gage	LP: DG 2713 012/2740 196
September 1976-		CD: DG (Japan) POCG 9022-9029
December 1977		CD: DG 437 9432/445 4952

Mignons Gesang (Kennst du das Land, wo die Zitronen blüh'n?)

Berlin	Gage	LP: DG 2713 012/2740 196
September 1976-		CD: DG (Japan) POCG 9022-9029
December 1977		CD: DG 437 9432/445 4952

Nachtstück (Wenn über Berge sich der Nebel breitet)

| Milan | Spencer | CD: Nuova Era NE 6860 |
| October 1989 | | |

Die Rose (Es lockte schöne Wärme)

Berlin	Gage	LP: DG 2713 012/2740 196
September 1976-		CD: DG (Japan) POCG 9022-9029
December 1977		CD: DG 437 9432 /445 4952

Schwestergruss (Im Mondenschein wall' ich auf und ab)

Berlin	Gage	LP: DG 2713 012/2740 196/2530 858
September 1976-		CD: DG (Japan) POCG 9022-9029
December 1977		CD: DG 437 9432/445 4952/447 3522

Suleika I & II: Was bedeutet die Bewegung?; Ach, um deine feuchten Schwingen

Berlin	Gage	LP: DG 2713 012/2740 196/2530 858
September 1976-		CD: DG (Japan) POCG 9022-9029
December 1977		CD: DG 437 9432/445 4952/447 3522

Schubert Lieder/concluded

Szene der Delphine (Ach, was soll ich beginnen vor Liebe?)

Berlin   Gage   LP: DG 2713 012/2740 196
September 1976–   CD: DG (Japan) POCG 9022-9029
December 1977   CD: DG 437 9432/445 4952

Thekla/Eine Geisterstimme (Wo ich sei und wo mich hingewendet), 1st and 2nd settings

Berlin   Gage   LP: DG 2713 012/2740 196
September 1976–   CD: DG (Japan) POCG 9022-9029
December 1977   CD: DG 445 4952

Vergiss mein nicht (Als der Frühling sich vom Herzen)

Berlin   Gage   LP: DG 2713 012/2740 196
September 1976–   CD: DG (Japan) POCG 9022-9029
December 1977   CD: DG 437 9432/445 4952

Vom Mitleiden Mariae (Als bei dem Kreuz Maria stand)

Berlin   Gage   LP: DG 2713 012/2740 196
September 1976–   CD: DG (Japan) POCG 9022-9029
December 1977   CD: DG 445 4952

Wiegenlied (Schlafe, schlafe, holder süsser Knabe)

Berlin   Gage   LP: DG 2713 012/2740 196
September 1976–   CD: DG (Japan) POCG 9022-9029
December 1977   CD: DG 437 9432/445 4952

Wiegenlied (Wie sich der Aeuglein kindlicher Himmel)

Berlin   Gage   LP: DG 2713 012/2740 196
September 1976–   CD: DG (Japan) POCG 9022-9029
December 1977   CD: DG 437 9432/445 4952

Der Winterabend (Es ist so still, so heimlich um mich)

Milan   Spencer   CD: Nuova Era NE 6860
October 1989

SPONTINI

La Vestale

Rome
1974

Role of Giulia
Baldani, Py,
Corradi, Ferrin
RAI Rome
Orchestra & Chorus
Lopez-Cobos

LP: MRF Records MRF 124

STOLZ

Die Rosen der Madonna

Vienna
1973

Role of Maria
Kmennt, Wächter,
Pernerstorfer
Austrian RO
Stolz

LP: BASF BB 20.212610

JOHANN STRAUSS

Die Fledermaus

Vienna
February 1971

Role of Rosalinde
Holm, Windgassen,
Kmennt, Wächter,
Holecek
Vienna Opera Chorus
VPO
Böhm

LP: Decca SET 540-541
VHS Video: Victor (Japan) JHC 0118
Excerpts
CD: Decca 421 8982

RICHARD STRAUSS

Arabella

Vienna
September 1976

Role of Arabella
Popp, Gruberova,
Bence, Cvejic,
Dallapozza,
Wächter, Helm
Vienna Opera Chorus
VPO
Hollreiser

VHS Video: Lyric (USA) 8636

Vienna
January 1977

Ghazarian,
Gruberova, Lilowa,
Mödl, Kollo,
Weikl, Rydl
Vienna Opera Chorus
VPO
Solti

VHS Video: Decca 071 4053
Laserdisc: Decca 071 4051

Arabella: Excerpt (Er ist der Richtige nicht/Aber der Richtige)

Munich
1968

Auger
Munich RO
Eichhorn

CD: Originals SH 832

Ariadne auf Naxos

Dresden
June and
July 1968

Role of Ariadne
Zylis-Gara, Geszty,
King, Schreier,
Adam, Prey, Vogel
Dresden
Staatskapelle
Kempe

LP: EMI SLS 936
CD: EMI CMS 764 1592
Excerpts
LP: EMI 1C 061 100 8241

Vienna
October 1977

T.Schmidt, Gruberova,
Kollo, Berry,
Zednik
VPO
Böhm

VHS Video: DG 072 4423

Capriccio

Munich
April 1971

Role of Countess
Troyanos, Auger,
Schreier, Prey,
Fischer-Dieskau,
Ridderbusch
Bavarian RO
Böhm

LP: DG 2709 038/2721 188/419 0231
CD: DG 419 0232/445 4912/445 3472
Excerpt
CD: DG 439 4672

Feuersnot

Berlin
May 1978

Role of Diemut
Krebs, Berger-Tuna,
Shirley-Quirk
RIAS & Tölz Choirs
Berlin RO
Leinsdorf

Unpublished radio broadcast

Die Frau ohne Schatten

Vienna
June 1964

Role of Empress
Kuchta, G.Hoffman,
Thomas, Wiener,
Kreppel
Vienna Opera Chorus
VPO
Karajan

Unpublished radio broadcast

Der Rosenkavalier

Salzburg
July 1978

Role of Marschallin
Minton, Popp,
Pavarotti, Moll,
Gutstein
Vienna Opera Chorus
VPO
Dohnanyi

Unpublished radio broadcast

Vienna
1982

Wise, Baltsa,
Hadley, Moll,
Hornik
Vienna Opera Chorus
VPO
Stein

Unpublished video recording

Der Rosenkavalier: Excerpt (Marie Theres'!/Hab' mir's gelobt)

Munich
1968

Auger, Troyanos
Munich RO
Eichhorn

CD: Originals SH 832

Befreit (Du wirst nicht weinen)

London	Academy of London	CD: Virgin VC 790 7942
April 1988–	Stamp	
November 1989		

Beim Schlafengehen/4 letzte Lieder (Nun der Tag mich müd' gemacht)

Rome	RAI Rome Orchestra	CD: Nuova Era NE 2217
April 1969	Celibidache	CD: Nuova Era NE 2393-2398
		CD: Hunt CD 570/CDHP 570
		CD: Cetra CDAR 2012
Berlin	BPO	LP: DG 2530 368
February 1973	Karajan	CD: DG 423 8882/439 4672
		CD: DG 447 3982/447 4222

Freundliche Vision (Nicht im Schlafe hab' ich das geträumt)

London	Academy of London	CD: Virgin VC 790 7942
April 1988–	Stamp	
November 1989		

Frühling/4 letzte Lieder (In dämm'rigen Grüften träumte ich lang)

Rome	RAI Rome Orchestra	CD: Nuova Era NE 2217
April 1969	Celibidache	CD: Nuova Era NE 2393-2398
		CD: Hunt CD 570/CDHP 570
		CD: Cetra CDAR 2012
Berlin	BPO	LP: DG 2530 368
February 1973	Karajan	CD: DG 423 8882/439 4672
		CD: DG 447 3982/447 4222

Die heil'gen drei Könige aus Morgenland

London	Academy of London	CD: Virgin VC 790 7942
April 1988–	Stamp	
November 1989		

Im Abendrot/4 letzte Lieder (Wir sind durch Not und Freude gegangen Hand in Hand)

Munich	Munich RO	CD: Originals SH 832
1968	Eichhorn	
Rome	RAI Rome Orchestra	CD: Nuova Era NE 2217
April 1969	Celibidache	CD: Nuova Era NE 2393-2398
		CD: Hunt CD 570/CDHP 570
		CD: Cetra CDAR 2012
Berlin	BPO	LP: DG 2530 368
February 1973	Karajan	CD: DG 423 8882/439 4672
		CD: DG 447 3982/447 4222

Meinem Kinde (Du schläfst und sachte neig' ich mich)

London	Academy of London	CD: Virgin VC 790 7942
April 1988-	Stamp	
November 1989		

Morgen (Und morgen wird die Sonne wieder scheinen)

London	Academy of London	CD: Virgin VC 790 7942
April 1988-	Stamp	
November 1989		

Ruhe meine Seele (Nicht ein Lüftchen regt sich leise)

London	Academy of London	CD: Virgin VC 790 7942
April 1988-	Stamp	
November 1989		

September/4 letzte Lieder (Der Garten trauert)

Munich	Munich RO	CD: Originals SH 832
1968	Eichhorn	

Rome	RAI Rome Orchestra	CD: Nuova Era NE 2217
April 1969	Celibidache	CD: Nuova Era NE 2393-2398
		CD: Hunt CD 570/CDHP 570
		CD: Cetra CDAR 2012

Berlin	BPO	LP: DG 2530 368
February 1973	Karajan	CD: DG 423 8882/439 4672
		CD: DG 447 3982/447 4222

Waldseligkeit (Der Wald beginnt zu rauschen)

London	Academy of London	CD: Virgin VC 790 7942
April 1988-	Stamp	
November 1989		

Wiegenlied (Träume, träume, du mein süsses Leben)

London	Academy of London	CD: Virgin VC 790 7942
April 1988-	Stamp	
November 1989		

Winterweihe (In diesen Wintertagen)

London	Academy of London	CD: Virgin VC 790 7942
April 1988-	Stamp	
November 1989		

TELEMANN

Ino, cantata

Hamburg March and April 1965	Hamburg Telemann Orchestra Boettcher	LP: DG APM 14 359/SAPM 198 359

VERDI

Attila

Berlin 1971	Role of Odabella Tagliavini, Van Dam, Wixell, Rundgren Deutsche Oper Orchestra & Chorus Patanè	LP: Estro armonico EA 036

Un Ballo in maschera

Munich December 1975	Role of Amelia Wewezow, Bini, Miller Bavarian State Orchestra & Chorus Gomez-Martinis	Unpublished radio broadcast

Don Carlo

Vienna October 1970	Role of Elisabetta Verrett, Corelli, Ghiaurov, Wächter, Talvela Vienna Opera Chorus VPO Stein	LP: Morgan MOR 7003 LP: Legendary LR 163 CD: Legato SRO 514 CD: Rodolophe RPC 32653-32655 CD: Panthéon PHE 6614-6616

Simone Boccanegra

Vienna March 1969	Role of Amelia Cossutta, Wächter, Ghiaurov, Kerns Vienna Opera Chorus VPO Krips	Unpublished radio broadcast Comè in quest' ora bruna CD: Legato SRO 814 CD: Memories HR 4289-4290

La Traviata

Vienna 1964	Role of Flora Moffo, Zampieri, Bastianini Vienna Opera Chorus VPO Klobucar	CD: Melodram CDM 27510

Requiem

Salzburg August 1970	C.Ludwig, Bergonzi, Raimondi Vienna Singverein VPO Karajan	Unpublished radio broadcast
Munich 1974	Fassbaender, Ilosfalvy, Ridderbusch Munich Philharmonic Orchestra & Chorus Kempe	Unpublished radio broadcast

WAGNER

Die Feen

| Vienna
February 1983 | Role of Ada
Tokody, Hopferwieser,
Helm, Sramek
Vienna Opera Chorus
VPO
Ehrling | Unpublished radio broadcast |

Götterdämmerung

| Berlin
October 1969 | Role of Gutrune
Dernesch, C.Ludwig,
Brilioth, Stewart,
Kelemen, Ridderbusch
Deutsche Oper Chorus
BPO
Karajan | LP: DG 2716 051/2720 019/2720 051
LP: DG 2740 148/2740 240
CD: DG 415 1552/435 2112 |
| Salzburg
March 1970 | Dernesch, C.Ludwig,
Thomas, Stewart,
Kelemen, Ridderbusch
Vienna Opera Chorus
BPO
Karajan | CD: Memories HR 4107-4121/
HR 4118-4121
CD: Hunt CDKAR 223 |

Lohengrin

| Munich
1971 | Role of Elsa
Jones, King,
Stewart, Nienstedt,
Ridderbusch
Bavarian Radio
Orchestra & Chorus
Kubelik | LP: DG 2713 005/2720 036
LP: DG 2740 141/419 0291
CD: DG (Japan) POCG 2874-2876
Excerpts
LP: DG 2537 026
CD: DG 445 0502 |

Lohengrin: Excerpts (Einsam in trüben Tagen; Euch Lüften, die mein Klagen)

| Berlin
March and
April 1967 | Deutsche Oper
Orchestra
Leitner | LP: DG SLPM 136 546
CD: DG 447 3522 |

Die Meistersinger von Nürnberg

Munich   Role of Eva   CD: Myto MCD 92569
November 1967   Fassbaender, Konya,
                  Unger, Stewart,
                  Hemsley, Crass
                  Bavarian Radio
                  Orchestra & Chorus
                  Kubelik

Salzburg   Meyer, Kollo,   Unpublished radio broadcast
April 1974   Schreier, Hendriks,
                  Ridderbusch, Leib
                  Vienna Opera Chorus
                  BPO
                  Karajan

Parsifal

Vienna   Role of Flower Maiden   CD: Hunt CDKAR 219
April 1961   C.Ludwig, Höngen,
                  Uhl, Hotter, Berry,
                  Wächter, Franc
                  Vienna Opera Chorus
                  VPO
                  Karajan

Bayreuth   Dalis, Thomas,   LP: Philips AL 3475-3479/
August 1962   London, Hotter,   SAL 3475-3479
                  Neidlinger, Talvela   LP: Philips 6747 242/6747 250/6723 001
                  Bayreuth Festival   CD: Philips 416 3902
                  Orchestra & Chorus
                  Knappertsbusch

Rienzi: Excerpt (Gerechter Gott! So ist's entschieden schon!)

Berlin   Deutsche Oper   LP: DG SLPM 136 546
March and   Orchestra   CD: DG 447 3522
April 1967   Leitner

Tannhäuser

Vienna January 1963	Role of Shepherd Brouwenstijn, C.Ludwig, Beirer, Kmennt, Equiluz, Wächter, Frick Vienna Opera Chorus VPO Karajan	LP: Melodram MEL 427 CD: Nuova Era NE 013.6307-6309 CD: Hunt CDKAR 204
Perugia October 1972	Role of Elisabeth Dunn, Kollo, Brendel, Schenk Orchestra & Chorus Sawallisch	Unpublished radio broadcast

Tannhäuser: Excerpts (Dich, teure Halle; Allmächt'ge Jungfrau)

Berlin March and April 1967	Deutsche Oper Orchestra Leitner	LP: DG SLPM 136 546 CD: DG 447 3522

Die Walküre

Berlin September 1966	Role of Sieglinde Crespin, Veasey, Vickers, Stewart, Talvela BPO Karajan	LP: DG LPM 19 229-19 233/ SLPM 139 229-139 233 LP: DG 2713 001/2720 051 LP: DG 2740 146/2740 240 CD: DG 415 1452/435 2112 Excerpts LP: DG SLPEM 136 435/2535 239 CD: DG 415 2562/429 1682
Salzburg March 1967	Crespin, C.Ludwig, Vickers, Stewart, Talvela BPO Karajan	CD: Memories HR 4107-4121/ HR 4107-4110 CD: Hunt CDKAR 223
Vienna June 1985	Bjoner, Schiml, Jersusalem, McIntyre, Moll VPO Schneider	Unpublished radio broadcast Excerpt VHS Video: Lyric (USA) 1832/8277

WEBER

Der Freischütz

Vienna May 1972	Role of Agathe Holm, King, Wächter, Ridderbusch, Crass, Jungwirth Vienna Opera Chorus VPO Böhm	CD: Hunt CDMP 457 CD: Foyer 2CF-2059
Dresden January and February 1973	Mathis, Schreier, Adam, Weikl, Crass, Vogel Leipzig Radio Chorus Dresden Staatskapelle C.Kleiber	LP: DG 2709 046 CD: DG 415 4322 Excerpts LP: DG 2537 020 CD: DG 439 4402

Der Freischütz: Excerpts (Leise, leise; Und ob die Wolke)

Berlin March and April 1967	Deutsche Oper Orchestra Leitner	LP: DG SLPM 136 546 CD: DG 447 3522

Oberon: Excerpts (Ozean, du Ungeheuer!; Traure, mein Herz)

Berlin March and April 1967	Deutsche Oper Orchestra Leitner	LP: DG SLPM 136 546 CD: DG 447 3522

Arias by Weber and other composers, sung by Janowitz at performances in Tokyo
in 1984, are reported to exist on VHS Video: Lyric (USA) 3303, but details
could not be confirmed at time of going to press

MISCELLANEOUS

Da capo Gundula Janowitz

Munich 1991	The singer in interview with August Everding	Unpublished video recording

Christa Ludwig
born 1928

with valuable assistance
from Clifford Elkin

Discography compiled by John Hunt

BACH

Christmas Oratorio

Munich February, March and June 1965	Janowitz, Wunderlich, Crass Munich Bach Orchestra & Chorus K.Richter	LP: DG APM 14 353-14 355/ SAPM 198 353-198 355 LP: DG 2710 004/2722 018/2723 063 CD: DG 413 6252/427 2362 Excerpts LP: DG 136 498 rehearsal extracts issued as a promotional LP

Mass in B minor

Salzburg August 1961	L.Price, Gedda, Souzay Vienna Singverein VPO Karajan	LP: Movimento musica 03.012
Berlin September and November 1973 and January 1974	Janowitz, Schreier, Kerns, Ridderbusch Vienna Singverein BPO Karajan	LP: DG 2740 112/415 0221 CD: DG 415 6222/439 6962

Saint John Passion

Berlin September 1961	Grümmer, Wunderlich, Traxel, Kohn, Fischer-Dieskau St.Hedwig's Choir Berlin SO Forster	LP: HMV ALP 1975-1977/ASD 526-528 LP: EMI 1C 147 28589-28591 CD: EMI CMS 764 2342 Excerpts LP: Electrola E 80727/STE 80727 CD: EMI CMS 764 0742

Saint Matthew Passion

London	Schwarzkopf, Gedda,	LP: Columbia 33CX 1799-1803/
November 1960	Pears, Berry,	SAX 2446-2450
and April, May,	Fischer-Dieskau	LP: EMI SLS 827
November and	Philharmonia	CD: EMI CMS 763 0582
December 1961	Orchestra & Chorus	Excerpts
	Klemperer	LP: Columbia 33CX 1881/SAX 2526
		CD: EMI CDEMX 2223
Vienna	Lipp, Wunderlich,	Unpublished private recording
April 1962	Wiener, Berry	
	Vienna Singverein	
	VSO	
	Böhm	
Berlin	Janowitz, Schreier,	LP: DG 2720 070
January 1972	Laubenthal, Berry,	CD: DG 419 7892
	Fischer-Dieskau,	Excerpts
	Diakov	LP: DG 2530 631
	Vienna Singverein	
	BPO	
	Karajan	

BARTOK

Bluebeard's Castle

London	Role of Judith	LP: Decca MET 311/SET 311
November 1965	Berry	LP: Decca 414 1671
	LSO	CD: Decca 414 1672/443 5712
	Kertesz	

BEETHOVEN

Symphony No 9 "Choral"

London October and November 1957	Nordmo-Löverberg, Kmennt, Hotter Philharmonia Orchestra & Chorus Klemperer	LP: Columbia 33CX 1574-1575/ SAX 2276-2277 LP: EMI SLS 788/SLS 790/SXDW 3051 LP: EMI ED 29 02721/EX 29 03793 CD: EMI CDC 747 1892/CDM 763 3592
Tokyo November 1963	Grümmer, King, Berry Deutsche Oper Orchestra & Chorus Böhm	CD: Canyon (Japan) D30L-0011
Berlin January 1968	Janowitz, Thomas, Berry Deutsche Oper Chorus BPO Karajan	CD: Claque GM 1003 CD: Curcio-Hunt CONB 1 Also unpublished video recording

Missa Solemnis

Vienna September 1958	Schwarzkopf, Gedda, Zaccaria Vienna Singverein Philharmonia Karajan	LP: Columbia 33CX 1634-1635 LP: World Records T 914-915/ ST 914-915 LP: EMI 1C 191 00627-00628 LP: EMI SLS 5198
Salzburg August 1959	L.Price, Gedda, Zaccaria Vienna Singverein VPO Karajan	LP: Melodram MEL 704 CD: Nuova Era NE 2262-2263
Berlin February 1966	Janowitz, Wunderlich, Berry Vienna Singverein BPO Karajan	LP: DG KL 95-96/SKL 95-96 LP: DG 2707 030/2720 013/2721 135 LP: DG 2726 048/410 5351 CD: DG 423 9132
Berlin February 1966	Janowitz, Wunderlich, Berry Vienna Singverein BPO Karajan	CD: Hunt CDKAR 214
Vienna October 1974	M.Price, Ochman, Talvela Vienna Opera Chorus VPO Böhm	LP: DG 2707 080 CD: DG 413 1911/437 9252

Fidelio

London February 1962	Role of Leonore Hallstein, Unger, Vickers, Frick, Berry, Crass Philharmonia Orchestra & Chorus Klemperer	LP: Columbia 33CX 1804-1806/ SAX 2451-2453 LP: EMI SLS 5006 CD: EMI CMS 769 3242 Excerpts LP: Columbia 33CX 1907/SAX 2547 LP: EMI SXLP 30307
Vienna May 1962	Janowitz, Kmennt, Vickers, Kreppel, Berry, Wächter Vienna Opera Chorus VPO Karajan	LP: Movimento musica 03.014
Berlin November 1962	Otto, Grobe, King, Greindl, Berry, Talvela Deutsche Oper Orchestra & Chorus Böhm	VHS Video: Canyon (Japan)
Munich December 1963	Steffek, Stolze, Uhl, Frick, Berry, Prey Bavarian State Orchestra & Chorus Karajan	CD: Hunt CDKAR 208

Fidelio: Excerpt (Gut, Söhnchen, gut!)

Salzburg August 1968	Mathis, Crass VPO Böhm	CD: Orfeo C365 941B

Egmont, Incidental music: Excerpts (Freudvoll und leidvoll; Die Trommel gerühret)

Vienna April 1994	Spencer	CD: RCA/BMG 09026 626522 VHS Video: RCA/BMG 09026 626523

Lieder: Ich liebe dich; In questa tomba oscura

Vienna April 1994	Spencer	CD: RCA/BMG 09026 626522 VHS Video: RCA/BMG 09026 626523

BELLINI

Norma

Milan	Role of Adalgisa	LP: Columbia 33CX 1766-1768/
September 1960	Callas, Corelli,	SAX 2412-2414
	Zaccaria	LP: EMI SLS 5186
	La Scala	CD: EMI CMS 763 0002
	Orchestra & Chorus	Excerpts
	Serafin	LP: EMI ASD 3908

BERG

7 frühe Lieder: Nacht; Schilflied; Die Nachtigall; Traumgekrönt; Im Zimmer;
Liebesode; Sommertage

Salzburg	Werba	CD: Orfeo C331 931B
July 1968		

BERNSTEIN

Symphony No 1 "Jeremiah"

Berlin	Israel PO	LP: DG 2530 968
August 1977	Bernstein	CD: DG 415 9642/445 2452

Candide

London	Role of Old Lady	CD: DG 429 7342
December 1989	Anderson, D.Jones,	Excerpts
	Gedda, Hadley,	CD: DG 435 4872/435 3282
	Green, Ollmann	
	LSO Chorus	
	LSO	
	Bernstein	

London	Anderson, D.Jones,	VHS Video: DG 072 4233
December 1989	Gedda, Hadley,	Laserdisc: DG 072 4231
(13 December)	Green, Ollmann	
	LSO Chorus	
	LSO	
	Bernstein	

Candide: Excerpt (Old Lady's Tango)

Tanglewood	Boston SO	Unpublished video recording
August 1988	Mauceri	

I hate music

Vienna	Spencer	CD: RCA/BMG 09026 626522
April 1994		VHS Video: RCA/BMG 09026 626523

BIZET

Carmen

Berlin	Role of Carmen	LP: Columbia (Germany) C 91176-91178
September 1961	Muszely, Schock,	LP: EMI 1C 183 30209-30211
	Prey	Excerpts
	Deutsche Oper Chorus	45: Columbia (Germany) C 50565/
	Berlin SO	STC 50565
	Stein	LP: EMI 1C 061 28170
	Sung in German	CD: EMI CDZ 252 2112/CZS 253 0472
		Excerpts also issued on LP by
		Angel/Seraphim

BRAHMS

Alto Rhapsody

London March 1962	Chorus Philharmonia Klemperer	LP: Columbia 33CX 1817/SAX 2487 LP: EMI SLS 821/ASD 2391 LP: EMI SXLP 27 00001 CD: EMI CDM 769 6502
Vienna June 1976	Vienna Singverein VPO Böhm	LP: DG 2530 992/2536 396/2543 175 LP: Contour CC 7536

Am jüngsten Tag

London May-June 1959	Moore	LP: Columbia 33CX 1693/SAX 2340

An eine Aeolsharfe (Angelehnt an die Efeuwand)

Haitzendorf January 1993	Spencer	CD: RCA/BMG 09026 615472

Auf dem See (Blauer Himmel, blaue Wogen)

London March- April 1969	Parsons	LP: EMI ASD 2555/1C 063 02015 CD: EMI CMS 764 0742

Dein blaues Auge hält so still

London March- April 1969	Parsons	LP: EMI ASD 2555/1C 063 02015 CD: EMI CMS 764 0742
Haitzendorf January 1993	Spencer	CD: RCA/BMG 09026 615472

Feldeinsamkeit (Ich ruhe still im hohen grünen Gras)

London May-June 1959	Moore	LP: Columbia 33CX 1693/SAX 2340 CD: EMI CMS 764 0742
Vienna May 1972	Bernstein	LP: CBS 76379 Also unpublished video recording

Brahms Lieder/continued

Geistliches Wiegenlied (Die ihr schwebt um diese Palmen)

London	Downes, viola	LP: Columbia 33CX 5274/SAX 5274
December 1965-	Parsons	LP: EMI ESD 100 6151
March 1966		CD: EMI CMS 764 0742

Gestillte Sehnsucht (In gold'nem Abendschein getauchet)

London	Downes, viola	LP: Columbia 33CX 5274/SAX 5274
December 1965-	Parsons	LP: EMI ESD 100 6151
March 1966		CD: EMI CMS 764 0742

Heimweh II (O wüsst' ich doch den Weg zurück)

London	Parsons	LP: EMI ASD 2555/1C 063 02015
March-		CD: EMI CMS 764 0742
April 1969		

Immer leiser wird mein Schlummer

London	Parsons	LP: EMI ASD 2555/1C 063 02015
March-		CD: EMI CMS 764 0742
April 1969		
Vienna	Bernstein	LP: CBS 76379
May 1972		Also unpublished video recording
Haitzendorf	Spencer	CD: RCA/BMG 09026 615472
January 1993		

In stiller Nacht/Deutsche Volkslieder

London	Parsons	LP: EMI ASD 2555/1C 063 02015
March-		CD: EMI CMS 764 0742
April 1969		

Liebestreu (O versenk', o versenk' dein Leid, mein Kind!)

London	Moore	LP: Columbia 33CX 1552
November 1957		CD: EMI CMS 764 0742
Vienna	Bernstein	LP: CBS 76379
May 1972		Also unpublished video recording

Brahms Lieder/continued

Das Mädchen spricht (Schwalbe, sagt mir an!)

London   Parsons   LP: EMI ASD 2555/1C 063 02015
March-   CD: EMI CMS 764 0742
April 1969

Mädchenlied (Auf die Nacht in der Spinnstub')

London   Moore   LP: Columbia 33CX 1693/SAX 2340
May-
June 1959

London   Parsons   LP: EMI ASD 2555/1C 063 02015
March-   CD: EMI CMS 764 0742
April 1969

Vienna   Bernstein   LP: CBS 76379
May 1972   Also unpublished video recording

Haitzendorf   Spencer   CD: RCA/BMG 09026 615472
January 1993

Die Mainacht (Wann der silberne Mond durch die Gesträuche blinkt)

London   Moore   LP: Columbia 33CX 1552
November 1957   CD: EMI CMS 764 0742

Salzburg   Werba   CD: Orfeo C331 931B
August 1963

Vienna   Bernstein   LP: CBS 76379
May 1972   Also unpublished video recording

Och Mod'r, ich well en Ding han!/Deutsche Volkslieder

Munich   Moore   LP: Columbia (Germany) C 80976/
November-   SMC 80976
December 1965   LP: Angel 60087
                                         CD: EMI CMS 764 0742

Ruhe, Süssliebchen, im Schatten

Vienna   Bernstein   LP: CBS 76379
May 1972   Also unpublished video recording

Sapphische Ode (Rosen brach ich nachts mir am dunklen Hage)

London   Moore   LP: Columbia 33CX 1552
November 1957   CD: EMI CMS 764 0742

Salzburg   Werba   CD: Orfeo C331 931B
August 1963

Vienna   Bernstein   LP: CBS 76379
May 1972   Also unpublished video recording

Brahms Lieder/continued

Der Schmied (Ich hör' meinen Schatz)

| London
November 1957 | Moore | LP: Columbia 33CX 1552
CD: EMI CMS 764 0742 |
| Haitzendorf
January 1993 | Spencer | CD: RCA/BMG 09026 615472 |

Schwesterlein, Schwesterlein, wann geh'n wir nach Haus'?/Deutsche Volkslieder

| London
March-
April 1969 | Parsons | LP: EMI ASD 2555/1C 063 02015
CD: EMI CMS 764 0742 |

Ständchen (Der Mond steht über dem Berge)

London May-June 1959	Moore	LP: Columbia 33CX 1693/SAX 2340
Salzburg August 1963	Werba	CD: Orfeo C331 931B
London March- April 1969	Parsons	LP: EMI ASD 2555/1C 063 02015 CD: EMI CMS 764 0742
Vienna May 1972	Bernstein	LP: CBS 76379 Also unpublished video recording
Haitzendorf January 1993	Spencer	CD: RCA/BMG 09026 615472

Der Tod, das ist die kühle Nacht

| London
March-
April 1969 | Parsons | LP: EMI ASD 2555/1C 063 02015
CD: EMI CMS 764 0742 |
| Vienna
May 1972 | Bernstein | LP: CBS 76379
Also unpublished video recording |

Vergebliches Ständchen (Guten Abend, mein Schatz!)

London May-June 1959	Moore	LP: Columbia 33CX 1693/SAX 2340
Munich November- December 1965	Moore	LP: Columbia (Germany) C 80976/ SMC 80976 LP: Angel 60087
London March- April 1969	Parsons	LP: EMI ASD 2555/1C 063 02015 CD: EMI CMS 764 0742
Haitzendorf January 1993	Spencer	CD: RCA/BMG 09026 615472

Brahms Lieder/concluded

Von ewiger Liebe (Dunkel, wie dunkel, in Wald und in Feld!)

Salzburg August 1963	Werba	CD: Orfeo C331 931B
London March– April 1969	Parsons	LP: EMI ASD 2555/1C 063 02015 CD: EMI CMS 764 0742
Vienna May 1972	Bernstein	LP: CBS 76379 Also unpublished video recording

Vorschneller Schwur

Salzburg August 1963	Werba	CD: Orfeo C331 931B

Wie komm' ich denn zur Tür herein?/Deutsche Volkslieder

Munich November– December 1965	Moore	LP: Columbia (Germany) C 80976/ SMC 80976 LP: Angel 60087 CD: EMI CMS 764 0742

Wie Melodien zieht es mir

London March– April 1969	Parsons	LP: EMI ASD 2555/1C 063 02015 CD: EMI CMS 764 0742

Wiegenlied (Guten Abend, gut' Nacht!)

Vienna April 1994	Spencer	CD: RCA/BMG 09026 626522 VHS Video: RCA/BMG 09026 626523

Zigeunerlieder

London May and June 1959	Moore	LP: Columbia 33CX 1693/SAX 2340 CD: EMI CMS 764 0742
Vienna May 1972	Bernstein	LP: CBS 76379 Also unpublished video recording

BRUCKNER

Mass No 3

Berlin 1962	Lorengar, Traxel, Berry St Hedwig's Choir Berlin SO Forster	LP: HMV ALP 1964/ASD 515 LP: Electrola E 80715/STE 80715 LP: EMI 1C 047 28962 Also issued on LP by World Records

DEBUSSY

Pelléas et Mélisande

Vienna
January 1991

Role of Genevieve
Ewing, Le Roux,
Van Dam, Courtis
Vienna Opera Chorus
VPO
Abbado

CD: DG 435 3442

EINEM

Der Besuch der alten Dame

Vienna
May 1971

Role of Claire
Zachanassian
Loose, Beirer,
Terkal, Wächter,
Hotter, Jungwirth
Vienna Opera Chorus
VPO
Stein

LP: Amadeo 419 5521

FRANCK

Nocturne for mezzo-soprano and orchestra

Paris
1975

Orchestre de Paris
Barenboim

LP: DG 2530 771

GIORDANO

Andrea Chenier

Walthamstow
August 1982

Role of Madelon
Caballé, Kuhlmann,
Varnay, Pavarotti,
Nucci, Krause
WNO Chorus
National PO
Chailly

LP: Decca 410 1171
CD: Decca 410 1172

GLUCK

Iphigenie in Aulis

| Salzburg
July 1962 | Role of Iphigenie
Borkh, King,
Berry, Edelmann
Vienna Opera Chorus
VPO
Böhm | LP: Penzance PR 25
Excerpt
CD: Orfeo C365 941B |

Iphigenie in Aulis: Excerpt (Lebwohl! Lass' dein Treu bewahren!)

| Berlin
1964 | Deutsche Oper
Orchestra
Hollreiser | LP: Eurodisc 71394KR/27991CR
LP: World Records CM 84/SCM 84 |

Orfeo ed Euridice: Excerpt (Che farò?)

| Berlin
March 1962 | Berlin SO
Stein
Sung in German | 45: Columbia (Germany) C 50570 |

HANDEL

Giulio Cesare

| Munich
July 1965 | Role of Cornelia
Popp, Wunderlich,
Berry, Ernst
Bavarian Radio Chorus
Munich PO
Leitner
Sung in German | CD: Melodram CDM 37059
Incorrectly dated March 1966 |

Giulio Cesare: Excerpt (V'adoro pupille)

| Berlin
March 1962 | Role of Cleopatra
Berlin SO
Stein
Sung in German | 45: Columbia (Germany) C 50570
CD: EMI CMS 764 0742 |

HAYDN

Die Schöpfung

| Berlin
February 1966 | Mezzo part in Final
Chorus
Janowitz, Wunderlich,
Krenn, Berry,
Fischer-Dieskau
Vienna Singverein
BPO
Karajan | LP: DG 643 515-643 516
LP: DG 2707 044/410 9511
CD: DG 435 0772
Excerpts
LP: DG SLPM 136 439
CD: DG 439 4542 |

HUMPERDINCK

Hänsel und Gretel

Munich 1974	Role of Knusperhexe Donath, Moffo, Auger, Popp, Berthold, Fischer-Dieskau Choirs Munich RO Eichhorn	LP: Eurodisc 85340XF CD: RCA/Eurodisc GD 69294 CD: RCA/Eurodisc 74321 252812 Excerpt LP: Eurodisc 27991CR
Cologne 1979	Role of Mother Cotrubas, Von Stade, Söderström, Welting, Kanawa, Nimsgern Cologne Opera Chorus Gürzenich-Orchester Pritchard	LP: CBS 79217 CD: Sony M2K 79217
Dresden January 1992	Role of Knusperhexe Murray, Gruberova, Jones, Bonney, Oelze, Grundheber Chorus Dresden Staatskapelle C.Davis	CD: Philips 438 0132 Excerpts CD: Philips 442 4352

MAHLER

Das Lied von der Erde

London February 1964 and July 1966	Wunderlich Philharmonia New Philharmonia Klemperer	LP: EMI AN 179/SAN 179/EL 29 04401 CD: EMI CDC 747 2312
Vienna 1967	Kmennt VSO C.Kleiber	CD: Nuova Era NE 2224 CD: Exclusive EX 92 T53
Berlin December 1970	Spiess, Laubenthal BPO Karajan	CD: Hunt CD 739
Tel Aviv May 1972	Kollo Israel PO Bernstein	LP: CBS 76105 CD: Sony SMK 47589 VHS Video: DG 072 1283 Laserdisc: DG 072 1281
Salzburg August 1972	Kollo BPO Karajan	Unpublished radio broadcast
Berlin December 1973	Kollo BPO Karajan	LP: DG 2707 082/2531 379/419 0581 CD: DG 419 0582
Prague April 1983	Moser Czech PO Neumann	CD: Praga PR 254.052

Kindertotenlieder

London October 1958	Philharmonia Vandernoot	LP: Columbia 33CX 1671/SAX 2321 LP: World Records T 703/ST 703 LP: EMI SXLP 143 6521 CD: EMI CDM 769 4992
Berlin May 1974	Berlin PO Karajan	LP: DG 2707 081/2531 147/419 4761 CD: DG 415 0962/439 6782

Lieder eines fahrenden Gesellen

London October 1958	Philharmonia Boult	LP: Columbia 33CX 1671/SAX 2321 LP: World Records T 703/ST 703 LP: EMI SXLP 143 6521 CD: EMI CDM 769 4992

Symphony No 2 "Resurrection"

Vienna February 1975	Cotrubas Vienna Opera Chorus VPO Mehta	LP: Decca SXL 6744-6745 CD: Decca 440 6152
New York 1987	Hendricks Westminster Choir NYPO Bernstein	CD: DG 423 3952/435 1622

Symphony No 3

Vienna 1975	Vienna Opera Chorus VPO Bernstein	VHS Video: DG 072 4153 Laserdisc: DG 072 4151
Prague December 1981	Prague Philharmonic Czech PO Neumann	CD: Denon (Japan) 60C 37 7288-7289 CD: Supraphon 11 19722
New York November 1987	New York Choral Artists NYPO Bernstein	CD: DG 427 3282/435 1622

Des Antonius von Padua Fischpredigt/Des Knaben Wunderhorn (Antonius zur Predigt die Kirche find't ledig)

London November 1957	Moore	LP: Columbia 33CX 1552 LP: EMI SXLP 30182 CD: EMI CMS 764 0742
Salzburg August 1963	Werba	CD: Orfeo C331 931B
New York October 1967 and February 1969	NYPO Bernstein	LP: CBS 72805/79355 CD: Sony SMK 47590
Vienna April 1968	Bernstein	LP: CBS 72716 CD: Sony SM2K 47170

Blicke mir nicht in die Lieder/Rückert-Lieder

Berlin May 1974	BPO Karajan	LP: DG 2707 082/2531 147/419 4761 CD: DG 415 0992/439 6782
Vienna 1992	VPO Muti	VHS Video: Sony SHV 48351 Laserdisc: Sony SLV 48351

Frühlingsmorgen (Es klopft ans Fenster der Lindenbaum)

London May 1959	Moore	LP: Columbia 33CX 1705/SAX 2358 LP: EMI SXLP 30182/SXLP 143 6521 CD: EMI CMS 764 0742
Vienna April 1994	Spencer	CD: RCA/BMG 09026 626522 VHS Video: RCA/BMG 09026 626523

Mahler Lieder/continued

Ging heut' morgen übers Feld/Lieder eines fahrenden Gesellen
See Lieder eines fahrenden Gesellen

Hans und Grete (Ringel, ringel Reih'n!)

London	Moore	LP: Columbia 33CX 1705/SAX 2358
May 1959		LP: EMI SXLP 30182/SXLP 143 6521
		CD: EMI CMS 764 0742

Ich atmet' einen linden Duft/Rückert-Lieder

London	Moore	LP: Columbia 33CX 1705/SAX 2358
May 1959		LP: EMI SXLP 30182
		CD: EMI CMS 764 0742
London	Philharmonia	LP: EMI ASD 2391/SXLP 27 00001
February 1964	Klemperer	CD: EMI CDM 769 4992
Berlin	BPO	LP: DG 2707 082/2531 147/419 4761
May 1974	Karajan	CD: DG 415 0992/439 6782
Vienna	VPO	VHS Video: Sony SHV 48351
1992	Muti	Laserdisc: Sony SLV 48351

Ich bin der Welt abhanden gekommen/Rückert-Lieder

London	Moore	LP: Columbia 33CX 1552
November 1957		LP: EMI SXLP 30182
		CD: EMI CMS 764 0742
Salzburg	Werba	CD: Orfeo C331 931B
August 1963		
London	Philharmonia	LP: EMI ASD 2391/SXLP 27 000001
February 1964	Klemperer	CD: EMI CDM 769 4992
Berlin	BPO	LP: DG 2707 082/2531 147/419 4761
May 1974	Karajan	CD: DG 415 0992/439 6782
Haitzendorf	Spencer	CD: RCA/BMG 09026 615472
January 1993		
Vienna	VPO	VHS Video: Sony SHV 48351
1992	Muti	Laserdisc: Sony SLV 48351

Ich ging mit Lust durch einen grünen Wald

London	Moore	LP: Columbia 33CX 1705/SAX 2358
May 1959		LP: EMI SXLP 30182/SXLP 143 6521
		CD: EMI CMS 764 0742
Salzburg	Werba	CD: Orfeo C331 931B
August 1963		
Vienna	Spencer	CD: RCA/BMG 09026 626522
April 1994		

Mahler Lieder/continued

Ich hab' ein glühend Messer/Lieder eines fahrenden Gesellen
See Lieder eines fahrenden Gesellen

In diesem Wetter, in diesem Braus/Kindertotenlieder
See Kindertotenlieder

Das irdische Leben/Des Knaben Wunderhorn (Mutter, ach Mutter, es hungert mich!)

London May 1959	Moore	LP: Columbia 33CX 1705/SAX 2358 CD: EMI CMS 764 0742
London February 1964	Philharmonia Klemperer	LP: EMI ASD 2391/SXLP 27 00001 CD: EMI CDM 769 4992
New York October 1967 and February 1969	NYPO Bernstein	LP: CBS 72805/79355 CD: Sony SMK 47590
Vienna April 1968	Bernstein	LP: CBS 72716 CD: Sony SM2K 47170
Haitzendorf January 1993	Spencer	CD: RCA/BMG 09026 615472

Liebst du um Schönheit/Rückert-Lieder

London May 1959	Moore	LP: Columbia 33CX 1705/SAX 2358 LP: EMI SXLP 143 6521 CD: EMI CMS 764 0742
Berlin May 1974	BPO Karajan	LP: DG 2707 082/2531 147/419 4761 CD: DG 415 0992/439 6782
Vienna 1992	VPO Muti	VHS Video: Sony SHV 48351 Laserdisc: Sony SLV 48351

Lied des Verfolgten im Turm/Des Knaben Wunderhorn (Die Gedanken sind frei)

New York October 1967 and February 1969	Berry NYPO Bernstein	LP: CBS 72805/79355 CD: Sony SMK 47590
Vienna April 1968	Berry Bernstein	LP: CBS 72716 CD: Sony SM2K 47170

Lob des hohen Verstandes/Des Knaben Wunderhorn (Einstmal in einem tiefen Tal)

London	Moore	LP: Columbia 33CX 1705/SAX 2358
May 1959		CD: EMI CMS 764 0742

Nun seh' ich wohl, warum so dunkle Flammen/Kindertotenlieder
See Kindertotenlieder

Nun will die Sonn' so hell aufgeh'n/Kindertotenlieder
See Kindertotenlieder

Oft denk' ich, sie sind nur ausgegangen/Kindertotenlieder
See Kindertotenlieder

Phantasie aus Don Juan (Das Mägdlein trat aus dem Fischerhaus)

Vienna	Spencer	CD: RCA/BMG 09026 626522
April 1994		VHS Video: RCA/BMG 09026 626523

Rheinlegendchen/Des Knaben Wunderhorn (Bald gras' ich am Neckar)

London	Moore	LP: Columbia 33CX 1552
November 1957		LP: EMI SXLP 30182
		CD: EMI CMS 764 0742
New York	NYPO	LP: CBS 72805/79355
October 1967	Bernstein	CD: Sony SMK 47590
and February		
1969		
Vienna	Bernstein	LP: CBS 72716
April 1968		CD: Sony SM2K 47170
Haitzendorf	Spencer	CD: RCA/BMG 09026 615472
January 1993		

Scheiden und Meiden (Es ritten drei Ritter zum Tore hinaus)

Vienna	Spencer	CD: RCA/BMG 09026 626522
April 1994		

Der Schildwache Nachtlied/Des Knaben Wunderhorn (Ich kann und mag nicht
fröhlich sein)

London May 1959	Moore	LP: Columbia 33CX 1705/SAX 2358 LP: EMI SXLP 143 6521 CD: EMI CMS 764 0742
New York October 1967 and February 1969	Berry NYPO Bernstein	LP: CBS 72805/79355 CD: Sony SMK 47590
Vienna April 1968	Berry Bernstein	LP: CBS 72716 CD: Sony SM2K 47170

Trost im Unglück/Des Knaben Wunderhorn (Wohlan, die Zeit ist kommen!)

New York October 1967 and February 1969	Berry NYPO Bernstein	LP: CBS 72805/79355 CD: Sony SMK 47590
Vienna April 1968	Berry Bernstein	LP: CBS 72716 CD: Sony SM2K 47170

Um Mitternacht/Rückert-Lieder

London May 1959	Moore	LP: Columbia 33CX 1705/SAX 2358 CD: EMI CMS 764 0742
London February 1964	Philharmonia Klemperer	LP: EMI ASD 2391/SXLP 27 00001 CD: EMI CDM 769 4992
Berlin May 1974	BPO Karajan	LP: DG 2707 082/2531 147/419 4761 CD: DG 415 0992/439 6782
Haitzendorf January 1993	Spencer	CD: RCA/BMG 09026 615472
Vienna 1992	VPO Muti	VHS Video: Sony SHV 48351 Laserdisc: Sony SLV 48351

Um schlimme Kinder artig zu machen/Des Knaben Wunderhorn (Es kamm ein Herr
zum Schlösseli)

London May 1959	Moore	LP: Columbia 33CX 1705/SAX 2358 LP: EMI HQM 1072/SXLP 30182 CD: EMI CMS 764 0742
Vienna April 1994	Spencer	CD: RCA/BMG 09026 626522 VHS Video: RCA/BMG 09026 626523

Mahler Lieder/continued

Urlicht/Des Knaben Wunderhorn (O Mensch, gib' acht!)

Salzburg August 1963	Werba	CD: Orfeo C331 931B
New York October 1967 and February 1969	NYPO Bernstein	LP: CBS 72805/79355 CD: Sony SMK 47590
Vienna April 1968	Bernstein	LP: CBS 72716 CD: Sony SM2K 47170

Verlor'ne Müh'/Des Knaben Wunderhorn (Büble, wir wolle ausse gehe!)

New York October 1967 and February 1969	Berry NYPO Bernstein	LP: CBS 72805/79355 CD: Sony SMK 47590
Vienna April 1968	Berry Bernstein	LP: CBS 72716 CD: Sony SM2K 47170

Wenn dein Mütterlein tritt zur Tür herein (Kindertotenlieder)
See Kindertotenlieder

Wenn mein Schatz Hochzeit macht/Lieder eines fahrenden Gesellen
See Lieder eines fahrenden Gesellen

Wer hat dies Liedlein erdacht/Des Knaben Wunderhorn (Dort oben am Berg in dem hohen Haus)

London May 1959	Moore	LP: Columbia 33CX 1705/SAX 2358 LP: EMI SXLP 143 6521 CD: EMI CMS 764 0742
New York October 1967 and February 1969	NYPO Bernstein	LP: CBS 72805/79355 CD: Sony SMK 47590
Vienna April 1968	Bernstein	LP: CBS 72716 CD: Sony SM2K 47170

Wo die schönen Trompeten blasen/Des Knaben Wunderhorn (Wer ist denn draussen und wer klopfet an?)

London May 1959	Moore	LP: Columbia 33CX 1705/SAX 2358 CD: EMI CMS 764 0742
London February 1964	Philharmonia Klemperer	LP: EMI ASD 2391/SXLP 27 00001 CD: EMI CDM 769 4992
New York October 1967 and February 1969	NYPO Bernstein	LP: CBS 72805/79355 CD: Sony SMK 47590
Vienna April 1968	Bernstein	LP: CBS 72716 CD: Sony SM2K 47170

Die zwei blauen Augen von meinem Schatz/Lieder eines fahrenden Gesellen
See Lieder eines fahrenden Gesellen

MONTEVERDI

L'Incoronazione di Poppea

Paris March 1978	Role of Ottavia Jones, Masterson, Vickers, Stilwell, Ghiaurov Paris Opéra Orchestra & Chorus Rudel	LP: Legendary LR 160 Also unpublished video recording

MOZART

Così fan tutte

Vienna May and June 1955	Role of Dorabella Della Casa, Loose, Dermota, Kunz, Schöffler Vienna Opera Chorus VPO Böhm	LP: Decca LXT 5107-5109 LP: Decca GOM 543-545/GOS 543-545 CD: Decca 417 1852 Excerpts LP: Decca ADD 208/SDD 208
Salzburg July 1960	Schwarzkopf, Sciutti, Kmennt, Prey, Dönch Vienna Opera Chorus VPO Böhm	LP: Melodram MEL 708 LP: Movimento musica 03.026
Salzburg August 1962	Schwarzkopf, Sciutti, Kmennt, Prey, Dönch Vienna Opera Chorus VPO Böhm	CD: Hunt CDMP 455
London September 1962	Schwarzkopf, Steffek, Kraus, Taddei, Berry Philharmonia Orchestra & Chorus Böhm	LP: EMI AN 103-106/SAN 103-106 LP: EMI SLS 5028 CD: EMI CMS 769 3302 Excerpts LP: EMI ALP 2265/ASD 2265 LP: EMI SXLP 30457
Vienna 1970	Janowitz, Miljakovic, Alva, Prey, Berry Vienna Opera Chorus VPO Böhm	Unpublished video recording

Così fan tutte, excerpts

Salzburg August 1958	Schwarzkopf, Sciutti, Alva, Panerai, Schmidt Vienna Opera Chorus VPO Böhm	LP: Gioielli della lirica GML 52

Così fan tutte: Excerpts (Prenderò quel brunettino; Il core vi dono)

Salzburg August 1959	Seefried, Panerai VPO Böhm	CD: Orfeo C365 941B

Don Giovanni

London June and July 1966	Role of Donna Elvira Watson, Freni, Gedda, Ghiaurov, Berry, Crass New Philharmonia Orchestra & Chorus Klemperer	LP: EMI AN 172-175/SAN 172-175 LP: EMI SLS 923/143 4623 CD: EMI CMS 763 8412 Excerpts LP: EMI ASD 2508 CD: EMI CDM 769 0552

Le Nozze di Figaro

Vienna April 1956	Role of Cherubino Jurinac, Streich, Berry, Schöffler Vienna Opera Chorus VSO Böhm	LP: Philips A 00357-00359 L LP: Philips GL 5777-5779 LP: Philips SFL 14012-14014 LP: Philips 6706 006 CD: Philips 438 6702 Excerpts LP: Philips GL 5666
Salzburg July 1957	Schwarzkopf, Seefried, Kunz, Fischer-Dieskau Vienna Opera Chorus VPO Böhm	LP: Melodram MEL 709 CD: Di Stefano GDS 310209 CD: Orfeo C296 923D Excerpts CD: Verona 27092-27094 CD: Orfeo C365 941B

Die Zauberflöte

Vienna May 1955	Role of 2nd Lady Güden, Lipp, Simoneau, Berry, Schöffler, Böhme Vienna Opera Chorus VPO Böhm	LP: Decca LXT 5085-5087/ SXL 2215-2217 LP: Decca GOM 501-503/GOS 501-503 CD: Decca 414 3622
London March and April 1964	Janowitz, Popp, Gedda, Berry, Frick, Crass Philharmonia Orchestra & Chorus Klemperer	LP: EMI AN 137-139/SAN 137-139 LP: EMI SLS 912 CD: EMI CMS 769 9712 Excerpts LP: EMI ALP 2314/ASD 2314 LP: EMI ESD 100 3261 CD: EMI CDM 763 4512

Ch'io mi scordi di te?, concert aria

Salzburg August 1963	Anda Mozarteum-Orchester Paumgartner	CD: Orfeo C330 031B

Mass in C minor

Vienna 1958	Lipp, Dickie, Berry Vienna Oratorio Choir VSO Grossmann	LP: Vox PL 10270 LP: Turnabout TV 34174 CD: Preiser 90053 CD: Vox 0013

Requiem

Vienna 1972	Janowitz, Schreier, Berry Vienna Opera Chorus VPO Böhm	Unpublished video recording
London September 1978	Donath, Tear, Lloyd Philharmonia Orchestra & Chorus Giulini	LP: EMI ASD 3723 CD: EMI CDZ 762 5182

OFFENBACH

Les contes d'Hoffmann

Paris 1988	Role of Antonia's Mother Gruberova, Domingo, Bacquier, Morris, Diaz ORTF Chorus Orchestre National Ozawa	CD: DG 427 6822

ORFF

De temporum fine comoedia

Leverkusen July 1973	Schreier, Greindl WDR & RIAS Choirs WDR Orchestra Karajan	LP: DG 2530 432 CD: DG 429 8592

PERGOLESI

Stabat mater

Berlin	Lear	LP: Philips SAL 3590/6586 010
1965	RIAS Choir	
	Berlin RO	
	Maazel	

PFITZNER

Palestrina

Vienna	Role of Silla	CD: Myto MCD 92259
December 1964	Jurinac, Janowitz,	
	Wunderlich, Stolze,	
	Kreppel, Wiener,	
	Welter	
	Vienna Opera Chorus	
	VPO	
	Heger	

Lieder: Gretel; Hast du von den Fischerkindern; Ist der Himmel darum im Lenz so blau?; Venus mater; Zum Abschied meiner Tochter

| Salzburg | Werba | CD: Orfeo C331 931B |
| July 1968 | | |

PUCCINI

Madama Butterfly

Vienna January 1974	Role of Suzuki Freni, Pavarotti, Kerns Vienna Opera Chorus VPO Karajan	LP: Decca SET 584-586 CD: Decca 417 5772 Excerpts LP: Decca SET 605 CD: Decca 421 2472
Vienna November 1974 (soundtrack) and·Salzburg December 1974 (picture)	Freni, Domingo, Kerns Vienna Opera Chorus VPO Karajan	VHS Video: Decca 071 4043 Laserdisc: Decca 071 4041

Suor Angelica

London 1978	Role of Principessa Sutherland London Opera Chorus National PO Bonynge	LP: Decca SET 627

RACHMANINOV

Songs: Cease thy singing, maiden fair!; Harvest of sorrow

London November 1965- March 1966	Parsons	LP: Columbia 33CX 5274/SAX 5274 LP: EMI ESD 100 6151 CD: EMI CMS 764 0742

RAVEL

3 Chansons madécasses: Nahandove; Aoua! Aoua!; Il est doux

London November 1965- March 1966	Whittaker, flute Fleming, cello Parsons	LP: Columbia 33CX 5274/SAX 5274 LP: EMI ESD 100 6151 CD: EMI CMS 764 0742

REGER

An die Hoffnung

London	New Philharmonia	EMI unpublished
July 1966	Mackerras	

Lieder: Der Brief; Waldeinsamkeit

Munich	Moore	LP: Columbia (Germany) C 80976/
October–		SMC 80976
December 1965		LP: Angel 60087
		CD: EMI CMS 764 0742

ROSSINI

La Cenerentola

Vienna	Role of Angelina	Unpublished radio broadcast
October 1959	Loose, D.Hermann,	
	Kmennt, Berry,	
	Dönch	
	Vienna Opera Chorus	
	VPO	
	Erede	

Il Barbiere di Siviglia: Excerpt (Una voce poco fa)

Berlin	Deutsche Oper	LP: Eurodisc 71394KR/27991CR
1964	Orchestra	LP: World Records CM 84/SCM 84
	Hollreiser	
	Sung in German	

Duetto buffo di due gatti

Munich	Berry	LP: Columbia (Germany) C 80976/
October–	Moore	SMC 80976
December 1965		LP: Angel 60087

La regata veneziana: Anzoleta avanti la regata; Anzoleta co passa la regata; Anzoleta dopo la regata

Munich	Moore	LP: Columbia (Germany) C 80976/
October–		SMC 80976
December 1965		LP: Angel 60087
		CD: EMI CMS 764 0742

SAINT-SAENS

Samson et Dalila

Munich	Role of Dalila	LP: Eurodisc XG 86977
1973	King, Weikl	LP: RCA ARL3-0662/LRL3-5017
	Bavarian Radio	CD: Eurodisc 352875
	Chorus	Excerpt
	Munich RO	LP: Eurodisc 27991CR
	Patanè	Also unpublished video recording

Une flûte invisible soupire dans les vergers

London	Whittaker, flute	LP: Columbia 33CX 5274/SAX 5274
November 1965–	Moore	LP: EMI ESD 100 6151
March 1966		CD: EMI CMS 764 0742

SCHUBERT

Winterreise

Vienna	Levine	CD: DG 423 3662/445 5212
December 1986		

Der Lindenbaum (Winterreise)

Vienna	Spencer	CD: RCA/BMG 09026 616522
April 1994		VHS Video: RCA/BMG 09026 626523

Die Allmacht (Gross ist Jehova, der Herr!)

London	Moore	LP: Columbia 33CX 1552
November 1957		CD: EMI CMS 764 0742

An den Mond (Füllest wieder Busch und Tal)

Vienna	Gage	LP: DG 2530 528
June and		CD: DG 431 4762
July 1974		CD: DG (Japan) POCG 9022-9029

An die Musik (Du holde Kunst, in wieviel grauen Stunden)

London	Parsons	LP: Columbia SAX 5272
November 1961		LP: EMI SXLP 30182
		CD: EMI CDZ 252 3732/CMS 764 0742

An die Nachtigall (Er liegt und schläft an meinem Herzen)

Vienna   Gage   LP: DG 2530 404
June 1973   CD: DG 431 4762
                                    CD: DG (Japan) POCG 9022-9029

Am Bach im Frühling (Du brachst sie nun, die kalte Rinde)

Vienna   Gage   LP: DG 2530 404/2740 188
June 1973   CD: DG 431 4762
                                    CD: DG (Japan) POCG 9022-9029

Auf dem Flusse/Winterreise (Der du so lustig rauschtest)
See Winterreise

Auf dem Wasser zu singen (Mitten im Schimmer der spiegelnden Wellen)

London   Parsons   LP: Columbia SAX 5272
November 1961   LP: EMI SXLP 30182
                                    CD: EMI CDZ 252 3732/CMS 764 0742

Auf der Donau (Auf der Wellen Spiegel schwimmt der Kahn)

Vienna   Gage   LP: DG 2530 404
June 1973   CD: DG 431 4762
                                    CD: DG (Japan) POCG 9022-9029

Bertas Lied in der Nacht (Nacht umhüllt mit wehendem Flügel)

Vienna   Gage   LP: DG 2530 528
June and   CD: DG 431 4762
July 1974   CD: DG (Japan) POCG 9022-9029

Dass sie hier gewesen (Dass der Ostwind Düfte)

Vienna   Gage   LP: DG 2530 528
June and   CD: DG 431 4762
July 1974   CD: DG (Japan) POCG 9022-9029

Einsamkeit/Winterreise (Wie eine trübe Wolke durch heit're Lüfte geht)
See Winterreise

Schubert Lieder/continued

Ellens Gesang III (Ave Maria! Jungfrau mild!)

London	Parsons	LP: Columbia SAX 5272
November 1961		LP: EMI SXLP 30182
		CD: EMI CDZ 252 3732/CMS 764 0742

Vienna	Gage	LP: DG 2530 404/2535 656
June 1973		CD: DG 431 4762
		CD: DG (Japan) POCG 9022-9029

Erlkönig (Wer reitet so spät durch Nacht und Wind?)

| London | Parsons | LP: Columbia SAX 5272 |
| November 1961 | | CD: EMI CDZ 252 3732/CMS 764 0742 |

Erstarrung/Winterreise (Ich such' im Schnee vergebens)
See Winterreise

Fischerweise (Den Fischer fechten Sorgen)

| London | Moore | LP: Columbia 33CX 1552 |
| November 1957 | | CD: EMI CMS 764 0742 |

Die Forelle (In einem Bächlein helle)

London	Parsons	LP: Columbia SAX 5272
November 1961		LP: EMI SXLP 30182
		CD: EMI CDZ 252 3732/CMS 764 0742

Frühlingsglaube (Die linden Düfte sind erwacht)

| London | Parsons | LP: Columbia SAX 5272 |
| November 1961 | | CD: EMI CDZ 252 3732/CMS 764 0742 |

Vienna	Gage	LP: DG 2530 404/2740 188
June 1973		CD: DG 431 4762
		CD: DG (Japan) POCG 9022-9029

| Vienna | Spencer | CD: RCA/BMG 09026 626522 |
| April 1994 | | VHS Video: RCA/BMG 09026 626523 |

Frühlingstraum/Winterreise (Ich träumte von bunten Blumen)
See Winterreise

Ganymed (Wie im Morgenglanze du rings mich anglühst)

| London | Parsons | LP: Columbia SAX 5272 |
| November 1961 | | CD: EMI CDZ 252 3732/CMS 764 0742 |

Schubert Lieder/continued

Gefror'ne Tränen fallen/Winterreise
See Winterreise

Geheimes (Sag' an, wer lehrt dich Lieder?)

Vienna	Gage	CD: RCA/BMG 09026 626522
April 1994		VHS Video: RCA/BMG 09026 626523

Der greise Kopf/Winterreise (Der Reif hat einen weissen Schein mir übers Haar gestreuet)
See Winterreise

Gretchen am Spinnrade (Meine Ruh' ist hin, mein Herz ist schwer!)

London	Parsons	LP: Columbia SAX 5272
November 1961		CD: EMI CDZ 252 3732/CMS 764 0742
Vienna	Gage	LP: DG 2530 404/2740 188
June 1973		CD: DG 431 4762
		CD: DG (Japan) POCG 9022-9029

Gute Nacht/Winterreise (Fremd bin ich eingezogen)
See Winterreise

Heidenröslein (Sah ein Knab' ein Röslein steh'n)

Vienna	Spencer	CD: RCA/BMG 09026 626522
April 1994		VHS Video: RCA/BMG 09026 626523

Der Hirt auf dem Felsen (Wenn auf dem höchsten Fels ich steh')

London	De Peyer, clarinet	LP: Columbia 33CX 5274/SAX 5274
November 1965	Parsons	LP: EMI SXLP 30182/ESD 100 6151
		CD: EMI CDZ 252 3732/CMS 764 0742

Im Abendrot (O wie schön ist deine Welt!)

Vienna	Gage	LP: DG 2530 404/2535 656
June 1973		CD: DG 431 4762
		CD: DG (Japan) POCG 9022-9029
Vienna	Spencer	CD: RCA/BMG 09026 626522
April 1994		VHS Video: RCA/BMG 09026 626523

Im Dorfe/Winterreise (Es bellen die Hunde, es rasseln die Ketten)
See Winterreise

Schubert Lieder/continued

Die junge Nonne (Wie braust durch die Wipfel der heulende Sturm)

Vienna	Gage	LP: DG 2530 404
June 1973		CD: DG 431 4762
		CD: DG (Japan) POCG 9022-9029

Klärchens Lied (Freudvoll und leidvoll)

Vienna	Gage	LP: DG 2530 528
June and		CD: DG 431 4762
July 1974		CD: DG (Japan) POCG 9022-9029

Der König in Thule (Es war ein König in Thule)

Vienna	Gage	LP: DG 2530 404/2740 188
June 1973		CD: DG 431 4762
		CD: DG (Japan) POCG 9022-9029

Die Krähe/Winterreise (Eine Krähe war mit mir aus der Stadt gezogen)
See Winterreise

Lachen und Weinen zu jeglicher Stunde

| London | Parsons | LP: Columbia SAX 5272 |
| November 1961 | | CD: EMI CDZ 252 3732/CMS 764 0742 |

Vienna	Gage	LP: DG 2530 404/2535 656/2740 188
June 1973		CD: DG 431 4762
		CD: DG (Japan) POCG 9022-9029

Der Leiermann/Winterreise (Drüben hinterm Dorfe steht ein Leiermann)
See Winterreise

Letzte Hoffnung/Winterreise (Hie und da ist an den Bäumen)
See Winterreise

Lied der Anne Lyle (Wärst du bei mir im Lebenstal)

Vienna	Gage	LP: DG 2530 528
June and		CD: DG 431 4762
July 1974		CD: DG (Japan) POCG 9022-9029

Schubert Lieder/continued

Lied der Mignon (Heiss mich nicht reden)

Vienna   Gage   LP: DG 2530 528
June and   CD: DG 431 4762
July 1974   CD: DG (Japan) POCG 9022-9029

Lied der Mignon (Nur wer die Sehnsucht kennt)

Vienna   Gage   LP: DG 2530 404
June 1973   CD: DG 431 4762
                                   CD: DG (Japan) POCG 9022-9029

Lied der Mignon (So lasst mich scheinen)

Vienna   Gage   LP: DG 2530 528
June and   CD: DG 431 4762
July 1974   CD: DG (Japan) POCG 9022-9029

Lilla an die Morgenröte (Wie schön bist du, du güld'ne Morgenröte!)

Vienna   Gage   LP: DG 2530 528
June and   CD: DG 431 4762
July 1974   CD: DG (Japan) POCG 9022-9029

Der Lindenbaum/Winterreise (Am Brunnen vor dem Tore)
See Winterreise

Litanei auf das Fest „Aller Seelen" (Ruh'n in Frieden alle Seelen)

London   Parsons   LP: Columbia SAX 5272
November 1961   CD: EMI CDZ 252 3732/CMS 764 0742

Das Mädchen (Wie so innig, möcht' ich sagen)

Vienna   Gage   LP: DG 2530 528
June and   CD: DG 431 4762
July 1974   CD: DG (Japan) POCG 9022-9029

Des Mädchens Klage (Der Eichwald braust)

Vienna   Gage   LP: DG 2530 404
June 1973   CD: DG 431 4762
                                   CD: DG (Japan) POCG 9022-9029

Schubert Lieder/continued

Mignons Gesang (Kennst du das Land, wo die Zitronen blüh'n?)

Vienna	Gage	LP: DG 2530 528/2740 188
June and		CD: DG 431 4762
July 1974		CD: DG (Japan) POCG 9022-9029

Der Musensohn (Durch Feld und Wald zu schweifen)

London	Parsons	LP: Columbia SAX 5272
November 1961		LP: EMI SXLP 30182
		CD: EMI CDZ 252 3732/CMS 764 0742
Vienna	Spencer	CD: RCA/BMG 09026 626522
June 1994		VHS Video: RCA/BMG 09026 626523

Mut!/Winterreise (Fliegt der Schnee mir ins Gesicht)
See Winterreise

Die Nebensonnen/Winterreise (Drei Sonnen sah ich am Himmel steh'n)
See Winterreise

Die Post/Winterreise (Von der Strasse her ein Posthorn klingt)
See Winterreise

Rast/Winterreise (Nun merk' ich erst, wie müd' ich bin)
See Winterreise

Romanze (Der Vollmond strahlt auf Bergeshöh'n)

Vienna	Gage	LP: DG 2530 404
June 1973		CD: DG 431 4762
		CD: DG (Japan) POCG 9022-9029

Die Rose (Es lockte schöne Wärme)

Vienna	Gage	LP: DG 2530 404
June 1973		CD: DG 431 4762
		CD: DG (Japan) POCG 9022-9029

Rückblick/Winterreise (Es brennt mir unter beiden Sohlen)
See Winterreise

Schubert Lieder/continued

Sehnsucht (Ach, aus dieses Tales Gründen)

Vienna June and July 1974	Gage	LP: DG 2530 528 CD: DG 431 4762 CD: DG (Japan) POCG 9022-9029

Vienna April 1994	Spencer	CD: RCA/BMG 09026 626522 VHS Video: RCA/BMG 09026 626523

Ständchen (Zögernd leise)

Vienna June and July 1974	ORF Choir Gage	LP: DG 2530 528 CD: DG 431 4762 CD: DG (Japan) POCG 9022-9029

Der stürmische. Morgen/Winterreise (Wie hat der Sturm zerrissen des Himmels graues Kleid!)
See Winterreise

Täuschung/Winterreise (Ein Licht tanzt freundlich vor mir her)
See Winterreise

Der Tod und das Mädchen (Vorüber, ach vorüber! Geh', wilder Knochenmann!)

London November 1961	Parsons	LP: Columbia SAX 5272 CD: EMI CDZ 252 3732/CMS 764 0742

Vienna June 1973	Gage	LP: DG 2530 404/2740 188 CD: DG 431 4762 CD: DG (Japan) POCG 9022-9029

Vienna April 1994	Spencer	CD: RCA/BMG 09026 626522 VHS Video: RCA/BMG 09026 626523

Schubert Lieder/concluded

Wasserflut/Winterreise (Manche Trän' aus meinen Augen)
See Winterreise

Der Wegweiser/Winterreise (Was vermeid' ich denn die Wege, wo die andren
Wandrer geh'n?)
See Winterreise

Wehmut (Wenn ich durch Wald und Fluren geh')

Vienna   Gage   LP: DG 2530 528
June and   CD: DG 431 4762
July 1974   CD: DG (Japan) POCG 9022-9029

Die Wetterfahne/Winterreise (Der Wind spielt mit der Wetterfahne)
See Winterreise

Das Wirtshaus/Winterreise (Auf einen Totenacker hat mich mein Weg gebracht)
See Winterreise

Der Zwerg (Im trüben Licht verschwinden schon die Berge)

Vienna   Gage   LP: DG 2530 528
June and   CD: DG 431 4762
July 1974   CD: DG (Japan) POCG 9022-9029

SCHUMANN

Frauenliebe und -Leben, song cycle

London June 1959	Moore	LP: Columbia 33CX 1693/SAX 2340 CD: EMI CMS 764 0742

Prague May 1966	Parsons	CD: Praga PR 254.052

Aus den hebräischen Gesängen (Mein Herz ist stumm)

Haitzendorf January 1993	Spencer	CD: RCA/BMG 09026 615472

Der Himmel hat eine Träne geweinet

Haitzendorf January 1993	Spencer	CD: RCA/BMG 09026 615472

Im Walde/Liederkreis op 39 (Es zog eine Hochzeit den Berg entlang)

Vienna 1968	Werba	LP: DG SLPM 139 386

Märzveilchen (Der Himmel wölbt sich rein und klar)

Haitzendorf January 1993	Spencer	CD: RCA/BMG 09026 615472

Mondnacht/Liederkreis op 39 (Es war, als hätt' der Himmel)

Vienna 1968	Werba	LP: DG SLPM 139 386

Haitzendorf January 1993	Spencer	CD: RCA/BMG 09026 615472

Schumann Lieder/concluded

Der Nussbaum (Es grünet ein Nussbaum vor dem Haus)

Haitzendorf   Spencer   CD: RCA/BMG 09026 615472
January 1993

Schöne Fremde/Liederkreis op 39 (Es rauschen die Wipfel und schauern)

Vienna   Werba   LP: DG SLPM 139 386
1968

Die Stille/Liederkreis op 39 (Es weiss und rät es doch keiner)

Vienna   Werba   LP: DG SLPM 139 386
1968

Haitzendorf   Spencer   CD: RCA/BMG 09026 615472
January 1993

Stille Tränen (Du bist vom Schlaf erstanden)

Haitzendorf   Spencer   CD: RCA/BMG 09026 615472
January 1993

Waldesgespräch/Liederkreis op 39 (Es ist schon spät, es ist schon kalt)

Vienna   Werba   LP: DG SLPM 139 386
1968

Wehmut/Liederkreis op 39 (Ich kann wohl manchmal singen)

Vienna   Werba   LP: DG SLPM 139 386
1968

SMETANA

The Bartered Bride, Querschnitt

Hamburg
February 1955

Role of Ludmila
Berger, Höffgen,
Schock, Frick,
Nissen
Hamburg Opera Chorus
NWD Philharmonie
Schüchter
Sung in German

LP: Electrola E 60063
LP: EMI 1C 047 28568M
Excerpt
78: Electrola DB 11582
45: Electrola E 30097

JOHANN STRAUSS

Die Fledermaus

London
June and
July 1959

Role of Orlofsky
Lipp, Scheyrer,
Terkal, Dermota,
Kunz, Berry,
Wächter
Philharmonia
Orchestra & Chorus
Ackermann

LP: Columbia 33CX 1688-1689/
SAX 2336-2337
LP: EMI 1C 147 01652-01653
LP: EMI CFPD 4702
CD: EMI CDCFPD 4702
Excerpts
LP: EMI XLP 20091/SXLP 20091

RICHARD STRAUSS

Ariadne auf Naxos: Excerpt (Seien wir wieder gut!)

| Salzburg
August 1955 | Role of Composer
Schöffler
VPO
Böhm | CD: Orfeo C365 941B |

Ariadne auf Naxos: Excerpt (Es gibt ein Reich)

| Salzburg
July 1964 | Role of Ariadne
VPO
Böhm | CD: Orfeo C365 941B |
| Berlin
1964 | Deutsche Oper
Orchestra
Hollreiser | LP: Eurodisc 71394KR/27991CR
LP: World Records CM 84/SCM 84 |

Capriccio

| London
September 1957 | Role of Clairon
Schwarzkopf, Moffo,
Gedda, Wächter,
Fischer-Dieskau,
Schmitt-Walter,
Hotter
Philharmonia
Sawallisch | LP: Columbia 33CX 1600-1602
LP: World Records OC 230-232
LP: EMI 143 5243
CD: EMI CDS 749 0148
Excerpts
LP: World Records OH 233 |
| Vienna
March 1964 | Della Casa, Popp,
Wunderlich, Kmennt,
Kerns, Berry,
Wiener
VPO
Prêtre | Unpublished private recording |

Elektra

| New York
December 1984 | Role of Klytemnestra
Vinzing, J.Meier,
Cassilly, Estes
Metropoloitan Opera
Orchestra & Chorus
Levine | Unpublished Met broadcast |
| Boston
November 1988 | Behrens, Secunde,
Ulfung, Hynninen
Tanglewood Chorus
Boston SO
Ozawa | CD: Philips 422 5742 |

Elektra: Excerpt (Was willst du, fremder Mensch?)

Berlin	Role of Elektra	LP: Eurodisc 71187KR/27991KR
1964	Berry	LP: World Records CM 70/SCM 70
	Deutsche Oper	
	Orchestra	
	Hollreiser	

Die Frau ohne Schatten

Vienna	Role of Färberin	CD: Nuova Era NE 2288-2290
June 1964	Rysanek, G.Hoffman,	CD: Hunt CDKAR 207
	Thomas, Berry	
	Vienna Opera Chorus	
	VPO	
	Karajan	

New York	Rysanek, Dalis,	Unpublished Met broadcast
December 1966	King, Berry	
	Metropolitan Opera	
	Orchestra & Chorus	
	Böhm	

New York	Rysanek, Dalis,	Unpublished Met broadcast
March 1969	King, Berry	
	Metropolitan Opera	
	Orchestra & Chorus	
	Böhm	

New York	Rysanek, Dalis,	Unpublished Met broadcast
January 1971	Nagy, Berry	
	Metropolitan Opera	
	Orchestra & Chorus	
	Böhm	

Salzburg	Rysanek, Hesse,	Unpublished radio broadcast
August 1974	King, Berry	Schweigt doch, ihr Stimmen/
	Vienna Opera Chorus	Barak mein Mann!
	VPO	CD: Orfeo C365 941B
	Böhm	

Die Frau ohne Schatten: Excerpt (Barak, mein Mann!)

Berlin	Berry	LP: Eurodisc 71187KR/27991CR
1964	Deutsche Oper	LP: World Records CM 70/SCM 70
	Orchestra	
	Hollreiser	

Der Rosenkavalier

London December 1956	Role of Oktavian Schwarzkopf, Stich-Randall, Gedda, Edelmann, Wächter Chorus Philharmonia Karajan	LP: Columbia 33CX 1492-1495/ SAX 2269-2272 LP: EMI SLS 810/EX 29 00453 CD: EMI CDS 749 3542 Excerpts LP: Columbia 33CX 1777/SAX 2423
New York December 1959	Della Casa, Söderström, Fernandi, Czerwenka, Herbert Metropolitan Opera Orchestra & Chorus Leinsdorf	Unpublished Met broadcast
New York February 1969	Rysanek, Grist, Gedda, Berry, Knoll Metropolitan Opera Orchestra & Chorus Böhm	Unpublished Met broadcast
New York February 1970	Rysanek, Popp, Gedda, Berry, Knoll Metropolitan Opera Orchestra & Chorus Böhm	Unpublished Met broadcast
Moscow October 1971	Rysanek, De Groote, Blankenship, Jungwirth, Kunz Vienna Opera Chorus VPO Krips	LP: Melodiya C10 28033 007 Guest performance by Vienna State Opera
Salzburg July 1969	Role of Marschallin Mathis, Troyanos, De Ridder, Adam, Wiener Vienna Opera Chorus VPO Böhm	CD: DG 445 3382/445 4912 Excerpt CD: Orfeo C365 941B
Vienna March and April 1971	Jones, Popp, Domingo, Berry, Gutstein Vienna Opera Cghorus VPO Bernstein	LP: CBS 77416 CD: Sony M3K 42564

Der Rosenkavalier, Querschnitt

Berlin 1964	Role of Annina Hillebrecht, Töpper, Köth, Curzi, Berry Deutsche Oper ·Orchestra Hollreiser	LP: Eurodisc 86820KR

Salome

Frankfurt   Role of Page   CD: Myto MCD 93592
1952   Borkh, Klose,
                  Lorenz, Fehringer,
                  Frantz
                  Hessischer Rundfunk
                  Orchestra
                  Schröder

Allerseelen (Stell' auf den Tisch die duftenden Reseden)

London   Moore   LP: Columbia 33CX 1552
November 1957   CD: EMI CMS 764 0742

Begegnung (Die Treppe hinunter gesprungen)

Haitzendorf   Spencer   CD: RCA/BMG 09026 615472
January 1993

Cäcilie (Wenn du es wüsstest)

Salzburg   Werba   CD: Orfeo C331 931B
July 1968

Du meines Herzens Krönelein

Salzburg   Werba   CD: Orfeo C331 931B
July 1968

Haitzendorf   Spencer   CD: RCA/BMG 09026 615472
January 1993

Gefunden (Ich ging im Walde so für mich hin)

Haitzendorf   Spencer   CD: RCA/BMG 09026 615472
January 1993

Morgen (Und morgen wird die Sonne wieder scheinen)

Haitzendorf   Spencer   CD: RCA/BMG 09026 615472
January 1993

Vienna   Spencer   CD: RCA/BMG 09026 626522
April 1994   VHS Video: RCA/BMG 09026 626523

Die Nacht (Aus dem Walde tritt die Nacht)

London November 1957	Moore	LP: Columbia 33CX 1552 CD: EMI CMS 764 0742
Salzburg July 1968	Werba	CD: Orfeo C331 931B
Haitzendorf January 1993	Spencer	CD: RCA/BMG 09026 615472

Ruhe meine Seele (Nicht ein Lüftchen regt sich leise)

Haitzendorf January 1993	Spencer	CD: RCA/BMG 09026 615472

Schlechtes Wetter (Das ist ein schlechtes Wetter)

Munich November- December 1965	Moore	LP: Columbia (Germany) C 80976/ SMC 80976 LP: Angel 60087 CD: EMI CMS 764 0742
Salzburg July 1968	Werba	CD: Orfeo C331 931B

TCHAIKOVSKY

The Queen of Spades

Vienna November 1982	Role of Countess Ligendza, Kollo, Hynninen, Hornik Vienna Opera Chorus VPO Kitaenko Sung in German	Unpublished video recording

Requiem

London September 1963- April 1964	Schwarzkopf, Gedda, Ghiaurov Philharmonia Orchestra & Chorus Giulini	LP: EMI AN 133-134/SAN 133-134 LP: EMI SLS 909 CD: EMI CDS 747 2578
Berlin January 1972	Freni, Cossutta, Ghiaurov Vienna Singverein BPO Karajan	LP: DG 2707 065/413 2151 CD: DG 413 2152

Aida: Excerpts (Quale insolita gioia; Alta cagion v'aduna; Chi mai fra gli inni; Fu la sorte dell' armi; L'aborrita rivale a me sfuggia; Ohimè, morir mi sento)

New York February 1970	Role of Amneris Amara, Tucker, Flagello, Karlsrud, MacWherter Metropolitan Opera Orchestra & Chorus Cleva	CD: Melodram MEL 26516

Un Ballo in maschera

London June 1982- May 1983	Role of Ulrica M.Price, Battle, Pavarotti, Bruson London Opera Chorus National PO Solti	LP: Decca 410 2101 CD: Decca 410 2102

Don Carlo

Salzburg August 1975	Role of Eboli Freni, Domingo, Cappuccilli, Ghiaurov Vienna Opera Chorus VPO Karajan	Unpublished radio broadcast

Don Carlo: Excerpts (Nel giardin del Bello; La regina!; A mezzanotte ai giardini della regina; Ciel! Che mai feci!; O don fatale)

Vienna May 1967	Jones, Domingo, Paskalis, Ghiaurov Vienna Opera Chorus VPO Klobucar	CD: Melodram MEL 26516

Falstaff

Vienna May 1980	Role of Quickly Kabaiwanska, Perry, T.Schmidt, Araiza, Taddei, Panerai Vienna Opera Chorus VPO Karajan	LP: Philips 6769 060 CD: Philips 412 2632 Excerpts LP: Philips 411 4231 CD: Philips 411 4232
Salzburg July 1982	Kabaiwanska, Perry, T.Schmidt, Araiza, Taddei, Panerai Vienna Opera Chorus VPO Karajan	VHS Video: Sony SHV 48422 Laserdisc: Sony SLV 48422

Macbeth

Vienna April 1970	Role of Lady Macbeth Cossutta, Milnes, Ridderbusch Vienna Opera Chorus VPO Böhm	LP: Morgan MORG 7001 CD: Legato LCD 143 CD: Foyer 2CF-2027 Excerpts CD: Hunt CDMP 457

Götterdämmerung

Vienna May, June, October and November 1964	Role of Waltraute Nilsson, Watson, Windgassen, Frick, Fischer-Dieskau, Neidlinger Vienna Opera Chorus VPO Solti	LP: Decca MET 292-297/SET 292-297 LP: Decca D100 D19/RING 1-22 LP: Decca 414 1001/414 1151 CD: Decca 414 1002/414 1152 Excerpt LP: Decca GRV 18
Berlin October 1969	Roles of Waltraute and Second Norn Dernesch, Janowitz, Brilioth, Stewart, Kelemen, Ridderbusch Deutsche Oper Chorus BPO Karajan	LP: DG 2716 051/2720 019/2720 051 LP: DG 2740 148/2740 240 CD: DG 415 1552/435 2112
Salzburg March 1970	Dernesch, Janowitz, Thomas, Stewart, Kelemen, Ridderbusch Vienna Opera Chorus BPO Karajan	CD: Memories HR 4107-4121/ HR 4118-4121 CD: Hunt CDKAR 223
New York 1990	Role of Waltraute Behrens, Lisowska, Jersualem, Rafell, Salminen, Wlaschiha Metropolitan Opera Orchestra & Chorus Levine	VHS Video: DG 072 4213/072 4223 Laserdisc: DG 072 4211

Götterdämmerung: Excerpt (Starke Scheite schichtet mir dort)

Hamburg March 1963	Role of Brünnhilde NDR Orchestra Knappertsbusch	LP: Discocorp RR 535 CD: Nuova Era NE 013.6304 CD: Seven Seas (Japan) KICC 2030
Berlin 1964	Deutsche Oper Orchestra Hollreiser	LP: Eurodisc 71395KR/27991CR LP: World Records CM 84/SCM 84

Lohengrin

Vienna November and December 1962	Role of Ortrud Grümmer, Thomas Fischer-Dieskau, Frick, Wiener, Vienna Opera Chorus VPO Kempe	LP: EMI AN 121-125/SAN 121-125 LP: EMI SLS 5072/EX 29 09553 CD: EMI CDS 749 0178
New York January 1967	Bjoner, Konya, Berry, Macurdy, Milnes Metropolitan Opera Orchestra & Chorus Böhm	Unpublished Met broadcast

Lohengrin: Excerpt (Euch Lüften, die mein Klagen/Ortrud! Bist du's?/Entweihte Götter!)

London May 1958	Schwarzkopf Philharmonia Süsskind	LP: Columbia 33CX 1658/SAX 2300 LP: EMI SXDW 3049 CD: EMI CDM 769 5012

Die Meistersinger von Nürnberg

Berlin April 1976	Role of Magdalene Ligendza, Domingo, Fischer-Dieskau, Laubenthal, Lagger, R.Hermann Deutsche Oper Orchestra & Chorus Jochum	LP: DG 2713 011/2740 149 CD: DG 415 2782 Excerpts LP: DG 2535 383/2537 041

Parsifal

Vienna January 1961	Role of Kundry Höngen (Acts 1 & 3), Uhl, Wächter, Berry, Hotter, Franc Vienna Opera Chorus VPO Karajan	CD: Hunt CDKAR 219 Ludwig sings the role in Act 2 scene 2 only
Vienna December 1971 and March and June 1972	Kollo, Hotter, Fischer-Dieskau, Kelemen, Frick Vienna Opera Chorus VPO Solti	LP: Decca SET 550-554 CD: Decca 417 1432 Excerpt LP: Decca GRV 18
New York April 1979	Vickers, Weikl, Talvela, Shinall, Plishka Metropolitan Opera Orchestra & Chorus Levine	Unpublished Met broadcast

Das Rheingold

New York April and May 1988	Role of Fricka Jersusalem, Zednik, Morris, Wlaschiha, Rootering, Moll Metropolitan Opera Orchestra Levine	CD: DG 445 2952/445 3542
New York 1990	Jersusalem, Zednik, Morris, Wlaschiha, Rootering, Salminen Metropolitan Opera Orchestra Levine	VHS Video: DG 072 4183/072 4223 Laserdisc: DG 072 4181

Tannhäuser

Vienna January 1963	Role of Venus Brouwenstijn, Janowitz, Beirer, Kmennt, Wächter, Frick Vienna Opera Chorus VPO Karajan	LP: Melodram MEL 427 CD: Nuova Era NE 013.6307-6309 CD: Hunt CDKAR 204
Vienna October 1970	Dernesch, Kollo, Hollweg, Braun, Sotin Vienna Opera Chorus VPO Solti	LP: Decca SET 506-509 CD: Decca 414 5812 Excerpt LP: Decca GRV 18

Tristan und Isolde

Bayreuth July and August 1966	Role of Brangäne Nilsson, Windgassen, Talvela, Wächter Bayreuth Festival Orchestra & Chorus Böhm	LP: DG SLPM 139 221-139 225 LP: DG 2713 001/2740 144/415 3951 LP: Philips 6747 243 CD: DG 415 3951/419 8892 CD: Philips 434 4202/434 4252 Excerpts LP: DG 2537 001 CD: DG 439 4692
Bayreuth August 1966	Nilsson, Windgassen, Talvela, Wächter, Bayreuth Festival Orchestra & Chorus Böhm	CD: Frequenz CML 3 Excerpts CD: Curcio-Hunt OPV 16
Berlin December 1971- January 1972	Dernesch, Vickers, Berry, Ridderbusch Deutsche Oper Chorus BPO Karajan	LP: EMI SLS 963 CD: EMI CMS 769 3192 Excerpts LP: EMI ASD 3354

Tristan und Isolde: Excerpt (Mild und leise)

London March 1962	Role of Isolde Philharmonia Klemperer	LP: Columbia 33CX 1817/SAX 2462 LP: EMI ASD 2391/SXLP 27 00001 CD: EMI CMS 764 0742
Hamburg March 1963	NDR Orchestra Knappertsbusch	LP: Discocorp RR 535 CD: Nuova Era NE 013.6304 CD: Seven Seas (Japan) KICC 2030

Die Walküre

Vienna October and November 1965	Role of Fricka Nilsson, Crespin, King, Hotter, Frick VPO Solti	LP: Decca MET 312-316/SET 312-316 LP: Decca D100 D19/RING 1-22 LP: Decca 414 1001/414 1051 CD: Decca 414 1002/414 1052 Excerpts LP: Decca SET 390/GRV 18 CD: Decca 421 8872
New York February 1968	Nilsson, Rysanek, Vickers, Stewart, Ridderbusch Metropolitan Opera Orchestra Klobucar	Unpublished Met broadcast
New York April 1987	Behrens, Norman, Lakes, Morris, Moll Metropolitan Opera Orchestra Levine	CD: DG 423 3892/445 3542
New York 1990	Behrens, Norman, Lakes, Morris, Moll Metropolitan Opera Orchestra Levine	VHS Video: DG 072 4193/072 4223 Laserdisc: DG 072 4191
New York March 1993	Jones, Gessendorf, Lakes, Morris, Salminen Metropolitan Opera Orchestra Levine	Unpublished Met broadcast Ludwig's final Met appearance

Der Engel/Wesendonk-Lieder (In der Kindheit frühen Tagen)

London March 1962	Philharmonia Klemperer	LP: Columbia 33CX 1817/SAX 2462 LP: EMI ASD 2391/SXLP 27 00001 CD: EMI CMS 764 0742

Im Treibhaus/Wesendonk-Lieder (Hochgewölbte Blätterkronen)

London October 1958	Philharmonia Boult	Columbia unpublished
London March 1962	Philharmonia Klemperer	LP: Columbia 33CX 1817/SAX 2462 LP: EMI ASD 2391/SXLP 27 00001 CD: EMI CMS 764 0742

Schmerzen/Wesendonk-Lieder (Sonne, weinest jeden Abend)

London March 1962	Philharmonia Klemperer	LP: Columbia 33CX 1817/SAX 2462 LP: EMI ASD 2391/SXLP 27 00001 CD: EMI CMS 764 0742

Stehe still/Wesendonk-Lieder (Sausendes brausendes Rad der Zeit)

London March 1962	Philharmonia Klemperer	LP: Columbia 33CX 1817/SAX 2462 LP: EMI ASD 2391/SXLP 27 00001 CD: EMI CMS 764 0742

Träume/Wesendonk-Lieder (Sag', welch' wunderbare Träume)

London March 1962	Philharmonia Klemperer	LP: Columbia 33CX 1817/SAX 2462 LP: EMI ASD 2391/SXLP 27 00001 CD: EMI CMS 764 0742

Anakreons Grab/Goethe-Lieder (Wo die Rose hier blüht)

| Vienna | Spencer | CD: RCA/BMG 09026 626522 |
| April 1994 | | VHS Video: RCA/BMG 09026 626523 |

Auch kleine Dinge können uns entzücken/Italienisches Liederbuch

Berlin	Barenboim	LP: DG 2707 114
June 1975		CD: DG 439 9752
		CD: DG (Japan) POCG 9013-9021

| Vienna | Spencer | CD: RCA/BMG 09026 626522 |
| April 1994 | | VHS Video: RCA/BMG 09026 626523 |

Auf einer Wanderung/Mörike-Lieder (In ein freundliches Städtchen tret' ich ein)

| London | Moore | LP: Columbia 33CX 1552 |
| November 1957 | | CD: EMI CMS 764 0742 |

Bedeckt mich mit Blumen/Spanisches Liederbuch

| Vienna | Spencer | CD: RCA/BMG 09026 626522 |
| April 1994 | | VHS Video: RCA/BMG 09026 626523 |

Du denkst, mit einem Fädchen mich zu fangen/Italienisches Liederbuch

Berlin	Barenboim	LP: DG 2707 114
June 1975		CD: DG 439 9752
		CD: DG (Japan) POCG 9013-9021

Du sagst mir, dass ich keine Fürstin sei/Italienisches Liederbuch

| Vienna | Spencer | CD: RCA/BMG 09026 626522 |
| April 1994 | | VHS Video: RCA/BMG 09026 626523 |

Der Gärtner/Mörike-Lieder (Auf ihrem Leibrösslein so weiss wie der Schnee)

| Vienna | Spencer | CD: RCA/BMG 09026 626522 |
| April 1994 | | VHS Video: RCA/BMG 09026 626523 |

Gesang Weylas/Mörike-Lieder (Du bist Orplid, mein land!)

| London | Moore | LP: Columbia 33CX 1552 |
| November 1957 | | CD: EMI CMS 764 0742 |

Gesegnet sei das Grün/Italienisches Liederbuch

Berlin June 1975	Barenboim	LP: DG 2707 114 CD: DG 439 9752 CD: DG (Japan) POCG 9013-9021
Vienna April 1994	Spencer	CD: RCA/BMG 09026 626522 VHS Video: RCA/BMG 09026 626523

Heimweh/Mörike-Lieder (Anders wird die Welt mit jedem Schritt)

Vienna April 1994	Spencer	CD: RCA/BMG 09026 626522 VHS Video: RCA/BMG 09026 626523

Ich esse nun mein Brot nicht trocken mehr/Italienisches Liederbuch

Berlin June 1975	Barenboim	LP: DG 2707 114 CD: DG 439 9752 CD: DG (Japan) POCG 9013-9021

Ich hab' in Penna einen Liebsten wohnen/Italienisches Liederbuch

Berlin June 1975	Barenboim	LP: DG 2707 114 CD: DG 439 9752 CD: DG (Japan) POCG 9013-9021

Ich liess mir sagen/Italienisches Liederbuch

Berlin June 1975	Barenboim	LP: DG 2707 114 CD: DG 439 9752 CD: DG (Japan) POCG 9013-9021

Ihr jungen Leute/Italienisches Liederbuch

Berlin June 1975	Barenboim	LP: DG 2707 114 CD: DG 439 9752 CD: DG (Japan) POCG 9013-9021

In dem Schatten meiner Locken/Spanisches Liederbuch

Vienna April 1994	Spencer	CD: RCA/BMG 09026 626522 VHS Video: RCA/BMG 09026 626523

Man sagt mir, deine Mutter wollt' es nicht/Italienisches Liederbuch

| Berlin
June 1975 | Barenboim | LP: DG 2707 114
CD: DG 439 9752
CD: DG (Japan) POCG 9013-9021 |

Mein Liebster hat zu Tische mich geladen/Italienisches Liederbuch

| Berlin
June 1975 | Barenboim | LP: DG 2707 114
CD: DG 439 9752
CD: DG (Japan) POCG 9013-9021 |
| Vienna
April 1994 | Spencer | CD: RCA/BMG 09026 626522
VHS Video: RCA/BMG 09026 626523 |

Mein Liebster ist so klein/Italienisches Liederbuch

| Berlin
June 1975 | Barenboim | LP: DG 2707 114
CD: DG 439 9752
CD: DG (Japan) POCG 9013-9021 |

Mein Liebster singt am Haus im Mondenscheine/Italienisches Liederbuch

| Berlin
June 1975 | Barenboim | LP: DG 2707 114
CD: DG 439 9752
CD: DG (Japan) POCG 9013-9021 |

Mignon/Goethe Lieder (Kennst du das Land?)

| Vienna
1968 | Werba | LP: DG SLPM 139 386 |

Mignon I-III/Goethe-Lieder (Heiss mich nicht reden; Nur wer die Sehnsucht kennt; So lasst mich scheinen)

| Vienna
1968 | Werba | LP: DG SLPM 139 386 |

Mir ward gesagt, du reisest in die Ferne/Italienisches Liederbuch

| Berlin
June 1975 | Barenboim | LP: DG 2707 114
CD: DG 439 9752
CD: DG (Japan) POCG 9013-9021 |

Nein, junger Herr!/Italienisches Liederbuch

| Berlin
June 1975 | Barenboim | LP: DG 2707 114
CD: DG 439 9752
CD: DG (Japan) POCG 9013-9021 |

O wär' dein Haus durchsichtig wie ein Glas/Italienisches Liederbuch

Berlin	Barenboim	LP: DG 2707 114
June 1975		CD: DG 439 9752
		CD: DG (Japan) POCG 9013-9021

Schweig' einal still/Italienisches Liederbuch

Berlin	Barenboim	LP: DG 2707 114
June 1975		CD: DG 439 9752
		CD: DG (Japan) POCG 9013-9021

Verschling' der Abgrund meines Liebsten Hütte/Italienisches Liederbuch

Berlin	Barenboim	LP: DG 2707 114
June 1975		CD: DG 439 9752
		CD: DG (Japan) POCG 9013-9021

Verschwiegene Liebe/Eichendorff-Lieder (Ueber Wipfel und Saaten)

| Vienna | Spencer | CD: RCA/BMG 09026 626522 |
| April 1994 | | VHS Video: RCA/BMG 09026 626523 |

Was soll der Zorn, mein Schatz?/Italienisches Liederbuch

Berlin	Barenboim	LP: DG 2707 114
June 1975		CD: DG 439 9752
		CD: DG (Japan) POCG 9013-9021

Wenn du, mein Liebster, steigst zum Himmel auf/Italienisches Liederbuch

Berlin	Barenboim	LP: DG 2707 114
June 1975		CD: DG 439 9752
		CD: DG (Japan) POCG 9013-9021

Wer rief dich denn?/Italienisches Liederbuch

Berlin	Barenboim	LP: DG 2707 114
June 1975		CD: DG 439 9752
		CD: DG (Japan) POCG 9013-9021

Wolf Lieder/concluded

Wie lange schon war immer mein Verlangen/Italienisches Liederbuch

Berlin June 1975	Barenboim	LP: DG 2707 114 CD: DG 439 9752 CD: DG (Japan) POCG 9013-9021
Vienna April 1994	Spencer	CD: RCA/BMG 09026 626522 VHS Video: RCA/BMG 09026 626523

Wie soll ich fröhlich sein?/Italienisches Liederbuch

Berlin June 1975	Barenboim	LP: DG 2707 114 CD: DG 439 9752 CD: DG (Japan) POCG 9013-9021

Wir haben beide lange Zeit geschwiegen/Italienisches Liederbuch

Berlin June 1975	Barenboim	LP: DG 2707 114 CD: DG 439 9752 CD: DG (Japan) POCG 9013-9021
Vienna April 1994	Spencer	CD: RCA/BMG 09026 626522 VHS Video: RCA/BMG 09026 626523

Wohl kenn' ich euren Stand/Italienisches Liederbuch

Berlin June 1975	Barenboim	LP: DG 2707 114 CD: DG 439 9752 CD: DG (Japan) POCG 9013-9021

MISCELLANEOUS

Da capo Christa Ludwig

Munich 1989	The singer in interview with August Everding	Unpublished video recording

Farewell to Vienna

Vienna April 1994	The singer in interview with Thomas Voigt	VHS Video: RCA/BMG 09026 626523

Another German TV programme was devoted to Christa Ludwig on the occasion of her final Berlin and Vienna recitals in 1993-1994

A recording of the Christmas carol Stille Nacht, in which Christa Ludwig was accompanied by either Geoffrey Parsons or the New Philharmonia Orchestra and Charles Mackerras, may have been made in London in July 1966; if so, it remains unpublished

Nicolai Gedda
born 1925

with valuable assistance from
Giovanna Visconti and Clifford Elkin

Discography compiled by John Hunt

ADAM

Le postillon de Lonjumeau, Querschnitt

Munich	Role of Chapelon	LP: EMI 1C 063 28502
June 1965	Pütz, Crass	CD: EMI CZS 253 0472/CDZ 252 2202
	Bavarian State	Excerpts
	Orchestra & Chorus	LP: EMI 1C 063 29064
	Lehan	LP: EMI 1C 187 29227-29228
	Sung in German	CD: EMI CDCFP 4561

Le postillon de Lonjumeau: Excerpt (Mes amis, écoutez l'histoire!)

Stockholm	Swedish RO	45: Odeon (Sweden) BEOS 2
April 1952	Rybrant	LP: Odeon (Sweden) MOAK 1001/PMES 536
	Sung in Swedish	LP: EMI 1C 137 78233-78236/SLS 5250
Paris	Orchestre National	LP: Columbia 33CX 1837/SAX 2481
September 1961	Prêtre	LP: EMI 1C 063 11272
		LP: Angel 34055/36106/3204
		CD: EMI CDM 769 5502

O holy night

Stockholm	Ellerstedt, organ	LP: Wisa WISLP 542
December 1977		

Du aer stilla ro

Stockholm November- December 1982	Eyron	LP: Bluebell BELL 182

Jag laengtar dig

Stockholm November- December 1982	Eyron	LP: Bluebell BELL 182

Lindagull, lindagull lilla

Stockholm 1952	YMCA Chorus Lidstram	LP: Odeon (Sweden) MOAK 1001/ PMES 536

Saa tag mit Hjerte

Stockholm November- December 1982	Eyron	LP: Bluebell BELL 182

Skogen sover

Stockholm May 1965	Stockholm PO Grevillius	LP: RCA LSC 10034
September 1968	Eyron	LP: EMI 1C 063 28023
London November 1971	Parsons	CD: Arkadia GI 8061
Stockholm November- December 1982	Eyron	LP: Bluebell BELL 182

Sommardofter

Stockholm November- December 1982	Eyron	LP: Bluebell BELL 182

ALTHEN

Land du vaelsignade

Stockholm May 1965	Stockholm PO Grevillius	LP: RCA LSC 10034
Stockholm September 1980	Ellerstedt	LP: Wisa WISLP 590

AQUILON

Songs: Folksvisa; Hoestens vaer

Stockholm May 1977	Aquilon	LP: Artemis ART 50103

AUBER

Fra Diavolo

Monte Carlo September 1983- June 1984	Role of Diavolo Mesplé, Berbie, Bastin Chorus Monte Carlo PO Soustrot	LP: EMI EX 27 00683 CD: EMI CDC 754 8102

Fra Diavolo: Excerpt (Je vois marcher)

New York October 1975	Musica Aeterna Orchestra Waldman	LP: MGS 106

La muette de Portici: Excerpt (Du pauvre seul)

London April 1953	Philharmonia Galliera	LP: Columbia 33CX 1130 LP: Angel 35096/3204 LP: EMI 1C 137 78233-78236/SLS 5250 CD: EMI CDM 769 5502
New York October 1975	Musica Aeterna Orchestra Waldman	LP: MGS 106

BACH

Mass in B minor

London July 1953	Schwarzkopf, Höffgen, Rehfuss Vienna Singverein Philharmonia Karajan	LP: Columbia 33CX 1121-1123 LP: World Records T 854-856 LP: EMI RLS 746/29 09743 CD: EMI CHS 763 5052 Choruses recorded in Vienna in November 1952
Salzburg August 1961	L.Price, C.Ludwig, Souzay Vienna Singverein VPO Karajan	LP: Movimento musica 03.012
London March, October and November 1967	Giebel, Baker, Prey, Crass BBC Chorus New Philharmonia Klemperer	LP: EMI SLS 930 CD: EMI CMS 763 3642
London November 1967	Giebel, Baker, Prey, Crass BBC Chorus New Philharmonia Klemperer	CD: Hunt CD 727

Saint Matthew Passion

London November 1960, January, April, May, November & December 1961	Schwarzkopf, C.Ludwig, Pears, Berry, Fischer-Dieskau Philharmonia Orchestra & Chorus Klemperer	LP: Columbia 33CX 1799-1803/ SAX 2446-2450 LP: EMI SLS 827 CD: EMI CMS 763 0582 Excerpts LP: Columbia 33CX 1881/SAX 2526 CD: EMI CDEMX 2223
Munich 1968-1969	Zylis-Gara, Hamari, Altmeyer, Prey, Crass, Sotin South German Madrigal Choir Consortium musicum Gönnenwein	LP: EMI SAN 228-231/SLS 942 LP: Angel 3735 LP: EMI 1C 197 28052-28055 CD: EMI CZS 762 5882 Excerpts LP: EMI SHZE 305/1C 047 29286 CD: EMI WHS 568 3962

Cantata No 55 "Ich armer Mensch, ich Sündenknecht"

1969-1970	Schola cantorum	LP: EMI 1C 063 29065
	Linde	

Cantata No 160 "Ich weiss, dass mein Erlöser lebet"

1969-1970	Schola cantorum	LP: EMI 1C 063 29065
	Linde	

Cantata No 189 "Meine Seele rühmt und preist"

1969-1970	Schola cantorum	LP: EMI 1C 063 29065
	Linde	

Ave Maria

Stockholm	E.Nilsson, organ	LP: Karp LP 1
March 1978		

BARBER

Vanessa

New York	Role of Anatol	LP: Victor LM 6138/LSC 6138
February-	Steber, Elias,	LP: RCA ARL2-2094/RL 02094
April 1958	Resnik, Tozzi,	CD: RCA/BMG RG 78992/GD 87899
	Cehanovsky	Excerpts
	Metropolitan Opera	LP: Victor LM 6062/LSC 6062
	Orchestra & Chorus	LP: RCA RL 85177
	Mitropoulos	

BEETHOVEN

Symphony No 9 "Choral"

Berlin	Brouwenstijn, Meyer,	LP: Electrola E 80034-80035
December 1957	Guthrie	LP: Angel 60079
	St Hedwig's Choir	LP: EMI XLP 30085/SXLP 30085
	BPO	LP: EMI CFP 40019/1C 063 11129
	Cluytens	Issued on CD in Japan
Munich	Koszut, Fassbaender,	LP: EMI SLS 892
1973	McIntyre	LP: EMI 1C 147 02506-02513
	Munich Philharmonic	LP: EMI 1C 125 02761-02762
	Orchestra & Chorus	LP: EMI 1C 145 02761-02762
	Kempe	

Missa Solemnis

Vienna	Schwarzkopf,	LP: Columbia 33CX 1634-1635
September 1958	C.Ludwig, Zaccaria	LP: Angel 3598
	Vienna Singverein	LP: World Records T 914-915/
	Philharmonia	ST 914-915
	Karajan	LP: EMI 1C 191 00627-00628
		LP: EMI SLS 5198
Salzburg	L.Price, C.Ludwig,	LP: Melodram MEL 704
August 1959	Zaccaria	CD: Nuova Era NE 2262-2263
	Vienna Singverein	
	VPO	
	Karajan	

Christus am Oelberge

Cologne	Deutekom, Sotin	LP: EMI 1C 063 29029
1969	Orchestra & Chorus	LP: Angel 36696
	of Beethovenhalle Bonn	
	Wangenheim	

Fidelio: Excerpt (Gott! Welch' Dunkel hier!)

Munich	Bavarian State	LP: EMI ASD 2364/SME 80814
June 1967	Orchestra	LP: Angel 36624
	Bender	LP: EMI 1C 063 28993
		LP: EMI 1C 187 29227-29228

Another version of the aria sung by Gedda, with orchestra and conductor
unidentified, can be heard on Ed Smith LP UORC 374

An die ferne Geliebte, song cycle

August 1969   Eyron   LP: EMI ASD 2601/1C 063 28520

Adelaide (Einsam wandelt dein Freund im Frühlingsgarten)

1953   Westermeier   LP: Melodram MEL 659

August 1969   Eyron   LP: EMI ASD 2601/1C 063 28520
                                        LP: EMI 1C 187 29227-29228

An die Geliebte (O dass ich dir vom stillen Auge)

August 1969   Eyron   LP: EMI ASD 2601/1C 063 28520

Andenken (Ich denke dein)

1953   Westermeier   LP: Melodram MEL 659

August 1969   Eyron   LP: EMI ASD 2601/1C 063 28520
                                        LP: EMI 5C 055 24368

Bitten/Gellert-Lieder (Gott, deine Güte reicht so weit)

Stockholm   E.Nilsson, organ LP: Karp LP 1
March 1978

Busslied/Gellert-Lieder (An dir allein, an dir hab' ich gesündigt)

Stockholm   E.Nilsson, organ LP: Karp LP 1
March 1978

Die Ehre Gottes aus der Natur/Gellert-Lieder (Die Himmel rühmen)

Stockholm   E.Nilsson, organ LP: Karp LP 1
March 1978

Stockholm   Ellerstedt   LP: Wisa WISLP 542
December 1977   Sung in Swedish

Stockholm   Ellerstedt, organ LP: Wisa WISLP 590
September 1980   Sung in Swedish

Flohlied (Es war einmal ein König)

August 1969   Eyron   LP: EMI 1C 163 28522-28523

Budapest   Pataki   CD: Bluebell ABCD 041
February 1984

Beethoven Lieder/continued

Gottes Macht und Vorsehung/Gellert-Lieder (Gott ist mein Lied!)

Stockholm March 1978	E.Nilsson, organ	LP: Karp LP 1

Der Kuss (Ich war bei Chloen ganz allein)

August 1969	Eyron	LP: EMI ASD 2601/1C 063 28520 LP: EMI 1C 187 29227-29228

Der Liebende (Welch ein wunderbares Leben)

August 1969	Eyron	LP: EMI ASD 2601/1C 063 28520

Lied aus der Ferne (Als mir noch die Träne)

August 1969	Eyron	LP: EMI ASD 2601/1C 063 28520

Mailied (Wie herrlich leuchtet mir die Natur)

August 1969	Eyron	LP: EMI ASD 2601/1C 063 28520 LP: EMI 1C 137 78233-78236

Mit einem gemalten Band (Kleine Blumen, kleine Blätter)

August 1969	Eyron	LP: EMI ASD 2601/1C 063 28520
Budapest February 1984	Pataki	CD: Bluebell ABCD 041

Beethoven Lieder/concluded

Neue Liebe, neues Leben (Herz, mein Herz, was soll das geben?)

August 1969	Eyron	LP: EMI ASD 2601/1C 063 28520
		LP: EMI 1C 137 78233-78236

O welch ein Leben!/Die schöne Schusterin

1967-1968	Convivium musicum	LP: EMI 1C 163 28522-28523
	Keller	

Sehnsucht (Was zieht mir das Herz so?)

August 1969	Eyron	LP: EMI ASD 2601/1C 063 28520

Vom Tode/Gellert-Lieder (Meine Lebenszeit verstreicht)

Stockholm	E.Nilsson, organ	LP: Karp LP 1
March 1978		

Wonne der Wehmut (Trocknet nicht, Tränen der ewigen Liebe)

August 1969	Eyron	LP: EMI ASD 2601/1C 063 28520
Budapest	Pataki	CD: Bluebell ABCD 041
February 1984		

Zärtliche Liebe (Ich liebe dich)

August 1969	Eyron	LP: EMI ASD 2601/1C 063 28520
		LP: EMI 5C 055 24368

Der Zufriedene (Zwar schuf das Glück hienieden)

August 1969	Eyron	LP: EMI 1C 163 28522-28523

BELLINI

I Capuleti e i Montecchi

London
June 1975

Role of Tebaldo
Sills, Baker,
Lloyd, Herincx
Alldis Choir
New Philharmonia
Patané

LP: EMI SLS 986
LP: Angel 3824

I Puritani

Philadelphia
April 1963

Role of Arturo
Sutherland,
Blanc, Diaz
American Opera Soc.
Bonynge

LP: MRF Records MRF 39
CD: Legato SRO 838

Florence
December 1970

Deutekom, Ferrin,
Bruscantini
Maggio Musicale
Orchestra & Chorus
Muti

CD: GOP Records GOP 735

London
August 1973

Sills, L.Quilico,
Plishka
Ambrosian Singers
LPO
Rudel

LP: ABC (USA) ATS 20016

La Sonnambula

New York
March 1963

Role of Elvino
Sutherland,
Flagello
Metropolitan Opera
Orchestra & Chorus
Varviso

LP: Melodram MEL 411
Excerpt
LP: Melodram MEL 659

La Sonnambula: Excerpt (Prendi! L'anel ti dono)

London
June 1966

Freni
New Philharmonia
Downes

LP: EMI ASD 2473
LP: Angel 36397
LP: EMI 1C 137 78233-78236

La Sonnambula: Excerpt (Son geloso del zefiro errante)

London
February-June
1966

Freni
New Philharmonia
Downes

LP: EMI ASD 2473
LP: Angel 36397

Songs: Bella Nice, che d'amore; Vanne, o rosa fortuna!

Stockholm
June 1981

Eyron

LP: Bluebell BELL 134
CD: Bluebell ABCD 004

Benvenuto Cellini

Geneva 1964	Role of Cellini Esposito, Cuenod, Vessières Chorus Suisse Romande Orchestra De Froment	LP: Ed Smith EJS 315 Excerpt LP: Ed Smith EJS 518
London December 1966	Vaughan, Minton, Massard Covent Garden Orchestra & Chorus Pritchard	LP: MRF Records MRF 77
London July 1973	Eda-Pierre, Cuenod, Bastin, Massard Covent Garden Chorus BBC SO C.Davis	LP: Philips 6709 019 CD: Philips 416 9552 Excerpts CD: Philips 416 8712

Benvenuto Cellini: Excerpt (Seul pour lutter)

Paris September 1961	Orchestre National Prêtre	LP: Columbia 33CX 1837/SAX 2481 LP: EMI 1C 063 11272/SLS 5250 LP: Angel 34055/36106/3204 LP: EMI 1C 137 78233-78236 CD: EMI CDM 769 5502

Benvenuto Cellini: Excerpt (Une heure encore)

Paris September 1961	Orchestre National Prêtre	LP: Columbia 33CX 1837/SAX 2481 LP: EMI 1C 063 11272 LP: Angel 34055/36106/3204 LP: EMI SLS 5250/ASD 2574 LP: EMI 1C 137 78233-78236 CD: EMI CDM 769 5502

La Damnation de Faust

Rome January 1969	Role of Faust Horne, Soyer, Petkov RAI Rome Orchestra & Chorus Prêtre	CD: Hunt CDMP 461 Excerpts CD: Hunt CDMP 462
Paris September and October 1969	Baker, Bacquier, Thau Paris Opéra Chorus Orchestre de Paris Prêtre	LP: EMI SLS 947 LP: Angel 3758
London July 1972	Veasey, Bastin, Van Allan Ambrosian Singers LSO C.Davis	LP: Philips 6703 042 CD: Philips 416 3952

La Damnation de Faust, excerpts

Paris 1959	Gorr, Souzay Paris Opéra Orchestra & Chorus Cluytens	LP: HMV ALP 1860/ASD 430 LP: Angel 35941

L'Enfance du Christ

Paris November 1965– September 1966	Role of Narrator De los Angeles, Blanc, Soyer Duclos Choir Paris Conservatoire Orchestra Cluytens	LP: EMI AN 170-171/SAN 170-171 LP: Angel 3680 Issued on CD in Japan

Lélio, ou le retour à la vie

Paris 1976	Burles Chorus Orchestre National Martinon	LP: EMI 2C 069 12880 LP: Angel 37139 LP: EMI 1C 187 52299-52300

Les Nuits d'été, song cycle

Stockholm 1970	Stockholm PO Ehrling	LP: MGS 106

Roméo et Juliette

Vienna February 1983	Fassbaender, Shirley-Quirk Vienna Opera Chorus Austrian RO Gardelli	LP: Orfeo S087 842H CD: Orfeo C087 842H

Les Troyens

Rome May 1969	Role of Aeneas Verrett, Horne, Lucchetti, Massard, Clabassi RAI Rome Orchestra & Chorus Prêtre	LP: HRE Records HRE 389 CD: Melodram MEL 37060 CD: Hunt CDMP 461 Excerpt CD: Hunt CDMP 462

BERNSTEIN

Candide

London December 1989	Roles of Governor, Vanderdendur and Roagotski Anderson, C.Ludwig, D.Jones, Hadley, Green, Ollmann LSO Chorus LSO Bernstein	CD: DG 429 7342 Excerpts CD: DG 435 3282/435 4872
London December 1989 (13 December)	Anderson, C.Ludwig, D.Jones, Hadley, Green, Ollmann LSO Chorus LSO Bernstein	VHS Video: DG 072 4233 Laserdisc: DG 072 4231

BERWALD

Vaggvisa

Stockholm February- November 1982	Eyron	LP: Bluebell BELL 151

BIXIO

Mamma

Munich 1968	Graunke SO Mattes	LP: Columbia (Germany) SMC 83884 LP: Angel 36314

BIZET

Carmen

Vienna October 1954	Role of Don José Simionato, Güden, Roux Vienna Singverein VSO Karajan	LP: GOP Records GFC 026-028 CD: Melodram MEL 27012 CD: Gala GL 100.603 Excerpt CD: Myto MCD 91646
Paris June 1958 and September 1959	De los Angeles, Micheau, Blanc French Radio Chorus Orchestre National Beecham	LP: HMV ALP 1762-1764/ASD 331-333 LP: Angel 3613 LP: EMI SLS 755/SLS 5021 CD: EMI CDC 754 3682 Excerpts 45: HMV 7ER 5214/RES 4297 LP: EMI ASD 2574
Paris July 1964	Callas, Guiot, Massard Duclos Choir Paris Opéra Orchestra Prêtre	LP: EMI AN 143-145/SAN 143-145/SLS 913 LP: Angel 3650 CD: EMI CDC 747 3138 Excerpts LP: EMI ALP 2282/ASD 2282 LP: Angel 36312 LP: EMI 1C 063 29064 LP: EMI 1C 187 29227-29228

Carmen, extracts

New York April 1959	Elias, Merritt Firestone Orchestra Wallenstein	VHS Video: VAI Audio VAIA 69131

Carmen: Excerpt (La fleur que tu m'avais jetée)

Livorno 1985	Soroga	CD: Fonè 85F-026

Les pêcheurs de perles

Paris October 1960	Role of Nadir Micheau, Blanc, Mars Opéra-Comique Orchestra & Chorus Dervaux	LP: Columbia 33CX 1795-1796/ SAX 2442-2443 LP: EMI SLS 877 CD: EMI CMS 769 7042 Excerpt LP: EMI 1C 063 29064
New York 1974	Eda-Pierre, Bruson Opera Chorus and Orchestra of New York Queler	LP: BJR Records RHR 504

Les pêcheurs de perles: Excerpt (Je crois entendre encore)

London	Philharmonia	78: Columbia LX 1614
April 1953	Galliera	45: Columbia SCD 2082/SCB 118
		LP: Columbia 33CX 1130
		LP: Angel 35096
		LP: EMI 1C 137 78233-78236

Leningrad	Andreeva	LP: Melodiya C20 16003-16004
October 1980	Folk Orchestra	CD: Olympia OCD 244
	Popov	

Livorno	Soroga	CD: Fonè 85F-026
1985		

Another version of the aria sung by Gedda, with orchestra and conductor
unidentified, can be heard on Ed Smith EJS 518/UORC 374

Les pêcheurs de perles: Excerpt (Leila! Dieu puissant!)

Paris	Mesplé	LP: EMI 2C 069 14010
1974	Paris Opéra Orchestra	LP: Angel 37143
	Dervaux	CD: EMI CZS 767 8132

Agnus Dei

Stockholm	Accompaniment not	45: Odeon (Sweden) BEOS 4
1958	identified	

Après l'hiver

1979	Wustman	LP: Glendale GLS 8007
Leningrad 1980	Werba	LP: Melodiya C10 14631-14632

Chanson d'avril

1979	Wustman	LP: Glendale GLS 8007
Leningrad 1980	Werba	LP: Melodiya C10 14631-14632

Le chanson du fou

Stockholm June 1981	Eyron	LP: Bluebell BELL 134 CD: Bluebell ABCD 004
Livorno 1985	Soroga	CD: Fonè 85F-026

Ouvre ton coeur

Stockholm June 1981	Eyron	LP: Bluebell BELL 134 CD: Bluebell ABCD 004
Livorno 1985	Soroga	CD: Fonè 85F-026

Pastorale

1979	Wustman	LP: Glendale GLS 8007
Leningrad 1980	Werba	LP: Melodiya C10 14631-14632

BJOERNSTROEM

Om hoesten, duet

Stockholm	Leanderson	LP: Bluebell BELL 166
October 1983	Eyron	

BOIELDIEU

La dame blanche

Hilversum	Role of Georges	LP: HRE Records HRE 249
1964	Spoorenberg, Vroons	CD: Melodram MEL 27053
	Chorus	Excerpts
	Hilversum RO	CD: Myto MCD 91646/90318
	Fournet	

BOITO

Mefistofele: Excerpts (Dai campi; Giunto sul passo)

Budapest	Pataki	CD: Bluebell ABCD 041
February 1984		

BONONCINI

Per la gloria di adorarvi

Livorno	Soroga	CD: Fonè 85F-026
1985		

BORODIN

Prince Igor: Excerpt (The light of day has lingered)

Stockholm	Stockholm Opera	LP: Odeon (Sweden) MOAK 1001
1952	Orchestra	
	Bendix	
	Sung in Swedish	
Stockholm	Stockholm Opera	45: Odeon (Sweden) BEOS 5
February 1962	Orchestra	LP: Electrola SHZE 223
	Grevillius	LP: EMI 1C 137 78233-78236
Berlin	Berlin SO	LP: Melodram MEL 659
1962	Stein	

BRITTEN

Serenade for tenor, horn and strings

New York	Musica Aeterna	Unpublished radio broadcast
April 1968	Orchestra	
	Waldman	

BRUCKNER

Te Deum

Vienna	Lipp, Höngen,	Unpublished radio broadcast
May 1962	Kreppel	
	Singverein	
	VPO	
	Karajan	

BULL

Seterjentens soendag

Stockholm	YMCA Chorus	LP: Odeon (Sweden) MOAK 1001/
1955	Lidstam	PMES 536

CACCINI

Amarilli

Stockholm	National Museum	LP: Polar POLS 321
August 1979	Chamber Orchestra	
	Génetay	

Livorno	Soroga	CD: Fonè 85F-026
1985		

CARNEVALI

Stornelli capricciosi

Berlin	Moore	LP: Columbia 33CX 5278/SAX 5278
July 1965		LP: Columbia (Germany) C 91439/
		SMC 91439/1C 063 28514
		LP: Angel 3204
		LP: EMI 1C 137 78233-78236/SLS 5250

Another version of this song, sung by Gedda with unidentified accompanist, can be heard on Ed Smith UORC 373-374

CASELLA

La storia della fanciulla rapita da pirati

Berlin	Moore	LP: Columbia 33CX 5278/SAX 5278
July 1965		LP: Columbia (Germany) C 91439/
		SMC 91439/1C 063 28514

Another version of this song, performed by Gedda with unidentified
accompanist, can be heard on Ed Smith UORC 373

CHARPENTIER

Louise

Paris	Role of Julien	LP: Angel 3846
1976	Sills, Dunn,	CD: EMI CMS 565 2992
	Van Dam	
	Paris Opéra	
	Orchestra & Chorus	
	Rudel	

CILEA

L'Arlesiana: Excerpt (E la solita storia)

London	Philharmonia	LP: Columbia 33CX 1130
April 1953	Galliera	LP: Angel 35096/3204
		LP: EMI 1C 137 78233-78236/SLS 5250
		CD: EMI CDM 769 5502

| Berlin | Berlin RO | Unpublished video recording |
| 1977 | Albrecht | |

Another version of this aria, sung by Gedda with unidentified orchestra
and conductor, can be heard on Ed Smith UORC 374

CIMAROSA

Il matrimonio segreto

Vienna
Date uncertain

Cast and orchestra
not confirmed
Sung in German

Unpublished video recording

CORNELIUS

Der Barbier von Bagdad

Watford and
London
May 1956

Role of Nureddin
Schwarzkopf,
G.Hoffman, Unger,
Wächter, Prey
Chorus
Philharmonia
Leinsdorf

LP: Columbia 33CX 1400-1401
LP: EMI 1C 147 01448-01449M
CD: EMI CMS 565 2842
Excerpt
LP: Columbia (Germany) C 70411

DANNSTROEM

Duets: Bachi barn; Duellanterna

Stockholm
October 1983

Leanderson
Eyron

LP: Bluebell BELL 166

Hur ljuvt det aer att komma till Herrans tempelgaerd

Stockholm
April 1985

Eyron

LP: Bluebell BELL 191

DARGOMITSKY

Rusalka: Excerpt (Mad Scene)

New York
December 1976

Hines
Russian Choral
Society
Rondenko

LP: Ed Smith UORC 374

DEBUSSY

Pelléas et Mélisande

New York December 1962	<u>Role of Pelléas</u> Moffo, London, Hines Metropolitan Opera Orchestra Ansermet	Unpublished Met broadcast
Munich November 1971	Donath, Meven, Fischer-Dieskau Bavarian RO Kubelik	CD: Orfeo C367 942I

Beau soir

Paris September 1967	Ciccolini	LP: Pathé 2C 063 10000

Fleur des blés

Paris September 1967	Ciccolini	LP: Pathé 2C 063 10000

Mandoline

Paris September 1967	Ciccolini	LP: Pathé 2C 063 10000 LP: EMI ASD 2574

Romance

Paris September 1967	Ciccolini	LP: Pathé 2C 063 10000

<u>Other recordings of Beau soir and Mandoline, sung by Gedda with unidentified accompanist, can be heard on Ed Smith UORC 373</u>

DE CURTIS

Non ti scordar di me

Munich	Graunke SO	LP: Columbia (Germany)
1968	Mattes	SMC 83884/SHZE 236
		LP: Angel 36314

DE FRUMIERE

20 Songs to poems by Lagerkvist: Det blir vackert daer du gaer; Det aer
vackrast naer det skymmer; Det kom ett brev; Det kanske var en dag som
alla andra; Du aer min Afrodite; En gaeng blir allting stilla; Fraen
mitt vaesens yta blaeser han bort den graea hinnan; Hemlaengtan; Intet
aer foergaeves; Kaellan; Kaerlekens visa; Laet mig gae vilse i ditt ljus;
Livsbaeten; Morgonen; Naer du sluter mina oegon; Nu aer det sommarmorgon;
Saliga vaentan; Som en vaeg skoeljt uppmot stranden; Stjaertimman; Ur
djupet av min sjael

Stockholm	Eyron	LP: Bluebell BELL 127
February 1981		

DELIBES

Lakmé

New York	Role of Gérald	LP: HRE Records HRE 425
1981	Devia, Plishka	CD: Legato awaiting publication
	Opera Chorus and	
	Orchestra of New York	
	Queler	

Lakmé, excerpts

Paris	D'Angelo, Berbie,	LP: Pathé CVT 3506
March 1961	Blanc	LP: EMI HQM 1027/HQS 1027
	Opéra-Comique	LP: Angel 34051/36167
	Orchestra & Chorus	
	Prêtre	

DENZA

Funiculi, funicula

Munich	Graunke SO	LP: Columbia (Germany)
1968	Mattes	SMC 83884/SHZE 236
		LP: Angel 36314

DONIZETTI

Don Pasquale: Excerpt (Povero Ernesto! Cercherò lontana!)

London	Role of Ernesto	LP: EMI ASD 2473
June 1966	New Philharmonia	LP: Angel 36397/3204
	Downes	LP: EMI 1C 037 02703/SLS 5250

Don Pasquale: Excerpt (Tornami a dir!)

London	Freni	LP: EMI ASD 2473
June 1966	New Philharmonia	LP: Angel 36397
	Downes	

L'Elisir d'amore

Rome	Role of Nemorino	LP: EMI AN 180-181/SAN 180-181
August 1966	Freni, Sereni,	LP: Angel 3701
	Capecchi	CD: EMI CMS 769 8972
	Rome Opera	Excerpts
	Orchestra & Chorus	LP: EMI ASD 2574/SME 81100
	Molinari-Pradelli	LP: Angel 36397/3204
		LP: EMI 1C 037 02703/1C 047 30638

L'Elisir d'amore: Excerpt (Una furtiva lagrima)

London	Philharmonia	LP: Columbia 33CX 1130
April 1953	Galliera	LP: Angel 35096
		LP: EMI SLS 5250

New York	Metropolitan Opera	VHS Video: Paramount (USA) 2365
October 1983	Orchestra	Laserdisc: Pioneer (USA) 34089/94046
	Levine	Performed at Met centennial gala

Germany	Unspecified	VHS Video: Bel Canto (USA) 658
1985	Orchestra & conductor	

Another recording of the aria by Gedda, with unidentified orchestra and conductor, can be heard on Melodram MEL 569

L'Elisir d'amore: Excerpt (Quanto è bella)

Livorno	Soroga	CD: Fonè 85F-026
1985		

La Favorita: Excerpt (Spirto gentil)

London	Role of Fernando	LP: Columbia 33CX 1130
April 1953	Philharmonia	LP: Angel 35096
	Galliera	CD: EMI CDM 769 5502

Another recording of the aria, sung by Gedda with unidentified orchestra and conductor, can be heard on Melodram MEL 569

Lucia di Lammermoor

New York	Role of Edgardo	Unpublished Met broadcast
February 1969	Moffo, Urdassy,	
	Saccomani, Giaiotti	
	Metropolitan Opera	
	Orchestra & Chorus	
	Franci	

New York	Sills, Ordassy,	Unpublished Met broadcast
January 1977	Edwards, Flagello	
	Metropolitan Opera	
	Orchestra & Chorus	
	Woitach	

Lucia di Lammermoor: Excerpt (Verrano a te)

London	Freni	LP: EMI ASD 2473
June 1966	New Philharmonia	LP: Angel 36397
	Downes	

Lucia di Lammermoor: Excerpt (Tombe degli avi miei/Fra poco a me ricovero)

London	New Philharmonia	LP: EMI ASD 2473
June 1966	Downes	LP: Angel 36397
		LP: EMI 1C 037 02703
		LP: EMI 1C 137 78233-78236

Lucia di Lammermoor: Excerpt (Chi mi frema in tal momento?)

New York	Sutherland, Miller	VHS Video: VAI Audio VAIA 69090
1968	Anthony, Gobbi, Hines	
	Bell Telephone	
	Orchestra	
	Vohees	

Songs: Ah rammenta, o bella Irene!; Le crépuscule

| Stockholm | Eyron | LP: Bluebell BELL 134 |
| June 1981 | | CD: Bluebell ABCD 004 |

DOSTAL

Bella Venezia

| Munich | Graunke SO | LP: EMI SME 74169/SHZE 236 |
| 1968 | Mattes | |

DUPARC

Mélodies: Chanson triste; L'invitation au voyage; Le manoir de Rosemonde;
Phidylé

| Salzburg | Werba | CD: EMI CDM 565 3522 |
| August 1961 | | |

Other recordings of Chanson triste, Le manoir de Rosemonde and Phidylé,
sung by Gedda with unidentified accompanist, can be heard on Ed Smith
UORC 373

DURANTE

Danza, danza, fanciulla, al mio cantar!; Vergine, tutto amor, o madre
di bontade

Stockholm	National Museum	LP: Polar POLS 321
August 1975	Chamber Orchestra	
	Génetay	

EKLOEF

Morgon

| Stockholm | Stockholm PO | LP: RCA LSC 10034 |
| May 1965 | Grevillius | |

ELGAR

The Dream of Gerontius

London
May-July
1975

Role of Gerontius
Watts, Lloyd
LPO & Alldis Choirs
New Philharmonia
Boult

LP: EMI SLS 987
CD: EMI CDC 747 2088

ELLERSTEDT

Froejda dig! (Advent Cantata)

Stockholm
December 1977

Choir and
Instrumentalists

LP: Wisa WISLP 542

ENESCU

Oedipe

Monte Carlo
June 1989

Role of Shepherd
Hendricks, Lipovsek,
Fassbaender,
Bacquier, Van Dam
Chorus
Monte Carlo
Philharmonic
Foster

CD: EMI CDS 754 0112

ERIKSSON

Stora och underbara aero dina verk

Stockholm
April 1985

Stockholm University
Singers
Jonsson

LP: Bluebell BELL 191

ERLING

Om aen aenglars spraek

Stockholm
April 1985

Stockholm University
Singers
Jonsson

LP: Bluebell BELL 191

FAURÉ

Adieu/Poème d'un jour

| Paris | Ciccolini | LP: Pathé 2C 063 10000 |
| September 1967 | | |

Après un rêve

| Paris | Ciccolini | LP: Pathé 2C 063 10000 |
| September 1967 | | LP: EMI ASD 2574 |

Chanson/Shylock

Toulouse	Capitole Orchestra	LP: EMI 2C 167 73071-73073
December 1979-	Plasson	CD: EMI CDC 747 9382
July 1981		

Clair de lune/Masques et bergamasques

Toulouse	Capitole Orchestra	LP: EMI 2C 167 73071-73073
December 1979-	Plasson	
July 1981		

Fleur jetée

| Paris | Ciccolini | LP: Pathé 2C 063 10000 |
| September 1967 | | |

Ici-bas!

| Paris | Ciccolini | LP: Pathé 2C 063 10000 |
| September 1967 | | |

Le plus doux chemin/Masques et bergamasques

Toulouse	Capitole Orchestra	LP: EMI 2C 167 73071-73073
December 1979-	Plasson	
July 1981		

Madrigal/Shylock

Toulouse	Capitole Orchestra	LP: EMI 2C 167 73071-73073
December 1979-	Plasson	
July 1981		

Nell

Paris	Ciccolini	LP: Pathé 2C 063 10000
September 1967		

Rencontre/Poème d'un jour

Paris	Ciccolini	LP: Pathé 2C 063 10000
September 1967		

Toujours/Poème d'un jour

Paris	Ciccolini	LP: Pathé 2C 063 10000
September 1967		

Other versions of the three songs comprising Poème d'un jour, with Gedda
and an unidentified accompanist, can be heard on Ed Smith UORC 373

FLOTOW

Martha

Munich	Role of Lyonel	LP: EMI SAN 246-248
March 1968	Rothenberger,	LP: EMI SMA 91748-91750
	Fassbaender, Prey	LP: EMI 1C 197 30241-30243
	Bavarian State	CD: EMI CMS 769 3392
	Orchestra & Chorus	Excerpt
	Heger	CD: EMI CDCFP 4561

Martha: Excerpt (Ach so fromm)

London	Philharmonia	78: Columbia LX 1617
April 1953	Galliera	LP: Columbia 33CX 1130
		LP: Angel 35096

Munich	Bavarian State	LP: EMI ASD 2364/1C 063 28993
June 1967	Orchestra	LP: Angel 36624
	Bender	LP: EMI SME 80814/SMC 81049
		LP: EMI 1C 063 29044/1C 047 60638

Alessandro Stradella: Excerpt (Jungfrau Maria!)

Munich	Bavarian State	LP: EMI ASD 2364/SME 80814
June 1967	Orchestra	LP: Angel 36624
	Bender	LP: EMI 1C 063 28993
		CD: EMI CDM 769 5502

FRANCK

La procession

| Stockholm September 1980 | Ellerstedt, organ | LP: Wisa WISLP 590 |

Panis angelicus

Stockholm 1958	Unidentified accompanist	45: Odeon (Sweden) BEOS 4
Stockholm December 1977	Ellerstedt, organ	LP: Wisa WISLP 542
Stockholm September 1980	Ellerstedt, organ Inge, violin Chorus	LP: Wisa WISLP 590

FRYKLOEF

Songs: Jag har varit; I droemmar traeden stae

| Stockholm November– December 1982 | Eyron | LP: Bluebell BELL 182 |

GADE

Kalanus

Copenhagen May 1986	Role of Alexander Rerholm, Mroz Collegium musicum Rasmussen	CD: Danacord DACOCD 310

GEIJER

7 Songs: Avskedet; Barndomsminnen; Den 56te foedelsedagen; Det forma hemmet; Min politik; Min musik; Till min dotter

Stockholm September- November 1982	Eyron	LP: Bluebell BELL 151

GIORDANI

Caro mio ben

Stockholm August 1979	National Museum Chamber Orchestra Génetay	LP: Polar POLS 321

GIORDANO

Fedora: Excerpt (Amor ti vieta)

Berlin 1977	Berlin RO Albrecht	Unpublished video recording
Livorno 1985	Soroga	CD: Fonè 85F-026
Vienna 1988	Austrian RO Guadagno	Unpublished video recording

GLINKA

A Life for the Tsar

Paris June, November and December 1957	Role of Sobinin Stich-Randall, Bugarinovic, Christoff Belgrade Opera Chorus Lamoureux Orchestra Markevitch	LP: HMV ALP 1613-1615 LP: Capitol GCR 7163 LP: EMI 2C 163 73011-73013 CD: EMI CMS 769 6982 Excerpt LP: EMI 1C 137 78233-78236

A Life for the Tsar: Excerpt (Brothers in the storm!)

Belgrade April 1969	Belgrade PO Zdravkovich	LP: EMI 1C 063 28070/1C 063 29044 LP: Angel 3204 LP: EMI 1C 047 30638/SLS 5250

Russlan and Ludmila: Excerpt (Opening scene)

Paris 1956	Micheau, Gorr, Depraz, Froumenly Paris Opéra Orchestra Fourestier	LP: HMV History of Music HLP 23

Do not sing, beauty!

Moscow March 1980	Mogilevskaya	LP: Melodiya C10 13977-13978 LP: Eurodisc 203 284.366

Doubt

Stockholm September 1968	Eyron	LP: EMI 1C 063 28023
London November 1971	Parsons	CD: Arkadia GI 8061
Moscow March 1980	Mogilevskaya	LP: Melodiya C10 13977-13978 LP: Eurodisc 203 284.366

I remember the wonderful moment

Stockholm September 1968	Eyron	LP: EMI 1C 063 28023
London November 1971	Parsons	CD: Arkadia GI 8061
Moscow March 1980	Mogilevskaya	LP: Melodiya C10 13977-13978 LP: Eurodisc 203 284.366

O you sweet, lovely maiden

Stockholm September 1968	Eyron	LP: EMI 1C 063 28023
London November 1971	Parsons	CD: Arkadia GI 8061

A young beauty

Moscow March 1980	Mogilevskaya	LP: Melodiya C10 13977-13978 LP: Eurodisc 203 284.366

GLUCK

Alceste

New York February 1961	Role of Admète Farrell, Cassel, Nagy Metropolitan Opera Orchestra & Chorus Adler	Unpublished Met broadcast
Munich June 1982	Norman, Gambill, Krause, Weikl, Nimsgern Bavarian Radio Orchestra & Chorus Baudo	LP: Orfeo S027 823F CD: Orfeo C027 823F

Alceste, excerpts

Paris April 1962	Rubio, Bianco Paris Opéra Orchestra & Chorus Prêtre	LP: HMV ALP 2027/ASD 576

Alceste: Excerpt (Bannis la crainte!)

Stockholm September 1980	National Museum Chamber Orchestra Génetay	LP: Polar POLS 323

Der betrogene Kadi

Munich 1974	Role of Nuradin Rothenberger, Donath, Hirte, Berry Bavarian State Orchestra & Chorus Suitner	LP: EMI 1C 065 28834

Iphigénie en Tauride, excerpts

Paris May 1961	Role of Pylade Gorr, Blanc, Quilico Paris Conservatoire Orchestra & Chorus Prêtre	LP: HMV ASD 465 LP: Angel 35632 LP: EMI 173 1881

Iphigénie en Tauride: Excerpts (Divintés des grandes ames; Unis dès la plus tendre enfance)

Stockholm September 1980	National Museum Chamber Orchestra Génetay	LP: Polar POLS 323

Orphée et Euridice

Paris	Role of Orphée	LP: Pathé 2C 153 12059-12060
March 1957	Berton, Micheau	LP: Angel 3659
	Aix Festival Chorus	CD: EMI CMS 769 8612
	Paris Conservatoire	Excerpts
	Orchestra	LP: Columbia (Germany) C 70411
	De Froment	LP: EMI 1C 137 78233-78236

Orphée et Euridice: Excerpt (J'ai perdu mon Euridice)

Stockholm	National Museum	LP: Polar POLS 323
September 1980	Chamber Orchestra	
	Génetay	

Orphée et Euridice: Excerpt (Viens, viens, Euridice, suis-moi!)

Paris	Mesplé	LP: EMI 2C 069 14010
1974	Paris Opéra Orchestra	LP: Angel 37143
	Dervaux	CD: EMI CZS 767 8132

Paride e Elena: Excerpt (O del mio dolce ardor)

Stockholm	National Museum	LP: Polar POLS 323
September 1980	Chamber Orchestra	
	Génetay	

GODARD

Berceuse de Jocelyn

Munich	Graunke SO	LP: Columbia (Germany) SMC 83884
1968	Mattes	LP: Angel 36314

GOLDMARK

Die Königin von Saba: Excerpt (Magische Töne)

Munich	Bavarian State	LP: EMI ASD 2364/ASD 2574/SLS 5250
June 1967	Orchestra	LP: EMI SME 80814/1C 063 28993
	Bender	LP: Angel 36624/3204
		LP: EMI 1C 137 78233-78236
		CD: EMI CDM 769 5502

GOUNOD

Faust

Paris October 1953	Role of Faust De los Angeles, Angelici, Christoff Borthayre Paris Opéra Orchestra & Chorus Cluytens	LP: HMV ALP 1162-1165 LP: Victor LM 6403 CD: EMI CMS 565 2562 Excerpts 45: HMV 7ER 5050/5059/5064 LP: Victor LM 1825
New York January 1958	Güden, Votipka, Hines, Guarrera Metropolitan Opera Orchestra & Chorus Morel	Unpublished Met broadcast
Paris September- October 1958	De los Angeles, Berton, Christoff, Blanc Paris Opéra Orchestra & Chorus Cluytens	LP: HMV ALP 1721-1724/ASD 307-310 LP: Angel 3622 LP: EMI SLS 816 CD: EMI CMS 769 9832 Excerpts LP: HMV ALP 1837/ASD 412
New York April 1966	Fenn, Kriese, Siepi, Walker Metropolitan Opera Orchestra & Chorus Prêtre	Unpublished Met broadcast
New York January 1969	Lorengar, Siepi, Merrill Metropolitan Opera Orchestra & Chorus Varviso	Unpublished Met broadcast
Paris 1972	Freni, Soyer, Krause Paris Opéra Orchestra & Chorus Mackerras	VHS Video: Bel Canto (USA) 586
New York December 1972	Boky, MacCurdy, Maneguerra Metropolitan Opera Orchestra & Chorus Benzi	Unpublished radio broadcast

Faust, Querschnitt

Berlin September 1973	Moser, Moll, Fischer-Dieskau RIAS Choir Berlin RO Patané Sung in German	LP: EMI 1C 063 28961

Faust: Excerpt (Salut demeure)

Berlin 1962	Berlin RO F.Walter	LP: Melodram MEL 659
London November 1967	Covent Garden Orchestra Patané	LP: EMI ASD 2445/1C 047 30638 LP: Angel 36623 LP: EMI 1C 187 29227-29228
Buenos Aires April 1971	Colòn Orchestra Gavazzeni	CD: Myto MCD 91646

Faust: Excerpt (Rien! En vain j'interroge)

Buenos Aires April 1971	Colòn Orchestra Gavazzeni	CD: Myto MCD 91646

Faust: Excerpt (Alerte, alerte/Anges purs)

New York 1968	Curtin, Hines Bell Telephone Orchestra Vohees	VHS Video: VAI Audio VAIA 69090
Paris 1972	Freni, Soyer Unidentified Orchestra & conductor	Unpublished video recording
New York 1982	Scotto, Ramey Unidentified Orchestra & conductor	Unpublished video recording

Mireille

Aix-en-Provence July 1954	Role of Vincent Vivalda, Dens Aix Festival Chorus Paris Conservatoire Orchestra Cluytens	LP: Columbia 33CX 1299-1301 LP: EMI 2C 153 10613-10615 CD: EMI CMS 764 3822 Excerpts LP: Pathé UCD 3162 LP: Columbia (Germany) C 70411 LP: EMI 1C 137 78233-78236/SLS 5250

Mireille: Excerpt (Anges du paradis)

Paris September 1961	Orchestre National Prêtre	LP: Columbia 33CX 1837/SAX 2481 LP: EMI 1C 063 11272 LP: Angel 34055/36106/3204 LP: EMI 1C 187 29227-29228

Mireille: Excerpt (Vincenette, à votre âge!)

Paris 1974	Mesplé Paris Opéra Orchestra Dervaux	LP: EMI 2C 069 14010 LP: Angel 37143 CD: EMI CZS 767 8132

Roméo et Juliette

New York April 1968	Role of Roméo Freni, MacCurdy, Reardon Metropolitan Opera Orchestra & Chorus Molinari-Pradelli	Unpublished Met broadcast

Roméo et Juliette, excerpts

Paris 1964	Carteri, Dens, Rouleau Paris Opéra Orchestra Lombard	LP: Columbia 33CX 1941/SAX 2580 LP: Pathé CVT 1026/2C 061 11688 LP: Angel 36287

Roméo et Juliette, unspecified extract

New York February 1963	Peters, Walker Firestone Orchestra	VHS Video: VAI Audio VAIA 69131

Roméo et Juliette: Excerpt (Lève-toi, soleil!)

London April 1953	Philharmonia Galliera	LP: Columbia 33CX 1130 LP: Angel 35096 CD: EMI CDM 769 5502
Berlin 1962	Berlin SO Stein	LP: Melodram MEL 659

Roméo et Juliette: Excerpt (Ange adorable)

Paris 1974	Mesplé Paris Opéra Orchestra Dervaux	LP: EMI 2C 069 14010 LP: Angel 37143 CD: EMI CZS 767 8132

Mélodies: Au rossignol; Envoi de fleurs; Où voulez-vous aller?

Berlin 1962	Singer	LP: Melodram MEL 659
Stockholm June 1981	Eyron	LP: Bluebell BELL 134 CD: Bluebell ABCD 004
Livorno 1985	Soroga	CD: Fonè 85F-026

GRÉTRY

Richard Coeur de Lion: Excerpt (Si l'univers entier m'oublie)

New York April 1968	Musica Aeterna Orchestra Waldman	LP: MGS 106

GRIEG

En drom

Stockholm September 1968	Eyron	LP: EMI 1C 063 28023
London November 1971	Parsons	CD: Arkadia GI 8061
New York 1979	Wustman	LP: Glendale GLS 8007
Leningrad 1980	Werba	LP: Melodiya C10 14631-14632

En svane

Stockholm September 1968	Eyron	LP: EMI 1C 063 28023
London November 1971	Parsons	CD: Arkadia GI 8061

Geheimnisvolle Liebe

Stockholm September 1968	Eyron	LP: EMI 1C 063 28023
London November 1971	Parsons	CD: Arkadia GI 8061

Jeg elsker dig

Stockholm September 1968	Eyron	LP: EMI 1C 063 28023/ASD 2574 LP: EMI 5C 055 24368
London November 1971	Parsons	CD: Arkadia GI 8061

Jeg giver mit digt til vaeren

New York 1979	Wustman	LP: Glendale GLS 8007
Leningrad 1980	Werba	LP: Melodiya C10 14631-14632

Vaeren

New York 1979	Wustman	LP: Glendale GLS 8007
Leningrad 1980	Werba	LP: Melodiya C10 14631-14632

HAEFFNER

Sippan

Stockholm September- November 1982	Eyron	LP: Bluebell BELL 151

HAEGGBOM

Aftonfrid, duet

Stockholm October 1983	Leanderson Eyron	LP: Bluebell BELL 166

HAEKANSON

Gammal ramsa; Till ett skoent barn

Stockholm November- December 1982	Eyron	LP: Bluebell BELL 182

HAHN

Ciboulette

Monte Carlo September 1981- June 1982	Role of Antonine Mesplé, Alliot-Lugaz, Le Roux, Van Dam Laforge Choir Monte Carlo Philharmonic Orchestra Diederich	LP: EMI 2C 167 73105-73106 CD: EMI CDS 749 8732

4 Chansons: D'une prison; L'allée est sans fin; L'heure exquise; Paysage

Paris September 1967	Ciccolini	LP: EMI 2C 063 10000 L'heure exquise only LP: EMI ASD 2574

HANDEL

Messiah

London	Schwarzkopf,	LP: EMI AN 146-148/SAN 146-148/SLS 915
February-	G.Hoffman, Hines	LP: Angel 3657
November 1964	Philharmonia	CD: EMI CMS 763 6212
	Orchestra & Chorus	Excerpts
	Klemperer	LP: EMI ALP 2288/ASD 2288

Atalanta: Excerpt (Cara selve)

Stockholm	National Museum	LP: Polar POLS 323
September 1980	Chamber Orchestra	
	Génetay	

Atalanta: Excerpt (Di ad Irene)

Salzburg	Werba	CD: EMI CDM 565 3522
August 1961		

Stockholm	National Museum	LP: Polar POLS 323
September 1980	Chamber Orchestra	
	Génetay	

Serse: Excerpt (Ombra mai fù)

Stockholm	National Museum	LP: Polar POLS 323
September 1980	Chamber Orchestra	
	Génetay	

Dank sei dir Herr, attrib.

Stockholm	National Museum	LP: Polar POLS 323
September 1980	Chamber Orchestra	
	Génetay	

HAQUINIUS

Songs: Dofta, dofta, vit syren; Skaergaerdso; En vaervisa

Stockholm	Eyron	LP: Bluebell BELL 182
November-		
December 1982		

Die Jahreszeiten

Munich October 1964– January 1965	Mathis, Crass South German Madrigal Choir Bavarian State Orchestra Gönnenwein	LP: Columbia (Germany) C 91388-91390/SMC 91388-91390 LP: EMI 1C 163 28531-28533 CD: EMI CMS 764 5482

Orfeo ed Euridice

Vienna May 1967	Role of Orfeo Sutherland, Malas Akademiechor VSO Bonynge	LP: MRF Records MRF 9
Edinburgh September 1967	Sutherland, Malas Scottish Opera Chorus Scottish National Orchestra Bonynge	CD: Myto MCD 90529

L'infedeltà delusa: Excerpt (Chi s'impaccia di moglie citadina)

Munich 1975	Bavarian State Orchestra Ungar	LP: EMI 1C 187 30221-30222

HEUBERGER

Der Opernball: Excerpt (Geh'n wir ins chambre separée)

Munich	Fassbaender	LP: EMI SHZE 450-451
1968	Graunke SO	
	Mattes	

Der Opernball: Excerpt (Man lebt nur einmal)

| Munich | Graunke SO | LP: EMI SHZE 236/SHZE 450-451 |
| 1968 | Mattes | |

JANACEK

Glagolithic Mass

New York	Pilarczyk, Martin,	LP: Columbia (USA) MS 6737
1964	Gaynes	CD: Sony SMK 47569
	Westminster Choir	
	NYPO	
	Bernstein	

JONSSON

Kom!

Stockholm	Stockholm University	LP: Bluebell BELL 191
April-	Singers	
September 1985	Jonsson	

KALMAN

Die Czardasfürstin

Munich	Role of Edwin	LP: EMI 1C 191 29066-29067
January 1971	Rothenberger,	Excerpts
	Miljakovic,	LP: EMI 1C 061 28817/1C 061 28818
	Anheisser,	LP: EMI 1C 187 30179-30180
	Brokmeier	CD: EMI CDM 769 6002
	Bavarian State Chorus	CD: EMI CMS 764 3092
	Graunke SO	
	Mattes	

Die Czardasfürstin: Excerpt (Machen wir's den Schwalben nach!)

Stockholm	Hallin-Bostrom	45: Odeon (Sweden) BEOS 2
1955	Stockholm Opera	LP: Odeon (Sweden) PMES 536/MOAK 1001
	Orchestra	
	Bendix	
	Sung in Swedish	

Gräfin Maritza

Munich	Role of Tassilo	LP: EMI 1C 191 29068-29069
January 1971	Rothenberger, Moser,	CD: EMI CMS 769 6752
	Brokmeier, Böhme	Excerpts
	Bavarian State Chorus	LP: EMI 1C 061 28818
	Graunke SO	CD: EMI CDM 769 5062/CDM 769 5992
	Mattes	CD: EMI CMS 764 3092

Die Zirkusprinzessin: Excerpt (Zwei Märchenaugen)

Stockholm	Stockholm Opera	45: Odeon (Sweden) BEOS 2
1955	Orchestra	LP: Odeon (Sweden) PMES 536/MOAK 1001
	Bendix	
	Sung in Swedish	

Das Veilchen von Montmartre: Excerpt (Heut' nacht hab' ich geträumt von dir)

Munich	Graunke SO	LP: EMI 1C 183 28811-28813
1968	Mattes	LP: EMI 1C 187 29227-29228
		LP: EMI 1C 187 30179-30180
		CD: EMI CMS 764 3092

KHACHATURIAN

Nina's song

Salzburg August 1961	Werba	CD: EMI CDM 565 3522

KIENZL

Der Evangelimann, Querschnitt

Munich August 1965	Role of Mathias Rothenberger, Höffgen, Lenz, Kusche, Crass Bavarian State Orchestra & Chorus Heger	LP: Columbia (Germany) C 80965/SMC 80965 LP: EMI 1C 063 29005 CD: EMI CZS 253 0472/CDZ 252 2122 Selig sind, die Verfolgung leiden LP: EMI ASD 2574/1C 063 29064

KOERLING

Aftonstaemning

Stockholm September- November 1982	Eyron	LP: Bluebell BELL 151

Sjung!, duet

Stockholm October 1983	Leanderson Eyron	LP: Bluebell BELL 166

KORNGOLD

Das Wunder der Heliane

Berlin   Role of Schwertrichter   CD: Decca 436 6362
February 1992   Tomowa-Sintov, Runkel,
                       Welker, De Haan, Pape
                       Rundfunkchor
                       Berlin RO
                       Mauceri

LALO

Le roi d'Ys: Excerpt (Vainement, ma bien-aimée)

Paris   Orchestre National   LP: Columbia 33CX 1837/SAX 2481
September 1961   Prêtre   LP: EMI 1C 063 11272/SLS 5250
                                            LP: Angel 34055/36106/3204
                                            CD: EMI CDM 769 5502

Another version of the aria, sung by Gedda with unidentified orchestra and
conductor, can be heard on Ed Smith UORC 374

Le roi d'Ys: Excerpt (Cher Mylio!)

Paris   Mesplé   LP: EMI 2C 069 14010
1974   Paris Opéra Orchestra LP: Angel 37143
                      Dervaux   CD: EMI CZS 767 8132

LANGE-MUELLER

En engel haer roert ved din Pande

Stockholm   YMCA Chorus   LP: Odeon (Sweden) MOAK 1001
1952   Lidstam

LARA

Granada

Munich   Graunke SO   LP: EMI SMC 83884
1968   Mattes   LP: Angel 36314

LEHAR

Frasquita: Excerpt (Hab' ich ein blaues Himmelbett)

Munich	Graunke SO	LP: EMI CSD 3676/1C 061 28184
1968	Mattes	LP: EMI 1C 187 28494-28495
		CD: EMI CDM 769 5062

Frasquita: Excerpt (Schatz, ich bitte dich, komm heut' nacht!)

Munich	Graunke SO	LP: EMI 1C 183 28811-28813
1968	Mattes	

Friederike: Excerpt (O Mädchen, mein Mädchen)

Munich	Graunke SO	LP: EMI CSD 3676/1C 061 28184
1968	Mattes	LP: EMI 1C 047 30630
		LP: EMI 1C 187 28494-28495

Giuditta

Munich	Role of Octavio	LP: EMI EX 27 02573
June 1983-	Moser	LP: Angel 3947
July 1984	Munich Radio	CD: EMI CMS 565 3782
	Orchestra & Chorus	
	Boskovsky	

Giuditta, Querschnitt

Munich	Rothenberger	LP: Electrola E 73941/SME 73941
June and	Gärtnerplatz Chorus	LP: EMI 1C 061 28197
July 1965	Graunke SO	Excerpts
	Mattes	LP: Electrola E 74169/SME 74169
		LP: EMI CSD 3676/1C 061 28184
		LP: EMI 1C 137 78233-78236/SHZE 181
		LP: EMI 1C 183 28811-28813/SHZE 236
		LP: EMI 1C 187 29227-29228
		CD: EMI CDM 769 5062

Der Graf von Luxemburg

Munich	Role of René	LP: EMI SME 81093-81094
August 1968	Popp, Litz, Holm,	LP: EMI 1C 163 28982-28983
	Brokmeier, Böhme	CD: EMI CMS 565 3752
	Bavarian State	Excerpts
	Chorus	LP: EMI 1C 061 28074
	Graunke SO	LP: EMI CSD 3676/1C 061 28184
	Mattes	CD: EMI CDM 769 5062

Das Land des Lächelns

London	Role of Sou-Chong	LP: Columbia 33CX 1114-1115
April and	Schwarzkopf,	LP: EMI SXDW 3044
June 1953	Loose, Kunz	CD: EMI CHS 769 5232
	BBC Chorus	Excerpts
	Philharmonia	LP: Columbia 33CX 1712
	Ackermann	LP: Angel 3204
		LP: EMI RLS 763/SLS 5250

Munich	Rothenberger,	LP: EMI 1C 163 28991-28992
June 1967	Holm, Friedauer	CD: EMI CMS 565 3722
	Bavarian Radio Chorus	Excerpts
	Graunke SO	LP: EMI 1C 061 28198
	Mattes	LP: EMI CSD 3676/1C 061 28184
		LP: EMI SHZE 450451/SLS 5250
		LP: EMI 1C 137 78233-78236
		LP: EMI 1C 183 28811-28813
		LP: EMI 1C 187 29227-29228
		CD: EMI CDM 769 5062

Das Land des Lächelns: Excerpt (Dein ist mein ganzes Herz)

Stockholm	Unidentified	LP: Odeon (Sweden) MOAK 1001
1952	orchestra & conductor	
	Sung in Swedish	

Stockholm	Bendix	LP: Bluebell BELL 154
October 1983	Sung in Swedish	

Die lustige Witwe

London April 1953	Role of Rosillon Schwarzkopf, Loose, Kunz BBC Chorus Philharmonia Ackermann	LP: Columbia 33CX 1051-1052 LP: EMI SXDW 3045 LP: Angel 3501 CD: EMI CDH 769 5202 Excerpts LP: Columbia 33CX 1712
London July 1962	Schwarzkopf, Steffek, Wächter Philharmonia Orchestra & Chorus Matacic	LP: EMI AN 101-102/SAN 101-102 LP: EMI SLS 823 LP: Angel 3630 CD: EMI CDS 747 1788 Excerpts LP: EMI ALP 2252/ASD 2252

Die lustige Witwe, Querschnitt

Munich June 1967	Role of Danilo Rothenberger, Köth, Ilosfalvy Bavarian Radio Chorus Graunke SO Mattes	LP: EMI SME 73934/1C 061 28194 CD: EMI CDM 769 0902 Excerpts LP: EMI SHZE 450-451 LP: EMI 1C 061 28184 LP: EMI 1C 183 28811-28813 LP: EMI 1C 187 28494-28495 LP: EMI 1C 187 29227-29228 CD: EMI CDM 769 5062

Paganini

Munich April and May 1977	Role of Paganini Rothenberger, Miljakovic, Lenz, Zednik, Kusche Bavarian State Orchestra & Chorus Boskovsky	LP: EMI SLS 5112 LP: EMI 1C 157 30752-30753 Excerpts LP: EMI 1C 061 30778/1C 061 30948 LP: EMI 1C 137 78233-78236 CD: EMI CDM 769 5062

Paganini: Excerpt (Gern hab' ich die Frau'n geküsst)

Munich 1968	Graunke SO Mattes	LP: EMI CSD 3676/1C 061 28184 LP: SHZE 236/1C 187 28494-28495 LP: EMI 5C 055 24366
Stockholm April 1987	Palm Court Orchestra Almgren	CD: Bluebell ABCD 014

Schön ist die Welt: Excerpt (Schön ist die Welt)

Munich	Graunke SO	LP: EMI CSD 3676/1C 061 28184
1968	Mattes	LP: EMI SHZE 450-451
		LP: EMI 1C 187 28494-28495

Schön ist die Welt: Excerpt (Liebste, glaub' an mich)

Munich	Graunke SO	LP: EMI CSD 3676/1C 061 28184
1968	Mattes	

Der Zarewitsch

Munich	Role of Alexei	LP: EMI 1C 163 29020-29021
June 1968	Streich, Reichart,	CD: EMI CMS 769 3662
	Friedauer	Excerpts
	Bavarian State Chorus	LP: EMI 1C 061 28073
	Graunke SO	LP: EMI CSD 3676/1C 061 28184
	Mattes	CD: EMI CDM 769 6012

Der Zarewitsch: Excerpt (Es steht ein Soldat am Wolgastrand)

Stockholm	Swedish RO	LP: Odeon (Sweden) MOAK 1001/PMES 536
1952	Rybrant	
	Sung in Swedish	

Unspecified arias from Giuditta, Land des Lächelns, Lustige Witwe and Paganini
on German TV recording from 1985, issued in USA on VHS Video Bel Canto 658

LEONCAVALLO

La mattinata

Stockholm	Eyron	LP: Bluebell BELL 134
June 1981		CD: Bluebell ABCD 004

LINDBLAD

En sommardag

Stockholm	Eyron	LP: Bluebell BELL 151
September-		
November 1982		

4 Heine songs: Im Rhein, im schönen Strome;   Du bist wie eine Blume;
Vergiftet sind meine Lieder;   Morgens steh' ich auf und frage

Stockholm   Roos   CD: Bluebell ABCD 021
May-December
1986

3 Sonetti di Petrarca: Pace non trovo;   Benedetto sia'l giorno;   I visi
in terra

Stockholm   Roos   CD: Bluebell ABCD 021
May-December
1986

3 Songs from Wilhelm Tell: Der Fischerknabe;   Der Hirt;   Der Alpenjäger

Stockholm   Roos   CD: Bluebell ABCD 021
May-December
1986

4 Victor Hugo songs: Comment disaient-ils?;   Quand je dors;   Enfant, si
j'étais roi;   S'il est un charmant gazon

Stockholm   Roos   CD: Bluebell ABCD 021
May-December
1986

3 Wartburg songs: Heinrich von Ofterdingen;   Walther von der Vogelweide;
Reimar der Alte

Stockholm   Roos   CD: Bluebell ABCD 021
May-December
1986

Songs: Angiolin dal biondo crin;   Bist du's?;   Der Glückliche;   Die drei
Zigeuner;   Es rauschen die Winde;   Es muss ein Wunderbares sein;   Gestorben
war ich;   Go not, happy day!;   Ich möchte hingeh'n;   Ich liebe dich;   In
Liebeslust;   Kling' leise, mein Lied;   O lieb', solang du lieben kannst;
Schwebe, schwebe, blaues Auge

Stockholm   Roos   CD: Bluebell ABCD 022
May-December
1986

LORTZING

Die Opernprobe

Munich 1974	Role of Johann Litz, Lövaas, Hirte, Berry Bavarian State Orchestra & Chorus Suitner	LP: EMI 1C 065 28835

Undine

Berlin September 1966	Role of Hugo Pütz, Rothenberger, Schreier, Prey, Frick RIAS Choir Berlin RO Heger	LP: EMI SMC 91635-91637 LP: EMI 1C 183 30218-30220 LP: EMI 1C 149 30218-30220 CD: EMI CMS 763 2082 Excerpts LP: EMI 1C 063 28528/1C 061 29044

Zar und Zimmermann

Dresden 1966	Role of Chateauneuf Köth, Burmeister, Schreier, Prey, Frick Leipzig Radio Chorus Dresden Staatskapelle Heger	LP: EMI 1C 183 29302-29304 LP: EMI 1C 149 29302-29304 LP: Angel 6020 CD: Berlin Classics Excerpts LP: EMI HQM 1059/HQS 1059 LP: EMI 1C 063 28171/1C 063 29064

MASSENET

Cendrillon

London June 1978	Role of Prince Welting, Von Stade, Berbie, Bastin Ambrosian Chorus Philharmonia Rudel	LP: CBS 79323 CD: Sony M2K 79323

Manon

New York December 1959	Role of Des Grieux De los Angeles, Cehanovsky, Herbert Metropolitan Opera Orchestra & Chorus Morel	Unpublished Met broadcast
New York December 1963	Moffo, Guarrera, Tozzi Metropolitan Opera Orchestra & Chorus Schippers	Unpublished Met broadcast
London July 1970	Sills, Bacquier, Souzay Ambrosian Chorus New Philharmonia Rudel	LP: EMI SLS 800 LP: EMI 2C 165 92282-92285 CD: EMI CMS 769 8312 Excerpt LP: MCA Records ATS 20018

Manon: Excerpt (En fermant les yeux)

London April 1953	Philharmonia Galliera	78: Columbia LX 1614 45: Columbia SEL 1590/SCD 2082/ SCB 118 LP: Columbia 33CX 1130 LP: Angel 35096
Paris September 1961	Orchestre National Prêtre	LP: Columbia 33CX 1837/SAX 2481 LP: EMI 1C 063 11272/SLS 5250 LP: Angel 34055/36106/3204 LP: EMI 1C 137 78233-78236/SLS 5250

Manon: Excerpt (Ah! Fuyez doux image!)

Paris September 1961	Orchestre National Prêtre	LP: Columbia 33CX 1837/SAX 2481 LP: EMI 1C 063 11272/1C 063 29044 LP: Angel 34055/36106/3204 LP: EMI 1C 137 78233-78236/SLS 5250

Manon: Excerpt (J'ai marqué l'heure du départ)

| Paris
1974 | Mesplé
Paris Opéra Orchestra
Dervaux | LP: EMI 2C 063 14010
LP: Angel 37143
CD: EMI CZS 767 8132 |

Thaïs

| London
June 1976 | Role of Nicias
Sills, Milnes,
Van Allan
Alldis Choir
New Philharmonia
Maazel | LP: EMI SLS 993
LP: Angel 3832 |

Werther

| Paris
September 1968-
June 1969 | Role of Werther
De los Angeles,
Mesplé, Soyer
ORTF Chorus
Orchestre de Paris
Prêtre | LP: EMI SLS 5105
LP: Angel 3736
CD: EMI CMS 763 9732
Excerpts
LP: EMI 1C 063 02054/1C 063 29044 |

Werther: Excerpt (Pourquoi me réveiller?)

| Salzburg
August 1961 | Werba | CD: EMI CDM 565 3522 |

| Paris
September 1961 | Orchestre National
Prêtre | LP: Columbia 33CX 1837/SAX 2481
LP: Angel 34055/36106/3204
LP: EMI 1C 063 11272/5C 055 24368
LP: EMI 1C 137 78233-78236/SLS 5250 |

| Livorno
1985 | Soroga | CD: Fonè 85F-026 |

Another version of this aria, sung by Gedda with unidentified orchestra and conductor, can be heard on Ed Smith UORC 374

Werther: Excerpt (Un autre est son époux)

| Paris
September 1961 | Orchestre National
Prêtre | LP: Columbia 33CX 1837/SAX 2481
LP: Angel 34055/36106/3204
LP: EMI 1C 063 11272/5C 055 24368
LP: EMI 1C 137 78233-78236/SLS 5250 |

Werther: Excerpts (O nature!; Oui! Ce qu'elle m'ordonne)

| Budapest
February 1984 | Pataki | CD: Bluebell ABCD 041 |

Elégie

| Stockholm
June 1981 | Eyron | LP: Bluebell BELL 134
CD: Bluebell ABCD 004 |

MAY

Ein Stern fällt vom Himmel

Munich	Graunke SO	LP: Columbia (Germany) SMC 83884
1968	Mattes	LP: Angel 36314

MEHUL

Joseph: Excerpt (Champs paternels)

New York	Musica Aeterna	LP: MGS 109
October 1975	Orchestra	
	Waldman	

MENDELSSOHN

Elijah

London	Jones, Baker,	LP: EMI SLS 935
July 1968	Fischer-Dieskau	LP: Angel 3738
	New Philharmonia	LP: EMI 1C 149 00107-00109
	Orchestra & Chorus	
	Frühbeck de Burgos	

MENOTTI

L'ultimo selvaggio

New York	Role of Kodanda	Unpublished Met broadcast
January 1964	Peters, Stratas,	
	Chookasian, London,	
	Flagello	
	Metropolitan Opera	
	Orchestra & Chorus	
	Schippers	

MERIKANTO

Daer bjoerkarna susa

Stockholm	Stockholm PO	LP: RCA VICS 1546
May 1965	Grevillius	

Saeg, minnes du psalmen, vi sjoengo?

Stockholm	Unidentified	45: Odeon (Sweden) BEOS 4
1958	accompaniment	
Stockholm	Chorus	LP: Wisa WISLP 542
December 1977	Ellerstedt, organ	
Stockholm	E.Nilsson, organ	LP: Karp LP 1
March 1978		
Stockholm	Chorus	LP: Wisa WISLP 590
September 1980	Flink, organ	

MEYER

Gute Nacht, mein holdes süsses Mädchen

Munich	Graunke SO	LP: Columbia (Germany) SMC 83884
1968	Mattes	LP: Angel 36314

MEYERBEER

L'Africaine: Excerpt (O paradis!)

London	Covent Garden	LP: EMI ASD 2445/1C 047 30638
November 1967	Orchestra	LP: Angel 36623
	Patané	LP: EMI 1C 187 29227-29228
		CD: EMI CDM 769 5502

Les Huguenots, abridged version

Vienna	Role of Raoul	LP: BJR Records BJR 124
February 1971	Tarres, Welting,	Excerpts
	Diaz	CD: Myto MCD 91646
	Austrian Radio	CD: Gala GL 100.603
	Orchestra & Chorus	
	Märzendorfer	

Les Huguenots: Excerpt (Beauté divine enchanteresse)

Paris	Mesplé	LP: EMI 2C 069 14010
1974	Paris Opéra Orchestra	LP: Angel 37143
	Dervaux	CD: EMI CZS 767 8132

Le Prophète

Turin	Role of Jean	LP: BJR Records BJR 121
July 1970	Scotto, Horne	CD: Myto MCD 90318
	RAI Turin	CD: Foyer 3CF-2035
	Orchestra & Chorus	CD: Claque GM 3013-3015
	H.Lewis	Excerpts
		CD: Myto MCD 91646
		CD: Gala GL 100.603

MIASKOVSKY

The moon and the mist

Salzburg	Werba	CD: EMI CDM 565 3522
August 1961		

MILLOECKER

Der Bettelstudent

| Munich
September 1967 | Role of Symon
Litz, Streich, Holm,
Unger, Prey
Bavarian Radio
Chorus
Graunke SO
Allers | LP: EMI 1C 191 30162-30163
CD: EMI CMS 565 3872
Excerpts
LP: 1C 061 28199
LP: EMI 1C 047 30630/SHZE 236
LP: EMI 1C 137 78233-78236
LP: EMI 1C 187 29227-29228
CD: EMI CDM 769 5062/CDM 769 6022 |

Die Dubarry: Excerpt (Es lockt die Nacht)

| Munich
June-July
1965 | Graunke SO
Mattes | LP: EMI SME 74169/1C 061 28818
LP: EMI 1C 183 28811-28813 |

MOZART

La Clemenza di Tito

| Cologne
December 1955 | Role of Tito
Zadek, Malaniuk,
Offermanns, Gröschel,
Wallenstein
WDR Orchestra
and Chorus
Keilberth | LP: Cetra LO 78 |

La Clemenza di Tito: Excerpt (Se all' impero)

| Paris
July 1957 | Paris Conservatoire
Orchestra
Cluytens | LP: Columbia 33CX 1528
LP: Angel 35510
LP: EMI 1C 137 78233-78236 |

La Clemenza di Tito: Excerpt (Del più sublime soglio)

| Amsterdam
1963 | Concertgebouw
Orchestra
Jochum | CD: Verona 28013 |

Cosi fan tutte

London	Role of Ferrando	LP: Philips 6707 025/6747 385
April and	Caballé, Baker,	CD: Philips 416 6332/422 5422
June 1974	Cotrubas, Ganzarolli,	
	Van Allan	
	Covent Garden	
	Orchestra & Chorus	
	C.Davis	

Cosi fan tutte: Excerpt (Un aura amorosa)

Paris	Paris Conservatoire	LP: Columbia 33CX 1528
July 1957	Orchestra	LP: Angel 35510/3204
	Cluytens	LP: EMI 1C 137 78233-78236/SLS 5250
Stockholm	National Museum	LP: Polar POLS 325
August 1970	Chamber Orchestra	
	Génetay	

Don Giovanni

Aix-en-Provence	Role of Don Ottavio	LP: Vox OPBX 162
July 1956	Stich-Randall,	CD: EMI CMS 764 3722
	Danco, Moffo, Cortis,	
	Arié, Campo	
	Aix Festival Chorus	
	Paris Conservatoire	
	Orchestra	
	Rosbaud	
New York	Steber, Della Casa,	Unpublished Met broadcast
January 1961	Hurley, Siepi,	
	Wildermann	
	Metropolitan Opera	
	Orchestra & Chorus	
	Leinsdorf	
London	Watson, C.Ludwig,	LP: EMI AN 172-175/SAN 172-175
June and	Freni, Ghiaurov,	LP: EMI SLS 923/SLS 143 4623
July 1966	Berry, Crass	CD: EMI CMS 763 8412
	New Philharmonia	Excerpts
	Orchestra & Chorus	LP: EMI ASD 2508
	Klemperer	CD: EMI CDM 769 0552
New York	Sutherland, Lorengar,	CD: Nuova Era 033.6708
January 1967	Hurley, Siepi,	Excerpts
	Flagello, Giaotti	CD: Memories HR 4585-4596
	Metropolitan Opera	
	Orchestra & Chorus	
	Böhm	
New York	Moser, Zylis-Gara,	Unpublished Met broadcast
March 1971	Pilou, Siepi,	
	Plishka, Corena	
	Metropolitan Opera	
	Orchestra & Chorus	
	Krips	

Don Giovanni: Excerpt (Dalla sua pace)

Paris July 1957	Paris Conservatoire Orchestra Cluytens	LP: Columbia 33CX 1528 LP: Angel 35510
Stockholm August 1970	National Museum Chamber Orchestra Génetay	LP: Polar POLS 325
Vienna June 1984	Austrian RO Hollreiser	LP: Amadeo 415 3111

Don Giovanni: Excerpt (Il mio tesoro)

Paris July 1957	Paris Conservatoire Orchestra Cluytens	LP: Columbia 33CX 1528 LP: Angel 35510
Stockholm August 1970	National Museum Chamber Orchestra Génetay	LP: Polar POLS 325

Don Giovanni: Excerpt (Ah, dovè il perfido?)

Munich August 1963	Hillebrecht, Jurinac, Rothenberger, Kusche, Peter Munich PO Keilberth	LP: Orfeo S120 841I

Die Entführung aus dem Serail

Aix-en-Provence July 1954	Role of Belmonte Stich-Randall, Prietto, Senéchal, Arié Aix Festival Chorus Paris Conservatoire Orchestra Rosbaud	LP: Melodram MEL 445 Excerpt CD: Verona 28012
Vienna February 1966	Rothenberger, Popp, Unger, Frick Vienna Opera Chorus VPO Krips	LP: EMI 1C 163 00070-00071 LP: Angel 6025 CD: EMI CMS 763 2632 Excerpts LP: EMI 1C 063 00844 Also issued on LP by World Records
London October 1967	Dobbs, Eddy, Fryatt, Mangin Bath Festival Orchestra & Chorus Menuhin Sung in English	LP: EMI SAN 201-203/SLS 932 LP: Angel 3741 CD: Priceless D 18398

Die Entführung aus dem Serail: Excerpts (O wie ängstlich, o wie feurig!; Wenn der Freude Tränen fliessen)

Paris	Paris Conservatoire	LP: Columbia 33CX 1528
July 1957	Orchestra	LP: Angel 35510
	Cluytens	

Die Entführung aus dem Serail: Excerpt (Im Mohrenland gefangen)

Paris	Role of Pedrillo	LP: Columbia 33CX 1528
July 1957	Paris Conservatoire	LP: Angel 35510/3204
	Orchestra	LP: EMI 1C 137 78233-78236/SLS 5250
	Cluytens	

Idomeneo

Dresden	Role of Idomeneo	LP: EMI SLS 965
May 1971	Rothenberger, Moser,	LP: EMI 1C 191 29271-29274
	Dallapozza, Schreier,	CD: EMI CMS 763 9902
	Büchner, Adam	CD: Berlin Classics
	Leipzig Radio Chorus	
	Dresden Staatskapelle	
	Schmidt-Isserdstedt	
Rome	Harper, Woodland,	CD: Myto MCD 91238
May 1971	Norman	
	RAI Rome	
	Orchestra & Chorus	
	C.Davis	

Idomeneo: Excerpt (Fuor del mar)

Paris	Paris Conservatoire	LP: Columbia 33CX 1528
July 1957	Orchestra	LP: Angel 35510
	Cluytens	LP: Columbia (Germany) C 70411
		LP: EMI 1C 137 78233-78236

Der Schauspieldirektor

Munich	Role of Vogelsang	LP: EMI 1C 065 30230
1975	Moser, Mesplé,	CD: EMI CDC 763 8262
	Hirte, Ustinov	
	Bavarian State	
	Orchestra	
	Schöner	

Die Zauberflöte

Rome December 1953	Role of Tamino Schwarzkopf, Streich, Noni, Taddei, Petri, Clabassi RAI Rome Orchestra & Chorus Karajan Sung in Italian	CD: Myto 89007 Excerpts CD: Hunt CD 535/CDHP 535 CD: Gala GL 317
Vienna May 1962	Lipp, Hallstein, Sciutti, Kunz, Frick, Wächter Vienna Opera Chorus VPO Karajan	LP: Movimento musica 03.015 CD: Movimento musica 051.028
London March and April 1964	Janowitz, Popp, Pütz, Berry, Frick, Crass Philharmonia Orchestra & Chorus Klemperer	LP: EMI AN 137-139/SAN 137-139/SLS 912 LP: Angel 3651 CD: EMI CMS 769 9712/CDS 755 1732 Excerpts LP: EMI ALP 2314/ASD 2314 LP: EMI ESD 100 3261 CD: EMI CDM 763 4512
Hamburg 1972	Mathis, Deutekom, Workman, Grundheber, Moll Philharmonisches Staatsorchester and Chorus Stein	VHS Video: Lyric (USA) LDV 1380

Die Zauberflöte: Excerpt (Dies Bildnis ist bezaubernd schön)

Stockholm 1952	Stockholm Opera Orchestra Bendix	LP: Odeon (Sweden) MOAK 1001
Paris July 1957	Paris Conservatoire Orchestra Cluytens	LP: Columbia 33CX 1528 LP: Angel 35510
Munich June 1967	Bavarian State Orchestra Bender	LP: EMI ASD 2364/SME 80814 LP: Angel 36624/3204 LP: EMI 1C 063 28993/1C 063 29044 LP: EMI 5C 055 24368/SLS 5250 LP: EMI 1C 137 78233-78236
Stockholm August 1970	National Museum Chamber Orchestra Génetay	LP: Polar POLS 325

Requiem

London July 1971	Armstrong, Baker, Fischer-Dieskau Alldis Choir English Chamber Orchestra Barenboim	LP: EMI ASD 2788/1C 065 02246 LP: Angel 36842 CD: EMI CZS 762 8922

Coronation Mass

Munich July 1976	Moser, Hamari, Fischer-Dieskau Bavarian Radio Orchestra & Chorus Jochum	LP: EMI ASD 3373 LP: Angel 37283 CD: EMI CDM 769 0232

Vesperae solennes de confessore

Munich July 1976	Moser, Hamari, Fischer-Dieskau Bavarian Radio Orchestra & Chorus Jochum	LP: EMI ASD 3373 LP: Angel 37283 CD: EMI CDM 769 0232

Clarice, cara mia sposa, duet

Munich	Schmidpeter	LP: EMI 1C 187 30221-30222
1975	Bavarian State	
	Orchestra	
	Ungar	

Con ossequio, con rispetto, concert aria

Munich	Bavarian State	LP: EMI 1C 187 30221-30222
1975	Orchestra	
	Ungar	

Misero o sogno!, concert aria

Stockholm	National Museum	LP: Polar POLS 323
August 1970	Chamber Orchestra	
	Génetay	

Müsst' ich durch tausend Drachen, concert aria

Munich	Bavarian State	LP: EMI 1C 187 30221-30222
1975	Orchestra	
	Ungar	

Per pietà non ricercate, concert aria

Paris	Paris Conservatoire	LP: Columbia 33CX 1528
July 1957	Orchestra	LP: Angel 35510
	Cluytens	LP: EMI 1C 137 78233-78236/SLS 5250
Stockholm	National Museum	LP: Polar POLS 323
August 1970	Chamber Orchestra	
	Génetay	

Das Veilchen

Budapest	Pataki	CD: Bluebell ABCD 041
February 1984		

MUSSORGSKY

Boris Godunov

Paris July 1952	Roles of Dimitri and Boyar Zareska, Bielecki, Christoff, Borg Choeurs russes Orchestre National Dobrowen	45: Victor WHMV 6400 LP: HMV ALP 1044-1047/SLS 5072 LP: Victor LHMV 6400 LP: Capitol GDR 7164 LP: Angel 6101 CD: EMI CHS 565 1922 Excerpts LP: HMV ALP 1323 LP: Victor LHMV 1052/LVT 1021
New York April 1963	Role of Dimitri Elias, Tozzi, Hines, Cassel Metropolitan Opera Orchestra & Chorus Solti	Unpublished Met broadcast
Warsaw 1976	Kinasz, Talvela, Haugland, Mroz Polish Radio Orchestra & Chorus Semkow	LP: EMI SLS 1000 LP: Angel 3844 LP: EMI 1C 155 02870-02873 CD: EMI CMS 754 3772 Excerpts LP: EMI ESD 143 6171
Washington July 1987	Role of Simpleton Vishnevskaya, Riegel, Raimondi, Plishka National Symphony Orchestra & Chorus Rostropovitch	CD: Erato 2292 454182

Boris Godunov: Excerpt (That wily Jesuit had caught me)

Belgrade April 1969	Role of Dimitri Belgrade PO Zdravkovitch	LP: EMI 1C 063 28070 LP: EMI 1C 137 78233-78236 LP: EMI 1C 187 29227-29228

Sorochintsky Fair: Excerpt (My heart, my poor heart!)

Belgrade April 1969	Belgrade PO Zdravkovitch	LP: EMI 1C 063 28070

The garden by the Don

Stockholm   Eyron   LP: EMI 1C 063 28023
September 1968

London   Parsons   CD: Arkadia GI 8061
November 1971

The He-Goat

Stockholm   Eyron   LP: EMI 1C 063 28023
September 1968

London   Parsons   CD: Arkadia GI 8061
November 1971

Moscow   Mogilewskaya   LP: Melodiya C10 13977-13978
March 1980   LP: Eurodisc 203 284.366

Song of the flea

Budapest   Pataki   CD: Bluebell ABCD 041
February 1984

Where art thou, little star?

Stockholm   Eyron   LP: EMI 1C 063 28023
September 1968

London   Parsons   CD: Arkadia GI 8061
November 1971

Moscow   Mogilewskaya   LP: Melodiya C10 13977-13978
March 1980   LP: Eurodisc 203 284.366

MYRBERG

Duets: Nattetid vid stranden; Vaerbaecken

Stockholm	Leanderson	LP: Bluebell BELL 166
October 1983	Eyron	

NAPRAVNIK

Dubrovsky: Excerpt (O give me oblivion)

Salzburg	Werba	CD: EMI CDM 565 3522
August 1961		
New York	Unidentified	Unpublished Met broadcast
November 1977	pianist	

NICOLAI

Die lustigen Weiber von Windsor: Excerpt (Horch', die Lerche singt im Hain)

Munich	Bavarian State	LP: EMI ASD 2364/SME 80814
June 1967	Orchestra	LP: Angel 36624
	Bender	LP: EMI 1C 047 30638
		LP: EMI 1C 137 78233-78236

NIN

Granadinas

Date and	Unidentified	LP: Ed Smith UORC 373
location	pianist	
uncertain		

NORDQVIST

Allenast i Gud soeker min sjael sin ro; Herren aer min herde

Stockholm   Stockholm University   LP: Bluebell BELL 191
April-September   Singers
1985   Jonsson

Boen; Till havs

Stockholm   Eyron   LP: Bluebell BELL 182
November-
December 1982

NORLEN

Visa vid midsommartid

Stockholm   Stockholm PO   LP: RCA LSC 10034
May 1965   Grevillius

NORMAN

Aennu "Till en saengare"; Foerargligt grannskap; Om vinten; Vi ses igen

Stockholm   Eyron   LP: Bluebell BELL 151
September-
November 1982

OFFENBACH

Les Contes d'Hoffmann

New York February 1959	Role of Hoffmann Dobbs, Elias, Amara, M.Miller, London Metropolitan Opera Orchestra & Chorus Morel	Unpublished Met broadcast
Paris September and October 1964	Schwarzkopf, De los Angeles, D'Angelo, Ghiuselev, London, Blanc Duclos Choir Paris Conservatoire Orchestra Cluytens	LP: EMI AN 154-156/SAN 154-156 LP: EMI 1C 157 00045-00047 LP: Angel 3667 CD: EMI CMS 763 2222 Excerpts LP: EMI SXLP 30538 LP: EMI 1C 063 01967/1C 063 29044 CD: EMI CDM 763 4482/CZS 568 1132
New York April 1971	Boky, Crespin, Amara, Bacquier, Franke, Plishka Metropolitan Opera Orchestra & Chorus Baudo	Unpublished Met broadcast
Miami 1980	Welting, Elias, Putnam, Van Dam Miami Opera Orchestra & Chorus De Almeida	LP: HRE Records HRE 330

Die schöne Helene

Munich 1979	Role of Paris Rothenberger, Fassbaender, Gruber, Orth, Kusche Bavarian Radio Orchestra & Chorus Mattes	LP: EMI 1C 157 45832-45833 CD: EMI CMS 565 3662 Excerpt CD: EMI CDM 769 5062

Die schöne Helene: Excerpt (Auf dem Berge Ida)

Stockholm 1962	Stockholm Opera Orchestra Jelving Sung in Swedish	LP: Odeon (Sweden) PMES 536

OLSSON

Saesom hjorten traengtar efter vattubaecken

Stockholm	Stockholm University	LP: Bluebell BELL 191
April-September	Singers	
1985	Jonsson	

OSCAR I

Songs: Beaucoup d'amour; Bergers et troubadours

Stockholm	Oestman	LP: Swedish Society SLT 33243
December 1975		

PALM

Under roenn och syren, duet

Stockholm	Leanderson	LP: Bluebell BELL 154
June 1983	Pataki	

Stockholm	Leanderson	LP: Bluebell BELL 166
October 1983	Eyron	

PEREZ

Schlaf' ein, mein blond' Engelein

Munich	Graunke SO	LP: Columbia (Germany) SMC 83884
1968	Mattes	LP: Angel 36314

PERGOLESI

Nina

Stockholm	Stockholm University	LP: Bluebell BELL 124
February and	Singers	
March 1981	Blohm	

PETERSON-BERGER

Songs: Aftonstaemning; Bland skogens hoega furnstammar; Ditt namm jag
hade slrivit; Ecce homo; En gammal dansrytm; Irmelin rose; Jungfrurosen;
Meine Rosen; Mitt trollslott; Naer jag foer mig sjaelv i moerka skogen gaer;
Semele; Sju rosor och sju eldar; Sommarnattsdagg; Under vintergatan;
Venedig; Vid aessjorna; Villemo; Zarathustras Rundgesang

Stockholm	Eyron	LP: Bluebell BELL 122
September 1980		

Songs: Aspaekerspolka; Boeljebyvais; Dagen flyr; Die letzte Nacht; Dina
oegon aero eldar; Du ler; En madrigal; Herr Ollondal; Intet aer som
vaetanstider; Laengtan heter min arvedel; Liebesreime; Liksom den unge
Zephyr; Maj i munga; Musik bewegt mich; Pae vaerdshuset kopparfloejeln;
Tvae klara stjaernor har himlen; Vackra barn daer vid ditt foernster;
Vorfrühling

Stockholm	Eyron	LP: Bluebell BELL 121
September 1980		

2 Songs on Swedish folk melodies

London	Parsons	CD: Arkadia GI 8061
November 1971		

Saeng efter skoedeanden; Fanjunkar Berg

Stockholm	Eyron	LP: Bluebell BELL 182
November-		
December 1982		

Als ich in dem Walde ging; Im Walde unter hohen Bäumen

Stockholm   Eyron   LP: EMI 1C 063 28023
September 1968

De tysta saengerna

Stockholm   Stockholm University LP: Bluebell BELL 124
February-   Singers
March 1981   Blohm

Jungfrun under lind

Stockholm   Stockholm PO   LP: RCA LSC 10034
May 1965   Grevillius

Leningrad   Werba   LP: Melodiya C10 14631-14632
1980

Stockholm   Eyron   LP: Bluebell BELL 122
September 1980

Som stjaernorna pae himmelen

Stockholm   Stockholm PO   LP: RCA LSC 10034
May 1965   Grevillius

Stockholm   Eyron   LP: Bluebell BELL 122
September 1980

Til majdag

Leningrad   Werba   LP: Melodiya C10 14631-14632
1980

Stockholm   Eyron   LP: Bluebell BELL 122
September 1980

The entire contents of the 2 LPs of songs by Peterson-Berger (Bluebell BELL
121 and BELL 122) have been re-issued on 2 CDs (Bluebell ABCD 034 and ABCD
035);   however, they are grouped in an entirely different sequence to that
of the LPs

PFITZNER

Palestrina

Munich	Role of Palestrina	LP: DG 2711 013/2740 223
January and	Donath, Fassbaender,	CD: DG 427 4172
February 1973	Weikl, Prey,	
	Fischer-Dieskau	
	Bavarian Radio	
	Orchestra & Chorus	
	Kubelik	

PICCINI

Le faux Lord: Excerpt (O nuit, déesse du mystère)

Stockholm	National Museum	LP: Polar POLS 321
August 1979	Chamber Orchestra	
	Génetay	

PLANQUETTE

Les cloches de Corneville: Excerpt (Skeppsgossevisa)

Stockholm	Stockholm Opera	LP: Odeon (Sweden) PMES 536
1962	Orchestra	
	Jelving	
	Sung in Swedish	

PONCHIELLI

La Gioconda: Excerpt (Cielo e mar)

London	Philharmonia	LP: Columbia 33CX 1130
April 1953	Galliera	LP: Angel 35096

London	Covent Garden	LP: EMI ASD 2445/SLS 5250
November 1967	Orchestra	LP: Angel 36623/3204
	Patané	LP: EMI 1C 063 02703/1C 047 30638
		CD: EMI CDM 769 5502

POULENC

A sa guitare

Paris September 1967	Ciccolini	LP: Pathé 2C 063 10000
Paris September 1974– February 1977	Baldwin	LP: EMI 2C 165 16231-16235 CD: EMI CMS 764 0872

Another version of the song, performed by Gedda with unidentified accompanist, can be heard on Ed Smith UORC 373

Air champêtre/Airs chantés

1960	Singer	LP: Melodram MEL 659
Paris September 1967	Ciccolini	LP: Pathé 2C 063 10000 LP: EMI ASD 2574

Air grave/Airs chantés

1960	Singer	LP: Melodram MEL 659
Salzburg August 1961	Werba	CD: EMI CDM 565 3522
Paris September 1967	Ciccolini	LP: Pathé 2C 063 10000

Bleuet

Paris September 1974– February 1977	Baldwin	LP: EMI 2C 165 16231-16235 CD: EMI CMS 764 0872

8 chansons polonaises

Paris	Baldwin	LP: EMI 2C 165 16231-16235
September 1974-	Sung in Polish	
February 1977		

Hôtel/Banalités

Paris	Ciccolini	LP: Pathé 2C 063 10000
September 1967		

2 poèmes de Guillaume Apollinaire: Hyde Park; Montparnasse

Paris	Baldwin	LP: EMI 2C 165 16231-16235
September 1974-		CD: EMI CMS 764 0872
February 1977		

Paganini/Métamorphoses

1960	Singer	LP: Melodram MEL 659

Paris	Ciccolini	LP: Pathé 2C 063 10000
September 1967		LP: EMI ASD 2574

Tel jour, telle nuit

Paris	Baldwin	LP: EMI 2C 165 16231-16235
September 1974-		CD: EMI CMS 764 0872
February 1977		

Voyage à Paris/Banalités

Paris	Ciccolini	LP: Pathé 2C 063 10000
September 1967		

Another version of the song, performed by Gedda with unidentified accompanist, can be heard on Ed Smith UORC 373

PRATELLA

La strada blanca

Berlin	Moore	LP: Columbia 33CX 5278/SAX 5278
July 1965		LP: Columbia (Germany) C 91439/
		SMC 91439/1C 063 28514

Another version of the song, performed by Gedda with unidentified accompanist, can be heard on Ed Smith UORC 373

PRINCE GUSTAV

Mina levnadstimmar stupa

Stockholm	Stockholm University	LP: Bluebell BELL 191
April-September	Singers	
1985	Jonsson	

Studentsaegen

Stockholm	Stockholm University	LP: Bluebell BELL 124
February-	Singers	
March 1981	Blohm	

PROKOFIEV

War and Peace

Paris	Role of Kuragin	CD: Erato ECD 75480/2292 453312
December 1986	Vishnevskaya, Ochman,	
	Miller, Ghiuselev	
	French Radio Chorus	
	Orchestre National	
	Rostropovich	

PUCCINI

La Bohème

Rome
July-August
1963

Role of Rodolfo
Freni, Adani,
Sereni, Basiola
Rome Opera
Orchestra & Chorus
Schippers

LP: EMI SLS 907
LP: Angel 3643
CD: EMI CMS 769 6572
Excerpts
LP: EMI SMC 80149/SLS 5250
LP: EMI 1C 063 00769/1C 063 00372
CD: EMI CDM 763 9322

La Bohème: Excerpt (Che gelida manina)

New York
November 1962

Firestone Orchestra
Pelletier

LP: Melodram MEL 659
VHS Video: VAI Audio VAIA 69136

London
November 1967

Covent Garden
Orchestra
Patané

LP: EMI ASD 2445
LP: Angel 36623/3204
LP: EMI 1C 063 02703/1C 063 29064

1977

Unidentified
Orchestra & conductor

LP: Ed Smith UORC 374

It is possible that the LP and VHS Video issues of the 1962 performance of
this aria could be two separate versions

La Bohème: Excerpt (O soave fanciulla)

New York
November 1962

Della Casa
Firestone Orchestra
Pelletier

LP: Melodram MEL 659
VHS Video: VAI Audio VAIA 69136

It is possible that the LP and VHS Video issues of this duet are two
separate performances

Madama Butterfly

Milan
August 1955

Role of Pinkerton
Callas, Danieli,
Borriello
La Scala
Orchestra & Chorus
Karajan

LP: Columbia 33CX 1296-1298
LP: EMI SLS 5015/EX 29 12653
LP: Angel 3523
CD: EMI CDS 747 9592
Excerpts
LP: Columbia 33CX 1787
LP: Columbia (Germany) C 70411/SHZE 110

Madama Butterfly, Querschnitt

Berlin August- September 1966	Rothenberger, Wagner, Prey, Günter RIAS Choir Deutsche Oper Orchestra Patané Sung in German	LP: EMI SME 81002/1C 063 29006 CD: EMI CDZ 252 3842

Madama Butterfly: Excerpt (Bimba dagli occhi)

Berlin 1977	Lorengar Berlin RO Albrecht	Unpublished video recording

Manon Lescaut: Excerpt (Donna non vidi mai)

London November 1967	Covent Garden Orchestra Patané	LP: EMI ASD 2445/SME 81100 LP: Angel 36623 LP: EMI 1C 063 02703/1C 063 29064 LP: EMI 5C 055 24368

Tosca: Excerpt (Recondita armonia)

London November 1967	Covent Garden Orchestra Patané	LP: EMI ASD 2445/SME 81100 LP: Angel 36623 LP: EMI 1C 063 29064/1C 047 30638 LP: EMI 1C 063 02703
Boston April 1972	Boston Opera Orchestra McConachy	LP: HRE Records HRE 377

Tosca: Excerpt (E lucevan le stelle)

London November 1967	Covent Garden Orchestra Patané	LP: EMI ASD 2445/SME 81100 LP: Angel 36623 LP: EMI 1C 063 02703
Vienna June 1984	Austrian RO Graf	LP: Amadeo 415 3111

Turandot: Excerpt (Nessun dorma)

London November 1967	Covent Garden Orchestra Patané	LP: EMI ASD 2445/SME 81100 LP: Angel 36623 LP: EMI 1C 063 02703/1C 047 30638

Aleko: Excerpt (Song of the young gypsy)

Salzburg August 1961	Werba	CD: EMI CDM 565 3522
Berlin July 1965	Moore	LP: Columbia 33CX 5278/SAX 5278 LP: Columbia (Germany) C 91439/ SMC 91439 LP: EMI 1C 063 28514/SLS 5250
Belgrade April 1969	Belgrade PO Zdravkovitch	LP: EMI 1C 063 28070/1C 047 30638 LP: Angel 3204 LP: EMI 1C 137 78233-78236
London November 1971	Parsons	CD: Arkadia GI 8061
Moscow October 1980	Andreeva Folk Orchestra Popov	LP: Melodiya C20 16003-16004 CD: Olympia OCD 244

Alone again

1979	Wustman	LP: Glendale GLS 8007
Leningrad 1980	Werba	LP: Melodiya C10 14631-14632

The answer

Paris June 1967- June 1969	Weissenberg	LP: EMI 2C 063 10585 CD: EMI CDM 763 7312

April, Feast day of Spring

Paris June 1967- June 1969	Weissenberg	LP: EMI 2C 063 10585 CD: EMI CDM 763 7312
1979	Wustman	LP: Glendale GLS 8007
Leningrad 1980	Werba	LP: Melodiya C10 14631-14632

Arion

Paris June 1967- June 1969	Weissenberg	LP: EMI 2C 063 10585 CD: EMI CDM 763 7312

Rachmaninov Songs/continued

By my window

Moscow	Mogilevskaya	LP: Melodiya C10 13977-13978
March 1980		LP: Eurodisc 203 284.366

Cease thy singing, maiden fair

Berlin	Moore	LP: Columbia 33CX 5278/SAX 5278
July 1965		LP: Columbia (Germany) C 91439/
		SMC 91439/1C 063 28514
Paris	Weissenberg	LP: EMI 2C 063 10585
June 1967-		CD: EMI CDM 763 7312
June 1969		

Christ is risen

Salzburg	Werba	CD: EMI CDM 565 3522
August 1961		
Paris	Weissenberg	LP: EMI 2C 063 10585
June 1967-		CD: EMI CDM 763 7312
June 1969		

A dream

Moscow	Mogilevskaya	LP: Melodiya C10 13977-13978
March 1980		LP: Eurodisc 203 284.366

Fragment by Alfred de Musset

Paris	Weissenberg	LP: EMI 2C 063 10585
June 1967-		CD: EMI CDM 763 7312
June 1969		

Happiness

Salzburg	Werba	CD: EMI CDM 565 3522
August 1961		

Harvest of sorrow

Paris	Weissenberg	LP: EMI 2C 063 10585
June 1967-		CD: EMI CDM 763 7312
June 1969		

Rachmaninov Songs/continued

How fair this spot

Berlin July 1965	Moore	LP: Columbia 33CX 5278/SAX 5278 LP: EMI 1C 063 28514 LP: Angel 3204 LP: EMI ASD 2574/SLS 5250
Paris June 1967– June 1969	Weissenberg	LP: EMI 2C 063 10585 CD: EMI CDM 763 7312
London November 1971	Parsons	CD: Arkadia GI 8061

In my garden

Paris June 1967– June 1969	Weissenberg	LP: EMI 2C 063 10585 CD: EMI CDM 763 7312

In the morn of life

Paris June 1967– June 1969	Weissenberg	LP: EMI 2C 063 10585 CD: EMI CDM 763 7312

In the silence of the night

Paris June 1967– June 1969	Weissenberg	LP: EMI 2C 063 10585 CD: EMI CDM 763 7312

Lilacs

Paris June 1967– June 1969	Weissenberg	LP: EMI 2C 063 10585 CD: EMI CDM 763 7312
Moscow March 1980	Mogilevskaya	LP: Melodiya C10 13977-13978 LP: Eurodisc 203 284.366

A little isle

Moscow March 1980	Mogilevskaya	LP: Melodiya C10 13977-13978 LP: Eurodisc 203 284.366

Rachmaninov Songs/concluded

No regrets

Paris June 1967- June 1969	Weissenberg	LP: EMI 2C 063 10585 CD: EMI CDM 763 7312

A passing breeze

Paris June 1967- June 1969	Weissenberg	LP: EMI 2C 063 10585 CD: EMI CDM 763 7312

Spring waters

Berlin July 1965	Moore	LP: Columbia 33CX 5278/SAX 5278 LP: Angel 3204 LP: EMI 1C 063 28514/SLS 5250
Paris June 1967- June 1969	Weissenberg	LP: EMI 2C 063 10585 CD: EMI CDM 763 7312
1979	Wustman	LP: Glendale GLS 8007
Leningrad 1980	Werba	LP: Melodiya C10 14631-14632

The storm

Paris June 1967- June 1969	Weissenberg	LP: EMI 2C 063 10585 CD: EMI CDM 763 7312

To the children

Paris June 1967- June 1969	Weissenberg	LP: EMI 2C 063 10585 CD: EMI CDM 763 7312

Vocalise

Paris June 1967- June 1969	Weissenberg	LP: EMI 2C 063 10585 CD: EMI CDM 763 7312

RALF

Sjung mig saenger; Vaggvisa

Stockholm 1967	Stockholm University Singers Ralf	LP: Odeon (Sweden) 4E 053 34012

RAMEAU

Platée

Aix-en-Provence July 1956	Roles of Thespis and Mercure Micheau, Sautereau, Sénéchal, Jansen, Benoît Aix Festival Chorus Paris Conservatoire Orchestra Rosbaud	LP: Pathé DTX 223-224 LP: EMI 2C 165 12503-12504 CD: EMI CMS 769 8612

Castor et Pollux: Excerpt: (Ariette de berceuse)

Stockholm April 1968	Musica Aeterna Orchestra Waldman	LP: MGS 106

Castor et Pollux: Excerpt (Eclatez, fières trompettes!)

Stockholm April 1968	Musica Aeterna Orchestra Waldman	LP: Ed Smith EJS 518 LP: MGS 106

RANGSTROEM

Songs: Bergakungen; Det finns vael sae maeng a i vaerlden; Du och jag;
En gammal nyaersvisa; En gammal dansrytm; Gammalsvenskt; I dina haenders
mjuka faegelbo; Melodie; Naecken; Pan; Paradisets born; Rondeau;
Serenad; Sjoefararen vid milan; Som ett blommande mandeltraed; Stormar;
Vi maenniskor; Vingar i natten

Stockholm	Eyron	LP: Bluebell BELL 171
November 1983–		
January 1984		

Songs: Avskedet; Boen till natten; Den moerka blomman; Den gamle; En
ballad om narren och doeden; En ballad om god soemn; Flickan fraen ffaerran;
Jordans oenskan; Kastaliskt; Orfeus; Stjaernornes troest; Sysorna; Till
smaerten; Traedet som doer; Tristans doed; Vaentan; Vildgaessen flytta;
Vinden och traedet

Stockholm	Eyron	LP: Bluebell BELL 172
November 1983–		
January 1984		

RESPIGHI

Notte

Berlin	Moore	LP: Columbia 33CX 5278/SAX 5278
July 1965		LP: EMI 1C 063 28514/SLS 5250
		LP: Angel 3204
		LP: EMI 1C 137 78233-78236

Stornellatrice

Berlin	Moore	LP: Columbia 33CX 5278/SAX 5278
July 1965		LP: EMI ASD 2574/1C 063 28514

Other versions of these two Respighi songs, performed by Gedda with unidentified
accompanist, can be heard on Ed Smith UORC 373

May Night: Excerpt (How calm, how marvellous the night)

Belgrade	Belgrade PO	LP: EMI 1C 063 28070/ASD 2574
April 1969	Zdravkovitch	

May Night: Excerpt (The sun is sinking)

Belgrade	Belgrade PO	LP: EMI 1C 063 28070/SLS 5250
April 1969	Zdravkovitch	LP: Angel 3204

Sadko: Excerpt (You dark, shadowy wood)

Belgrade	Belgrade PO	LP: EMI 1C 063 28070
April 1969	Zdravkovitch	

Sadko: Excerpt (Song of the Indian Guest)

Stockholm	Stockholm Opera	45: Odeon (Sweden) BEOS 5
February 1962	Orchestra	
	Grevillius	
Berlin	Berlin RO	LP: Melodram MEL 659
1962	F.Walter	
Munich	Bavarian State	LP: EMI 1C 063 29064/SHZE 223
1966	Orchestra	
	Eichhorn	
	Sung in German	

A fir tree and a palm tree

Berlin	Singer	LP: Melodram MEL 659
1960		
Moscow	Mogilevskaya	LP: Melodiya C10 13977-13978
March 1980		LP: Eurodisc 203 284.366

It is not the breeze of wind

1979	Wustman	LP: Glendale GLS 8007
Leningrad	Werba	LP: Melodiya C10 14631-14632
1980		

It was in early spring

1979	Wustman	LP: Glendale GLS 8007
Leningrad 1980	Werba	LP: Melodiya C10 14631-14632

Return to the past

Berlin 1960	Singer	LP: Melodram MEL 659

Spring

Berlin 1960	Singer	LP: Melodram MEL 659

Song of the lark

1979	Wustman	LP: Glendale GLS 8007
Leningrad 1980	Werba	LP: Melodiya C10 14631-14632

Your wreath is freshly scented

1979	Wustman	LP: Glendale GLS 8007
Leningrad 1980	Werba	LP: Melodiya C10 14631-14632

ROMAN

Aria on Dixit Dominus; 59th Psalm of David; 51st Psalm of David; Jag vet
att min foerlossare lever; Vi love, vi love dig

Stockholm	Stockholm University	LP: Bluebell BELL 191
April-September	Singers	
1985	Jonsson	

ROSSINI

Armida: Excerpt (Grata quest' alma)

1967	Grist	LP: Ed Smith UORC 374
	Unidentified orchestra	
	and conductor	

Il Barbiere di Siviglia

London	Role of Almaviva	LP: EMI SLS 985
August 1974-	Sills, Milnes,	LP: Angel 3761
May 1975	Raimondi, Capecchi	Excerpt
	Alldis Choir	LP: EMI 1C 137 78233-78236
	LSO	
	Levine	

Guilleaume Tell

London	Role of Arnold	LP: EMI SLS 970
July 1972	Caballé, Mesplé,	LP: Angel 3793
	Bacquier, Hendriks	CD: EMI CMS 769 9512
	Ambrosian Chourus	Excerpt
	RPO	LP: Angel 3204
	Gardelli	

Guilleaume Tell, excerpts

Paris	Guiot, Blanc	LP: EMI 2C 061 10899/1C 063 10899
October 1967	Paris Opéra	Excerpts
	Orchestra & Chorus	LP: EMI SHZE 271/SLS 5250
	Lombard	LP: EMI 1C 137 78233-78236

Il Turco in Italia

Milan August and September 1954	Role of Narciso Callas, Stabile, Rossi-Lemeni La Scala Orchestra & Chorus Gavazzeni	LP: Columbia 33CX 1289-1291 LP: Angel 3535/6095 LP: EMI SLS 5148 CD: EMI CDS 749 3442 Excerpt LP: Columbia (Germany) C 70411

Petite messe solennelle

Cambridge August 1984 and London December 1984	Popp, Fassbaender, Kavrakos Labecq Sisters Kings College Choir Cleobury	LP: EMI EX 27 03169 LP: Angel 3976

La chanson de bébé; La lontananza

Stockholm June 1981	Eyron	LP: Bluebell BELL 134 CD: Bluebell ABCD 004

La danza

Munich 1968	Graunke SO Mattes	LP: EMI SHZE 236 LP: Angel 36314

Duetto buffo degli due gatti

Stockhom October 1983	Kirstenson Pataki	LP: Bluebell BELL 154

ROTTER

Ich küsse Ihre Hand, Madame

Munich 1968	Graunke SO Mattes	LP: EMI SMC 83884 LP: Angel 36314

ROUSSEAU

Le devin du village

Paris 1957	Role of Colin Micheau, Roux De Froment Chamber Orchestra De Froment	LP: Columbia (France) LP: Angel 35421 Excerpt LP: Columbia (Germany) C 70411

ROUSSEL

Padmâvatî

Toulouse	Role of Ratan-Sen	LP: EMI EX 173 1773
1982	Horne, Berbie,	LP: Angel 3948
	Burles, Van Dam	CD: EMI CDS 747 8918
	Orféon Donostiarra	
	Toulouse Capitole	
	Orchestra	
	Plasson	

Evocations

Toulouse	Stutzmann, Van Dam	LP: EMI 27 05431
June-October	Orféon Donostiarra	CD: EMI CDC 747 8872
1986	Toulouse Capitole	
	Orchestra	
	Plasson	

Details of 2 Roussel songs on Pathé LP 2C 051 12797 could not be traced

SATIE

4 petites mélodies; Tendrement

Paris	Ciccolini	LP: Pathé 2C 063 10749
Date uncertain		CD: EMI CDC 749 1672

ALESSANDRO SCARLATTI

Già il sole dal Gange; Sento nel core certo dolore

Stockholm	National Museum	LP: Polar POLS 321
August 1975	Chamber Orchestra	
	Génetay	

Le violette

Stockholm	National Museum	LP: Polar POLS 321
August 1975	Chamber Orchestra	
	Génetay	
Livorno	Soroga	CD: Fonè 85F-026
1985		

Die Zwillingsbrüder

| Munich
January 1975 | Role of Anton
Donath,
Fischer-Dieskau
Bavarian State
Orchestra
Sawallisch | LP: EMI 1C 065 28833/
1C 151 53043-53045 |

Die schöne Müllerin

| London
March 1955 | Moore | Columbia unpublished |
| 1971 | Eyron | LP: EMI 1C 037 29048 |

Die Advokaten (Mein Herr, ich komm', mich anzufragen)

| 1973 | Anheisser, Berry
Werba | LP: EMI 1C 187 30196-30197 |

Ave Maria

New York 1967	Firestone Orchestra Kostal	LP: Firestone CSLP 7015
Stockholm March 1978	E.Nilsson, organ	LP: Karp LP 1
Stockholm September 1980	Ellerstedt	LP: Wisa WISLP 590

Der Doppelgänger/Schwanengesang (Still ist die Nacht, es ruhen die Gassen)

| 1960 | Singer | LP: Melodram MEL 659 |

Erster Verlust (Ach, wer bringt die schönen Tage?)

| Budapest
February 1984 | Pataki | CD: Bluebell ABCD 041 |

Das Fischermädchen/Schwanengesang (Du schönes Fischermädchen)

| 1960 | Singer | LP: Melodram MEL 659 |

Der Hochzeitsbraten (Ach liebes Herz, ach Theobold!)

| 1973 | Rothenberger, Berry
Werba | LP: EMI 1C 187 30196-30197 |

Ihr Bild/Schwanengesang (Ich stand in dunklen Träumen)

| 1960 | Singer | LP: Melodram MEL 659 |

Die Liebe hat gelogen

| Salzburg
August 1961 | Werba | CD: EMI CDM 565 3522 |

Nacht und Träume (Heil'ge Nacht, du sinkest nieder)

| 1960 | Singer | LP: Melodram MEL 659 |
| Salzburg
August 1961 | Werba | CD: EMI CDM 565 3522 |

Nachthelle (Die Nacht ist heiter und ist rein)

| 1973 | Werba | LP: EMI 1C 187 30196-30197 |

Rastlose Liebe (Dem Schnee, dem Regen, dem Wind entgegen)

| Salzburg
August 1961 | Werba | CD: EMI CDM 565 3522 |
| Budapest
February 1984 | Pataki | CD: Bluebell ABCD 041 |

Schäfers Klagelied (Da droben auf jenem Berge)

| Budapest
February 1984 | Pataki | CD: Bluebell ABCD 041 |

Der Schiffer (Das Wasser rauscht', das Wasser schwoll)

| Salzburg
August 1961 | Werba | CD: EMI CDM 565 3522 |
| Budapest
February 1984 | Pataki | CD: Bluebell ABCD 041 |

Schubert Lieder/concluded

Des Teufels Lustschloss (Ich lach', ich wein')

1973   Moser, Berry   LP: EMI 1C 187 30196-30197
                       Bavarian State
                       Chorus
                       Ungar

Trinklied (Brüder, unser Erdenwallen)

1973   Bavarian State   LP: EMI 1C 187 30196-30197
                       Chorus
                       Werba

Die Verschworenen (Sie ist's, er ist's!)

1973   Moser   LP: EMI 1C 187 30196-30197
                       Bavarian State
                       Chorus
                       Ungar

Wanderers Nachtlied I (Ueber allen Gipfeln)

Budapest   Pataki   CD: Bluebell ABCD 041
February 1984

SCHUMANN

Paradies und die Peri

Düsseldorf   Moser, Fassbaender,   LP: EMI 1C 193 30187-30188
August 1973   Tripp   CD: EMI CMS 764 4472
                       Düsseldorf Symphony
                       Orchestra & Chorus
                       Czyz

Requiem

Düsseldorf   Donath, Soffel,   LP: EMI 146 7561
July 1983   Fischer-Dieskau   CD: EMI CZS 767 8192
                       Düsseldorf SO
                       Klee

Szenen aus Goethes „Faust"

Düsseldorf   Mathis, Lövaas,   LP: EMI 1C 165 46435-46436
April 1981   Fischer-Dieskau,   CD: EMI CMS 769 4502
                       Berry
                       Düsseldorf Symphony
                       Orchestra & Chorus
                       Klee

An den Sonnenschein (O Sonnenschein!)

1979   Wustman   LP: Glendale GLS 8007

Leningrad   Werba   LP: Melodiya C10 14631-14632
1980

Auf ihrem Grab, da steht eine Linde/Tragödie

1976   Werba   LP: EMI 1C 165 30692-30693

Blaue Augen hat das Mädchen/Spanische Liebeslieder

1976   Werba   LP: EMI 1C 165 30692-30693

Dunkler Lichtglanz, blinder Blick/Spanische Liebeslieder

1976   Moser, Schwarz,   LP: EMI 1C 165 30692-30693
                        Berry
                        Werba

Entflieh' mit mir/Tragödie

1976   Werba   LP: EMI 1C 165 30692-30693

Erstes Grün (Du junges Grün, du frisches Gras!)

1979   Wustman   LP: Glendale GLS 8007

Leningrad   Werba   LP: Melodiya C10 14631-14632
1980

Es ist verraten/Spanisches Liederspiel

1976   Werba   LP: EMI 1C 165 30692-30693

Flügel! Flügel! Um zu fliegen/Liebesfrühling

1976   Werba   LP: EMI 1C 165 30692-30693

1979   Wustman   LP: Glendale GLS 8007

Leningrad   Werba   LP: Melodiya C10 14631-14632
1980

Schumann Lieder/continued

Geständnis/Spanisches Liederspiel

1976   Werba   LP: EMI 1C 165 30692-30693

Der Himmel hat eine Träne geweint/Liebesfrühling

1976   Werba   LP: EMI 1C 165 30692-30693

1979   Wustman   LP: Glendale GLS 8007

Leningrad   Werba   LP: Melodiya C10 14631-14632
1980

Ich bin geliebt/Spanisches Liederspiel

1976   Moser, Schwarz,   LP: EMI 1C 165 30692-30693
                       Berry
                       Werba

Ich hab' in mich gesogen/Liebesfrühling

1976   Werba   LP: EMI 1C 165 30692-30693

1979   Wustman   LP: Glendale GLS 8007

Leningrad   Werba   LP: Melodiya C10 14631-14632
1980

In der Nacht/Spanisches Liederspiel

1976   Moser   LP: EMI 1C 165 30692-30693
                       Werba

Intermezzo/Spanisches Liederspiel

1976   Berry   LP: EMI 1C 165 30692-30693
                       Werba

Liebste, was kann uns denn scheiden?/Liebesfrühling

1976   Werba   LP: EMI 1C 165 30692-30693

Mein schöner Stern/Minnespiel

1976   Werba   LP: EMI 1C 165 30692-30693

Schumann Lieder/ concluded

Meine Töne, still und heiter/Minnespiel

1976   Werba   LP: EMI 1C 165 30692-30693

O Sonn', o Meer, o Rose/Liebesfrühling

1976   Werba   LP: EMI 1C 165 30692-30693

1979   Wustman   LP: Glendale GLS 8007

Leningrad   Werba   LP: Melodiya C10 14631-14632
1980

O wie lieblich ist das Mädchen/Spanische Liebeslieder

1976   Werba   LP: EMI 1C 165 30692-30693

Schön ist das Fest des Lenzes/Liebesfrühling

1976   Moser   LP: EMI 1C 165 30692-30693
                Werba

Schön ist das Fest des Lenzes/Minnespiel

1976   Moser, Schwarz,   LP: EMI 1C 165 30692-30693
                Berry
                Werba

So wahr die Sonne scheinet/Liebesfrühling

1976   Werba   LP: EMI 1C 165 30692-30693

So wahr die Sonne scheinet/Minnespiel

1976   Werba   LP: EMI 1C 165 30692-30693

Die tausend Grüsse/Minnespiel

1976   Moser   LP: EMI 1C 165 30692-30693
                Werba

Weh, wie zornig ist das Mädchen!/Spanisches Liederspiel

1976   Werba   LP: EMI 1C 165 30692-30693

SHOSTAKOVICH

Katerina Ismailova

London	Role of Sergei	LP: EMI SLS 5157
1979	Vishnevskaya,	LP: Angel 3866
	Petkov	CD: EMI CDS 749 9552
	Ambrosian Chorus	
	LPO	
	Rostropovitch	

SIBELIUS

Jubal

London	Parsons	CD: Arkadia GI 8061
November 1971		

Saev, saev, susa

Stockholm	Eyron	LP: EMI ASD 2574/1C 063 28023
September 1968		

London	Parsons	CD: Arkadia GI 8061
November 1971		

Svarta rosor

Stockholm	Eyron	LP: EMI ASD 2574/1C 063 28023
September 1968		

London	Parsons	CD: Arkadia GI 8061
November 1971		

SJOEBERG

Tonerna

Stockholm May 1965	Stockholm PO Grevillius	LP: RCA LSC 10034
Stockholm September 1968	Eyron	LP: EMI 1C 063 28023
London November 1971	Parsons	CD: Arkadia GI 8061
Stockholm September 1980	Ellerstedt	LP: Wisa WISLP 590
Stockholm June 1983	Pataki	LP: Bluebell BELL 154

SJOEGREN

Songs: Agnes, min dejlige sommerfugl; Den laenga dagen; Det foerste moede;
Tannhäuser-Lieder op 3 ; Dulgt kjaierlighed; Holder du af mig; Ich ging
in der Sommernacht ganz allein; Jeg giver mit digt til vaeren; Prinsessen;
Ro, ro, oegonsten; Sover du, min sjaed?

Stockholm January 1982	Eyron	LP: Bluebell BELL 141

Songs: Blanche de Namur; 5 Lieder an Eine; Det komma skallen sorgestund;
Tannhäuser-Lieder op 12; En vaervintervisa; Min hustru; O saeg, du ende
kaera; Sommarnattens sista ros; Vaersaeng

Stockholm January 1982	Eyron	LP: Bluebell BELL 142

I de sidste Oeiblikke

Stockholm September- November 1982	Eyron	LP: Bluebell BELL 151

I droemmen du aer mig naera

Stockholm May 1965	Stockholm PO Grevillius	LP: RCA LSC 10034
Stockholm January 1982	Eyron	LP: Bluebell BELL 141

Oktoberstaemning

Stockholm November- December 1982	Eyron	LP: Bluebell BELL 182

SMETANA

The Bartered Bride

New York November 1978	Role of Jenik Stratas, Boky, Vickers, Talvela, Hammond-Stroud Metropolitan Opera Orchestra & Chorus Levine Sung in English	Unpublished video recording
New York December 1978	Stratas, Boky, Vickers, Talvela, Hammond-Stroud Metropolitan Opera Orchestra & Chorus Levine Sung in English	Unpublished Met broadcast

Dalibor

New York January 1977	Role of Dalibor Kubiak, Sormova, Monk, Plishka New York Opera Orchestra & Chorus Queler	LP: Ed Smith UORC 324

SOEDERMAN

Songs: Ballad; Det var Maj, den skoena Maj; Frost foell pae blommor; Jag har dig aelskat; Kom fly med mig till fjaerran land; Kunde aen en gaeng jag; Min aelskling din hand pae mitt hjaerta laegg; O laegg din kind intill min kind

Stockholm September- November 1982	Eyron	LP: Bluebell BELL 151

Hymn

Stockholm March 1978	E.Nilsson, organ	LP: Karp LP 1
Stockholm April-September 1985	Stockholm University Singers Jonsson	LP: Bluebell BELL 191

STENHAMMAR,P.

Denne aer min kaere son

Stockholm   Stockholm University   LP: Bluebell BELL 191
April-September   Singers
1985   Jonsson

STENHAMMAR,W.

Adagio; Ballad; Det far ett skepp; Flickan knyter i Johannenatten; Fylgia;
Gammal Nederlaendare; Guld och groena skogar; I skogen; I loennens
skymning; Jungfru blond och jungfru brunett; Jutta kommer till Folkungarna;
Lycklandresan; Maenljuset; Maensken; Naer solen gaer ner; Vandraren;
Varfoer till ro sae braett; Vid foenstret; Vore jag ett litet barn

Stockhkolm   Eyron   LP: Bluebell BELL 147
September 1982

En positivvisa

Stockholm   Eyron   LP: Bluebell BELL 182
November-
December 1982

Stjaernoega

Stockholm   Stockholm PO   LP: RCA LSC 10034
May 1965   Grevillius

Stockholm   Eyron   LP: Bluebell BELL 147
September 1982

Sverige

Stockholm   Stockholm PO   LP: RCA LSC 10034
May 1965   Grevillius

STOLZ

Arrivederci, bella Italia!

Munich	Graunke SO	LP: EMI SHZE 335
1970	Stolz	LP: EMI 1C 183 28811-28813
		LP: EMI 1C 188 28056-28057

Drei von der Donau: Excerpt (Servus Du!)

| Munich | Graunke SO | LP: EMI SHZE 335 |
| 1970 | Stolz | |

Frag' nicht, warum ich gehe

| Munich | Graunke SO | LP: EMI SHZE 335 |
| 1970 | Stolz | LP: EMI 1C 188 28056-28057 |

Frühjahrsparade: Excerpt (Schenk' mir dein Herz heute nacht!)

| Munich | Graunke SO | LP: EMI SHZE 335 |
| 1970 | Stolz | |

Frühling im Prater: Excert (Du bist auf dieser Welt)

Munich	Rothenberger	LP: EMI 1C 061 28818
1970	Graunke SO	LP: EMI 1C 188 28056-28057
	Stolz	

Ich liebe die Welt

| Munich | Graunke SO | LP: EMI SHZE 335 |
| 1970 | Stolz | LP: EMI 1C 188 28056-28057 |

Ich sing' mein Lied heut' nur für dich

| Munich | Graunke SO | LP: EMI SHZE 335 |
| 1970 | Stolze | LP: EMI 1C 188 28056-28057 |

In Wien hab' ich einmal ein Mädel geliebt

| Munich | Graunke SO | LP: EMI SHZE 335 |
| 1970 | Stolz | LP: EMI 1C 188 28056-28057 |

Ob blond oder braun, ich lieb' alle Frau'n

| Munich | Graunke SO | LP: EMI SHZE 335/1C 061 30225 |
| 1970 | Stolz | LP: EMI 1C 188 28056-28057 |

Tanzgräfin: Excerpt (Ich bin verliebt in meine eigene Frau)

| Munich | Graunke SO | LP: EMI SHZE 335 |
| 1970 | Stolz | LP: EMI 1C 187 28848-28849 |

Tanzgräfin: Excerpt (Mein Herz ruft immer nur nach dir)

Munich	Graunke SO	LP: EMI SHZE 335
1970	Stolz	LP: EMI 1C 187 28848-28849
		LP: EMI 1C 188 28056-28057

Wenn die kleinen Veilchen blüh'n: Excerpt (Du, du, schliess' deine Augen zu!)

| Munich | Graunke SO | LP: EMI SHZE 335 |
| 1970 | Stolz | LP: EMI 1C 187 28848-28849 |

Wenn die kleinen Veilchen blüh'n: Excerpt (Wenn die kleinen Veilchen blüh'n)

| Munich | Graunke SO | LP: EMI 1C 187 28848-28849 |
| 1970 | Stolz | |

Zauber der Bohème: Excerpt (Ich liebe dich)

Munich	Graunke SO	LP: EMI SHZE 335
1970	Stolz	LP: EMI 1C 183 28811-28813
		LP: EMI 1C 188 28056-28057

Zwei Herzen im Dreivierteltakt: Excerpt (Zwei Herzen im Dreivierteltakt)

Munich	Rothenberger	LP: EMI 1C 061 28818
1970	Graunke SO	LP: EMI 1C 188 28056-28057
	Stolz	

STRADELLA

Se nel ben sempre incostante

Stockholm	National Museum	LP: Polar POLS 321
August 1979	Chamber Orchestra	
	Génetay	

OSCAR STRAUS

Ein Walzertraum

Munich 1969	Role of Niki Rothenberger, Moser, Fassbaender, Brokmeier, Anheisser Bavarian State Chorus Graunke SO Mattes	LP: EMI 1C 163 29041-29042 Excerpts LP: EMI 1C 061 28809 CD: Laserlight 16042

Ein Walzertraum: Excerpt (Da draussen im düftigen Garten)

Stockholm 1952	Stockholm Opera Orchestra Bendix Sung in Swedish	LP: Odeon (Sweden) MOAK 1001

JOHANN STRAUSS

Casanova: Excerpt (Ich steh' zu dir)

Munich 1968	Rothenberger Graunke SO Mattes	LP: EMI SME 74169/1C 061 28818

Die Fledermaus

London April 1955	Role of Eisenstein Schwarzkopf, Streich, Krebs, Christ, Kunz Chorus Philharmonia Karajan	LP: Columbia 33CX 1309-1310 LP: Angel 3539 LP: EMI RLS 728 CD: EMI CHS 769 5312 Excerpts LP: Columbia 33CX 1516
Vienna November- December 1971	Rothenberger, Holm, Dallapozza, Berry, Fischer-Dieskau Vienna Opera Chorus VSO Boskovsky	LP: EMI SLS 964 LP: Angel 3790 CD: EMI CMS 769 3542 Excerpts CD: EMI CDM 769 5982

Der lustige Krieg: Excerpts (Der Klügere gibt nach; Ein Blitz, ein Knall;
Nur für Natur)

Stockholm	Musica Sveciae	LP: Fermat FLPS 43
November 1981	Verde	

Eine Nacht in Venedig

London	Role of Urbino	LP: Columbia 33CX 1224-1225
May and	Schwarzkopf, Loose,	LP: Angel 3530
September 1954	Kunz, Dönch	LP: EMI SXDW 3043
	Chorus	CD: EMI CDH 769 5302
	Philharmonia	
	Ackermann	
Munich	Rothenberger,	LP: EMI SME 81051-81052
September 1967	Streich, Curzi, Prey	LP: EMI 1C 157 29095-29096
	Bavarian Radio Chorus	CD: EMI CMS 769 3632
	Graunke SO	Excerpts
	Allers	LP: EMI SHZE 236/1C 063 28200
		LP: EMI 1C 137 78233-78236
		LP: EMI 1C 187 29227-29228
		CD: EMI CDM 769 5062

Eine Nacht in Venedig: Excerpt (Ach, wie so herrlich zu schau'n)

Munich	Graunke SO	LP: EMI E 74169/SME 74169
June-July	Mattes	
1965		

Eine Nacht in Venedig: Excerpt (Der Mond hat schwere Klag' erhoben)

Stockholm	Musica Sveciae	LP: Fermat FLPS 43
November 1981	Verde	

Eine Nacht in Venedig: Excerpt (Komm' in die Gondel)

Munich	Graunke SO	LP: EMI E 74169/SME 74169/SHZE 236
June-July	Mattes	
1965		
Stockholm	Musica Sveciae	LP: Fermat FLPS 43
November 1981	Verde	

Eine Nacht in Venedig: Excerpt (Sei mir gegrüsst, du holdes Venezia!)

Munich	Graunke SO	LP: EMI E 74169/SME 74169
June-July	Mattes	
1965		
Stockholm	Palm Court Orchestra	CD: Bluebell ABCD 014
April 1987	Almgren	

Wiener Blut

London May 1954	Role of Zedlau Schwarzkopf, Köth, Loose, Kunz, Dönch Chorus Philharmonia Ackermann	LP: Columbia 33CX 1186-1187 LP: Angel 3519 LP: EMI SXDW 3042 CD: EMI CDH 769 5292
1975	Rothenberger, Holm, Zednik, Hirte Philharmonia Hungarica & Chorus Boskovsky	LP: EMI 1C 193 30688-30689 LP: Angel 3831 CD: EMI CMS 769 9432 Excerpts CD: EMI CDM 769 5062

Wiener Blut, Querschnitt

Munich June-July 1965	Rothenberger, Görner, Kuchar Gärtnerplatz Chorus Graunke SO Mattes	LP: EMI E 73941/SME 73941 LP: EMI 1C 061 28197 Excerpts LP: EMI 1C 061 28818 LP: EMI 1C 187 30200-30201 CD: Laserlight 16048

Wiener Blut: Excerpt (Ich bin ein echtes Wiener Blut)

Stockholm April 1987	T.Gedda Palm Court Orchestra Almgren	CD: Bluebell ABCD 014

Der Zigeunerbaron

London May and September 1954	Role of Barinkay Schwarzkopf, Köth, Kunz, Prey Chorus Philharmonia Ackermann	LP: Columbia 33CX 1329-1330 LP: Angel 3566 LP: EMI SXDW 3046 CD: EMI CDH 769 5262 Excerpts LP: EMI 1C 137 78233-78236/SLS 5250
New York December 1959	Della Casa, Resnik, Hurley, Franke Metropolitan Opera Orchestra & Chorus Leinsdorf	Unpublished Met broadcast
Munich July-October 1969	Bumbry, Litz, Anheisser, Prey, Böhme Bavarian State Orchestra & Chorus Allers	LP: EMI 1C 163 28354-28355 Excerpts LP: EMI 1C 061 28200 LP: EMI 1C 187 29227-29228 CD: EMI CDM 769 5062

RICHARD STRAUSS

Arabella, excerpts

London September- October 1954	Role of Matteo Schwarzkopf, Felbermayer, Metternich, Berry Philharmonia Matacic	LP: Columbia 33CX 1226/33CX 1897 LP: World Records OH 199 LP: EMI RLS 751 CD re-issue does not contain Gedda's part

Capriccio

London September 1957	Role of Flamand Schwarzkopf, Moffo, C.Ludwig, Wächter, Fischer-Dieskau, Hotter Philharmonia Sawallisch	LP: Columbia 33CX 1600-1602 LP: Angel 3580 LP: World Records OC 230-232 LP: EMI 143 5243 CD: EMI CDS 749 0148 Excerpts LP: World Records OH 233 LP: EMI 1C 137 78233-78236

Der Rosenkavalier

London December 1956	Role of Sänger Schwarzkopf, Stich-Randall, C.Ludwig, Wächter, Edelmann Chorus Philharmonia Karajan	LP: Columbia 33CX 1492-1495/ SAX 2269-2272 LP: Angel 3563 LP: EMI SLS 810/EX 29 00453 CD: EMI CDS 749 3542 Excerpts LP: Columbia 33CX 1777/SAX 2423 LP: EMI 1C 187 29227-29228
New York February 1969	Rysanek, Grist, C.Ludwig, Berry, Knoll Metropolitan Opera Orchestra & Chorus Böhm	Unpublished Met broadcast
New York February 1970	Rysanek, Popp, C.Ludwig, Berry, Knoll Metropolitan Opera Orchestra & Chorus Böhm	Unpublished Met broadcast

Befreit (Du wirst nicht weinen)

Berlin	Moore	LP: Columbia 33CX 5278/SAX 5278
July 1965		LP: Angel 3204
		LP: EMI 1C 063 28514/SLS 5250
		LP: EMI 1C 137 78233-78236
		LP: EMI 1C 187 29227-29228

Heimkehr (Leiser schwanken die Aeste)

Salzburg	Werba	CD: EMI CDM 565 3522
August 1961		

Heimliche Aufforderung (Auf hebe die funkelnde Schale!)

Salzburg	Werba	CD: EMI CDM 565 3522
August 1961		
Berlin	Moore	LP: Columbia 33CX 5278/SAX 5278
July 1965		LP: Angel 3204
		LP: EMI 1C 063 28514/SLS 5250
		LP: EMI 1C 137 78233-78236

Herr Lenz springt heute durch die Stadt

1979	Wustman	LP: Glendale GLS 8007

Liebeshymnus (Heil jenem Tag!)

Salzburg	Werba	CD: EMI CDM 565 3522
August 1961		
Berlin	Moore	LP: Columbia 33CX 5278/SAX 5278
July 1965		LP: Angel 3204
		LP: EMI 1C 063 28514/SLS 5250

Die Nacht (Aus dem Walde tritt die Nacht)

Salzburg	Werba	CD: EMI CDM 565 3522
August 1961		
Berlin	Moore	LP: Columbia 33CX 5278/SAX 5278
July 1965		LP: Angel 3204
		LP: EMI 1C 063 28514/SLS 5250
		LP: EMI 1C 137 78233-78236

Ständchen (Mach auf', doch leise, mein Kind!)

Berlin	Moore	LP: Columbia 33CX 5278/SAX 5278
July 1965		LP: EMI 1C 063 28514/ASD 2574
		LP: EMI 1C 187 29227-29228

STRAVINSKY

Oedipus rex

Rome December 1952	Role of Oedipus Laszlo, Petri RAI Rome Orchestra & Chorus Karajan	CD: Datum DAT 12311
Stockholm May 1991	Role of Shepherd Von Otter, Cole, Estes Swedish Radio Orchestra & Chorus Salonen	CD: Sony SK 48057

Perséphone

Paris January 1955	Role of Eumolpe Nollier Paris Conservatoire Orchestra Cluytens	LP: Columbia (France) FCX 412

SZYMANOWSKI

Song of the beloved Muezzin

1960	Singer	LP: Melodram MEL 659

TAUBER

Du bist die Welt für mich

Munich 1968	Graunke SO Mattes	LP: Columbia (Germany) SMC 83884 LP: Angel 36314

Eugene Onegin

Boston October 1976	Role of Lensky Vishnevskaya, Luxon, Davidson, Plishka Tanglewood Chorus Boston SO Ozawa	Unpublished radio broadcast
New York February 1978	Zylis-Gara, I.Jones, Milnes, Plishka Metropolitan Opera Orchestra & Chorus Levine	Unpublished Met broadcast
New York December 1979	Kabaiwanska, I.Jones, Masurok, Plishka Metropolitan Opera Orchestra & Chorus Tchakarov	Unpublished Met broadcast
Sofia January 1988	Tomowa-Sintov, Lilowa Masurok, Ghiuselev Sofia Festival Orchestra & Chorus Tchakarov	CD: Sony S2K 45539
Swansea June and July 1992	Role of M. Triquet Kanawa, Rosenshein, Hampson, Connell Welsh National Opera Orchestra & Chorus Mackerras	CD: EMI CDS 555 0042

Eugene Onegin: Excerpt (Where have you gone?)

London April 1953	Role of Lensky Philharmonia Galliera	LP: Columbia 33CX 1130 LP: Angel 35096 LP: Columbia (Germany) C 70411
Stockholm 1962	Unidentified Orchestra & conductor	45: Odeon (Sweden) BEOS 5
Berlin 1962	Berlin RO F.Walter	LP: Melodram MEL 659
London November 1967	Covent Garden Orchestra Patané	LP: EMI ASD 2445/SLS 5250 LP: Angel 36623/3204 LP: EMI 1C 137 78233-78236 CD: EMI CDM 769 5502
Belgrade April 1969	Belgrade PO Zdravkovich	LP: EMI 1C 063 28070/1C 063 29044 LP: EMI 5C 055 24368
New York 1981-1982	Rostropovich	LP: RCA ARL1-4667
Germany 1985	Unspecified accompaniment	VHS Video: Bel Canto (USA) 658
Livorno 1985	Soroga	CD: Fonè 85F-026
Vienna 1988	Austrian RO Guadagno	Unpublished video recording

Another version of the aria, sung by Gedda with unidentified orchestra and conductor, can be heard on Ed Smith UORC 374

Iolanta

Paris December 1984	Role of Vaudémont Vishnevskaya, Grönroos, Petkov, Krause Groupe vocale Orchestre de Paris Rostropovich	LP: Erato 75207 CD: Erato 2292 459732

The Queen of Spades: Excerpt (Forgive me, bright celestial vision)

Belgrade	Role of Hermann	LP: EMI 1C 063 28070
April 1969	Belgrade PO	
	Zdravkovitch	

The Queen of Spades: Excerpt (What is our life?)

Berlin	Berlin RO	LP: Melodram MEL 659
1962	Stein	
Belgrade	Belgrade PO	LP: EMI 1C 063 28070/1C 063 29064
April 1969	Zdravkovitch	LP: EMI 1C 137 78233-78236

At the ball

Stockholm	Eyron	LP: EMI 1C 187 29227-29228
September 1968		
London	Moore	LP: EMI SAN 255/1C 061 01961
April 1969		LP: Angel 36640/3204
		LP: EMI 1C 137 78233-78236/SLS 5250
London	Parsons	CD: Arkadia GI 8061
November 1971		
Moscow	Mogilevskaya	LP: Melodiya C10 13977-13978
March 1980		LP: Eurodisc 203 284.366

Don Juan's Serenade

Stockholm	Eyron	LP: EMI 1C 063 28023/ASD 2574
September 1968		
London	Moore	LP: EMI SAN 255/1C 061 01961
April 1969		LP: Angel 36640/3204
		LP: EMI 1C 137 78233-78236/SLS 5250
London	Parsons	CD: Arkadia GI 8061
November 1971		

Expostilarion on the Dormition of the Mother of God

Helsinki	Upenski Cathedral	CD: Ikon IKO 9002
1986	Choir	
	Mirolybov	

Legend

Stockholm September 1968	Eyron	LP: EMI 1C 063 28023
London November 1971	Parsons	CD: Arkadia GI 8061

None but the lonely heart

Budapest February 1984	Pataki	CD: Bluebell ABCD 041

On this moonlit night

Stockholm September 1968	Eyron	LP: EMI 1C 063 28023 LP: EMI 1C 187 29227-29228
London November 1971	Parsons	CD: Arkadia GI 8061

Why?

Moscow March 1980	Mogilevskaya	LP: Melodiya C10 13977-13978 LP: Eurodisc 203 284.366

TCHEREPNIN

7 Songs to poems from the Chinese

Paris December 1973	Tcherepnin	LP: EMI 2C 065 14028

The lake of Tsarskoie Sela

Paris December 1973	Tcherepnin	LP: EMI 2C 065 14028 CD: EMI CDM 763 7312

Mystic Legends: 3 Tombs; Mother solitude

Paris December 1973	Tcherepnin	LP: EMI 2C 065 14028 CD: EMI CDM 763 7312

10 Songs to poems by Guillot

Paris December 1973	Tcherepnin	LP: EMI 2C 065 14028 Excerpts CD: EMI CDM 763 7312

THOMAS

Mignon: Excerpt (Adieu, Mignon!)

Paris	Orchestre National	LP: Columbia 33CX 1837/SAX 2481
September 1961	Prêtre	LP: Angel 34055/36106
		LP: EMI 1C 063 11272/5C 055 24368

Budapest	Pataki	CD: Bluebell ABCD 041
February 1984		

Mignon: Excerpt (Elle ne croyait pas)

Paris	Orchestre National	LP: Columbia 33CX 1837/SAX 2481
September 1961	Prêtre	LP: Angel 34055/36106/3204
		LP: EMI 1C 063 11272/SLS 5250

Budapest	Pataki	CD: Bluebell ABCD 041
February 1984		

TURINA

Poema en forma de canciones: Cantares; Los dos miedos; Nunca olvida

Berlin	Moore	LP: Columbia 33CX 5278/SAX 5278
July 1965		LP: EMI 1C 063 28514

Another version of this cycle, sung by Gedda with unidentified accompanist, can be heard on Ed Smith UORC 373

VERACINI

Rosalinda: Excerpt (Meco verrai)

Berlin	Moore	LP: Columbia 33CX 5278/SAX 5278
July 1965		LP: EMI 1C 063 28514/SLS 5250
		LP: Angel 3204
		LP: EMI 1C 137 78233-78236

Stockholm	National Museum	LP: Polar POLS 321
August 1979	Chamber Orchestra	
	Génetay	

VERDI

Requiem

London	Schwarzkopf,	LP: EMI AN 133-134/SAN 133-134
September 1963-	C.Ludwig, Ghiaurov,	LP: EMI SLS 909
April 1964	Philharmonia	LP: Angel 3649
	Orchestra & Chorus	CD: EMI CDS 747 2578
	Giulini	Excerpt
		CD: EMI CDCFP 4532

Aida: Excerpt (Celeste Aida)

London	Covent Garden	LP: EMI ASD 2445/SME 81100
November 1967	Orchestra	LP: Angel 36623
	Patané	LP: EMI 1C 063 02703/1C 047 30638

Un Ballo in maschera: Excerpt (Di tu se fedele)

London	Covent Garden	LP: EMI ASD 2445/SME 81100
November 1967	Orchestra	LP: Angel 36623
	Patané	LP: EMI 1C 063 02703

Un Ballo in machera: Excerpt (Ma se m'è forza)

London	Covent Garden	LP: EMI ASD 2445/SME 81100
November 1967	Orchestra	LP: Angel 36623/3204
	Patané	LP: EMI 1C 963 02703/SLS 5250

Don Carlo, Querschnitt

Berlin	Role of Carlos	LP: EMI 1C 063 28960
September 1973	Moser, Fassbaender,	
	Fischer-Dieskau,	
	Moll	
	Berlin RO	
	Patané	
	Sung in German	

La Forza del destino, Querschnitt

Dresden	Role of Alvaro	LP: Columbia (Germany) C 80966/
August 1965	Bumbry, Dernesch,	SMC 80966
	Prey, Vogel, Frick	LP: EMI 1C 063 28168
	Dresden Staatskapelle	CD: Berlin Classics 20252
	and Chorus	Excerpts
	Patané	LP: Angel 3204
	Sung in German	LP: EMI 1C 063 29064
		LP: EMI 1C 137 78233-78236

Rigoletto

Stockholm January 1959	Role of Duke Hallin, Meyer, Hasslo Stockholm Opera Orchestra & Chorus Ehrling	LP: Bis BISLP 296
New York April 1967	Peters, Amparan, MacNeil Metropolitan Opera Orchestra & Chorus Gardelli	Unpublished Met broadcast
Rome July 1967	Grist, Stasio, MacNeil Rome Opera Orchestra & Chorus Molinari-Pradelli	LP: EMI SAN 204-206 LP: Angel 3718 CD: EMI CDCFP 4700 Excerpts LP: EMI 1C 063 29044/1C 063 00700

Rigoletto: Excerpt (Questa o quella)

Location uncertain	Unidentified Orchestra & conductor	LP: Ed Smith UORC 374

Rigoletto: Excerpt (Parmi veder)

London April 1953	Philharmonia Galliera	78: Columbia LX 1617 LP: Columbia 33CX 1130 LP: Angel 35096

Another version of the aria, sung by Gedda with unidentified orchestra and conductor, can be heard on Ed Smith UORC 374

Rigoletto: Excerpt (La donna è mobile)

Munich June 1967	Bavarian State Orchestra Bender	LP: EMI SMC 81049/SHZE 212 LP: EMI 1C 047 30638 LP: EMI 1C 187 29227-29228

Another version of the aria, sung by Gedda with unidentified orchestra and conductor, can be heard on Ed Smith UORC 374

Rigoletto: Excerpt (Bella figlia dell' amore)

New York 1968	Sutherland, Miller, Gobbi Bell Telephone Orchestra Vohees	VHS Video: VAI Audio VAIA 69090

La Traviata

London July 1971	Role of Alfredo Sills, Panerai Alldis Choir RPO Ceccato	LP: EMI SLS 960 LP: Angel 3780 CD: EMI CMS 769 8272 Excerpts LP: EMI 1C 063 29044
Vienna December 1971	Cotrubas, MacNeil Vienna Opera Chorus VPO Krips	LP: Estro armonico EA 003 CD: Hunt CDMP 462
London June 1972	Caballé, Braun Covent Garden Orchestra & Chorus Cillario	CD: Foyer 2CF-2049

I Vespri siciliani

New York March 1974	Role of Arrigo Caballé, MacNeil, Diaz Metropolitan Opera Orchestra & Chorus Levine	LP: HRE Records HREV 819 Excerpts LP: HRE Records HRE 202

Ad una stella; Lo spazzacamino

Stockholm June 1981	Eyron	LP: Bluebell BELL 134 CD: Bluebell ABCD 004

WAGNER

Lohengrin

Stockholm	Nordmo-Lövberg,	Unpublished radio broadcast
January 1966	Ericson, Rundgren,	
	Jupither, Wixell	
	Stockholm Opera	
	Orchestra & Chorus	
	Varviso	

Lohengrin: Excerpt (In fernem Land)

Munich	Bavarian State	LP: EMI ASD 2364/SME 80814
June 1967	Orchestra	LP: Angel 36624
	Bender	LP: EMI 1C 063 28993/1C 047 30638
		LP: EMI 1C 049 30659

Lohengrin: Excerpt (Mein lieber Schwan!)

Munich	Bavarian State	LP: EMI ASD 2364/SME 80814
June 1967	Orchestra	LP: Angel 36624/3204
	Bender	LP: EMI 1C 063 28993/SLS 5250
		LP: EMI 1C 187 29227-29228
		CD: EMI CDM 769 5502

Die Meistersinger von Nürnberg: Excerpt (Selig wie die Sonne)

New York	Curtin, Miller,	VHS Video: VAI Audio VAIA 69090
1968	Anthony, Hines	
	Bell Telephone	
	Orchestra	
	Vohees	

Les 2 grenadiers

Stockholm	Eyron	LP: Bluebell BELL 134
June 1981		CD: Bluebell ABCD 004

WEBER

Abu Hassan

| Munich
1974 | Role of Abu Hassan
Moser, Moll
Bavarian State
Orchestra & Chorus
Sawallisch | LP: EMI 1C 065 30148 |

Euryanthe

| Dresden
June and
July 1974 | Role of Adolar
Norman, Hunter,
Krause, Vogel
Leipzig Radio Chorus
Dresden Staatskapelle
Janowski | LP: EMI SLS 983
CD: EMI CMS 763 5092
CD: Berlin Classics BC 0011082 |

Der Freischütz

| Munich
July 1969 | Role of Max
Nilsson, Köth,
Berry, Crass
Bavarian State
Orchestra & Chorus
Heger | LP: EMI 1C 165 28351-28353
LP: Angel 3748
Excerpts
LP: EMI 1C 063 29023/1C 063 29044
LP: EMI 1C 047 30629 |

Oberon: Excerpt (Vater! Hör' mich!)

| Munich
June 1967 | Role of Huon
Bavarian State
Orchestra
Bender | LP: EMI ASD 2364/SME 80814
LP: Angel 36624
LP: EMI 1C 063 28993
LP: EMI 1C 137 78233-78236
LP: EMI 1C 187 29227-29228
CD: EMI CDM 769 5502 |

Oberon: Excerpt (Von Jugend auf)

| Munich
June 1967 | Bavarian State
Orchestra
Bender | LP: EMI ASD 2364/SME 80814
LP: EMI 1C 063 28993/SLS 5250
LP: Angel 36624/3204
LP: EMI 1C 137 78233-78236
CD: EMI CDM 769 5502 |

WENNERBERG

Det aer en kostelig ting; Lova herren min sjael; Min sjael laengtar och traengtar

Stockholm	Stockholm University	LP: Bluebell BELL 191
April-September	Singers	
1985	Jonsson	

Goeren portarne hoega

Stockholm	Ellerstedt, organ	LP: Wisa WISLP 542
December 1977		

Stockholm	Stockholm University	LP: Bluebell BELL 191
April-September	Singers	
1985	Jonsson	

Gluntarne, song cycle

Stockholm	Leanderson	LP: Bluebell BELL 166
October 1983	Eyron	

WIDEN

Serenade

Stockholm	YMCA Chorus	LP: Odeon (Sweden) MOAK 1001
1952	Lidstam	

Stockholm	Stockholm University	LP: Bluebell BELL 124
February-	Singers	
March 1981	Blohm	

WINKLER

Chianti-Lied

Munich	Graunke SO	LP: EMI SME 74169/SHZE 236
1968	Mattes	

WOLF

Lieder: Anakreons Grab; Der Schäfer; Frühling übers Jahr

Budapest	Pataki	CD: Bluebell ABCD 041
February 1984		

Er ist's

1979	Wustman	LP: Glendale GLS 8007

ZELLER

Der Vogelhändler: Excerpt (Schenkt man sich Rosen im Tirol)

Stockholm	Stockholm Opera	45: Odeon (Sweden) BEOS 2
1955	Orchestra	LP: Odeon (Sweden) MOAK 1001/
	Bendix	PMES 536
	Sung in Swedish	

Der Vogelhändler: Excerpt (Wie mein Ahn'l zwanzig Jahr')

Stockholm	Stockholm Opera	45: Odeon (Sweden) BEOS 2
1955	Orchestra	LP: Odeon (Sweden) MOAK 1001
	Bendix	
	Sung in Swedish	

MISCELLANEOUS

Ack vaermeland du skoena

Stockholm May 1965	Stockholm PO	LP: RCA LSC 10034

Allt under himmelens faeste

Stockholm May 1965	Stockholm PO Grevillius	LP: RCA LSC 10034

Bethlehems stjarna

London June 1966	Parsons	LP: Electrola SHZE 244

Chi sà le mie pene

Stockholm August 1979	National Museum Chamber Orchestra Génetay	LP: Polar POLS 321

Du gamla, du fria

Stockholm May 1965	Stockholm PO Grevillius	LP: RCA LSC 10034

Good Christian men rejoice

New York 1967	Firestone Chorus Kostal	LP: Firestone CSLP 7015

Hylands loerna

Stockholm March 1983	T.Gedda Palm Court Orchestra Almgren	LP: Fermat FLPS 43 Also unpublished video recording

Nar det leder mot ful

London June 1966	Parsons	LP: Electrola SHZE 244

Och hoer du unga dora

Stockholm May 1965	Stockholm PO Grevillius	LP: RCA LSC 10034

Red jumper

Stockholm 1967	Stockholm University Singers Blohm	LP: Odeon (Sweden) 4E 053 34012

4 saenger foer manskor med tenor solo

Date uncertain	Chorus	45: Odeon (Sweden) BEOS 3

Samtala

Stockholm October 1983	Bendix	LP: Bluebell BELL 154

Silent night

New York 1967	Firestone Chorus Kostal	LP: Firestone CSLP 7015

Till himmelen di laengtar jag

Stockholm April-September 1985	Stockholm University Singers Jonsson	LP: Bluebell BELL 191

Tiritomba

Munich 1968	Graunke SO Mattes	LP: EMI SMC 83884/SHZE 236 LP: Angel 36314

Uti din naed

Stockholm April-September 1985	Stockholm University Singers Jonsson	LP: Bluebell BELL 191

Christmas Songs

Stockholm   CD: Bluebell ABCS 3001

The World of Nicolai Gedda

New York   WNET TV   Unpublished video recording
1972   Channel 13
                  documentary

Portrait of a great tenor

Germany   German TV   Unpublished video recording
May 1972   documentary
                  produced by Krüger
                  and Finnern

Nicolai Gedda master classes

Stockholm   Swedish TV   Unpublished video recording
August 1981

Concert of unspecified songs and arias

Moscow   Chorus   VHS Video: Bel Canto (USA) 583
1980   Orchestra   Incorrectly dated 1984

Also many German TV appearances in programmes hosted by Anneliese Rothenberger and Hermann Prey

Ah thou my soul/Ah my darling!

Moscow October 1980	Russian Academic Orchestra Nekrasov	LP: Melodiya C20 15749-15750 CD: Olympia OCD 244

Alone I pass along the lonely road

Moscow 1980	USSR TV Chorus Yermakova	LP: Melodiya C20 16183-16184

Along the river

Moscow 1980	USSR TV Chorus Yermakova	LP: Melodiya C20 16183-16184

Caucasian Melody

1963	Balalaika Orchestra & Chorus Kolbouss	LP: Electrola SHZE 140 LP: Capitol SP 8597 LP: Angel 60225
New York May 1976	Russian Choral Society Rodenko	LP: Ed Smith UORC 374 Performed with two different endings

Cradle Song/Lullaby

Munich 1992	Russian Soloists Ensemble Ciolkovich	CD: Polydor 446 2482/521 2912

Evening bells

Stockholm 1957	YMCA Chorus Lidstam	LP: Odeon (Sweden) PMES 536
1963	Balalaika Orchestra & Chorus Kolbouss	45: Columbia SCD 2247 LP: Electrola SHZE 140 LP: Capitol SP 8597 LP: Angel 60225
Leningrad October 1980	Andreeva Orchestra Leningrad TV Choir Popov	LP: Melodiya C20 16003-16004 CD: Olympia OCD 244
Moscow 1980	USSR TV Chorus Yermakova	LP: Melodiya C20 16183-16184
Stockholm June 1983	Instrumental Ensemble	LP: Bluebell BELL 154
Munich 1992	Russian Soloists Ensemble Ciolkovich	CD: Polydor 446 2482/521 2912

Farewell, Joy!

Moscow October 1980	Russian Academic Orchestra Nekrasov	LP: Melodiya C20 15749-15750 CD: Olympia OCD 244

Foggy morning

1963	Balalaika Orchestra & Chorus Kolbouss	LP: Electrola SHZE 140 LP: Capitol SP 8597 LP: Angel 60225
Moscow October 1980	Russian Academic Orchestra Nekrasov	LP: Melodiya C20 15749-15750 CD: Olympia OCD 244

Homeland

Leningrad October 1980	Andreeva Orchestra Popov	LP: Melodiya C20 16003-16004 CD: Olympia OCD 244
Moscow October 1980	Russian Academic Orchestra Nekrasov	LP: Melodiya C20 15749-15750

Russian Songs and Romances/continued

How I go on the rapid river

| Leningrad
October 1980 | Andreeva Orchestra
Popov | LP: Melodiya C20 16003-16004
CD: Olympia OCD 244 |

| Moscow
1980 | USSR TV Chorus
Yermakova | LP: Melodiya C20 16183-16184 |

I pray to the power of Love

| Munich
1992 | Russian Soloists
Ensemble
Ciolkovich | CD: Polydor 446 2482/521 2912 |

Ja vstretil vas

| Munich
1992 | Russian Soloists
Ensemble
Ciolkovich | CD: Polydor 446 2482/521 2912 |

Like a nightingale of passage

| Moscow
October 1980 | Russian Academic
Orchestra
Nekrasov | LP: Melodiya C29 15749-15750
CD: Olympia OCD 244 |

| Munich
1992 | Russian Soloists
Ensemble
Ciolkovich | CD: Polydor 446 2482/521 2912 |

Little farmstead

| Moscow
October 1980 | Russian Academic
Orchestra
Nekrasov | LP: Melodiya C20 15749-15750
CD: Olympia OCD 244 |

Mecelitza

| Munich
1992 | Russian Soloists
Ensemble
Ciolkovich | CD: Polydor 446 2482/521 2912 |

Russian Songs and Romances/continued

Monotonously chimes the little bell

Stockholm 1957	YMCA Chorus Lidstam	LP: Odeon (Sweden) PMES 536
1963	Balalaika Orchestra & Chorus Kolbouss	45: Columbia SCD 2247 LP: Electrola SHZE 140 LP: Capitol SP 8597 LP: Angel 60225 LP: EMI 5C 055 24368
Leningrad October 1980	Andreeva Orchestra Leningrad TV Choir Popov	LP: Melodiya C20 16003-16004 CD: Olympia OCD 244
Moscow 1980	USSR TV Chorus Yermakova	LP: Melodiya C20 16183-16184
Munich 1992	Russian Soloists Ensemble Ciolkovich	CD: Polydor 446 2482/521 2912

Night

Moscow October 1980	Russian Academic Orchestra Nekrasov	LP: Melodiya C20 15749-15750 CD: Olympia OCD 244
Leningrad October 1980	Andreeva Orchestra Popov	LP: Melodiya C20 16003-16004

Notschenka

Munich 1992	Russian Soloists Ensemble Ciolkovich	CD: Polydor 446 2482/521 2912

O could I express in song!

Salzburg August 1961	Werba	CD: EMI CDM 565 3522
1963	Balalaika Orchestra & Chorus Kolbouss	LP: Electrola SHZE 140 LP: Capitol SP 8597 LP: Angel 60225
Moscow October 1980	Russian Academic Orchestra Nekrasov	LP: Melodiya C20 15749-15750 CD: Olympia OCD 244
Leningrad October 1980	Andreeva Orchestra Leningrad TV Choir Popov	LP: Melodiya C20 16003-16004

Russian Songs and Romances/continued

Serenade

Munich 1992	Russian Soloists Ensemble Ciolovich	CD: Polydor 446 2482/521 2912

Snow-covered Russia

1963	Balalaika Orchestra & Chorus Kolbouss	LP: Electrola SHZE 140 LP: Capitol SP 8597 LP: Angel 60225

Soldiers farewell

1963	Balalaika Orchestra & Chorus Kolbouss	LP: Electrola SHZE 140 LP: Capitol SP 8597 LP: Angel 60225

Steppe and steppe all around

Moscow 1980	USSR TV Chorus Yermakova	LP: Melodiya C20 16183-16184

Stillness

Leningrad October 1980	Andreeva Orchestra Popov	LP: Melodiya C20 16003-16004 CD: Olympia OCD 244

The storm

1963	Balalaika Orchestra & Chorus Kolbouss	LP: Electrola SHZE 140 LP: Capitol SP 8597 LP: Angel 60225
Moscow October 1980	Russian Academic Orchestra Nekrasov	LP: Melodiya C20 15749-15750 CD: Olympia OCD 244
Leningrad October 1980	Andreeva Orchestra Popov	LP: Melodiya C20 16003-16004
Moscow 1980	USSR TV Chorus Yermakova	LP: Melodiya C20 16183-16184

Russian Songs and Romances/concluded

Troika

1963	Balalaika Orchestra & Chorus Kolbouss	LP: Electrola SHZE 140 LP: Capitol SP 8597 LP: Angel 60225
Stockholm 1967	Stockholm University Singers Ralf	LP: Odeon (Sweden) 4E 053 34012
Leningrad October 1980	Andreeva Orchestra Leningrad TV Choir Popov	LP: Melodiya C20 16003-16004 CD: Olympia OCD 244
Moscow 1980	USSR TV Chorus Yermakova	LP: Melodiya C20 16183-16184

Weeping willow's dream

1963	Balalaika Orchestra & Chorus Kolbouss	LP: Electrola SHZE 140 LP: Capitol SP 8597 LP: Angel 60225
Leningrad October 1980	Andreeva Orchestra Popov	LP: Melodiya C20 16003-16004 CD: Olympia OCD 244
Moscow October 1980	Russian Academic Orchestra Nekrasov	LP: Melodiya C20 15749-15750

The young pedlar

1963	Balalaika Orchestra & Chorus Kolbouss	LP: Electrola SHZE 140 LP: Capitol SP 8597 LP: Angel 60225
Leningrad October 1980	Andreeva Orchestra Leningrad TV Choir Popov	LP: Melodiya C20 16003-16004 CD: Olympia OCD 244
Moscow October 1980	Russian Academic Orchestra Nekrasov	LP: Melodiya C20 15749-15750

RUSSIAN LITURGICAL MUSIC

Before thy cross

Munich   Russian Soloists   CD: Philips 445 3922
1994   Ensemble
                      Ciolovich

Bless the Lord, o my soul!

Paris   Russian Orthodox   LP: Philips 6504 135
February 1975   Cathedral Choir   CD: Philips 434 1742
                      Evetz

Cherubic Hymn

London   Russian Orthodox   LP: Ikon IKOS 10
August 1979   Choir   CD: Ikon IKO 9002
                      Fortounatto

Munich   Russian Soloists   CD: Philips 445 3922
1994   Ensemble
                      Ciolovich

Christ has risen

Munich   Russian Soloists   CD: Philips 445 3922
1994   Ensemble
                      Ciolovich

Come and let us bless Joseph

London   Russian Orthodox   LP: Ikon IKOS 10
August 1979   Choir   CD: Ikon IKO 9002
                      Fortounatto

Dogmatic, tone 6

Helsinki   Uspenski Cathedral   CD: Ikon IKO 9002
1986   Choir
                      Mirolybov

Dogmatic, tone 8

Helsinki   Haekkaelae   CD: Ikon IKO 9002
1986   Uspenski Cathedral
                      Choir
                      Mirolybov

Russian Liturgical music/continued

Exapostilarion on the Mother of God

London   Russian Orthodox   LP: Ikon IKOS 6
August 1977   Choir   CD: Ikon IKO 9001
                    Fortounatto   CD: Fidelis FIDCD 100

Exapostilarion on Good Friday

London   Russian Orthodox   LP: Ikon IKOS 6
August 1977   Choir   CD: Ikon IKOS 9001
                    Fortounatto   CD: Fidelis FIDCD 100

Give us rest with the righteous!

London   Russian Orthodox   LP: Ikon IKOS 10
August 1979   Choir   CD: Ikon IKO 9002
                    Fortounatto

God is with us: know this, ye nations!

Paris   Russian Orthodox   LP: Philips 6504 135
February 1975   Cathedral Choir   CD: Philips 434 1742
                    Evetz

Munich   Russian Soloists   CD: Philips 445 3922
1994   Ensemble
                    Ciolovich

Holy God

Munich   Russian Soloists   CD: Philips 445 3922
1994   Ensemble
                    Ciolovich

House of the Euphrates

Munich   Russian Soloists   CD: Philips 445 3922
1994   Ensemble
                    Ciolovich

I see thy bridal chamber

London   Russian Orthodox   LP: Ikon IKOS 10
August 1979   Choir   CD: Ikon IKO 9002
                    Fortounatto

Let my prayer be set forth

London August 1979	Russian Orthodox Choir Fortounatto	LP: Ikon IKOS 10 CD: Ikon IKO 9002

Litany

Munich 1994	Russian Soloists Ensemble Ciolovich	CD: Philips 445 3922

Lord, now lettest thou thy servant depart in peace!

Paris February 1975	Russian Orthodox Cathedral Choir Evetz	LP: Philips 6504 135 CD: Philips 434 1742

The Lord's prayer

Paris February 1975	Russian Orthodox Cathedral Choir	LP: Philips 6504 135 CD: Philips 434 1742

Nunc dimittis

London August 1977	Russian Orthodox Choir Fortounatto	LP: Ikon IKOS 6 CD: Ikon IKO 9001 CD: Fidelis FIDCD 100
London August 1979	Russian Orthodox Choir Fortounatto	LP: Ikon IKOS 10 CD: Ikon IKO 9002

Psalm 1; Psalm 135

Munich 1994	Russian Soloists Ensemble Ciolovich	CD: Philips 445 3922

Putevoy Chant

London August 1977	Russian Orthodox Choir Fortounatto	LP: Ikon IKOS 6 CD: Ikon IKO 9001 CD: Fidelis FIDCD 100

Rejoice, ye people!

Munich	Russian Soloists	CD: Philips 445 3922
1994	Ensemble	
	Ciolovich	

Requiem aeternam

Munich	Russian Soloists	CD: Philips 445 3922
1994	Ensemble	
	Ciolovich	

Sedalion on Sunday of the Prodigal Son/Sunday of Saint Thomas

London	Russian Orthodox	LP: Ikon IKOS 6
August 1977	Choir	CD: Ikon IKOS 9001
	Fortounatto	CD: Fidelis FIDCD 100

Seligpreisungen

Munich	Russian Soloists	CD: Philips 445 3922
1994	Ensemble	
	Ciolovich	

Thy birth

Munich	Russian Soloists	CD: Philips 445 3922
1994	Ensemble	
	Ciolovich	

Royal Opera House Covent Garden
House Manager Trevor Jones

Royal Opera House Covent Garden Limited

General Administrator JOHN TOOLEY

in association with

The Friends of Covent Garden and Lies Askonas

present

NICOLAI GEDDA

Tenor

GEOFFREY PARSONS

Piano

Sunday 9 March 1975

The Royal Opera House Covent Garden Limited receives financial assistance from
The Arts Council of Great Britain

Dietrich Fischer-Dieskau
born 1925

with valuable assistance
from Clifford Elkin

Discography compiled by John Hunt

Drawing by Brian Pinder

ADAM

Vernimm', o Welt, gekommen ist die Stunde

Berlin November 1970	Demus	LP: DG 2530 219

ANNA AMALIE VON SACHSEN-WEIMAR

Auf dem Land und in die Stadt; Sie scheinen zu spielen

Berlin September 1972	Demus, fortepiano	LP: DG 2533 149

APOSTEL

Nacht (Dunkle Schwester)

Berlin March 1974	Reimann	LP: EMI 1C 065 02677/ 1C 161 02673-02677

ARNIM

O schaudre nicht

Berlin September 1972	Demus, fortepiano	LP: DG 2533 149

C.P.E.BACH

Ueber die Finsternis; Kurz vor dem Tode

Berlin November 1969	Demus	LP: DG 2533 058

J.C.BACH

Ah, lamenta la bella Irene

Berlin December 1960	Moore De los Angeles	LP: HMV ALP 1891/ASD 459 CD: EMI CMS 565 0612

BACH

Magnificat BWV 243

Munich	Stader, Töpper,	LP: DG AP 13 078/SAP 195 078
April 1961	Haefliger	LP: DG APM 14 197/SAPM 198 197
	Munich Bach	LP: DG 2722 018
	Orchestra	CD: DG 419 4662
	and Chorus	
	K.Richter	

Mass in B minor BWV 232

Munich	Stader, Töpper,	LP: DG APM 14 190-14 192/
February and	Haefliger, Engen	SAPM 198 190-198 192
April 1961	Munich Bach	LP: DG 2710 001/2722 017/2723 065
	Orchestra	CD: DG 427 1552
	and Chorus	Excerpts
	K.Richter	LP: DG LPEM 19 300/SLPEM 136 300
		LP: DG 2535 313

Easter Oratorio BWV 249

Stuttgart	Zylis-Gara,	LP: HMV ALP 2076/ASD 626
March 1964	P.Johnson, Altmeyer	LP: EMI 1C 053 00255/ED 100 2551
	South-West German	
	Chamber Orchestra	
	Madrigalchor	
	Gönnenwein	

Christmas Oratorio BWV 248

Leipzig	Giebel, Höffgen,	LP: HMV ALP 1950-1953/ASD 501-504
December 1958	Traxel	LP: EMI 1C 147 28583-28585
	Gewandhaus-Orchester	CD: Berlin Classics BC 0021912
	Thomanerchor	Excerpts
	Thomas	LP: EMI 1C 047 28592/ED 29 03661
London	Ameling, Baker,	LP: EMI SLS 5098
August 1976	Tear	
	Academy of Saint	
	Martins	
	Kings College Choir	
	Ledger	

In all versions of the Saint John and Saint Matthew Passions listed on the opposite page, Fischer-Dieskau sings the part of Christus, except in the 1958 Karl Richter edition on DG, in which he performs the bass arias

Saint John Passion BWV 245

Berlin September 1961	Grümmer, Otto, C.Ludwig, Traxel, Wunderlich, Kohn Berlin SO St Hedwig's Choir Forster	LP: HMV ALP 1975-1977/ASD 526-528 LP: EMI 1C 147 28589-28591 CD: EMI CMS 764 2342 Excerpts LP: Electrola E 80727/STE 80727
Stuttgart April 1984	Auger, Hamari, Schreier, Huttenlocher Bach Collegium Gächinger Kantorei Rilling	CD: Sony M2K 39694

Saint Matthew Passion BWV 244

Berlin 1949	Trötschel, Eustrati, Krebs, Haertel Berlin Radio Orchestra & Chorus Lehmann	78: Discophiles français LP: Vox (USA) DL 6070 Also published pseudonymously on Royale and Gramophone LPs
Vienna April 1954	Grümmer, Höffgen, Dermota, Edelmann VPO Singverein Furtwängler	LP: Cetra LO 508/FE 34 LP: Movimento Musica 03.008 CD: Movimento Musica 013.005 CD: Virtuoso 269.9212 CD: EMI CHS 565 5092 All issues taken from unapproved tapes, but it is understood that the EMI edition will be from a newly edited and approved tape
Munich June-August 1958	Seefried, Töpper, Haefliger, Engen Munich Bach Orchestra & Chorus K.Richter	LP: DG APM 14125-14128/ SAPM 198 009-198 012 LP: DG 2722 010 CD: DG 439 3382 Excerpts LP: DG LPEM 19 233/SLPEM 136 233 LP: DG 2535 220
London November 1960- December 1961	Schwarzkopf, C.Ludwig, Pears, Gedda, Berry Philharmonia Orchestra & Chorus Klemperer	LP: Columbia 33CX 1799-1803/ SAX 2446-2450 LP: EMI SLS 827 CD: EMI CMS 763 0582
Berlin January 1972	Janowitz, C.Ludwig, Schreier, Berry BPO Wiener Singverein Karajan	LP: DG 2711 012/2720 070 CD: DG 419 7892
Munich June-August 1979	Mathis, Baker, Schreier, Salminen Munich Bach Orchestra & Chorus K.Richter	LP: DG 2712 005/2723 067 CD: DG 413 6132

Cantata No 1 "Wie schön leuchtet der Morgenstern"

Munich	Munich Bach	LP: DG 198 465/2547 064
July 1968	Orchestra & Chorus	LP: DG 2722 022/2722 028
	K.Richter	CD: DG 439 3742/439 3682
	Mathis, Haefliger	

Cantata No 4 "Christus lag in Todesbanden"

July and	Göttingen Bach	LP: DG APM 14046/APM 14079
August 1950	Orchestra	
	Frankfurt Chorus	
	Lehmann	

Munich	Munich Bach	LP: DG 198 465/2722 022
July 1968	Orchestra & Chorus	CD: DG 413 6462/427 1282
	K.Richter	CD: DG 439 3742/439 3682

Cantata No 5 "Wo soll ich fliehen hin?"

Munich	Mathis, T.Schmidt,	LP: DG 2722 030
October 1977-	Schreier	CD: DG 439 3942/439 3682
May 1978	Munich Bach	
	Orchestra & Chorus	
	K.Richter	

Cantata No 6 "Bleib' bei uns, denn es will Abend werden"

Munich	Reynolds, Schreier	LP: DG 2722 022
May 1973-	Munich Bach	CD: DG 439 3742/439 3682
January 1974	Orchestra & Chorus	
	K.Richter	

Cantata No 8: Excerpt (Doch weichet, ihr tollen vergeblichen Sorgen!)

Berlin	Nicolet, flute	LP: HMV ALP 1703/ASD 342
February 1958	Poppen, cello	LP: Electrola E 90022/STE 90022/
	Picht-Axenfeld,	E 70415/STE 70415
	harpsichord	LP: EMI EX 29 04353
	BPO	
	Forster	

Bach Cantatas/continued

Cantata No 9 "Es ist das Heil uns kommen her"

Munich	Mathis, Hamari,	LP: DG 2722 028
March 1975-	Schreier	CD: DG 439 3872/439 3682
June 1977	Munich Bach	
	Orchestra & Chorus	
	K.Richter	

Cantata No 11 "Lobet Gott in seinen Reichen" (Ascension Oratorio)

Munich	Mathis, Reynolds,	LP: DG 2533 355/2722 025
May 1973-	Schreier	LP: DG 439 3802/439 3682
January 1975	Munich Bach	
	Orchestra & Chorus	
	K.Richter	

Cantata No 13 "Meine Seufzer, meine Tränen"

Munich	Mathis, Reynolds,	LP: DG 2722 005
June and	Schreier	CD: DG 439 3692/439 3682
July 1971	Munich Bach	
	Orchestra & Chorus	
	K.Richter	

Cantata No 13: Excerpt (So sei nun, Seele, seine)

Berlin	BPO	LP: HMV ALP 1703/ASD 342
February 1958	Forster	LP: Electrola E 90022/STE 90022

Cantata No 13: Excerpt (Aechzen und erbärmlich weinen)

Berlin	Rampal, flute	LP: EMI ASD 2903/1C 063 02328
1971	Neilz, cello	
	Veyron-Lacroix,	
	harpsichord	

An excerpt from this cantata, performed with Menuhin and Rostropovich in New York in May 1976, may exist as an unpublished CBS recording

Cantata No 17 "Wer Dank opfert, der preiset mich"

Munich	Mathis, Hamari,	LP: DG 2722 028
March 1976-	Schreier	CD: DG 439 3872/439 3682
June 1977	Munich Bach	
	Orchestra & Chorus	
	K.Richter	

Cantata No 21 "Ich hatte viel Bekümmernis"

Munich	Mathis, Haefliger	LP: DG 2533 049
July 1969	Munich Bach	CD: DG 439 3802/439 3682
	Orchestra & Chorus	
	K.Richter	

Bach Cantatas/continued

Cantata No 24 "Ein ungefärbt Gemüte"

Munich	Reynolds, Schreier	LP: DG 2533 329/2722 025
May 1974 and	Munich Bach	CD: DG 439 3802/439 3682
January 1975	Orchestra & Chorus	
	K.Richter	

Cantata No 26 "Ach wie flüchtig, ach wie nichtig"

Munich	Munich Bach	LP: DG 2722 005/2722 030
October 1976 and	Orchestra & Chorus	CD: DG 413 6462/427 1302
February 1978	K.Richter	

Cantata No 27 "Wer weiss, wie nahe mir mein Ende"

Munich	Mathis, Hamari,	LP: DG 2722 028
March 1976-	Schreier	
June 1977	Munich Bach	
	Orchestra & Chorus	
	K.Richter	

Cantata No 28 "Gottlob! Nun geht das Jahr zu Ende"

Munich	Mathis, Töpper,	LP: DG 2722 005
June 1970-	Schreier	CD: DG 439 3692/439 3682
April 1972	Munich Bach	
	Orchestra & Chorus	
	K.Richter	

Cantata No 30 "Freue dich, erlöste Schar"

Munich	Mathis, Reynolds,	LP: DG 2533 330/2722 025
March 1974-	Schreier	CD: DG 439 3802/439 3682
January 1975	Munich Bach	
	Orchestra & Chorus	
	K.Richter	

Cantata No 33 "Allein zu dir, Herr Jesu Christ"

Munich	Hamari, Schreier	LP: DG 2722 028
March 1976-	Munich Bach	CD: DG 439 3872/439 3682
June 1977	Orchestra & Chorus	
	K.Richter	

Bach Cantatas/continued

Cantata No 34 "O ewiges Feuer, o Ursprung der Liebe"

Munich	Reynolds, Schreier	LP: DG 2533 306/2722 025
March 1974-	Munich Bach	CD: DG 439 3802/439 3682
January 1975	Orchestra & Chorus	
	K.Richter	

Cantata No 38 "Aus tiefer Not schrei' ich zu dir"

Munich	Mathis, T.Schmidt,	LP: DG 2722 030
October 1977-	Schreier	CD: DG 439 3942/439 3682
May 1978	Munich Bach	
	Orchestra & Chorus	
	K.Richter	

Cantata No 39 "Brich dem Hungrigen das Brot"

Munich	Mathis, Reynolds	LP: DG 2722 025
January 1974-	Munich Bach	CD: DG 439 3802/439 3682
January 1975	Orchestra & Chorus	
	K.Richter	

Cantata No 44 "Sie werden euch in den Bann tun"

Munich	Mathis, Reynolds	LP: DG 2533 355/2722 025
October 1973-	Munich Bach	CD: DG 439 3802/439 3682
January 1975	Orchestra & Chorus	
	K.Richter	

Cantata No 56 "Ich will den Kreuzstab gerne tragen"

Berlin	Berlin Chamber	LP: DG APM 14 004/2548 128
June 1951	Orchestra and	
	Motettenchor	
	Ristenpart	
Lucerne	Lucerne Festival	LP: DG LPM 18 969/SLPM 138 969
August 1963	and Chorus	LP: DG 2535 283
	Baumgartner	
Munich	Munich Bach	LP: DG 198 477/2547 072
July 1969	Orchestra & Chorus	CD: DG 413 6462/427 1283
	K.Richter	CD: DG 439 3942/439 3682
Stuttgart	Bach Collegium	LP: Hänssler 98 756
July 1983	Gächinger Kantorei	CD: Hänssler 98 903
	Rilling	CD: Novalis 15 00292
		CD: Laudate 98 855

Cantata No 58 "Ach Gott, wie manches Herzeleid"

Munich	Armstrong	LP: DG 2722 005
June and	Munich Bach	CD: DG 439 3692/439 3682
July 1970	Orchestra & Chorus	
	K.Richter	

Cantata No 61 "Nun komm' der Heiden Heiland"

Munich	Mathis, Schreier	LP: DG 2722 005
July 1970 and	Munich Bach	CD: DG 413 6462/439 3692/439 3682
July 1971	Orchestra & Chorus	
	K.Richter	

Cantata No 63 "Christen, ätzet diesen Tag"

Munich	Mathis, Reynolds,	LP: DG 2722 005
June 1970-	Schreier	CD: DG 439 3692/439 3682
April 1972	Munich Bach	
	Orchestra & Chorus	
	K.Richter	

Cantata No 64 "Sehet, welch' eine Liebe hat uns der Vater erzeiget"

Munich	Mathis, Reynolds	LP: DG 2722 005
June 1970-	Munich Bach	CD: DG 439 3692/439 3682
April 1972	Orchestra & Chorus	
	K.Richter	

Cantata No 67 "Halt im Gedächtnis Jesum Christ"

Munich	Reynolds, Schreier	LP: DG 2722 022
May 1973-	Munich Bach	CD: DG 439 3742/439 3682
January 1974	Orchestra & Chorus	
	K.Richter	

Cantata No 68 "Also hat Gott die Welt geliebt"

Munich	Mathis	LP: DG 2533 306/2722 025
May 1974 and	Munich Bach	CD: DG 439 3802/439 3682
January 1975	Orchestra & Chorus	

Cantata No 70 "Wachet! Betet! Seid bereit allezeit!"

Munich	Mathis, T.Schmidt,	LP: DG 2722 030
February 1977-	Schreier	CD: DG 439 3942/439 3682
May 1978	Munich Bach	
	Orchestra & Chorus	
	K.Richter	

Cantata No 73: Excerpt (Herr, so du willst)

Berlin	BPO	LP: HMV ALP 1703/ASD 342/ASD 2549
February 1958	Forster	LP: Electrola E 90022/STE 90022/
		SHZE 173

Cantata No 80 "Ein' feste Burg ist unser Gott"

Munich	Mathis, T.Schmidt,	LP: DG 2533 459/2722 030
February 1977-	Schreier	CD: DG 413 6462/427 1302
June 1978	Munich Bach	CD: DG 439 3942/439 3682
	Orchestra & Chorus	
	K.Richter	

Cantata No 81 "Jesus schläft, was soll ich hoffen?"

Munich	Reynolds, Schreier	LP: DG 2722 005
March and	Munich Bach	CD: DG 439 3692/439 3682
April 1972	Orchestra & Chorus	
	K.Richter	

Cantata No 82 "Ich habe genug"

Berlin	Berlin Chamber	LP: DG APM 14 004/2548 128
June 1951	Orchestra	
	Ristenpart	

Munich	Munich Bach	LP: DG 198 477/2722 005
July 1968	Orchestra	CD: DG 427 1282/439 3692/439 3682
	K.Richter	

Stuttgart	Bach Collegium	LP: Hänssler 98 756
July 1983	Rilling	CD: Hänssler 98 903
		CD: Novalis 15 00282
		CD: Laudate 98 855

Cantata No 87 "Bisher habt ihr nichts gegeben"

Munich	Reynolds, Schreier	LP: DG 2533 313/2722 022
May 1973-	Munich Bach	CD: DG 439 3742/439 3682
January 1974	Orchestra & Chorus	
	K.Richter	

Cantata No 92 "Ich hab' in Gottes Herz und Sinn"

Munich	Mathis, Schreier	LP: DG 2533 312/2722 022
May 1973-	Munich Bach	CD: DG 439 3742/439 3682
January 1974	Orchestra & Chorus	
ł	K.Richter	

Cantata No 93 "Wer nur den lieben Gott lässt walten"

Munich	Mathis, T.Schmidt,	LP: DG 2722 030
January 1974-	Schreier	CD: DG 439 3942/439 3682
January 1975	Munich Bach	
	Orchestra & Chorus	
	K.Richter	

Cantata No 96 "Herr Christ, der ein'ge Gottessohn"

Munich	Mathis, Reynolds,	LP: DG 2722 025
October 1977-	Schreier	CD: DG 427 1152/439 3802/439 3682
May 1978	Munich Bach	
	Orchestra & Chorus	
	K.Richter	

Cantata No 100 "Was Gott tut, das ist wohlgetan"

Munich	Mathis, Hamari,	LP: DG 2722 028
March 1976-	Schreier	CD: DG 439 3872/439 3682
June 1977	Munich Bach	
	Orchestra & Chorus	
	K.Richter	

Cantata No 102 "Herr, deine Augen sehen nach dem Glauben"

Munich	Hamari, Schreier	LP: DG 2722 028
March 1975-	Munich Bach	CD: DG 439 3872/439 3682
June 1977	Orchestra & Chorus	
	K.Richter	

Cantata No 104 "Du Hirte Israel, höre"

Munich	Schreier	LP: DG 2722 022
May-October	Munich Bach	CD: DG 439 3742/439 3682
1973	Orchestra & Chorus	
	K.Richter	

Cantata No 105 "Herr, gehe nicht ins Gericht"

Munich	Mathis, Hamari,	LP: DG 2722 028
March 1976-	Schreier	CD: DG 439 3872/439 3682
June 1977	Munich Bach	
	Orchestra & Chorus	
	K.Richter	

Cantata No 115 "Mache dich, mein Geist, bereit"

Munich	Mathis, T.Schmidt,	LP: DG 2722 030
October 1977-	Schreier	CD: DG 439 3942/439 3682
May 1978	Munich Bach	
	Orchestra & Chorus	
	K.Richter	

Cantata No 116 "Du Friedensfürst, Herr Jesu Christ"

Munich	Mathis, T.Schmidt,	LP: DG 2722 030
February 1977-	Schreier	CD: DG 427 1302/439 3942/439 3682
June 1978	Munich Bach	
	Orchestra & Chorus	
	K.Richter	

Cantata No 121 "Christum wir sollen loben schon"

Munich	Mathis, Reynolds,	LP: DG 2722 005
June 1971-	Schreier	CD: DG 439 3692/439 3682
March 1972	Munich Bach	
	Orchestra & Chorus	
	K.Richter	

Cantata No 123: Excerpt (Lass, o Welt, mich aus Verachtung)

Berlin	Rampal, flute	LP: EMI ASD 2903/1C 063 02328
1971	Neilz, cello	
	Veyron-Lacroix,	
	harpsichord	

Cantata No 129 "Gelobet sei der Herr, mein Gott"

Munich	Mathis, Reynolds	LP: DG 2722 025
January 1974-	Munich Bach	CD: DG 427 1152/439 3802/439 3682
January 1975	Orchestra & Chorus	
	K.Richter	

Cantata No 130 "Herr Gott, dich loben wir alle"

Munich	Mathis, T.Schmidt,	LP: DG 2722 030
March 1975-	Schreier	CD: DG 439 3942/439 3682
February 1978	Munich Bach	
	Orchestra & Chorus	
	K.Richter	

Cantata No 135 "Ach Herr, mich armen Sünder"

Munich	Reynolds, Schreier	LP: DG 2533 329/2722 025
March 1974-	Munich Bach	CD: DG 439 3802/439 3682
January 1975	Orchestra & Chorus	
	K.Richter	

Cantata No 137 "Lobet den Herrn, den mächtigen König"

Munich	Mathis, Hamari,	LP: DG 2722 028
March 1975-	Schreier	CD: DG 439 3872/439 3682
June 1977	Munich Bach	
	Orchestra & Chorus	
	K.Richter	

Cantata No 139 "Wohldem, der sich auf seinen Gott"

Munich	Mathis, T.Schmidt,	LP: DG 2722 030
October 1977-	Schreier	CD: DG 439 3942/439 3682
May 1978	Munich Bach	
	Orchestra & Chorus	
	K.Richter	

Cantata No 140 "Wachet auf, ruft uns die Stimme"

Munich	Mathis, Schreier	LP: DG 2533 459/2722 030
October 1977-	Munich Bach	CD: DG 419 4662/439 3942/439 3682
May 1978	Orchestra & Chorus	
	K.Richter	

Cantata No 157: Excerpts (Meinen Jesum lass' ich nicht; Ja, ich halte Jesum feste)

| Berlin | BPO | LP: HMV ALP 1703/ASD 342 |
| February 1958 | Forster | LP: Electrola E 90022/STE 90022 |

Cantata No 158 "Der Friede sei mit dir"

Munich	Munich Bach	LP: DG 2722 022
July 1969	Orchestra & Chorus	CD: DG 439 3742/439 3682
	K.Richter	

Cantata No 158: Excerpt (Der Friede sei mit dir)

| Berlin | BPO | LP: HMV ALP 1703/ASD 342 |
| February 1958 | Forster | LP: Electrola E 90022/STE 90022 |

Cantata No 159: Excerpt (Es ist vollbracht)

Berlin	Koch, oboe	LP: HMV ALP 1703/ASD 342
February 1958	Poppen, cello	LP: Electrola E 90022/STE 90022
	Picht-Axenfeld,	LP: EMI EX 29 04353
	harpsichord	
	BPO	
	Forster	

Cantata No 171 "Gott, wie dein Name, so ist dein Ruhm"

Munich	Mathis, Töpper,	LP: DG 2722 005
June 1970-	Schreier	CD: DG 439 3692/439 3682
July 1971	Munich Bach	
	Orchestra & Chorus	
	K.Richter	

Cantata No 175 "Er rufet seinen Schafen mit Namen"

Munich	Reynolds, Schreier	LP: DG 2533 306/2722 025
February 1974-	Munich Bach	CD: DG 439 3802/439 3682
January 1975	Orchestra & Chorus	
	K.Richter	

Cantata No 178 "Wo Gott, der Herr, nicht bei uns hält"

Munich	Mathis, Hamari,	LP: DG 2722 028
March 1975-	Schreier	CD: DG 439 3872/439 3682
June 1977	Munich Bach	
	Orchestra & Chorus	
	K.Richter	

Cantata No 179 "Siehe zu, dass deine Gottesfurcht nicht Heuchelei sei"

Munich	Mathis, Schreier	LP: DG 2722 028
March 1976-	Munich Bach	CD: DG 439 3872/439 3682
June 1977	Orchestra & Chorus	
	K.Richter	

Cantata No 180 "Schmücke dich, o liebe Seele"

Munich	Mathis, T.Schmidt,	LP: DG 2722 030
October 1977-	Schreier	CD: DG 439 3942/439 3682
May 1978	Munich Bach	
	Orchestra & Chorus	
	K.Richter	

Bach Cantatas/concluded

Cantata No 187 "Es wartet alles auf dich"

Munich	Mathis, Hamari	LP: DG 2722 028
March 1976-	Munich Bach	CD: DG 439 3872/439 3682
June 1977	Orchestra & Chorus	
	K.Richter	

Cantata No 208 "Was mir behagt, ist die muntre Jagd"

Berlin	Kupper, Köth,	LP: HMV ALP 1985/ASD 534
March 1962	Wunderlich	LP: EMI 1C 063 28160/ED 29 03701
	St Hedwig's Choir	
	Berlin SO	
	Forster	

Cantata No 211 "Schweigt stille, plaudert nicht" (Coffee Cantata)

Berlin	Otto, Traxel	LP: HMV ALP 1888/ASD 457
October 1960	BPO	LP: EMI 1C 063 29014/ED 29 03701
	Forster	Also published on LP by
		World Records

London	Varady, Baldin	LP: Philips 412 8821
November 1981	Academy of	CD: Philips 412 8822
	Saint Martin's	
	Marriner	

Cantata No 212 "Mer hahn en neue Oberkeet" (Peasant Cantata)

Berlin	Otto, Traxel	LP: HMV ALP 1888/ASD 457
October 1960	BPO	LP: EMI 1C 063 29014
	Forster	Also published on LP by
		World Records
		Dein Wachstum sei feste
		LP: Electrola E 70415/STE 70415
		LP: EMI EX 29 04353

London	Varady, Baldin	LP: Philips 412 8821
November 1981	Academy of	CD: Philips 412 8822
	Saint Martin's	
	Marriner	

Cantata No 213 "Amore traditore"

Berlin	Poppen, cello	LP: HMV ALP 1804/ASD 397
February 1960	Picht-Axenfeld,	CD: EMI CZS 568 5092
	harpsichord	

BARBER

Dover Beach

New York April 1967	Juilliard String Quartet	LP: CBS 72687/KS 7131/61898 CD: Sony MPK 46727

BARTOK

Bluebeard's Castle

Berlin October 1958	Role of Bluebeard Töpper Berlin RO Fricsay Sung in German	LP: DG LPM 18 565/SLPM 138 030 LP: DG 2535 703 Excerpt LP: DG 2705 001
Munich March and April 1979	Role of Bluebeard Varady Bavarian State Orchestra Sawallisch	LP: DG 2531 172 CD: DG 423 2362

Im Tale

Berlin May 1970	Reutter	LP: EMI 1C 065 02676/ 1C 161 02673-02677

Cantata profana

Berlin September 1951	Krebs Berlin RO St Hedwig's and RIAS Choirs Fricsay Sung in German	CD: DG 445 4022/445 4002

BECK

Herbst (Die Blätter fallen)

Berlin March 1974	Reimann	LP: EMI 1C 065 02677/ 1C 161 02673-02677

BEETHOVEN

Fidelio

Munich May, June and July 1957	Role of Pizarro Rysanek, Seefried, Haefliger, Lenz, Frick, Engen Bavarian State Orchestra & Chorus Fricsay	LP: DG LPM 18 390-18 391/ SLPM 138 390-138 391 LP: DG 2726 088/2727 006 CD: DG 437 3452 Excerpts 45: DG EPL 30 408/SEPL 30 408 LP: DG LPEM 19 215/SLPEM 136 215 LP: DG LPEM 19 460/SLPEM 139 460 LP: DG LPE 17 168/135 018/135 113 LP: DG 2535 298/2535 631 LP: DG 2548 118/2705 001 CD: IMP IMPX 9021/DG 447 6782
Vienna January, February and April 1978	Role of Fernando Janowitz, Popp, Kollo, Dallapozza, Jungwirth, Sotin Vienna Opera Chorus VPO Bernstein	LP: DG 2709 082/2740 191 CD: DG 419 4362 Excerpts LP: DG 2537 048

Symphony No 9 "Choral"

Berlin December 1957 and January and April 1958	Seefried, Forrester Haefliger St Hedwig's Choir BPO Fricsay	LP: DG LPM 18 512-18 513/ SLPM 138 002-138 003 LP: DG 2700 108/89 727-89 728 LP: DG 2730 015/2535 203 CD: DG 445 4012/445 4002

An die ferne Geliebte, song cycle (Auf dem Hügel sitz' ich spähend; Wo die Berge so blau; Leichte Segler in den Höhen; Diese Wolken in den Höhen; Es kehret der Maien; Nimm' sie hin denn, diese Lieder)

London October 1951	Moore	78: HMV DB 21347-21348/ DB 9681-9682 auto 45: HMV 7ER 5326 45: Electrola E 50074 45: Victor WHMV 1046 LP: HMV ALP 1066 LP: Electrola E 90052 LP: Victor LHMV 1046 CD: EMI CZS 568 5092
Salzburg August 1965	Moore	LP: Orfeo S140 855R CD: Orfeo C140 501A/C339 930T
Berlin April 1966	Demus	LP: DG 139 197/139 216-139 218 LP: DG 2709 022/2720 017/2721 138 CD: DG 415 1892
Berlin November 1982- March 1984	Höll	LP: EMI EX 27 00423

Beethoven Lieder/continued

Abendlied unterm gestirnten Himmel (Wenn die Sonne niedersinket)

Berlin November- December 1954	Klust	LP: HMV ALP 1318 LP: Electrola E 90006 LP: EMI EX 29 04293 CD: Testament SBT 1057
Berlin April 1966	Demus	LP: DG 139 216-139 218/2709 022 LP: DG 2720 017/2721 138
Berlin November 1982- March 1984	Höll	LP: EMI EX 27 00423

Adelaide (Einsam wandelt dein Freund)

Berlin November- December 1954	Klust	LP: HMV ALP 1317 LP: Electrola E 90005 LP: EMI 1C 053 01138M/EX 29 04293 CD: Testament SBT 1057
Salzburg August 1965	Moore	LP: Orfeo S140 855R CD: Orfeo C140 501A/C339 930T
Berlin April 1966	Demus	LP: DG 139 197/139 216-139 218 LP: DG 2709 022/2720 017/2721 138
Berlin November 1982- March 1984	Höll	LP: EMI EX 27 00423

Als die Geliebte sich trennen wollte (Der Hoffnung letzter Schimmer sinkt dahin)

Berlin April 1966	Demus	LP: DG 139 197/139 216-139 218 LP: DG 2709 022/2720 017/2721 138
Berlin November 1982- March 1984	Höll	LP: EMI EX 27 00423

An die Geliebte (O dass ich dir vom stillen Auge)

Berlin April 1966	Demus	LP: DG 139 197/139 216-139 218 LP: DG 2709 022/2720 017/2721 138
Berlin November 1982- March 1984	Höll	LP: EMI EX 27 00423

An die Hoffnung (Die du so gern in heiligen Nächten)

Berlin November 1982- March 1984	Höll	LP: EMI EX 27 00423

An die Hoffnung (Ob ein Gott sei?)

Berlin November- December 1954	Klust	LP: HMV ALP 1317 LP: Electrola E 90005 LP: EMI 1C 053 01138M CD: Testament SBT 1057
Salzburg August 1965	Moore	LP: Orfeo S140 855R CD: Orfeo C140 501A/C339 930T
Berlin April 1966	Demus	LP: DG 139 216-139 218/2709 022 LP: DG 2720 017/2721 138
Berlin November 1982- March 1984	Höll	LP: EMI EX 27 00423

Andenken (Ich denke dein)

Berlin November- December 1954	Klust	LP: HMV ALP 1317 LP: Electrola E 90005 LP: EMI 1C 053 01138M CD: Testament SBT 1057
Berlin April 1966	Demus	LP: DG 139 197/139 216-139 218 LP: DG 2709 022/2720 017/2721 138
Berlin November 1982- March 1984	Höll	LP: EMI EX 27 00423

2 Ariette (Dimmi, ben mio/Hoffnung; T'intendo sì, mio cor/Liebesklage

Berlin April 1966	Demus	LP: DG 139 197/139 216-139 218 LP: DG 2709 022/2720 017/2721 138
Berlin November 1982- March 1984	Höll	LP: EMI EX 27 00423

Beethoven Lieder/continued

2 Ariette/L'amante impatiente (Stille Frage; Liebesungeduld)

Berlin November- December 1954	Klust	LP: HMV ALP 1318 LP: Electrola E 90006
Berlin April 1966	Demus	LP: DG 139 197/139 216-139 218 LP: DG 2709 022/2720 017/2721 138 CD: DG 415 1892
Berlin November 1982- March 1984	Höll	LP: EMI EX 27 00423

Der Bardengeist

Berlin April 1966	Demus	LP: DG 139 216-139 218/2709 022 LP: DG 2720 017/2721 138
Berlin November 1982- March 1984	Höll	LP: EMI EX 27 00423

Behold my love/Scottish folksongs

Berlin 1970	Mathis Engel Rohn, violin Donderer, cello	LP: DG 2530 262/2721 138

Bitten/Gellert-Lieder (Gott, deine Güte reicht so weit)
See Gellert-Lieder

Das Blümchen Wunderhold (Es blüht ein Blümchen irgendwo)

Berlin April 1966	Demus	LP: DG 139 216-139 218/2709 022 LP: DG 2720 017/2721 138
Berlin November 1982- March 1984	Höll	LP: EMI EX 27 00423

Bonny laddie, highland laddie/Scottish folksongs

Berlin January 1983	Höll Menuhin, violin	LP: EMI EX 27 00451

Busslied/Gellert Lieder (An dir allein, an dir hab' ich gesündigt)
See Gellert-Lieder

Come draw we round a cheerful song/Folksongs

Berlin 1961	Engel Heller, violin Nicolet, flute Poppen, cello	LP: DG LPM 18 706/SLPM 138 706 LP: DG 2721 138

Come fill, my good fellow/Scottish folksongs

Berlin 1961	Engel Heller, violin Nicolet, flute Poppen, cello	LP: DG LPM 18 706/SLPM 138 706
Berlin 1970	Engel Rohn, violin Donderer, cello	LP: DG 2530 262/2721 138
Berlin January 1983	Höll Menuhin, violin	LP: EMI EX 27 00451

Could this ill world have been contriv'd/Scottish folksongs

Berlin January 1983	Höll Menuhin, violin	LP: EMI EX 27 00451

The Dream/Welsh folksongs

Berlin December 1960	De los Angeles Moore Drolc, violin Poppen, cello	LP: HMV ALP 1891/ASD 459 CD: EMI CMS 565 0612

Duncan Gray/Scottish folksongs

Berlin 1970	Mathis, Young Engel Rohn, violin Donderer, cello	LP: DG 2530 262/2721 138

Die Ehre Gottes aus der Natur/Gellert-Lieder (Die Himmel rühmen des Ewigen Ehre)
See Gellert-Lieder

Beethoven Lieder/continued

Faithful Johnie/Scottish folksongs

Berlin 1961	Engel Heller, violin Nicolet, flute Poppen, cello	LP: DG LPM 18 706/SLPM 138 706
Berlin 1970	Mathis Engel Rohn, violin	LP: DG 2530 262/2721 138
Berlin January 1983	Höll Menuhin, violin	LP: EMI EX 27 00451

Feuerfarb' (Ich weiss eine Farbe)

| Berlin
November 1982-
March 1984 | Höll | LP: EMI EX 27 00423 |

Flohlied/Aus Goethes Faust

Berlin November- December 1954	Klust	LP: HMV ALP 1317 LP: Electrola E 90005 LP: EMI 1C 053 01138M/1C 047 01247 CD: Testament SBT 1057
Salzburg August 1965	Moore	LP: Orfeo S140 855R CD: Orfeo C140 501A/C339 930T
Berlin April 1966	Demus	LP: DG 139 216-139 218/2709 022 LP: DG 2720 017/2721 138 CD: DG 415 1892
Berlin November 1982- March 1984	Höll	LP: EMI EX 27 00423

Gedenke mein

| Berlin
November 1982-
March 1984 | Höll | LP: EMI EX 27 00423 |

Das Geheimnis (Wo blüht das Blümchen, das nie verblüht?)

| Berlin
April 1966 | Demus | LP: DG 139 216-139 218/2709 022
LP: DG 2720 017/2721 138 |
| Berlin
November 1982-
March 1984 | Höll | LP: EMI EX 27 00423 |

Beethoven Lieder/continued

6 Gellert-Lieder (Bitten; Liebe des Nächsten; Vom Tode; Die Ehre Gottes aus der Natur; Gottes Macht und Vorsehung; Busslied)

Berlin November- December 1954	Klust	LP: HMV ALP 1318 LP: Electrola E 90006 LP: EMI 1C 053 01138M CD: Testament SBT 1057
Salzburg August 1965	Moore	LP: Orfeo S140 855R CD: Orfeo C140 501A/C339 930T
Berlin April 1966	Demus	LP: DG 139 197/139 216-139 216 LP: DG 2709 022/2720 017/2721 138
Berlin November 1982- March 1984	Höll	LP: EMI EX 27 00423

Das Glück der Freundschaft (Der lebt ein Leben wonniglich)

Berlin April 1966	Demus	LP: DG 139 197/139 216-139 218 LP: DG 2709 022/2720 017/2721 138

La gondoletta/Folksongs (Oh leave thy soft pillow)

Berlin 1961	Engel Heller, violin Nicolet, flute Poppen, cello	LP: DG LPM 18 706/SLPM 138 706 LP: DG 2721 138
Berlin January 1983	Höll Menuhin, violin	LP: EMI EX 27 00454

Good Night/Welsh folksongs

Berlin January 1983	Höll Menuhin, violin	LP: EMI EX 27 00454

Gottes Macht und Vorsehung/Gellert-Lieder (Gott ist mein Lied!)
See Gellert-Lieder

He promised me at parting/Irish folksongs

Berlin December 1960	De los Angeles Moore Drolc, violin Poppen, cello	LP: HMV ALP 1891/ASD 459 CD: EMI CMS 565 0612

Horch' auf, mein Liebchen/Folksongs

Berlin 1961	Engel Heller, violin Nicolet, flute Poppen, cello	LP: DG LPM 18 706/SLPM 138 706 LP: DG 2721 138

Beethoven Lieder/continued

In questa tomba oscura

Berlin November- December 1954	Klust	LP: HMV ALP 1317 LP: Electrola E 90005 CD: Testament SBT 1057
Salzburg August 1965	Moore	LP: Orfeo S140 855R CD: Orfeo C140 501A/C339 930T
Berlin April 1966	Demus	LP: DG 139 197/139 216-139 218 LP: DG 2709 022/2720 017/2721 138 CD: DG 415 1892
Berlin November 1982- March 1984	Höll	LP: EMI EX 27 00423

Der Jüngling in der Fremde (Der Frühling entblüht dem Schoss der Natur)

Berlin April 1966	Demus	LP: DG 139 216-139 218/2709 022 LP: DG 2720 017/2721 138
Berlin November 1982- March 1984	Höll	LP: EMI EX 27 00423

Der Kuss (Ich war bei Chloen ganz allein)

Berlin November- December 1954	Klust	LP: HMV ALP 1317 LP: Electrola E 90005 LP: EMI 1C 053 01138M/1C 047 01247
Berlin April 1966	Demus	LP: DG 139 216-139 218/2709 022 LP: DG 2720 017/2721 138
Berlin November 1982- March 1984	Höll	LP: EMI EX 27 00423

Die laute Klage (Turteltaube, du klagest so laut)

Berlin April 1966	Demus	LP: DG 139 216-139 218/2709 022 LP: DG 2720 017/2721 138
Berlin November 1982- March 1984	Höll	LP: EMI EX 27 00423

Beethoven Lieder/continued

Die Liebe (Ohne Liebe lebe, wer da kann)

Berlin	Klust	LP: HMV ALP 1318
November-		LP: Electrola E 90006
December 1954		CD: Testament SBT 1057

| Berlin | Demus | LP: DG 139 216-139 218/2709 022 |
| April 1966 | | LP: DG 2720 017/2721 138 |

Berlin	Höll	LP: EMI EX 27 00423
November 1982-		
March 1984		

Die Liebe des Nächsten/Gellert-Lieder (So jemand spricht: Ich liebe Gott!)
See Gellert-Lieder

Der Liebende (Welch ein wunderbares Leben)

| Berlin | Demus | LP: DG 139 216-139 218/2709 022 |
| April 1966 | | LP: DG 2720 017/2721 138 |

Berlin	Höll	LP: EMI EX 27 00423
November 1982-		
March 1984		

Lied aus der Ferne (Als mir noch die Träne der Sehnsucht nicht floss)

Berlin	Klust	LP: HMV ALP 1318
November-		LP: Electrola E 90006
December 1954		LP: EMI 1C 053 01138M
		CD: Testament SBT 1057

| Berlin | Demus | LP: DG 139 216-139 218/2709 022 |
| April 1966 | | LP: DG 2720 017/2721 138 |

Berlin	Höll	LP: EMI EX 27 00423
November 1982-		
March 1984		

Das Liedchen von der Ruhe (Im Arm der Liebe ruht sich's wohl)

Berlin	Klust	LP: HMV ALP 1318
November-		LP: Electrola E 90006
December 1954		CD: Testament SBT 1057

| Berlin | Demus | LP: DG 139 216-139 218/2709 022 |
| April 1966 | | LP: DG 2720 017/2721 138 |

Berlin	Höll	LP: EMI EX 27 00423
November 1982-		
March 1984		

Beethoven Lieder/continued

Mailied (Wie herrlich leuchtet mir die Natur)

Berlin November- December 1954	Klust	LP: HMV ALP 1317 LP: Electrola E 90005 LP: EMI 1C 053 01138M CD: Testament SBT 1057
Salzburg August 1965	Moore	LP: Orfeo S140 855R CD: Orfeo C140 501A/C339 930T
Berlin April 1966	Demus	LP: DG 139 216-139 218/2709 022 LP: DG 2720 017/2721 138 CD: DG 415 1892
Berlin November 1982- March 1984	Höll	LP: EMI EX 27 00423

Marmotte (Ich komme schon durch manches Land)

Berlin November- December 1954	Klust	LP: HMV ALP 1317 LP: Electrola E 90005/1C 053 01138M CD: Testament SBT 1057
Berlin April 1966	Demus	LP: DG 139 216-139 218/2709 022 LP: DG 2720 017/2721 138
Berlin November 1982- March 1984	Höll	LP: EMI EX 27 00423

Miller of Dee/Folksongs

Berlin 1970	Mathis, Young Engel Rohn, violin Donderer, cello	LP: DG 2530 262/2721 138

Mit einem gemalten Band (Kleine Blumen, kleine Blätter)

Berlin November- December 1954	Klust	LP: HMV ALP 1317 LP: Electrola E 90005/1C 053 01138M CD: Testament SBT 1057
Berlin April 1966	Demus	LP: DG 139 216-139 218/2709 022 LP: DG 2720 017/2721 138
Berlin November 1982- March 1984	Höll	LP: EMI EX 27 00423

Beethoven Lieder/continued

Mit Mädchen sich vertragen

| Berlin
September 1972 | Demus, fortepiano | LP: DG 2533 149 |

The morning air plays on my face/Irish folksongs

| Berlin
January 1983 | Höll
Menuhin, violin | LP: EMI EX 27 00454 |

Neue Liebe, neues Leben (Herz, mein Herz, was soll das geben)

| Berlin
November-
December 1954 | Klust | LP: HMV ALP 1317
LP: Electrola E 90005/1C 053 01138M
CD: Testament SBT 1057 |

| Salzburg
August 1965 | Moore | LP: Orfeo S140 855R
CD: Orfeo C140 501A/C339 930T |

| Berlin
April 1966 | Demus | LP: DG 139 216-139 218/2709 022
LP: DG 2720 017/2721 138 |

| Berlin
November 1982-
March 1984 | Höll | LP: EMI EX 27 00423 |

O had my fate been joined with thine/Scottish folksongs

| Berlin
1970 | Engel
Rohn, violin
Donderer, cello | LP: DG 2530 262/2721 138 |

| Berlin
January 1983 | Höll
Menuhin, violin | LP: EMI EX 27 00454 |

O Harp of Erin/Irish folksongs

| Berlin
January 1983 | Höll
Menuhin, violin | LP: EMI EX 27 00454 |

Once more I hail thee/Irish folksongs

| Berlin
January 1983 | Höll
Menuhin, violin | LP: EMI EX 27 00454 |

Opferlied (Die Flamme lodert)

| Berlin
April 1966 | Demus | LP: DG 139 216-139 218/2709 022
LP: DG 2720 017/2721 138 |

| Berlin
November 1982-
March 1984 | Höll | LP: EMI EX 27 00423 |

O sweet were the hours/Scottish folksongs

| Berlin 1966 | Engel Heller, violin Nicolet, flute Poppen, cello | LP: DG LPM 18 706/SLPM 138 706 |

| Berlin 1970 | Engel Rohn, violin Donderer, cello | LP: DG 2530 262/2721 138 |

| Berlin January 1983 | Höll Menuhin, violin | LP: EMI EX 27 00454 |

O would I were but that sweet linnet/Irish folksongs

| Berlin December 1960 | De los Angeles Moore Drolc, violin Poppen, cello | LP: HMV ALP 1891/ASD 459 LP: EMI EX 29 04353 CD: EMI CMS 565 0612 |

La partenza (Ecco quel fiero istante!)

| Berlin April 1966 | Demus | LP: DG 139 197/139 216-139 218 LP: DG 2709 022/2720 017/2721 138 |

| Berlin November 1982- March 1984 | Höll | LP: EMI EX 27 00423 |

The parting kiss/Welsh folksongs

| Berlin January 1983 | Höll Menuhin, violin | LP: EMI EX 27 00454 |

The pulse of an Irishman/Irish folksongs

| Berlin 1970 | Engel Rohn, violin Donderer, cello | LP: DG 2530 262/2721 138 |

| Berlin January 1983 | Höll Menuhin, violin | LP: EMI EX 27 00454 |

Put round the bright wine/Folksongs

| Berlin 1970 | Engel Rohn, violin Donderer, cello | LP: DG 2530 262/2721 138 |

Beethoven Lieder/continued

Resignation (Lisch' aus, mein Licht!)

Berlin November- December 1954	Klust	LP: HMV ALP 1318 LP: Electrola E 90006/EX 29 04293 CD: Testament SBT 1057
Berlin April 1966	Demus	LP: DG 139 216-139 218/2709 022 LP: DG 2720 017/2721 138
Berlin November 1982- March 1984	Höll	LP: EMI EX 27 00423

The Return to Ulster/Irish folksongs

| Berlin
January 1983 | Höll
Menuhin, violin | LP: EMI EX 27 00454 |

Ruf vom Berge (Wenn ich ein Vöglein wäre)

| Berlin
April 1966 | Demus | LP: DG 139 197/139 216-139 218
LP: DG 2709 022/2720 017/2721 138 |

Schilderung eines Mädchens (Schildern willst du, Freund)

| Berlin
April 1966 | Demus | LP: DG 139 197/139 216-139 218
LP: DG 2709 022/2720 017/2721 138 |
| Berlin
November 1982-
March 1984 | Höll | LP: EMI EX 27 00423 |

Sehnsucht (Die stille Nacht umdunkelt)

| Berlin
April 1966 | Demus | LP: DG 139 197/139 216-139 218
LP: DG 2709 022/2720 017/2721 138 |
| Berlin
November 1982-
March 1984 | Höll | LP: EMI EX 27 00423 |

Sehnsucht (Was ziehet mir das Herz so?)

Berlin November- December 1954	Klust	LP: HMV ALP 1317 LP: Electrola E 90005/1C 053 01138M CD: Testament SBT 1057
Salzburg August 1965	Moore	LP: Orfeo S140 855R CD: Orfeo C140 501A/C339 930T
Berlin April 1966	Demus	LP: DG 139 197/139 216-139 218 LP: DG 2709 022/2720 017/2721 138
Berlin November 1982- March 1984	Höll	LP: EMI EX 27 00423

Beethoven Lieder/continued

Ein Selbstgespräch (Ich, der mit flatterndem Sinn)

Berlin November 1982- March 1984	Höll	LP: EMI EX 27 00423

Seufzer eines Ungeliebten und Gegenliebe (Hast du nicht Liebe zugemessen?)

Berlin April 1966	Demus	LP: DG 139 216-139 218/2709 022 LP: DG 2720 017/2721 138
Berlin November 1982- March 1984	Höll	LP: EMI EX 27 00423

The Soldier's Dream/Irish folksongs

Berlin January 1983	Höll Menuhin, violin	LP: EMI EX 27 00454

Sunset/Scottish folksongs

Berlin January 1983	Höll Menuhin, violin	LP: EMI EX 27 00454

They bid me slight my Dermot dear/Irish folksongs

Berlin December 1960	De los Angeles Moore Drolc, violin Poppen, cello	LP: HMV ALP 1891/ASD 459 CD: EMI CMS 565 0612

Urians Reise um die Welt (Wenn jemand eine Reise tut)

Berlin April 1966	Demus	LP: DG 139 216-139 218/2709 022 LP: DG 2720 017/2721 138

Vom Tode/Gellert-Lieder (Meine Lebenszeit verstreicht)
See Gellert-Lieder

Der Wachtelschlag (Horch', wie schallt's dorten so lieblich hervor!)

Berlin November- December 1954	Klust	LP: HMV ALP 1318 LP: Electrola E 90006 CD: Testament SBT 1057
Salzburg August 1965	Moore	LP: Orfeo S140 855R CD: Orfeo C140 501A/C339 930T
Berlin April 1966	Demus	LP: DG 139 216-139 218/2709 022 LP: DG 2720 017/2721 138
Berlin November 1982- March 1984	Höll	LP: EMI EX 27 00423

Wonne der Wehmut (Trocknet nicht, Tränen der ewigen Liebe)

Berlin November- December 1954	Klust	LP: HMV ALP 1317 LP: Electrola E 90005/1C 053 01138M CD: Testament SBT 1057
Salzburg August 1965	Moore	LP: Orfeo S140 855R CD: Orfeo C140 501A/C339 930T
Berlin April 1966	Demus	LP: DG 139 216-139 218/2709 022 LP: DG 2720 017/2721 138
Berlin November 1982- March 1984	Höll	LP: EMI EX 27 00423

Zärtliche Liebe (Ich liebe dich)

Berlin November- December 1954	Klust	LP: HMV ALP 1317 LP: Electrola E 90005/1C 053 01138M CD: Testament SBT 1057
Berlin April 1966	Demus	LP: DG 139 197/139 216-139 218 LP: DG 2709 022/2720 017/2721 138 CD: DG 415 1892
Berlin November 1982- March 1984	Höll	LP: EMI EX 27 00423

Der Zufriedene (Zwar schuf das Glück hienieder)

Berlin November- December 1954	Klust	LP: HMV ALP 1318 LP: Electrola E 90006 CD: Testament SBT 1057
Berlin April 1966	Demus	LP: DG 139 216-218/2709 022 LP: DG 2720 017/2721 138
Berlin November 1982- March 1984	Höll	LP: EMI EX 27 00423

BERG

Lulu

Berlin	Role of Dr Schön	LP: DG 139 273-139 275/2709 029
February 1968	Lear, Johnson,	LP: DG 413 7971/413 8071
	Grobe, Driscoll,	CD: DG 435 7052
	Greindl, Feldhoff	
	Deutsche Oper	
	Orchestra	
	Böhm	

Wozzeck

Berlin	Role of Wozzeck	LP: DG LPM 18 991-18 992/
March and	Lear, Melchert,	SLPM 138 991-138 992
April 1965	Wunderlich, Stolze	LP: DG 2707 023
	Deutsche Oper	LP: DG 413 7971/413 8041
	Orchestra	CD: DG 435 7052
	Böhm	

Abschied

Berlin	Reimann	LP: EMI EL 27 01951
October 1984		

Am Strande

Berlin	Reimann	LP: EMI EL 27 01951
October 1984		CD: EMI CDM 763 5702

Erster Verlust

Berlin	Reimann	LP: EMI EL 27 01951
October 1984		CD: EMI CDM 763 5702

Es klagt, dass der Frühling so kurz blüht

Berlin	Reimann	LP: EMI EL 27 01951
October 1984		CD: EMI CDM 763 5702

Es wandelt, was will schauen

Berlin	Reimann	LP: EMI EL 27 01951
October 1984		CD: EMI CDM 763 5702

Ferne Lieder

Berlin	Reimann	LP: EMI EL 27 01951
October 1984		CD: EMI CDM 763 5702

Berg Lieder/continued

Geliebte Schöne

Berlin   Reimann   LP: EMI EL 27 01951
October 1984   CD: EMI CDM 763 5702

Grabschrift

Berlin   Reimann   LP: EMI EL 27 01951
October 1984   CD: EMI CDM 763 5702

Grenzen der Menschheit

Berlin   Reimann   LP: EMI EL 27 01951
October 1984

Ich liebe dich

Berlin   Reimann   LP: EMI EL 27 01951
October 1984   CD: EMI CDM 763 5702

Im Morgengrauen

Berlin   Reimann   LP: EMI EL 27 01951
October 1984   CD: EMI CDM 763 5702

Nun ich der Riesen stärksten überwand

Berlin   Reimann   LP: DG 2530 107/413 8021
October 1970   CD: DG 431 7442

Regen

Berlin   Reimann   LP: EMI EL 27 01951
October 1984   CD: EMI CDM 763 5702

Schattenleben

Berlin   Reimann   LP: EMI EL 27 01951
October 1984   CD: EMI CDM 763 5702

Schlafen, schlafen

Berlin   Reimann   LP: DG 2530 107/413 8021
October 1970   CD: DG 431 7442

Schlafend trägt man mich

Berlin   Reimann   LP: DG 2530 107/413 8021
October 1970   CD: DG 431 7442

Berg Lieder/concluded

Schlummerlose Nächte

| Berlin | Reimann | LP: EMI EL 27 01951 |
| October 1984 | | CD: EMI CDM 763 5702 |

Sehnsucht II

| Berlin | Reimann | LP: EMI EL 27 01951 |
| October 1984 | | CD: EMI CDM 763 5702 |

Sehnsucht III

| Berlin | Reimann | LP: EMI EL 27 01951 |
| October 1984 | | CD: EMI CDM 763 5702 |

Spaziergang

| Berlin | Reimann | LP: EMI EL 27 01951 |
| October 1984 | | CD: EMI CDM 763 5702 |

Traurigkeit

| Berlin | Reimann | LP: EMI EL 27 01951 |
| October 1984 | | CD: EMI CDM 763 5702 |

Ueber den Bergen

| Berlin | Reimann | LP: EMI EL 27 01951 |
| October 1984 | | CD: EMI CDM 763 5702 |

Vielgeliebte, schöne Frau

| Berlin | Reimann | LP: EMI EL 27 01951 |
| October 1984 | | CD: EMI CDM 763 5702 |

Warm die Lüfte

| Berlin | Reimann | LP: DG 2530 107/413 8021 |
| October 1970 | | CD: DG 437 7442 |

Winter

| Berlin | Reimann | LP: EMI EL 27 01951 |
| October 1984 | | CD: EMI CDM 763 5702 |

Wo der Goldregen steht

| Berlin | Reimann | LP: EMI EL 27 01951 |
| October 1984 | | |

Béatrice et Bénédict

Paris July 1979- October 1981	Role of Somarone Cotrubas, Minton, Domingo Orchestre de Paris Choirs Barenboim	LP: DG 2707 130

La Damnation de Faust

Paris January and July 1978	Role of Mephisto Minton, Domingo, Bastin Orchestre de Paris Choirs Barenboim	LP: DG 2709 087/2740 199

Le jeune pâtre breton

Munich August 1983	Höll Klöcker, clarinet Wallendorf, horn	LP: Orfeo S153 861A CD: Orfeo C153 861A

Sur les lagunes

Berlin March 1971	Reimann	LP: EMI 1C 065 02674/ 1C 161 02673-02677

Le trébuchet/Les fleurs des landes

Berlin December 1960	De los Angeles Moore	LP: HMV ALP 1891/ASD 459 LP: EMI EX 29 05583 CD: EMI CMS 565 0612

Harold en Italie

Prague 1976	Suk Czech PO Fischer-Dieskau conducts	LP: Supraphon LP: Eurodisc KK 27970

BIZET

Carmen: Excerpt (Votre toast)

Berlin	Berlin RO	LP: DG LPM 18 700/SLPM 138 700
January 1961	Fricsay	LP: DG 135 008

Les Pêcheurs de perles: Excerpt (L'orage s'est calmé/O Nadir)

Berlin	Berlin RO	LP: DG LPM 18 700/SLPM 138 700
January 1961	Fricsay	LP: DG 2705 001

Les Pêcheurs de perles: Excerpt (Au fond du temple saint)

Munich	Bergonzi	LP: Orfeo S028 821A
July 1982	Bavarian RO	CD: Orfeo C028 821A
	Lopez-Cobos	

La chanson du fou

Munich	Höll	LP: Teldec 643.754
April 1984		CD: Teldec 843.754

BLACHER

Apreslude nach Gottfried Benn

Berlin	Reutter	LP: EMI 1C 065 02676/
May 1970		1C 161 02673-02677

3 Psalmen (Ich schreie zum Herrn; Herr, ich rufe zu dir; Ich hebe meine Augen auf)

Berlin	Reimann	LP: Electrola E 91189/STE 91189
November 1961		CD: EMI CZS 568 5092

Ein deutsches Requiem

Vienna January 1951	Seefried Singakademie VPO Furtwängler	LP: Japan AT 01-02 CD: Refrain (Japan) DR 920021 Part of „Denn wir haben hier" taken from a performance with Alfred Poell, and not conducted by Furtwängler
Berlin June 1955	Grümmer St Hedwig's Choir BPO Kempe	LP: HMV ALP 1351-1352 LP: EMI XLP 30073-30074 LP: EMI 1C 147 28550-28551 CD: EMI CDH 764 7052
London March, April and May 1961	Schwarzkopf Philharmonia Orchestra & Chorus Klemperer	LP: Columbia 33CX 1781-1782/ SAX 2430-2431 LP: EMI SLS 821 CD: EMI CDC 747 2382
Edinburgh September 1972	Mathis Edinburgh Festival Chorus LPO Barenboim	LP: DG 2707 066 CD: DG 445 0352

Symphony No 4

Prague 1976	Czech PO Fischer-Dieskau conducts	LP: Supraphon SUAST 410 2077 LP: Eurodisc HK 25923

4 ernste Gesänge (Denn es gehet dem Menschen wie dem Vieh; Ich wandte mich und sahe an alle; O Tod, wie bitter bist du; Wenn ich mit Menschen- und Engelszungen redete)

Berlin September 1949	Klust	78: DG LM 68414-68415 LP: DG LPE 17 047
Salzburg August 1958	Moore	LP: Orfeo S140 855R CD: Orfeo C140 201B/C339 930T
Berlin October 1958	Demus	LP: DG LPM 18 644/SLPM 138 644 LP: DG 135 161 CD: DG 415 1892
Berlin March 1972	Barenboim	LP: DG 2530 298/2707 066/2740 279
Salzburg August 1973	Sawallisch	LP: EMI SLS 5002 LP: EMI 1C 191 50379-50385 CD: EMI CMS 764 8202

Die schöne Magelone, 15 Romances to poems by Tieck (Keinen hat es noch gereut;
Traun! Bogen und Pfeil!; Sind es Schmerzen; Liebe kam aus fernen Landen; So
willst du Armen; Wie soll ich die Freude; War es dir, dem diese Lippen bebten?;
Wir müssen uns trennen; Ruhe, Süssliebchen; So tönet dann schäumende Wellen;
Wie schnell verschwindet; Muss es eine Trennung geben?; Geliebter, wo
zaudert; Wie froh und frisch; Treue Liebe dauert lange)

Berlin April 1957	Demus	LP: DG LPM 18 388-18 389/LPM 18 800 LPM 18 388-18 389 also contained Tieck's additional narrative spoken by Fischer-Dieskau
Salzburg August 1964	Moore	CD: EMI CMS 763 1672
Aldeburgh June 1965	Richter	CD: AS-Disc AS 337
Munich July 1970	Richter	LP: EMI SAN 291 CD: EMI CMS 764 8202
Berlin February 1978- September 1982	Barenboim	LP: DG 2740 279

3 Vocal Quartets op 31: Wechsellied zum Tanz; Neckereien; Gang zum Liebchen

| Berlin
September 1981 | Mathis, Fassbaender,
Schreier
Engel, Sawallisch | LP: DG 2740 280 |

3 Vocal quartets op 64 (An die Heimat; Der Abend; Fragen)

| Berlin
September 1981 | Mathis, Fassbaender,
Schreier
Engel, Sawallisch | LP: DG 2740 280/2532 094
CD: DG 423 1332 |

4 Vocal Quartets op 92: O schöne Nacht; Spätherbst; Abendlied; Warum?

| Berlin
September 1981 | Mathis, Fassbaender,
Schreier
Engel, Sawallisch | LP: DG 2740 280 |

6 Vocal Quartets op 112: Sehnsucht; Nächtens; Himmel strahlt so helle und
klar; Rote Rosenknospen; Brennessel steht am Wegesrand; Lieb' Schwalbe,
kleine Schwalbe

| Berlin
September 1981 | Mathis, Fassbaender,
Schreier
Engel, Sawallisch | LP: DG 2740 280 |

Brahms Lieder/continued

4 Vocal duets op 28 (Die Nonne und der Ritter; Vor der Tür; Es rauschet das Wasser; Der Jäger und sein Liebchen)

Berlin May 1967	Meyer Demus	LP: DG 139 328
London August 1969	Baker Barenboim	LP: EMI ASD 2553/1C 063 02041 Es rauschet das Wasser LP: EMI EX 29 04293
Berlin September 1981	Fassbaender Engel	LP: DG 2740 280

Abenddämmerung (Sei willkommen, Zwielichtsstunde!)

Berlin February 1958	Demus	LP: DG LPM 18 504/SLPM 138 011
Salzburg August 1958	Moore	LP: Orfeo S140 855R CD: Orfeo C140 201B/C339 930T
Salzburg August 1973	Sawallisch	LP: EMI SLS 5002 LP: EMI 1C 191 50379-50385 CD: EMI CMS 764 8202
Berlin February 1978- September 1982	Barenboim	LP: DG 2740 279
Munich ca. 1986	Höll	LP: Bayer BR 30 006 CD: Bayer BR 100 006

Abendregen (Langsam und schimmernd fiel ein Regen)

Salzburg March 1972	Barenboim	LP: EMI SLS 5002 LP: EMI 1C 191 50379-50385 CD: EMI CMS 764 8202
Berlin February 1978- September 1982	Barenboim	LP: DG 2740 279
Munich ca. 1986	Höll	LP: Bayer BR 30 006 CD: Bayer BR 100 006

Abschied (Ach, mich hält der Gram gefangen)

Salzburg March 1972	Barenboim	LP: EMI SLS 5002 LP: EMI 1C 191 50379-50385 CD: EMI CMS 764 8202
Berlin February 1978- September 1982	Barenboim	LP: DG 2740 279

Brahms Lieder/continued

Ach, englische Schäferin/Deutsche Volkslieder

Berlin	Schwarzkopf	LP: EMI AN 163-164/SAN 163-164
August-	Moore	LP: EMI 1C 193 00054-00055
September 1965		CD: EMI CDS 749 5252

Ach Gott, wie weh tut Scheiden/Deutsche Volkslieder

Berlin	Moore	LP: EMI AN 163-164/SAN 163-164
August-		LP: EMI 1C 193 00054-00055
September 1965		CD: EMI CDS 749 5252

Ach, könnt' ich diesen Abend/Deutsche Volkslieder

Berlin	Schwarzkopf	LP: EMI AN 163-164/SAN 163-164
August-	Moore	LP: EMI 1C 193 00054-00055
September 1965		CD: EMI CDS 749 5252

Ach, wende diesen Blick

Salzburg	Sawallisch	LP: EMI SLS 5002
August 1973		LP: EMI 1C 191 50379-50385
		CD: EMI CMS 764 8202

Berlin	Barenboim	LP: DG 2740 279
February 1978-		
September 1982		

Ade! (Wie schienen die Sternlein so hell, so hell)

Salzburg	Barenboim	LP: EMI SLS 5002
March 1972		LP: EMI 1C 191 50379-50385
		CD: EMI CMS 764 8202

Berlin	Barenboim	LP: DG 2740 279
February 1978-		
September 1982		

All' mein' Gedanken/Deutsche Volkslieder

Berlin	Moore	LP: EMI AN 163-164/SAN 163-164
August-		LP: EMI 1C 193 00054-00055
September 1965		CD: EMI CDS 749 5252

Brahms Lieder/continued

Alte Liebe (Es kehrt die dunkle Schwalbe)

Berlin February 1958	Demus	LP: DG LPM 18 504/SLPM 138 011 CD: DG 415 1892
Salzburg March 1972	Barenboim	LP: EMI SLS 5002 LP: EMI 1C 191 50379-50385 CD: EMI CMS 764 8202
Berlin February 1978- September 1982	Barenboim	LP: DG 2740 279

Am Sonntag Morgen, zierlich angetan

Salzburg August 1973	Sawallisch	LP: EMI SLS 5002 LP: EMI 1C 191 50379-50385 CD: EMI CMS 764 8202
Berlin February 1978- September 1982	Barenboim	LP: DG 2740 279

An den Mond (Silbermond mit bleichen Strahlen)

Salzburg March 1972	Barenboim	LP: EMI SLS 5002 LP: EMI 1C 191 50379-50385 CD: EMI CMS 764 8202
Berlin February 1978- September 1982	Barenboim	LP: DG 2740 279

An die Nachtigall (Geuss' nicht so laut der liebentflammten Lieder)

Salzburg August 1973	Sawallisch	LP: EMI SLS 5002 LP: EMI 1C 191 50379-50385 CD: EMI CMS 764 8202
Berlin February 1978- September 1982	Barenboim	LP: DG 2740 279

An die Stolze (Und gleich kann ich anders nicht)

Salzburg August 1973	Sawallisch	LP: EMI SLS 5002 LP: EMI 1C 191 50379-50385 CD: EMI CMS 764 8202
Berlin February 1978- September 1982	Barenboim	LP: DG 2740 279

Brahms Lieder/continued

An die Tauben (Fliegt nur aus, geliebte Tauben)

Salzburg August 1973	Sawallisch	LP: EMI SLS 5002 LP: EMI 1C 191 50379-50385 CD: EMI CMS 764 8202
Berlin February 1978- September 1982	Barenboim	LP: DG 2740 279

An ein Bild (Was schaustdu mich so freundlich an?)

Salzburg August 1973	Sawallisch	LP: EMI SLS 5002 LP: EMI 1C 191 50379-50385 CD: EMI CMS 764 8202
Berlin February 1978- September 1982	Barenboim	LP: DG 2740 279

An ein Veilchen (Birg', o Veilchen)

Salzburg August 1973	Sawallisch	LP: EMI SLS 5002 LP: EMI 1C 191 50379-50385 CD: EMI CMS 764 8202
Berlin February 1978- September 1982	Barenboim	LP: DG 2740 279

An eine Aeolsharfe (Angelehnt an die Efeuwand)

Berlin May 1967	Demus	LP: DG 139 328
Salzburg August 1973	Sawallisch	LP: EMI SLS 5002 LP: EMI 1C 191 50379-50385 CD: EMI CMS 764 8202
Berlin February 1978- September 1982	Barenboim	LP: DG 2740 279
Munich ca. 1986	Höll	LP: Bayer BR 30 006 CD: Bayer BR 100 006

Anklänge (Horch' über stillen Höhen)

Berlin March 1964	Moore	LP: EMI ALP 2083/ASD 630/SLS 5002 LP: EMI 1C 191 50379-50385 CD: EMI CMS 764 8202
Berlin February 1978- September 1982	Barenboim	LP: DG 2740 279

Brahms Lieder/continued

Auf dem Kirchhofe (Der Tag ging regenschwer und sturmbewegt)

Berlin February 1958	Demus	LP: DG LPM 18 504/SLPM 138 011 CD: DG 415 1892
Salzburg August 1958	Moore	LP: Orfeo S140 855R CD: Orfeo C140 201B/C339 930T
Salzburg August 1973	Sawallisch	LP: EMI SLS 5002 LP: EMI 1C 191 50379-50385 CD: EMI CMS 764 8202
Berlin February 1978- September 1982	Barenboim	LP: DG 2740 279
Munich ca. 1986	Höll	LP: Bayer BR 30 006 CD: Bayer BR 100 006

Auf dem Schiffe (Ein Vögelein fliegt über den Rhein)

Salzburg August 1973	Sawallisch	LP: EMI SLS 5002 LP: EMI 1C 191 50379-50385 CD: EMI CMS 764 8202
Berlin February 1978- September 1982	Barenboim	LP: DG 2740 279

Auf dem See (An dies Schifflein schmiege)

Berlin February 1958	Demus	LP: DG LPM 18 504/SLPM 138 011
Salzburg August 1958	Moore	LP: Orfeo S140 855R CD: Orfeo C140 201B/C339 930T
Salzburg August 1964	Moore	CD: EMI CMS 763 1672
Salzburg August 1973	Sawallisch	LP: EMI SLS 5002 LP: EMI 1C 191 50379-50385 CD: EMI CMS 764 8202
Berlin February 1978- September 1982	Barenboim	LP: DG 2740 279
Munich ca. 1986	Höll	LP: Bayer BR 30 006 CD: Bayer BR 100 006

Brahms Lieder/continued

Auf dem See (Blauer Himmel, blaue Wogen)

| Salzburg
August 1973 | Sawallisch | LP: EMI SLS 5002
LP: EMI 1C 191 50379-50385
CD: EMI CMS 764 8202 |
| Berlin
February 1978-
September 1982 | Barenboim | LP: DG 2740 279 |

Bei dir sind meine Gedanken

Salzburg March 1972	Barenboim	LP: EMI SLS 5002 LP: EMI 1C 191 50379-50385 CD: EMI CMS 764 8202
Berlin February 1978- September 1982	Barenboim	LP: DG 2740 279
Munich ca. 1986	Höll	LP: Bayer BR 30 006 CD: Bayer BR 100 006

Beim Abschied (Ich müh' mich ab und kann's nicht verschmerzen)

| Salzburg
August 1973 | Sawallisch | LP: EMI SLS 5002
LP: EMI 1C 191 50379-50385
CD: EMI CMS 764 8202 |
| Berlin
February 1978-
September 1982 | Barenboim | LP: DG 2740 279 |

Bitteres zu sagen denkst du

| Berlin
March 1964 | Moore | LP: EMI ALP 2083/ASD 630/SLS 5002
LP: EMI 1C 191 50379-50385
CD: EMI CMS 764 8202 |
| Berlin
February 1978-
September 1982 | Barenboim | LP: DG 2740 279 |

Blinde Kuh (Im Finstern geh' ich suchen)

| Salzburg
August 1973 | Sawallisch | LP: EMI SLS 5002
LP: EMI 1C 191 50379-50385
CD: EMI CMS 764 8202 |
| Berlin
February 1978-
September 1982 | Barenboim | LP: DG 2740 279 |

Brahms Lieder/continued

Botschaft (Wehe, Lüftchen, lind und lieblich)

Berlin March 1957	Engel	LP: HMV ALP 1584 CD: EMI CZS 568 5092
Salzburg August 1958	Moore	LP: Orfeo S140 855R CD: Orfeo C140 201B/C339 930T
Salzburg August 1973	Sawallisch	LP: EMI SLS 5002 LP: EMI 1C 191 50379-50385 CD: EMI CMS 764 8202
Berlin February 1978- September 1982	Barenboim	LP: DG 2740 279

Da unten im Tale/Deutsche Volkslieder

Berlin August- September 1965	Schwarzkopf Moore	LP: EMI AN 163-164/SAN 163-164 LP: EMI 1C 193 00054-00055 CD: EMI CDS 749 5252

Another setting of Da unten im Tale recorded by Fischer-Dieskau under the song title Trennung

Dämm'rung senkte sich von oben

Salzburg August 1973	Sawallisch	LP: EMI SLS 5002 LP: EMI 1C 191 50379-50385 CD: EMI CMS 764 8202
Berlin February 1978- September 1982	Barenboim	LP: DG 2740 279

Dein blaues Auge hält so still

Berlin March 1957	Engel	LP: HMV ALP 1584 CD: EMI CZS 568 5092
Salzburg August 1973	Sawallisch	LP: EMI SLS 5002 LP: EMI 1C 191 50379-50385 CD: EMI CMS 764 8202

Denn es gehet dem Menschen wie dem Vieh/4 ernste Gesänge
See 4 ernste Gesänge

Brahms Lieder/continued

Des Abends kann ich nicht schlafen geh'n/Deutsche Volkslieder

Berlin	Schwarzkopf	LP: EMI AN 163-164/SAN 163-164
August-	Moore	LP: EMI 1C 193 00054-00055
September 1965		CD: EMI CDS 749 5252

Du mein einzig Licht/Deutsche Volkslieder

Berlin	Moore	LP: EMI AN 163-164/SAN 163-164
August-		LP: EMI 1C 193 00054-00055
September 1965		LP: EMI CDS 749 5252

Du sprichst, dass ich mich täuschte

Berlin	Klust	LP: HMV ALP 1270
May 1955		LP: Electrola E 90106
		CD: EMI CZS 568 5092

Berlin	Moore	LP: EMI ALP 2083/ASD 630/SLS 5002
March 1964		LP: EMI 1C 191 50379-50385
		CD: EMI CMS 764 8202

Berlin	Barenboim	LP: DG 2740 279
February 1978-		
September 1982		

Eine gute, gute Nacht

Berlin	Engel	LP: HMV ALP 1584
March 1957		CD: EMI CZS 568 5092

Salzburg	Sawallisch	LP: EMI SLS 5002
August 1973		LP: EMI 1C 191 50379-50385
		CD: EMI CMS 764 8202

Berlin	Barenboim	LP: DG 2740 279
February 1978-		
September 1982		

Entführung (O Lady Judith, spröder Schatz)

Salzburg	Sawallisch	LP: EMI SLS 5002
August 1973		LP: EMI 1C 191 50379-50385
		CD: EMI CMS 764 8202

Berlin	Barenboim	LP: DG 2740 279
February 1978-		
September 1982		

Brahms Lieder/continued

Erinnerung (Ihr wunderschönen Augenblicke)

Salzburg   Sawallisch   LP: EMI SLS 5002
August 1973   LP: EMI 1C 191 50379-50385
                                       CD: EMI CMS 764 8202

Berlin   Barenboim   LP: DG 2740 279
February 1978-
September 1982

Erlaube mir, fein's Mädchen/Deutsche Volkslieder

Berlin   Moore   LP: EMI AN 163-164/SAN 163-164
August-   LP: EMI 1C 193 00054-00055
September 1965   LP: EMI 1C 047 01247/EX 29 04293
                                       CD: EMI CDS 749 5252

Es hing ein Reif im Lindenbaum

Salzburg   Sawallisch   LP: EMI SLS 5002
August 1973   LP: EMI 1C 191 50379-50385
                                       CD: EMI CMS 764 8202

Berlin   Barenboim   LP: DG 2740 279
February 1978-
September 1982

Es liebt sich so lieblich

Vienna   Demus   45: DG EPL 30 313
February 1957   LP: DG LPM 18 370

Salzburg   Barenboim   LP: EMI SLS 5002
March 1972   LP: EMI 1C 191 50379-50385
                                       CD: EMI CMS 764 8202

Berlin   Barenboim   LP: DG 2740 279
February 1978-
September 1982

Munich   Höll   LP: Bayer BR 30 006
ca. 1986   CD: Bayer BR 100 006

Es reit' ein Herr und auch sein Knecht/Deutsche Volkslieder

Berlin   Moore   LP: EMI AN 163-164/SAN 163-164
August-   LP: EMI 1C 191 00054-00055
September 1965   CD: EMI CMS 764 8202

Brahms Lieder/continued

Es ritt ein Ritter/Deutsche Volkslieder

Berlin	Schwarzkopf	LP: EMI AN 163-164/SAN 163-164
August-	Moore	LP: EMI 1C 193 00054-00055
September 1965		CD: EMI CDS 749 5252

Es schauen die Blumen

Vienna	Demus	45: DG EPL 30 313
February 1957		LP: DG LPM 18 370

Salzburg	Sawallisch	LP: EMI SLS 5002
August 1973		LP: EMI 1C 191 50379-50385
		CD: EMI CMS 764 8202

Berlin	Barenboim	LP: DG 2740 279
February 1978-		
September 1982		

Munich	Höll	LP: Bayer BR 30 006
ca. 1986		CD: Bayer BR 100 006

Es träumte mir, ich sei dir teuer

Berlin	Engel	LP: HMV ALP 1584
March 1957		LP: EMI EX 29 04293
		CD: EMI CZS 568 5092

Salzburg	Moore	LP: Orfeo S140 855R
August 1958		CD: Orfeo C140 201B/C339 930T

Salzburg	Sawallisch	LP: EMI SLS 5002
August 1973		LP: EMI 1C 191 50379-50385
		CD: EMI CMS 764 8202

Berlin	Barenboim	LP: DG 2740 279
February 1978-		
September 1982		

Es war eine schöne Jüdin/Deutsche Volkslieder

Berlin	Schwarzkopf	LP: EMI AN 163-164/SAN 163-164
August-	Moore	LP: EMI 1C 193 00054-00055
September 1965		CD: EMI CDS 749 5252

Feinsliebchen, du sollst mir nicht barfuss geh'n/Deutsche Volkslieder

Berlin	Schwarzkopf	LP: EMI AN 163-164/SAN 163-164
August-	Moore	LP: EMI 1C 193 00054-00055
September 1965		CD: EMI CDS 749 5252

Feldeinsamkeit (Ich ruhe still im hohen grünen Gras)

Berlin February 1958	Demus	LP: DG LPM 18 504/SLPM 138 011 LP: DG 135 026 CD: DG 415 1892
Salzburg August 1964	Moore	CD: EMI CMS 763 1672
Salzburg March 1972	Barenboim	LP: EMI SLS 5002 LP: EMI 1C 191 50379-50385 CD: EMI CMS 764 8202
Berlin February 1978- September 1982	Barenboim	LP: DG 2740 279
Munich ca. 1986	Höll	LP: Bayer BR 30 006 CD: Bayer BR 100 006

Der Frühling (Es lockt und säuselt um den Baum)

Berlin May 1967	Demus	LP: DG 139 328
Salzburg August 1973	Sawallisch	LP: EMI SLS 5002 LP: EMI 1C 191 50379-50385 CD: EMI CMS 764 8202
Berlin February 1978- September 1982	Barenboim	LP: DG 2740 279

Frühlingslied (Mit geheimnisvollen Düften)

Berlin February 1958	Demus	LP: DG LPM 18 504/SLPM 138 011 LP: DG 135 026
Salzburg March 1972	Barenboim	LP: EMI SLS 5002 LP: EMI 1C 191 50379-50385 CD: EMI CMS 764 8202
Berlin February 1978- September 1982	Barenboim	LP: DG 2740 279

Brahms Lieder/continued

Frühlingstrost (Es weht um mich Narzissenduft)

| Salzburg
August 1973 | Sawallisch | LP: EMI SLS 5002
LP: EMI 1C 191 50379-50385
CD: EMI CMS 764 8202 |
| Berlin
February 1978-
September 1982 | Barenboim | LP: DG 2740 279 |

Der Gang zum Liebchen (Es glänzt der Mond nieder)

Berlin March 1957	Engel	LP: HMV ALP 1584 CD: EMI CZS 568 5092
Salzburg August 1958	Moore	LP: Orfeo S140 855R CD: Orfeo C140 201B/C339 930T
Salzburg August 1973	Sawallisch	LP: EMI SLS 5002 LP: EMI 1C 191 50379-50385 CD: EMI CMS 764 8202
Berlin February 1978- September 1982	Barenboim	LP: DG 2740 279
Munich ca. 1986	Höll	LP: Bayer BR 30 006 CD: Bayer BR 100 006

Gang zur Liebsten (Des Abends kann ich nicht schlafen geh'n)

Berlin May 1967	Demus	LP: DG 139 328
Salzburg August 1973	Sawallisch	LP: EMI SLS 5002 LP: EMI 1C 191 50379-50385 CD: EMI CMS 764 8202
Berlin February 1978- September 1982	Barenboim	LP: DG 2740 279

Gar lieblich hat sich gesellet/Deutsche Volkslieder

| Berlin
August-
September 1965 | Moore | LP: EMI AN 163-164/SAN 163-164
LP: EMI 1C 193 00054-00055
LP: EMI 1C 047 01247
CD: EMI CDS 749 5252 |

Brahms Lieder/continued

Geheimnis (O Frühlings-Abenddämmerung)

Berlin March 1957	Engel	LP: HMV ALP 1584 CD: EMI CZS 568 5092
Salzburg August 1958	Moore	LP: Orfeo S140 855R CD: Orfeo C140 201B/C339 930T
Salzburg March 1972	Barenboim	LP: EMI SLS 5002 LP: EMI 1C 191 50379-50385 CD: EMI CMS 764 8202
Berlin February 1978- September 1982	Barenboim	LP: DG 2740 279
Munich ca. 1986	Höll	LP: Bayer BR 30 006 CD: Bayer BR 100 006

Guten Abend, mein tausiger Schatz/Deutsche Volkslieder

Berlin August- September 1965	Schwarzkopf Moore	LP: EMI AN 163-164/SAN 163-164 LP: EMI 1C 191 50379-50385 CD: EMI CDS 749 5252

Heimkehr (O brich' nicht, Steg)

Berlin March 1957	Engel	LP: HMV ALP 1584 CD: EMI CZS 568 5092
Berlin May 1967	Demus	LP: DG 139 328
Salzburg August 1973	Sawallisch	LP: EMI SLS 5002 LP: EMI 1C 191 50379-50385 CD: EMI CMS 764 8202
Berlin February 1978- September 1982	Barenboim	LP: DG 2740 279

Heimweh I (Wie traulich war das Fleckchen)

Salzburg August 1973	Sawallisch	LP: EMI SLS 5002 LP: EMI 1C 191 50379-50385 CD: EMI CMS 764 8202
Berlin February 1978- September 1982	Barenboim	LP: DG 2740 279

Brahms Lieder/continued

Heimweh II (O wüsst' ich doch den Weg zurück)

Berlin   Demus   LP: DG LPM 18 504/SLPM 138 011
February 1958   LP: DG 135 026
                               CD: DG 415 1892

Salzburg   Sawallisch   LP: EMI SLS 5002
August 1973   LP: EMI 1C 191 50379-50385
                               LP: EMI CMS 764 8202

Berlin   Barenboim   LP: DG 2740 279
February 1978-
September 1982

Heimweh III (Ich sah als Knabe Blumen blühn)

Salzburg   Sawallisch   LP: EMI SLS 5002
August 1973   LP: EMI 1C 191 50379-50385
                               CD: EMI CMS 764 8202

Berlin   Barenboim   LP: DG 2740 279
February 1978-
September 1982

Herbstgefühl (Wie wenn im frost'gen Windhauch tödlich)

Berlin   Demus   LP: DG LPM 18 504/SLPM 138 011
February 1958

Salzburg   Moore   LP: Orfeo S140 855R
August 1958   CD: Orfeo C140 201B/C339 930T

Salzburg   Sawallisch   LP: EMI SLS 5002
August 1973   LP: EMI 1C 191 50379-50385
                               CD: EMI CMS 764 8202

Berlin   Barenboim   LP: DG 2740 279
February 1978-
September 1982

Ich schell' mein Horn ins Jammertal

Salzburg   Sawallisch   LP: EMI SLS 5002
August 1973   LP: EMI 1C 191 50379-50385
                               CD: EMI CMS 764 8202

Berlin   Barenboim   LP: DG 2740 279
February 1978-
September 1982

Ich schleich' umher betrübt und stumm

Berlin May 1955	Klust	LP: HMV ALP 1270 LP: Electrola E 90106 CD: EMI CZS 568 5092
Berlin March 1964	Moore	LP: EMI ALP 2083/ASD 630/SLS 5002 LP: EMI 1C 191 50379-50385 CD: EMI CMS 764 8202
Berlin February 1978- September 1982	Barenboim	LP: DG 2740 279

Ich wandte mich und sahe an alle/4 ernste Gesänge
See 4 ernste Gesänge

Ich weiss mir'n Maidlein/Deutsche Volkslieder

Berlin August- September 1965	Moore	LP: EMI AN 163-164/SAN 163-164 LP: EMI 1C 193 00054-00055 LP: EMI EX 29 04293 CD: EMI CDS 749 5252

Im Garten am Seegestade

Salzburg March 1972	Barenboim	LP: EMI SLS 5002 LP: EMI 1C 191 50379-50385 CD: EMI CMS 764 8202
Berlin February 1978- September 1982	Barenboim	LP: DG 2740 279

In der Ferne (Will ruhen unter den Bäumen hier)

Berlin March 1964	Moore	LP: EMI ALP 2083/ASD 630/SLS 5002 LP: EMI 1C 191 50379-50385 CD: EMI CMS 764 8202
Berlin February 1978- September 1982	Barenboim	LP: DG 2740 279

In der Fremde (Aus der Heimat hinter den Blitzen rot)

Berlin March 1964	Moore	LP: EMI ALP 2083/ASD 630/SLS 5002 LP: EMI 1C 191 50379-50385 CD: EMI CMS 764 8202
Berlin February 1978- September 1982	Barenboim	LP: DG 2740 279

Brahms Lieder/continued

In der Gasse (Ich blicke hinab in die Gasse)

Salzburg August 1973	Sawallisch	LP: EMI SLS 5002 LP: EMI 1C 191 50379-50385 CD: EMI CMS 764 8202
Berlin February 1978- September 1982	Barenboim	LP: DG 2740 279

In meiner Nächte Sehnen

Salzburg August 1973	Sawallisch	LP: EMI SLS 5002 LP: EMI 1C 191 50379-50385 CD: EMI CMS 764 8202
Berlin February 1978- September 1982	Barenboim	LP: DG 2740 279

In Waldeinsamkeit (Ich sass zu deinen Füssen)

Berlin March 1957	Engel	LP: HMV ALP 1584 CD: EMI CZS 568 5092
Salzburg March 1972	Barenboim	LP: EMI SLS 5002 LP: EMI 1C 191 50379-50385 CD: EMI CMS 764 8202
Berlin February 1978- September 1982	Barenboim	LP: DG 2740 279

Juchhe! (Wie ist doch die Erde so schön!)

Berlin May 1967	Demus	LP: DG 139 328
Salzburg August 1973	Sawallisch	LP: EMI SLS 5002 LP: EMI 1C 191 50379-50385 CD: EMI CMS 764 8202
Berlin February 1978- September 1982	Barenboim	LP: DG 2740 279

Junge Lieder I (Meine Liebe ist grün wie der Fliederbusch)

Berlin March 1957	Engel	LP: HMV ALP 1584 /EX 29 04293 LP: Electrola E 90015 CD: EMI CZS 568 5092
Salzburg August 1973	Sawallisch	LP: EMI SLS 5002 LP: EMI 1C 191 50379-50385 CD: EMI CMS 764 8202
Berlin February 1978- September 1982	Barenboim	LP: DG 2740 279

Brahms Lieder/continued

Junge Lieder III (Wenn um den Hollunder der Abendwind kost)

| Salzburg
August 1973 | Sawallisch | LP: EMI SLS 5002
LP: EMI 1C 191 50379-50385
CD: EMI CMS 764 8202 |
| Berlin
February 1978-
September 1982 | Barenboim | LP: DG 2740 279 |

Jungfräulein, soll ich mit euch geh'n/Deutsche Volkslieder

| Berlin
August-
September 1965 | Schwarzkopf
Moore | LP: EMI AN 163-164/SAN 163-164
LP: EMI 1C 193 00054-00055
CD: EMI CDS 749 5252 |

Kein Haus, keine Heimat

Berlin February 1958	Demus	LP: DG LPM 18 504/SLPM 138 011
Salzburg March 1972	Barenboim	LP: EMI SLS 5002 LP: EMI 1C 191 50379-50385 CD: EMI CMS 764 8202
Berlin February 1978- September 1982	Barenboim	LP: DG 2740 279

Keinen hat es noch gereut/Die schöne Magelone
See Die schöne Magelone

Die Klage (Fein's Liebchen, trau' du nicht)

| Salzburg
August 1973 | Sawallisch | LP: EMI SLS 5002
LP: EMI 1C 191 50379-50385
CD: EMI CMS 764 8202 |

Brahms Lieder/continued

Komm' bald (Warum denn warten von Tag zu Tag?)

Berlin March 1957	Engel	LP: HMV ALP 1584 CD: EMI CZS 568 5092
Salzburg August 1964	Moore	CD: EMI CMS 763 1672
Salzburg August 1973	Sawallisch	LP: EMI SLS 5002 LP: EMI 1C 191 50379-50385 CD: EMI CMS 764 8202
Berlin February 1978- September 1982	Barenboim	LP: DG 2740 279

Die Kränze (Hier ob dem Eingang seid befestigt)

Salzburg August 1973	Sawallisch	LP: EMI SLS 5002 LP: EMI 1C 191 50379-50385 CD: EMI CMS 764 8202
Berlin February 1978- September 1982	Barenboim	LP: DG 2740 279

Der Kuss (Unter Bluten des Mai's spielt' ich mit ihrer Hand)

Berlin March 1964	Moore	LP: EMI ALP 2083/ASD 630/SLS 5002 LP: EMI 1C 191 50379-50385 CD: EMI CMS 764 8202
Berlin February 1978- September 1982	Barenboim	LP: DG 2740 279

Lerchengesang (Aetherische ferne Stimmen)

Salzburg March 1972	Barenboim	LP: EMI SLS 5002 LP: EMI 1C 191 50379-50385 CD: EMI CMS 764 8202
Berlin February 1978- September 1982	Barenboim	LP: DG 2740 279

Liebe kam aus fernen Landen/Die schöne Magelone
See Die schöne Magelone

Brahms Lieder/continued

Liebe und Frühling (Wie sich Rebenranken schwingen)

Berlin March 1964	Moore	LP: EMI ALP 2083/ASD 630/SLS 5002 LP: EMI 1C 191 50379-50385 CD: EMI CMS 764 8202
Berlin February 1978- September 1982	Barenboim	LP: DG 2740 279

Liebe und Frühling (Ich muss hinaus, ich muss zu dir)

Berlin March 1964	Moore	LP: EMI ALP 2083/ASD 630/SLS 5002 LP: EMI 1C 191 50379-50385 CD: EMI CMS 764 8202
Berlin February 1978- September 1982	Barenboim	LP: DG 2740 279

Liebesglut (Die Flamme hier, die wilde, zu verhehlen)

Salzburg August 1973	Sawallisch	LP: EMI SLS 5002 LP: EMI 1C 191 50379-50385 CD: EMI CMS 764 8202
Berlin February 1978- September 1982	Barenboim	LP: DG 2740 279

Liebeslieder-Walzer

Berlin September 1981	Mathis, Fassbaender, Schreier Engel, Sawallisch	LP: DG 2740 280/2532 094 CD: DG 423 1332

Lied (Lindes Rauschen in den Wipfeln)

Berlin March 1964	Moore	LP: EMI ALP 2083/ASD 630/SLS 5002 LP: EMI 1C 191 50379-50385 CD: EMI CMS 764 8202
Berlin February 1978- September 1982	Barenboim	LP: DG 2740 279

Brahms Lieder/continued

Lied (Weit über das Feld durch die Lüfte hoch)

| Salzburg
August 1973 | Sawallisch | LP: EMI SLS 5002
LP: EMI 1C 191 50379-50385
CD: EMI CMS 764 8202 |

| Berlin
February 1978-
September 1982 | Barenboim | LP: DG 2740 279 |

Lied aus dem Gedicht „Ivan"

| Berlin
February 1978-
September 1982 | Barenboim | LP: DG 2740 279 |

Lied vom Herrn von Falkenstein

| Berlin
February 1978-
September 1982 | Barenboim | LP: DG 2740 279 |

Magyarisch (Sah dem edlen Bildnis allzu süssen Wunderschein)

| Salzburg
August 1973 | Sawallisch | LP: EMI SLS 5002
LP: EMI 1C 191 50379-50385
CD: EMI CMS 764 8202 |

| Berlin
February 1978-
September 1982 | Barenboim | LP: DG 2740 279 |

Maienkätzchen, erster Gruss

| Salzburg
August 1973 | Sawallisch | LP: EMI SLS 5002
LP: EMI 1C 191 50379-50385
CD: EMI CMS 764 8202 |

| Berlin
February 1978-
September 1982 | Barenboim | LP: DG 2740 279 |

| Munich
ca. 1986 | Höll | LP: Bayer BR 30.006
CD: Bayer BR 100.006 |

Die Mainacht (Wann der silberne Mond durch die Gesträuche blinkt)

| Berlin
March 1957 | Engel | LP: HMV ALP 1584
LP: Electrola E 90015
CD: EMI CZS 568 5092 |

| Salzburg
August 1973 | Sawallisch | LP: EMI SLS 5002
LP: EMI 1C 191 50379-50385
CD: EMI CMS 764 8202 |

| Berlin
February 1978-
September 1982 | Barenboim | LP: DG 2740 279 |

Brahms Lieder/continued

Meerfahrt (Mein Liebchen, wir sassen beisammen)

Vienna February 1957	Demus	45: DG EPL 30313 LP: DG LPM 18 370
Salzburg August 1958	Moore	LP: Orfeo S140 855R CD: Orfeo C140 201B/C339 930J
Salzburg March 1972	Barenboim	LP: EMI SLS 5002/EX 29 04293 LP: EMI 1C 191 50379-50385 CD: EMI CMS 764 8202
Berlin February 1978- September 1982	Barenboim	LP: DG 2740 279
Munich ca. 1986	Höll	LP: Bayer BR 30.006 CD: Bayer BR 100.006

Mein Herz ist schwer

Berlin February 1958	Demus	LP: DG LPM 18 504/SLPM 138 011
Salzburg March 1972	Barenboim	LP: EMI SLS 5002 LP: EMI 1C 191 50379-50385 CD: EMI CMS 764 8202
Berlin February 1978- September 1982	Barenboim	LP: DG 2740 279

Mein Mädel hat einen Rosenmund/Deutsche Volkslieder

Berlin August- September 1965	Moore	LP: EMI AN 163-164/SAN 163-164 LP: EMI 1C 193 00054-00055 LP: EMI 1C 047 01247 CD: EMI CDS 749 5252

Mein wundes Herz verlangt nach dir

Berlin March 1957	Engel	LP: HMV ALP 1584 LP: Electrola E 90015 CD: EMI CZS 568 5092
Salzburg August 1973	Sawallisch	LP: EMI SLS 5002 LP: EMI 1C 191 50379-50385 CD: EMI CMS 764 8202
Berlin February 1978- September 1982	Barenboim	LP: DG 2740 279

Brahms Lieder/continued

Meine Lieder (Wenn mein Herz beginnt zu klingen)

Salzburg August 1973	Sawallisch	LP: EMI SLS 5002 LP: EMI 1C 191 50379-50385 CD: EMI CMS 764 8202
Berlin February 1978- September 1982	Barenboim	LP: DG 2740 279

Minnelied (Holder klingt der Vogelsang)

Berlin March 1957	Engel	LP: HMV ALP 1584 LP: Electrola E 90015 CD: EMI CZS 568 5092
Salzburg March 1972	Barenboim	LP: EMI SLS 5002 LP: EMI 1C 191 50379-50385 CD: EMI CMS 764 8202
Berlin February 1978- September 1982	Barenboim	LP: DG 2740 279

Mir ist ein schön's braun's Maidelein/Deutsche Volkslieder

Berlin August- September 1965	Moore	LP: EMI AN 163-164/SAN 163-164 LP: EMI 1C 193 00054-00055 CD: EMI CDS 749 5252

Mit 40 Jahren ist der Berg erstiegen

Berlin February 1958	Demus	LP: DG LPM 18 504/SLPM 138 011
Salzburg March 1972	Barenboim	LP: EMI SLS 5002 LP: EMI 1C 191 50379-50385 CD: EMI CMS 764 8202
Berlin February 1978- September 1982	Barenboim	LP: DG 2740 279

Mondenschein (Nacht liegt auf den fremden Wegen)

Vienna February 1957	Demus	45: DG EPL 30 313 LP: DG LPM 18 370
Salzburg August 1958	Moore	LP: Orfeo S140 855R CD: Orfeo C140 201B/C339 930T
Salzburg March 1972	Barenboim	LP: EMI SLS 5002 LP: EMI 1C 191 50379-50385 CD: EMI CMS 764 8202
Berlin February 1978- September 1982	Barenboim	LP: DG 2740 279

Mondnacht (Es war, als hätt' der Himmel)

Berlin May 1967	Demus	LP: DG SLPM 139 328
Salzburg August 1973	Sawallisch	LP: EMI SLS 5002 LP: EMI 1C 191 50379-50385 CD: EMI CMS 764 8202
Berlin February 1978- September 1982	Barenboim	LP: DG 2740 279

Murrays Ermordung (O Hochland und o Südland)

Berlin May 1967	Demus	LP: DG SLPM 139 328
Salzburg August 1973	Sawallisch	LP: EMI SLS 5002 LP: EMI 1C 191 50379-50385 CD: EMI CMS 764 8202
Berlin February 1978- September 1982	Barenboim	LP: DG 2740 279

Muss es eine Trennung geben?/Die schöne Magelone
See Die schöne Magelone

Nachklang (Regentropfen aus den Bäumen)

Berlin February 1958	Demus	LP: DG LPM 18 504/SLPM 138 011 LP: DG 135 020 CD: DG 415 1892
Salzburg August 1973	Sawallisch	LP: EMI SLS 5002 LP: EMI 1C 191 50379-50385 CD: EMI CMS 764 8202
Berlin February 1978- September 1982	Barenboim	LP: DG 2740 279

Nachtigall (O Nachtigall, dein süsser Schall)

Salzburg August 1973	Sawallisch	LP: EMI SLS 5002 LP: EMI 1C 191 50379-50385 CD: EMI CMS 764 8202
Berlin February 1978- September 1982	Barenboim	LP: DG 2740 279

Brahms Lieder/continued

Nachtigallen schwingen lustig

| Berlin
March 1964 | Moore | LP: EMI ALP 2083/ASD 630/ASD 2549
LP: EMI SLS 5002
LP: EMI 1C 191 50379-50385
CD: EMI CMS 764 8202 |
| Berlin
February 1978-
September 1982 | Barenboim | LP: DG 2740 279 |

Nachtwandler (Störe nicht den leisen Schlummer)

| Salzburg
March 1972 | Barenboim | LP: EMI SLS 5002
LP: EMI 1C 191 50379-50385
CD: EMI CMS 764 8202 |
| Berlin
February 1978-
September 1982 | Barenboim | LP: DG 2740 279 |

Nachwirkung (Sie ist gegangen, die Wonnen versanken)

Berlin May 1967	Demus	LP: DG SLPM 139 328
Salzburg August 1973	Sawallisch	LP: EMI SLS 5002 LP: EMI 1C 191 50379-50385 CD: EMI CMS 764 8202
Berlin February 1978- September 1982	Barenboim	LP: DG 2740 279

Neue Liebeslieder-Walzer

| Berlin
September 1981 | Mathis, Fassbander,
Schreier
Engel, Sawallisch | LP: DG 2740 280/2532 094
CD: DG 423 1332 |

Nicht mehr zu dir zu gehen

Berlin May 1955	Klust	LP: HMV ALP 1270 LP: Electrola E 90106 CD: EMI CZS 568 5092
Berlin March 1964	Moore	LP: EMI ALP 2083/ASD 630/SLS 5002 LP: EMI 1C 191 50379-50385 CD: EMI CMS 764 8202
Berlin February 1978- September 1982	Barenboim	LP: DG 2740 279
Munich ca. 1986	Höll	LP: Bayer BR 30.006 CD: Bayer BR 100.006

Brahms Lieder/continued

Nur ein Gesicht auf Erden lebt/Deutsche Volkslieder

Berlin	Moore	LP: EMI AN 163-164/SAN 163-164
August-		LP: EMI 1C 193 00054-00055
September 1965		CD: EMI CDS 749 5252

O komme, holde Sommernacht

Salzburg	Sawallisch	LP: EMI SLS 5002
August 1973		LP: EMI 1C 191 50379-50385
		CD: EMI CMS 764 8202

Berlin	Barenboim	LP: DG 2740 279
February 1978-		
September 1982		

O kühler Wald, wo rauschest du?

Salzburg	Barenboim	LP: EMI SLS 5002
March 1972		LP: EMI 1C 191 50379-50385
		CD: EMI CMS 764 8202

Berlin	Barenboim	LP: DG 2740 279
February 1978-		
September 1982		

O liebliche Wangen, ihr macht mir Verlangen

Salzburg	Sawallisch	LP: EMI SLS 5002
August 1973		LP: EMI 1C 191 50379-50385
		CD: EMI CMS 764 8202

Berlin	Barenboim	LP: DG 2740 279
February 1978-		
September 1982		

O Tod, wie bitter bist du/4 ernste Gesänge
See 4 ernste Gesänge

Parole (Sie stand wohl am Fensterbogen)

Berlin	Moore	LP: EMI ALP 2083/ASD 630/SLS 5002
March 1964		LP: EMI 1C 191 50379-50385
		CD: EMI CMS 764 8202

Berlin	Barenboim	LP: DG 2740 279
February 1978-		
September 1982		

Brahms Lieder/continued

Regenlied (Walle Regen, walle nieder)

Berlin February 1958	Demus	LP: DG LPM 18 504/SLPM 138 011

Salzburg August 1973	Sawallisch	LP: EMI SLS 5002 LP: EMI 1C 191 50379-50385 CD: EMI CMS 764 8202

Berlin February 1978- September 1982	Barenboim	LP: DG 2740 279

Der Reiter/Deutsche Volkslieder

Berlin August- September 1965	Schwarzkopf Moore	LP: EMI AN 163-164/SAN 163-164 LP: EMI 1C 193 00054-00055 CD: EMI CDS 749 5252

Ruhe, Süssliebchen/Die schöne Magelone
See Die schöne Magelone

Sagt mir, o schöne Schäf'rin mein/Deutsche Volkslieder

Berlin August- September 1965	Schwarzkopf Moore	LP: EMI AN 163-164/SAN 163-164 LP: EMI 1C 193 00054-00055 CD: EMI CDS 749 5252

Salamander (Es sass ein Salamander)

Berlin March 1957	Engel	LP: HMV ALP 1584 LP: Electrola E 90015 CD: EMI CZS 568 5092

Salzburg August 1958	Moore	LP: Orfeo S140 855R CD: Orfeo C140 201B/C339 930T

Salzburg August 1973	Sawallisch	LP: EMI SLS 5002 LP: EMI 1C 191 50379-50385 CD: EMI CMS 764 8202

Berlin February 1978- September 1982	Barenboim	LP: DG 2740 279

Die Schale der Vergessenheit (Eine Schale des Stroms, welcher Vergessenheit)

Salzburg August 1973	Sawallisch	LP: EMI SLS 5002 LP: EMI 1C 191 50379-50385 CD: EMI CDS 749 5252

Berlin February 1978- September 1982	Barenboim	LP: DG 2740 279

Brahms Lieder/continued

Scheiden und Meiden (So soll ich dich nur meiden)

| Berlin
May 1967 | Demus | LP: DG SLPM 139 328 |

| Salzburg
August 1973 | Sawallisch | LP: EMI SLS 5002
LP: EMI 1C 191 50379-50385
CD: EMI CMS 764 8202 |

| Berlin
February 1978-
September 1982 | Barenboim | LP: DG 2740 279 |

Schön war, das ich dir weihte

| Salzburg
March 1972 | Barenboim | LP: EMI SLS 5002
LP: EMI 1C 191 50379-50385
CD: EMI CMS 764 8202 |

| Berlin
February 1978-
September 1982 | Barenboim | LP: DG 2740 279 |

Schöner Augen schöne Strahlen/Deutsche Volkslieder

| Berlin
August-
September 1965 | Schwarzkopf
Moore | LP: EMI AN 163-164/SAN 163-164
LP: EMI 1C 193 00054-00055
CD: EMI CDS 749 5252 |

Schönster Schatz, mein Engel/Deutsche Volkslieder

| Berlin
August-
September 1965 | Moore | LP: EMI AN 163-164/SAN 163-164
LP: EMI 1C 193 00054-00055
CD: EMI CDS 749 5252 |

Die Schnur, die Perl' an Perle

| Salzburg
August 1973 | Sawallisch | LP: EMI SLS 5002
LP: EMI 1C 191 50379-50385
CD: EMI CMS 764 8202 |

| Berlin
February 1978-
September 1982 | Barenboim | LP: DG 2740 279 |

Schwermut (Mir ist so weh ums Herz)

Salzburg August 1973	Sawallisch	LP: EMI SLS 5002 LP: EMI 1C 191 50379-50385 CD: EMI CMS 764 8202
Berlin February 1978- September 1982	Barenboim	LP: DG 2740 279

Schwesterlein/Deutsche Volkslieder

Berlin August- September 1965	Schwarzkopf Moore	LP: EMI AN 163-164/SAN 163-164 LP: EMI 1C 193 50379-50385 CD: EMI CDS 749 5252

Sehnsucht (Hinter jenen dichten Wäldern)

Salzburg August 1973	Sawallisch	LP: EMI SLS 5002 LP: EMI 1C 191 50379-50385 CD: EMI CMS 764 8202
Berlin February 1978- September 1982	Barenboim	LP: DG 2740 279

Sehnsucht(Mein Schatz ist nicht da)

Berlin May 1967	Demus	LP: DG SLPM 139 328
Salzburg August 1973	Sawallisch	LP: EMI SLS 5002 LP: EMI 1C 191 50379-50385 CD: EMI CMS 764 8202
Berlin February 1978- September 1982	Barenboim	LP: DG 2740 279

Serenade (Leise, um dich nicht zu wecken)

Berlin March 1957	Engel	LP: HMV ALP 1584 LP: Electrola E 90015 CD: EMI CZS 568 5092
Salzburg August 1973	Sawallisch	LP: EMI SLS 5002 LP: EMI 1C 191 50379-50385 CD: EMI CMS 764 8202
Berlin February 1978- September 1982	Barenboim	LP: DG 2740 279

Brahms Lieder/continued

Serenade (Liebliches Kind)

Salzburg March 1972	Barenboim	LP: EMI SLS 5002 LP: EMI 1C 191 50379-50385 CD: EMI CMS 764 8202
Berlin February 1978- September 1982	Barenboim	LP: DG 2740 279
Munich ca. 1986	Höll	LP: Bayer BR 30.006 CD: Bayer BR 100.006

Sind es Schmerzen, sind es Freuden/Die schöne Magelone
See Die schöne Magelone

So stehn wir, ich und meine Weide

Berlin March 1964	Moore	LP: EMI ALP 2083/ASD 630/SLS 5002 LP: EMI 1C 191 50379-50385 CD: EMI CMS 764 8202
Berlin February 1978- September 1982	Barenboim	LP: DG 2740 279

So will ich frisch und fröhlich sein/Deutsche Volkslieder

Berlin August- September 1965	Moore	LP: EMI AN 163-164/SAN 163-164 LP: EMI 1C 193 00054-00055 CD: EMI CDS 749 5252

So willst du des Armen dich gnädig erbarmen/Die schöne Magelone
See Die schöne Magelone

So wünsch' ich ihr ein' gute Nacht/Deutsche Volkslieder

Berlin August- September 1965	Moore	LP: EMI AN 163-164/SAN 163-164 LP: EMI 1C 193 00054-00055 CD: EMI CDS 749 5252

Soll sich der Mond nicht heller scheinen/Deutsche Volkslieder

Berlin August- September 1965	Schwarzkopf Moore	LP: EMI AN 163-164/SAN 163-164 LP: EMI 1C 193 00054-00055 CD: EMI CDS 749 5252

Brahms Lieder /continued

Sommerabend (Dämmernd liegt der Sommerabend)

Vienna February 1957	Demus	45: DG EPL 30 313 LP: DG LPM 18 370
Salzburg March 1972	Barenboim	LP: EMI SLS 5002 LP: EMI 1C 191 50379-50385 CD: EMI CMS 764 8202
Berlin February 1978- September 1982	Barenboim	LP: DG 2740 279

Sommerfäden hin und wieder

Salzburg March 1972	Barenboim	LP: EMI SLS 5002 LP: EMI 1C 191 50379-50385 CD: EMI CMS 764 8202
Berlin February 1978- September 1982	Barenboim	LP: DG 2740 279

Ein Sonett (Ach könnt' ich, könnte vergessen sie)

Berlin March 1957	Engel	LP: HMV ALP 1584 LP: Electrola E 90015 CD: EMI CZS 568 5092
Berlin May 1967	Demus	LP: DG SLPM 139 328
Salzburg August 1973	Sawallisch	LP: EMI SLS 5002 LP: EMI 1C 191 50379-50385 CD: EMI CMS 764 8202
Berlin February 1978- September 1982	Barenboim	LP: DG 2740 279

Sonntag (So hab' ich doch die ganze Woche)

Berlin March 1957	Engel	LP: HMV ALP 1584 LP: Electrola E 90015 CD: EMI CZS 568 5092
Salzburg August 1973	Sawallisch	LP: EMI SLS 5002 LP: EMI 1C 191 50379-50385 CD: EMI CMS 764 8202
Berlin February 1978- September 1982	Barenboim	LP: DG 2740 279

Die Spröde (Ich sah eine Tigrin im dunklen Haine)

Salzburg August 1973	Sawallisch	LP: EMI SLS 5002 LP: EMI 1C 191 50379-50385 CD: EMI CMS 764 8202
Berlin February 1978- September 1982	Barenboim	LP: DG 2740 279

Ständchen (Gut' Nacht, gut' Nacht, mein liebster Schatz)

Berlin May 1967	Demus	LP: DG SLPM 139 328
Salzburg August 1973	Sawallisch	LP: EMI SLS 5002 LP: EMI 1C 191 50379-50385 CD: EMI CMS 764 8202
Berlin February 1978- September 1982	Barenboim	LP: DG 2740 279

Ständchen (Der Mond steht über dem Berge)

Berlin March 1957	Engel	LP: HMV ALP 1584 LP: Electrola E 90015 CD: EMI CZS 568 5092
Salzburg August 1958	Moore	LP: Orfeo S140 855R CD: Orfeo C140 201B/C339 930 T
Salzburg August 1973	Sawallisch	LP: EMI SLS 5002 LP: EMI 1C 191 50379-50385 CD: EMI CMS 764 8202
Berlin February 1978- September 1982	Barenboim	LP: DG 2740 279

Steig' auf, geliebter Schatten

Berlin February 1958	Demus	LP: DG LPM 18 504/SLPM 138 011
Salzburg March 1972	Barenboim	LP: EMI SLS 5002 LP: EMI 1C 191 50379-50385 CD: EMI CMS 764 8202
Berlin February 1978- September 1982	Barenboim	LP: DG 2740 279

Brahms Lieder/continued

Strahlt zuweilen auch ein mildes Licht

Salzburg August 1973	Sawallisch	LP: EMI SLS 5002 LP: EMI 1C 191 50379-50385 CD: EMI CMS 764 8202
Berlin February 1978- September 1982	Barenboim	LP: DG 2740 279

Der Strom, der neben mir verrauschte

Berlin May 1955	Klust	LP: HMV ALP 1270 LP: Electrola E 90106 CD: EMI CZS 568 5092
Salzburg August 1958	Moore	LP: Orfeo S140 855R CD: Orfeo C140 201B/C339 930 T
Berlin March 1964	Moore	LP: EMI ALP 2083/ASD 630/SLS 5002 LP: EMI 1C 191 50379-50385 CD: EMI CMS 764 8202
Berlin February 1978- September 1982	Barenboim	LP: DG 2740 279
Munich ca. 1986	Höll	LP: Bayer BR 30.006 CD: Bayer BR 100.006

Sulima/Die schöne Magelone (Geliebter, wo zaudert dein irrender Fuss)
See Die schöne Magelone

Tambourliedchen (Den Wirbel schlag' ich gar so stark)

Salzburg March 1972	Barenboim	LP: EMI SLS 5002 LP: EMI 1C 191 50379-50385 CD: EMI CMS 764 8202
Berlin February 1978- September 1982	Barenboim	LP: DG 2740 279
Munich ca. 1986	Höll	LP: Bayer BR 30.006 CD: Bayer BR 100.006

Brahms Lieder/continued

Therese (Du milchjunger Knabe, wie schaust du mich an?)

Salzburg March 1972	Barenboim	LP: EMI SLS 5002/EX 29 04293 LP: EMI 1C 191 50379-50385 CD: EMI CMS 764 8202
Munich ca. 1986	Höll	LP: Bayer BR 30.006 LP: Bayer BR 100.006

Der Tod, das ist die kühle Nacht

Vienna February 1957	Demus	45: DG EPL 30 313 LP: DG LPM 18 370
Salzburg March 1972	Barenboim	LP: EMI SLS 5002 LP: EMI 1C 191 50379-50385 CD: EMI CMS 764 8202
Berlin February 1978- September 1982	Barenboim	LP: DG 2740 279

Todessehnen (Ach, wer nimmt von meiner Seele)

Salzburg March 1972	Barenboim	LP: EMI SLS 5002 LP: EMI 1C 191 50379-50385 CD: EMI CMS 764 8202

Traun, Bogen und Pfeil sind gut für den Feind/Die schöne Magelone
See Die schöne Magelone

Trennung (Da unten im Tale)

Salzburg August 1973	Sawallisch	LP: EMI SLS 5002 LP: EMI 1C 191 50379-50385 CD: EMI CMS 764 8202
Berlin February 1978- September 1982	Barenboim	LP: DG 2740 279

Trennung (Wach auf, wach auf, du junger Gesell')

Salzburg August 1973	Sawallisch	LP: EMI SLS 5002 LP: EMI 1C 191 50379-50385 CD: EMI CMS 764 8202
Berlin February 1978- September 1982	Barenboim	LP: DG 2740 279

Brahms Lieder/continued

Treue Liebe (Ein Mägdlein sass am Meeresstrand)

Berlin May 1967	Demus	LP: DG SLPM 139 328
Salzburg August 1973	Sawallisch	LP: EMI SLS 5002 LP: EMI 1C 191 50379-50385 CD: EMI CMS 764 8202
Berlin February 1978- September 1982	Barenboim	LP: DG 2740 279

Treue Liebe dauert lange/Die schöne Magelone
See Die schöne Magelone

Trost in Tränen (Wie kommt's, dass du so traurig bist?)

Salzburg August 1973	Sawallisch	LP: EMI SLS 5002 LP: EMI 1C 191 50379-50385 CD: EMI CMS 764 8202
Berlin February 1978- September 1982	Barenboim	LP: DG 2740 279

Ueber die Heide hallt mein Schritt

Salzburg March 1972	Barenboim	LP: EMI SLS 5002 LP: EMI 1C 191 50379-50385 CD: EMI CMS 764 8202
Berlin February 1978- September 1982	Barenboim	LP: DG 2740 279

Ueber die See, fern über die See

Salzburg March 1972	Barenboim	LP: EMI SLS 5002 LP: EMI 1C 191 50379-50385 CD: EMI CMS 764 8202
Berlin February 1978- September 1982	Barenboim	LP: DG 2740 279

Brahms Lieder/continued

Der Ueberläufer (In den Garten wollen wir gehen aus)

Salzburg	Sawallisch	LP: EMI SLS 5002
August 1973		LP: EMI 1C 191 50379-50385
		CD: EMI CMS 764 8202

Berlin	Barenboim	LP: DG 2740 279
February 1978-		
September 1982		

Unbewegte laue Luft

Salzburg	Sawallisch	LP: EMI SLS 5002
August 1973		LP: EMI 1C 191 50379-50378
		CD: EMI CMS 764 8202

Berlin	Barenboim	LP: DG 2740 279
February 1978-		
September 1982		

Unüberwindlich (Hab' ich tausendmal geschworen)

Salzburg	Barenboim	LP: EMI SLS 5002
March 1972		LP: EMI 1C 191 50379-50385
		CD: EMI CMS 764 8202

Berlin	Barenboim	LP: DG 2740 279
February 1978-		
December 1982		

| Munich | Höll | LP: Bayer BR 30.006 |
| ca. 1986 | | CD: Bayer BR 100.006 |

Vergangen ist mir Glück und Heil

Salzburg	Sawallisch	LP: EMI SLS 5002
August 1973		LP: EMI 1C 191 50379-50385
		CD: EMI CMS 764 8202

Berlin	Barenboim	LP: DG 2740 279
February 1978-		
September 1982		

Brahms Lieder/continued

Verrat (Ich stand in einer lauen Nacht)

Salzburg	Sawallisch	LP: EMI SLS 5002
August 1973		LP: EMI 1C 191 50379-50385
		CD: EMI CMS 764 8202

Berlin   Barenboim   LP: DG 2740 279
February 1978-
September 1982

Versunken (Es brausen der Liebe Wogen)

Salzburg   Barenboim   LP: EMI SLS 5002
March 1972   LP: EMI 1C 191 50379-50385
                                    CD: EMI CMS 764 8202

Berlin   Barenboim   LP: DG 2740 279
February 1978-
September 1982

Verzagen (Ich sitz' am Strande der rauschenden See)

Berlin   Demus   LP: DG LPM 18 504/SLPM 138 011
February 1958   CD: DG 415 1892

Salzburg   Barenboim   LP: EMI SLS 5002
March 1972   LP: EMI 1C 191 50379-50385
                                    CD: EMI CMS 764 8202

Berlin   Barenboim   LP: DG 2740 279
February 1978-
September 1982

Verzweiflung/Die schöne Magelone (So tönet denn, schäumende Wellen)
See Die schöne Magelone

Volkslied (Die Schwalbe ziehet fort)

Berlin   Demus   LP: DG SLPM 139 328
May 1967

Salzburg   Sawallisch   LP: EMI SLS 5002
August 1973   LP: EMI 1C 191 50379-50385
                                    CD: EMI CMS 764 8202

Berlin   Barenboim   LP: DG 2740 279
February 1978-
September 1982

Brahms Lieder/continued

Vom verwundeten Knaben (Es wollt' ein Mädchen früh aufstehn)

Berlin May 1967	Demus	LP: DG SLPM 139 328
Salzburg August 1973	Sawallisch	LP: DG SLS 5002 LP: EMI 1C 191 50379-50385 CD: EMI CMS 764 8202
Berlin February 1978- September 1982	Barenboim	LP: DG 2740 279

Von ewiger Liebe (Dunkel, wie dunkel, in Wald und in Flur)

Berlin March 1957	Engel	LP: HMV ALP 1584 LP: Electrola E 90015 CD: EMI CZS 568 5092
Salzburg August 1973	Sawallisch	LP: EMI SLS 5002 LP: EMI 1C 191 50379-50385 CD: EMI CMS 764 8202
Berlin February 1978- September 1982	Barenboim	LP: DG 2740 279

Vor dem Fenster (Soll sich der Mond nicht heller scheinen)

Berlin May 1967	Demus	LP: DG SLPM 139 328
Salzburg August 1973	Sawallisch	LP: EMI SLS 5002 LP: EMI 1C 191 50379-50385 CD: EMI CMS 764 8202
Berlin February 1978- September 1982	Barenboim	LP: DG 2740 279

Vorüber (Ich legte mich unter den Lindenbaum)

Salzburg August 1973	Sawallisch	LP: EMI SLS 5002 LP: EMI 1C 191 50379-50385 CD: EMI CMS 764 8202
Berlin February 1978- September 1982	Barenboim	LP: DG 2740 279

Wach auf, mein Herzensschöne/Deutsche Volkslieder

Berlin	Moore	LP: EMI AN 163-164/SAN 163-164
August-		LP: EMI 1C 193 00054-00055
September 1965		LP: EMI 1C 047 01247
		CD: EMI CDS 749 5252

Wach auf, mein Hort/Deutsche Volkslieder

Berlin	Schwarzkopf	LP: EMI AN 163-164/SAN 163-164
August-	Moore	LP: EMI 1C 193 00054-00055
September 1965		CD: EMI CDS 749 5252

Während des Regens (Voller, dichter, tropft ums Dach da)

Salzburg	Sawallisch	LP: EMI SLS 5002
August 1973		LP: EMI 1C 191 50379-50385
		CD: EMI CMS 764 8202
Berlin	Barenboim	LP: DG 2740 279
February 1978-		
September 1982		

Ein Wanderer (Hier, wo sich die Strassen scheiden)

Salzburg	Sawallisch	LP: EMI SLS 5002
August 1973		LP: EMI 1C 191 50379-50385
		CD: EMI CMS 764 8202
Berlin	Barenboim	LP: DG 2740 279
February 1978-		
September 1982		

War es dir, dem diese Lippen bebten/Die schöne Magelone
See Die schöne Magelone

Wehe, so willst du mich wieder

Berlin	Klust	LP: HMV ALP 1270
May 1955		LP: Electrola E 90106
		CD: EMI CZS 568 5092
Salzburg	Moore	LP: Orfeo S140 855R
August 1958		CD: Orfeo C140 201B/C339 930T
Berlin	Moore	LP: EMI ALP 2083/ASD 630/SLS 5002
March 1964		LP: EMI 1C 191 50379-50385
		CD: EMI CMS 764 8202
Berlin	Barenboim	LP: DG 2740 279
February 1978-		
September 1982		
Munich	Höll	LP: Bayer BR 30.006
ca. 1986		CD: Bayer BR 100.006

Brahms Lieder/continued

Wenn du nur zuweilen lächelst

Salzburg August 1973	Sawallisch	LP: EMI SLS 5002 LP: EMI 1C 191 50379-50385 CD: EMI CMS 764 8202
Berlin February 1978- September 1982	Barenboim	LP: DG 2740 279

Wenn ich mit Menschen- und mit Engelszungen redete/4 ernste Gesänge
See 4 ernste Gesänge

Wie bist du, meine Königin?

Berlin May 1955	Klust	LP: HMV ALP 1270 LP: Electrola E 90106 CD: EMI CZS 568 5092
Salzburg August 1958	Moore	LP: Orfeo S140 855R CD: Orfeo C140 201B/C339 930T
Berlin March 1964	Moore	LP: EMI ALP 2083/ASD 630/SLS 5002 LP: EMI 1C 191 50379-50385 CD: EMI CMS 764 8202
Salzburg August 1964	Moore	CD: EMI CMS 763 1672
Berlin February 1978- September 1982	Barenboim	LP: DG 2740 279
Munich ca. 1986	Höll	LP: Bayer BR 30.006 CD: Bayer BR 100.006

Wie die Wolken nach der Sonne

Berlin May 1967	Demus	LP: DG SLPM 139 328
Salzburg August 1973	Sawallisch	LP: EMI SLS 5002 LP: EMI 1C 191 50379-50385 CD: EMI CMS 764 8202
Berlin February 1978- September 1982	Barenboim	LP: DG 2740 279

Brahms Lieder/continued

Wie froh und frisch mein Sinn sich hebt/Die schöne Magelone
See Die schöne Magelone

Wie komm' ich denn zur Tür herein?/Deutsche Volkslieder

Berlin	Schwarzkopf	LP: EMI AN 163-164/SAN 163-164
August-	Moore	LP: EMI 1C 193 00054-00055
September 1965		CD: EMI CDS 749 5252

Wie Melodien zieht es mir

Salzburg	Sawallisch	LP: EMI SLS 5002
August 1973		LP: EMI 1C 191 50379-50385
		CD: EMI CMS 764 8202

Wie rafft' ich mich auf in der Nacht

Berlin	Klust	LP: HMV ALP 1270
May 1955		LP: Electrola E 90106
		CD: EMI CZS 568 5092
Salzburg	Moore	LP: Orfeo S140 855R
August 1958		CD: Orfeo C140 201B/C339 930T
Berlin	Moore	LP: EMI ALP 2083/ASD 630
March 1964		LP: EMI SLS 5002/EX 29 04293
		LP: EMI 1C 191 50379-50385
		CD: EMI CMS 764 8202
Berlin	Barenboim	LP: DG 2740 279
February 1978-		
September 1982		
Munich	Höll	LP: Bayer BR 30.006
ca. 1986		CD: Bayer BR 100.006

Wie schnell verschwindet so Licht als Glanz/Die schöne Magelone
See Die schöne Magelone

Wie soll ich die Freude, die Wonne denn tragen/Die schöne Magelone
See Die schöne Magelone

Wiegenlied (Guten Abend, gut' Nacht)

Salzburg	Sawallisch	LP: EMI SLS 5002
August 1973		LP: EMI 1C 191 50379-50385
		CD: EMI CMS 764 8202
Berlin	Barenboim	LP: DG 2740 279
February 1978-		
September 1982		

Brahms Lieder/concluded

Willst du, dass ich geh'? (Auf der Heide weht der Wind)

Salzburg March 1972	Barenboim	LP: EMI SLS 5002 LP: EMI 1C 191 50379-50385 CD: EMI CMS 764 8202
Berlin February 1978- September 1982	Barenboim	LP: DG 2740 279

Wir müssen uns trennen, geliebtes Saitenspiel/Die schöne Magelone
See Die schöne Magelone

Wir wandelten, wir zwei zusammen

Berlin March 1957	Engel	LP: HMV ALP 1584 LP: Electrola E 90015 CD: EMI CZS 568 5092
Salzburg August 1958	Moore	LP: Orfeo S140 855R CD: Orfeo C140 201B/C339 930T
Salzburg March 1972	Barenboim	LP: EMI SLS 5002 LP: EMI 1C 191 50379-50385 CD: EMI CMS 764 8202
Berlin February 1978- September 1982	Barenboim	LP: DG 2740 279

Wo gehst du hin, du Stolze?/Deutsche Volkslieder

Berlin August- September 1965	Moore	LP: EMI AN 163-164/SAN 163-164 LP: EMI 1C 193 00054-00055 LP: EMI 1C 047 01247 CD: EMI CDS 749 5252

At the time of going to press DG announces the issue on CD of
Fischer-Dieskau's 1978-1982 Brahms Lieder recordings with Barenboim:
catalogue number 447 5012

BRITTEN

War Requiem

London January 1963	Vishnevskaya, Pears Bach & Highgate Choirs Melos Ensemble LSO Britten	LP: Decca MET 252-253/SET 252-253 CD: Decca 414 3832 Excerpts LP: Decca GRV 7

Cantata misericordium

London December 1963	Pears LSO Chorus LSO Britten	LP: Decca LXT 6175/SXL 6175/SXL 6640 CD: Decca 425 1002

Songs and Proverbs of William Blake

London December 1965	Britten	LP: Decca SXL 6391 CD: Decca 417 4282

ADOLF BUSCH

Lieder: Nun die Schatten dunkeln; Wonne der Wehmut; Aus den Himmelsaugen

Berlin May 1964	Nel, viola Demus	LP: DG LPM 18 946/SLPM 138 946

BUSONI

Doktor Faust

Munich May 1969	Role of Faust Hillebrecht, Cochran, De Ridder, Kohn Bavarian Radio Orchestra & Chorus Leitner	LP: DG 2709 032 CD: DG 427 4132

4 Lieder nach Gedichten von Goethe: Lied des Unmuts; Zigeunerlied; Schlechter Trost; Lied des Mephistopheles

London May 1962	Moore	CD: Intaglio INCD 7461
Berlin May 1964	Demus	LP: DG LPM 18 946/SLPM 138 946

BUXTEHUDE

2 geistliche Kantaten: Ich bin eine Blume zu Saron; Ich suche des Nachts

Berlin	Krebs	LP: DG APM 14 088
March 1957	Gorvin Chamber	
	Ensemble	
	Gorvin	

CHABRIER

3 Mélodies: L'île heureuse; Vilanelle des petits canards; Les cigales

Berlin	Höll	LP: Teldec 643 754
April 1984		CD: Teldec 843 754/4509 974572

CHAUSSON

2 Mélodies: Le temps des lilas; Les papillons

Berlin	Höll	LP: Teldec 643 754
April 1984		CD: Teldec 843 754/4509 974572

CIMAROSA

Il Matrimonio segreto

Edinburgh	Role of Geronimo	LP: DG 2709 069/2740 171
August and	Auger, Varady,	CD: DG 437 6962
September 1975	Hamari, Davies	
and London	English Chamber	
August 1976	Orchestra	
	Barenboim	

CLÉREMBAULT

Orphée, cantata

Berlin	Nicolet, flute	LP: EMI 1C 063 02258
August 1969	Toyoda, violin	Excerpt
	Picht-Axenfeld,	LP: EMI EX 29 04353
	harpsichord	
	Donderer, cello	
	Nowak, double-bass	

CORNELIUS

Auf ein schlummerndes Kind

Berlin	Reutter	LP: EMI 1C 065 01251
1970		CD: EMI CZS 568 5092

Auf eine Unbekannte

Berlin	Reutter	LP: EMI 1C 065 01251
1970		CD: EMI CZS 568 5092

Der beste Liebesbrief

London	Baker	LP: EMI ASD 2553/1C 063 02041
August 1969	Barenboim	

Christbaum/Weihnachtslieder

Berlin	Moore	LP: EMI ASD 2630/1C 065 01251
February 1966		CD: EMI CZS 568 5092

Christkind/Weihnachtslieder

Berlin	Moore	LP: EMI ASD 2630
February 1966		LP: EMI 1C 065 01251/SHZE 244
		CD: EMI CZS 568 5092

Christus der Kinderfreund/Weihnachtslieder

Berlin	Moore	LP: EMI ASD 2630
February 1966		LP: EMI 1C 065 01251/SHZE 244
		CD: EMI CZS 568 5092

Geheiligt werde dein Name

Berlin	Reutter	LP: EMI 1C 065 01251
1970		CD: EMI CZS 568 5092

Heimatgedanken

London	Baker	LP: EMI ASD 2553/1C 063 02041
August 1969	Barenboim	

Die Hirten/Weihnachtslieder

Berlin	Moore	LP: EMI ASD 2630/EX 29 04293
February 1966		LP: EMI 1C 065 01251/SHZE 244
		CD: EMI CZS 568 5092

Cornelius Lieder/concluded

Ich und du

London	Baker	LP: EMI ASD 2553/1C 063 02041
August 1969	Barenboim	

Komm, wir wandeln zusammen

Berlin	Reutter	LP: EMI 1C 065 01251
1970		CD: EMI CZS 568 5092

Die Könige/Weihnachtslieder

Berlin	Moore	LP: EMI ASD 2630/1C 065 01251
February 1966		CD: EMI CZS 568 5092

Liebe ohne Heimat (Meine Liebe, lange wie die Taube)

Berlin	Reimann	LP: EMI 1C 065 02674/
March 1971		1C 161 02673-02677

Simeon/Weihnachtslieder

Berlin	Moore	LP: EMI ASD 2630
February 1966		LP: EMI 1C 065 01251/SHZE 244
		CD: EMI CZS 568 5092

Sonnenuntergang (Wo bist du?)

Berlin	Reimann	LP: EMI 1C 065 02674/
March 1971		1C 161 02673-02677

Trauer und Trost, 6 Lieder op 3: Trauer; Angedenken; Ein Ton; An den Traum; Treue; Trost

Berlin	Reutter	LP: EMI 1C 065 01251
1970		CD: EMI CZS 568 5092

Vater unser (Zu uns komme dein Reich)

Berlin	Demus	LP: DG 2530 219
November 1970		

Vergib' uns unsere Schuld

Berlin	Reutter	LP: EMI 1C 065 01251
1970		CD: EMI CZS 568 5092

Verratene Liebe

London	Baker	LP: EMI ASD 2553/1C 063 02041
August 1969	Barenboim	

COUPERIN

Lecons des ténèbres pour le mercredi, cantata

Berlin	Poppen, cello	LP: HMV ALP 2066/ASD 615
1963	Picht-Axenfeld,	LP: Electrola E 80822/STE 80822

CREUSSOLD

Abschied im Herbst

Munich	Klöcker, clarinet	LP: Orfeo S153 861A
August 1983	Wallendorf, horn	CD: Orfeo C153 861A
	Höll	

General Administrator: Sir John Tooley

in association with

Scott Concert
Promotions Ltd.
and
Ibbs & Tillett

Sunday
10 February
1980

presents

Dietrich Fischer-Dieskau
Baritone

Wolfgang Sawallisch
Piano

The Royal Opera House Covent Garden
Limited receives financial assistance from
The Arts Council of Great Britain.

ROYAL FESTIVAL HALL

General Manager: T. E. Bean, C.B.E.

PHILHARMONIA CONCERT SOCIETY

ARTISTIC DIRECTOR:
WALTER LEGGE

PHILHARMONIA ORCHESTRA

Leader: HUGH BEAN

DIETRICH FISCHER-DIESKAU

GERALD MOORE

Leslie Fyson   Neil Howlett   John Frost

OTAKAR KRAUS

BUSONI
Comedy Overture
Four Songs with Piano
Geharnischte Suite

———

Doktor Faustus:

First Vorspiel; Cortège;
Sarabande; Traum der Jugend

Tanzwalzer

SIR ADRIAN BOULT

Monday, May 14, 1962, at 8 p.m.

DEBUSSY

Pelléas et Mélisande

Munich November 1971	Role of Golaud Donath, Schiml, Gedda, Meven Bavarian RO Kubelik	CD: Orfeo C367 924I

L'enfant prodigue

Stuttgart August and September 1981	Norman, Carreras SDR Orchestra Bertini	LP: Orfeo S012 821A CD: Orfeo C012 821A CD: Pro Arte CDD 128

3 Ballades de Francois Villon: Faulse beauté; Dame du ciel; Quoy qu'on tien

Berlin October 1959	Engel	LP: DG LPM 18 615/SLPM 138 115

Paris October 1979	Orchestre de Paris Barenboim	LP: DG 2531 263

Mélodies: Beau soir; Chevaux de bois; Clair de lune; Colloque sentimental; Les cloches; Dans le jardin; De soir; Fantoches; Le faune; Fleur des blés; L'échelonnement; Green; Le jet d'eau; Les ingénues; Le merle; Le son du cor; Recueillement; En sourdine

Berlin February 1988	Höll	CD: Claves CD 50 8809

Mandoline

Berlin October 1959	Engel	LP: DG LPM 18 615/SLPM 138 115

Berlin February 1988	Höll	CD: Claves CD 50 8809

La grotte

Berlin October 1959	Engel	LP: DG LPM 18 615/SLPM 138 115

Le temps à laissé son manteau

Berlin May 1970	Reutter	LP: EMI 1C 065 02676/EX 29 04293 LP: EMI 1C 161 02673-02677 CD: EMI CZS 568 5092

Pour ce que plaisance est morte

Berlin May 1970	Reutter	LP: EMI 1C 065 02676/ 1C 161 02673-02677 CD: EMI CZS 568 5092

DESSAU

Lieder: Noch bin ich eine Stadt; Such' nicht mehr, Frau

Berlin	Reimann	LP: EMI 1C 065 02677/
March 1974		1C 161 02673-02677

D'INDY

Mélodies: Madrigal; Lied maritime

Berlin	Höll	LP: Teldec 643 754
April 1984		CD: Teldec 843 754/4509 974572

DONIZETTI

Lucia di Lammermoor

Berlin	Role of Enrico	Unpublished radio broadcast
January 1953	Stader, Wagner,	
	Häfliger, Schlott,	
	Wilhelm, Van Dyk	
	RIAS Choir	
	Berlin RO	
	Fricsay	

L'amor funesto

Munich	Klöcker, clarinet	LP: Orfeo S153 861A
August 1983	Wallendorf, horn	CD: Orfeo C153 861A
	Höll	

DVORAK

6 Biblical Songs: Rings um den Himmel; Gott erhöre mein inniges Flehen; Gott
ist mein Hirte; An den Wassern zu Babylon; Wende dich zu mir; Singet ein
neues Lied

Berlin	Demus	LP: DG LPM 18 644/SLPM 138 644
April 1960	Sung in German	CD: DG 437 3772

Duets: Möglichkeit; Der Apfel

Berlin	De los Angeles	LP: HMV ALP 1891/ASD 459
December 1960	Moore	CD: EMI CMS 565 0612
	Sung in German	

A group of Dvorak songs with orchestra (?Biblical Songs), in which Fischer-
Dieskau is accompanied by the Malmö Symphony Orchestra, may have been
published on the LP Big Ben 861; confirmation of this could not be found

EINEM

An die Nachgeborenen, cantata

Vienna	Hamari	LP: DG 666 543
October-	Singverein	Special issue for United Nations
November 1975	VSO	
	Giulini	

Leb' wohl, Frau Welt, song-cycle

Berlin	Engel	LP: DG 2530 877
March 1977		

Lieder: In der Fremde; Ein junger Dichter denkt an die Geliebte

Berlin	Reimann	LP: EMI 1C 065 02677/
March 1974		1C 161 02673-02677

EULENBURG

Liebessehnsucht (Umwallt vom Weben der Sommernacht)

Berlin	Reimann	LP: EMI 1C 065 02674/
March 1971		1C 161 02673-02677

EISLER

Hollywood Song Book/Songs of Exile, song-cycle

Berlin December 1987	Reimann	CD: Teldec 844 092/4509 974592

Hollywood Song Book: Excerpts (An die Hoffnung; In der Frühe; Spruch 1939)

Berlin March 1974	Reimann	LP: EMI 1C 065 02677/ 1C 161 02673-02677

FAURÉ

Requiem

Paris February and March 1962	De los Angeles Brasseur Choir Paris Conservatoire Orchestra Cluytens	LP: EMI AN 107/SAN 107/CFP 40234 CD: EMI CDC 747 8362 Excerpt LP: EMI EX 29 04353
Paris 1974	Armstrong Edinburgh Festival Chorus Orchestre de Paris Barenboim	LP: EMI ASD 3065 /SXLP 102 5681 CD: EMI CDM 769 0382/CDM 764 6342

La bonne chanson, song-cycle

Berlin May 1958	Moore	LP: HMV BLP 1106 CD: EMI CZS 568 5092
Berlin 1975	Sawallisch	LP: BASF 22 7650

Pleurs d'or

Berlin December 1960	De los Angeles Moore	LP: HMV ALP 1891/ASD 459 CD: EMI CMS 565 0612

Mélodies: Au cimetière; Clair de lune; Lydia

Berlin April 1984	Höll	LP: Teldec 643 754 CD: Teldec 843 754/4509 974572

FORTNER

The Creation, to a poem by James Weldon Johnson

Hamburg	NDR Orchestra	LP: DG LPM 18 405
March 1957	Schmidt-Isserstedt	

Abbitte/Hölderlin-Gesänge

Berlin	Reimann	LP: Electrola E 91189/STE 91189
November 1961		CD: EMI CZS 568 5092

Berlin	Reutter	LP: EMI 1C 065 02676/
May 1970		1C 161 02673-02677

An die Parzen/Hölderlin-Gesänge

Berlin	Reimann	LP: Electrola E 91189/STE 91189
November 1961		CD: EMI CZS 568 5092

Geh' unter, schöne Sonne/Hölderlin-Gesänge

Berlin	Reimann	LP: Electrola E 91189/STE 91189
November 1961		CD: EMI CZS 568 5092

Hyperions Schicksalslied/Hölderlin-Gesänge

Berlin	Reimann	LP: Electrola E 91189/STE 91189
November 1961		CD: EMI CZS 568 5092

Berlin	Reutter	LP: EMI 1C 065 02676/
May 1970		1C 161 02673-02677

Lied vom Weidenbaum

Berlin	Reutter	LP: EMI 1C 065 02676/
May 1970		1C 161 02673-02677

FRANCK

Mélodies: Le mariage des roses; Roses et papillons; Nocturne

| Berlin | Höll | LP: Teldec 643 754 |
| April 1984 | | CD: Teldec 843 754/4509 974572 |

FRANZ

Lieder: Auf dem Meere I; Wie des Mondes Abbild; Gewitternacht; Bitte;
Für Musik; Abends; Auf dem Meere II; Wonne der Wehmut; Masilied; Auf
dem Meere III

Berlin	Reimann	LP: EMI 1C 065 02673/
March 1974		1C 161 02673-02677
		Wonne der Wehmut also on
		LP: EMI EX 29 04293

GIORDANO

Andrea Chenier: Excerpt (Nemico della patria)

| Berlin | Berlin RO | LP: DG LPM 19 700/SLPM 138 700 |
| April 1961 | Fricsay | LP: DG 2705 001 |

GLUCK

Iphigenia in Aulis

Berlin December 1951	Role of Agamemmnon Musial, Blatter, Krebs, Greindl Berlin Radio Orchestra & Chorus Rother	LP: Melodram MEL 048
Munich 1972	Moffo, T.Schmidt, Spiess, Stewart Bavarian Radio Orchestra & Chorus Eichhorn	LP: Eurodisc XF 86271 CD: Eurodisc 352988 Also issued on LP by RCA

Iphigénie en Tauride

Munich 1982	Role of Thoas Lorengar, Bonisolli, Grönroos Bavarian Radio Orchestra & Chorus Gardelli	LP: Orfeo S052 832H CD: Orfeo C052 832H

Orfeo ed Euridice

Berlin September 1956	Role of Orfeo Stader, Streich Berlin Radio Orchestra & Chorus Fricsay Sung in German	LP: DG LPM 18 343-18 344/ LPM 18 345-18 346 LP: DG 2700 103 CD: DG 439 7112 Excerpts 45: DG EPL 30405/30444/30650 LP: DG LPEM 19 411
New York April 1967	Schwarzkopf, Popp American Opera Society Orchestra & Chorus Perlea	Unpublished radio broadcast
Munich August 1967	Janowitz, Moser Munich Bach Orchestra & Chorus K.Richter	LP: DG 2707 033/2726 043 Excerpts LP: DG 136 556/2705 001/2721 084

GOUNOD

Faust: Excerpt (Avant de quitter ces lieux)

Berlin	Berlin RO	LP: DG LPM 18 700/SLPM 138 700
September 1961	Fricsay	LP: DG 2705 001
Berlin	Berlin RO	LP: EMI 1C 063 28961/EX 29 04323
September 1973	Patané	
	Sung in German	

Faust: Excerpt (Death of Valentin)

Berlin	Moser, Groenewold	LP: EMI 1C 063 28961
September 1973	RIAS Choir	
	Berlin RO	
	Patané	
	Sung in German	

Sérénade

Munich	Klöcker, clarinet	LP: Orfeo S153 861A
August 1983	Wallendorf, horn	CD: Orfeo C153 861A
	Höll	

Solitude

Berlin	Höll	LP: Teldec 643 754
April 1984		CD: Teldec 843 754/4509 974572

GRIEG

Songs: Morgentau; Abschied; Jägerlied; Wo sind si hin?; Hör' ich das Liedchen klingen; Dereinst, dereinst, Gedanke mein; Lauf der Welt

Berlin	Reimann	LP: EMI 1C 065 02673/
1974		1C 161 02673-02677
		With the exception of Hör' ich das Liedchen klingen, these Grieg settings are of original German texts

HAAS

Die bewegliche Musica

Berlin	Demus	LP: DG 2530 219
November 1970		

HAHN

Mélodies: L'heure exquise; Si mers vers avaient des ailes

| Berlin | Höll | LP: Teldec 643 754 |
| April 1984 | | CD: Teldec 843 754/4509 974572 |

HANDEL

Alexander's Feast: Excerpt (Revenge Timotheus cries)

Munich	Munich Chamber	LP: DG 2530 979
August-	Orchestra	
October 1977	Stadlmair	

Agrippina: Excerpt (Pur ritorno a rimiarvi)

Munich	Munich Chamber	LP: DG 2530 979
August-	Orchestra	
October 1977	Stadlmair	

Apollo e Dafne, cantata

Berlin	Giebel	LP: DG SLPM 139 153
January 1966	BPO	
	Weissenborn	

Belsazar: Excerpts (O memory, still bitter to my soul; Opprest with never ceasing grief)

Munich	Munich Chamber	LP: DG 2530 979
August-	Orchestra	
October 1977	Stadlmair	

Berenice: Excerpt (Si, tra i cappi)

Munich	Munich Chamber	LP: DG 2530 979
August-	Orchestra	
October 1977	Stadlmair	

Cuopra tal volta il cielo, cantata

Berlin	Nicolet, flute	LP: HMV ALP 1804/ASD 397
February 1960	Koch, oboe	LP: EMI EX 29 04353/ED 29 03641
	Poppen, cello	
	Picht-Axenfeld,	
	harpsichord	

Dalla guerra amorosa, cantata

Berlin	Nicolet, flute	LP: HMV ALP 1804/ASD 397
February 1960	Koch, oboe	LP: EMI ED 29 03641
	Poppen, cello	Excerpt
	Picht-Axenfeld,	LP: Electrola E 70415/STE 70415
	harpsichord	

Giulio Cesare

Munich	Role of Cesare	LP: DG 2711 009
April 1969	Troyanos, Hamari,	
	Schreier	
	Munich Bach	
	Orchestra & Chorus	
	K.Richter	

Giulio Cesare, excerpts

Berlin	Role of Cesare	LP: DG LPM 18 637/SLPM 138 637
April 1960	Seefried	CD: DG (Japan) DO 1042
	Berlin RO	
	Böhm	

Giù nei Tartarei regni, duet

London	Baker	LP: EMI ASD 2710
February 1970	Heath, cello	
	Malcolm, harpsichord	

Judas Maccabaeus

Berlin	Stader, Hartwig,	LP: Melodram MEL
May 1954	Häfliger, Van Dyk	
	Berlin Radio	
	Orchestra & Chorus	
	Fricsay	

Messiah: Excerpt (Hallelujah Chorus)

New York	Bernstein, Horowitz,	LP: CBS 79200
May 1976	Menuhin, Stern,	CD: Sony SM2K 46743
	Rostropovich	
	Oratorio Society	
	NYPO members	

Ottone: Excerpts (Con gelosi sospetti; Dopo l'orore d'un cielo turbato)

Munich	Munich Chamber	LP: DG 2530 979
August-	Orchestra	
October 1977	Stadlmair	

Quando in calma ride il mare, duet

London   Baker   LP: EMI ASD 2710
February 1970   Heath, cello
                        Malcolm, harpsichord

Rinaldo: Excerpt (Caro spose)

Berlin   Rampal, flute   LP: EMI ASD 2903/1C 063 02328
1971   Neilz, cello
                        Veyron-Lacroix,
                          harpsichord

Salomo: Excerpts (Prais'd be the Lord; When the sun o'er yonder hills)

Munich   Munich Chamber   LP: DG 2530 979
August-   Orchestra
October 1977   Stadlmair

Samson: Excerpt (Honour and arms)

Munich   Munich Chamber   LP: DG 2530 979
August-   Orchestra
October 1977   Stadlmair

Saul

Vienna   Varady, Gale,   LP: Teldec 635 687
April 1985   Esswood,   CD: Teldec 835 687
                        Rolfe-Johnson
                        Vienna Opera Chorus
                        Concentus musicus
                        Harnoncourt

Saul: Excerpts (To him ten thousands; With rage I shall burst)

Munich	Munich Chamber	LP: DG 2530 979
August-	Orchestra	
October 1977	Stadlmair	

Serse: Excerpts (Frondi tenere e belle; Ombra mai fù)

Munich	Munich Chamber	LP: DG 2530 979
August-	Orchestra	
October 1977	Stadlmair	

Susanna: Excerpts (Down my old cheeks; Peace crowned with roses)

Munich	Munich Chamber	LP: DG 2530 979
August-	Orchestra	
October 1977	Stadlmair	

HARTMANN

Gesangsszene für Bariton und Orchester

| Munich | Bavarian RO | LP: Wergo WER 60061 |
| 1968 | Kubelik | |

HAUER

Lieder: Der gefesselte Strom; An die Parzen

| Berlin | Reimann | LP: EMI 1C 065 02677/ |
| March 1974 | | 1C 161 02673-02677 |

Die Jahreszeiten

| London
December 1980 | Mathis, Jerusalem
Academy St Martins
Orchestra & Choir
Marriner | LP: Philips 6769 068
CD: Philips 411 4282/438 7152 |

Die Schöpfung

| Berlin
February 1966,
September and
November 1968
& April 1969 | Janowitz, C.Ludwig,
Wunderlich, Krenn,
Berry
Singverein
BPO
Karajan | LP: DG 643 515-643 516
LP: DG 2707 044/410 9511
CD: DG 435 0772
Excerpts
LP: DG 136 439
CD: DG 439 4542 |

| London
December 1980 | Mathis, Baldin
Academy St Martins
Orchestra & Choir
Marriner | LP: Philips 6769 047
CD: Philips 416 4492 |

Acide e Galatea: Excerpt (Tergi i vezzosi rai)

| Vienna
October 1969 | Vienna Haydn
Orchestra
Peters | LP: Decca SXL 6490/GRV 7
CD: Decca 440 4832 |

La vera costanza: Excerpt (Spann' deine langen Ohren)

| Vienna
October 1969 | Vienna Haydn
Orchestra
Peters | LP: Decca SXL 6490/GRV 7 |

Abschiedslied (Nimm dies kleine Angedenken)

| Berlin
June 1959 | Moore | LP: HMV ALP 1829
LP: Electrola E 90988/STE 90988
LP: EMI 1C 053 01436 |

Afton Water (Fliess leise, mein Bächlein)

| Berlin
June 1961 | Nicolet, flute
Heller, violin
Poppen, cello
Engel | LP: DG LPM 18 706/SLPM 138 706 |

An den Vetter (Ja, Vetter, ja!)

London   Schwarzkopf,   LP: EMI AN 182-183/SAN 182-183
February 1967   De los Angeles   LP: EMI SLS 926/ASD 143 5941
                  Moore   CD: EMI CDC 749 2382/CDEMX 2233

Auch die Sprödeste der Schönen

Berlin   Moore   LP: HMV ALP 1829
June 1959   LP: Electrola E 90988/STE 90988
                                       LP: EMI 1C 053 01436

Un cor si tenero

Vienna   Vienna Haydn   LP: Decca SXL 6490/GRV 7
October 1969   Orchestra
                  Peters

Damon and Sylvia (Dort, wo durchs Ried)

Berlin   Nicolet, flute   LP: DG LPM 18 706/SLPM 138 706
June 1961   Heller, violin
                  Poppen, cello
                  Engel

Daphnens einziger Fehler (Sie hat das Auge)

London   Schwarzkopf,   LP: EMI AN 182-183/SAN 182-183
February 1967   De los Angeles   LP: EMI SLS 926/ASD 143 5941
                  Moore   CD: EMI CDC 749 2382/CDEMX 2233

Dice benissimo

Vienna   Vienna Haydn   LP: Decca SXL 6490/GRV 7
October 1969   Orchestra
                  Peters

Eine sehr gewöhnliche Geschichte (Philine stand jüngst vor Babetts Tür)

Berlin   Moore   LP: HMV ALP 1829
June 1959   LP: Electrola E 90988/STE 90988
                                       LP: EMI 1C 053 01436/1C 047 01247

Fidelty (Wenn hohl erdröht)

Berlin   Moore   LP: HMV ALP 1829
June 1959   LP: Electrola E 90988/STE 90988
                                       LP: EMI 1C 053 01436

Gegenliebe (Wüsst' ich)

Berlin	Moore	LP: HMV ALP 1829
June 1959		LP: Electrola E 90988/STE 90988
		LP: EMI 1C 053 01436

Geistliches Lied (Dir nah' ich mich)

Berlin	Moore	LP: HMV ALP 1829
June 1959		LP: Electrola E 90988/STE 90988
		LP: EMI 1C 053 01436

Der Gleichsinn (Solt' ich voller Sorg' und Pein)

Berlin	Moore	LP: HMV ALP 1829
June 1959		LP: Electrola E 90988/STE 90988
		LP: EMI 1C 053 01436

Heimkehr (My ain' kind dearie o')

Berlin	Nicolet, flute	LP: DG LPM 18 706/SLPM 138 706
June 1961	Heller, violin	
	Poppen, cello	
	Engel	

Das Kaiserlied (Gott erhalte Franz den Kaiser)

Berlin	Moore	LP: HMV ALP 1829
June 1959		LP: Electrola E 90988/STE 90988
		LP: EMI 1C 053 01436

Das Leben ist ein Traum

Berlin	Moore	LP: HMV ALP 1829
June 1959		LP: Electrola E 90988/STE 90988
		LP: EMI 1C 053 01436

Lob der Faulheit (Faulheit, endlich muss ich dir)

Berlin	Moore	LP: HMV ALP 1829
June 1959		LP: Electrola E 90988/STE 90988
		LP: EMI 1C 053 01436/1C 047 01247

Lover's morning salute to his mistress (Schläfst oder wachst du)

Berlin	Nicolet, flute	LP: DG LPM 18 706/SLPM 138 706
June 1961	Heller, violin	
	Poppen, cello	
	Engel	

Maggy Lauder

Berlin	Nicolet, flute	LP: DG LPM 18 706/SLPM 138 706
June 1961	Heller, violin	
	Poppen, cello	
	Engel	

Piercing eyes (Du kannst mich fragen ob ich liebe)

Berlin	Moore	LP: HMV ALP 1829
June 1959		LP: Electrola E 90988/STE 90988
		LP: EMI 1C 053 01436

Recollection (Der Mond erscheint)

Berlin	Moore	LP: HMV ALP 1829
June 1961		LP: Electrola E 90988/STE 90988
		LP: EMI 1C 053 01436

Sailor's Song (Hoch klimmt der Seemann auf den Mast)

Berlin	Moore	LP: HMV ALP 1829/ASD 2549
June 1959		LP: Electrola E 90988/STE 90988
		LP: Electrola E 70415/STE 70415
		LP: EMI 1C 053 01436

Schlaf in deiner engen Kammer

Berlin	De los Angeles	LP: HMV ALP 1891/ASD 459
December 1960	Drolc, ciolin	LP: EMI EX 29 05583/EX 29 04353
	Poppen, cello	CD: EMI CMS 565 0612
	Moore	

She never told her love (Stets barg sie ihre Liebe)

Berlin	Moore	LP: HMV ALP 1829/ASD 2549
June 1959		LP: Electrola E 90988/STE 90988
		LP: Electrola E 70415/STE 70415
		LP: EMI EX 29 04293/1C 053 01436

The Spirit's song (Horch, was dein Treuer spricht)

Berlin	Moore	LP: HMV ALP 1829
June 1959		LP: Electrola E 90988/STE 90988
		LP: EMI 1C 053 01436

The Wanderer (Wir wandeln alleine)

Berlin   Moore   LP: HMV ALP 1829
June 1959   LP: Electrola E 90988/STE 90988
                                         LP: EMI EX 29 04293/1C 053 01436

Zufriedenheit (Ich bin vergnügt)

Berlin   Moore   LP: HMV ALP 1829
June 1959   LP: Electrola E 90988/STE 90988
                                         LP: EMI 1C 053 01436

Die zu späte Ankunft der Mutter (Beschattet von blühenden Aesten)

Berlin   Moore   LP: HMV ALP 1829
June 1959   LP: Electrola E 90988/STE 90988
                                         LP: EMI 1C 053 01436

HENZE

Elegie für junge Liebende, excerpts

Berlin   Role of Mittenhofer   LP: DG LPM 18 876/SLPM 138 876
May 1963   Gayer, Mödl,
                Dubin, Hemsley
                Berlin Radio and
                Deutsche Oper
                Orchestras
                Henze

Das Floss der Medusa

Hamburg   Moser, Regnier   LP: DG 2707 041
December 1968   NDR & RIAS Choirs
                NDR Orchestra
                Henze

5 Neapolitanische Lieder

Berlin   BPO   LP: DG LPM 18 406
December 1956   Kraus

HERRMANN

Lieder: Erfüllung; Du bist wie eine Blume; Ich denke dein

Munich	Klöcker, clarinet	LP: Orfeo S153 861A
August 1983	Wallendorf, horn	CD: Orfeo C153 861A
	Höll	

HILLER

Gebet (Herr, den ich tief im Herzen trage)

| Berlin | Reimann | LP: EMI 1C 065 02673/ |
| March 1974 | | 1C 161 02673-02677 |

HINDEMITH

Cardillac

Cologne	Role of Cardillac	LP: DG 2707 042/2721 246
June 1968	Söderström,	CD: DG 431 7412
	Kirschstein, Grobe	Excerpts
	WDR Orchestra	LP: DG 2705 001
	and Chorus	
	Keilberth	

Mathis der Maler

Munich	Role of Mathis	LP: EMI SLS 5182
June and	Wagemann, Koszut,	LP: EMI 1C 165 03515-03517
September	King, Cochran,	CD: EMI CDS 555 2372
1977	Meven	
	Bavarian Radio	
	Orchestra & Chorus	
	Kubelik	

Mathis der Maler, scenes

Berlin	Role of Mathis	LP: DG LPM 18 769/SLPM 138 769
November 1961	Lorengar, Grobe	CD: DG 431 7412
	Berlin RO	Excerpt
	L.Ludwig	LP: DG LPEM 19 460/SLPEM 136 460

Requiem "For those we love"

Munich	Fassbaender	LP: Orfeo S112 851A
November 1983	Vienna Opera Chorus	CD: Orfeo C112 851A
	VSO	
	Sawallisch	

Fragment (Das Angenehme dieser Welt)

Berlin	Reutter	LP: EMI 1C 065 02676/
May 1970		1C 161 02673-02677
Tutzing	Reimann	LP: Orfeo S156 861A
February 1984		CD: Orfeo C156 861A

Lieder: Sonnenuntergang: The wild flowers' song; Sing on there in the swamp; On hearing "The last rose of summer"; Ehmals und jetzt; Brautgesang; Singet leise; Das Ganze, nicht das Einzelne; Des Morgens; Der Tod; Ich will nicht klagen mehr; Hymne; Abendphantasie; O nun heb' du an in deinem Moor; Vor dir schein' ich aufgewacht; Die Sonne sinkt; An die Parzen

Tutzing	Reimann	LP: Orfeo S156 861A
February 1984		CD: Orfeo C156 861A

HUMMEL

Zur Logenfeier/Goethe-Lieder

Berlin	Demus, fortepiano	LP: DG 2533 149
September 1972		

HUMPERDINCK

Hänsel und Gretel

Munich	Role of Father	LP: RCA ARL2-0637
1971	Moffo, Donath,	CD: RCA GD 69294
	Auger, Popp,	CD: Eurodisc 74321 252812
	C.Ludwig, Berthold	Also issued on LP by Eurodisc
	Tölz Choir	
	Bavarian RO	
	Eichhorn	

An das Christkind

Berlin	Demus	LP: DG 2530 219
November 1970		

IVES

Songs: At the river; Elegy; Ann Street; A Christmas carol; From "The Swimmers"; West London; A farewell to land; Abide with me; Where the eagle cannot see; Disclosure; The white gulls; The childrens' hour; The little flowers; Autumn; Tom sails away; Ich grolle nicht; Feldeinsamkeit; Weil' auf mir; In Flanders' fields

Berlin   Ponti   LP: DG 2530 696
December 1975

JENSEN

Lehn' deine Wang' an meine Wang'

Berlin   Reimann   LP: EMI 1C 065 02673/
March 1974   1C 161 02673-02677

WILHELM KEMPFF

4 Lieder to poems by C.F. Meyer: Lied der Seele; Es sprach der Geist; Gesang des Meeres; In einer Sturmnacht

Berlin   Kempff   LP: DG LPM 18 946/SLPM 138 946
May 1964

KIRCHNER

Lieder: Frühlingslied (Leise zieht durch mein Gemüt); Sie weiss es nicht; Frühlingslied (In dem Walde spriesst und grünt es); Frühlingslied (Ich liebe eine Blume)

Berlin   Reimann   LP: EMI 1C 065 02673/
March 1974   1C 161 02673-02677

KNAB

Marienkind

Berlin   Demus   LP: DG 2530 219
November 1970

KRENEK

Lieder: Erinnerung; Die frühen Gräber

Berlin   Reimann   LP: EMI 1C 065 02677/
March 1974   1C 161 02673-02677

KREUTZER

Ein Bettler vor dem Tor/Goethe-Lieder

Berlin   Demus, fortepiano   LP: DG 2533 149
September 1972

Das Mühlrad

Munich   Klöcker, clarinet   LP: Orfeo S153 861A
August 1983   Wallendorf, horn   CD: Orfeo C153 861A
                     Höll

LAWES

Duets: Dialogue on a kiss; Dialogue between Charon and Philomel; Dialogue
between Daphne and Strephon

London   Baker   LP: HMV ASD 2710
February 1970   Heath, cello
                     Malcolm, harpsichord

LEONCAVALLO

I Pagliacci: Excerpt (Prologue)

Berlin   Berlin RO   LP: DG LPM 18 700/SLPM 138 700
April 1961   Fricsay   LP: DG 135 008

LILIUS

Tua Jesu delictio, duet

London   Baker   LP: HMV ASD 2710
February 1970   Heath, cello
                     Malcolm, harpsichord

Der Alpenjäger (Es donnern die Höh'n, es zittert der Steg)

Berlin November 1961	Demus	LP: DG LPM 18 793/SLPM 138 793
Berlin November 1979- January 1981	Barenboim	LP: DG 2740 254

Anfangs wollt' ich fast verzagen

Berlin November 1979- January 1981	Barenboim	LP: DG 2740 254

Angiolin dal biondo crin

Berlin November 1979- January 1981	Barenboim	LP: DG 2740 254

Arbeiterchor

Amsterdam October 1989	Netherlands Chamber Choir Jansen	CD: Globus GLO 5070

Benedetto sia 'l giorno /Sonetti di Petrarca

Berlin November 1961	Demus	LP: DG LPM 18 793/SLPM 138 793 LP: DG 2530 332
Berlin November 1979- January 1981	Barenboim	LP: DG 2740 254

Blume und Duft (Im Frühlings-Heiligtume)

Berlin November 1961	Demus	LP: DG LPM 18 793/SLPM 138 793
Berlin November 1979- January 1981	Barenboim	LP: DG 2740 254

Sankt Christoph

Amsterdam October 1989	Netherlands Chamber Choir Jansen	CD: Globus GLO 5070

Liszt Lieder/continued

Comment, disaient-ils

| Berlin
November 1979-
January 1981 | Barenboim | LP: DG 2740 254 |

Der du von dem Himmel bist

| Berlin
November 1979-
January 1981 | Barenboim | LP: DG 2740 254 |

Die drei Zigeuner (Drei Zigeuner fand ich einmal)

| Berlin
November 1961 | Demus | LP: DG LPM 18 793/SLPM 138 793 |
| Berlin
November 1979-
January 1981 | Barenboim | LP: DG 2740 254 |

Du bist wie eine Blume

| Berlin
November 1979-
January 1981 | Barenboim | LP: DG 2740 254 |

Enfant, si j'étais roi

| Berlin
November 1979-
January 1981 | Barenboim | LP: DG 2740 254 |

Es muss ein Wunderbares sein

| Berlin
November 1961 | Demus | LP: DG LPM 18 793/SLPM 138 793
LP: DG 135 026 |
| Berlin
November 1979-
January 1981 | Barenboim | LP: DG 2740 254 |

Es rauschen die Winde

| Berlin
March 1971 | Reimann | LP: EMI 1C 065 02674/EX 29 04293
LP: EMI 1C 161 02673-02677 |
| Berlin
November 1979-
January 1981 | Barenboim | LP: DG 2740 254 |

Liszt Lieder/continued

Es war einmal ein König

Amsterdam	Netherlands	CD: Globus GLO 5070
October 1989	Chamber Choir	
	Jansen	

Ein Fichtenbaum steht einsam

Berlin	Barenboim	LP: DG 2740 254
November 1979-		
January 1981		

Der Fischerknabe (Es lächelt der See, er ladet zum Bade)

Berlin	Barenboim	LP: DG 2740 254
November 1979-		
January 1981		

Gastibelza

Berlin	Barenboim	LP: DG 2740 254
November 1979-		
January 1981		

Gestorben war ich

Berlin	Barenboim	LP: DG 2740 254
November 1979-		
January 1981		

Der Hirt (Ihr Matten, lebt wohl)

Berlin	Barenboim	LP: DG 2740 254
November 1979-		
January 1981		

Hohe Liebe (In Liebesarmen ruht ihr trunken)

Berlin	Barenboim	LP: DG 2740 254
November 1979-		
January 1981		

I vidi in terra/Sonetti di Petrarca

| Berlin | Demus | LP: DG LPM 18 793/SLPM 138 793 |
| November 1961 | | LP: DG 2530 332 |

Berlin	Barenboim	LP: DG 2740 254
November 1979-		
January 1981		

Ich möchte hingeh'n

Berlin   Barenboim   LP: DG 2740 254
November 1979-
January 1981

Ihr Glocken von Marling

Berlin   Demus   LP: DG LPM 18 793/SLPM 138 793
November 1961

Berlin   Barenboim   LP: DG 2740 254
November 1979-
January 1981

Im Rhein, im schönen Strome

Berlin   Barenboim   LP: DG 2740 254
November 1979-
January 1981

In Liebeslust

Berlin   Barenboim   LP: DG 2740 254
November 1979-
January 1981

Lasst mich ruhen

Berlin   Barenboim   LP: DG 2740 254
November 1979-
January 1981

O lieb', so lang du lieben kannst

Berlin   Barenboim   LP: DG 2740 254
November 1979-
January 1981

Die Loreley (Ich weiss nicht, was soll's bedeuten)

Berlin   Barenboim   LP: DG 2740 254
November 1979-
January 1981

Morgens steh' ich auf und frage

Berlin   Barenboim   LP: DG 2740 254
November 1979-
January 1981

Liszt Lieder/continued

Oh, quand je dors

Berlin November 1961	Demus	LP: DG LPM 18 793/SLPM 138 793
Berlin November 1979- January 1981	Barenboim	LP: DG 2740 254

Pace non trovo/Sonetti di Petrarca

Berlin November 1961	Demus	LP: DG LPM 18 793/SLPM 138 793 LP: DG 2530 332
Berlin November 1979- January 1981	Barenboim	LP: DG 2740 254

Psalm 129 (De profundis)

Amsterdam October 1989	Jansen	CD: Globus GLO 5070

Qui Mariam absolvisti

Amsterdam October 1989	Netherlands Chamber Choir Jansen	CD: Globus GLO 5070

Rosario

Amsterdam October 1989	Netherlands Chamber Choir	CD: Globus GLO 5070

Schwebe, schwebe, blaues Auge

Berlin November 1979- January 1981	Barenboim	LP: DG 2740 254

Die Seligkeiten

Amsterdam October 1989	Netherlands Chamber Choir	CD: Globus GLO 5070

S'il est un charmant gazon

Berlin November 1979- January 1981	Barenboim	LP: DG 2740 254

Die stille Wasserrose

Berlin   Barenboim   LP: DG 2740 254
November 1979-
January 1981

Des Tages laute Stimmen schweigen

Berlin   Barenboim   LP: DG 2740 254
November 1979-
January 1981

La tombe et la rose (La tombe dit à la rose)

Berlin   Barenboim   LP: DG 2740 254
November 1979-
January 1981

Ständchen (Kling leise, mein Lied)

Berlin   Reimann   LP: EMI 1C 065 02674/
March 1971   1C 161 02673-02677

Berlin   Barenboim   LP: DG 2740 254
November 1979-
January 1981

Der traurige Mönch (In Schweden steht ein grauer Turm)

Berlin   Barenboim   LP: DG 2740 254
November 1979-
January 1981

Tristesse (J'ai perdu ma force et ma vie)

Berlin   Demus   LP: DG LPM 18 793/SLPM 138 793
November 1961

Berlin   Barenboim   LP: DG 2740 254
November 1979-
January 1981

Ueber allen Gipfeln

Berlin   Reimann   LP: EMI 1C 065 02674/
March 1971   1C 161 02673-02677

Berlin   Barenboim   LP: DG 2740 254
November 1979-
January 1981

Liszt Lieder/concluded

Die Vätergruft (Es ging wohl über die Heide)

| Berlin
November 1961 | Demus | LP: DG LPM 18 793/SLPM 138 793 |
| Berlin
November 1979-
January 1981 | Barenboim | LP: DG 2740 254 |

Vergiftet sind meine Lieder

| Berlin
November 1961 | Demus | LP: DG LPM 18 793/SLPM 138 793 |
| Berlin
November 1979-
January 1981 | Barenboim | LP: DG 2740 254 |

Via crucis

| Berlin
September 1984 | Berlin Radio
Choir
Reimann | CD: Schwann Musica Sacra AMS 3553 |

Le vieux vagabond (Dans ce fossé cessons de vivre)

| Berlin
November 1979-
January 1981 | Barenboim | LP: DG 2740 254 |

Wer nie sein Brot mit Tränen ass

| Berlin
November 1979-
January 1981 | Barenboim | LP: DG 2740 254 |

Wie singt die Lerche schön

| Berlin
November 1979-
January 1981 | Barenboim | LP: DG 2740 254 |

Wieder möcht' ich dir begegnen

| Berlin
March 1971 | Reimann | LP: EMI 1C 065 02674/
1C 161 02673-02677 |
| Berlin
November 1979-
January 1981 | Barenboim | LP: DG 2740 254 |

At the time of going to press DG announces the issue on CD of
Fischer-Dieskau's Liszt song recordings with Barenboim: catalogue
number 447 5082

LLOYD

Annette

Munich	Klöcker, clarinet	LP: Orfeo S153 861A
August 1983	Wallendorf, horn	CD: Orfeo C153 861A
	Höll	

LOEWE

Der alte Goethe (Als ich ein junger Geselle war)

Berlin	Höll	CD: Teldec 843 753/4509 974582
1987		

Archibald Douglas (Ich hab' es getragen sieben Jahr')

Berlin	Moore	LP: EMI ASD 2423/1C 063 00388
1967		LP: EMI E 91665/STE 91665

Der Asra

Berlin	Höll	CD: Teldec 843 753/4509 974582
1987		

Bauernregel (Im Sommer auch ein Liebchen dir)

Berlin	Höll	CD: Teldec 843 753/4509 974582
1967		

Busslied

Berlin	Demus	LP: DG 2531 376
November 1979		

Canzonette

Berlin	Demus	LP: DG 2530 052/2535 214/2726 056
November 1969		

Die drei Lieder (In der hohen Hall' sass König Heinrich)

Munich	Demus	LP: DG 139 416/2726 056
July 1968		

Das dunkle Auge

Berlin	Höll	CD: Teldec 853 753/4509 974582
1987		

Loewe Lieder and Ballads/continued

Edward (Dein Schwert, wie ist's von Blut so rot?)

Berlin 1967	Moore	LP: EMI ASD 2423/1C 063 00388 LP: EMI E 91665/STE 91665 CD: EMI CZS 568 5092
Berlin November 1979	Demus	LP: DG 2531 376

Elvershöh

Munich July 1968	Demus	LP: DG 139 416/2726 056

Erlkönig (Wer reitet so spät durch Nacht und Wind?)

London 1952	Moore	78: HMV DA 5524 45: HMV 7ER 5044
Berlin 1967	Moore	LP: EMI ASD 2423/1C 063 00388 LP: EMI E 91665/STE 91665 CD: EMI CZS 568 5092
Berlin November 1979	Demus	LP: DG 2531 376

Fredericus rex (Fredericus rex, unser König und Herr)

Berlin 1987	Höll	CD: Teldec 843 753/4509 974582

Freibeuter

Berlin November 1969	Demus	LP: DG 2530 052/2535 214/2726 056

Frühzeitiger Frühling

Berlin November 1969	Demus	LP: DG 2530 052/2535 214/2726 056

Der gefangene Admiral

Berlin 1987	Höll	CD: Teldec 843 753/4509 974582

Der getreue Eckhart (O wären wir weiter)

Berlin November 1969	Demus	LP: DG 2530 052/2535 214/2726 056

Gottes ist der Orient

Berlin November 1969	Demus	LP: DG 2530 052/2535 214/2726 056

Graf Eberstein (Zu Speier im Saale)

| Berlin
1987 | Höll | CD: Teldec 843 753/4509 974582 |

Die Gruft der Liebenden (Da wo des Tajo grünlich blauer Strom)

| Munich
July 1968 | Demus | LP: DG 139 416/2726 056 |

Gruss vom Meere (Sei mir gegrüsst in deiner Pracht)

| Berlin
1987 | Höll | CD: Teldec 843 753/4509 974582 |

Gutmann und Gutweib (Und morgen fällt Sankt Martins Fest)

| Berlin
November 1969 | Demus | LP: DG 2530 052/2535 214/2726 056 |

Der heilige Franziskus

| Munich
July 1968 | Demus | LP: DG 139 416/2726 056 |

Heinrich der Vogler (Herr Heinrich sitzt am Vogelherd)

| Munich
July 1968 | Demus | LP: DG 139 416/2726 056 |

Herr Oluf (Herr Oluf reitet spät und weit)

| Berlin
1967 | Moore | LP: EMI ASD 2423/1C 063 00388
LP: EMI E 91665/STE 91665
CD: EMI CZS 568 5092 |
| Berlin
November 1979 | Demus | LP: DG 2531 376 |

Hinkende Jamben (Ein Liebchen hatt' ich)

| Berlin
November 1979 | Demus | LP: DG 2531 375 |

Der Hirten Lied am Krippelein

| Berlin
November 1970 | Demus | LP: DG 2530 219 |
| Berlin
November 1979 | Demus | LP: DG 2531 376 |

Loewe Lieder and Ballads/continued

Hochzeitlied

Munich July 1968	Demus	LP: DG 139 416/2726 056

Ich bin ein guter Hirte

Berlin 1987	Höll	CD: Teldec 843 753/4509 974582

Ich denke dein

Berlin November 1969	Demus	LP: DG 2530 052/2535 214/2726 056

Im Vorübergehen

Berlin November 1969	Demus	LP: DG 2530 052/2535 214/2726 056

Jordans Ufer

Berlin 1987	Höll	CD: Teldec 843 753/4509 974582

Kleiner Haushalt (Einen Haushalt klein und fein)

Berlin 1967	Moore	LP: EMI ASD 2423/1C 063 00388 LP: EMI E 91665/STE 91665 CD: EMI CZS 568 5092
Berlin November 1979	Demus	LP: DG 2531 376

Lynceus der Türmer auf Fausts Sternwarte singend

Berlin November 1969	Demus	LP: DG 2530 052/2535 214/2726 056

Meeresleuchten (Wieviel Sonnenstrahlen fielen goldenschwer)

Berlin November 1979	Demus	LP: DG 2531 376

Mein Geist ist trüb

Berlin 1987	Höll	CD: Teldec 843 753/4509 974582

Der Mohrenfürst auf der Messe

Berlin 1967	Moore	LP: EMI ASD 2423/1C 063 00388 LP: EMI E 91665/STE 91665 CD: EMI CZS 568 5092
Berlin November 1979	Demus	LP: DG 2531 376

Der Nöck (Es tönt des Nöcken Harfenschall)

Munich July 1968	Demus	LP: DG 139 416/2726 056

Odins Meeresritt (Meister Olof, der Schmied auf Helgoland)

Munich July 1968	Demus	LP: DG 139 416/2726 052

Prinz Eugen (Zelte, Posten, Wer-da-Rufer)

Munich July 1968	Demus	LP: DG 139 416/2726 056

Der selt'ne Beter (Im Abendgolde glänzt zu Bärenburg das Schloss)

Berlin 1987	Höll	CD: Teldec 843 753/4509 974582

Der Schatzgräber (Arm am Beutel, krank am Herzen)

Berlin 1967	Moore	LP: EMI ASD 2423/1C 063 00388 LP: EMI E 91665/STE 91665 CD: EMI CZS 568 5092
Berlin November 1979	Demus	LP: DG 2531 376

Die Sonne der Schlaflosen

Berlin 1987	Höll	CD: Teldec 843 753/4509 974582

Süsses Begräbnis (Schäferin, ach wie haben sie dich so süss begraben)

Berlin 1967	Moore	LP: EMI ASD 2423/1C 063 00388 LP: EMI E 91665/STE 91665
Berlin November 1979	Demus	LP: DG 2531 376

Loewe Lieder and Ballads/continued

Tom der Reimer (Der Reimer Thomas lag am Bach)

Berlin 1948	L.Stein	78: Electrola number uncertain See Lieder on Record, ed. Blyth page 100 (Cambridge University Press 1986)
Berlin 1967	Moore	LP: EMI ASD 2423/1C 063 00388 LP: EMI E 91665/STE 91665 CD: EMI CZS 568 5092

Der Totentanz (Der Türmer, der schaut zu mitten der Nacht)

Berlin November 1969	Demus	LP: DG 2530 052/2535 214/2726 056

Trommel-Ständchen

Munich July 1968	Demus	LP: DG 139 416/2726 056

Turmwächter Lynceus zu den Füssen der Helena

Berlin November 1969	Demus	LP: DG 2530 052/2535 214/2726 056

Die Ueberfahrt (Ueber diesen Strom vor Jahren)

Berlin 1987	Höll	CD: Teldec 843 753/4509 974582

Die Uhr (Ich trage, wo ich gehe)

Berlin 1948	L.Stein	78: Electrola number uncertain See Lieder on Record, ed. Blyth page 100 (Cambridge University Press 1986)
Munich July 1968	Demus	LP: DG 139 416/2726 056

Die wandelnde Glocke (Es war ein Kind, das wollte nie)

Berlin November 1969	Demus	LP: DG 2530 052/2535 214/2726 056

Wandrers Nachtlied

Berlin November 1969	Demus	LP: DG 2530 052/2535 214/2726 056

Loewe Lieder and Ballads/concluded

Der Weichdorn

Berlin   Höll   CD: Teldec 843 753/4509 974582
1987

Wenn alle untreu werden

Munich   Demus   LP: DG 2531 376
November 1979

Wenn der Blüten Frühlingsregen

Berlin   Demus   LP: DG 2530 052/2535 214/2726 056
November 1969

Wenn ich ihn nur habe

Berlin   Demus   LP: DG 2531 376
November 1979

Der Wirtin Töchterlein (Es zogen drei Burschen wohl über den Rhein)

Berlin   Höll   CD: Teldec 843 753/4509 974582
1987

Das Wunder auf der Flucht

Berlin   Höll   CD: Teldec 843 753/4509 974582
1987

Der Zauberlehrling (Hat der alte Hexenmeister)

Berlin   Demus   LP: DG 2530 052/2535/2726 056
November 1969

LORTZING

Undine: Excerpt (Nun ist's vollbracht/O kehr' zurück)

Berlin	Streich	78: HMV DB 11550
May 1953	BPO	45: Electrola 7RW 501
	Schüchter	LP: EMI 1C 047 28181M

Der Wildschütz: Excerpt (Wie freundlich strahlt/Heiterkeit und Fröhlichkeit)

Berlin	BPO	LP: Electrola
December 1955	Schüchter	LP: EMI EX 29 04323

Zar und Zimmermann, scenes

Bamberg	Hallstein,	LP: DG 136 432/2537 004
September 1966	Wunderlich, Lenz,	CD: DG 445 0472
	Kohn	445 0472 contains additional
	Bavarian Radio	numbers not on the original
	Chorus	issue
	Bamberg SO	
	Gierster	

Zar und Zimmermann: Excerpt (Sonst spielt' ich mit Zepter und Krone)

Berlin	BPO	LP: Electrola
December 1955	Schüchter	LP: EMI EX 29 04323

LOTHAR

Musik des Einsamen, song-cycle

Berlin	Chamber Ensemble	LP: Electrola SME 91660
1967	Lothar	

LUTOSLAWSKI

Les espaces du sommeil

Berlin	BPO	CD: Philips 416 3872
1986	Lutoslawski	

MAHLER

Symphony No 8 "Symphony of a Thousand"

Munich June 1970	Parts of baritone soloist and Pater Ecstaticus Arroyo, Mathis, Spoorenberg, Hamari, Procter, Grobe, Crass Choruses Bavarian RO Kubelik	LP: DG 2720 063/2726 053 CD: DG 419 4332/429 0422/447 5292

Das Lied von der Erde

London October 1959	Dickie Philharmonia Kletzki	LP: HMV ALP 1773-1774/ASD 351-352 LP: EMI 30165/EMX 41 20731 CD: EMI CZS 762 7072 Excerpts LP: EMI ASD 2549/EX 29 04353
Bamberg April 1964	Wunderlich Bamberg SO Keilberth	Unpublished private recording
Vienna June 1964	Wunderlich VSO Keilberth	Unpublished radio broadcast
Vienna April 1966	King VPO Bernstein	LP: Decca MET 331/SET 331/JB 13 CD: Decca 417 7832 Excerpts LP: Decca GRV 7 CD: Decca 440 4082

Kindertotenlieder: Nun will die Sonn' so hell aufgehn; Nun seh' ich wohl, warum so dunkle Flammen; Wenn dein Mütterlein tritt zur Tür herein; Oft denk' ich, sie sind nur ausgegangen; In diesem Wetter, in diesem Braus

Berlin June 1955	BPO Kempe	LP: HMV BLP 1081/1C 063 00898 CD: EMI CDC 747 6572
Berlin 1960	Berlin RO Maazel	Unpublished video recording
Salzburg August 1962	BPO Böhm	LP: Melodram MEL 712
Berlin April 1963	BPO Böhm	LP: DG LPM 18 879/SLPM 138 879 LP: DG 2531 375/2726 066 LP: DG 2543 182/413 6311 CD: DG 415 1912

Lieder eines fahrenden Gesellen: Wenn mein Schatz Hochzeit macht; Ging heut'
morgen übers Feld; Ich hab' ein glühend Messer; Die zwei blauen Augen von
meinem Schatz

Salzburg August 1951	VPO Furtwängler	LP: Cetra LO 510/FE 29 LP: Rococo 2105 LP: Discocorp IGI 382/RR 314 LP: German Furtwängler Society F667.497-667.498 CD: Priceless D 18355 CD: Cetra CDE 1045 CD: Palette PAL 1075 CD: Virtuoso 269 7392 CD: Orfeo C336 931B
London June 1952	Philharmonia Furtwängler	LP: HMV ALP 1270/XLP 30044 LP: Electrola E 90106/SHZE 338 LP: EMI 1C 063 00898/EX 29 04353 LP: Toshiba WF 60032/GR 70041 CD: EMI CDH 747 6572
New York November 1968	Bernstein	CD: Sony SM2K 47170 CD: Myto MCD 89008
Munich December 1968	Bavarian RO Kubelik	LP: DG 2707 056/2530 630/2726 064 CD: DG 415 1912
Berlin February 1978	Barenboim	LP: EMI SLS 5173 LP: EMI 1C 165 03446-03448
Berlin April 1989	BPO Barenboim	CD: Sony SK 44935

Ablösung im Sommer/Lieder und Gesänge aus der Jugendzeit (Kukuk hat sich zu
Tode gefallen)

Berlin June 1959	Engel	LP: DG LPM 18 590/SLPM 138 058
New York November 1968	Bernstein	LP: CBS 72973 CD: Sony SM2K 47170/M2K 42196 CD: Myto MCD 89008
Salzburg August 1976	Sawallisch	CD: Orfeo C333 931B/C339 930T
Berlin February 1978	Barenboim	LP: EMI SLS 5173 LP: EMI 1C 165 03446-03448

Des Antonius von Padua Fischpredigt/Des Knaben Wunderhorn (Antonius zur Predigt die Kirche find't ledig)

Berlin June 1959	Engel	LP: DG LPM 18 590/SLPM 138 058
London March 1968	LSO Szell	LP: EMI SAN 218/ASD 143 4424 CD: EMI CDC 747 2772
Salzburg August 1976	Sawallisch	CD: Orfeo C333 931B/C339 930T
Berlin February 1978	Barenboim	LP: EMI SLS 5173 LP: EMI 1C 165 03446-03448
Berlin April 1989	BPO Barenboim	CD: Sony SK 44935

Aus, aus/Lieder und Gesänge aus der Jugendzeit (Heute marschieren wir)

Berlin February 1978	Barenboim	LP: EMI SLS 5173 LP: EMI 1C 165 03446-03448

Blicke mir nicht in die Lieder/Rückert-Lieder

Berlin June 1959	Engel	LP: DG LPM 18 590/SLPM 138 058
Berlin April 1963	BPO Böhm	LP: DG LPM 18 879/SLPM 138 879 LP: DG 2726 065/2531 375/2543 182 CD: DG 415 1912
Salzburg August 1967	VPO Mehta	CD: Orfeo C336 931B
New York November 1968	Bernstein	LP: CBS 72973 CD: Sony SM2K 47170/M2K 42196 CD: Myto MCD 89008
Salzburg August 1976	Sawallisch	CD: Orfeo C333 931B/C339 930T
Berlin February 1978	Barenboim	LP: EMI SLS 5173 LP: EMI 1C 165 03446-03448 CD: EMI CDC 747 6572

Erinnerung/Lieder und Gesänge aus der Jugendzeit (Es wecket meine Liebe)

New York November 1968	Bernstein	CD: Sony SM2K 47170 CD: Myto MCD 89008
Berlin February 1978	Barenboim	LP: EMI SLS 5173 LP: EMI 1C 165 03446-03448

Mahler Lieder/continued

Frühlingsmorgen/Lieder und Gesänge aus der Jugendzeit (Es klopft an das Fenster der Lindenbaum)

New York   Bernstein   CD: Sony SM2K 47170
November 1968   CD: Myto MCD 89008

Salzburg   Sawallisch   CD: Orfeo C333 931B/C339 930T
August 1976

Berlin   Barenboim   LP: EMI SLS 5173
February 1978   LP: EMI 1C 165 03466-03448

Ging heut' morgen übers Feld/Lieder eines fahrenden Gesellen
See Lieder eines fahrenden Gesellen

Hans und Grete/Lieder und Gesänge aus der Jugendzeit (Ringel Ringel Reihn)

Berlin   Barenboim   LP: EMI SLS 5173
February 1978   LP: EMI 1C 165 03446-03448

Ich atmet' einen linden Duft/Rückert-Lieder

Berlin   Engel   LP: DG LPM 18 590/SLPM 138 058
June 1959

Berlin   BPO   LP: DG LPM 18 879/SLPM 138 879
April 1963   Böhm   LP: DG 2726 065/2531 375/2543 182
                                     CD: DG 415 1912

Salzburg   VPO   CD: Orfeo C336 931B
August 1967   Mehta

New York   Bernstein   LP: CBS 72973
November 1968   CD: Sony SM2K 47170/M2K 42196
                                     CD: Myto MCD 89008

Salzburg   Sawallisch   CD: Orfeo C333 931B/C339 930T
August 1976

Berlin   Barenboim   LP: EMI SLS 5173
February 1978   LP: EMI 1C 165 03446-03448
                                     CD: EMI CDC 747 6572

Ich bin der Welt abhanden gekommen/Rückert-Lieder

Berlin June 1959	Engel	LP: DG LPM 18 590/SLPM 138 058
Berlin April 1963	BPO Böhm	LP: DG LPM 18 879/SLPM 138 879 LP: DG 2726 065/2531 375/2543 182 CD: DG 415 1912
Salzburg August 1967	VPO Mehta	CD: Orfeo C336 931B
New York November 1968	Bernstein	LP: CBS 72973 CD: Sony SM2K 47170/M2K 42196 CD: Myto MCD 89008
Berlin February 1978	Barenboim	LP: EMI SLS 5173/1C 165 03446-03448 LP: EMI CDC 747 6572

Ich ging mit Lust durch einen grünen Wald/Lieder und Gesänge aus der Jugendzeit

New York November 1968	Bernstein	CD: Sony SM2K 47170 CD: Myto MCD 89008
Berlin February 1978	Barenboim	LP: EMI SLS 5173 LP: EMI 1C 165 03446-03448

Ich hab' ein glühend Messer/Lieder eines fahrenden Gesellen
See Lieder eines fahrenden Gesellen

In diesem Wetter, in diesem Braus/Kindertotenlieder
See Kindertotenlieder

Das irdische Leben/Des Knaben Wunderhorn (Mutter, ach Mutter, es hungert mich)

Salzburg August 1976	Sawallisch	CD: Orfeo C339 931B/C339 930T
Berlin February 1978	Barenboim	LP: EMI SLS 5173 LP: EMI 1C 165 03446-03448
Berlin April 1989	BPO Barenboim	CD: Sony SK 44935

Liebst du um Schönheit/Rückert-Lieder

Salzburg August 1967	VPO Mehta	CD: Orfeo C336 931B
Berlin February 1978	Barenboim	LP: EMI SLS 5173/1C 165 03446-03448 CD: EMI CDC 747 6572

Lied des Verfolgten im Turm/Des Knaben Wunderhorn (Die Gedanken sind frei)

London March 1968	Schwarzkopf LSO Szell	LP: EMI SAN 218/ASD 143 4424 CD: EMI DCD 747 2772
Salzburg August 1976	Sawallisch	CD: Orfeo C333 931B/C339 930T
Berlin February 1978	Barenboim	LP: EMI SLS 5173 LP: EMI 1C 165 03446-03448
Berlin April 1989	BPO Barenboim	CD: Sony SK 44935

Lob des hohen Verstandes/Des Knaben Wunderhorn (Einstmals in einem tiefen Tal)

Berlin February 1978	Barenboim	LP: EMI SLS 5173 LP: EMI 1C 165 03446-03448
Berlin April 1989	BPO Barenboim	CD: Sony SK 44935

Nicht wiedersehen!/Lieder und Gesänge aus der Jugendzeit (Und nun ade, mein herzallerliebster Schatz)

New York November 1968	Bernstein	LP: CBS 72973 CD: Sony SM2K 47170/M2K 42196 CD: Myto MCD 89008
Salzburg August 1976	Sawallisch	CD: Orfeo C333 931B/C339 930T
Berlin February 1978	Barenboim	LP: EMI SLS 5173 LP: EMI 1C 165 03446-03448

Nun will die Sonn' so hell aufgehn/Kindertotenlieder
See Kindertotenlieder
Nun seh' ich wohl, warum so dunkle Flammen/Kindertotenlieder
See Kindertotenlieder
Oft denk' ich, sie sind nur ausgegangen/Kindertotenlieder
See Kindertotenlieder

Phantasie aus Don Juan/Lieder und Gesänge aus der Jugendzeit (Das Mägdlein trat aus dem Fischerhaus)

Berlin June 1959	Engel	LP: DG LPM 18 590/SLPM 138 058
New York November 1968	Bernstein	LP: CBS 72973 CD: Sony SM2K 47170/M2K 42196 CD: Myto MCD 89008
Salzburg August 1976	Sawallisch	CD: Orfeo C333 931B/C339 930T
Berlin February 1978	Barenboim	LP: EMI SLS 5173 LP: EMI 1C 165 03446-03448

Mahler Lieder/continued

Revelge/Des Knaben Wunderhorn (Des Morgens zwischen drei'n und vieren)

London March 1968	LSO Szell	LP: EMI SAN 218/ASD 143 4424 CD: EMI CDC 747 2772
Salzburg August 1976	Sawallisch	CD: Orfeo C333 931B/C339 930T
Berlin February 1978	Barenboim	LP: EMI SLS 5173 LP: EMI 1C 165 03446-03448

Rheinlegendchen/Des Knaben Wunderhorn (Bald gras' ich am Neckar)

Salzburg August 1976	Sawallisch	CD: Orfeo C333 931B/C339 930T
Berlin February 1978	Barenboim	LP: EMI SLS 5173 LP: EMI 1C 165 03446-03448
Berlin April 1989	BPO Barenboim	CD: Sony SK 44935

Scheiden und Meiden/Lieder und Gesänge aus der Jugendzeit (Es ritten drei Ritter zum Tore hinaus)

New York November 1968	Bernstein	LP: CBS 72973 CD: Sony SM2K 47170/M2K 42196 CD: Myto MCD 89008
Salzburg August 1976	Sawallisch	CD: Orfeo C333 931B/C339 930T
Berlin February 1978	Barenboim	LP: EMI SLS 5173 LP: EMI 1C 165 03446-03448

Der Schildwache Nachtlied/Des Knaben Wunderhorn (Ich kann und mag nicht fröhlich sein)

London March 1968	Schwarzkopf LSO Szell	LP: EMI SAN 218/ASD 143 4424 CD: EMI CDC 747 2772
Salzburg August 1976	Sawallisch	CD: Oreo C333 931B/C339 930T
Berlin February 1978	Barenboim	LP: EMI SLS 5173 LP: EMI 1C 165 03446-03448
Berlin April 1989	BPO Barenboim	CD: Sony SK 44935

Mahler Lieder/continued

Selbstgefühl/Lieder und Gesänge aus der Jugendzeit (Ich weiss nicht, wie mir ist

Berlin June 1959	Engel	LP: DG LPM 18 590/SLPM 138 058
New York November 1968	Bernstein	LP: CBS 72973 LP: Sony SM2K 47170/M2K 42196 CD: Myto MCD 89008
Salzburg August 1976	Sawallisch	CD: Orfeo C333 931B/C339 930T
Berlin February 1978	Barenboim	LP: EMI SLS 5173 LP: EMI 1C 165 03446-03448

Serenade aus Don Juan/Lieder und Gesänge aus der Jugendzeit (Ist's dein Wille, süsse Maid)

New York November 1968	Bernstein	CD: Sony SM2K 47170 CD: Myto MCD 89008
Berlin February 1978	Barenboim	LP: EMI SLS 5173 LP: EMI 1C 165 03446-03448

Starke Einbildungskraft/Lieder und Gesänge aus der Jugendzeit (Hast gesagt, du willst mich nehmen)

Berlin February 1978	Barenboim	LP: EMI SLS 5173 LP: EMI 1C 165 03446-03448

Der Tambourg'sell/Des Knaben Wunderhorn (Ich armer Tambourg'sell)

London March 1968	LSO Szell	LP: EMI SAN 218/ASD 143 4424 CD: EMI CDC 747 2772
Salzburg August 1976	Sawallisch	CD: Orfeo C333 931B/C339 930T
Berlin February 1978	Barenboim	LP: EMI SLS 5173 LP: EMI 1C 165 03446-03448
Berlin April 1989	BPO Barenboim	CD: Sony SK 44935

Trost im Unglück/Des Knaben Wunderhorn (Wohlan! Die Zeit ist kommen!)

London March 1968	Schwarzkopf LSO Szell	LP: EMI SAN 218/ASD 143 4424 CD: EMI CDC 747 2772
Berlin February 1978	Barenboim	LP: EMI SLS 5173 LP: EMI 1C 165 03446-03448
Berlin April 1989	BPO Barenboim	CD: Sony SK 44935

Um Mitternacht/Rückert-Lieder

Berlin April 1963	BPO Böhm	LP: DG LPM 18 879/SLPM 138 879 LP: DG 2726 065/2531 375/2543 182 CD: DG 415 1912
Salzburg August 1967	VPO Mehta	CD: Orfeo C336 931B
New York November 1968	Bernstein	LP: CBS 72973 CD: Sony SM2K 47170/M2K 42196 CD: Myto MCD 89008
Berlin February 1978	Barenboim	LP: EMI SLS 5173/1C 165 03446-03448 CD: EMI CDC 747 6572

Um schlimme Kinder artig zu machen/Lieder und Gesänge aus der Jugendzeit (Es kam ein Herr zum Schlösseli)

New York November 1968	Bernstein	CD: Sony SM2K 47170 CD: Myto MCD 89008
Salzburg August 1976	Sawallisch	CD: Orfeo C333 931B/C339 930T
Berlin February 1978	Barenboim	LP: EMI SLS 5173 LP: EMI 1C 165 03446-03448

Verlor'ne Müh'/Des Knaben Wunderhorn (Büble, wir wollen aussegehe!)

London March 1968	Schwarzkopf LSO Szell	LP: EMI SAN 218/ASD 143 4424 CD: EMI CDC 747 2772
Berlin February 1978	Barenboim	LP: EMI SLS 5173 LP: EMI 1C 165 03446-03448
Berlin April 1989	BPO Barenboim	CD: Sony SK 44935

Wenn mein Schatz Hochzeit macht/Lieder eines fahrenden Gesellen
See Lieder eines fahrenden Gesellen

Wenn dein Mütterlein tritt zur Tür herein/Kindertotenlieder
See Kindertotenlieder

Wer hat dies Liedlein erdacht?/Des Knaben Wunderhorn (Dort oben am Berg in dem
hohen Haus)

London March 1968	LSO Szell	LP: EMI SAN 218/ASD 143 4424 CD: EMI CDC 747 2772
Salzburg August 1976	Sawallisch	CD: Orfeo C333 931B/C339 930T
Berlin February 1978	Barenboim	LP: EMI SLS 5173 LP: EMI 1C 165 03446-03448
Berlin April 1989	BPO Barenboim	CD: Sony SK 44935

Wo die schönen Trompeten blasen/Des Knaben Wunderhorn (Wer ist denn draussen
und wer klopfet an?)

London March 1968	Schwarzkopf LSO Szell	LP: EMI SAN 218/ASD 143 4424 CD: EMI CDC 747 2772
Berlin May 1970	Reutter	LP: EMI 1C 065 02676/ 1C 161 02673-02677
Salzburg August 1976	Sawallisch	CD: Orfeo C333 931B/C339 930T
Berlin February 1978	Barenboim	LP: EMI SLS 5173 LP: EMI 1C 165 03446-03448
Berlin April 1989	BPO Barenboim	CD: Sony SK 44935

Die zwei blauen Augen von meinem Schatz/Lieder eines fahrenden Gesellen
See Lieder eines fahrenden Gesellen

Zu Strassburg auf der Schanz'/Lieder und Gesänge aus der Jugendzeit

Berlin June 1959	Engel	LP: DG LPM 18 590/SLPM 138 058 LP: DG 135 026
New York November 1968	Bernstein	LP: CBS 72973 CD: Sony SM2K 47170/M2K 42196 CD: Myto MCD 89008
Salzburg August 1976	Sawallisch	CD: Orfeo C333 931B/C339 930T
Berlin February 1978	Barenboim	LP: EMI SLS 5173 LP: EMI 1C 165 03446-03448

MAINARDI

Songs: Uomo del mio tempo; Con una fronda di mirto

Berlin   Demus   LP: DG LPM 18 946/SLPM 138 946
May 1964

MARTIN

Monologe aus „Jedermann"

Geneva   Suisse Romande   CD: Cascavelle VEL 2001
March 1961   Orchestra
                    Ansermet

Berlin   BPO   LP: DG LPM 18 871/SLPM 138 871
May 1963   Martin   LP: DG 2530 630

Salzburg   Austrian RO   CD: Orfeo C336 931B
August 1983   Zender

Der Sturm, Fragmente

Berlin   BPO   LP: DG LPM 18 871/SLPM 138 871
May 1963   Martin

MASSENET

Que l'heure est donc brève

Berlin   Höll   LP: Teldec 643 754
April 1984   CD: Teldec 843 754/4509 974572

MATTHUS

Holofernes, Porträt für Bariton und Orchester

Leipzig   Gewandhaus-Orchester   LP: Eterna 827 698
November 1981   Masur   CD: Berlin Classics BC 20722

Nachtlieder für Bariton, Streichquartett und Harfe

Berlin   Cherubini Quartet   CD: EMI CDC 754 5202
December 1990   Graf, harp

MATTIESEN

Lieder: Herbstgefühl; Heimgang in der Frühe

Berlin   Reimann   LP: EMI 1C 065 02675/
May 1971   1C 161 02673-02677

MENDELSSOHN

Elijah

London   Jones, Baker   LP: EMI SLS 935/1C 149 00107-00109
July 1968   Gedda   Excerpts
                     Wandsworth and New   LP: EMI ASD 2549/EX 29 04353
                     Philharmonia Choirs LP: EMI 1C 063 00908
                     New Philharmonia   CD: EMI CDCFP 4532
                     Frühbeck de Burgos

Paulus

Düsseldorf   Donath, Schwarz,   LP: EMI 1C 157 30701-30703
October 1976-   Hollweg   CD: EMI CMS 764 0052
January 1977   Düsseldorf SO   Excerpt
                     and Chorus   LP: EMI EX 29 04353
                     Frühbeck de Burgos

Die beiden Pädagogen

Munich   Role of Dorfschul-   LP: EMI 1C 065 45416
1980   meister
                     Laki, Fuchs,
                     Hirte, Dallapozza
                     Bavarian Radio
                     Chorus & Orchestra
                     Wallberg

Die Heimkehr aus der Fremde

Munich   Role of Kauz   LP: EMI 1C 065 30741
1977   Donath, Schwarz,
                     Schreier, Kusche
                     Bavarian Radio
                     Chorus & Orchestra
                     Wallberg

Lieder: Allnächtlich im Traume; Altdeutsches Lied; An die Entfernte; Auf
der Wanderschaft; Bei der Wiege; Der Blumenkranz; Da lieg' ich unter den
Bäumen; Erntelied; Erster Verlust; Das erste Veilchen; Es lauschte das
Laub; 3 Frühlingslieder; Hexenlied; Hirtenlied; Jagdlied; 2 Minnelieder;
Der Mond; Neue Liebe; O Jugend; 2 Reiselieder; Schilflied; Schlafloser
Augen Leuchte; Tröstung; Wanderlied; Warnung vor dem Rhein; Wenn sich zwei
Herzen scheiden; Winterlied

Berlin	Sawallisch	LP: EMI SLS 805/1C 157 02180-02181
September 1970		LP: EMI 1C 193 02180-02181
		CD: EMI CMS 764 8272

Lieder: Der Verlassene; Ich weiss mir'n Mädchen; Mary's Dream; We've a
bonny wee flower; Minnelied im Mai; Pilgerspruch; Maienlied; Im Grünen;
Abendlied; Wartend; Im Frühling; Im Herbst; Frühlingsglaube; Das
Schilflein; Lieblingsplätzchen; Altdeutsches Frühlingslied; Minnelied;
Meerfahrt; Weiter rastlos; Der Blumenstrauss; Frühlingslied; Herbstlied;
Erntelied

Berlin	Höll	CD: Claves CD 50 9009
June 1989-		
March 1991		

Auf Flügeln des Gesanges

Berlin	Sawallisch	LP: EMI SLS 805/1C 157 02180-02181
September 1970		LP: EMI 1C 047 01247
		LP: EMI 1C 193 02180-02181
		CD: EMI CMS 764 8272

Gruss (Leise zieht durch mein Gemüt)

Berlin	Sawallisch	LP: EMI SLS 805/1C 157 02180-02181
September 1970		LP: EMI 1C 047 01247
		LP: EMI 1C 193 02180-02181
		CD: EMI CMS 764 8272

Morgengruss (Ueber die Berge steigt schon die Sonne)

Berlin	Sawallisch	LP: EMI SLS 805/1C 157 02180-02181
September 1970		LP: EMI 1C 193 02180-02181
		LP: EMI EX 29 04293
		CD: EMI CMS 764 8272

Nachtlied (Vergangen ist der lichte Tag)

Berlin	Sawallisch	LP: EMI SLS 805/1C 157 02180-02181
September 1970		LP: EMI 1C 193 02180-02181
		CD: EMI CMS 764 8272
Salzburg	Sawallisch	CD: Orfeo C185 891A/C339 930T
August 1975		

Mendelssohn Lieder/concluded

Pagenlied (Wenn die Sonne lieblich schiene)

Berlin September 1970	Sawallisch	LP: EMI SLS 805/1C 157 02180-02181 LP: EMI 1C 193 02180-02181 CD: EMI CMS 764 8272
Salzburg August 1975	Sawallisch	CD: Orfeo C185 891A/C339 930T

Scheidend (Wie so gelinde die Flut bewegt)

Berlin September 1970	Sawallisch	LP: EMI SLS 805/1C 157 02180-02181 LP: EMI 1C 193 02180-02181 LP: EMI EX 29 04293 CD: EMI CMS 764 8272

Venezianisches Gondellied (Wenn durch die Piazetta)

Berlin September 1970	Sawallisch	LP: EMI SLS 805/1C 157 02180-02181 LP: EMI 1C 193 02180-02181 LP: EMI EX 29 04292 CD: EMI CMS 764 8272

Volkslied (Es ist bestimmt in Gottes Rat)

Berlin September 1970	Sawallisch	LP: EMI SLS 805/1C 157 02180-02181 LP: EMI 1C 047 01247 LP: EMI 1C 193 02180-02181 CD: EMI CMS 764 8272

Das Waldschloss (Wo noch kein Wanderer gegangen)

Berlin September 1970	Sawallisch	LP: EMI SLS 805/1C 157 02180-02181 LP: EMI 1C 193 02180-02181 CD: EMI CMS 764 8272
Salzburg August 1975	Sawallisch	CD: Orfeo C185 891A/C339 930T

Duets: Abendlied; Ich wollt' meine Lieb'; Lied aus Ruy Blas; Wasserfahrt; Gruss

London February 1967	De los Angeles Moore	LP: EMI SAN 182-183/SLS 926/ASD 143 5941 CD: EMI CDC 749 2382/CDEMX 2233

Duets: Abschiedslied der Zugvögel; Herbstlied; Wie kann ich froh und lustig sein ich froh und lustig sein

London August 1969	Baker Barenboim	LP: EMI ASD 2553/1C 063 02041

Duet: Suleika und Hatem

London February 1967	De los Angeles Moore	EMI unpublished
London August 1969	Baker Barenboim	LP: EMI ASD 2553/1C 063 02041

MERGNER

Weihnachtslied

Berlin
November 1970

Demus

LP: DG 2530 219

MESSIAEN

Saint François d'Assise: Excerpt (Frères oiseaux, en tous temps et lieux)

Salzburg
August 1985

Austrian RO
Zagrosek

CD: Orfeo C335 931B

MEYERBEER

Lieder: Menschenfeindlich; Hör' ich das Liedchen klingen; Die Rose, die Lilie; Komm'; Der Garten des Herzens; Sie und ich; Sicilienne; Ständchen; Die Rosenblätter; Le chant du dimanche; Le poète mourant; Cantique du trappiste; Sarocco; Mina

Berlin
December 1974

Demus

LP: DG 2533 295

MILHAUD

Lamentation

Berlin
May 1970

Reutter

LP: EMI 1C 065 02676/
     1C 161 02673-02677
CD: EMI CZS 568 5092

MONTEVERDI

L'Orfeo

Munich
July 1983

This recording, planned with the participation of Fischer-Dieskau, either did not take place or it remains unpublished; the recording company was Orfeo

MOZART

Così fan tutte

Berlin December 1962 and April 1963	Role of Alfonso Seefried, Merriman, Köth, Häfliger, Prey RIAS Choir BPO Jochum	LP: DG LPM 18 861-18 863/ SLPM 138 861-138 863 LP: DG 2709 012/2728 010 Excerpts LP: DG LPM 18 792/SLPM 138 792 LP: DG LPEM 19 278/SLPEM 136 278 LP: DG 2535 300/2535 624 CD: Belart 450 1832
Salzburg July 1972	Role of Alfonso Janowitz, Grist, Fassbaender, Schreier, Prey Vienna Opera Chorus VPO/Böhm	CD: Foyer 2CF 2066 Excerpt CD: Orfeo C335 931B

Così fan tutte: Excerpt (Soave sia il vento)

London February 1967	Schwarzkopf, De los Angeles Moore	EMI unpublished

Don Giovanni

Berlin September 1958	Role of Giovanni Stader, Jurinac, Seefried, Häfliger, Kohn, Kreppel RIAS Choir Berlin RO Fricsay	LP: DG LPM 18 850-18 852/ SLPM 138 050-138 052 LP: DG 2711 006/2728 003/2730 014 CD: DG 437 3412 Excerpts LP: DG LPEM 19 380/SLPEM 139 380 LP: DG 135 004/135 008/2705 001
Berlin September 1961	Role of Giovanni Grümmer, Lorengar, Köth, Grobe, Berry, Greindl Deutsche Oper Chorus & Orchestra Fricsay Sung in German	Unpublished radio broadcast and video recording Opening performance of the re-built Deutsche Oper
Prague February and March 1967	Role of Giovanni Arroyo, Nilsson, Grist, Schreier, Flagello, Talvela Prague National Chorus & Orchestra Böhm	LP: DG 139 260-139 263/2711 006 LP: DG 2740 119/2740 108 LP: DG 2740 205/2740 222 CD: DG 429 8702/435 3942 Excerpts LP: DG 136 282/2537 014 CD: DG 445 0482/447 6782

Don Giovanni, Querschnitt

Berlin February 1963	Salemka, Watson, Streich, Häfliger, Berry Berlin RO/Löwlein Sung in German	LP: DG LPEM 19 415/SLPEM 136 415 LP: DG 2535 278/2535 627/2548 230 Excerpts LP: DG LPEM 19 456 LP: DG LPEM 19 460/SLPEM 136 460 CD: DG 447 8122

La finta giardiniera: Excerpt (Nach der Welschen Art)

Vienna October 1969	Vienna Haydn Orchestra Peters	LP: Decca SXL 6940/GRV 7

Le Nozze di Figaro

Salzburg July 1957	Role of Almaviva Schwarzkopf, Seefried, C.Ludwig, Kunz Vienna Opera Chorus VPO Böhm	LP: Melodram MEL 709 CD: Di Stefano GDS 31039 CD: Orfeo C296 923D Excerpts CD: Verona 27092-27094
Berlin September 1960	Stader, Seefried, Töpper, Capecchi RIAS Choir Berlin RO Fricsay	LP: DG LPM 18 697-18 699/ SLPM 138 697-138 699 LP: DG 2728 004/2730 014 CD: DG 437 6712 Excerpts LP: DG LPEM 19 272/SLPEM 136 272 LP: DG 135 040/2535 710
Salzburg July 1963	Güden, Sciutti, Lear, G.Evans Vienna Opera Chorus VPO Böhm	LP: Movimento musica 03.025 CD: Movimento musica 013.004
Tokyo October 1963	Grümmer, Köth, Mathis, Berry Deutsche Oper Chorus & Orchestra Böhm	CD: Canyon Classics (Japan) PCCL 00059
Berlin March 1968	Janowitz, Mathis, Troyanos, Prey Deutsche Oper Chorus & Orchestra Böhm	LP: DG 2711 007/2740 108/2740 139 LP: DG 2740 202/2740 204/2740 222 LP: DG 415 5201 CD: DG 415 5202/429 8692/435 3942 Excerpts LP: DG 2537 023
Vienna December 1975 (soundtrack) and June 1976 (picture)	Kanawa, Freni, Ewing, Prey Vienna Opera Chorus VPO Böhm	VHS Video: DG 072 4033 Laserdisc: DG 072 4031
London August 1976	Harper, Blegen, Berganza, G.Evans Alldis Choir English Chamber Orchestra Barenboim	LP: EMI SLS 995 CD: EMI CMS 763 6462 Excerpt LP: EMI EX 29 04323

Le Nozze di Figaro: Excerpt (Tutto è como lasciai/Esci omai garzon malnana)

Salzburg	Schwarzkopf,	CD: Orfeo C335 931B
July 1958	Seefried, Kunz	
	VPO	
	Böhm	

Le Nozze di Figaro: Excerpt (Crudel, perchè finora)

Salzburg	Seefried	CD: Orfeo C335 931B
August 1960	VPO	
	Böhm	
Berlin	Streich	LP: DG LPEM 19 406/SLPEM 136 406
December 1961	BPO	LP: DG 2535 279
	Leitner	CD: DG 423 8742
	Sung in German	

Le Nozze di Figaro: Excerpt (Hai già vinta la causa)

Salzburg	VPO	CD: Orfeo C335 931B
August 1960	Böhm	
Berlin	BPO	LP: DG LPEM 19 406/SLPEM 136 406
December 1961	Leitner	LP: DG LPEM 19 460/SLPEM 136 460
	Sung in German	LP: DG 2535 279
		CD: DG 423 8742/447 6782
Vienna	Vienna Haydn	LP: Decca SXL 6940/GRV 7
October 1969	Orchestra	CD: Decca 440 4092
	Peters	

L'Oca del Cairo

Berlin	Role of Pippo	CD: Philips 422 5392
January 1990	Nielsen, Wiens,	
	Coburn, Schreier	
	CPE Bach Chamber	
	Orchestra	
	Schreier	

Die Zauberflöte

Berlin
June 1956
	Role of Papageno
	Stader, Streich,
	Otto, Häfliger,
	Greindl, Borg
	RIAS Choir
	Berlin RO
	Fricsay
		LP: DG LPM 18 264-18 266/
		    LPM 18 267-18 269
		LP: DG 2701 003/2728 009/2730 014
		LP: DG 89 662-89 664
		CD: DG 435 7412
		Excerpts
		45: DG EPL 30 202/EPL 30 237
		LP: DG LPM 18 554-18 555
		LP: DG LPE 17 074/LPEM 19 194
		LP: DG 89 539/89 653/CD: DG 447 6782/44
		                           46

Berlin June 1964	Role of Papageno Lear, Peters, Otto, Wunderlich, Crass, Hotter RIAS Choir BPO Böhm	LP: DG LPM 18 981-18 983/ SLPM 138 981-138 983 LP: DG 2709 017/2720 058/2740 207 LP: DG 2740 222/2740 108 CD: DG 419 5662/429 8772/435 3952 Excerpts LP: DG 136 440/2537 003/2705 001
Tokyo 1966	Role of Sprecher Güden, Gayer, Häfliger, McDaniel, Talvela Deutsche Oper Chorus & Orchestra Jochum	Unpublished video recording
Vienna September and October 1969	Role of Sprecher Lorengar, Deutekom, Holm, Burrows, Prey, Talvela Vienna Opera Chorus VPO Solti	LP: Decca SET 479-481 CD: Decca 414 5682
Hamburg 1972	Role of Sprecher Mathis, Deutekom, Gedda, Fliether, Sotin Philharmonisches Staatsorchester and Chorus Stein	VHS Video: Lyric Distribution (USA) LDV 1380

Requiem

| London
July 1971 | Armstrong, Baker,
Gedda
Alldis Choir
English Chamber
Orchestra
Barenboim | LP: EMI ASD 2788/1C 065 02246
CD: EMI CZS 762 8922 |

Coronation Mass

| Munich
July 1976 | Moser, Hamari,
Gedda
Bavarian Radio
Chorus & Orchestra
Jochum | LP: EMI ASD 3373
CD: EMI CDM 769 0232 |

Vesperae solennes de confessore

| Munich
July 1976 | Moser, Hamari,
Gedda
Bavarian Radio
Chorus & Orchestra
Jochum | LP: EMI ASD 3373
CD: EMI CDM 769 0232 |

Abendempfindung (Abend ist's, die Sonne ist verschwunden)

| London
July 1971 | Barenboim | LP: EMI ASD 2824/1C 065 02261
LP: EMI EX 29 04293 |

An Chloe (Wenn die Lieb')

| London
July 1971 | Barenboim | LP: EMI ASD 2824/1C 065 02261 |

An die Freundschaft (O heiliges Band)

| London
July 1971 | Barenboim | LP: EMI ASD 2824/1C 065 02261 |

An die Hoffnung (Ich würd' auf meinem Pfad)

| London
July 1971 | Barenboim | LP: EMI ASD 2824/1C 065 02261 |

Un baco di mano, concert aria

| Vienna
October 1969 | Vienna Haydn
Orchestra
Peters | LP: Decca SXL 6940 |

Die betrogene Welt (Der reiche Tor)

| London
July 1971 | Barenboim | LP: EMI ASD 2824/1C 065 02261 |

Caro bell' idol mio, canon

| London
February 1967 | Schwarzkopf,
De los Angeles
Moore | EMI unpublished |

Così dunque tradisci, concert aria

| Vienna
October 1969 | Vienna Haydn
Orchestra
Peters | LP: Decca SXL 6940 |

Die ihr des unermesslichen Weltalls

| London
July 1971 | Barenboim | LP: EMI ASD 2824/1C 065 02261 |

Geheime Liebe (Was ich in Gedanken küsse)

| London
July 1971 | Barenboim | LP: EMI ASD 2824/1C 065 02261 |

Gesellenreise (Die ihr einem neuen Grade)

| London
July 1971 | Barenboim | LP: EMI ASD 2824/1C 065 02261 |

Die grossmütige Gelassenheit (Ich hab' es längst gesagt)

| London
July 1971 | Barenboim | LP: EMI ASD 2824/1C 065 02261 |

Ich möchte wohl der Kaiser sein

| Vienna
October 1969 | Vienna Haydn
Orchestra
Peters | LP: Decca SXL 6940 |

Lied der Freiheit (Wer unter eines Mädchens Hand)

| London
July 1971 | Barenboim | LP: EMI ASD 2824/1C 065 02261 |

Lied der Trennung (Die Engel Gottes weinen)

| London
July 1971 | Barenboim | LP: EMI ASD 2824/1C 065 02261 |

Männer suchen stets zu naschen

Vienna	Vienna Haydn	LP: Decca SXL 6940
October 1969	Orchestra	
	Peters	

Mentre ti lascio o figlia, concert aria

Vienna	Vienna Haydn	LP: Decca SXL 6940
October 1969	Orchestra	CD: Decca 440 4832
	Peters	

La partenza, trio

London	Schwarzkopf,	LP: EMI AN 182-183/SAN 182-183
February 1967	De los Angeles	LP: EMI SLS 926/EX 29 04353
	Moore	CD: EMI CMS 565 0612

Più non si trovano, trio

London	Schwarzkopf,	LP: EMI AN 182-183/SAN 182-183
February 1967	De los Angeles	LP: EMI SLS 926/EX 29 04353/ASD 143 5941
	Moore	CD: EMI CDC 749 2382/CDEMX 2233

Das Traumbild (Wo bist du, Bild?)

London	Barenboim	LP: EMI ASD 2824/1C 065 02261
July 1971		LP: EMI EX 29 02493

Das Veilchen (Ein Veilchen auf der Wiese stand)

London	Barenboim	LP: EMI ASD 2824/1C 065 02261
July 1971		

Wie unglücklich bin ich nit

London	Barenboim	LP: EMI ASD 2824/1C 065 02261
July 1971		

Die Zufriedenheit (Wie sanft)

London	Barenboim	LP: EMI ASD 2824/1C 065 02261
July 1971		

Die Zufriedenheit im niedrigen Stande (Ich trachte nicht nach solchen Dingen)

London	Barenboim	LP: EMI ASD 2824/1C 065 02261
July 1971		

NEEFE

Serenade/Goethe-Lieder

Berlin	Demus, fortepiano	LP: DG 2533 149
September 1972		

NEUKOMM

Poor Adele

Munich	Klöcker, clarinet	LP: Orfeo S153 861A
August 1983	Wallendorf, horn	CD: Orfeo C153 861A
	Höll	

NICOLAI

Die lustigen Weiber von Windsor: Excerpt (Gott grüss' Euch Sir/In einem Wasch-
korb/Wie freu' ich mich)

Berlin	Köth, Wilhelm,	LP: HMV BLP 1098
April 1955	Frick	LP: Electrola WBLP 1510
	BPO	LP: EMI 1C 187 30150-30151
	Schüchter	LP: EMI EX 29 04323

NIETZSCHE

Nachspiel/7 Lieder

Berlin　　　　　　　Reimann
March 1971

LP: EMI 1C 065 02674/
1C 161 02673-02677

Verwelkt (Du warst ja meine einz'ge)

Berlin　　　　　　　Reimann
March 1971

LP: EMI 1C 065 02674/EX 29 04293
LP: EMI 1C 161 02673-02677

Wie sich Rebenschranken schwingen

Berlin　　　　　　　Reimann
March 1971

LP: EMI 1C 065 02674/
1C 161 02673-02677

OFFENBACH

Les contes d'Hoffmann

Munich　　　　　　Roles of Lindorf,
January 1979　　　Coppelius, Mirakel
　　　　　　　　　and Dappertutto
　　　　　　　　　Scovotti, Sharp,
　　　　　　　　　Varady, Jerusalem,
　　　　　　　　　Orth, Moll
　　　　　　　　　Bavarian Radio
　　　　　　　　　Chorus
　　　　　　　　　Munich RO
　　　　　　　　　Wallberg
　　　　　　　　　Sung in German

LP: EMI 1C 157 45351-45353
Excerpt
LP: EMI EX 29 04323

ORFF

Carmina burana

Berlin　　　　　　Janowitz, Stolze
October 1967　　　Deutsche Oper
　　　　　　　　　Chorus & Orchestra
　　　　　　　　　Jochum

LP: DG 139 362/2726 510
CD: DG 423 8862/427 8782
Excerpts
LP: DG 2705 001

Carmina burana, excerpts

Berlin　　　　　　Schlemm
January 1950　　　St Hedwig's Choir
　　　　　　　　　Berlin RO
　　　　　　　　　Fricsay

Unpublished radio broadcast

Palestrina

Munich January and February 1973	Role of Borromeo Donath, Fassbaender, Gedda, Weikl, Ridderbusch, Prey Bavarian Radio Chorus & Orchestra Kubelik	LP: DG 2711 013/2740 223 CD: DG 427 4172

Abendrot

Munich June 1982	Höll	LP: Orfeo S036 821A CD: Orfeo C036 821A

Abschied (Abendlich schon rauscht der Wald)

Berlin September 1969	Engel	LP: EMI 1C 065 29036 CD: EMI CDM 763 5692

Das Alter (Hoch mit den Wolken geht der Vögel Reise)

Berlin September 1969	Engel	LP: EMI 1C 065 29036 CD: EMI CDM 763 5692

An den Mond (Füllest wieder Busch und Tal)

Berlin September 1970	Reimann	LP: EMI 1C 065 02675/ 1C 161 02673-02677 CD: EMI CDM 763 5692
Munich March 1979	Bavarian RO Sawallisch	LP: EMI 1C 065 45616
Munich June 1982	Höll	LP: Orfeo S036 821A CD: Orfeo C036 821A

An die Mark (Bereifte Kiefern, atemlose Seen)

Berlin June 1959	Engel	LP: DG LPM 18 590/SLPM 138 058
Munich March 1979	Bavarian RO Sawallisch	LP: EMI 1C 065 45616/EX 29 04353

Pfitzner Lieder/continued

Dietrichs Erzählung (Auf grüne Wipfel lacht nun wonnig der Lenz)

| Munich | Bavarian RO | LP: EMI 1C 065 45616 |
| March 1979 | Sawallisch | |

Eingelegte Ruder

| Berlin | Engel | LP: DG LPM 18 590/SLPM 138 058 |
| June 1959 | | |

Der Einsame (Wär's dunkel, ich läg' im Walde)

| Berlin | Engel | LP: EMI 1C 065 29036 |
| September 1969 | | CD: EMI CDM 769 5692 |

Es glänzt so schön die sinkende Sonee

| Munich | Höll | LP: Orfeo S036 821A |
| June 1982 | | CD: Orfeo C036 821A |

Der Gärtner (Wohin ich geh' und schaue)

| Berlin | Engel | LP: EMI 1C 065 29036 |
| September 1959 | | CD: EMI CDM 763 5692 |

Gebet

| Munich | Höll | LP: Orfeo S036 821A |
| June 1982 | | CD: Orfeo C036 821A |

Gegenliebe

| Munich | Höll | LP: Orfeo S036 821A |
| June 1982 | | CD: Orfeo C036 821A |

Herr Oluf reitet spät und weit

| Munich | Bavarian RO | LP: EMI 1C 065 45616 |
| March 1979 | Sawallisch | |

Hussens Kerker (Es geht mit mir zu Ende)

| Berlin | Engel | LP: DG LPM 18 590/SLPM 138 058 |
| June 1959 | | |

Berlin	Reutter	LP: EMI 1C 065 02676/
May 1970		1C 161 02673-02677
		CD: EMI CDM 763 5692

Ich aber weiss

| Munich | Höll | LP: Orfeo SO36 821A |
| June 1982 | | CD: Orfeo CO36 821A |

Ich und du (Wir träumten von einander)

| Munich | Höll | LP: Orfeo SO36 821A |
| June 1982 | | CD: Orfeo CO36 821A |

Im Herbst (Der Wald wird falb, die Blätter fallen)

| Berlin | Engel | LP: EMI 1C 065 29036/EX 29 04293 |
| September 1969 | | CD: EMI CDM 763 5692 |

| Salzburg | Sawallisch | CD: Orfeo C185 891A/C339 930T |
| August 1975 | | |

In Danzig (Dunkle Giebel, hohe Fenster)

| Berlin | Engel | LP: DG LPM 18 590/SLPM 138 058 |
| June 1959 | | |

| Berlin | Engel | LP: EMI 1C 065 29036 |
| September 1969 | | |

Ist der Himmel darum im Lenz so blau?

| Munich | Höll | LP: Orfeo SO36 821A |
| June 1982 | | CD: Orfeo CO36 821A |

Der Kühne (Und wo noch kein Wanderer gegangen)

| Berlin | Engel | LP: EMI 1C 065 29036 |
| September 1969 | | CD: EMI CDM 763 5692 |

Leierkastenmann

| Munich | Höll | LP: Orfeo SO36 821A |
| June 1982 | | CD: Orfeo CO36 821A |

Lethe (Jüngst im Traume sah ich auf den Fluten)

| Munich | Bavarian RO | LP: EMI 1C 065 45616/EX 29 04353 |
| March 1979 | Sawallisch | |

Pfitzner Lieder/continued

Lockung (Hörst du nicht die Bäume rauschen?)

Berlin September 1969	Engel	LP: EMI 1C 065 29036 CD: EMI CDM 763 5692
Salzburg August 1975	Sawallisch	CD: Orfeo C185 891A/C339 930T

Mailied (Wie herrlich leuchtet mir die Natur)

Berlin September 1970	Reimann	LP: EMI 1C 065 02675/ 1C 161 02673-02677 CD: EMI CDM 763 5692

Michaelskirchplatz

Munich June 1982	Höll	LP: Orfeo S036 821A CD: Orfeo C036 821A

Müde

Munich June 1982	Höll	LP: Orfeo S036 821A CD: Orfeo C036 821A

Die Nachtigallen (Möcht' wissen, was sie schlagen)

Berlin September 1969	Engel	LP: EMI 1C 065 29036 CD: EMI CDM 763 5692

Nachts (Ich stehe in Waldesschatten)

Berlin September 1969	Engel	LP: EMI 1C 065 29036 CD: EMI CDM 763 5692
Salzburg August 1975	Sawallisch	CD: Orfeo C185 891A/C339 930T

Nachtwanderer (Er reitet nachts auf einem braunen Ross)

Berlin September 1969	Engel	LP: EMI 1C 065 29036 CD: EMI CDM 763 5692

Neue Liebe (Herz, mein Herz, warum so fröhlich?)

Berlin September 1969	Engel	LP: EMI 1C 065 29036

Säerspruch

Berlin June 1959	Engel	LP: DG LPM 18 590/SLPM 138 058

Schön Suschen

| Munich | Höll | LP: Orfeo S036 821A |
| June 1982 | | CD: Orfeo C036 821A |

Sehnsucht

| Munich | Höll | LP: Orfeo S036 821A |
| June 1982 | | CD: Orfeo C036 821A |

Sie haben heut' abend Gesellschaft

| Berlin | Engel | LP: DG LPM 18 590/SLPM 138 058 |
| June 1959 | | |

| Munich | Bavarian RO | LP: EMI 1C 065 45616 |
| March 1979 | Sawallisch | |

Sonst (Es glänzt der Tulpenflor)

| Berlin | Engel | LP: EMI 1C 065 29036 |
| September 1969 | | |

Stimme der Sehnsucht

| Munich | Höll | LP: Orfeo S036 821A |
| June 1982 | | CD: Orfeo C036 821A |

Studentenfahrt (Die Jäger zieh'n in grünen Wald)

| Berlin | Engel | LP: EMI 1C 065 29036 |
| September 1969 | | CD: EMI CDM 763 5692 |

Tragische Geschichte

| Berlin | Engel | LP: DG LPM 18 590/SLPM 138 058 |
| June 1959 | | |

| Munich | Höll | LP: Orfeo S036 821A |
| June 1982 | | CD: Orfeo C036 821A |

Der verspätete Wanderer (Wo aber werd' ich sein im künft'gen Lenze?)

| Berlin | Engel | LP: EMI 1C 065 29036/EX 29 04293 |
| September 1969 | | CD: EMI CDM 763 5692 |

Pfitzner Lieder/concluded

Voll jener Süsse, die nicht auszudrücken

Berlin September 1972	Demus	LP: DG 2530 332

Wasserfahrt

Munich June 1982	Höll	LP: Orfeo S036 821A CD: Orfeo C036 821A

Zorn (Seh' ich im verfall'nen dunklen Haus)

Berlin June 1959	Engel	LP: DG LPM 18 590/SLPM 138 058
Berlin September 1969	Engel	LP: EMI 1C 065 29036 CD: EMI CDM 763 5692
Munich March 1979	Bavarian RO Sawallisch	LP: EMI 1C 065 45616

Zum Abschied meiner Tochter (Der Herbstwind schüttelt die Linde)

Berlin June 1959	Engel	LP: DG LPM 18 590/SLPM 138 058
Berlin September 1969	Engel	LP: EMI 1C 065 29036 CD: EMI CDM 763 5692
Salzburg August 1975	Sawallisch	CD: Orfeo C185 891A/C339 930T

PIERNE

Sérénade

Berlin April 1984	Höll	LP: Teldec 643 754 CD: Teldec 843 754/4509 974572

PONCHIELLI

La Gioconda: Excerpt (Enzo Grimaldo, Principe di Santofior)

Munich July 1982	Bergonzi Bavarian RO Lopez-Cobos	LP: Orfeo S028 821A CD: Orfeo C028 821A

POULENC

Le bal masqué, song cycle

Berlin 1975	BPO soloists Sawallisch	LP: RCA/BASF EA 22.7650

PUCCINI

La Bohème

Berlin June 1961	Role of Marcello Lorengar, Streich, Konya, Günter Deutsche Staatsoper & Komische Oper Choruses Staatskapelle Erede Sung in German	LP: DG LPM 18 720-18 721/ SLPM 138 720-138 721 LP: DG 2726 059 Excerpts LP: DG 136 404/2535 007/2535 427 CD: DG 423 8752

La Bohème, Querschnitt

Berlin September 1954	Berger, Köth, Schock, Prey, Frick Deutsche Oper Chorus Berlin SO Schüchter Sung in German	LP: Electrola E 80003 LP: EMI 1C 047 28572

La Bohème: Excerpt (Addio dolce svegliare alla mattina)

Berlin September 1949	Trötschel, Streich, Fehenberger Komische Oper Orchestra Schmitz Sung in German	78: DG LM 68 435 45: DG NL 32 048

La Bohème: Excerpt (Che penna infame!)

Munich July 1982	Bergonzi Bavarian RO Lopez-Cobos	LP: Orfeo S 028 821A CD: Orfeo C 028 821A

Gianni Schicchi

Cologne December 1975	Role of Schicchi Zeumer, Lipp, Töpper, Ilosfalvy WDR Orchestra Erede Sung in German	Promotional LP issued by Westdeutscher Rundfunk

Madama Butterfly, Querschnitt

Berlin September 1954	Role of Sharpless Berger, S.Wagner, Schock Deutsche Oper Orchestra & Chorus Schüchter Sung in German	LP: Electrola E 60062 LP: EMI 1C 047 28570

Tosca

Rome June 1966	Role of Scarpia Nilsson, Corelli Santa Cecilia Orchestra & Chorus Maazel	LP: Decca MET 341-342/SET 341-342 CD: Decca 440 0512 Excerpt LP: Decca GRV 7 CD: Decca 440 4832

Tosca, Querschnitt

Rome June 1966	Silja, King Santa Cecilia Orchestra & Chorus Sung in German	LP: Decca (Germany) SX 21213

PURCELL

When night her purple veil, cantata

Berlin August 1969	Nicolet, flute Toyoda, violin Donderer, cello Nowak, double-bass Picht-Axenfeld, harpsichord	LP: EMI 1C 063 02258 CD: EMI CZS 568 5092 Excerpt LP: EMI EX 29 04353

Duets: Let us wander; Lost is my quiet

Berlin December 1960	De los Angeles Moore	LP: HMV ALP 1891/ASD 459 CD: EMI CMS 565 0612

Duets: No, resistance is but vain; My dearest, my fairest; Shepherd, leave decoying; Sound the trumpet

London August 1969	Baker Barenboim	LP: EMI ASD 2553/1C 063 02041

RAFF

Unter Palmen

Berlin	Reimann	LP: EMI 1C 065 02674/
March 1971		1C 161 02673-02677

RAMEAU

Thétis, cantata

London	Rampal, flute	LP: EMI ASD 2903/1C 063 02328
October 1971	Neilz, cello	CD: EMI CZS 568 5092
	Veyron-Lacroix,	
	harpsichord	

RAVEL

3 chansons madécasses: Nahandove; Aoua! Aoua!; Il est doux de se coucher

Berlin	Nicolet, flute	LP: DG LPM 18 615/SLPM 138 115
October 1959	Poppen, cello	
	Engel	

Berlin	Zöller, flute	LP: RCA/BASF EA 22.7650
1975	Böttcher, cello	
	Sawallisch	

Don Quichotte à Dulcinée: Chanson romanesque; Chanson épique; Chanson à boire

Berlin	Engel	LP: DG LPM 18 615/SLPM 138 115
October 1959		

Munich	Höll	LP: Orfeo S061 831A
March 1983		CD: Orfeo C061 831A

5 mélodies populaires grecques: Réveille-toi!; Là-bas, vers l'église; Quel galant; O joi de mon âme; Tout gai!

Berlin	Engel	LP: DG LPM 18 615/SLPM 138 115
October 1959		

Munich	Höll	LP: Orfeo S061 831A
March 1983		CD: Orfeo C061 831A

Mélodies: Un grand sommeil noir; 2 épigrammes; Histoires naturelles; Ronsard à son âme; Rêves

Munich	Höll	LP: Orfeo S061 831A
March 1983		CD: Orfeo C061 831A

Aeolsharfe

Berlin   Weissenborn   LP: DG 139 127/135 026
November 1965

An die Hoffnung

Hamburg   Philharmonisches   CD: Orfeo C209 901A
July 1989   Staatsorchester
                      Albrecht

Das Blatt im Buche

Berlin   Weissenborn   LP: DG 139 127
November 1965

Christkindleins Wiegenlied

Berlin   Demus   LP: DG 2530 219
November 1970

Ein Drängen

Berlin   Weissenborn   LP: DG 139 127
November 1965

Einsamkeit

Berlin   Weissenborn   LP: DG 139 127
November 1965

Der Einsiedler

Hamburg   Philharmonisches   CD: Orfeo C209 901A
July 1989   Staatsorchester
                      Albrecht

Flieder

Berlin   Weissenborn   LP: DG 139 127
November 1965

Glückes genug

Berlin   Weissenborn   LP: DG 139 127
November 1965

Grablied

| Berlin
November 1965 | Weissenborn | LP: DG 139 127 |

Gottes Segen

| Berlin
November 1965 | Weissenborn | LP: DG 139 127 |

Heimat

| Berlin
November 1965 | Weissenborn | LP: DG 139 127 |

Der Himmel hat eine Träne geweinet

| Berlin
November 1965 | Weissenborn | LP: DG 139 127 |

Hymnus der Liebe

| Hamburg
July 1989 | Philharmonisches
Staatsorchester
Albrecht | CD: Orfeo C209 901A |

Im April

| Berlin
November 1965 | Weissenborn | LP: DG 139 127/135 007 |

Ihr, ihr Herrlichen

| Berlin
November 1965 | Weissenborn | LP: DG 139 127 |

Mariae Wiegenlied

| Berlin
November 1970 | Demus | LP: DG 2530 219 |

Minnelied

| Berlin
November 1965 | Weissenborn | LP: DG 139 127 |

Nelken

| Berlin
November 1965 | Weissenborn | LP: DG 139 127 |

Requiem

Hamburg July 1989	Philharmonisches Staatsorchester Albrecht	CD: Orfeo C209 901A

Schlecht Wetter

Berlin November 1965	Weissenborn	LP: DG 139 127

Sommernacht

Berlin September 1970	Reimann	LP: EMI 1C 065 02675/ 1C 161 02673-02677 LP: EMI EX 29 04293

Das sterbende Kind

Berlin November 1965	Weissenborn	LP: DG 139 127

Traum durch die Dämmerung

Berlin November 1965	Weissenborn	LP: DG 139 127

Trost

Berlin November 1965	Weissenborn	LP: DG 139 127

Uns ist ein Kind geboren

Berlin November 1970	Demus	LP: DG 2530 219

Waldeinsamkeit

Berlin November 1965	Weissenborn	LP: DG 139 127

Reger Lieder/concluded

Warnung

Berlin   Reimann   LP: EMI 1C 065 02675/
September 1970   1C 161 02673-02677

Winterahnung

Berlin   Weissenborn   LP: DG 139 127/135 026
November 1965

Der zerrissene Grabkreuz

Berlin   Weissenborn   LP: DG 139 127
November 1965

REICHARDT

6 Petrarch Sonnets: Canzon s'al dolce loco la donna nostra vedi; Erano i
capei d'oro; O poggi, o valli, o fiume, so selve, o campi; Più volte già
dal bel sembiante umano; Di tempo in tempo mi si fa men dura; Or che' l
ciel a la terra, e'l vento tace

Berlin   Demus   LP: DG 2530 332
September 1972

Lieder: Gott; Feiger Gedanken; Die schöne Nacht; Einziger Augenblick;
Einschränkung; Mut; Rhapsodie; An Lotte; Aus Euphrosyne

Berlin   Demus, fortepiano   LP: DG 2533 149
September 1972

Lieder: Aeneas zu Dido; Der Alpenjäger; An Belinden; Aus Alexis und Dora;
Aus Euphrosne; Aus Harzreise im Winter; Berglied; Geister meiner Toten;
Gott; Hoffnung und Erinnerung; Der Ideale; Johanna Sebus; Klage; Kophtisch
Lied; Letztes Lied des Harfenspielers; Mut; Nachtgesang; Prometheus; Die
schöne Nacht; Wechsel

Recording details   Graf, harp   CD: Orfeo C245 921A
not confirmed

REIMANN

Lear

Munich October 1978	Role of Lear Varady, Lorand, Dernesch, Boysen Bavarian State Orchestra & Chorus	LP: DG 2709 089
Munich 1982	Varady, Lorand, Dernesch, Boysen Bavarian State Orchestra & Chorus Albrecht Albrecht	Unpublished video recording

Requiem

Berlin January 1983	Varady, Dernesch RIAS Choir Berlin RO Albrecht	LP: EMI

5 Gedichte von Paul Celan: Blume; Auge der Zeit; Tenebrae; Heut' und Morgen; Ein Lied in der Wüste

Berlin November 1961	Reimann	LP: Electrola E 91189/STE 91189 CD: EMI CZS 568 5092 Auge der Zeit LP: EMI EX 29 04293

3 poemi di Michelangelo: Sol io ardendo; Che fie di me?; L'alma inquieta e confusa

Berlin October 1986	Reimann	LP: Teldec 643 7142 CD: Teldec 4509 974602

Shine and Dark, for baritone and piano left hand

Berlin   Reimann   CD: Orfeo C212 901A
December 1988

Unrevealed, for baritone and string quartet

Berlin   Cherubini Quartet   CD: Orfeo C212 901A
December 1988   Reimann

REINECKE

Weihnachtslied

Berlin   Demus   LP: DG 2530 219
November 1970

REISSIGER

Abendständchen an die Geliebte;   Heimweh

Munich   Klöcker, clarinet   LP: Orfeo S153 861A
August 1983   Wallendorf, horn   CD: Orfeo C153 861A
                      Höll

REUTTER

Bankelsänger/Meine dunklen Hände

Berlin	Reimann	LP: Electrola E 91189/STE 91189
November 1961		CD: EMI CZS 568 5092

Lied für ein dunkles Mädchen/Meine dunklen Hände

Berlin	Reimann	LP: Electrola E 91189/STE 91189
November 1961		CD: EMI CZS 568 5092
Berlin	Reutter	LP: EMI 1C 065 02676/
May 1970		1C 161 02673-02677

Johannes Kepler

Berlin	Reutter	LP: EMI 1C 065 02676/
May 1970		1C 161 02673-02677

Schwarzes Mädchen/Meine dunklen Hände

Berlin	Reimann	LP: Electrola E 91189/STE 91189
November 1961		CD: EMI CZS 568 5092

Trommel/Meine dunklen Hände

Berlin	Reimann	LP: Electrola E 91189/STE 91189
November 1961		CD: EMI CZS 568 5092
Berlin	Reutter	LP: EMI 1C 065 02676/
May 1970		1C 161 02673-02677

Wenn Susanna Jones trägt rot/Meine dunklen Hände

Berlin	Reimann	LP: Electrola E 99189/STE 91189
November 1961		CD: EMI CZS 568 5092

Weihnachtskantilene

Berlin	Demus	LP: DG 2530 219
November 1970		

REZNICEK

4 Bet- und Bussgesänge nach Worten der Heiligen Schrift

Berlin March 1960	Weissenborn	LP: Electrola

RHEINBERGER

Der Stern von Bethlehem

Munich September and October 1968	Streich Bavarian Radio Chorus Graunke Orchestra Heger	LP: EMI ASD 2630/146 7951 CD: Carus (USA) 83111 Excerpt LP: EMI EX 29 04353

REUTTER

Primula veris

Berlin March 1971	Reimann	LP: EMI 1C 065 02674/ 1C 161 02673-02677

ROSENMÜLLER

Von den himmlischen Freuden, cantata

Berlin August 1969	Donderer, cello Nowak, double bass Picht-Axenfeld, harpsichord	LP: EMI 1C 063 02258 CD: EMI CZS 568 5092

ROSSINI

Guilleaume Tell

Milan April 1956	Role of Tell Jaia, Cerquetti, Mancini, Borelli, Modesti, Sardi RAI Milan Orchestra & Chorus Rossi Sung in Italian	LP: Morgan 5601 LP: MRF Records MRF 69 LP: Replica ARPL 32429 CD: Foyer FO 1037 CD: Claque 300 103

Guilleaume Tell: Excerpt (Reste immobile)

Berlin April 1961	Berlin RO Fricsay Sung in Italian	LP: DG LPM 18 700/SLPM 138 700

Petite messe solennelle

Baumburg/Chiemgau July 1972	Lövaas, Fassbaender, Schreier Munich Vocal Soloists Harmonium & piano Sawallisch	LP: RCA/Ariola MLDS 60006 CD: Eurodisc 610. 263 232

ANTON RUBINSTEIN

Es blinkt der Tau

Berlin 1974	Reimann	LP: EMI 1C 065 02673/ 1C 161 02673-02677

SAINT-SAENS

Pastorale

Berlin	De los Angeles	LP: HMV ALP 1891/ASD 459
December 1960	Moore	LP: EMI EX 29 05583
		CD: EMI CMS 565 0612

La cloche; Clair de lune; L'attente; Le pas d'armes

Berlin	Höll	LP: Teldec 643 754
April 1984		CD: Teldec 843 754/4509 974572

ALESSANDRO SCARLATTI

Infirmata vulnerata, cantata

Berlin	Nicolet, flute	LP: HMV ALP 2066/ASD 615
February 1963	Heller, violin	CD: EMI CZS 568 5092
	Poppen, cello	
	Picht-Axenfeld,	
	harpsichord	

SCHEIN

Duets: Christe, der du bist Tag und Licht; Gott der Vater wohnt bei uns

London	Baker	LP: EMI ASD 2710
February 1970	Heath, cello	
	Malcolm, harpsichord	

SCHILLINGS

Freude soll in deinen Werken sein

Berlin	Reimann	LP: EMI 1C 065 02674/
March 1971		1C 161 02673-02677

SCHOECK

Das holde Bescheiden, song cycle

Berlin 1990	Höll	CD: Claves 50 9308-50 9309

Lebendig begraben, song cycle to poems by Keller

Berlin March 1962	Berlin RO Rieger	LP: DG LPM 18 821/SLPM 138 821 CD: DG 437 0332

Notturno, for voice and string quartet

New York April 1967	Juilliard Quartet	LP: CBS 72687
Berlin May 1991	Cherubini Quartet	CD: EMI CDC 754 5202

Das stille Leuchten, song cycle to poems by Meyer

Berlin February 1988	Höll	CD: Claves 50 8910

Unter Sternen, song cycle to poems by Keller

Berlin February 1986	Höll	CD: Claves 50 8606

Ein Tagewerk I and II/Unter Sternen

Berlin April 1958	M.Weber	LP: DG LPM 18 511/SLPM 138 013

Abends

Berlin March 1977	Engel	LP: DG 2530 877

Abendwolken

Berlin May 1971	Reutter	LP: EMI 1C 065 02675/ 1C 161 02673-02677

Schoeck Lieder/continued

Aber wie schön ist Nacht und Dämmerschein

| Berlin
April 1958 | M.Weber | LP: DG LPM 18 511/SLPM 138 013 |

Auf ein Kind

| Berlin
April 1958 | M.Weber | LP: DG LPM 18 511/SLPM 138 013 |

Aus 2 Tälern

| Berlin
March 1977 | Engel | LP: DG 2530 877 |

Auskunft

| Berlin
March 1977 | Engel | LP: DG 2530 877 |

Blauer Schmetterling

| Berlin
March 1977 | Engel | LP: DG 2530 877 |

Dämm'rung senkte sich von oben

| Berlin
April 1958 | M.Weber | LP: DG LPM 18 511/SLPM 138 013 |

Das Ende des Festes

| Berlin
April 1958 | M.Weber | LP: DG LPM 18 511/SLPM 138 013 |

Frühgesicht

| Berlin
April 1958 | M.Weber | LP: DG LPM 18 511/SLPM 138 013 |

Für Nino

| Berlin
March 1977 | Engel | LP: DG 2530 877 |

Höre den Rat

| Berlin
April 1958 | M.Weber | LP: DG LPM 18 511/SLPM 138 013 |

Im Kreuzgang von Santo Stefano

Berlin March 1977	Engel	LP: DG 2530 877

Im Nebel

Berlin March 1977	Engel	LP: DG 2530 877

Jetzt rede du!

Berlin April 1958	M.Weber	LP: DG LPM 18 511/SLPM 138 013

Jugendgedenken

Berlin April 1958	M.Weber	LP: DG LPM 18 511/SLPM 138 013

Kennst du das auch?

Berlin March 1977	Engel	LP: DG 2530 877

Keine Rast

Berlin March 1977	Engel	LP: DG 2530 877

Kindheit

Berlin March 1977	Engel	LP: DG 2530 877

Magier der Farben

Berlin March 1977	Engel	LP: DG 2530 877

Mittag im September

Berlin March 1977	Engel	LP: DG 2530 877

Schoeck Lieder/continued

Nachklang

Berlin   M.Weber   LP: DG LPM 18 511/SLPM 138 013
April 1958

Nachruf

Berlin   M.Weber   LP: DG LPM 18 511/SLPM 138 013
April 1958

Nachtgefühl

Berlin   Engel   LP: DG 2530 877
March 1977

Peregrina II

Berlin   M.Weber   LP: DG LPM 18 511/SLPM 138 013
April 1958

Berlin   Reutter   LP: EMI 1C 065 02676/
May 1970   1C 161 02673-02677
                                       LP: EMI EX 29 04293

Pfeifer

Berlin   Engel   LP: DG 2530 877
March 1977

Ravenna I

Berlin   Engel   LP: DG 2530 877
March 1977

Reisephantasie

Berlin   M.Weber   LP: DG LPM 18 511/SLPM 138 013
April 1958

Reiselied

Berlin   Reutter   LP: EMI 1C 065 02675/
May 1971   1C 161 02673-02677

Sommernacht

Berlin   Engel   LP: DG 2530 877
March 1977

Schoeck Lieder/concluded

Venezianisches Epigramm

Berlin   M.Weber   LP: DG LPM 18 511/SLPM 138 013
April 1958

Vergänglichkeit

Berlin   Engel   LP: DG 2530 877
March 1977

Verwelkende Rosen

Berlin   Engel   LP: DG 2530 877
March 1977

Das Ziel

Berlin   Engel   LP: DG 2530 877
March 1977

SCHOENBERG

Abschied/Der Wanderer

| Berlin | Reimann | CD: EMI CDM 763 5702 |
| January 1983 | | Also on an EMI LP |

Am Strande

| Berlin | Reimann | CD: EMI CDM 763 5702 |
| January 1983 | | Also on an EMI LP |

Die Aufgeregten (Welche tiefbewegten Lebensläufchen)

Berlin	Reimann	LP: DG 2530 107
October 1970		CD: DG 431 7442
Berlin	Reimann	CD: EMI CDM 763 5702
January 1983		Also on an EMI LP

Deinem Blick mich zu bequemen

| Berlin | Reimann | CD: EMI CDM 763 5702 |
| January 1983 | | Also on an EMI LP |

Erwartung (Aus dem meergrünen Teiche)

Berlin	Reimann	LP: DG 2530 107
October 1970		CD: DG 431 7442
Berlin	Reimann	CD: EMI CDM 763 5702
January 1983		Also on an EMI LP

Geübtes Herz (Weise nicht von dir mein schlichtes Herz)

Berlin	Reimann	LP: DG 2530 107
October 1970		CD: DG 431 7442
Berlin	Reimann	CD: EMI CDM 763 5702
January 1983		Also on an EMI LP

Ich darf nicht dankend

Berlin	Reimann	LP: DG 2530 107
October 1970		CD: DG 431 7442
Berlin	Reimann	CD: EMI CDM 763 5702
January 1983		Also on an EMI LP

Schoenberg Lieder/continued

Sommermüd (Wenn du schon glaubst, es ist ewige Nacht)

Berlin October 1970	Reimann	LP: DG 2530 107 CD: DG 431 7442
Berlin January 1983	Reimann	CD: EMI CDM 763 5702 Also on an EMI LP

Schenk' mir deinen goldenen Kamm

Berlin January 1983	Reimann	CD: EMI CDM 763 5702 Also on an LP EMI

Tot (Ist alles eins, was liegt daran!)

Berlin October 1970	Reimann	LP: DG 2530 107 CD: DG 431 7442
Berlin January 1983	Reimann	CD: EMI CDM 763 5702 Also on an EMI LP

Traumleben (Um meinen Nacken)

Berlin 1974	Reimann	LP: EMI 1C 065 02677/ 1C 161 02673-02677
Berlin January 1983	Reimann	CD: EMI CDM 763 5702 Also on an EMI LP

Verlassen (In Morgengrauen schritt ich fort)

Berlin October 1970	Reimann	LP: DG 2530 107 CD: DG 431 7442
Berlin January 1983	Reimann	CD: EMI CDM 763 5702 Also on an EMI LP

Schoenberg Lieder/concluded

Der verlorene Haufen (Trink' aus, ihr zechtet zum letzten Mal)

Berlin October 1970	Reimann	LP: DG 2530 107 CD: DG 431 7442
Berlin January 1983	Reimann	CD: EMI CDM 763 5702 Also on an EMI LP

Warnung (Mein Hund)

Berlin 1974	Reimann	LP: EMI 1C 065 02677/ 1C 161 02673-02677
Berlin January 1983	Reimann	CD: EMI CDM 763 5702 Also on an EMI LP

Wie Georg von Frundsberg von sich selber sang

Berlin January 1983	Reimann	CD: EMI CDM 763 5702 Also on an EMI LP

SCHREKER

Die Dunkelheit sinkt schwer wie Blei

Berlin May 1971	Reimann	LP: EMI 1C 065 02675/ 1C 161 02673-02677

SCHUBART

Weihnachtslied der Hirten

Berlin November 1970	Demus	LP: DG 2530 219/2545 051/2721 213

SCHUBERT

Symphony No 5

London February 1973	New Philharmonia Fischer-Dieskau conducts	LP: EMI ASD 2942/1C 063 02429

Symphony No 8 "Unfinished"

London February 1973	New Philharmonia Fischer-Dieskau conducts	LP: EMI ASD 2942/1C 063 02429

Mass in F D105

Munich January 1980- December 1981	Popp, Donath, Fassbaender, Schreier, Dallapozza Bavarian Radio Orchestra & Chorus Sawallisch	LP: EMI SLS 5254 CD: EMI CMS 764 7782

Mass in B flat D324

Munich January 1980- December 1981	Popp, Fassbaender, Dallapozza Bavarian Radio Orchestra & Chorus Sawallisch	LP: EMI SLS 5254 CD: EMI CMS 764 7782

Mass in C D452

Munich January 1980- December 1981	Donath, Fassbaender, Schreier Bavarian Radio Orchestra & Chorus Sawallisch	LP: EMI SLS 5278 LP: EMI CDM 769 2222/CMS 764 7782

Mass in A flat D678

Munich June 1983	Popp, Fassbaender, Araiza Bavarian Radio Orchestra & Chorus Sawallisch	LP: EMI SLS 143 6073 CD: EMI CDM 769 2222/CMS 764 7782

Magnificat in C D486

Munich 1981-1983	Popp, Fassbaender, Dallapozza Bavarian Radio Orchestra & Chorus Sawallisch	LP: EMI SLS 143 6073 CD: EMI CMS 764 7832

Psalm 92

Munich	Capella Bavariae	LP: EMI ASD 4415/1C 067 43383
June 1983	Sawallisch, piano	CD: EMI CDC 747 4072/CMS 764 7832

Kyrie in D minor D49

Munich	Popp, Fassbaender,	LP: EMI SLS 5254
January 1980-	Dallapozza	CD: EMI CMS 764 7782
December 1981	Bavarian Radio	
	Orchestra & Chorus	
	Sawallisch	

Lazarus D689

Munich	Donath, Popp,	LP: EMI SLS 143 6073
June 1983	Venuti, Protschka,	CD: EMI CMS 764 7832
	Tear	Excerpt
	Bavarian Radio	LP: EMI EX 29 04353
	Orchestra & Chorus	
	Sawallisch	

Stabat mater D383

Munich	Bavarian Radio	LP: EMI SLS 143 6073
June 1983	Orchestra & Chorus	CD: EMI CMS 764 7782
	Sawallisch	Excerpt
		LP: EMI EX 29 04353

Tantum ergo in E flat D962

Munich	Popp, Fassbaender,	LP: EMI SLS 5254
January 1980-	Dallapozza	CD: EMI CDM 769 2232/CMS 764 7782
December 1981	Bavarian Radio	
	Orchestra & Chorus	
	Sawallisch	

Trinklied D75

Munich	Capella Bavariae	LP: EMI SLS 5220/1C 039 143 2541
June 1983	Sawallisch, piano	

Zur guten Nacht D903

Munich	Capella Bavariae	LP: EMI SLS 5220
June 1983	Sawallisch, piano	

Alfonso und Estrella

Berlin January and February 1978	Role of Froila Mathis, Schreier, Prey, Adam Rundfunkchor Staatskapelle Suitner	LP: EMI 1C 157 30816-30818 CD: Berlin Classics BC 21562 Excerpt LP: EMI EX 29 04323

Der vierjährige Posten

Munich 1977	Role of Dorfrichter Donath, Schreier Bavarian Radio Chorus Munich RO Wallberg	LP: EMI 1C 065 30742/ 1C 151 53043-53045

Die Zwillingsbrüder

Munich January 1975	Role of Friedrich Donath, Gedda, Moll Bavarian State Orchestra & Chorus Sawallisch	LP: EMI 1C 065 28833/ 1C 151 53043-53045 Excerpt LP: EMI EX 29 04323

Die schöne Müllerin

London October 1951	Moore	78: HMV DB 21388-21395/ DB 9719-9726 auto LP: HMV ALP 1036-1037 LP: Victor LHMV 6 LP: EMI 1C 175 01764-01766M CD: EMI CMS 763 5592 Excerpts LP: EMI RLS 766
Berlin 1961	Moore	LP: HMV ALP 1913/ASD 481/SLS 840 LP: Electrola E 91187-91188/ STE 91187-91188/1C 065 00202 CD: EMI CDC 747 1732
Berlin December 1971	Moore	LP: DG 2530 544/2720 059/2740 188 CD: DG 415 1862 CD: DG 437 2142/437 2352

Winterreise

Berlin January 1948	Billing	LP: Movimento musica 02.013 <u>Excerpts</u> <u>CD:</u> Verona 27064
Berlin 1952	Reutter	CD: Verona 2702
Berlin 1953	Klust	CD: Melodram CDM 18016
Berlin 1955	Moore	LP: HMV ALP 1298-1299 LP: Electrola E 90001-90002 LP: Electrola 1C 175 01764-01766M CD: EMI CMS 763 5592
Berlin 1961	Moore	LP: HMV ALP 2001-2002/ASD 551-552 LP: Electrola E 91239-91240/ STE 91239-91240 LP: EMI SLS 840
Berlin May 1965	Demus	LP: DG 139 201-139 202/2707 028 LP: DG 2726 058 CD: DG 447 4212
London August 1969	Barenboim	EMI unpublished
Berlin August 1971	Moore	LP: DG 2720 059/2740 188/2726 523 CD: DG 413 1872/437 2142/437 2352
Salzburg August 1978	Pollini	Unpublished radio broadcast
Berlin January 1979	Barenboim	LP: DG 2707 118 CD: DG 439 4322
Berlin July 1985	Brendel	LP: Philips 411 4631 CD: Philips 411 4632 Also unpublished video recording
Berlin July 1990	Perahia	CD: Sony SK 48237 VHS Video: Sony SHV 46374 Laserdisc: Sony SLV 46374

Der Abend (Der Abend blüht, Temora glüht)

Berlin	Moore	LP: DG 2720 022
December 1966–		CD: DG 437 2152/437 2142
February 1968		

Der Abend (Purpur malt die Tannenhügel)

Berlin	Moore	LP: DG 2720 022
December 1966–		CD: DG 437 2152/437 2142
February 1968		

Abendbilder (Still beginnt's im Hain zu tauen)

Berlin	Moore	LP: DG 2720 006/2530 229
February–		CD: DG 437 2252/437 2142
March 1969		

Tours	Richter	LP: DG 2530 988
July 1977		CD: DG 445 7172

Salzburg	Richter	CD: Orfeo C334 931B/C339 930T
August 1977		

Abendlied (Gross und rotentflammend schwebet noch die Sonn')

Berlin	Moore	LP: DG 2720 022
December 1966–		CD: DG 437 2152/437 2142
February 1968		

Abendlied (Der Mond ist aufgegangen)

Berlin	Moore	LP: DG 2720 022
December 1966–		CD: DG 437 2152/437 2142
February 1968		

Schubert Lieder/continued

Abendlied (Sanft glänzt die Abendsonne)

Berlin	Moore	LP: DG 2720 022
December 1966-		CD: DG 437 2152/437 2142
February 1968		

Abendlied für die Entfernte (Hinaus, mein Blick!)

Berlin	Moore	LP: DG 2720 006
February-		CD: DG 437 2252/437 2142
March 1969		

Das Abendrot (Du heilig, glühend Abendrot)

Berlin	Moore	LP: DG 2720 006
February-		CD: DG 437 2252/437 2142
March 1969		

Die Abendröte (Tiefer sinket schon die Sonne)

Berlin	Moore	LP: DG 2720 006
February-		CD: DG 437 2252/437 2142
March 1969		

Abends unter der Linde (Woher, o namenloses Sehnen?)

Berlin	Moore	LP: DG 2720 022
December 1966-		CD: DG 437 2152/437 2142
February 1968		

Abendständchen an Lina (Sei sanft wie ihre Seele)

Berlin	Moore	LP: DG 2720 022
December 1966-		CD: DG 437 2152/437 2142
February 1968		

Abendstern (Was weilst du einsam an dem Himmel?)

Berlin	Engel	LP: HMV ALP 1850
1959		LP: Electrola E 91024

Berlin	Moore	LP: DG 2720 006
February-		CD: DG 437 2252/437 2142
March 1969		

Die abgeblühte Linde (Wirst du halten, was du schwurst?)

Berlin	Moore	LP: DG 2720 022
December 1966-		CD: DG 437 2152/437 2142
February 1968		

Schubert Lieder/continued

Abschied/Schwanengesang (Ade, du muntre, du fröhliche Stadt, ade!)

Berlin January 1948	Billing	CD: Verona 27064 CD: Melodram CDM 18017
London May 1955	Moore	LP: HMV ALP 1295 LP: Electrola E 90121 LP: EMI 1C 175 01764-01766M CD: EMI CMS 763 5592
Salzburg August 1957	Moore	LP: Orfeo S140 855R CD: Orfeo C140 101A/C339 930T
Berlin 1961	Moore	LP: HMV ALP 1993/ASD 544/SLS 840 LP: Electrola E 91222/STE 91222 CD: EMI CDC 749 0812
London February 1967	Moore	LP: AN 182-183/SAN 182-183 LP: EMI SLS 926 /ASD 143 5941 CD: EMI CDC 749 2382/CDEMX 2233
Berlin March 1972	Moore	LP: DG 2720 059/2531 383 CD: DG 415 1882/437 2352/437 2142
Salzburg August 1977	Richter	CD: Orfeo C334 931B/C339 930T
Berlin August 1982	Brendel	LP: Philips 6514 383 CD: Philips 411 0512/432 0532
Nürnberg May 1992	Höll	CD: Erato 4509 984932 Also unpublished video recording

Abschied (Lebe wohl, du lieber Freund!)

Berlin February- March 1969	Moore	LP: DG 2720 006 CD: DG 437 2252/437 2142

Abschied (Ueber die Berge zieht ihr fort)

Berlin December 1966- February 1968	Moore	LP: DG 2720 022 CD: DG 437 2152/437 2142

Abschied von der Erde (Leb' wohl, du schöne Erde!)

Berlin February- March 1969	Moore	LP: DG 2720 006 CD: DG 437 2252/437 2142

Schubert Lieder/continued

Abschied von der Harfe (Noch einmal tön', o Harfe)

| Berlin
December 1966-
February 1968 | Moore | LP: DG 2720 022
CD: DG 437 2152/437 2142 |

Adelaide (Einsam wandelt der Freund)

| Berlin
December 1966-
February 1968 | Moore | LP: DG 2720 022
CD: DG 437 2152/437 2142 |

Die Advokaten (Mein Herr, ich komm' mich anzufragen)

| Berlin
March-
April 1972 | Schreier,
Laubenthal,
Moore | LP: DG 2530 361/2726 083
CD: DG 435 5962 |

Alinde (Die Sonne sinkt ins tiefe Meer)

| Berlin
May 1958 | Moore | LP: HMV ALP 1827
LP: Electrola E 90921
CD: EMI CMS 763 5662 |

| Berlin
December 1966-
February 1968 | Moore | LP: DG 2720 022
CD: DG 437 2152/437 2142 |

Alles um Liebe (Was ist es, das die Seele füllt?)

| Berlin
December 1966-
February 1968 | Moore | LP: DG 2720 022
CD: DG 437 2152/437 2142 |

Die Allmacht (Gross ist Jehova, der Herr)

| Berlin
February-
March 1969 | Moore | LP: DG 2720 006
CD: DG 437 2252/437 2142 |

Der Alpenjäger (Auf hohem Bergesrücken, wo frischer alles grünt)

| Berlin
December 1966-
February 1968 | Moore | LP: DG 2720 022
CD: DG 437 2152/437 2142 |

Der Alpenjäger (Willst du nicht das Lämmlein hüten?)

| Berlin
1959 | Engel | LP: HMV ALP 1850
LP: Electrola E 91024 |

| Berlin
February-
March 1969 | Moore | LP: DG 2720 006
CD: DG 437 2252/437 2142 |

Als ich sie erröten sah (All mein Wirken, all mein Leben)

Berlin	Moore	LP: DG 2720 022
December 1966-		CD: DG 437 2152/437 2142
February 1968		

Alte Liebe rostet nie

Berlin	Moore	LP: DG 2720 022
December 1966-		CD: DG 437 2152/437 2142
February 1968		

Am Bach im Frühling (Du brachst sie nun, die kalte Rinde)

Berlin	Moore	LP: DG 2720 022
December 1966-		CD: DG 437 2152/437 2142
February 1968		

Am Feierabend/Die schöne Müllerin (Hätt' ich tausend Arme zu rühren)
See Die schöne Müllerin

Am Fenster (Ihr lieben Mauern hold und traut)

Berlin	Moore	LP: DG 2720 006
February-		CD: DG 437 2252/437 2142
March 1969		
Tours	Richter	LP: DG 2530 988
July 1977		CD: DG 445 7172
Salzburg	Richter	CD: Orfeo C334 931B/C339 930T
August 1977		
Nürnberg	Höll	CD: Erato 4509 984932
May 1992		Also unpublished video recording

Am Flusse (Verfliesset, vielgeliebte Lieder), 1st setting

Berlin	Moore	LP: DG 2720 022
December 1966-		CD: DG 437 2152/437 2142
February 1968		

Am Flusse (Verfliesset, vielgeliebte Lieder), 2nd setting

Berlin	Moore	LP: DG 2720 006
February-		CD: DG 437 2252/437 2142
March 1969		

Schubert Lieder/continued

Am Grabe Anselmos (Dass ich dich verloren habe)

| Berlin
December 1966-
February 1968 | Moore | LP: DG 2720 022
CD: DG 437 2152/437 2142 |

Am Meer/Schwanengesang (Das Meer erglänzte weit hinaus)

Berlin   Billing   CD: Verona 27064
January 1948   CD: Melodram CDM 18017

London   Moore   78: HMV DB 21491/DB 21586
October 1951   45: Victor WHMV 1046
                                    LP: HMV ALP 1066
                                    LP: Victor LHMV 1046
                                    LP: Electrola E 90052
                                    LP: EMI 1C 175 01764-01766M
                                    CD: EMI CMS 763 5592

Salzburg   Moore   LP: Orfeo S140 855R
August 1956   CD: Orfeo C294 921B/C339 930T

Berlin   Moore   LP: HMV ALP 1993/ASD 544/SLS 840
1961   LP: Electrola E 91204/E 91222/
                                        STE 91204/STE 91222
                                    CD: EMI CDC 749 0812

Berlin   Moore   LP: DG 2720 059/2531 383
March 1972   CD: DG 415 1882/437 2352/437 2142

Berlin   Brendel   LP: Philips 6514 383
August 1982   CD: Philips 411 0512/432 0532

Am See (In des Sees Wogenspiele)

Berlin   Moore   LP: DG 2720 006/2530 347
February-   CD: DG 437 2252/437 2142
March 1969

Am See (Sitz' ich im Gras am glatten See)

Berlin   Moore   LP: DG 2720 022
December 1966-   CD: DG 437 2152/437 2142
February 1968

Am Strome (Ist mir's doch, als sei mein Leben)

Berlin   Engel   LP: HMV ALP 1850
1959   LP: Electrola E 91024

Berlin   Moore   LP: DG 2720 022
December 1966-   CD: DG 437 2152/437 2142
February 1968

Amphiaros (Vor Thebens siebenfach gähnenden Toren)

Berlin	Moore	LP: DG 2720 022
December 1966-		CD: DG 437 2152/437 2142
February 1968		

An Chloen (Bei der Liebe reinsten Flammen glänzt)

Berlin	Moore	LP: DG 2720 022
December 1966-		CD: DG 437 2152/437 2142
February 1968		

An den Frühling (Willkommen, schöner Jüngling!)

Berlin	Moore	LP: DG 2720 022/2530 306
December 1966-		CD: DG 437 2152/437 2142
February 1968		

An den Mond (Füllest wieder Busch und Tal), 1st setting

Berlin	Moore	LP: DG 2720 022
December 1966-		CD: DG 437 2152/437 2142
February 1968		

An den Mond (Füllest wieder Busch und Tal), 2nd setting

| Berlin | Demus | LP: DG LPM 18 617/SLPM 138 117 |
| September 1959 | | LP: DG 2535 104 |

Berlin	Moore	LP: DG 2720 022/2530 229
December 1966-		CD: DG 437 2152/437 2142
February 1968		

An den Mond (Geuss', lieber Mond, geuss' deine Silberflimmen)

Berlin	Moore	LP: DG 2720 022
December 1966-		CD: DG 437 2152/437 2142
February 1968		

An den Mond (Was schauest du so hell und klar?)

Berlin	Moore	LP: DG 2720 022/2530 229
December 1966-		CD: DG 437 2152/437 2142
February 1968		

An den Mond in einer Herbstnacht (Freundlich ist dein Antlitz)

Berlin	Moore	LP: DG 2720 006
February-		CD: DG 437 2252/437 2142
March 1969		

An den Schlaf (Komm' und senke die umflorten Schwingen)

Berlin	Moore	LP: DG 2720 022
December 1966-		CD: DG 437 2152/437 2142
February 1968		

An den Tod (Tod, du Schrecken der Natur)

Berlin	Moore	LP: DG 2720 006
February-		CD: DG 437 2252/437 2142
March 1969		

An die Apfelbäume, wo ich Julien erblickte (Ein heilig Säuseln)

Berlin	Moore	LP: DG 2720 022
December 1966-		CD: DG 437 2152/437 2142
February 1968		

An die Entfernte (So hab' ich wirklich dich verloren?)

Berlin	Moore	LP: HMV ALP 2273/ASD 2273
February-		CD: EMI CDM 769 5032/CMS 763 5662
March 1965		

Berlin	Moore	LP: DG 2720 006
February-		CD: DG 437 2252/437 2142
March 1969		

An die Freude (Freude, schöner Götterfunken)

Berlin	Moore	LP: DG 2720 022/2530 306
December 1966-		CD: DG 437 2152/437 2142
February 1968		

An die Freunde (Im Wald, im Wald da grabt mich ein)

| Berlin | Engel | LP: HMV ALP 1850 |
| 1959 | | LP: Electrola E 91024 |

Berlin	Moore	LP: DG 2720 006
February-		CD: DG 437 2252/437 2142
March 1969		

Schubert Lieder/continued

An die Geliebte (O dass ich dir vom stillen Auge)

Berlin	Moore	LP: DG 2720 022
December 1966-		CD: DG 437 2152/437 2142
February 1968		

An die Laute (Leiser, leiser, kleine Laute)

Berlin	Moore	LP: HMV ALP 2263/ASD 2263
February-		LP: Electrola 1C 063 00292
March 1965		CD: EMI CMS 763 5662

Berlin	Moore	LP: DG 2720 022
December 1966-		CD: DG 437 2152/437 2142
February 1968		

An die Leier (Ich will von Atreus Söhnen)

| Berlin | Demus | LP: DG LPM 18 715/SLPM 138 715 |
| November 1961 | | LP: DG 9108/109 108 |

Berlin	Moore	LP: DG 2720 006
February-		LP: DG 437 2252/437 2142/431 0852
March 1969		

An die Musik (Du holde Kunst, in wieviel grauen Stunden)

| Berlin | Moore | LP: HMV ALP 1677/XLP 30095 |
| 1958 | | LP: Electrola E 90021 |

Berlin	Moore	LP: DG 2720 006
February-		LP: DG 415 1882/437 2252/437 2142
March 1969		

An die Nachtigall (Geuss' nicht so laut der liebentflammten Lieder)

Berlin	Moore	LP: DG 2720 022
December 1966-		CD: DG 437 2152/437 2142
February 1968		

An die Natur (Süsse, heilige Natur)

Berlin	Moore	LP: DG 2720 022
December 1966-		CD: DG 437 2152/437 2142
February 1968		

Schubert Lieder/continued

An die Sonne (Königliche Morgensonne, sei gegrüsst in deiner Wonne)

Berlin	Moore	LP: DG 2720 022
December 1966-		CD: DG 437 2152/437 2142
February 1968		

An die Sonne (O Sonne, Königin der Welt)

Berlin	Ameling, Baker,	LP: DG 2530 409/2726 083
March-	Schreier,	CD: DG 435 5962
April 1972	Moore	

An die untergehende Sonne (Sonne, du sinkst, sink' in Frieden)

Berlin	Moore	LP: DG 2720 022
December 1966-		CD: DG 437 2152/437 2142
February 1968		

An eine Quelle (Du kleine grünumwachsne Quelle)

Berlin	Moore	LP: DG 2720 022
December 1966-		CD: DG 437 2152/437 2142
February 1968		

An Emma (Weit in nebelgrauer Ferne)

Berlin	Moore	LP: DG 2720 022
December 1966-		CD: DG 437 2152/437 2142
February 1968		

An Laura, als sie Klopstocks Auferstehungslied sang (Herzen, die gen Himmel sich erheben)

Berlin	Moore	LP: DG 2720 022
December 1966-		CD: DG 437 2152/437 2142
February 1968		

An mein Herz (O Herz, sei endlich stille!)

Berlin	Moore	LP: DG 2720 006
February-		CD: DG 437 2252/437 2142
March 1969		

An mein Klavier (Sanftes Klavier, welche Entzückungen schaffest du mir)

Berlin	Moore	LP: DG 2720 022
December 1966-		CD: DG 437 2152/437 2142
February 1968		

An Mignon (Ueber Tal und Fluss getragen)

Berlin	Moore	LP: DG 2720 022
December 1966-		CD: DG 437 2152/437 2142
February 1968		

Schubert Lieder/continued

An Rosa I (Warum bist du nicht hier?)

Berlin	Moore	LP: DG 2720 022
December 1966- February 1968		CD: DG 437 2152/437 2142

An Rosa II (Rosa, du denkst an mich?)

Berlin	Moore	LP: DG 2720 022
December 1966- February 1968		CD: DG 437 2152/437 2142

An Schwager Kronos (Spute dich, Kronos!)

Salzburg   Moore   LP: Orfeo S140 855R
August 1957   CD: Orfeo C140 101A/C339 930T

Berlin   Demus   LP: DG LPM 18 617/SLPM 138 117
September 1959   LP: DG 2535 104

Berlin   Moore   LP: DG 2720 022
December 1966-   CD: DG 431 0852/437 2152/437 2142
February 1968

Nürnberg   Höll   CD: Erato 4509 984932
May 1992   Also unpublished video recording

An Sie (Zeit, Verkündigerin der besten Freundin)

Berlin   Moore   LP: DG 2720 022
December 1966-   CD: DG 437 2152/437 2142
February 1968

An Silvia (Was ist Silvia, saget an?)

Berlin   Moore   45: HMV 7ER 5213
1958   LP: HMV ALP 1677/XLP 30095
                                      LP: Electrola E 90021

Berlin   Moore   LP: DG 2720 006
February-   CD: DG 415 1882/437 2252/437 2142
March 1969

Schubert Lieder/continued

Andenken (Ich denke dein)

Berlin	Moore	LP: DG 2720 022
December 1966-		CD: DG 437 2152/437 2142
February 1968		

Antigone und Oedip (Ihr hohen Himmlischen erhöret)

Berlin	Baker	LP: DG 2530 328/2726 083
March-	Moore	CD: DG 435 5962
April 1972		

Der Atlas/Schwanengesang (Ich unglücksel'ger Atlas!)

Berlin	Billing	CD: Verona 27064
January 1948		CD: Melodram MEL 18017

London	Moore	78: HMV DA 2049
October 1951		45: Victor WHMV 1046
		LP: HMV ALP 1066
		LP: Victor LHMV 1046
		LP: Electrola E 90052
		LP: EMI 1C 175 01764-01766M
		CD: EMI CMS 763 5592

Salzburg	Moore	LP: Orfeo S140 855R
August 1956		CD: Orfeo C294 921B/C339 930T

Berlin	Moore	LP: HMV ALP 1993/ASD 544/SLS 840
1961		LP: Electrola E 91204/E 91222/
		STE 91204/STE 91222
		CD: EMI CDC 749 0812

Berlin	Moore	LP: DG 2720 059/2531 383
March 1972		CD: DG 415 1882/437 2352/437 2142

Berlin	Brendel	LP: Philips 6514 383
August 1982		CD: Philips 411 0512/432 0532

Atys (Der Knabe seufzt über's grüne Meer)

Berlin	Moore	LP: DG 2720 006
February-		CD: DG 437 2252/437 2142
March 1969		

Auf dem Flusse/Winterreise (Der du so lustig rauschtest)
See Winterreise

Schubert Lieder/continued

Auf dem See (Und frische Nahrung, neues Blut)

Berlin September 1959	Demus	LP: DG LPM 18 617/SLPM 138 117 LP: DG 2535 104
Berlin December 1966- February 1968	Moore	LP: DG 2720 022 CD: DG 437 2152/437 2142

Auf dem Wasser zu singen (Mitten im Schimmer der spiegelnden Wellen)

Berlin February- March 1965	Moore	LP: HMV ALP 2273/ASD 2273/ASD 2549 LP: EMI SXLP 30553/SHZE 148 CD: EMI CDM 769 5032/CMS 763 5662
Berlin February- March 1969	Moore	LP: DG 2720 006 CD: DG 431 0852/437 2252/437 2142

Auf den Tod einer Nachtigall (Sie ist dahin, die Maienlieder tönte)

Berlin December 1966- February 1968	Moore	LP: DG 2720 022 CD: DG 437 2152/437 2142

Auf der Bruck (Frisch trabe sonder Ruh' und Rast)

Berlin 1958	Moore	LP: HMV ALP 1677/XLP 30095/HQM 1072 LP: Electrola E 90021
Berlin February- March 1969	Moore	LP: DG 2720 006 CD: DG 437 2252/437 2142
Tours July 1977	Richter	LP: DG 2530 988 CD: DG 445 7172
Salzburg August 1977	Richter	CD: Orfeo C334 931B/C339 930T
Nürnberg May 1992	Höll	CD: Erato 4509 984932 Also unpublished video recording

Auf der Donau (Auf der Wellen Spiegel schwimmt der Kahn)

Berlin 1959	Engel	LP: HMV ALP 1850 LP: Electrola E 91024
Berlin February- March 1969	Moore	LP: DG 2720 006 CD: DG 437 2252/437 2142
Tours July 1977	Richter	LP: DG 2530 988 CD: DG 445 7172
Salzburg August 1977	Richter	CD: Orfeo C334 931B/C339 930T
Nürnberg May 1992	Höll	CD: Erato 4509 984932 Also unpublished video recording

Schubert Lieder/continued

Auf der Riesenkoppe (Hoch auf dem Gipfel deiner Gebirge)

Berlin	Moore	LP: HMV ALP 2263/ASD 2263
February-		LP: Electrola 1C 063 00292
March 1965		CD: EMI CMS 763 5662

Berlin	Moore	LP: DG 2720 006
February-		CD: DG 437 2252/437 2142
March 1969		

Auf einem Kirchhof (Sei gegrüsst, geweihte Stille)

Berlin	Moore	LP: DG 2720 022
December 1966-		CD: DG 437 2152/437 2142
February 1968		

Aufenthalt/Schwanengesang (Rauschender Strom, brausender Wald)

| Berlin | Billing | CD: Verona 27064 |
| January 1948 | | CD: Melodram CDM 18017 |

Berlin	Moore	45: HMV 7ER 5194
May 1958		LP: HMV ALP 1827
		LP: Electrola E 90921
		LP: EMI 1C 175 01764-01766M
		CD: EMI CMS 763 5592

Berlin	Moore	LP: HMV ALP 1993/ASD 544/SLS 840
1961		LP: Electrola E 91222/STE 91222
		CD: EMI CDC 749 0812

| Berlin | Moore | LP: DG 2720 059 /2531 383 |
| March 1972 | | CD: DG 415 1882/437 2352/437 2142 |

| Berlin | Brendel | LP: Philips 6514 383 |
| August 1982 | | CD: Philips 411 0512/432 0532 |

Auflösung (Verbirg' dich, Sonne)

| London | Moore | LP: HMV ALP 1295 |
| May 1955 | | LP: Electrola E 90121 |

Berlin	Moore	LP: DG 2720 006/2530 347
February-		CD: DG 437 2252/437 2142
March 1969		

| Berlin | Brendel | LP: Philips 6514 383 |
| August 1982 | | CD: Philips 411 4212 |

Schubert Lieder/continued

Augenlied (Süsse Augen, klare Bronnen!)

Berlin	Moore	LP: DG 2720 022
December 1966-		CD: DG 437 2152/437 2142
February 1968		

Aus Heliopolis I (Im kalten rauhen Norden)

| Berlin | Engel | LP: HMV ALP 1850 |
| 1959 | | LP: Electrola E 91024 |

| Berlin | Demus | LP: DG LPM 18 715/SLPM 138 715 |
| November 1961 | | LP: DG 9108/109 108 |

Berlin	Moore	LP: DG 2720 006
February-		CD: DG 437 2252/437 2142
March 1969		

Aus Heliopolis II (Fels auf Felsen hingewälzt)

| Berlin | Engel | LP: HMV ALP 1850 |
| 1959 | | LP: Electrola E 91024 |

| Berlin | Demus | LP: DG LPM 18 715/SLPM 138 715 |
| November 1961 | | LP: DG 9108/109 108 |

Berlin	Moore	LP: DG 2720 006
February-		CD: DG 437 2252/437 2142
March 1969		

| Tours | Richter | LP: DG 2530 988 |
| July 1977 | | CD: DG 445 7172 |

| Salzburg | Richter | CD: Orfeo C334 931B/C339 930T |
| August 1977 | | |

Des Baches Wiegenlied/Die schöne Müllerin (Gute Ruh'! Gute Ruh'!)
See Die schöne Müllerin

Schubert Lieder/continued

Ballade (Ein Fräulein schaut vom hohen Turm)

Berlin	Moore	LP: DG 2720 022
December 1966-		CD: DG 437 2152/437 2142
February 1968		

Begräbnislied (Begrabt den Leib in seine Gruft)

Berlin	Ameling, Baker,	LP: DG 2530 409/2726 083
March-	Schreier,	CD: DG 435 5962
April 1972	Moore	

Bei dem Grabe meines Vaters (Friede sei um diesen Grabstein her!)

Berlin	Moore	LP: DG 2720 022
December 1966-		CD: DG 437 2152/437 2142
February 1968		

Bei dir allein empfind' ich, dass ich lebe

Berlin	Moore	LP: DG 2720 006
February-		CD: DG 437 2252/437 2142
March 1969		

Beim Winde (Es träumen die Wolken)

Berlin	Engel	LP: HMV ALP 1850
1959		LP: Electrola E 91024

Berlin	Moore	LP: DG 2720 006
February-		CD: DG 437 2252/437 2142
March 1969		

Die Berge (Sieht uns der Blick gehoben)

Berlin	Moore	LP: DG 2720 022
December 1966-		CD: DG 437 2152/437 2142
February 1968		

Die Betende (Laura betet!)

Berlin	Moore	LP: DG 2720 022
December 1966-		CD: DG 437 2152/437 2142
February 1968		

Das Bild (Ein Mädchen ist's, das früh und spät)

Berlin	Moore	LP: DG 2720 022
December 1966-		CD: DG 437 2152/437 2142
February 1968		

Schubert Lieder/continued

Der blinde Knabe (O sagt, ihr Lieben, mir einmal)

Berlin   Moore   LP: DG 2720 006/2530 347
February-   CD: DG 437 2252/437 2142
March 1969

Blondel zu Marien (In düst'rer Nacht, wenn Gram mein fühlend Herz umziehet)

Berlin   Moore   LP: DG 2720 006
February-   CD: DG 437 2252/437 2142
March 1969

Der Blumen Schmerz (Wie tönt es mir so schaurig)

Berlin   Moore   LP: DG 2720 006
February-   CD: DG 437 2252/437 2142
March 1969

Der Blumenbrief (Euch Blümlein will ich senden)

Berlin   Moore   LP: DG 2720 006
February-   CD: DG 437 2252/437 2142
March 1969

Blumenlied (Es ist ein halbes Himmelreich)

Berlin   Moore   LP: DG 2720 022
December 1966-   CD: DG 437 2152/437 2142
February 1968

Die Blumensprache (Es deuten die Blumen des Herzens Gefühl)

Berlin   Moore   LP: DG 2720 022
December 1966-   CD: DG 437 2152/437 2142
February 1968

Die böse Farbe/Die schöne Müllerin (Ich möchte zieh'n in die Welt hinaus)
See Die schöne Müllerin

Schubert Lieder/continued

Bundeslied (In allen guten Stunden)

Berlin	Moore	LP: DG 2720 022
December 1966-		CD: DG 437 2152/437 2142
February 1968		

Die Bürgschaft (Zu Dionys, dem Tyrannen)

Berlin	Engel	LP: Electrola E 91023/STE 91023
January and		LP: Electrola SHZE 219
June 1959		CD: EMI CMS 763 5662

Berlin	Moore	LP: DG 2720 022/2530 306
December 1966-		CD: DG 437 2152/437 2142
February 1968		

Cronnan (Ich sitz' bei der moosigen Quelle)

Berlin	Baker,	LP: DG 2530 328/2726 083
March-	Moore	CD: DG 435 5962
April 1972		

Danksagung an den Bach/Die schöne Müllerin (War es also gemeint?)
See Die schöne Müllerin

Das war ich (Jüngst träumte mir, ich sah auf lichten Höhen)

Berlin	Moore	LP: DG 2720 022
December 1966-		CD: DG 437 2152/437 2142
February 1968		

Dass sie hier gewesen (Dass der Ostwind Düfte hauchet in die Lüfte)

Berlin	Moore	LP: HMV ALP 2263/ASD 2263
February-		LP: Electrola E 91204/STE 91204
March 1965		LP: Electrola 1C 063 00292
		CD: EMI CMS 763 5662

Berlin	Moore	LP: DG 2720 006
February-		CD: DG 437 2252/437 2142
March 1969		

Dithyrambe (Nimmer, das glaubt mir, erscheinen die Götter)

Berlin	Moore	LP: DG 2720 006
February-		CD: DG 437 2252/437 2142
March 1969		

Der Doppelgänger/Schwanengesang (Still ist die Nacht, es ruhen die Gassen)

London October 1951	Moore	78: HMV DB 21491/DB 21586 45: Victor WHMV 1046 LP: HMV ALP 1066 LP: Victor LHMV 1046 LP: Electrola E 90052 LP: EMI 1C 175 01764-01766M CD: EMI CMS 763 5592
Berlin January 1948	Billing	CD: Verona 27064 CD: Melodram MEL 18017
Salzburg August 1956	Moore	LP: Orfeo CD: Orfeo C294 921B/C339 930T
Berlin 1961	Moore	LP: HMV ALP 1993/ASD 544/SLS 840 LP: Electrola E 91204/E 91222/ STE 91204/STE 91222 CD: EMI CDC 749 0812
Berlin March 1972	Moore	LP: DG 2720 059 /2531 383 CD: DG 415 1882/437 2352/437 2142
Berlin August 1982	Brendel	LP: Philips 6514 383 CD: Philips 411 0512/432 0532

Drang in die Ferne (Vater, du glaubst es nicht)

Berlin February- March 1969	Moore	LP: DG 2720 006 CD: DG 437 2252/437 2142

Du bist die Ruh'

London October 1951	Moore	78: HMV DB 21349 CD: EMI CMS 763 5592
Berlin February- March 1965	Moore	LP: HMV ALP 2263/ASD 2263 LP: Electrola E 91204/STE 91204 LP: Electrola 1C 063 00292 LP: EMI SXLP 30553/SHZE 148 CD: EMI CDM 769 5032/CMS 763 5662
Berlin February- March 1969	Moore	LP: DG 2720 006 CD: DG 431 0852/437 2252/437 2142

Schubert Lieder/continued

Du liebst mich nicht (Mein Herz ist zerrissen)

Berlin	Moore	LP: DG 2720 006
February-		CD: DG 437 2252/437 2142
March 1969		

Eifersucht und Stolz/Die schöne Müllerin (Wohin so schnell, so kraus und wild?)
See Die schöne Müllerin

Der Einsame (Wann meine Grillen schwirren)

| London | Moore | LP: HMV ALP 1295 |
| May 1955 | | LP: Electrola E 90121 |

| London | Moore | LP: EMI AN 182-183/SAN 182-183 |
| February 1967 | | LP: EMI SLS 926 |

Berlin	Moore	LP: DG 2720 006
February-		CD: DG 431 0852/437 2252/437 2142
March 1969		

| Salzburg | Richter | CD: Orfeo C334 931B/C339 930T |
| August 1977 | | |

| Berlin | Brendel | CD: Philips 411 4212 |
| August 1982 | | |

| Nürnberg | Höll | CD: Erato 4509 984932 |
| May 1992 | | Also unpublished video recording |

Einsamkeit (Gib' mir die Fülle der Einsamkeit)

| Berlin | Engel | LP: Electrola E 91023/STE 91023 |
| 1958 | | |

Berlin	Moore	LP: DG 2720 006
February-		CD: DG 437 2252/437 2142
March 1969		

Einsamkeit/Winterreise (Wie eine trübe Wolke)
See Winterreise

Die Einsiedelei (Es rieselt klar und wehend)

Berlin	Moore	LP: DG 2720 022
December 1966-		CD: DG 437 2152/437 2142
February 1968		

Elysium (Vorüber die stöhnende Klage!)

Berlin	Moore	LP: DG 2720 006
February-		CD: DG 437 2252/437 2142
March 1969		

Schubert Lieder/continued

Der Entfernten (Wohl denk' ich allenthalben)

Berlin	Moore	LP: DG 2720 022
December 1966- February 1968		CD: DG 437 2152/437 2142

Der entsühnte Orest (Zu meinen Füssen brichst du dich)

Berlin November 1961	Demus	LP: DG LPM 18 715/SLPM 138 715
Berlin February- March 1969	Moore	LP: DG 2720 006 CD: DG 437 2252/437 2142

Entzückung (Tag voll Himmel!)

Berlin	Moore	LP: DG 2720 022
December 1966- February 1968		CD: DG 437 2152/437 2142

Die Entzückung an Laura (Laura, über diese Welt zu flüchten)

Berlin	Moore	LP: DG 2720 022
December 1966- February 1968		CD: DG 437 2152/437 2142

Erinnerung (Ich lag auf grünen Matten)

Berlin	Moore	LP: DG 2720 022
December 1966- February 1968		CD: DG 437 2152/437 2142

Erinnerungen (Am Seegestad in lauen Vollmondsnächten)

Berlin	Moore	LP: DG 2720 022
December 1966- February 1968		CD: DG 437 2152/437 2142

Erlafsee (Mir ist so wohl, so weh)

Berlin 1959	Engel	LP: HMV ALP 1850 LP: Electrola E 91024
Berlin February- March 1969	Moore	LP: DG 2720 006 CD: DG 437 2252/437 2142

Schubert Lieder/continued

Erlkönig (Wer reitet so spät durch Nacht und Wind?)

| London | Moore | 78: HMV DB 21350 |
| October 1951 | | CD: EMI CMS 763 5592 |

Berlin	Moore	45: HMV 7ER 5194
May 1958		LP: HMV ALP 1827/ASD 2549
		LP: Electrola E 90921/1C 047 01247
		LP: Electrola SHZE 148/SHZE 219
		LP: EMI SXLP 30553
		CD: EMI CDM 769 5032

Berlin	Moore	LP: DG 2720 022/2740 188
December 1966-		LP: DG 2530 229/2535 656
February 1968		CD: DG 431 0852/437 2152/437 2142

Erntelied (Sicheln schallen, Aehren fallen)

Berlin	Moore	LP: DG 2720 022
December 1966-		CD: DG 437 2152/437 2142
February 1968		

Erstarrung/Winterreise (Ich such' im Schnee vergebens)
See Winterreise

Die erste Liebe füllt das Herz mit Sehnen

Berlin	Moore	LP: DG 2720 022
December 1966-		CD: DG 437 2152/437 2142
February 1968		

Erster Verlust (Ach, wer bringt die schönen Tage)

| Berlin | Demus | LP: DG LPM 18 617/SLPM 138 117 |
| September 1959 | | LP: DG 2535 104 |

Berlin	Moore	LP: DG 2720 022
December 1966-		CD: DG 437 2152/437 2142
February 1968		

Die Erwartung (Hör' ich das Pförtchen nicht gehen?)

| Berlin | Engel | LP: HMV ALP 1767/ASD 337 |
| 1959 | | LP: World Records T 671/ST 671 |

Berlin	Moore	LP: DG 2720 022
December 1966-		CD: DG 437 2152/437 2142
February 1968		

Fahrt zum Hades (Der Nachen dröhnt, Zypressen flüstern)

Berlin	Demus	LP: DG LPM 18 715/SLPM 138 715
November 1961		

Berlin	Moore	LP: DG 2720 022
December 1966-		CD: DG 437 2152/437 2142
February 1968		

Das Finden (Ich hab' ein Mädchen funden)

Berlin	Moore	LP: DG 2720 022
December 1966-		CD: DG 437 2152/437 2142
February 1968		

Der Fischer (Das Wasser rauscht, das Wasser schwoll)

Berlin	Engel	LP: Electrola E 91023/STE 91023
January and		LP: Electrola SHZE 219
June 1959		CD: EMI CMS 763 5662

Berlin	Moore	LP: DG 2720 022/2530 229
December 1966-		CD: DG 437 2152/437 2142
February 1968		

Fischerlied (Das Fischergewerbe gibt rüstigen Mut), 1st setting

Berlin	Moore	LP: DG 2720 022
December 1966-		CD: DG 437 2152/437 2142
February 1968		

Fischerlied (Das Fischergewerbe gibt rüstigen Mut), 2nd setting

Berlin	Moore	LP: DG 2720 006
February-		CD: DG 437 2252/437 2142
March 1969		

Schubert Lieder/continued

Das Fischermädchen/Schwanengesang (Du schönes Fischermädchen)

Berlin January 1948	Billing	CD: Verona 27064 CD: Melodram CDM 18017
London October 1951	Moore	78: HMV DA 2045 45: Victor WHMV 1046/EHA 8 LP: HMV ALP 1066 LP: Victor LHMV 1046 LP: Electrola E 90052 LP: EMI 1C 175 01764-01766M/RLS 766 CD: EMI CMS 763 5592
Salzburg August 1956	Moore	LP: Orfeo CD: Orfeo C294 921B/C339 930T
Berlin 1961	Moore	LP: HMV ALP 1993/ASD 544/SLS 840 LP: Electrola E 91204/E 91222 STE 91204/STE 91222 CD: EMI CDC 749 0812
Berlin March 1972	Moore	LP: DG 2720 059 /2531 383 CD: DG 415 1882/437 2352/437 2142
Berlin August 1982	Brendel	LP: Philips 6514 383 CD: Philips 411 0512/432 0532

Des Fischers Liebesglück (Dort blinket durch Weiden und winket ein Schimmer)

Berlin February- March 1965	Moore	LP: HMV ALP 2263/ASD 2263 LP: EMI 1C 063 00292/EX 29 04293 CD: EMI CMS 763 5662
Berlin February- March 1969	Moore	LP: DG 2720 006 CD: DG 437 2252/437 2142
Nürnberg May 1992	Höll	CD: Erato 4509 984932 Also unpublished video recording

Fischerweise (Den Fischer fechten Sorgen)

Berlin February- March 1965	Moore	LP: HMV ALP 2263/ASD 2263 LP: EMI 1C 063 00292 CD: EMI CMS 763 5662
Berlin February- March 1969	Moore	LP: DG 2720 006 CD: DG 437 2252/437 2142
Tours July 1977	Richter	LP: DG 2530 988 CD: DG 445 7172
Salzburg August 1977	Richter	CD: Orfeo C334 931B/C339 930T
Nürnberg May 1992	Höll	CD: Erato 4509 984932 Also unpublished video recording

Schubert Lieder/continued

Der Flüchtling (Frisch atmet des Morgens lebendiger Hauch)

Berlin	Moore	LP: DG 2720 022
December 1966-		CD: DG 437 2152/437 2142
February 1968		

Der Flug der Zeit (Es floh die Zeit im Wirbelfluge)

Berlin	Moore	LP: DG 2720 022
December 1966-		CD: DG 437 2152/437 2142
February 1968		

Der Fluss (Wie rein Gesang sich windet)

Berlin	Moore	LP: DG 2720 006
February-		CD: DG 437 2252/437 2142
March 1969		

Die Forelle (In einem Bächlein helle)

Berlin	Moore	LP: HMV ALP 2263/ASD 2263
February-		LP: EMI 1C 063 00292/1C 047 01247
March 1965		LP: EMI SXLP 30553/SHZE 148
		CD: EMI CDM 769 5032/CMS 763 5662

Berlin	Moore	LP: DG 2720 006/2740 188
February-		CD: DG 415 1882/431 0852
March 1969		CD: DG 437 2252/437 2142

Fragment aus dem Aischylos (So wird der Mann, der sonder Zwang gerecht ist)

Berlin	Demus	LP: DG LPM 18 715/SLPM 138 715
November 1961		

Berlin	Moore	LP: DG 2720 022
December 1966-		CD: DG 437 2152/437 2142
February 1968		

Schubert Lieder/continued

Freiwilliges Versinken (Wohin, o Helios? Wohin?)

| Berlin
November 1961 | Demus | LP: DG LPM 18 715/SLPM 138 715 |

| Berlin
February-
March 1969 | Moore | LP: DG 2720 006
CD: DG 437 2252/437 2142 |

| Nürnberg
May 1992 | Höll | CD: Erato 4509 984932
Also unpublished video recording |

Freude der Kinderjahre (Freude, die im frühen Lenze)

| Berlin
December 1966-
February 1968 | Moore | LP: DG 2720 022
CD: DG 437 2152/437 2142 |

Frohsinn (Ich bin von lockrem Schlage)

| Berlin
December 1966-
February 1968 | Moore | LP: DG 2720 022
CD: DG 437 2152/437 2142 |

Die Fröhlichkeit (Wess' Adern leichtes Blut durchspringt)

| Berlin
December 1966-
February 1968 | Moore | LP: DG 2720 022
CD: DG 437 2152/437 2142 |

Die frühe Liebe (Schon im bunten Knabenkleide)

| Berlin
December 1966-
February 1968 | Moore | LP: DG 2720 022
CD: DG 437 2152/437 2142 |

Die frühen Gräber (Willkommen, o silberner Mond!)

| Berlin
December 1966-
February 1968 | Moore | LP: DG 2720 022
CD: DG 437 2152/437 2142 |

Frühlingsglaube (Die linden Düfte sind erwacht)

| Berlin
1958 | Moore | 45: HMV 7ER 5213
LP: HMV ALP 1677/XLP 30095
LP: Electrola E 90021 |

| Berlin
February-
March 1969 | Moore | LP: DG 2720 006
CD: DG 437 2252/437 2142 |

Schubert Lieder/continued

Frühlingslied (Die Luft ist blau, das Tal ist grün)

Berlin May 1965	Demus	LP: DG 2707 028/2726 058
Berlin December 1966- February 1968	Moore	LP: DG 2720 022 CD: DG 437 2152/437 2142

Frühlingssehnsucht/Schwanengesang (Säuselnde Lüfte wehend so mild)

Berlin January 1948	Billing	CD: Verona 27064 CD: Melodram CDM 18017
London May 1955	Moore	HMV unpublished
Salzburg August 1957	Moore	LP: Orfeo S140 855R CD: Orfeo C140 101A/C339 930T
London September 1957	Moore	LP: HMV ALP 1295 LP: Electrola E 90121 LP: EMI 1C 175 01764-01766M CD: EMI CMS 763 5592
Berlin 1961	Moore	LP: HMV ALP 1993/ASD 544/SLS 840 LP: Electrola E 91222/STE 91222 CD: EMI CDC 749 0812
Berlin March 1972	Moore	LP: DG 2720 059 /2531 383 CD: DG 415 1882/437 2352/437 2142
Berlin August 1982	Brendel	LP: Philips 6514 383 CD: Philips 411 0512/432 0532

Frühlingstraum/Winterreise (Ich träumte von bunten Blumen)
See Winterreise

Fülle der Liebe (Ein sehnend Streben teilt mir das Herz)

Berlin February- March 1969	Moore	LP: DG 2720 006 CD: DG 437 2252/437 2142

Schubert Lieder/continued

Furcht der Geliebten (Cidli, du weinst und ich schlummre sicher)

Berlin   Moore   LP: DG 2720 022
December 1966-   CD: DG 437 2152/437 2142
February 1968

Ganymed (Wie im Morgenglanze du rings mich anglühst)

Berlin   Demus   LP: DG LPM 18 617/SLPM 138 117
September 1959   LP: DG 2535 104

Berlin   Moore   LP: DG 2720 022/2740 188
December 1966-   CD: DG 437 2152/437 2142
February 1968

Gebet (Du Urquell aller Güte)

Berlin   Ameling, Baker, LP: DG 2530 409/2726 083
March-   Schreier,   CD: DG 435 5962
April 1972   Moore

Geburtstagshymne (Schicksalslenker, blicke nieder)

Berlin   Ameling, Baker, LP: DG 2530 409/2726 083
March-   Schreier,   CD: DG 435 5962
April 1972   Moore

Die Gebüsche (Es wehet kühl und leise)

Berlin   Moore   LP: DG 2720 006
February-   CD: DG 437 2252/437 2142
March 1969

Die gefangenen Sänger (Hörst du von den Nachtigallen)

Berlin   Moore   LP: DG 2720 006
February-   CD: DG 437 2252/437 2142
March 1969

Gefror'ne Tränen/Winterreise (Gefror'ne Tränen fallen von meinen Wangen ab)
See Winterreise

Schubert Lieder/continued

Geheimes (Ueber meines Liebchens Aeugeln)

London May 1955	Moore	LP: HMV ALP 1295 LP: Electrola E 90121
Salzburg August 1957	Moore	LP: Orfeo S140 855R CD: Orfeo C140 101A/C339 930T
Berlin February- March 1969	Moore	LP: DG 2720 006 CD: DG 437 2252/2142
Salzburg August 1977	Richter	CD: Orfeo C334 931B/C339 930T

Das Geheimnis (Sie konnte mir kein Wörtchen sagen), 1st setting

| Berlin
December 1966-
February 1968 | Moore | LP: DG 2720 022
CD: DG 437 2152/437 2142 |

Das Geheimnis (Sie konnte mir kein Wörtchen sagen), 2nd setting

| Berlin
February-
March 1969 | Moore | LP: DG 2720 006/2530 306
CD: DG 437 2252/437 2142 |

Geheimnis an Franz Schubert (Sag' an, wer lehrt dich Lieder?)

| Berlin
December 1966-
February 1968 | Moore | LP: DG 2720 022
CD: DG 437 2152/437 2142 |

Geist der Liebe (Der Abend schleiert Flur und Hain)

| Berlin
December 1966-
February 1968 | Moore | LP: DG 2720 022
CD: DG 437 2152/437 2142 |

Geist der Liebe (Wer bist du, Geist der Liebe?)

| Berlin
December 1966-
February 1968 | Moore | LP: DG 2720 022
CD: DG 437 2152/437 2142 |

Schubert Lieder/continued

Geisternähe (Der Dämm'rung Schein durchblinkt den Hain)

Berlin	Moore	LP: DG 2720 022
December 1966-		CD: DG 437 2152/437 2142
February 1968		

Der Geistertanz (Die bretterne Kammer der Toten erbebt)

Berlin	Moore	LP: DG 2720 022
December 1966-		CD: DG 437 2152/437 2142
February 1968		

Geistesgruss (Hoch auf dem alten Turme)

Berlin	Moore	LP: DG 2720 022
December 1966-		CD: DG 437 2152/437 2142
February 1968		

Genügsamkeit (Dort raget ein Berg aus den Wolken hehr)

Berlin	Moore	LP: DG 2720 022
December 1966-		CD: DG 437 2152/437 2142
February 1968		

Gesang aus der Harmonie (Schöpferin beseelter Töne!)

Berlin	Moore	LP: DG 2720 022
December 1966-		CD: DG 437 2152/437 2142
February 1968		

Gesänge des Harfners I-III: Wer sich der Einsamkeit ergibt; An die Türen will ich schleichen; Wer nie sein Brot mit Tränen ass

Berlin	Demus	LP: DG LPM 18 617/SLPM 138 117
September 1959		LP: DG 2535 104
Berlin	Moore	LP: DG 2720 022/2530 229
December 1966-		CD: DG 437 437 2152/437 2142
February 1968		
Berlin	Brendel	CD: Philips 411 4212
August 1982		

Schubert Lieder/continued

Die Gestirne (Es tönet sein Lob Feld und Wald)

Berlin   Moore   LP: DG 2720 022
December 1966-   CD: DG 437 2152/437 2142
February 1968

Das gestörte Glück (Ich hab' ein heisses junges Blut)

Berlin   Moore   LP: DG 2720 022
December 1966-   CD: DG 437 2152/437 2142
February 1968

Glaube, Hoffnung und Liebe (Glaube, hoffe, liebe!)

Berlin   Moore   LP: DG 2720 006
February-   CD: DG 437 2252/437 2142
March 1969

Der Goldschmiedsgesell (Es ist doch meine Nachbarin ein allerliebstes Mädchen)

Berlin   Moore   LP: DG 2720 022
December 1966-   CD: DG 437 2152/437 2142
February 1968

Gondelfahrer (Es tanzen Mond und Sterne)

Berlin   Moore   LP: DG 2720 006
February-   CD: DG 437 2252/437 2142
March 1969

Gott der Weltschöpfer (Zu Gott flieg' ich hoch über alle Sphären)

Berlin   Ameling, Baker,   LP: DG 2530 409/2726 083
March-   Schreier,   CD: DG 435 5962
April 1972   Moore

Schubert Lieder/continued

Gott im Frühlinge (In seinen schimmernden Gewand)

Berlin	Moore	LP: DG 2720 022
December 1966-		CD: DG 437 2152/437 2142
February 1968		

Gott im Ungewitter (Du Schrecklicher, er kann von dir)

Berlin	Ameling, Baker,	LP: DG 2530 409/2726 083
March-	Schreier,	CD: DG 435 5962
April 1972	Moore	

Die Götter Griechenlands (Schöne Welt, wo bist du?)

Berlin	Engel	LP: HMV ALP 1767/ASD 337
January 1959		LP: World Records T 671/ST 671
		LP: EMI EX 29 04293
		CD: EMI CMS 763 5662

Berlin	Moore	LP: DG 2720 006/2530 306
February-		CD: DG 437 2252/437 2142
March 1969		

| Nürnberg | Höll | CD: Erato 4509 984932 |
| May 1992 | | Also unpublished video recording |

Das Grab (Das Grab ist tief und stille)

Berlin	Moore	LP: DG 2720 006
February-		CD: DG 437 2252/437 2142
March 1969		

Grablied (Er fiel dem Tod fürs Vaterland)

Berlin	Moore	LP: DG 2720 022/2530 347
December 1966-		CD: DG 437 2152/437 2142
February 1968		

Grablied für die Mutter (Hauche milder, Abendluft)

Berlin	Moore	LP: DG 2720 006
February-		CD: DG 437 2252/437 2142
March 1969		

Der greise Kopf/Winterreise (Der Reif hatt' einen weissen Schein)
See Winterreise

Schubert Lieder/continued

Greisengesang (Der Frost hat mir bereifet des Hauses Dach)

Berlin May 1958	Moore	LP: HMV ALP 1827/EX 29 04293 LP: Electrola E 90921 CD: EMI CMS 763 5662
Berlin February- March 1969	Moore	LP: DG 2720 006 CD: DG 437 2252/437 2142

Grenzen der Menschheit (Wenn der uralte heilige Vater)

Berlin February- March 1969	Moore	LP: DG 2720 006 CD: DG 437 2252/437 2142

Das grosse Halleluja (Ehre sei dem Hocherhabnen)

Berlin December 1966- February 1968	Moore	LP: DG 2720 022 CD: DG 437 2152/437 2142

Gruppe aus dem Tartarus (Horch', wie Murmeln des empörten Meeres)

Berlin January 1959	Engel	LP: HMV ALP 1767/ASD 337 LP: World Records T 671/ST 671
Berlin February- March 1969	Moore	LP: DG 2720 006/2530 306 CD: DG 437 2252/437 2142
Berlin August 1982	Brendel	CD: Philips 411 4212

Der gute Hirte (Was sorgest du? Sei stille, meine Seele!)

Berlin December 1966- February 1968	Moore	LP: DG 2720 022 CD: DG 437 2152/437 2142

Gute Nacht/Winterreise (Fremd bin ich eingezogen)
See Winterreise

Schubert Lieder/continued

Halt!/Die schöne Müllerin (Eine Mühle seh' ich blinken aus der Erlen heraus)
See Die schöne Müllerin

Hänflings Liebeswerbung (Ahidi, ich liebe!)

Berlin February- March 1969	Moore	LP: DG 2720 006 CD: DG 437 2252/437 2142

Heidenröslein (Sah ein Knab' ein Röslein stehn)

Berlin February- March 1965	Moore	LP: HMV ALP 2263/ASD 2263 LP: EMI 1C 063 00292/1C 047 01247 LP: EMI SXLP 30553/SHZE 148 CD: EMI CDM 769 5032/CMS 763 5662
Berlin December 1966- February 1968	Moore	LP: DG 2720 022/2530 229/2535 656 CD: DG 415 1882/431 0852 CD: DG 437 2152/437 2142

Das Heimweh (Ach, der Gebirgssohn hängt mit kindlicher LIeb' an der Heimat)

Berlin February- March 1969	Moore	LP: DG 2720 006 CD: DG 437 2252/437 2142

Das Heimweh (Oft in einsam stillen Stunden)

Berlin February- March 1965	Moore	LP: HMV ALP 2273/ASD 2273 CD: EMI CDM 769 5032/CMS 763 5662
Berlin December 1966- February 1968	Moore	LP: DG 2720 022 CD: DG 437 2152/437 2142

Hektors Abschied (Will sich Hektor ewig von mir wenden)

Berlin March- April 1972	Baker, Moore	LP: DG 2530 328/2726 083 CD: DG 435 5962

Herbst (Es rauschen die Winde so herbstlich und kalt)

Berlin February- March 1969	Moore	LP: DG 2720 006 CD: DG 437 2252/437 2142
Berlin August 1982	Brendel	CD: Philips 411 4212

Schubert Lieder/continued

Der Kreuzzug (Ein Mönch steht in seiner Zell' am Fenstergitter grau)

Berlin January 1948	Billing	CD: Verona 27064

London May 1955	Moore	LP: HMV ALP 1295 LP: Electrola E 90121

Salzburg August 1957	Moore	LP: Orfeo S140 855R CD: Orfeo C140 101A/C339 930T

Berlin May 1965	Demus	LP: DG 2707 028/2726 058

Berlin February- March 1969	Moore	LP: DG 2720 006 CD: DG 437 2252/437 2142

Nürnberg May 1992	Höll	CD: Erato 4509 984932 Also unpublished video recording

Kriegers Ahnung/Schwanengesang (In tiefer Ruh' liegt um mich her der Waffenbrüder Kreis)

Berlin January 1948	Billing	CD: Verona 27064 CD: Melodram CDM 18017

Berlin May 1958	Moore	LP: HMV ALP 1677/XLP 30095 LP: Electrola E 90021 LP: EMI 1C 175 01764-01766M CD: EMI CMS 763 5592

Berlin 1961	Moore	LP: HMV ALP 1993/ASD 544/SLS 840 LP: Electrola E 91222/STE 91222 CD: EMI CDC 749 0812

Berlin March 1972	Moore	LP: DG 2720 059/2531 383 CD: DG 415 1882/437 2352/437 2142

Berlin August 1982	Brendel	LP: Philips 6514 383 CD: Philips 411 0512/432 0532

Labetrank der Liebe (Wenn im Spiele leiser Töne)

Berlin December 1966- February 1968	Moore	LP: DG 2720 022 CD: DG 437 2152/437 2142

Schubert Lieder/continued

Lachen und Weinen zu jeglicher Stunde

Berlin   Moore   LP: HMV ALP 2263/ASD 2263
February-   LP: Electrola E 91204/STE 91204
March 1965   LP: EMI 1C 063 00292/SHZE 148
                                    LP: EMI SXLP 30553
                                    CD: EMI CMS 763 5662

Berlin   Moore   LP: DG 2720 006
February-   CD: DG 431 0852/437 2252/437 2142
March 1969

Die Laube (Nimmer werd' ich dein vergessen)

Berlin   Moore   LP: DG 2720 022
December 1966-   CD: DG 437 2152/437 2142
February 1968

Laura am Klavier (Wenn dein Finger durch die Saiten meistert)

Berlin   Moore   LP: DG 2720 022
December 1966-   CD: DG 437 2152/437 2142
February 1968

Lebenslied (Kommen und Scheiden, Suchen und Meiden)

Berlin   Moore   LP: DG 2720 022
December 1966-   CD: DG 437 2152/437 2142
February 1968

Lebenslust (Wer Lebenslust fühlet)

Berlin   Ameling, Baker,   LP: DG 2530 409/2726 083
March-   Schreier,   CD: DG 435 5962
April 1972

Lebensmut (O wie dringt das junge Leben kräftig mir durch Sinn und Herz!)

Berlin   Moore   LP: DG 2720 006
February-   CD: DG 437 2252/437 2142
March 1969

Eine Leichenphantasie (Mit erstorb'nem Scheinen steht der Mond)

Berlin   Moore   LP: DG 2720 022
December 1966-   Cd: DG 437 2152/437 2142
February 1968

Schubert Lieder/continued

Der Herbstabend (Abendglockenhalle zittern dumpf durch Moorgedüfte hin)

Berlin   Moore   LP: DG 2720 022
December 1966-   CD: DG 437 2152/437 2142
February 1968

Herbstlied (Bunt sind schon die Wälder)

Berlin   Moore   LP: DG 2720 022
December 1966-   CD: DG 437 2152/437 2142
February 1968

Hermann und Thusnelda (Dort kommt er mit Schweiss)

Berlin   Baker,   LP: DG 2530 328/2726 083
March-   Moore   CD: DG 435 5962
April 1972

Herrn Josef Spaun ((Und nimmer schreibst du?)

Berlin   Moore   LP: DG 2720 006/2530 347
February-   CD: DG 437 2252/437 2142
March 1969

Himmelsfunken (Der Odem Gottes weht)

Berlin   Moore   LP: DG 2720 006
February-   CD: DG 437 2252/437 2142
March 1969

Hippolits Lied (Lasst mich, ob ich auch still verglüh')

Berlin   Moore   LP: DG 2720 006
February-   CD: DG 437 2252/437 2142
March 1969

Berlin   Brendel   CD: Philips 411 4212
August 1982

Schubert Lieder/continued

Der Hirt (Du Turm! Zu meinem Leide ragst du so hoch empor)

Berlin	Moore	LP: DG 2720 022
December 1966-		CD: DG 437 2152/437 2142
February 1968		

Hoffnung (Es reden, träumen die Menschen viel)

Berlin	Moore	LP: DG 2720 006
February-		CD: DG 437 2252/437 2142
March 1969		

Hoffnung (Schaff' das Tagwerk meiner Hände hohes Glück)

Berlin	Moore	LP: DG 2720 022
December 1966-		CD: DG 437 2152/437 2142
February 1968		

Nürnberg	Höll	CD: Erato 4509 984932
May 1992		Also unpublished video recording

Hochzeitslied (Will singen euch im alten Ton)

Berlin	Moore	LP: DG 2720 022
December 1966-		CD: DG 437 2152/437 2142
February 1968		

Der Hochzeitsbraten (Ach liebes Herz, ach Theobald!)

Berlin	Ameling, Schreier,	LP: DG 2530 361/2726 083
March-	Moore	CD: DG 435 5962
April 1972		

Huldigung (Ganz verloren, ganz versunken)

Berlin	Moore	LP: DG 2720 022
December 1966-		CD: DG 437 2152/437 2142
February 1968		

Hymnen I-IV: Wenige wissen das Geheimnis der Liebe; Wenn ich ihn nur habe;
Wenn alle untreu werden; Ich sag' es jedem, dass er lebt

Berlin	Moore	LP: DG 2720 006
February-		CD: DG 437 2252/437 2142
March 1969		

Schubert Lieder/continued

Hymne an den Unendlichen (Zwischen Himmel und Erd')

| Berlin March- April 1972 | Ameling, Baker, Schreier, Moore | LP: DG 2530 409/2726 083 CD: DG 435 5962 |

Ihr Bild/Schwanengesang (Ich stand in dunklen Träumen)

| Berlin January 1948 | Billing | CD: Verona 27064 CD: Melodram CDM 18017 |

| London October 1951 | Moore | 78: HMV DA 2049 LP: HMV ALP 1066 LP: Electrola E 90052 LP: EMI 1C 175 01764-01766M CD: EMI CMS 763 5592 |

| Salzburg August 1956 | Moore | LP: Orfeo S140 855R CD: Orfeo C294 921B/C339 930T |

| Berlin 1961 | Moore | LP: HMV ALP 1993/ASD 544/SLS 840 LP: Electrola E 91204/E 91222/ STE 91204/STE 91222 CD: EMI CDC 749 0812 |

| Berlin March 1972 | Moore | LP: DG 2720 059/2531 383 CD: DG 415 1882/437 2352/437 2142 |

| Berlin August 1982 | Brendel | LP: Philips 6514 383 CD: Philips 411 0512/432 0532 |

Ihr Grab (Dort ist ihr Grab, die einst im Schmelz der Jugend glühte)

| Berlin February- March 1969 | Moore | LP: DG 2720 006 CD: DG 437 2252/437 2142 |

Im Abendrot (O wie schön ist diese Welt)

| London May 1955 | Moore | LP: HMV ALP 1295 LP: Electrola E 90121 |

| London February 1967 | Moore | LP: EMI AN 182-183/SAN 182-183 LP: EMI SLS 926/ASD 143 5941 CD: EMI CDC 749 2382/CDEMX 2233 |

| Berlin February- March 1969 | Moore | LP: DG 2720 006/2740 188 CD: DG 415 1882/431 0852 CD: DG 437 2252/437 2142 |

| Berlin August 1982 | Brendel | CD: Philips 411 4212 |

| Nürnberg May 1992 | Höll | CD: Erato 4509 984932 Also unpublished video recording |

Schubert Lieder/continued

Im Dorfe/Winterreise (Es bellen die Hunde, es rasseln die Ketten)
See Winterreise

Im Freien (Draussen in der weiten Nacht)

Berlin February- March 1969	Moore	LP: DG 2720 006 CD: DG 437 2252/437 2142

Im Frühling (Still sitz' ich an des Hügels Hang)

Salzburg August 1957	Moore	LP: Orfeo CD: Orfeo C140 101A/C339 930T
Berlin 1958	Moore	LP: HMV ALP 1677/XLP 30095 LP: Electrola E 90021
London February 1967	Moore	EMI unpublished
Berlin February- March 1969	Moore	LP: DG 2720 006 CD: DG 437 2252/437 2142
Tours July 1977	Richter	LP: DG 2530 988 CD: DG 445 7172
Salzburg August 1977	Richter	CD: Orfeo C334 931B/C339 930T

Im Haine (Sonnenstrahlen durch die Tannen)

Berlin February- March 1969	Moore	LP: DG 2720 006/2530 347 CD: DG 437 2252/437 2142

Im Walde (Ich wand're über Berg und Tal)

Berlin February- March 1969	Moore	LP: DG 2720 006 CD: DG 437 2252/437 2142

Im Walde (Windes Rauschen, Gottes Flügel)

Berlin February- March 1965	Moore	LP: HMV ALP 2263/ASD 2263 LP: Electrola E 91204/STE 91204 LP: EMI 1C 063 00292 CD: EMI CMS 763 5662
Berlin February- March 1969	Moore	LP: DG 2720 006 CD: DG 437 2252/437 2142

Schubert Lieder/continued

In der Ferne/Schwanengesang (Wehe, den Fliehenden, Welt hinaus ziehenden!)

Berlin   Billing   CD: Verona 27064
January 1948   CD: Melodram CDM 18017

Berlin   Moore   LP: HMV ALP 1827
May 1958   LP: Electrola E 90921
                                CD: EMI CMS 763 5592

Berlin   Moore   LP: HMV ALP 1993/ASD 544/SLS 840
1961   LP: Electrola E 91222/STE 91222
                                CD: EMI CDC 749 0812

Berlin   Moore   LP: DG 2720 059/2531 383
March 1972   CD: DG 415 1882/437 2352/437 2142

Berlin   Brendel   LP: Philips 6514 383
August 1982   CD: Philips 411 0512/432 0532

In der Mitternacht (Todesstille deckt das Tal)

Berlin   Moore   LP: DG 2720 022
December 1966-   CD: DG 437 2152/437 2142
February 1968

L'incanto degli occhi (Da voi, cari lumi, di pende il mio stato)

Berlin   Moore   LP: DG 2720 006
February-   CD: DG 437 2252/437 2142
March 1969

Irdisches Glück (So mancher sieht mit finst'rer Miene)

Berlin   Moore   LP: DG 2720 006
February-   CD: DG 437 2252/437 2142
March 1969

Irrlicht/Winterreise (In die tiefsten Felsengründe)
See Winterreise

Der Jäger/Die schöne Müllerin (Was sucht denn der Jäger am Mühlbach hier?)
See Die schöne Müllerin

Schubert Lieder/continued

Jägers Abendlied (Im Felde schleich' ich, still und wild)

Berlin September 1959	Demus	LP: DG LPM 18 617/SLPM 138 117 LP: DG 2535 104
Berlin December 1966- February 1968	Moore	LP: DG 2720 022/2740 188 CD: DG 431 0852/437 2152/437 2142

Jägers Liebeslied (Ich schiess' den Hirsch im grünen Forst)

Berlin May 1965	Demus	LP: DG 2707 028/2726 058
Berlin February- March 1969	Moore	LP: DG 2720 006 CD: DG 437 2252/437 2142

Julius an Theone (Nimmer, nimmer darf ich dir gestehen)

Berlin December 1966- February 1968	Moore	LP: DG 2720 022 CD: DG 437 2152/437 2142

Der Jüngling am Bache (An der Quelle sass der Knabe), 1st setting

Berlin December 1966- February 1968	Moore	LP: DG 2720 022 CD: DG 437 2152/437 2142

Der Jüngling am Bache (An der Quelle sass der Knabe), 2nd setting

Berlin December 1966- February 1968	Moore	LP: DG 2720 022 CD: DG 437 2152/437 2142

Der Jüngling am Bache (An der Quelle sass der Knabe), 3rd setting

Berlin February- March 1969	Moore	LP: DG 2720 006/2530 306 CD: DG 437 2252/437 2142

Der Jüngling an der Quelle (Leise, rieselnder Quell!)

Berlin February- March 1965	Moore	LP: HMV ALP 2263/ASD 2263 LP: EMI 1C 063 00292 LP: EMI SXLP 30553/EX 29 04293 CD: EMI CDM 769 5032/CMS 763 5662
Berlin February- March 1969	Moore	LP: DG 2720 006 CD: DG 437 2252/437 2142

Schubert Lieder/continued

Der Jüngling auf dem Hügel (Ein Jüngling auf dem Hügel mit seinem Kummer sass)

Berlin   Moore   LP: DG 2720 006/2530 347
February-   CD: DG 437 2252/437 2142
March 1969

Der Jüngling und der Tod (Die Sonne sinkt, o könnt' ich mit ihr scheiden!)

Berlin   Moore   LP: HMV ALP 2273/ASD 2273
February-   LP: EMI EX 29 04293
March 1965   CD: EMI CDM 769 5032/CMS 763 5662

Berlin   Moore   LP: DG 2720 022/2530 347
December 1966-   CD: DG 437 2152/437 2142
February 1968

Der Kampf (Nein, länger werd' ich diesen Kampf nicht kämpfen!)

Berlin   Moore   LP: DG 2720 006
February-   CD: DG 437 2252/437 2142
March 1969

Kantate zum Geburtstag J.M.Vogels (Sänger, der vom Herzen singet)

Berlin   Ameling, Schreier,   LP: DG 2530 361/2726 083
March-   Moore   CD: DG 435 5962
April 1972

Kantate zur fünfzigjährigen Jubelfeier Salieris (Gütigster! Bester!)

Berlin   Schreier,   LP: DG 2530 361/2726 083
March-   Laubenthal,   CD: DG 435 5962
April 1972   Moore

Klage (Die Sonne steigt, die Sonne sinkt)

Berlin   Moore   LP: DG 2720 022
December 1966-   CD: DG 437 2152/437 2142
February 1968

Schubert Lieder/continued

Klage (Trauer umfliesst mein Leben)

Berlin	Moore	LP: DG 2720 022
December 1966-		CD: DG 437 2152/437 2142
February 1968		

Klage an den Mond (Dein Silber schien durch Eichengrün)

Berlin	Moore	LP: DG 2720 022
December 1966-		CD: DG 437 2152/437 2142
February 1968		

Der Knabe (Wenn ich nur ein Vöglein wäre)

Berlin	Moore	LP: DG 2720 006
February-		CD: DG 437 2252/437 2142
March 1969		

Der Knabe in der Wiege (Er schläft so süss)

Berlin	Moore	LP: DG 2720 006/2530 347
February-		CD: DG 437 2252/437 2142
March 1969		

Die Knabenzeit (Wie glücklich, wem das Knabenkleid noch um die Schultern fliegt)

Berlin	Moore	LP: DG 2720 022
December 1966-		CD: DG 437 2152/437 2142
February 1968		

Der König in Thule (Es war ein König in Thule)

Berlin	Moore	LP: DG 2720 022
December 1966-		CD: DG 431 0852/437 2152/437 2142
February 1968		

Die Krähe/Winterreise (Eine Krähe war mit mir aus der Stadt gezogen)
See Winterreise

Schubert Lieder/continued

Leiden der Trennung (Vom Meere trennt sich die Welle)

Berlin	Moore	LP: DG 2720 022/2530 347
December 1966-		CD: DG 437 2152/437 2142
February 1968		

Der Leidende (Nimmer trag' ich länger dieser Leiden Last)

Berlin	Moore	LP: DG 2720 022
December 1966-		CD: DG 437 2152/437 2142
February 1968		

Der Leiermann/Winterreise (Drüben hinterm Dorfe steht ein Leiermann)
See Winterreise

Letzte Hoffnung/Winterreise (Hie und da ist an den Bäumen)
See Winterreise

Liane („Hast du Lianen gesehen?")

Berlin	Moore	LP: DG 2720 022
December 1966-		CD: DG 437 2152/437 2142
February 1968		

Licht und Liebe (Liebe ist ein süsses Licht)

Berlin	Baker,	LP: DG 2530 328/2726 083
March-	Moore	CD: DG 435 5962
April 1972		

Die Liebe (Wo weht der Liebe hoher Geist?)

Berlin	Moore	LP: DG 2720 022
December 1966-		CD: DG 437 2152/437 2142
February 1968		

Die liebe Farbe/Die schöne Müllerin (In Grün will ich mich kleiden)
See Die schöne Müllerin

Schubert Lieder/continued

Die Liebe hat gelogen

Berlin	Moore	LP: DG 2720 006
February-		CD: DG 437 2252/437 2142
March 1969		

Der Liebende (Beglückt, wer dich erblickt)

Berlin	Moore	LP: DG 2720 022
December 1966-		CD: DG 437 2152/437 2142
February 1968		

Liebesbotschaft/Schwanengesang (Rauschendes Bächlein, so silbern und hell)

Berlin	Billing	CD: Verona 27064
January 1948		CD: Melodram CDM 18017
London	Moore	HMV unpublished
May 1955		
London	Moore	LP: HMV ALP 1295
September 1957		LP: Electrola E 90121
		LP: EMI 1C 175 01764-01766M
		CD: EMI CMS 763 5592
Berlin	Moore	LP: HMV ALP 1993/ASD 544/SLS 840
1961		LP: Electrola E 91222/STE 91222
		CD: EMI CDC 749 0812
Berlin	Moore	LP: DG 2720 059/2531 383
March 1972		CD: DG 415 1882/437 2352/437 2142
Berlin	Brendel	LP: Philips 6514 383
August 1982		CD: Philips 411 0512/432 0532

Die Liebesgötter (Cypris, meiner Phyllis gleich)

Berlin	Moore	LP: DG 2720 022
December 1966-		CD: DG 437 2152/437 2142
February 1968		

Liebeslauschen (Hier unten steht ein Ritter im hellen Mondenstrahl)

Berlin	Moore	LP: DG 2720 006
February-		CD: DG 437 2252/437 2142
March 1969		
Tours	Richter	LP: DG 2530 988
July 1977		CD: DG 445 7172
Salzburg	Richter	CD: Orfeo C334 931B/C339 930T
August 1977		

Liebesrausch (Dir, Mädchen, schlägt mit leisem Beben mein Herz)

Berlin	Moore	LP: DG 2720 022
December 1966-		CD: DG 437 2152/437 2142
February 1968		

Liebeständelei (Süsses Liebchen, komm' zu mir!)

Berlin	Moore	LP: DG 2720 022
December 1966-		CD: DG 437 2152/437 2142
February 1968		

Der liebliche Stern (Ihr Sternlein, still in der Höhe)

Berlin	Moore	LP: DG 2720 006
February-		CD: DG 437 2252/437 2142
March 1969		

Lied (Ferne von der grossen Stadt nimm' mich auf in deine Stille)

Berlin	Moore	LP: DG 2720 022
December 1966-		CD: DG 437 2152/437 2142
February 1968		

Lied (Ich bin vergnügt)

Berlin	Moore	LP: DG 2720 022
December 1966-		CD: DG 437 2152/437 2142
February 1968		

Lied (Ins stille Land? Wer leitet uns hinüber?)

Berlin	Moore	LP: DG 2720 022
December 1966-		CD: DG 437 2152/437 2142
February 1968		

Lied aus der Ferne (Wenn in des Abends letztem Scheine)

Berlin	Moore	LP: DG 2720 022
December 1966-		CD: DG 437 2152/437 2142
February 1968		

Schubert Lieder/continued

Lied der Liebe (Durch Fichten am Hügel)

Berlin	Moore	LP: DG 2720 022
December 1966-		CD: DG 437 2152/437 2142
February 1968		

Lied des gefangenen Jägers (Mein Ross so müd' in dem Stalle sich steht)

Berlin	Moore	LP: HMV ALP 1827
May 1958		LP: Electrola E 90921
		CD: EMI CMS 763 5662

Berlin	Moore	LP: DG 2720 006
February-		CD: DG 437 2252/437 2142
March 1969		

Lied eines Schiffers an den Dioskuren (Dioskuren, Zwillingsbrüder)

| Berlin | Demus | LP: DG LPM 18 715/SLPM 138 715 |
| November 1961 | | LP: DG 9108/109 108/135 026 |

Berlin	Moore	LP: DG 2720 022
December 1966-		CD: DG 437 2152/437 2142
February 1968		

Das Lied im Grünen (Ins Grüne, ins Grüne, da lockt uns der Frühling)

Berlin	Moore	LP: HMV ALP 2273/ASD 2273
February-		LP: EMI SXLP 30553/EX 29 04293
March 1965		CD: EMI CDM 769 5032/CMS 763 5662

Berlin	Moore	LP: DG 2720 006
February-		CD: DG 437 2252/437 2142
March 1969		

Lied nach dem Falle Nathos (Beugt euch aus euren Wolken nieder!)

Berlin	Moore	LP: DG 2720 022
December 1966-		CD: DG 437 2152/437 2142
February 1968		

Das Lied vom Reifen (Seht meine lieben Bäume an)

Berlin	Moore	LP: DG 2720 022
December 1966-		CD: DG 437 2152/437 2142
February 1968		

Schubert Lieder/continued

Liedesend (Auf seinem goldnen Throne der graue König sitzt)

Berlin 1959	Engel	LP: HMV ALP 1850 LP: Electrola E 91024

Berlin December 1966- February 1968	Moore	LP: DG 2720 022 CD: DG 437 2152/437 2142

Der Liedler (Gib, Schwester, mir die Harf' herab!)

Berlin December 1966- February 1968	Moore	LP: DG 2720 022 CD: DG 437 2152/437 2142

Der Lindenbaum/Winterreise (Am Brunnen vor dem Tore)
See Winterreise

Litanei auf das Fest Allerseelen (Ruh'n in Frieden alle Seelen)

Berlin February- March 1965	Moore	LP: HMV ALP 2273/ASD 2273 LP: EMI SXLP 30553/ASD 2549 CD: EMI CDM 769 5032/CMS 763 5662

Berlin February- March 1969	Moore	LP: DG 2720 006 CD: DG 437 2252/437 2142

Lob der Tränen (Laue Lüfte, Blumendüfte)

Berlin December 1966- February 1968	Moore	LP: DG 2720 022 CD: DG 437 2152/437 2142

Lob des Tokayers (O köstlicher Tokayer, o königlicher Wein)

Berlin December 1966- February 1968	Moore	LP: DG 2720 022 CD: DG 437 2152/437 2142

Lodas Gespenst (Der bleiche, kalte Mond erhob sich im Osten)

Berlin December 1966- February 1968	Moore	LP: DG 2720 022 CD: DG 437 2152/437 2142

Die Macht der Liebe (Ueberall wohin mein Auge blickt)

Berlin	Moore	LP: DG 2720 022
December 1966-		CD: DG 437 2152/437 2142
February 1968		

Das Mädchen aus der Fremde (In einem Tal bei armen Hirten)

Berlin	Moore	LP: DG 2720 022/2530 306
December 1966-		CD: DG 437 2152/437 2142
February 1968		

Das Mädchen von Inistore (Mädchen Inistores, wein' auf dem Felsen der stürmischen Winde)

Berlin	Moore	LP: DG 2720 022
December 1966-		CD: DG 437 2152/437 2142
February 1968		

Die Mainacht (Wann der silberne Mond durch die Gesträuche blinkt)

Berlin	Moore	LP: DG 2720 022
December 1966-		CD: DG 437 2152/437 2142
February 1968		

Marie (Ich sehe dich in tausend Bildern)

Berlin	Moore	LP: DG 2720 006
February-		CD: DG 437 2252/437 2142
March 1969		

Das Marienbild (Sei gegrüsst, du Frau der Huld)

Berlin	Moore	LP: DG 2720 006
February-		CD: DG 437 2252/437 2142
March 1969		

Meeres Stille (Tiefe Stille herrscht im Wasser)

| Salzburg | Moore | LP: Orfeo S140 855R |
| August 1957 | | CD: Orfeo C140 101A/C339 930T |

| Berlin | Demus | LP: DG LPM 18 617/SLPM 138 117 |
| September 1959 | | LP: DG 2535 104 |

Berlin	Moore	LP: DG 2720 022/2530 229
December 1966-		CD: DG 437 2152/437 2142
February 1968		

Schubert Lieder/continued

Mein!/Die schöne Müllerin (Bächlein, lass dein Rauschen sein!)
See Die schöne Müllerin

Mein Gruss an den Mai (Sei mir gegrüsst, o Mai)

Berlin	Moore	LP: DG 2720 022
December 1966-		CD: DG 437 2152/437 2142
February 1968		

Memnon (Den Tag hindurch nur einmal mag ich sprechen)

| Berlin | Demus | LP: DG LPM 18 715/SLPM 138 715 |
| November 1961 | | LP: DG 9108/109 108 |

Berlin	Moore	LP: DG 2720 022
December 1966-		CD: DG 437 2152/437 2142
February 1968		

Mignon und der Harfner (Nur wer die Sehnsucht kennt)

| Berlin | De los Angeles | LP: HMV ALP 1891/ASD 459 |
| December 1960 | Moore | CD: EMI CMS 565 0612 |

Berlin	Baker	LP: DG 2530 328/2726 083
March-	Moore	CD: DG 435 5962
April 1972		

Minnelied (Holder klingt der Vogelsang)

Berlin	Moore	LP: DG 2720 022
December 1966-		CD: DG 437 2152/437 2142
February 1968		

Mit dem grünen Lautenbande/Die schöne Müllerin (Schad' um das schöne grüne Band)
See Die schöne Müllerin

Il modo di prender moglie (Or sù! non si pensiamo)

Berlin	Moore	LP: DG 2720 006
February-		CD: DG 437 2252/437 2142
March 1969		

Schubert Lieder/continued

Der Mondabend (Rein und freundlich lacht der Himmel)

Berlin	Moore	LP: DG 2720 022
December 1966-		CD: DG 437 2152/437 2142
February 1968		

Die Mondnacht (Siehe, wie die Mondesstrahlen Busch und Flur in Silber malen)

Berlin	Moore	LP: DG 2720 022
December 1966-		CD: DG 437 2152/437 2142
February 1968		

Morgengruss/Die schöne Müllerin (Guten Morgen, schöne Müllerin!)
See Die schöne Müllerin

Der Morgenkuss nach einem Ball (Durch eine ganze Nacht sich nah zu sein)

Berlin	Moore	LP: DG 2720 022
December 1966-		CD: DG 437 2152/437 2142
February 1968		

Morgenlied (Eh' die Sonne früh aufsteht)

Berlin	Moore	LP: DG 2720 006
February-		CD: DG 437 2252/437 2142
March 1969		

Morgenlied (Die frohe Neubelebte singt ihrem Schöpfer Dank)

Berlin	Moore	LP: DG 2720 022
December 1966-		CD: DG 437 2152/437 2142
February 1968		

Morgenlied (Willkommen, rotes Morgenlicht!)

Berlin	Moore	LP: DG 2720 022
December 1966-		CD: DG 437 2152/437 2142
February 1968		

Der Müller und das Bach/Die schöne Müllerin (Wo ein treues Herze in Liebe vergeht)
See Die schöne Müllerin

Des Müllers Blumen/Die schöne Müllerin (Am Bach viel kleine Blumen steh'n)
See Die schöne Müllerin

Schubert Lieder/continued

Der Musensohn (Durch Feld und Wald zu schweifen)

| Berlin | Demus | LP: DG LPM 18 617/SLPM 138 117 |
| September 1959 | | LP: DG 135 005/135 026/2535 104 |

Berlin	Moore	LP: DG 2720 006
February-		CD: DG 415 1882/431 0852
March 1969		CD: DG 437 2252/437 2142

Mut/Winterreise (Fliegt der Schnee mir ins Gesicht)
See Winterreise

Die Mutter Erde (Des Lebens Tag ist schwer und schwül)

Berlin	Moore	LP: DG 2720 006
February-		CD: DG 437 2252/437 2142
March 1969		

Nach einem Gewitter (Auf den Blumen flimmern Perlen)

Berlin	Moore	LP: DG 2720 006
February-		CD: DG 437 2252/437 2142
March 1969		

Die Nacht (Du verstörst uns nicht, o Nacht!)

Berlin	Moore	LP: DG 2720 022
December 1966-		CD: DG 437 2152/437 2142
February 1968		

Nacht und Träume (Heil'ge Nacht, du sinkest nieder)

London	Moore	78: HMV DB 21517
October 1951		LP: EMI RLS 766
		CD: EMI CMS 763 5592

Berlin	Moore	LP: DG 2720 006
February-		CD: DG 437 2252/437 2142
March 1969		

| Salzburg | Richter | CD: Orfeo C334 931B/C339 930T |
| August 1977 | | |

| Berlin | Brendel | CD: Philips 411 4212 |
| August 1982 | | |

Schubert Lieder/continued

Nachtgesang (O gib, vom weichen Pfühle, träumend ein halb Gehör!)

Berlin	Moore	LP: DG 2720 022/2530 229
December 1966-		CD: DG 437 2152/437 2142
February 1968		

Nachtgesang (Tiefe Feier schauert um die Welt)

Berlin	Moore	LP: HMV ALP 2273/ASD 2273
February-		CD: EMI CDM 769 5032/CMS 763 5662
March 1965		
Berlin	Moore	LP: DG 2720 022
December 1966-		CD: DG 437 2152/437 2142
February 1968		

Nachthymne (Hinüber wall' ich)

Berlin	Moore	LP: DG 2720 006
February-		CD: DG 437 2252/437 2142
March 1969		

Nachtstück (Wenn über Berge sich der Nebel breitet)

Berlin	Moore	LP: HMV ALP 1827
May 1958		LP: Electrola E 90921/E 70415/ STE 70415
		CD: EMI CMS 763 5662
Berlin	Moore	LP: DG 2720 006
February-		CD: DG 437 2252/437 2142
March 1969		
Berlin	Brendel	CD: Philips 411 4212
August 1982		

Nachtviolen, dunkle Augen

London	Moore	LP: HMV ALP 1295
May 1955		LP: Electrola E 90121
Salzburg	Moore	LP: Orfeo S140 855R
August 1957		CD: Orfeo C140 101A/C339 930T
London	Moore	LP: EMI AN 182-183/SAN 182-183
February 1967		LP: EMI SLS 926 /ASD 143 5941
		CD: EMI CDC 749 2382/CDEMX 2233
Berlin	Moore	LP: DG 2720 006
February-		CD: DG 437 2252/437 2142
March 1969		
Salzburg	Richter	CD: Orfeo C334 931B/C339 930T
August 1977		

Schubert Lieder/continued

Nähe des Geliebten (Ich denke dein, wenn mir der Sonne Schimmer)

Berlin May 1958	Moore	45: HMV 7ER 5194 LP: HMV ALP 1827 LP: Electrola E 90921 CD: EMI CMS 763 5662
Berlin December 1966- February 1968	Moore	LP: DG 2720 022/2530 229/2535 656 CD: DG 437 2152/437 2142

Naturgenuss (Im Abendschimmer wallt der Quell)

Berlin December 1966- February 1968	Moore	LP: DG 2720 022 CD: DG 437 2152/437 2142

Die Nebensonnen/Winterreise (Drei Sonnen sah ich am Himmel steh'n)
See Winterreise

Der Neugierige/Die schöne Müllerin (Ich frage keine Blume)
See Die schöne Müllerin

Normans Gesang (Die Nacht bricht bald herein)

Berlin May 1958	Moore	LP: HMV ALP 1827/EX 29 04293 LP: Electrola E 90921/SHZE 219 CD: EMI CMS 763 5662
Berlin February- March 1969	Moore	LP: DG 2720 006 CD: DG 437 2252/437 2142

Orest auf Tauris (Ist dies Tauris, wo der Eumeniden Wut?)

Berlin November 1961	Demus	LP: DG LPM 18 715/SLPM 138 715
Berlin February- March 1969	Moore	LP: DG 2720 006 CD: DG 437 2252/437 2142

Schubert Lieder/continued

Orpheus (Wälze dich hinweg, du wildes Feuer!)

Berlin November 1961	Demus	LP: DG LPM 18 715/SLPM 138 715
Berlin December 1966- February 1968	Moore	LP: DG 2720 022 CD: DG 437 2152/437 2142

Pause/Die schöne Müllerin (Meine Laute hab' ich gehängt an die Wand)
See Die schöne Müllerin

Pax vobiscum („Der Friede sei mit euch!")

Berlin February- March 1969	Moore	LP: DG 2720 006 CD: DG 437 2252/437 2142

Pensa che questo istante

Berlin December 1966- February 1968	Moore	LP: DG 2720 022 CD: DG 437 2152/437 2142

Die Perle (Es ging ein Mann zur Frühlingszeit)

Berlin December 1966- February 1968	Moore	LP: DG 2720 022 CD: DG 437 2152/437 2142

Pflügerlied (Arbeitsam und wacker pflügen wir den Acker)

Berlin December 1966- February 1968	Moore	LP: DG 2720 022 CD: DG 437 2152/437 2142

Philoktet (Da sitz' ich ohne Bogen)

Berlin November 1961	Demus	LP: DG LPM 18 715/SLPM 138 715
Berlin December 1966- February 1968	Moore	LP: DG 2720 022 CD: DG 437 2152/437 2142

Schubert Lieder/continued

Pilgerweise (Ich bin ein Waller auf der Erde)

| Berlin
February-
March 1969 | Moore | LP: DG 2720 006
CD: DG 437 2252/437 2142 |

Der Pilgrim (Noch in meines Lebens Lenze war ich)

| Berlin
February-
March 1969 | Moore | LP: DG 2720 006/2530 306
CD: DG 437 2252/437 2142 |

Die Post/Winterreise (Von der Strasse her ein Posthorn klingt)
See Winterreise

Prometheus (Bedecke deinen Himmel, Zeus)

Salzburg August 1957	Moore	LP: Orfeo S140 855R CD: Orfeo C140 101A/C339 930T
Berlin September 1959	Demus	LP: DG LPM 18 617/SLPM 138 117 LP: DG 2535 104
Berlin February- March 1969	Moore	LP: DG 2720 006 CD: DG 437 2252/437 2142

Punschlied (Vier Elemente innig gesellt)

| Berlin
March-
April 1972 | Schreier,
Laubenthal,
Moore | LP: DG 2530 361/2726 083
CD: DG 435 5962 |

Rast/Winterreise (Nun merk' ich erst, wie müd' ich bin)
See Winterreise

Schubert Lieder/continued

Rastlose Liebe (Dem Schnee, dem Regen, dem Wind entgegen)

Berlin January 1948	Billing	CD: Verona 27064

London May 1955	Moore	LP: HMV ALP 1295 LP: Electrola E 90121

Salzburg August 1957	Moore	LP: Orfeo S140 855R CD: Orfeo C140 101A/C339 930T

Berlin December 1966- February 1968	Moore	LP: DG 2720 022/2530 229 CD: DG 431 0852/437 2152/437 2142

Der Rattenfänger (Ich bin der wohlbekannte Sänger)

Berlin December 1966- February 1968	Moore	LP: DG 2720 022 CD: DG 437 2152/437 2142

Romanze (Ein Fräulein klagt im finstern Turm)

Berlin December 1966- February 1968	Moore	LP: DG 2720 022 CD: DG 437 2152/437 2142

Romanze des Richard Löwenherz (Grosser Taten tat der Ritter)

Berlin February- March 1969	Moore	LP: DG 2720 006 CD: DG 437 2252/437 2142

Das Rosenband (Im Frühlingsgarten fand ich sie)

Berlin December 1966- February 1968	Moore	LP: DG 2720 022 CD: DG 437 2152/437 2142

Rückblick/Winterreise (Es brennt mir unter beiden Sohlen)
See Winterreise

Schubert Lieder/continued

Rückweg (Zum Donaustrom, zur Kaiserstadt)

Berlin   Moore   LP: DG 2720 022
December 1966-   CD: DG 437 2152/437 2142
February 1968

Der Sänger (Was hör' ich draussen vor dem Tor?)

Berlin   Engel   LP: Electrola E 91023/STE 91023
1958

Berlin   Moore   LP: DG 2720 022/2530 229
December 1966-   CD: DG 437 2152/437 2142
February 1968

Der Sänger am Felsen (Klage, meine Flöte, klage)

Berlin   Moore   LP: DG 2720 022
December 1966-   CD: DG 437 2152/437 2142
February 1968

Des Sängers Habe (Schlagt mein ganzes Glück im Splitter)

Berlin   Moore   LP: DG 2720 006
February-   CD: DG 437 2252/437 2142
March 1969

Tours   Richter   LP: DG 2530 988
July 1977   CD: DG 445 7172

Salzburg   Richter   CD: Orfeo C334 931B/C339 930T
August 1977

Nürnberg   Höll   CD: Erato 4509 984932
May 1992   Also unpublished video recording

Sängers Morgenlied (Süsses Licht! Aus goldnen Pforten brichst du)

Berlin   Moore   LP: DG 2720 022
December 1966-   CD: DG 437 2152/437 2142
February 1968

Der Schäfer und der Reiter (Ein Schäfer sass im Grünen)

Berlin   Moore   LP: DG 2720 022
December 1966-   CD: DG 437 2152/437 2142
February 1968

Schubert Lieder/continued

Schäfers Klagelied (Da droben auf jedem Berge)

Berlin	Moore	LP: DG 2720 022/2530 229
December 1966-		CD: DG 437 2152/437 2142
February 1968		

Die Schatten (Freunde, deren Grüfte sich schon bemoosten)

Berlin	Moore	LP: DG 2720 022
December 1966-		CD: DG 437 2152/437 2142
February 1968		

Der Schatzgräber (Arm am Beutel, krank am Herzen)

Berlin	Moore	LP: DG 2720 022
December 1966-		CD: DG 437 2152/437 2142
February 1968		

Schatzgräbers Begehr (In tiefster Erde ruht ein alt Gesetz)

Berlin	Moore	LP: DG 2720 006
February-		CD: DG 437 2252/437 2142
March 1969		

Der Schiffer (Friedlich lieg' ich hingegossen)

Berlin	Moore	LP: DG 2720 006
February-		CD: DG 437 2252/437 2142
March 1969		

Der Schiffer (Im Winde, im Sturme befahr' ich den Fluss)

Berlin	Moore	LP: HMV ALP 2273/ASD 2273
February-		CD: EMI CDM 769 5032/CMS 763 5662
March 1965		

Berlin	Moore	LP: DG 2720 006
February-		CD: DG 437 2252/437 2142
March 1969		

| Tours | Richter | LP: DG 2530 988 |
| July 1977 | | CD: DG 445 7172 |

| Salzburg | Richter | CD: Orfeo C334 931B/C339 930T |
| August 1977 | | |

Schubert Lieder/continued

Schiffers Scheidelied (Die Wogen am Gestade schwellen)

| Berlin
May 1965 | Demus | LP: DG 2707 038/2726 058 |
| Berlin
February-
March 1969 | Moore | LP: DG 2720 006
CD: DG 437 2252/437 2142 |

Schlaflied (Es mahnt der Wald, es ruft der Strom)

| Berlin
December 1966-
February 1968 | Moore | LP: DG 2720 022
CD: DG 437 2152/437 2142 |

Der Schmetterling (Wie soll ich nicht tanzen?)

| Berlin
December 1966-
February 1968 | Moore | LP: DG 2720 022
CD: DG 437 2152/437 2142 |

Schwanengesang (Endlich steh'n die Pforten offen)

| Berlin
December 1966-
February 1968 | Moore | LP: DG 2720 022
CD: DG 437 2152/437 2142 |

Schwanengesang (Wie klag' ich's aus, das Sterbegefühl?)

| Berlin
February-
March 1969 | Moore | LP: DG 2720 006
CD: DG 437 2252/437 2142 |

Sehnsucht (Ach, aus dieses Tales Gründen), 1st setting

| Berlin
December 1966-
February 1968 | Moore | LP: DG 2720 022/2530 306
CD: DG 437 2152/437 2142 |

Sehnsucht (Ach, aus dieses Tales Gründen), 2nd setting

| Berlin
1959 | Engel | LP: HMV ALP 1767/ASD 337
LP: World Records T 671/ST 671 |
| Berlin
February-
March 1969 | Moore | LP: DG 2720 006
CD: DG 437 2252/437 2142 |

Sehnsucht (Der Lerche wolkennahe Lieder)

Berlin	Moore	LP: DG 2720 006
February-		CD: DG 437 2252/437 2142
March 1969		

Sehnsucht (Die Scheibe friert, der Wind ist rauh)

Berlin	Engel	LP: HMV ALP 1850
1959		LP: Electrola E 91024
Berlin	Moore	LP: DG 2720 006
February-		CD: DG 437 2252/437 2142
March 1969		

Sehnsucht (Was zieht mich das Herz so?)

Berlin	Moore	LP: DG 2720 022
December 1966-		CD: DG 437 2152/437 2142
February 1968		

Sehnsucht der Liebe (Wie die Nacht mit heil'gem Beben)

Berlin	Moore	LP: DG 2720 022
December 1966-		CD: DG 437 2152/437 2142
February 1968		

Sei mir gegrüsst (O du Entriss'ne mir und meinem Kusse!)

Berlin	Moore	LP: HMV ALP 2263/ASD 2263
February-		LP: Electrola E 91204/STE 91204
March 1965		LP: EMI 1C 063 00292/SXLP 30553
		CD: EMI CDM 769 5032/CMS 763 5662
Berlin	Moore	LP: DG 2720 006/2740 188/2535 656
February-		CD: DG 431 0852/437 2252/437 2142
March 1969		

Selige Welt (Ich treibe auf des Lebens Meer)

Berlin	Moore	LP: DG 2720 006
February-		CD: DG 437 2252/437 2142
March 1969		

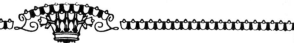

Deutsche Grammophon Gesellschaft

Dietrich Fischer-Dieskau

FRANZ SCHUBERT
Ein Schubert-Goethe-Liederabend
mit Jörg Demus, Klavier
18 617 - DM 24,— · 138 117 (Stereo) - DM 26,—

ROBERT SCHUMANN
Dichterliebe op. 48

JOHANNES BRAHMS
Sommerabend · Mondenschein
Es liebt sich so lieblich
Meerfahrt · Es schauen die Blumen
Der Tod, das ist die kühle Nacht
mit Jörg Demus, Klavier
18 370 · DM 24,—

HUGO WOLF
Italienisches Liederbuch
mit Irmgard Seefried
Klavierbegleitung: Jörg Demus und Erik Werba
18 568/69 - DM 48,— · 138 035/36 (Stereo) - DM 52,—

ROBERT SCHUMANN
Lieder aus dem Spanischen und aus „Myrten"
mit Jörg Demus, Klavier
18 655 .- DM 24,— · 138 655 (Stereo) - DM 26,—

JOHANNES BRAHMS
Ein Johannes-Brahms-Liederabend
mit Jörg Demus, Klavier
18 504 - DM 24,— · 138 011 (Stereo) - DM 26,—

Vorführung weiterer Aufnahmen des Künstlers in jedem guten Fachgeschäft

Dietrich Fischer-Dieskau

singt Lieder

JOSEPH HAYDN
Lieder und Canzonetten

LUDWIG VAN BEETHOVEN
An die ferne Geliebte op. 98 - Gellert-Lieder
Ausgewählte Lieder, Folge 1 und 2

FRANZ SCHUBERT
Die schöne Müllerin - Die Winterreise - Schwanengesang Nr. 8 - 13
Ausgewählte Lieder, Folge 1 bis 6

ROBERT SCHUMANN
Liederkreis op. 39 (Eichendorff) - Ausgewählte Lieder (Heine)

JOHANNES BRAHMS
Lieder aus op. 32 - Von ewiger Liebe (ausgewählte Lieder)

HUGO WOLF
Eichendorff-Lieder - Goethe-Lieder, Folge 1 und 2 - Mörike-Lieder, Folge 1 - 3
Aus dem Spanischen Liederbuch - Lieder nach verschiedenen Dichtern

RICHARD STRAUSS
Ausgewählte Lieder

GABRIEL FAURÉ
La bonne Chanson op. 61

DUETTE MIT VICTORIA DE LOS ANGELES
von Purcell, Haydn, J. S. Bach, Beethoven, Schubert, Berlioz, Dvorak,
Tschaikowsky, Saint-Saëns, Fauré

Im Vertrieb der ELECTROLA Ges. M. B. H. Köln

Schubert Lieder/continued

Seligkeit (Freuden sonder Zahl)

Berlin	Moore	LP: HMV ALP 2263/ASD 2263
February-		LP: EMI 1C 063 00292/SXLP 30553
March 1965		CD: EMI CMS 763 5662

Berlin	Moore	LP: DG 2720 022
December 1966-		CD: DG 431 0852/437 2152/437 2142
February 1968		

Selma und Selmar (Weine du nicht, o die ich innig liebe)

Berlin	Baker,	LP: DG 2530 328/2726 083
March-	Moore	CD: DG 435 5962
April 1972		

Seufzer (Die Nachtigall singt überall)

Berlin	Moore	LP: DG 2720 022
December 1966-		CD: DG 437 2152/437 2142
February 1968		

Der Sieg (O unbewölktes Leben!)

| Berlin | Engel | LP: HMV ALP 1850 |
| 1959 | | LP: Electrola E 91024 |

Berlin	Moore	LP: DG 2720 006
February-		CD: DG 437 2252/437 2142
March 1969		

Singübungen

Berlin	Baker,	LP: DG 2530 328/2726 083
March-	Moore	CD: DG 435 5962
April 1972		

Schubert Lieder/continued

Skolie (Lasst im Morgenstrahl des Mai'n uns der Blume Leben freu'n)

Berlin	Moore	LP: DG 2720 022
December 1966-		CD: DG 437 2152/437 2142
February 1968		

Skolie (Mädchen entsiegelten, Brüder, die Flaschen)

Berlin	Moore	LP: DG 2720 022
December 1966-		CD: DG 437 2152/437 2142
February 1968		

Die Sommernacht (Wenn der Schimmer von dem Monde nun herab)

Berlin	Moore	LP: DG 2720 022
December 1966-		CD: DG 437 2152/437 2142
February 1968		

Sonett I-III: Apollo, lebet noch dein hold Verlangen; Allein, nachdenklich, wie gelähmt vom Krampfe; Nunmehr, du Himmel, Erde schweigt und Winde

Berlin	Moore	LP: DG 2720 006/2530 332
February-		CD: DG 437 2252/437 2142
March 1969		

Sprache der Liebe (Lass' dich mit gelinden Schlägen rühren)

Berlin	Moore	LP: DG 2720 022
December 1966-		CD: DG 437 2152/437 2142
February 1968		

Die Stadt/Schwanengesang (Am fernen Horizonte)

| Berlin | Billing | CD: Verona 27064 |
| January 1948 | | CD: Melodram CDM 18017 |

London	Moore	78: HMV DA 2045
October 1951		LP: HMV ALP 1066
		LP: Electrola E 90052
		LP: EMI 1C 175 01764-01766M
		CD: EMI CMS 763 5592

| Salzburg | Moore | LP: Orfeo S140 855R |
| August 1956 | | CD: Orfeo C294 921B/C339 930T |

Berlin	Moore	LP: HMV ALP 1993/ASD 544/SLS 840
1961		LP: Electrola E 91204/E 91222/
		STE 91204/STE 91222
		CD: EMI CDC 749 0812

| Berlin | Moore | LP: DG 2720 059 /2531 383 |
| March 1972 | | CD: DG 415 1882/437 2352/437 2142 |

| Berlin | Brendel | LP: Philips 6514 383 |
| August 1982 | | CD: Philips 411 0512/432 0532 |

Schubert Lieder/continued

Ständchen (Horch', horch', die Lerch'!)

London October 1951	Moore	78: HMV DB 21349

Berlin February- March 1965	Moore	LP: HMV ALP 2263/ASD 2263 LP: EMI 1C 063 00292/SHZE 148 LP: EMI SXLP 30553 CD: EMI CMS 763 5662

Berlin February- March 1969	Moore	LP: DG 2720 006 CD: DG 431 0852/437 2252/437 2142

Ständchen/Schwanengesang (Leise flehen meine Lieder)

Berlin January 1948	Billing	CD: Verona 27064 CD: Melodram CDM 18017

Berlin May 1958	Moore	45: HMV 7ER 5194 LP: HMV ALP 1827/SXLP 30553 LP: Electrola E 90921/SHZE 148 LP: EMI 1C 175 01764-01766M CD: EMI CMS 763 5592

Berlin 1961	Moore	LP: HMV ALP 1993/ASD 544/SLS 840 LP: Electrola E 91222/STE 91222 CD: EMI CDC 749 0812

Berlin March 1972	Moore	LP: DG 2720 059/2531 383 CD: DG 415 1882/431 0852 CD: DG 437 2352/437 2142

Berlin August 1982	Brendel	LP: Philips 6514 383 CD: Philips 411 0512/432 0532

Die Sterne (Du staunest, o Mensch, was heilig wir strahlen?)

Berlin February- March 1969	Moore	LP: DG 2720 006 CD: DG 437 2252/437 2142

Schubert Lieder/continued

Die Sterne (Was funkelt ihr so mild mich an?)

Berlin 1958	Moore	LP: HMV ALP 1677/XLP 30095 LP: Electrola E 90021
Berlin December 1966- February 1968	Moore	LP: DG 2720 022 CD: DG 437 2152/437 2142

Die Sterne (Wie blitzen die Sterne so hell durch die Nacht!)

Berlin February- March 1969	Moore	LP: DG 2720 006 CD: DG 437 2252/437 2142
Tours July 1977	Richter	LP: DG 2530 988 CD: DG 445 7172
Salzburg August 1977	Richter	CD: Orfeo C334 931B/C339 930T
Nürnberg May 1992	Höll	CD: Erato 4509 984932 Also unpublished video recording

Die Sterne (Wie wohl ist mir im Dunkeln!)

Berlin December 1966- February 1968	Moore	LP: DG 2720 022 CD: DG 437 2152/437 2142

Die Sternennächte (In monderhellten Nächten)

Berlin February- March 1969	Moore	LP: DG 2720 006 CD: DG 437 2252/437 2142

Die Sternenwelten (Oben drehen sich die grossen unbekannten Welten dort)

Berlin December 1966- February 1968	Moore	LP: DG 2720 022 CD: DG 437 2152/437 2142

Stimme der Liebe (Meine Selinde!)

Berlin December 1966- February 1968	Moore	LP: DG 2720 022 CD: DG 437 2152/437 2142

Stimme der Liebe (Abendgewölke schweben hell)

Berlin December 1966- February 1968	Moore	LP: DG 2720 022 CD: DG 437 2152/437 2142

Der Strom (Mein Leben wälzt sich murrend fort)

Berlin February- March 1965	Moore	LP: HMV ALP 2273/ASD 2273 CD: EMI CDM 769 5032/CMS 763 5662
Berlin February- March 1969	Moore	LP: DG 2720 006 CD: DG 437 2252/437 2142
Tours July 1977	Richter	LP: DG 2530 988 CD: DG 445 7172
Salzburg August 1977	Richter	CD: Orfeo C334 931B/C339 930T
Nürnberg May 1992	Höll	CD: Erato 4509 984932 Also unpublished video recording

Der stürmische Morgen/Winterreise (Wie hat der Sturm zerrissen)
See Winterreise

Szene aus dem Schauspiel „Lacrimas" (Nun, da Schatten niedergleiten)

Berlin February- March 1969	Moore	LP: DG 2720 006 CD: DG 437 2252/437 2142

Szene aus „Faust" (Wie anders, Gretchen)

Berlin March- April 1972	Baker RIAS Choir Moore	LP: DG 2530 328/2726 083 CD: DG 435 5962

Der Tanz (Es redet und träumet die Jugend so viel)

Berlin March- April 1972	Ameling, Baker, Schreier, Moore	LP: DG 2530 409/2726 083 CD: DG 435 5962

Täglich zu singen (Ich danke Gott und freue mich)

Berlin December 1966- February 1968	Moore	LP: DG 2720 022 CD: DG 437 2152/437 2142

Schubert Lieder/continued

Die Taubenpost/Schwanengesang (Ich hab' eine Brieftaub' in meinem Sold)

Berlin January 1948	Billing	CD: Verona 27064 CD: Melodram CDM 18017
London September 1957	Moore	LP: HMV ALP 1677/XLP 30095 LP: Electrola E 90021 LP: EMI 1C 175 01764-01766M CD: EMI CMS 763 5592
Berlin 1961	Moore	LP: HMV ALP 1993/ASD 544/SLS 840 LP: Electrola E 91222/STE 91222 CD: EMI CDC 749 0812
Berlin March 1972	Moore	LP: DG 2720 059 /2531 383 CD: DG 415 1882/437 2352/437 2142
Berlin August 1982	Brendel	LP: Philips 6514 383 CD: Philips 411 0512/432 0532

Der Taucher (Wer wagt es, Rittersmann oder Knapp?)

Berlin 1959	Engel	LP: HMV ALP 1767/ASD 337 LP: World Records T 671/ST 671
Berlin December 1966- February 1968	Moore	LP: DG 2720 022 CD: DG 437 2152/437 2142

Täuschung/Winterreise (Ein Licht tanzt freundlich vor mir her)
See Winterreise

Die Täuschung (Im Erlenbusch, im Tannenhain)

Berlin December 1966- February 1968	Moore	LP: DG 2720 022 CD: DG 437 2152/437 2142

Tiefes Leid (Ich bin von aller Ruh' geschieden)

Berlin February- March 1969	Moore	LP: DG 2720 006 CD: DG 437 2252/437 2142

Tischlerlied (Mein Handwerk geht durch alle Welt)

Berlin December 1966- February 1968	Moore	LP: DG 2720 022 CD: DG 437 2152/437 2142

Schubert Lieder/continued

Tischlied (Mich ergreift, ich weiss nicht wie, himmlisches Behagen)

Berlin	Moore	LP: DG 2720 022
December 1966-		CD: DG 437 2152/437 2142
February 1968		

Der Tod und das Mädchen (Vorüber, ach vorüber! Geh', wilder Knochenmann!)

Berlin	Moore	LP: HMV ALP 2273/ASD 2273
February-		LP: EMI SXLP 30553/SHZE 148
March 1965		CD: EMI CDM 769 5032/CMS 763 5662
Berlin	Moore	LP: DG 2720 022
December 1966-		CD: DG 415 1882/437 2152/437 2142
February 1968		

Todesmusik (In des Todes Feierstunde)

Berlin	Moore	LP: DG 2720 006
February-		CD: DG 437 2252/437 2142
March 1969		

Totengräbers Heimweh (O Menschheit, o Leben! Was soll's?)

London	Moore	LP: HMV ALP 1295
May 1955		LP: Electrola E 90121
Salzburg	Moore	LP: Orfeo S140 855R
August 1957		CD: Orfeo C140 101A/C339 930T
Berlin	Moore	LP: DG 2720 006/2530 347
February-		CD: DG 437 2252/437 2142
March 1969		
Tours	Richter	LP: DG 2530 988
July 1977		CD: DG 445 7172
Salzburg	Richter	CD: Orfeo C334 931B/C339 930T
August 1977		
Nürnberg	Höll	CD: Erato 4509 984932
May 1992		Also unpublished video recording

Totengräberlied (Grabe, Spaten, grabe!)

Berlin	Moore	LP: DG 2720 022
December 1966-		CD: DG 437 2152/437 2142
February 1968		

Schubert Lieder/continued

Totengräberweise (Nicht so düster und so bleich)

Berlin	Moore	LP: DG 2720 006
February- March 1969		CD: DG 437 2252/437 2142

Totenkranz für ein Kind (Sanft weh'n im Hauch der Abendluft)

Berlin	Moore	LP: DG 2720 022
December 1966- February 1968		CD: DG 437 2152/437 2142

Totenopfer (Kein Rosenschimmer leuchtet dem Tag zur Ruh'!)

Berlin	Moore	LP: DG 2720 022
December 1966- February 1968		CD: DG 437 2152/437 2142

Il traditor deluso (Ahimè, io tremo!)

Berlin	Moore	LP: DG 2720 006
February- March 1969		CD: DG 437 2252/437 2142

Tränenregen/Die schöne Müllerin (Wir sassen so traulich beisammen)
See Die schöne Müllerin

Der Traum (Mir träumt', ich war ein Vögelein)

Berlin	Moore	LP: DG 2720 022
December 1966- February 1968		CD: DG 437 2152/437 2142

Trauer der Liebe (Wo die Taub' in stillen Buchen)

Berlin	Moore	LP: DG 2720 022
December 1966- February 1968		CD: DG 437 2152/437 2142

Trinklied (Bacchus, feister Fürst des Weins!)

Berlin	Moore	LP: DG 2720 006
February- March 1969		CD: DG 437 2252/437 2142

Trinklied (Brüder! Unser Erdenwallen)

Berlin	Schreier,	LP: DG 2530 361/2726 083
March-	Laubenthal,	CD: DG 435 5962
April 1972	Moore	

Trinklied (Ihr Freunde und du, gold'ner Wein)

Berlin	Moore	LP: DG 2720 022
December 1966-		CD: DG 437 2152/437 2142
February 1968		

Trockne Blumen/Die schöne Müllerin (Ihr Blümlein alle, die sie mir gab)
See Die schöne Müllerin

Trost (Hörnerklänge rufen klagend aus des Forstes grüner Nacht)

Berlin	Moore	LP: DG 2720 006
February-		CD: DG 437 2252/437 2142
March 1969		

Trost (Nimmer lange weil' ich hier)

Berlin	Engel	LP: HMV ALP 1850
1959		LP: Electrola E 91024

Berlin	Moore	LP: DG 2720 022
December 1966-		CD: DG 437 2152/437 2142
February 1968		

Trost an Elisa (Lehnst du deine bleichgehärmte Wange)

Berlin	Moore	LP: DG 2720 022
December 1966-		CD: DG 437 2152/437 2142
February 1968		

Trost im Liede (Braust des Unglücks Sturm empor)

Berlin	Moore	LP: DG 2720 022
December 1966-		CD: DG 437 2152/437 2142
February 1968		

Schubert Lieder/continued

Trost in Tränen (Wie kommt's, dass du so traurig bist?)

Berlin	Moore	LP: DG 2720 022
December 1966-		CD: DG 437 2152/437 2142
February 1968		

Ueber Wildemann (Die Winde sausen am Tannenhang)

London	Moore	LP: HMV ALP 1295
May 1955		LP: Electrola E 90121
Salzburg	Moore	LP: Orfeo S140 855R
August 1957		CD: Orfeo C140 101A/C339 930T
Berlin	Moore	LP: DG 2720 006
February-		CD: DG 437 2252/437 2142
March 1969		
Berlin	Brendel	CD: Philips 411 4212
August 1982		

Um Mitternacht (Keine Stimme hör' ich schallen)

Berlin	Moore	LP: DG 2720 006
February-		CD: DG 437 2252/437 2142
March 1969		

Dem Unendlichen (Wie erhebt sich das Herz)

Salzburg	Moore	LP: Orfeo S140 855R
August 1957		CD: Orfeo C140 101A/C339 930T
Berlin	Moore	LP: HMV ALP 1677/XLP 30095
1958		LP: Electrola E 90021
Berlin	Moore	LP: DG 2720 022
December 1966-		CD: DG 437 2152/437 2142
February 1968		

Ungeduld/Die schöne Müllerin (Ich schnitt' es gern in alle Rinden ein)
See Die schöne Müllerin

Der Unglückliche (Die Nacht bricht an)

Berlin	Moore	LP: DG 2720 006
February-		CD: DG 437 2252/437 2142
March 1969		

Der Vater mit seinem Kind (Dem Vater liegt das Kind im Arm)

Berlin	Moore	LP: DG 2720 006/2530 347
February-		CD: DG 437 2252/437 2142
March 1969		

Schubert Lieder/continued

Der Vatermörder (Ein Vater starb von des Sohnes Hand)

Berlin	Moore	LP: DG 2720 022
December 1966-		CD: DG 437 2152/437 2142
February 1968		

Vergebliche Liebe (Ja, ich weiss es, diese treue Liebe)

Berlin	Moore	LP: DG 2720 022
December 1966-		CD: DG 437 2152/437 2142
February 1968		

Verklärung (Lebensfunke, vom Himmel entglüht)

Berlin	Moore	LP: DG 2720 022
December 1966-		CD: DG 437 2152/437 2142
February 1968		

Verschwunden sind die Schmerzen

Berlin	Schreier,	LP: DG 2530 361/2726 083
March-	Laubenthal	CD: DG 435 5962
April 1972		

Versunken (Voll Lockenkraus ein Haupt so rund!)

Berlin	Moore	LP: DG 2720 006
February-		CD: DG 437 2252/437 2142
March 1969		

| Salzburg | Richter | CD: Orfeo C334 931B/C339 930T |
| August 1977 | | |

Die vier Weltalter (Wohl perlet im Glase der purpurne Wein)

Berlin	Moore	LP: DG 2720 022
December 1966-		CD: DG 437 2152/437 2142
February 1968		

Viola (Schneeglöcklein, in den Auen läutest du)

Berlin	Moore	LP: DG 2720 006
February-		CD: DG 437 2252/437 2142
March 1969		

Die Vögel (Wie lieblich und fröhlich zu schweben, zu singen)

Berlin February- March 1969	Moore	LP: DG 2720 006 CD: DG 437 2252/437 2142
Salzburg August 1977	Richter	CD: Orfeo C334 931B/C339 930T

Vom Mitleiden Mariae (Als bei dem Kreuz Maria stand)

Berlin February- March 1969	Moore	LP: DG 2720 006 CD: DG 437 2252/437 2142

Vor meiner Wiege (Das also ist der enge Schrein)

Berlin May 1965	Demus	LP: DG 2707 028/2726 058
Berlin February- March 1969	Moore	LP: DG 2720 006 CD: DG 437 2252/437 2142

Der Wachtelschlag (Ach, mir schallt's dorten so lieblich hervor)

Berlin February- March 1969	Moore	LP: DG 2720 006 CD: DG 437 2252/437 2142

Der Wallensteiner, Lanzknecht beim Trunk (He! Schenket mir im Helme ein!)

Berlin February- March 1969	Moore	LP: DG 2720 006 CD: DG 437 2252/437 2142

Der Wanderer (Ich komme vom Gebirge her)

Berlin 1958	Moore	45: HMV 7ER 5213 LP: HMV ALP 1677/XLP 30095 LP: Electrola E 90021
Berlin December 1966- February 1968	Moore	LP: DG 2720 022 CD: DG 431 0852/437 2152/437 2142
Berlin August 1982	Brendel	CD: Philips 411 4212

Schubert Lieder/continued

Der Wanderer (Wie deutlich des Mondes Licht zu mir spricht)

Berlin February- March 1965	Moore	LP: HMV ALP 2273/ASD 2273 LP: EMI SXLP 30553 CD: EMI CDM 769 5032/CMS 763 5662
Berlin February- March 1969	Moore	LP: DG 2720 006 CD: DG 437 2252/437 2142
Tours July 1977	Richter	LP: DG 2530 988 CD: DG 445 7172
Salzburg August 1977	Richter	CD: Orfeo C334 931B/C339 930T
Nürnberg May 1992	Höll	CD: Erato 4509 984932 Also unpublished video recording

Der Wanderer an den Mond (Ich auf der Erd', am Himmel du)

London May 1955	Moore	LP: HMV ALP 1295 LP: Electrola E 90121
Salzburg August 1957	Moore	LP: Orfeo S140 855R CD: Orfeo C140 101A/C339 930T
Berlin February- March 1969	Moore	LP: DG 2720 006 CD: DG 437 2252/437 2142
Berlin August 1982	Brendel	CD: Philips 411 4212

Das Wandern/Die schöne Müllerin (Das Wandern ist des Müllers Lust)
See Die schöne Müllerin

Wandrers Nachtlied I (Der du von dem Himmel bist)

Berlin September 1959	Demus	LP: DG LPM 18 617/SLPM 138 117 LP: DG 2535 104
Berlin December 1966- February 1968	Moore	LP: DG 2720 022/2530 229 CD: DG 431 0852/437 2152/437 2142

Wandrers Nachtlied II (Ueber allen Gipfeln ist Ruh')

Berlin September 1959	Demus	LP: DG LPM 18 617/SLPM 138 117 LP: DG 135 026/2535 104
Berlin February- March 1969	Moore	LP: DG 2720 006/2740 188 CD: DG 431 0852/437 2252/437 2142

Wasserflut/Winterreise (Manche Trän' aus meinen Augen)
See Winterreise

Der Wegweiser/Winterreise (Was vermeid' ich denn die Wege)
See Winterreise

Der Weiberfreund (Noch fand von Evens Töchterscharen ich keine)

Berlin	Moore	LP: DG 2720 022
December 1966-		CD: DG 437 2152/437 2142
February 1968		

Wehmut (Mit leisen Harfentönen sei, Wehmut, mir gegrüsst)

Berlin	Moore	LP: DG 2720 022/2530 347
December 1966-		CD: DG 437 2152/437 2142
February 1968		

Wehmut (Wenn ich durch Wald und Fluren geh')

| Salzburg | Moore | LP: Orfeo S140 855R |
| August 1957 | | CD: Orfeo C140 101A/C339 930T |

| Berlin | Moore | LP: HMV ALP 1677/XLP 30095 |
| 1958 | | LP: Electrola E 90021 |

Berlin	Moore	LP: DG 2720 006
February-		CD: DG 437 2252/437 2142
March 1969		

| Tours | Richter | LP: DG 2530 988 |
| July 1977 | | CD: DG 445 7172 |

| Salzburg | Richter | CD: Orfeo C334 931B/C339 930T |
| August 1977 | | |

| Nürnberg | Höll | CD: Erato 4509 984932 |
| May 1992 | | Also unpublished video recording |

Das Weinen (Gar tröstlich kommt geronnen der Tränen heil'ger Quell)

| Berlin | Demus | LP: DG 2707 028/2726 058 |
| May 1965 | | |

Berlin	Moore	LP: DG 2720 006
February-		CD: DG 437 2252/437 2142
March 1969		

Wer kauft Liebesgötter? (Von allen schönen Waren)

Berlin	Moore	LP: DG 2720 022
December 1966-		CD: DG 437 2152/437 2142
February 1968		

Schubert Lieder/continued

Die Wetterfahne/Winterreise (Der Wind spielt mit der Wetterfahne)
See Winterreise

Widerschein (Harrt ein Fischer auf der Brücke)

Berlin	Moore	LP: DG 2720 006
February-		CD: DG 437 2252/437 2142
March 1969		

Wie Ulfru fischt (Die Angel zuckt, die Rute bebt)

| Berlin | Engel | LP: HMV ALP 1850 |
| 1959 | | LP: Electrola E 91024 |

Berlin	Moore	LP: DG 2720 022
December 1966-		CD: DG 437 2152/437 2142
February 1968		

Wiedersehen (Der Frühlingssonne holdes Lächeln)

Berlin	Moore	LP: DG 2720 006
February-		CD: DG 437 2252/437 2142
March 1969		

Wiegenlied (Wie sich der Aeuglein kindischer Himmel)

Berlin	Moore	LP: DG 2720 006
February-		CD: DG 437 2252/437 2142
March 1969		

Willkommen und Abschied (Es schlug mein Herz, geschwind zu Pferde!)

Berlin	Moore	LP: DG 2720 006
February-		CD: DG 437 2252/437 2142
March 1969		

Der Winterabend (Es ist so still, so heimlich um mich)

Berlin	Moore	LP: HMV ALP 2273/ASD 2273
February-		CD: EMI CDM 769 5032/CMS 763 5662
March 1965		

Berlin	Moore	LP: DG 2720 006
February-		CD: DG 437 2252/437 2142
March 1969		

Schubert Lieder/continued

Winterlied(Keine Blumen blüh'n, nur das Wintergrün)

Berlin	Moore	LP: DG 2720 022
December 1966-		CD: DG 437 2152/437 2142
February 1968		

Das Wirtshaus/Winterreise (Auf einen Totenacker hat mich mein Weg gebracht)
See Winterreise

Wohin?/Die schöne Müllerin (Ich hört' ein Bächlein rauschen)
See Die schöne Müllerin

Wonne der Wehmut (Trocknet nicht, Tränen der ewigen Liebe!)

Berlin	Moore	LP: DG 2720 022
December 1966-		CD: DG 437 2152/437 2142
February 1968		

Der Zufriedene (Zwar schuf das Glück hienieden)

Berlin	Moore	LP: DG 2720 022
December 1966-		CD: DG 437 2152/437 2142
February 1968		

Das Zügenglöcklein (Kling' durch die Nacht, klinge!)

Berlin	Moore	LP: HMV ALP 2273/ASD 2273
February-		CD: EMI CDM 769 5032/CMS 763 5662
March 1965		
Berlin	Moore	LP: DG 2720 006
February-		CD: DG 437 2252/437 2142
March 1969		
Tours	Richter	LP: DG 2530 988
July 1977		CD: DG 445 7172
Salzburg	Richter	CD: Orfeo C334 931B/C339 930T
August 1977		
Nürnberg	Höll	CD: Erato 4509 984932
May 1992		Also unpublished video recording

Schubert Lieder/concluded

Zum Punsche (Woget brausend Harmonien, kehre wieder alte Zeit)

Berlin 1959	Engel	LP: HMV ALP 1850 LP: Electrola E 91024
Berlin December 1966- February 1968	Moore	LP: DG 2720 022 CD: DG 437 2152/437 2142

Der zürnende Barde (Wer wagt's, wer will mir die Leier zerbrechen?)

Berlin February- March 1965	Moore	LP: HMV ALP 2273/ASD 2273 CD: EMI CDM 769 5032/CMS 763 5662
Berlin February- March 1969	Moore	LP: DG 2720 006/2530 347 CD: DG 437 2252/437 2142

Der zürnenden Diana (Ja, spanne nur den Bogen, mich zu töten!)

Berlin November 1961	Demus	LP: DG LPM 18 715/SLPM 138 715
Berlin February- March 1969	Moore	LP: DG 2720 006 CD: DG 437 2252/437 2142

Der Zwerg (Im trüben Licht verschwinden schon die Berge)

Berlin January 1948	Billing	CD: Verona 27064
Salzburg August 1957	Moore	LP: Orfeo S140 855R CD: Orfeo C140 101A/C339 930T
Berlin 1958	Moore	LP: HMV ALP 1677/XLP 30095 LP: Electrola E 90021
Berlin February- March 1969	Moore	LP: DG 2720 006/2530 347 CD: DG 437 2252/437 2142
Nürnberg May 1992	Höll	CD: Erato 4509 984932 Also unpublished video recording

SCHUMANN

Symphony No 2

Bamberg	Bamberg SO	LP: BASF/Acanta DC 22704
1975	Fischer-Dieskau	
	conducts	

Symphony No 3 "Rhenish"

Bamberg	Bamberg SO	LP: BASF/Acanta DC 22705
1975	Fischer-Dieskau	
	conducts	

Piano Concerto

London	LPO	LP: EMI ASD 3053/1C 065 02530
June 1974	Barenboim	CD: EMI CDM 764 6262/CZS 767 5212
	Fischer-Dieskau	
	conducts	

Introduction and Allegro appassionato

London	LPO	LP: EMI ASD 3053/1C 065 02530
June 1974	Barenboim	CD: EMI CDM 764 6262
	Fischer-Dieskau	
	conducts	

Manfred Overture

Bamberg	Bamberg SO	LP: BASF/Acanta DC 22705
1975	Fischer-Dieskau	
	conducts	

Genoveva

Leipzig	Role of Count	LP: EMI 1C 157 02914-02916
October 1976	Siegfried	CD: Berlin Classics BC 022 0056
	Moser, Schröter,	Excerpt
	Schreier, Lorenz	LP: EMI EX 29 04323
	Berlin Radio Choir	
	Leipzig Gewandhaus	
	Orchestra	
	Masur	

Requiem in D flat

Düsseldorf July 1983	Donath, Soffel, Gedda Düsseldorf Civic Orchestra & Chorus Klee	LP: EMI ASD 146 7561 CD: EMI CZS 767 8192

Requiem für Mignon

Düsseldorf July 1983	Lindner, Andonian, Georg Düsseldorf Civic Orchestra & Chorus Klee	LP: EMI ASD 146 7561 CD: EMI CZS 767 8192

Szenen aus Goethes „Faust"

Snape September 1972	Role of Faust Harwood, Vyvyan, Pears, Shirley-Quirk Aldeburgh Festival Singers English CO Britten	LP: Decca SET 567-568 CD: Decca 425 7052 Excerpts LP: Decca GRV 7 CD: Decca 440 4832
London March 1973	Mathis, Robinson, Burrows, Howell BBC Choruses BBC SO Boulez	CD: Memories HR 4489-4490
Düsseldorf April 1981	Mathis, Lövaas, Gedda, Berry Düsseldorf Civic Orchestra & Chorus Klee	LP: EMI 1C 165 46435-46436 CD: EMI CMS 764 4502

Szenen aus Goethes „Faust": Excerpts (Des Lebens Pulse schlagen frisch; Die Nacht scheint tiefer hereinzudringen; Ein Sumpf zieht am Gebirge hin)

Salzburg July 1961	VPO Sawallisch	CD: Orfeo C336 931B

Dichterliebe

Salzburg August 1956	Moore	LP: Orfeo CD: Orfeo C294 921B/C339 930T
Vienna February 1957	Demus	LP: DG LPM 18 370 Excerpts 45: DG EPL 30 319
Berlin May 1965	Demus	LP: DG SLPM 139 109 Excerpts LP: DG 135 014/135 026
Berlin 1974-1976	Eschenbach	LP: DG 2709 079/2740 185/2531 290 CD: DG 415 1902/439 4172/445 6602
New York May 1976	Horowitz	LP: CBS 79200 CD: Sony SM2K 46743
Berlin July 1985	Brendel	LP: Philips 416 3521 CD: Philips 416 3522
Nürnberg May 1992	Höll	CD: Erato 4509 984922 Also unpublished video recording

Liederkreis op 24

Berlin September 1956	Klust	LP: HMV ALP 1551 LP: Electrola WALP 525/E 90014 LP: EMI 1C 053 01340M CD: EMI CZS 568 5092
Berlin May 1965	Demus	LP: DG SLPM 139 109
Berlin 1974	Eschenbach	LP: DG 2709 079/2740 185/2530 543 CD: DG 445 6602
Nürnberg May 1992	Höll	CD: Erato 4509 984922 Also unpublished video recording

Liederkreis op 39

London June 1952	Moore	HMV unpublished
London March 1954	Moore	LP: HMV BLP 1068 LP: Victor LM 6036 LP: Electrola E 70042 CD: EMI CZS 568 5092
Salzburg August 1956	Moore	LP: Orfeo S140 855R CD: Orfeo C294 921B/C339 930T Only 2 of the songs performed
Salzburg July 1959	Moore	LP: Orfeo S140 855R CD: Orfeo C140 301B/C339 930T
Berlin March 1964	Moore	LP: HMV ALP 2103/ASD 650 LP: Electrola 1C 063 00274
Berlin 1974-1975	Eschenbach	LP: DG 2709 074/2740 167/2531 290 CD: DG 415 1902/445 6602
Salzburg August 1975	Sawallisch	CD: Orfeo C185 891A/C339 930T Only 5 of the songs performed
Berlin July 1985	Brendel	LP: Philips 416 3521 CD: Philips 416 3522

Mondnacht (Liederkreis op 39)

London October 1951	Moore	78: HMV DB 21517 45: Victor WHMV 1046 LP: Victor LHMV 1046 LP: EMI EX 769 7411 CD: EMI CHS 769 7412

Schöne Fremde (Liederkreis op 39)

Nürnberg May 1992	Höll	CD: Erato 4509 984922 Also unpublished video recording

Schumann Lieder/continued

Abendlied (Es ist so still geworden)

Berlin	Eschenbach	LP: DG 2709 079/2740 185
1975-1977		CD: DG 445 6602

Abends am Strand (Wir sassen am Fischerhause)

Berlin	Klust	LP: HMV ALP 1551
September 1956		LP: Electrola WALP 525/E 90014
		LP: EMI 1C 053 01340M
		CD: EMI CZS 568 5092
Berlin	Demus	LP: DG SLPM 139 110
May 1965		
Berlin	Eschenbach	LP: DG 2709 079/2740 185
1974-1976		CD: DG 439 4172/445 6602
Nürnberg	Höll	CD: Erato 4509 984922
May 1992		Also unpublished video recording

Abschied vom Walde (Nun scheidet vom sterbenden Walde)

Berlin	Eschenbach	LP: DG 2709 079/2740 185
1975-1977		CD: DG 445 6602

Allnächtlich im Traume/Dichterliebe
See Dichterliebe

Alte Laute (Hörst du nicht die Vögel singen?)

Vienna	Weissenborn	LP: DG LPM 18 380
January 1957		
Salzburg	Moore	LP: Orfeo S140 855R
July 1959		CD: Orfeo C140 301B/C339 930T
Berlin	Eschenbach	LP: DG 2709 079/2740 185
1974-1976		CD: DG 445 6602

Die alten bösen Lieder/Dichterliebe
See Dichterliebe

Am leuchtenden Sommermorgen/Dichterliebe
See Dichterliebe

An Anna (Lange harrt' ich)

Berlin	Eschenbach	LP: DG 2709 088/2740 200
1975-1977		CD: DG 445 6602

Schumann Lieder/continued

An den Mond (Schlafloser Sonne melancholischer Stern!)

Berlin	Eschenbach	LP: DG 2709 079/2740 185
1975-1977		CD: DG 445 6602

An den Sonnenschein (O Sonnenschein, wie scheinst du mir ins Herz hinein!)

Berlin	Demus	LP: DG SLPM 139 326
June 1967		
Berlin	Eschenbach	LP: DG 2709 074/2740 167
1974-1975		CD: DG 445 6602

An die Türen will ich schleichen

Berlin	Eschenbach	LP: DG 2709 088/2740 200
1975-1977		CD: DG 445 6602

Anfangs wollt' ich fast verzagen/Liederkreis op 24
See Liederkreis op 24

Der arme Peter: Der Hans und die Grete tanzen herum; In meiner Brust, da sitzt ein Weh; Der arme Peter wankt vorbei

Berlin	Klust	LP: HMV ALP 1551
September 1956		LP: Electrola WALP 525/E 90014
		LP: EMI 1C 053 01340M
		CD: EMI CZS 568 5092
Berlin	Demus	LP: DG SLPM 139 110
May 1965		
Berlin	Eschenbach	LP: DG 2709 079/2740 185
1974-1976		CD: DG 445 6602

Auf das Trinkglas eines verstorbenen Freundes (Du herrlich Glas, nun stehst du leer)

Vienna	Weissenborn	45: DG EPL 30 320
January 1957		LP: DG LPM 18 380
Salzburg	Moore	LP: Orfeo S140 855R
July 1959		CD: Orfeo C140 301B/C339 930T
Berlin	Eschenbach	LP: DG 2709 079/2740 185
1974-1975		CD: DG 445 6602

Auf dem Rhein (Auf deinem Grunde haben sie an verborgnem Ort)

Berlin	Eschenbach	LP: DG 2709 079/2740 185
1974-1976		CD: DG 445 6602

Auf einer Burg/Liederkreis op 39 (Eingeschlafen auf der Lauer)
See Liederkreis op 39

Schumann Lieder/continued

Aufträge (Nicht so schnelle, nicht so schnelle!)

| Berlin | Eschenbach | LP: DG 2709 079/2740 185 |
| 1974-1975 | | CD: DG 445 6602 |

Aus alten Märchen winkt es/Dichterliebe
See Dichterliebe

Aus dem Schenkenbuch des Westöstlichen Divans I/Myrthen (Sitz' ich allein,
wo kann ich besser sein?)

| Berlin | Demus | LP: DG LPM 18 655/SLPM 138 655 |
| April 1960 | | |

| Berlin | Eschenbach | LP: DG 2709 074/2740 167/2530 543 |
| 1974 | | CD: DG 445 6602 |

| Nürnberg | Höll | CD: Erato 4509 984922 |
| May 1992 | | Also unpublished video recording |

Aus dem Schenkenbuch des Westöstlichen Divans II/Myrthen (Setze mir nicht,
du Grobian!)

| Berlin | Demus | LP: DG LPM 18 655/SLPM 138 655 |
| April 1960 | | |

| Berlin | Eschenbach | LP: DG 2709 074/2740 167/2530 543 |
| 1974 | | CD: DG 445 6602 |

Aus den östlichen Rosen/Myrthen (Ich sende einen Gruss wie Duft der Rosen)

| Berlin | Demus | LP: DG SLPM 139 326 |
| June 1967 | | |

| Berlin | Eschenbach | LP: DG 2709 074/2740 167/2530 543 |
| 1974 | | CD: DG 445 6602 |

Aus meinen Tränen spriessen/Dichterliebe
See Dichterliebe

Ballade des Harfners (Was hör' ich draussen vor der Tür?)

| Berlin | Eschenbach | LP: DG 2709 088/2740 200 |
| 1975-1977 | | CD: DG 445 6602 |

Ballade vom Heideknaben (Der Knabe träumt)

Berlin	Eschenbach	LP: DG 2709 088/2740 200
1975-1977	Fischer-Dieskau	CD: DG 445 6602
	recites	

Bedeckt mich mit Blumen

Berlin	Varady	LP: DG 2531 204
1980	Eschenbach	

Die beiden Grenadiere (Nach Frankreich zogen zwei Grenadier')

London	Moore	78: HMV DB 21350
October 1951		45: HMV 7P 384
		45: Victor WHMV 1046
		LP: Victor LHMV 1046
		LP: EMI RLS 154 7003/1C 053 01340M
		CD: EMI CZS 568 5092
Berlin	Demus	LP: DG SLPM 139 110/135 026
May 1965		
Berlin	Eschenbach	LP: DG 2709 079/2740 185
1974-1975		CD: DG 439 4172/445 6602

Belsatzar (Die Mitternacht zog näher schon)

Berlin	Klust	LP: HMV ALP 1551
September 1956		LP: Electrola WALP 525/E 90014
		LP: EMI 1C 053 01340M/EX 29 04293
		CD: EMI CZS 568 5092
Berlin	Demus	LP: DG SLPM 139 110
May 1965		
Berlin	Eschenbach	LP: DG 2709 079/2740 185
1974-1975		CD: DG 445 6602

Berg und Burgen schau'n herunter/Liederkreis op 24
See Liederkreis op 24

Blaue Augen hat das Mädchen

Berlin	Varady	LP: DG 2531 204
1980	Eschenbach	

Blondels Lied (Spähend nach dem Eisengitter)

Berlin	Eschenbach	LP: DG 2709 079/2740 185
1974-1976		CD: DG 445 6602

Schumann Lieder/continued

Der Contrabandiste (Ich bin der Contrabandiste)

Berlin April 1960	Demus	LP: DG LPM 18 655/SLPM 138 655

Berlin 1974-1976	Eschenbach	LP: DG 2709 079/2740 185 CD: DG 439 4172/445 6602

Nürnberg May 1992	Höll	CD: Erato 4509 984922 Also unpublished video recording

Da liegt der Feinde gestreckte Schar

Berlin 1975-1977	Eschenbach	LP: DG 2709 088/2740 200 CD: DG 445 6602

Das ist ein Flöten und Geigen/Dichterliebe
See Dichterliebe

Dein Angesicht, so lieb und schön

Berlin May 1965	Demus	LP: DG SLPM 139 110

Berlin 1975-1977	Eschenbach	LP: DG 2709 088/2740 200 CD: DG 445 6602

Dem roten Röslein gleicht mein Lieb

Berlin June 1967	Demus	LP: DG SLPM 139 326

Berlin 1974	Eschenbach	LP: DG 2709 074/2740 167 CD: DG 445 6602

Dichters Genesung (Und wieder hatt' ich der Schönsten gedacht)

Berlin June 1967	Demus	LP: DG SLPM 139 326

Berlin 1974-1975	Eschenbach	LP: DG 2709 074/2740 167 CD: DG 445 6602

Schumann Lieder/continued

Du bist wie eine Blume/Myrten

London October 1951	Moore	HMV unpublished
Salzburg August 1956	Moore	LP: Orfeo CD: Orfeo C294 921B/C339 930T
Berlin September 1956	Klust	45: HMV 7P 384 LP: HMV ALP 1551 LP: Electrola WALP 525/E 90014 LP: EMI 1C 053 01340M CD: EMI CZS 568 5092
Berlin May 1965	Demus	LP: DG SLPM 139 110/135 014
Berlin 1974	Eschenbach	LP: DG 2709 074/2740 167/2530 543 CD: DG 415 1902/445 6602
Nürnberg May 1992	Höll	CD: Erato 4509 984922 Also unpublished video recording

Einsamkeit (Wildverwachs'ne dunkle Fichten)

Berlin 1975-1977	Eschenbach	LP: DG 2709 088/2740 200 CD: DG 445 6602

Der Einsiedler (Komm, Trost der Welt, du stille Nacht!)

Berlin March 1964	Moore	LP: HMV ALP 2103/ASD 650 LP: Electrola 1C 063 00274
Salzburg August 1975	Sawallisch	CD: Orfeo C185 891A/C339 930T
Berlin 1975-1977	Eschenbach	LP: DG 2709 088/2740 200 CD: DG 445 6602

Er ist's (Frühling lässt sein blaues Band)

Berlin 1974-1976	Eschenbach	LP: DG 2709 079/2740 185 CD: DG 445 6602

Schumann Lieder/continued

Er und sie (Seh' ich das stille Tal)

London February 1967	Schwarzkopf Moore	LP: EMI AN 182-183/SAN 182-183 LP: EMI SLS 926/ASD 143 5941 CD: EMI CDC 749 2382/CDEMX 2233
London August 1969	Baker Barenboim	LP: EMI ASD 2553/1C 063 02041
Berlin 1980	Varady Eschenbach	LP: DG 2531 204

Erinnerung (Glück der Engel, wo geblieben?)

Berlin 1975-1977	Eschenbach	LP: DG 2709 088/2740 200 CD: DG 445 6602

Erstes Grün (Du junges Grün, du frisches Gras!)

Salzburg August 1956	Moore	CD: Orfeo C294 301B/C339 930T
Vienna January 1957	Weissenborn	45: DG EPL 30 320 LP: DG LPM 18 380
Salzburg July 1959	Moore	LP: Orfeo CD: Orfeo C140 301B/C339 930T
Berlin 1974-1976	Eschenbach	LP: DG 2709 079/2740 185 CD: DG 439 4172/445 6602
Nürnberg May 1992	Höll	CD: Erato 4509 984922 Also unpublished video recording

Es leuchtet meine Liebe

Berlin May 1965	Demus	LP: DG SLPM 139 110
Berlin 1975-1977	Eschenbach	LP: DG 2709 088/2740 200 CD: DG 445 6602
Nürnberg May 1992	Höll	CD: Erato 4509 984922 Also unpublished video recording

Es stürmet am Abendhimmel

Berlin 1975-1977	Eschenbach	LP: DG 2709 088/2740 200 CD: DG 445 6602

Es treibt mich hin, es treibt mich her!/Liederkreis op 24
See Liederkreis op 24

Schumann Lieder/continued

Familien-Gemälde (Grossvater und Grossmutter, die sassen im Gartenhag)

Berlin	Schreier	LP: DG 2531 204
1980	Eschenbach	

Die feindlichen Brüder (Oben auf des Berges Spitze)

Berlin	Klust	LP: HMV ALP 1551
September 1956		LP: Electrola WALP 525/E 90014
		LP: EMI 1C 053 01340M
		CD: EMI CZS 568 5092

Berlin	Demus	LP: DG SLPM 139 110
May 1965		

Berlin	Eschenbach	LP: DG 2709 079/2740 185
1974-1976		CD: DG 439 4172/445 6602

Die Flüchtlinge (Der Hagel klirret nieder)

Berlin	Eschenbach	LP: DG 2709 088/2740 200
1975-1977	Fischer-Dieskau recites	CD: DG 445 6602

Flügel! Flügel! Um zu fliegen!

Berlin	Eschenbach	LP: DG 2709 074/2740 167
1974-1975		CD: DG 445 6602

Frage (Wärst du nicht, heil'ger Abendschein!)

Vienna	Weissenborn	LP: DG LPM 18 380
January 1957		

Salzburg	Moore	LP: Orfeo S140 855R
July 1959		CD: Orfeo C140 301B/C339 930T

Berlin	Eschenbach	LP: DG 2709 079/2740 185
1974-1976		CD: DG 445 6602

Freisinn/Myrten (Lasst mich nur auf meinem Sattel gelten!)

Vienna	Weissenborn	45: DG EPL 30 314
January 1957		LP: DG LPM 18 380

Berlin	Demus	LP: DG SLPM 139 326
June 1967		

Berlin	Eschenbach	LP: DG 2709 074/2740 167/2530 543
1974		CD: DG 415 1902/445 6602

Schumann Lieder/continued

Der frohe Wandersmann (Wem Gott will rechte Gunst erweisen)

Berlin   Moore   LP: HMV ALP 2103/ASD 650
March 1964   LP: Electrola 1C 063 00274

Berlin   Eschenbach   LP: DG 2709 074/2740 167
1974-1975   CD: DG 445 6602

Frühlingsfahrt (Es zogen zwei rüst'gen Gesellen)

Berlin   Moore   LP: HMV ALP 2103/ASD 650
March 1964   LP: Electrola 1C 063 00274/SHZE 219
                                         LP: EMI EX 29 04293

Berlin   Eschenbach   LP: DG 2709 074/2740 167
1974-1975   CD: DG 445 6602

Frühlingslied (Schneeglöckchen klingen wieder)

Berlin   Varady   LP: DG 2531 204
1980   Eschenbach

Frühlingsnacht/Liederkreis op 39 (Ueber Gärten durch die Lüfte)
See Liederkreis op 39

Der Gärtner (Auf ihrem Leibrösslein so weiss wie der Schnee)

Berlin   Eschenbach   LP: DG 2709 088/2740 200
1975-1977   CD: DG 445 6602

Gesanges Erwachen (Könnt' ich einmal wieder singen)

Berlin   Eschenbach   LP: DG 2709 088/2740 200
1975-1977   CD: DG 445 6602

Geständnis (Also lieb' ich Euch, Geliebte!)

Berlin   Demus   LP: DG LPM 18 655/SLPM 138 655
April 1960

Berlin   Eschenbach   LP: DG 2709 079/2740 185
1974-1976   CD: DG 445 6602

Das Glück (Vöglein vom Zweig)

Berlin   Varady   LP: DG 2531 204
1980   Eschenbach

Schumann Lieder/continued

Den grünen Zeigern, den roten Wangen

| Berlin | Eschenbach | LP: DG 2709 088/2740 200 |
| 1975-1977 | | CD: DG 445 6602 |

Der Handschuh(Vor seinem Löwengarten)

| Berlin | Eschenbach | LP: DG 2709 088/2740 200 |
| 1975-1977 | | CD: DG 445 6602 |

Hauptmanns Weib/Myrthen (Hoch zu Pferd!)

| Berlin | Demus | LP: DG SLPM 139 326 |
| June 1967 | | |

| Berlin | Eschenbach | LP: DG 2709 074/2740 167/2530 543 |
| 1974 | | CD: DG 445 6602 |

Heimliches Verschwinden (Nachts zu unbekannter Stunde)

| Berlin | Eschenbach | LP: DG 2709 088/2740 200 |
| 1975-1977 | | CD: DG 445 6602 |

Herbstlied (Durch die Tannen und die Linde)

| Berlin | Eschenbach | LP: DG 2709 088/2740 200 |
| 1975-1977 | | CD: DG 445 6602 |

Herbstlied (Das Laub fällt von den Bäumen)

| London | Baker | LP: EMI ASD 2553/1C 063 02041 |
| August 1969 | Barenboim | LP: EMI EX 29 04293 |

| Berlin | Schreier | LP: DG 2531 204 |
| 1980 | Eschenbach | |

Der Hidalgo (Es ist so süss zu scherzen)

| Berlin | Demus | LP: DG LPM 18 655/SLPM 138 655 |
| April 1960 | | LP: DG 9108/109 108 |

| Berlin | Eschenbach | LP: DG 2709 074/2740 167 |
| 1974-1975 | | CD: DG 445 6602 |

Der Himmel hat eine Träne geweinet

| Berlin
1974-1975 | Eschenbach | LP: DG 2709 074/2740 167
CD: DG 445 6602 |

Hochländers Abschied/Myrthen (Mein Herz ist im Hochland)

| Berlin
June 1967 | Demus | LP: DG SLPM 139 326 |
| Berlin
1974 | Eschenbach | LP: DG 2709 074/2740 167/2530 543
CD: DG 415 1902/445 6602 |

Hör' ich das Liedchen klingen/Dichterliebe
See Dichterliebe

Der Husar, trara!

| Berlin
1975-1977 | Eschenbach | LP: DG 2709 088/2740 200
CD: DG 445 6602 |

Husarenabzug (Aus dem dunklen Tor wallt kein Zug von Mücklein)

| Berlin
1975-1977 | Eschenbach | LP: DG 2709 088/2740 200
CD: DG 445 6602 |

Ich bin dein Baum

| London
August 1969 | Baker
Barenboim | LP: EMI ASD 2553/1C 063 02041 |
| Berlin
1980 | Varady
Eschenbach | LP: DG 2531 204 |

Ich denke dein

| London
February 1967 | Schwarzkopf
Moore | LP: EMI AN 182-183/SAN 182-183
LP: EMI SLS 926 |
| Berlin
1980 | Varady
Eschenbach | LP: DG 2531 204 |

Ich grolle nicht/Dichterliebe
See Dichterliebe

Schumann Lieder/continued

Ich hab' im Traum geweinet/Dichterliebe
See Dichterliebe

Ich hab' in mich gesogen

Berlin   Eschenbach   LP: DG 2709 074/2740 167
1974-1975   CD: DG 445 6602

Ich wandelte unter den Bäumen/Liederkreis op 24
See Liederkreis op 24

Ich will meine Seele tauchen/Dichterliebe
See Dichterliebe

Ihre Stimme (Lass' tief in dir mich lesen)

Berlin   Eschenbach   LP: DG 2709 088/2740 200
1975-1977   CD: DG 445 6602

Im Rhein, im heiligen Strome/Dichterliebe
See Dichterliebe

Im Walde/Liederkreis op 39 (Es zog eine Hochzeit den Berg entlang)
See Liederkreis op 39

Im wunderschönen Monat Mai/Dichterliebe
See Dichterliebe

In der Fremde/Liederkreis op 39 (Aus der Heimat hinter den Blitzen rot)
See Liederkreis op 39

In der Fremde/Liederkreis op 39 (Ich hör' die Bächlein rauschen)
See Liederkreis op 39

Schumann Lieder/continued

In der Nacht (Alle gingen, Herz, zur Ruh')

London	Schwarzkopf	LP: EMI AN 182-183/SAN 182-183
February 1967	Moore	LP: EMI SLS 926
Berlin	Schreier	LP: DG 2531 204
1980	Eschenbach	

Ins Freie (Mir ist's so eng allüberall!)

Berlin	Eschenbach	LP: DG 2709 088/2740 200
1975-1977		CD: DG 445 6602

Intermezzo/Liederkreis op 39 (Dein Bildnis wunderselig)
See Liederkreis op 39

Intermezzo (Und schläfst du, mein Mädchen)

Berlin	Schreier	LP: DG 2531 204
1980	Eschenbach	

Jasminenstrauch (Grün ist der Jasminenstrauch)

Berlin	Demus	LP: DG SLPM 139 326
June 1967		
Berlin	Eschenbach	LP: DG 2709 074/2740 167
1974-1975		CD: DG 445 6602

Jung Volkers Lied (Und die mich trug im Mutterarm)

Berlin	Eschenbach	LP: DG 2709 088/2740 200
1975-1977		CD: DG 445 6602

Ein Jüngling liebt ein Mädchen/Dichterliebe
See Dichterliebe

Der Knabe mit dem Wunderhorn (Ich bin ein lust'ger Geselle)

Berlin	Demus	LP: DG SLPM 139 326
June 1967		
Berlin	Eschenbach	LP: DG 2709 074/2740 167
1974-1975		CD: DG 445 6602

Schumann Lieder/continued

Kommen und Scheiden (So oft sie kam)

Berlin	Eschenbach	LP: DG 2709 088/2740 200
1975-1977		CD: DG 445 6602

Kurzes Erwachen (Ich bin im Mai gegangen)

Berlin	Eschenbach	LP: DG 2709 088/2740 200
1975-1977		CD: DG 445 6602

Ländliches Lied (Und wenn die Primel schneeweiss blickt am Bach)

Berlin	Schreier	LP: DG 2531 204
1980	Eschenbach	

Lehn' deine Wang' an meine Wang'

Berlin	Demus	LP: DG SLPM 139 110
May 1965		

Berlin	Eschenbach	LP: DG 2709 088/2740 200
1975-1977		CD: DG 445 6602

Der leidige Frieden hat lange gewährt

Berlin	Eschenbach	LP: DG 2709 088/2740 200
1975-1977		CD: DG 445 6602

Lieb' Liebchen, leg's Händchen aufs Herze mein/Liederkreis op 24
See Liederkreis op 24

Liebesbotschaft (Wolken, die ihr nach Osten eilt)

Berlin	Demus	LP: DG SLPM 139 326
June 1967		

Berlin	Eschenbach	LP: DG 2709 074/2740 167
1974-1975		CD: DG 445 6602

Liebesgarten (Die Liebe ist ein Rosenstrauch)

Berlin	Schreier	LP: DG 2531 204
1980	Eschenbach	

Liebesgram (Dereinst, dereinst, o Gedanke mein!)

Berlin	Schreier	LP: DG 2531 204
1980	Eschenbach	

Liebhabers Ständchen (Wachst du noch, Liebchen?)

London	Schwarzkopf	EMI unpublished
February 1967	Moore	
Berlin	Schreier	LP: DG 2531 204
1980	Eschenbach	

Lied Lynceus' des Türmers (Zum Sehen geboren, zum Schauen bestellt)

Berlin	Eschenbach	LP: DG 2709 079/2740 185
1974-1976		CD: DG 445 6602

Lied eines Schmiedes (Fein Rösslein, ich beschlage dich)

Berlin	Eschenbach	LP: DG 2709 088/2740 200
1975-1977		CD: DG 445 6602

Loreley (Es flüstern und rauschen die Wogen)

Berlin	Eschenbach	LP: DG 2709 079/2740 185
1974-1976		CD: DG 445 6602

Die Lotosblume/Myrthen (Die Lotosblume ängstigt)

London	Moore	LP: EMI RLS 154 7003
October 1951		
Berlin	Demus	LP: DG LPM 18 655/SLPM 138 655
April 1960		LP: DG 9108/109 108
Berlin	Demus	LP: DG SLPM 139 110/135 026
May 1965		
Berlin	Eschenbach	LP: DG 2709 074/2740 167/2530 543
1974		CD: DG 415 1902/445 6602

Die Lotosblume, version for duet

Berlin	Varady	LP: DG 2531 204
1980	Eschenbach	

Schumann Lieder/continued

Die Löwenbraut (Mit der Myrthe geschmückt und dem Brautgeschmeid)

Berlin June 1967	Demus	LP: DG SLPM 139 326
Berlin 1974-1975	Eschenbach	LP: DG 2709 074/2740 167 CD: DG 445 6602

Lust der Sturmnacht (Wenn durch Berg und Tale draussen)

Vienna January 1957	Weissenborn	LP: DG LPM 18 380
Salzburg July 1959	Moore	LP: Orfeo S140 855R CD: Orfeo C140 301B/C339 930T
Berlin 1974-1976	Eschenbach	LP: DG 2709 079/2740 185 CD: DG 445 6602

Mailied (Komm', lieber Mai!)

Berlin 1980	Varady Eschenbach	LP: DG 2531 204

Marienwürmchen, setze dich auf meine Hand

Berlin 1974-1976	Eschenbach	LP: DG 2709 079/2740 185 CD: DG 445 6602

Märzveilchen (Der Himmel wölbt sich rein und blau)

Berlin 1974-1975	Eschenbach	LP: DG 2709 074/2740 167 CD: DG 445 6602

Die Meerfee (Helle Silberglöcklein klingen)

Berlin 1975-1977	Eschenbach	LP: DG 2709 088/2740 200 CD: DG 445 6602

Mein Herz ist schwer/Myrthen

Berlin April 1960	Demus	LP: DG LPM 18 655/SLPM 138 655 LP: DG 9108/109 108
Berlin 1974	Eschenbach	LP: DG 2709 074/2740 167/2530 543 CD: DG 445 6602

Schumann Lieder/continued

Mein schöner Stern, ich bitte dich

Berlin April 1960	Demus	LP: DG LPM 18 655/SLPM 138 655
Berlin 1975-1977	Eschenbach	LP: DG 2709 088/2740 200 CD: DG 445 6602

Mein Wagen rollet langsam

Berlin September 1956	Klust	LP: HMV ALP 1551 LP: Electrola WALP 525/E 90014 LP: EMI 1C 053 01340M CD: EMI CZS 568 5092
Berlin May 1965	Demus	LP: DG SLPM 139 110
Berlin 1975-1977	Eschenbach	LP: DG 2709 088/2740 200 CD: DG 439 4172/445 6602
Nürnberg May 1992	Höll	CD: Erato 4509 984922 Also unpublished video recording

Meine Rose (Dem holden Lenzgeschmeide)

Berlin 1975-1977	Eschenbach	LP: DG 2709 088/2740 200 CD: DG 445 6602

Melancholie (Wann erscheint der Morgen?)

Berlin April 1960	Demus	LP: DG LPM 18 655/SLPM 138 655
Berlin 1974-1976	Eschenbach	LP: DG 2709 079/2740 185 CD: DG 445 6602

Mondnacht/Liederkreis op 39 (Es war, als hätt' der Himmel)
See Liederkreis op 39

Morgens steh' ich auf und frage/Liederkreis op 24
See Liederkreis op 24

Mit Myrthen und Rosen/Liederkreis op 24
See Liederkreis op 24

Schumann Lieder/continued

Muttertraum (Die Mutter betet herzig)

Berlin	Eschenbach	LP: DG 2709 074/2740 167/2539 543
1974-1975		CD: DG 445 6602

Nachtlied (Ueber allen Gipfeln ist Ruh')

Berlin	Eschenbach	LP: DG 2709 088/2740 200
1975-1977		CD: DG 445 6602

Nichts Schöneres (Als ich zuerst dich hab' geseh'n)

Berlin	Demus	LP: DG SLPM 139 326
June 1967		

Berlin	Eschenbach	LP: DG 2709 074/2740 200
1974-1975		CD: DG 445 6602

Niemand/Myrthen (Ich hab' mein Weib allein)

Berlin	Demus	LP: DG SLPM 139 326
June 1967		

Berlin	Eschenbach	LP: DG 2709 074/2740 167/2530 543
1974		CD: DG 445 6602

Nur ein lächelnder Blick

Berlin	Demus	LP: DG SLPM 139 326
June 1967		

Berlin	Eschenbach	LP: DG 2709 074/2740 167
1974-1975		CD: DG 445 6602

Der Nussbaum/Myrthen (Es grünet ein Nussbaum vor dem Haus)

Berlin	Demus	LP: DG LPM 18 655/SLPM 138 655/9108
April 1960		LP: DG 109 108/135 007/135 026

Berlin	Eschenbach	LP: DG 2709 074/2740 167/2530 543
1974		CD: DG 415 1902/445 6602

Schumann Lieder/continued

O wie herrlich ist das Mädchen

Berlin April 1960	Demus	LP: DG LPM 18 655/SLPM 138 655
Berlin 1975-1977	Eschenbach	LP: DG 2709 088/2740 200 CD: DG 445 6602

Der Page (Da ich nun entsagen müssen)

Berlin 1974-1975	Eschenbach	LP: DG 2709 074/2740 167 CD: DG 445 6602

Provencalisches Lied (In den Talen der Provence)

Berlin 1975-1977	Eschenbach	LP: DG 2709 088/2740 200 CD: DG 445 6602

Rätsel/Myrthen (Es flüstert's der Himmel, es murrt es die Hölle)

Berlin June 1967	Demus	LP: DG SLPM 139 326
Berlin 1974	Eschenbach	LP: DG 2709 074/2740 167/2530 543 CD: DG 445 6602

Requiem (Ruh' von schmerzensreichen Mühen)

Berlin 1975-1977	Eschenbach	LP: DG 2709 088/2740 200 CD: DG 445 6602

Resignation (Lieben, von ganzer Seele)

Berlin 1975-1977	Eschenbach	LP: DG 2709 088/2740 200 CD: DG 445 6602

Romanze (Flutenreicher Ebro)

Berlin April 1960	Demus	LP: DG LPM 18 655/SLPM 138 655
Berlin 1975-1977	Eschenbach	LP: DG 2709 088/2740 200 CD: DG 445 6602

Schumann Lieder/continued

Die Rose, die Lilie, die Taube, die Sonne/Dichterliebe
See Dichterliebe

Rose, Meer und Sonne

| Berlin | Eschenbach | LP: DG 2709 074/2740 167 |
| 1974-1975 | | CD: DG 445 6602 |

Die rote Hanne (Den Säugling an der Brust)

| Berlin | Eschenbach | LP: DG 2709 074/2740 167 |
| 1974-1975 | | CD: DG 445 6602 |

Sag' an, o lieber Vogel mein

| Berlin | Demus | LP: DG SLPM 139 326 |
| June 1967 | | |

| Berlin | Eschenbach | LP: DG 2709 074/2740 167 |
| 1974-1975 | | CD: DG 445 6602 |

Der Schatzgräber (Wenn alle Wälder schliefen)

| Berlin | Moore | LP: HMV ALP 2103/ASD 650 |
| March 1964 | | LP: Electrola 1C 063 00274 |

| Berlin | Eschenbach | LP: DG 2709 074/2740 167 |
| 1974-1975 | | CD: DG 445 6602 |

Schneeglöckchen (Der Schnee, der gestern noch in Flöckchen)

| Vienna | Weissenborn | 45: DG EPL 30 314 |
| January 1957 | | LP: DG LPM 18 380 |

| Berlin | Eschenbach | LP: DG 2709 079/2740 185 |
| 1974-1976 | | CD: DG 445 6602 |

Schneeglöckchen (Die Sonne sah die Erde an)

| Berlin | Eschenbach | LP: DG 2709 088/2740 200 |
| 1975-1977 | | CD: DG 445 6602 |

Schumann Lieder/continued

Schön Blümelein (Ich bin hinausgegangen)

Berlin	Schreier	LP: DG 2531 204
1980	Eschenbach	

Schön Hedwig (Im Kreise der Vasallen)

Berlin	Eschenbach	LP: DG 2709 088/2740 200
1975-1977	Fischer-Dieskau	CD: DG 445 6602
	recites	

Schön ist das Fest des Lenzes

London	Baker	LP: EMI ASD 2553/1C 063 02041
August 1969	Barenboim	

Berlin	Schreier	LP: DG 2531 204
1980	Eschenbach	

Schöne Fremde/Liederkreis op 39 (Es rauschen die Wipfel und schauern)
See Liederkreis op 39

Schöne Wiege meiner Leiden/Liederkreis op 24
See Liederkreis op 24

Die Schwalben (Es fliegen zwei Schwalben)

Berlin	Varady	LP: DG 2531 204
1980	Eschenbach	

Der schwere Abend (Die dunklen Wolken hingen)

Berlin	Eschenbach	LP: DG 2709 088/2740 200
1975-1977		CD: DG 445 6602

Sehnsucht (Sterne der blauen himmlischen Auen)

Berlin	Demus	LP: DG LPM 18 655/SLPM 138 655
April 1960		

Berlin	Eschenbach	LP: DG 2709 088/2740 200
1975-1977		CD: DG 445 6602

Schumann Lieder/continued

Sehnsucht nach der Waldgegend (Wär' ich nie aus euch gegangen)

| Vienna | Weissenborn | 45: DG EPL 30 320 |
| January 1957 | | LP: DG LPM 18 380 |

| Salzburg | Moore | LP: Orfeo |
| July 1959 | | CD: Orfeo C140 301B/C339 930T |

| Berlin | Eschenbach | LP: DG 2709 074/2740 167 |
| 1974-1975 | | CD: DG 445 6602 |

Des Sennen Abschied (Ihr Matten, lebt wohl!)

| Vienna | Weissenborn | LP: DG LPM 18 380 |
| January 1957 | | |

| Berlin | Eschenbach | LP: DG 2709 079/2740 185 |
| 1974-1976 | | CD: DG 445 6602 |

Die Sennin (Schöne Sennin noch einmal)

| Berlin | Eschenbach | LP: DG 2709 088/2740 200 |
| 1975-1977 | | CD: DG 445 6602 |

So wahr die Sonne scheint

| Berlin | Schreier | LP: DG 2531 204 |
| 1980 | Eschenbach | |

Der Soldat (Es geht bei gedämpfter Trommel Klang)

| Berlin | Eschenbach | LP: DG 2740 074/2740 167 |
| 1974-1975 | | CD: DG 445 6602 |

Sommerruh', wie schön bist du

| Berlin | Varady | LP: DG 2531 204 |
| 1980 | Eschenbach | |

Sonntags am Rhein (Des Sonntags in der Morgenstund')

| Berlin | Demus | LP: DG SLPM 139 326 |
| June 1967 | | |

| Berlin | Eschenbach | LP: DG 2709 074/2740 167 |
| 1974-1975 | | CD: DG 445 6602 |

Schumann Lieder/continued

Der Spielmann (Im Städtchen gibt es des Jubels viel)

Berlin	Eschenbach	LP: DG 2709 074/2740 167
1974-1975		CD: DG 445 6602

Ständchen (Komm' in die stille Nacht)

Vienna	Weissenborn	45: DG EPL 30 314
January 1957		LP: DG LPM 18 380
Berlin	Eschenbach	LP: DG 2709 074/2740 167
1974-1975		CD: DG 445 6602

Die Stille/Liederkreis op 39 (Es weiss und rät es doch keiner)
See Liederkreis op 39

Stille Liebe (Könnt' ich dich in Liedern preisen)

Vienna	Weissenborn	45: DG EPL 30 320
January 1957		LP: DG LPM 18 380
Salzburg	Moore	LP: Orfeo
July 1959		CD: Orfeo C140 301B/C339 930T
Berlin	Eschenbach	LP: DG 2709 074/2740 167
1974-1975		CD: DG 445 6602

Stille Tränen (Du bist vom Schlaf erstanden)

Vienna	Weissenborn	LP: DG LPM 18 380
January 1957		
Salzburg	Moore	LP: Orfeo
July 1959		CD: Orfeo C140 301B/C339 930T
Berlin	Eschenbach	LP: DG 2709 074/2740 167
1974-1976		CD: DG 445 6602

Stirb, Lieb' und Freud'! (Zu Augsburg steht ein hohes Haus)

Vienna	Weissenborn	LP: DG LPM 18 380
January 1957		
Salzburg	Moore	LP: Orfeo
July 1959		CD: Orfeo C140 301B/C339 930T
Berlin	Eschenbach	LP: DG 2709 074/2740 167
1974-1976		CD: DG 445 6602

Schumann Lieder/continued

Talismane/Myrthen (Gottes ist der Orient!)

Vienna January 1957	Weissenborn	45: DG EPL 30 314 LP: DG LPM 18 380
Berlin June 1967	Demus	LP: DG SLPM 139 326
Berlin 1974	Eschenbach	LP: DG 2709 074/2740 167/2530 543 CD: DG 415 1902/445 6602

Tanzlied (Eija, wie flattert der Kranz!)

London February 1967	Schwarzkopf Moore	LP: EMI AN 182-183/SAN 182-183 LP: EMI SLS 926/ASD 143 5941 CD: EMI CDC 749 2382/CDEMX 2233
London August 1969	Baker Barenboim	LP: EMI ASD 2553/1C 063 02041 LP: EMI EX 29 04293
Berlin 1980	Schreier Eschenbach	LP: DG 2531 204

Die tausend Grüsse, die wir dir senden

Berlin 1980	Varady Eschenbach	LP: DG 2531 204

Tief im Herzen trag' ich Pein

Berlin April 1960	Demus	LP: DG LPM 18 655/SLPM 138 655
Berlin 1975-1977	Eschenbach	LP: DG 2709 088/2740 200 CD: DG 445 6602

Tragödie I & II: Entflieh' mit mir und sei mein Weib!; Es fiel ein Reif

Berlin September 1956	Klust	LP: HMV ALP 1551 LP: Electrola WALP 525/E 90014 LP: EMI 1C 053 01340M CD: EMI CZS 568 5092
Berlin May 1965	Demus	LP: DG SLPM 139 110
Berlin 1974-1976	Eschenbach	LP: DG 2709 079/2740 185 CD: DG 439 4172/445 6602

Schumann Lieder/continued

Trost im Gesang (Der Wanderer, dem verschwunden)

Berlin	Eschenbach	LP: DG 2709 088/2740 200
1975-1977		CD: DG 445 6602

Und wüssten's die Blumen/Dichterliebe
See Dichterliebe

Unterm Fenster (Wer ist vor meiner Kammertür?)

London	Schwarzkopf	EMI unpublished
February 1967	Moore	
Berlin	Schreier	LP: DG 2531 204
1980	Eschenbach	

Venezianische Lieder I & II/Myrthen: Leis' rudern hier, mein Gondolier;
Wenn durch die Piazetta die Abendluft weht

Vienna	Weissenborn	45: DG EPL 30 314
January 1957		LP: DG LPM 18 380
Berlin	Demus	LP: DG SLPM 139 326
June 1967		
Berlin	Eschenbach	LP: DG 2709 074/2740 167/2530 543
1974		CD: DG 445 6602

Verratene Liebe (Da nachts wir uns küssten, o Mädchen)

Berlin	Eschenbach	LP: DG 2709 074/2740 167
1974-1975		CD: DG 445 6602

Waldesgespräch/Liederkreis op 39 (Es ist schon spät, es ist schon kalt)
See Liederkreis op 39

Wanderlied (Wohlauf! Noch getrunken den funkelnden Wein)

Vienna	Weissenborn	45: DG EPL 30 320
January 1957		LP: DG LPM 18 380
Salzburg	Moore	LP: Orfeo
July 1959		CD: Orfeo C140 301B/C339 930T
Berlin	Eschenbach	LP: DG 2709 074/2740 167
1974-1976		CD: DG 445 6602

Schumann Lieder/continued

Die wandelnde Glocke (Es war ein Kind, das wollte nie)

Berlin	Eschenbach	LP: DG 2709 079/2740 185
1974-1976		CD: DG 445 6602

Wanderung (Wohlauf und frisch gewandert ins unbekannte Land)

Vienna	Weissenborn	LP: DG LPM 18 380
January 1957		
Salzburg	Moore	LP: Orfeo S140 855R
July 1959		CD: Orfeo C140 301B/C339 930T
Berlin	Eschenbach	LP: DG 2709 074/2740 167
1974-1975		CD: DG 445 6602

Warnung (Es geht der Tag zur Neige)

Berlin	Eschenbach	LP: DG 2709 088/2740 200
1975-1977		CD: DG 445 6602

Warte, warte, wilder Schiffmann/Liederkreis op 24
See Liederkreis op 24

Was soll ich sagen? (Mein Aug' ist trüb)

Berlin	Demus	LP: DG SLPM 139 326
June 1967		
Berlin	Eschenbach	LP: DG 2709 074/2740 167
1974-1975		CD: DG 445 6602

Was will die einsame Träne?/Myrthen

Berlin	Demus	LP: DG SLPM 139 110
May 1965		
Berlin	Eschenbach	LP: DG 2709 074/2740 167/2530 543
1974		CD: DG 445 6602

Weh, wie zornig ist das Mädchen

Berlin	Demus	LP: DG LPM 18 655/SLPM 138 655
April 1960		
Berlin	Eschenbach	LP: DG 2709 088/2740 200
1975-1977		CD: DG 445 6602

Wehmut/Liederkreis op 39 (Ich kann wohl manchmal singen)
See Liederkreis op 39

Schumann Lieder/continued

Die Weinende (Ich sah dich weinen, ach!)

Berlin	Eschenbach	LP: DG 2709 088/2740 200
1975-1977		CD: DG 445 6602

Wenn ich ein Vöglein wär'

Berlin	Schreier	LP: DG 2531 204
1980	Eschenbach	

Wenn ich in deine Augen seh'/Dichterliebe
See Dichterliebe

Wer machte dich so krank? (Dass du so krank geworden)

Vienna	Weissenborn	LP: DG LPM 18 380
January 1957		
Salzburg	Moore	LP: Orfeo S140 855R
July 1959		CD: Orfeo C140 301B/C339 930T
Berlin	Eschenbach	LP: DG 2709 074/2740 167
1974-1976		CD: DG 445 6602

Wer nie sein Brot mit Tränen ass

Berlin	Eschenbach	LP: DG 2709 088/2740 200
1975-1977		CD: DG 445 6602

Wer sich der Einsamkeit ergibt

Berlin	Eschenbach	LP: DG 2709 088/2740 200
1975-1977		CD: DG 445 6602

Widmung/Myrthen (Du meine Seele, du mein Herz)

Salzburg	Moore	LP: Orfeo S140 855R
August 1956		CD: Orfeo C294 921B/C339 930T
Berlin	Demus	LP: DG LPM 18 655/SLPM 138 655
April 1960		LP: DG 135 014
Berlin	Eschenbach	LP: DG 2709 074/2740 167/2530 543
1974		CD: DG 415 1902/445 6602

Schumann Lieder/concluded

Wiegenlied (Schlaf', Kindlein, schlaf')

London	Baker	LP: EMI ASD 2553
August 1969	Barenboim	LP: EMI 1C 063 02041/SHZE 326
Berlin	Varady	LP: DG 2531 204
1980	Eschenbach	

Zigeunerliedchen I & II: Unter die Soldaten ist ein Zigeunerbub' gegangen;
Jeden Morgen in der Frühe

Berlin	Demus	LP: DG LPM 18 655/SLPM 138 655
April 1960		
Berlin	Eschenbach	LP: DG 2709 079/2740 185
1974-1976		CD: DG 439 4172/445 6602

Zum Schluss/Myrthen (Hier in diesen erdbeklomm'nen Lüften)

Berlin	Demus	LP: DG LPM 18 655/SLPM 138 655
April 1960		
Berlin	Eschenbach	LP: DG 2709 074/2740 185/2530 543
1974		CD: DG 445 6602

Zwielicht/Liederkreis op 39 (Dämm'rung will die Flügel spreiten)
See Liederkreis op 39

A Schumann Lieder recital, recorded live at Munich in 1958 and accompanied
by Weissenborn, was announced as a Melodram LP but may not have appeared

SCHÜTZ

Matthäus-Passion

Berlin	J.Richter, Schulz,	LP: DG APM 14 174/SAPM 198 174
February 1961	L.Fischer-Dieskau	LP: DG 2547 018
	Distler Choir	
	K.Fischer-Dieskau	

Duets: Der Herr schauet vom Himmel; Cerbum caro factum est

London	Baker	LP: EMI ASD 2710
February 1970	Heath, cello	
	Malcolm, organ	

SCHWARZ-SCHILLING

Bist du manchmal auch verstimmt/Der wandernde Musikant

Berlin November 1961	Reimann	LP: Electrola E 91189/STE 91189 CD: EMI CZS 568 5092
Salzburg August 1975	Sawallisch	CD: Orfeo C185 891A/C339 930T

Durch Feld und Buchenhallen/Der wandernde Musikant

Berlin November 1961	Reimann	LP: Electrola E 91189/STE 91189 CD: EMI CZS 568 5092

Kurze Fahrt (Posthorn, wie so keck und fröhlich)

Berlin 1965	Moore	Details of publication could not be traced
Salzburg August 1975	Sawallisch	CD: Orfeo C185 891A/C339 930T

Marienlied (Wenn im Land die Wetter hängen)

Berlin 1965	Moore	Details of publication could not be traced
Salzburg August 1975	Sawallisch	CD: Orfeo C185 891A/C339 930T

Todeslust

Berlin 1965	Moore	Details of publication could not be traced

Wandern lieb' ich für mein Leben/Der wandernde Musikant

Berlin November 1961	Reimann	LP: Electrola E 91189/STE 91189 CD: EMI CZS 568 5092

Wenn die Sonne lieblich schiene/Der wandernde Musikant

Berlin November 1961	Reimann	LP: Electrola E 91189/STE 91189 CD: EMI CZS 568 5092

SECKENDORFF

Romanze aus „Claudine"

Berlin   Demus, fortepiano   LP: DG 2533 149
September 1972

SHOSTAKOVICH

Symphony No 14

Amsterdam   Varady   LP: Decca SXDL 7532
December 1980   Concertgebouw   CD: Decca 425 0742/444 4302
                          Orchestra
                          Haitink

Suite on verses of Michelangelo

Berlin   Reimann   LP: Teldec 643.7142
October 1986   CD: Teldec 843.7142/4509 974602

Berlin   Berlin RO   CD: Decca 433 3192
January 1991   Ashkenazy

Suite on verses of Captain Lebyadkin

Berlin   Ashkenazy   LP: Decca 433 3192
January 1991

SJOEGREN

Der Mond schon wandelt am Himmelszelt

Munich   Klöcker, clarinet   LP: Orfeo S153 861A
August 1983   Wallendorf, horn   CD: Orfeo C153 861A
                          Höll

Jessonda

| Hamburg
July 1990 | Role of Tristan
Varady, Moser,
Moll
Choir and
Philharmonisches
Staatsorchester
Albrecht | CD: Orfeo C240 912H |

A recording of Spohr's opera "Faust", with Fischer-Dieskau in the cast, was planned by Orfeo to take place in July 1984 but the plan does not appear to have been realised

Abendfeier (Leise schleich' ich mich am Abend)

| Berlin
April 1984 | Sitkovetsky, violin
Höll | LP: Orfeo S103 841A
CD: Orfeo C103 841A |

Abendstille (Der Tag hat sich zur Ruh' gelegt)

| Berlin
April 1984 | Sitkovetsky, violin
Höll | LP: Orfeo S103 841A
CD: Orfeo C103 841A |

An Mignon (Ueber Tal und Fluss getragen)

| Berlin
July 1984 | Höll | LP: Orfeo S103 841A
CD: Orfeo C103 841A |

Erlkönig (Wer reitet so spät durch Nacht und Wind?)

| Berlin
April 1984 | Sitkovetsky, violin
Höll | LP: Orfeo S103 841A
CD: Orfeo C103 841A |

Jagdlied (Seht ihr's dort funkelnd! in rötlicher Pracht?)

| Berlin
April 1984 | Sitkovetsky, violin
Höll | LP: Orfeo S103 841A
CD: Orfeo C103 841A |

Lied beim Rundtanz (Auf! Es dunkelt!)

| Berlin
July 1984 | Höll | LP: Orfeo S103 841A
CD: Orfeo C103 841A |

Schlaflied (Ruhe, süss' Liebchen)

| Berlin | Höll | LP: Orfeo S103 841A |
| July 1984 | | CD: Orfeo C103 841A |

Schottisch Lied (Mir ist, als müsst' ich dir was sagen)

| Berlin | Höll | LP: Orfeo S103 841A |
| April 1984 | | CD: Orfeo C103 841A |

Der Spielmann und seine Geige (Vor Gottes Aug', dem Abendrot)

| Berlin | Sitkovetsky, violin | LP: Orfeo S103 841A |
| April 1984 | Höll | CD: Orfeo C103 841A |

Töne (Worte hab' ich nicht, um dir zu sagen)

| Berlin | Sitkovetsky, violin | LP: Orfeo S103 841A |
| April 1984 | Höll | CD: Orfeo C103 841A |

Vanitas (Ich hab' meine Sach' auf nichts gestellt)

| Berlin | Höll | LP: Orfeo S103 841A |
| July 1984 | | CD: Orfeo C103 841A |

Zigeunerlied (Im Nebelgeriesel, im tiefen Schnee)

| Berlin | Höll | LP: Orfeo S103 841A |
| April 1984 | | CD: Orfeo C103 841A |

SPONTINI

Olympie

Berlin	Role of Antigonus	LP: Orfeo S137 862H
February 1984	Varady, Toczyska,	CD: Orfeo C137 862H
	Tagliavini, Fortune	
	RIAS Choir	
	Berlin RO	
	Albrecht	

STEPHAN

Liebeszauber für Bariton und Orchester

Berlin	Berlin RO	LP: Schwann VMS 1623
April 1983	Zender	

STÖLZEL

Aus der Tiefe rufe ich, cantata

Lucerne	Lucerne Festival	LP: DG LPM 18 969/SLPM 138 969
August 1963	Strings	
	Baumgartner	

JOHANN STRAUSS

Die Fledermaus

Vienna	Role of Falke	LP: EMI SLS 964
November-	Rothenberger, Holm,	CD: EMI CMS 769 3542
December 1971	Fassbaender, Gedda,	Excerpts
	Dallapozza, Berry	LP: EMI 1C 047 30630/EX 29 04323
	Vienna Opera Chorus	CD: EMI CDM 769 5982
	VSO	
	Boskovsky	

Der Zigeunerbaron

Munich	Role of Homonay	CD: EMI CDS 749 2318
June 1986	Varady, Lindner,	
	Gramatzki, Schwarz,	
	Protschka, Berry	
	Bavarian Radio Chorus	
	Munich RO	
	Boskovsky	

RICHARD STRAUSS

Arabella

Munich July 1963	Role of Mandryka Della Casa, Rothenberger, Paskuda, Kohn Bavarian State Orchestra & Chorus Keilberth	LP: DG LPM 18 883-18 885/ SLPM 138 883-138 885 LP: DG 2709 013/2721 163 CD: DG 437 7002 Excerpts LP: DG 136 419/2705 001
Munich July 1980	Varady, Donath, Dallapozza, Berry Bavarian State Orchestra & Chorus Sawallisch	LP: EMI 1C 165 64456-64458 LP: Orfeo S169 882H CD: Orfeo C169 882H

Arabella: Excerpts (Mandryka! Der reiche Kerl!; Sie woll'n mich heiraten?)

Salzburg July 1958	Della Casa, Edelmann VPO Keilberth	CD: Orfeo C335 931A

Ariadne auf Naxos

Munich September 1969	Role of Music Master Hillebrecht, Grist, Troyanos, Thomas Bavarian State Orchestra Böhm	LP: LP 2709 013/2721 189
Leipzig January 1988	Norman, Gruberova, Varady, Frey Leipzig Gewandhaus Orchestra Masur	CD: Philips 422 0842

Capriccio

London September 1957	Role of Olivier Schwarzkopf, C.Ludwig, Gedda, Schmitt-Walter, Wächter Philharmonia Sawallisch	LP: Columbia 33CX 1600-1602 LP: World Records OC 230-232 LP: EMI 143 5243 CD: EMI CDS 749 0148 Excerpts LP: World Records OH 233
Munich April 1971	Role of Count Janowitz, Troyanos, Schreier, Prey, Ridderbusch Bavarian State Orchestra Böhm	LP: DG 2709 038/2721 188 LP: DG 419 0231 CD: DG 419 0232/445 3472/445 4912

Elektra

Dresden October 1960	Role of Orest Borkh, Schech, Madeira, Uhl, Böhme Dresden Staatskapelle Böhm	LP: DG LPM 18 690-18 691/ SLPM 138 690-138 691 LP: DG 2707 011/2721 187 CD: DG 431 7372/445 3292/445 4912
Vienna April and June 1981	Rysanek, Ligendza, Varnay, Beirer, Greindl VPO Böhm	VHS Video: Decca 071 4003 Laserdisc: Decca 071 4001

Die Frau ohne Schatten

Munich November 1963	Role of Barak Borkh, Bjoner, Mödl, Thomas Bavarian State Orchestra & Chorus Keilberth	LP: DG LPM 18 911-18 914/ SLPM 138 911-138 914 LP: DG 2721 161 Excerpts LP: DG 136 422
Munich September 1976	Nilsson, Bjoner, Varnay, King Bavarian State Orchestra & Chorus Sawallisch	CD: Legendary LRCD 1029 Also issued by Legendary on LP

Intermezzo

Munich January 1980	Role of Storch Popp, Dallapozza, Moll Bavarian RO Sawallisch	LP: EMI SLS 5204 LP: EMI 1C 165 30983-30985 CD: EMI CDS 749 3372 Excerpt LP: EMI EX 29 04323

Der Rosenkavalier

Dresden December 1958	Role of Faninal Schech, Streich, Seefried, Francl, Böhme Dresden Staatskapelle and Chorus Böhm	LP: DG LPM 18 570-18 573/ SLPM 138 040-138 043 LP: DG 2711 001/2721 162/419 1201 Excerpts LP: DG LPM 18 656/SLPM 138 656 LP: DG LPEM 19 410/SLPEM 136 410 LP: DG 2537 013 Complete opera published on CD by DG in Japan

Salome

Hamburg November 1970	Role of Jokanaan Jones, Dunn, Cassilly, Ochman Philharmonisches Staatsorchester Böhm	LP: DG 2707 052/2721 186 CD: DG 445 3192/445 4912
Munich July 1971	Rysanek, Varnay, Stolze, Ochman Bavarian State Orchestra Leitner	LP: Legendary LR 204 CD: Melodram CDM 27098

Deutsche Motette for 4 soloists and unaccompanied chorus

Berlin 1984	Studer, Pell, Schreckenbach RIAS Choir Gronostay	CD: Deutsche Schallplatten CD 10022 Also published on LP by Deutsche Schallplatten

Enoch Arden, Melodrama for reciter and piano

Berlin February and March 1964	Demus	LP: DG LPM 18 915/SLPM 138 915 LP: DG 104 273

Krämerspiegel, song cycle

Berlin February and March 1964	Demus	LP: DG LPM 18 916/SLPM 138 916
Berlin November 1969	Moore	LP: EMI SLS 792/1C 065 02089 LP: EMI 1C 163 50043-50051 CD: EMI CMS 763 9952 Excerpt LP: EMI EX 29 04293

Ach Lieb', ich muss nun scheiden

Berlin June 1968	Moore	LP: EMI SLS 792/1C 063 01939 LP: EMI 1C 163 50043-50051 CD: EMI CMS 763 9952
Munich and Berlin October 1981- September 1983	Sawallisch	LP: DG 413 4551/415 4701 CD: DG 415 4702

Ach weh mir unglückhaftem Mann

Berlin December 1955	Moore	LP: HMV ALP 1487 LP: Electrola E 90007
Berlin June 1968	Moore	LP: EMI SLS 792/1C 063 01939 LP: EMI 1C 163 50043-50051 CD: EMI CMS 763 9952
Munich and Berlin October 1981- September 1983	Sawallisch	LP: DG 413 4551/415 4701 CD: DG 415 4702

All' mein Gedanken

Berlin December 1955	Moore	LP: HMV ALP 1487 LP: Electrola E 90007
Berlin June 1968	Moore	LP: EMI SLS 792/1C 063 01939 LP: EMI 1C 163 50043-50051 CD: EMI CMS 763 9952
Munich and Berlin October 1981- September 1983	Sawallisch	LP: DG 413 4551/415 4701 CD: DG 415 4702

Strauss Lieder/continued

Allerseelen (Stell' auf den Tisch die duftenden Reseden)

Berlin	Moore	LP: EMI ASD 2399/SLS 792
September 1967		LP: EMI 1C 063 00380
		LP: EMI 1C 163 50043-50051
		CD: EMI CMS 763 9952

Die Allmächtige (Die höchste Macht der Erde)

Berlin	Moore	LP: EMI SLS 792
November 1969		LP: EMI 1C 163 50043-50051
		CD: EMI CMS 763 9952

Als mir dein Lied erklang

Berlin	Moore	LP: EMI SLS 792
November 1969		LP: EMI 1C 163 50043-50051
		CD: EMI CMS 763 9952

Am Ufer (Die Welt verstummt)

Berlin	Moore	LP: EMI SLS 792
July 1969		LP: EMI 1C 163 50043-50051
		CD: EMI CMS 763 9952

An die Nacht (Heilige Nacht!)

Berlin	Moore	LP: EMI SLS 792
July 1969		LP: EMI 1C 163 50043-50051
		CD: EMI CMS 763 9952

An Sie (Zeit, Verkündigerin der besten Freuden)

Berlin	Moore	LP: EMI SLS 792
July 1969		LP: EMI 1C 163 50043-50051
		CD: EMI CMS 763 9952

Anbetung (Die Liebste steht mir vor dem Gedanken)

Berlin	Moore	LP: EMI SLS 792/1C 065 01940
June 1968		LP: EMI 1C 163 50043-50051
		CD: EMI CMS 763 9952

Munich and	Sawallisch	LP: DG 413 4551
Berlin		
October 1981-		
September 1983		

Der Arbeitsmann (Wir haben ein Bett)

| Berlin | Demus | LP: DG LPM 18 916/SLPM 138 916 |

Berlin
February and
March 1964

Berlin   Moore   LP: EMI SLS 792
July 1969   LP: EMI 1C 163 50043-50051
                                CD: EMI CMS 763 9952

Auf ein Kind (Aus der Bedrängnis)

Berlin   Moore   LP: EMI SLS 792
July 1969   LP: EMI 1C 163 50043-50051
                                CD: EMI CMS 763 9952

Aus den Liedern der Trauer I & II: Dem Herzen ähnlich;   Von dunklem Schleier
umsponnen

Berlin   Moore   LP: EMI ASD 2399/SLS 792
September 1967   LP: EMI 1C 063 00380
                                LP: EMI 1C 163 50043-50051
                                CD: EMI CMS 763 9952

Das Bächlein (Du Bächlein silberhell und klar)

Berlin   Moore   LP: EMI SLS 792
May 1970   LP: EMI 1C 163 50043-50051
                                CD: EMI CMS 763 9952

Barkarole (Um der fallenden Ruder Spitzen)

Berlin   Moore   LP: EMI ASD 2399/SLS 792
September 1967   LP: EMI 1C 063 00380
                                LP: EMI 1C 163 50043-50051
                                CD: EMI CMS 763 9952

Befreit (Du wirst nicht weinen)

Berlin   Moore   LP: HMV ALP 1487
December 1955   LP: Electrola E 90007

Berlin   Moore   LP: EMI SLS 792
July 1969   LP: EMI 1C 163 50043-50051
                                CD: EMI CMS 763 9952

Blauer Sommer (Ein blauer Sommer glanz- und glutenschwer)

Berlin	Moore	LP: EMI SLS 792/1C 065 01940
June 1968		LP: EMI 1C 163 50043-50051
		CD: EMI CMS 763 9952

Blick vom oberen Belvedere (Fülle du!)

Berlin	Moore	LP: EMI SLS 792
May 1970		LP: EMI 1C 163 50043-50051
		CD: EMI CMS 763 9952

Blindenklage (Wenn ich dich frage)

Berlin	Demus	LP: DG LPM 18 916/SLPM 138 916
February and		
March 1964		

Berlin	Moore	LP: EMI SLS 792
July 1969		LP: EMI 1C 163 50043-50051
		CD: EMI CMS 763 9952

Breit' über mein Haupt dein schwarzes Haar

Berlin	Moore	LP: EMI SLS 792/1C 063 01939
June 1968		LP: EMI 1C 163 50043-50051
		CD: EMI CMS 763 9952

Munich and	Sawallisch	LP: DG 413 4551
Berlin		
October 1981-		
September 1983		

Bruder Liederlich (Die Feder am Strohhut)

Berlin	Moore	LP: EMI SLS 792
July 1969		LP: EMI 1C 163 50043-50051
		CD: EMI CMS 763 9952

Cäcilie (Wenn du es wüsstest)

Berlin	Moore	LP: EMI SLS 792/1C 063 01939
June 1968		LP: EMI 1C 163 50043-50051
		CD: EMI CMS 763 9952

Strauss Lieder/continued

Des Dichters Abendgang (Ergehst du dich im Abendlicht)

| Berlin | Moore | LP: EMI SLS 792/1C 163 50043-50051 |
| July 1969 | | CD: EMI CMS 763 9952 |

Drei Masken sah ich am Himmel steh'n/Krämerspiegel
See Krämerspiegel

Du meines Herzens Krönelein

Berlin	Moore	LP: EMI SLS 792/1C 063 01939
June 1968		LP: EMI 1C 163 50043-50051
		CD: EMI CMS 763 9952

Berlin and	Sawallisch	LP: DG 413 4551/415 4701
Munich		CD: DG 415 4702
October 1981-		
September 1983		

Durch allen Schall und Klang

| Berlin | Moore | LP: EMI SLS 792/1C 163 50043-50051 |
| May 1970 | | CD: EMI CMS 763 9952 |

Einerlei (Ihr Mund ist stets derselbe)

Berlin	Demus	LP: DG LPM 18 916/SLPM 138 916
February and		
March 1964		

| Berlin | Moore | LP: EMI SLS 792/1C 163 50043-50051 |
| November 1969 | | CD: EMI CMS 763 9952 |

Munich and	Sawallisch	LP: DG 413 4551
Berlin		
October 1981-		
September 1983		

Einkehr (Bei einem Wirte wundermild)

| Berlin | Moore | LP: EMI SLS 792/1C 163 50043-50051 |
| July 1969 | | CD: EMI CMS 763 9952 |

Einst kam der Bock als Bote/Krämerspiegel
See Krämerspiegel

Strauss Lieder/continued

Epheu (Aber Epheu nenn' ich jene Mädchen)

| Berlin
June 1968 | Moore | LP: EMI SLS 792/1C 063 01939
LP: EMI 1C 163 50043-50051
CD: EMI CMS 763 9952 |

Es liebte einst ein Hase/Krämerspiegel
See Krämerspiegel

Es war einmal ein Bock/Krämerspiegel
See Krämerspiegel

Es war einmal eine Wanze/Krämerspiegel
See Krämerspiegel

Die Frauen sind oft fromm und still

| Berlin
June 1968 | Moore | LP: EMI SLS 792/1C 063 01939
LP: EMI 1C 163 50043-50051
CD: EMI CMS 763 9952 |
| Munich and
Berlin
October 1981-
September 1983 | Sawallisch | LP: DG 413 4551/415 4701
CD: DG 415 4702 |

Freundliche Vision (Nicht im Schlafe hab' ich das geträumt)

| Berlin
December 1955 | Moore | LP: HMV ALP 1487
LP: Electrola E 90007 |
| Berlin
July 1969 | Moore | LP: EMI SLS 792/EX 29 04293
LP: EMI 1C 163 50043-50051
CD: EMI CMS 763 9952 |

Frühlingsfeier (Das ist des Frühlings traurige Lust)

| Berlin
July 1969 | Moore | LP: EMI SLS 792/1C 163 50043-50051
CD: EMI CMS 763 9952 |

Frühlingsgedränge (Frühlingskinder im bunten Gedränge)

| Berlin
June 1968 | Moore | LP: EMI SLS 792/1C 063 01939
LP: EMI 1C 163 50043-50051
CD: EMI CMS 763 9952 |
| Munich and
Berlin
October 1981-
September 1983 | Sawallisch | LP: DG 413 4551 |

Strauss Lieder/continued

Geduld (Geduld, sagst du, und zeigst mit weissem Finger)

Berlin	Moore	LP: EMI ASD 2399/SLS 792
September 1967		LP: EMI 1C 063 00380
		LP: EMI 1C 163 50043-50051
		CD: EMI CMS 763 9952

Munich and	Sawallisch	LP: DG 413 4551
Berlin		
October 1981-		
September 1983		

Gefunden (Ich ging im Walde so für mich hin)

Berlin	Demus	LP: DG LPM 18 916/SLPM 138 916
February and		
March 1964		

| Berlin | Moore | LP: EMI SLS 792/1C 163 50043-50051 |
| July 1969 | | CD: EMI CMS 763 9952 |

Munich	Sawallisch	LP: DG 413 4551/415 4701
and Berlin		CD: DG 415 4702
October 1981-		
September 1983		

Das Geheimnis (Du fragst mich, Mädchen)

Berlin	Moore	LP: EMI ASD 2399/SLS 792
September 1967		LP: EMI 1C 063 00380
		LP: EMI 1C 163 50043-50051
		CD: EMI CMS 763 9952

Die Georgine (Warum so spät erst, Georgine?)

Berlin	Moore	LP: EMI ASD 2399/SLS 792
September 1967		LP: EMI 1C 063 00380
		LP: EMI 1C 163 50043-50051
		CD: EMI CMS 763 9952

Munich and	Sawallisch	LP: DG 413 4551
Berlin		
October 1981-		
September 1983		

Gestern war ich Atlas

| Berlin | Moore | LP: EMI SLS 792/1C 163 50043-50051 |
| July 1969 | | CD: EMI CMS 763 9952 |

Glückes genug (Wenn sanft du mir im Arme schliefst)

Berlin June 1968	Moore	LP: EMI SLS 792/1C 065 01940 LP: EMI 1C 163 50043-50051 CD: EMI CMS 763 9952
Munich and Berlin October 1981- September 1983	Sawallisch	LP: DG 413 4551

Hab' ich euch denn je geraten?

Berlin June 1959	Engel	LP: DG LPM 18 590/SLPM 138 058
Berlin November 1969	Moore	LP: EMI SLS 792/1C 163 50043-50051 CD: EMI CMS 763 9952

Die Händler und die Macher/Krämerspiegel
See Krämerspiegel

Hast du ein Tongedicht vollbracht?/Krämerspiegel
See Krämerspiegel

Die heiligen 3 Könige aus Morgenland

Berlin July 1969	Moore	LP: EMI SLS 792/1C 163 50043-50051 CD: EMI CMS 763 9952

Heimkehr (Leiser schwanken die Aeste)

Berlin February and March 1964	Demus	LP: DG LPM 18 916/SLPM 138 916
Berlin September 1967	Moore	LP: EMI ASD 2399/SLS 792 LP: EMI 1C 063 00380 LP: EMI 1C 163 50043-50051 CD: EMI CMS 763 9952
Munich and Berlin October 1981- September 1983	Sawallisch	LP: DG 413 4551/415 4701 CD: DG 415 4702

Heimliche Aufforderung (Auf, hebe die funkelnde Schale!)

Berlin December 1955	Moore	78: HMV DA 5536 (Germany only) LP: HMV ALP 1487 LP: Electrola E 90007
Berlin June 1968	Moore	LP: EMI SLS 792/1C 063 01939 LP: EMI 1C 163 50043-50051 CD: EMI CMS 763 9952
Munich and Berlin October 1981- September 1983	Sawallisch	LP: DG 413 4551/415 4701 CD: DG 415 4702

Herr Lenz springt heute durch die Stadt

Berlin December 1955	Moore	LP: HMV ALP 1487 LP: Electrola E 90007
Berlin June 1968	Moore	LP: EMI SLS 792/1C 065 01940 LP: EMI 1C 163 50043-50051 CD: EMI CMS 763 9952
Munich and Berlin October 1981- September 1983	Sawallisch	LP: DG 413 4551/415 4701 CD: DG 415 4702

Himmelsboten (Der Mondschein, der ist schon verblichen)

Berlin June 1968	Moore	LP: EMI SLS 792/1C 065 01940 LP: EMI 1C 163 50043-50051 CD: EMI CMS 763 9952
Munich and Berlin October 1981- September 1983	Sawallisch	LP: DG 413 4551/415 4701 CD: DG 415 4702

Hochzeitlich Lied (Lass' Akaziendüfte schaukeln)

Berlin June 1968	Moore	LP: EMI SLS 792/1C 065 01940 LP: EMI 1C 163 50043-50051 CD: EMI CMS 763 9952
Munich and Berlin October 1981- September 1983	Sawallisch	LP: DG 413 4551

Hoffen und wieder verzagen

Berlin June 1968	Moore	LP: EMI SLS 792/1C 063 01939 LP: EMI 1C 163 50043-50051 CD: EMI CMS 763 9952
Munich and Berlin October 1981- September 1983	Sawallisch	LP: DG 413 4551

Die Huldigung (Die Perlen meiner Seele)

Berlin November 1969	Moore	LP: EMI SLS 792/1C 163 50043-50051 CD: EMI CMS 763 9952

Ich liebe dich (Vier ad'lige Rosse)

Berlin December 1955	Moore	LP: HMV ALP 1487 LP: Electrola E 90007
Berlin June 1968	Moore	LP: EMI SLS 792/1C 065 01940 LP: EMI 1C 163 50043-50051 CD: EMI CMS 763 9952
Munich and Berlin October 1981- September 1983	Sawallisch	LP: DG 413 4551/415 4701 CD: DG 415 4702

Ich schwebe wie auf Engelsschwingen

Berlin July 1969	Moore	LP: EMI SLS 792/1C 163 50043-50051 CD: EMI CMS 763 9952

Ich sehe wie in einem Spiegel

Berlin July 1969	Moore	LP: EMI SLS 792/1C 163 50043-50051 CD: EMI CMS 763 9952

Ich trage meine Minne

Berlin June 1968	Moore	LP: EMI SLS 792/1C 065 01940 LP: EMI 1C 163 50043-50051 CD: EMI CMS 763 9952
Munich and Berlin October 1981- September 1983	Sawallisch	LP: DG 413 4551/415 4701 CD: DG 415 4702

Ihre Augen (Deine gewölbten Brauen)

Berlin November 1969	Moore	LP: EMI SLS 792/1C 163 50043-50051 CD: EMI CMS 763 9952

Im Sonnenschein (Noch eine Stunde lasst mich)

Berlin November 1969	Moore	LP: EMI SLS 792/1C 163 50043-50051 CD: EMI CMS 763 9952
Munich and Berlin October 1981- September 1983	Sawallisch	LP: DG 413 4551

Im Spätboot (Aus der Schiffsbank mach' ich meinen Pfühl)

Berlin July 1969	Moore	LP: EMI SLS 792/1C 163 50043-50051 CD: EMI CMS 763 9952
Munich and Berlin October 1981- September 1983	Sawallisch	LP: DG 413 4551

In der Campagna (Ich grüsse die Sonne)

Berlin July 1969	Moore	LP: EMI SLS 792/1C 163 50043-50051 CD: EMI CMS 763 9952

In goldener Fülle (Wir schreiten in goldener Fülle)

Berlin July 1969	Moore	LP: EMI SLS 792/1C 163 50043-50051 CD: EMI CMS 763 9952

Strauss Lieder/continued

Junggesellenschwur (Weine nur nicht)

| Berlin
July 1969 | Moore | LP: EMI SLS 792/1C 163 50043-50051
CD: EMI CMS 763 9952 |

| Munich
and Berlin
October 1981-
September 1983 | Sawallisch | LP: DG 413 4551 |

Junghexenlied (Als nachts ich überm Gebirge ritt)

| Berlin
July 1969 | Moore | LP: EMI SLS 792/1C 163 50043-50051
CD: EMI CMS 763 9952 |

Kling! (Meine Seele gibt reinen Ton)

| Berlin
July 1969 | Moore | LP: EMI SLS 792/1C 163 50043-50051
CD: EMI CMS 763 9952 |

Kornblumen nenn' ich die Gestalten

| Berlin
June 1968 | Moore | LP: EMI SLS 792/1C 063 01939
LP: EMI 1C 163 50043-50051
CD: EMI CMS 763 9952 |

Die Künstler sind die Schöpfer/Krämerspiegel
See Krämerspiegel

Leise Lieder sing' ich dir

| Berlin
July 1969 | Moore | LP: EMI SLS 792/1C 163 50043-50051
CD: EMI CMS 763 9952 |

Leises Lied (In einem stillen Garten)

| Berlin
July 1969 | Moore | LP: EMI SLS 792/1C 163 50043-50051
CD: EMI CMS 763 9952 |

Liebesgeschenke (Ich pflücke eine kleine Pfirsischblüte)

| Berlin
November 1969 | Moore | LP: EMI SLS 792/1C 163 50043-50051
CD: EMI CMS 763 9952 |

Strauss Lieder/continued

Liebeshymnus (Heil jenem Tag!)

Berlin	Moore	LP: EMI SLS 792/1C 065 01940
June 1968		LP: EMI 1C 163 50043-50051
		CD: EMI CMS 763 9952

Munich	Sawallisch	LP: DG 413 4551/415 4701
and Berlin		CD: DG 415 4702
October 1981-		
September 1983		

Liebesliedchen (Hör' mein Liebesliedchen zieh'n)

Berlin	Moore	LP: EMI SLS 792/1C 163 50043-50051
May 1970		CD: EMI CMS 763 9952

Lied an meinen Sohn (Der Sturm behorcht mein Vaterhaus)

Berlin	Moore	LP: EMI SLS 792/1C 163 50043-50051
July 1969		CD: EMI CMS 763 9952

Das Lied des Steinklopfers (Ich bin kein Minister)

Berlin	Moore	LP: EMI SLS 792/1C 163 50043-50051
July 1969		CD: EMI CMS 763 9952

Lob des Leidens (O schmäht des Lebens Leiden nicht!)

Berlin	Moore	LP: EMI ASD 2399/SLS 792
September 1967		LP: EMI 1C 063 00380
		LP: EMI 1C 163 50043-50051
		CD: EMI CMS 763 9952

Madrigal (Ins Joch beug' ich den Nacken)

Berlin	Moore	LP: EMI ASD 2399/SLS 792
September 1967		LP: EMI 1C 063 00380
		LP: EMI 1C 163 50043-50051
		CD: EMI CMS 763 9952

Mein Herz ist stumm, mein Herz ist kalt

Berlin	Moore	LP: EMI SLS 792/1C 063 01939
June 1968		LP: EMI 1C 163 50043-50051
		CD: EMI CMS 763 9952

Munich	Sawallisch	LP: DG 413 4551
and Berlin		
October 1981-		
September 1983		

Strauss Lieder/continued

Meinem Kinde (Du schläfst, und sachte neig' ich mich)

Berlin	Moore	LP: EMI SLS 792/1C 065 01940
June 1968		LP: EMI 1C 163 50043-50051
		CD: EMI CMS 763 9952

Mit deinen blauen Augen

| Berlin | Moore | LP: EMI SLS 792/1C 163 50043-50051 |
| July 1969 | | CD: EMI CMS 763 9952 |

Mohnblumen sind die runden

Berlin	Moore	LP: EMI SLS 792/1C 063 01939
June 1968		LP: EMI 1C 163 50043-50051
		CD: EMI CMS 763 9952

Morgen (Und morgen wird die Sonne wieder scheinen)

| Berlin | Moore | LP: HMV ALP 1487 |
| December 1955 | | LP: Electrola E 90007 |

Berlin	Moore	LP: EMI SLS 792/1C 063 01939
June 1968		LP: EMI 1C 163 50043-50051
		CD: EMI CMS 763 9952

Munich	Sawallisch	LP: DG 413 4551/415 4701
and Berlin		CD: DG 415 4702
October 1981-		
September 1983		

Morgenrot (Dort, wo der Morgenstern hergeht)

| Berlin | Moore | LP: EMI SLS 792/1C 163 50043-50051 |
| July 1969 | | CD: EMI CMS 763 9952 |

Die Nacht (Aus dem Walde tritt die Nacht)

| Berlin | Moore | LP: HMV ALP 1487 |
| December 1955 | | LP: Electrola E 90007 |

Berlin	Moore	LP: EMI ASD 2399/SLS 792
September 1967		LP: EMI 1C 063 00380
		LP: EMI 1C 163 50043-50051
		CD: EMI CMS 763 9952

Munich	Sawallisch	LP: DG 413 4551/415 4701
and Berlin		CD: DG 415 4702
October 1981-		
September 1983		

Strauss Lieder/continued

Nachtgang (Wir gingen durch die stille milde Nacht)

Berlin December 1955	Moore	LP: HMV ALP 1487 LP: Electrola E 90007
Berlin June 1968	Moore	LP: EMI SLS 792/1C 065 01940 LP: EMI 1C 163 50043-50051 CD: EMI CMS 763 9952
Munich and Berlin October 1981- September 1983	Sawallisch	LP: DG 413 4551

Nichts (Nennen soll ich, sagt ihr)

Berlin September 1967	Moore	LP: EMI ASD 2399/SLS 792 LP: EMI 1C 063 00380 LP: EMI 1C 163 50043-50051 CD: EMI CMS 763 9952
Munich and Berlin October 1981- September 1983	Sawallisch	LP: DG 413 4551/415 4701 CD: DG 415 4702

Nur Mut (Lass' das Zagen, trage mutig deine Sorgen)

Berlin September 1967	Moore	LP: EMI ASD 2399/SLS 792 LP: EMI 1C 063 00380 LP: EMI 1C 163 50043-50051 CD: EMI CMS 763 9952

O lieber Künstler, sei ermahnt!/Krämerspiegel
See Krämerspiegel

O Schröpferschwamm, o Händlerkreis!/Krämerspiegel
See Krämerspiegel

O süsser Mai

Berlin June 1968	Moore	LP: EMI SLS 792/1C 065 01940 LP: EMI 1C 163 50043-50051 CD: EMI CMS 763 9952
Munich and Berlin October 1981- September 1983	Sawallisch	LP: DG 413 4551/415 4701 CD: DG 415 4702

Strauss Lieder/continued

O wärst du mein!

Berlin December 1955	Moore	LP: HMV ALP 1487 LP: Electrola E 90007
Berlin June 1968	Moore	LP: EMI SLS 792/1C 063 01939 LP: EMI 1C 163 50043-50051 CD: EMI CMS 763 9952
Munich and Berlin October 1981- September 1983	Sawallisch	LP: DG 413 4551

Ein Obdach gegen Sturm und Regen

Berlin July 1969	Moore	LP: EMI SLS 792/1C 163 50043-50051 CD: EMI CMS 763 9952

Der Pokal (Freunde, weihet den Pokal!)

Berlin November 1969	Moore	LP: EMI SLS 792/1C 163 50043-50051 CD: EMI CMS 763 9952

Das Rosenband (Im Frühlingsschatten fand ich sie)

Berlin February and March 1964	Demus	LP: DG LPM 18 916/SLPM 138 916
Berlin June 1968	Moore	LP: EMI SLS 792/1C 065 01940 LP: EMI 1C 163 50043-50051 CD: EMI CMS 763 9952
Munich and Berlin October 1981- September 1983	Sawallisch	LP: DG 413 4551

Rote Rosen (Weisst du die Rose, die du mir gegeben?)

Berlin May 1970	Moore	LP: EMI SLS 792/1C 163 50043-50051 CD: EMI CMS 763 9952

Strauss Lieder/continued

Rückleben (An ihrem Grabe kniet' ich fest gebunden)

Berlin	Moore	LP: EMI SLS 792/1C 163 50043-50051
July 1969		CD: EMI CMS 763 9952

Ruhe meine Seele (Nicht ein Lüftchen regt sich leise)

Berlin	Moore	LP: HMV ALP 1487
December 1955		LP: Electrola E 90007

Berlin	Moore	LP: EMI SLS 792/1C 063 01939
June 1968		LP: EMI 1C 163 50043-50051
		CD: EMI CMS 763 9952

Munich	Sawallisch	LP: DG 413 4551/415 4701
and Berlin		CD: DG 415 4702
October 1981-		
September 1983		

Schlechtes Wetter (Das ist ein schlechtes Wetter)

Berlin	Moore	LP: EMI SLS 792/1C 163 50043-50051
November 1969		CD: EMI CMS 763 9952

Munich	Sawallisch	LP: DG 413 4551/415 4701
and Berlin		CD: DG 415 4702
October 1981-		
September 1983		

Schön sind, doch kalt die Himmelssterne

Berlin	Moore	LP: EMI SLS 792/1C 063 01939
June 1968		LP: EMI 1C 163 50043-50051
		CD: EMI CMS 763 9952

Munich	Sawallisch	LP: DG 413 4551
and Berlin		
October 1981-		
September 1983		

Schwung (Gebt mir meinen Becher!)

Berlin	Moore	LP: EMI SLS 792/1C 163 50043-50051
November 1969		CD: EMI CMS 763 9952

Strauss Lieder/continued

Sehnsucht (Ich ging den Weg entlang)

Berlin	Moore	LP: EMI SLS 792/1C 065 01940
June 1968		LP: EMI 1C 163 50043-50051
		CD: EMI CMS 763 9952

Munich	Sawallisch	LP: DG 413 4551/415 4701
and Berlin		CD: DG 415 4702
October 1981-		
September 1983		

Seitdem dein Aug' in meines schaute

Berlin	Moore	LP: EMI ASD 2399/SLS 792
September 1967		LP: EMI 1C 063 00380
		LP: EMI 1C 163 50043-50051
		CD: EMI CMS 763 9952

Sie wissen's nicht (Es wohnt ein kleines Vögelein)

Berlin	Moore	LP: EMI SLS 792/1C 163 50043-50051
July 1969		CD: EMI CMS 763 9952

Die sieben Siegel (Weil ich dich nicht legen kann)

Berlin	Moore	LP: EMI SLS 792/1C 163 50043-50051
July 1969		CD: EMI CMS 763 9952

Sinnspruch (Alle Menschen gross und klein)

Berlin	Moore	LP: EMI SLS 792/1C 163 50043-50051
May 1970		CD: EMI CMS 763 9952

Ständchen (Mach' auf, mach' auf, doch leise, mein Kind!)

Berlin	Moore	78: HMV DA 5537 (Germany only)
December 1955		LP: HMV ALP 1487
		LP: Electrola E 90007

Berlin	Moore	LP: EMI ASD 2399/ASD 2549/SLS 792
September 1967		LP: EMI 1C 063 00380/1C 047 01247
		LP: EMI 1C 163 50043-50051
		CD: EMI CMS 763 9952

Munich	Sawallisch	LP: DG 413 4551/415 4701
and Berlin		CD: DG 415 4702
October 1981-		
September 1983		

Strauss Lieder/continued

Der Stern (Ich sehe ihn wieder)

Berlin November 1969	Moore	LP: EMI SLS 792/1C 163 50043-50051 CD: EMI CMS 763 9952

Stiller Gang (Der Abend graut)

Berlin February and March 1964	Demus	LP: DG LPM 18 916/SLPM 138 916
Berlin June 1968	Moore	LP: EMI SLS 792/1C 065 01940 LP: EMI 1C 163 50043-50051 CD: EMI CMS 763 9952
Munich and Berlin October 1981- September 1983	Sawallisch	LP: DG 413 4551

Traum durch die Dämmerung (Weite Wiesen im Dämmergrau)

Berlin December 1955	Moore	78: HMV DA 5535 (Germany only) LP: HMV ALP 1487 LP: Electrola E 90007
Berlin June 1968	Moore	LP: EMI SLS 792 LP: EMI 1C 065 01940/1C 047 01247 LP: EMI 1C 163 50043-50051 CD: EMI CMS 763 9952
Munich and Berlin October 1981- September 1983	Sawallisch	LP: DG 413 4551/415 4701 CD: DG 415 4702

Und dann nicht mehr (Ich sah sie nur ein einzigmal)

Berlin November 1969	Moore	LP: EMI SLS 792/1C 163 50043-50051 CD: EMI CMS 763 9952
Munich and Berlin October 1981- September 1983	Sawallisch	LP: DG 413 4551

Die Ulme zu Hirsau (Zu Hirsau in den Trümmern)

Berlin July 1969	Moore	LP: EMI SLS 792/1C 163 50043-50051 CD: EMI CMS 763 9952

Strauss Lieder/continued

Unser Feind/Krämerspiegel
See Krämerspiegel

Die Verschwiegenen (Ich habe wohl, es sei hier laut)

Berlin	Moore	LP: EMI ASD 2399/SLS 792
September 1967		LP: EMI 1C 063 00380
		LP: EMI 1C 163 50043-50051
		CD: EMI CMS 763 9952

Munich	Sawallisch	LP: DG 413 4551
and Berlin		
October 1981-		
September 1983		

Vom künftigen Alter (Der Frost hat mir bereifet)

Berlin	Moore	LP: EMI SLS 792/1C 163 50043-50051
November 1969		CD: EMI CMS 763 9952

Munich	Sawallisch	LP: DG 413 4551
and Berlin		
October 1981-		
September 1983		

Von den sieben Zechbrüdern (Ich kenne sieben lust'ge Brüder)

Berlin	Moore	LP: EMI SLS 792/1C 163 50043-50051
July 1969		CD: EMI CMS 763 9952

Von Händlern wird die Kunst bedroht/Krämerspiegel
See Krämerspiegel

Waldesfahrt (Mein Wagen rollet langsam)

Berlin	Moore	LP: EMI SLS 792/1C 163 50043-50051
November 1969		CD: EMI CMS 763 9952

Munich	Sawallisch	LP: DG 413 4551/415 4701
and Berlin		CD: DG 415 4702
October 1981-		
September 1983		

Waldseligkeit (Der Wald beginnt zu rauschen)

Berlin	Moore	LP: EMI SLS 792/1C 163 50043-50051
July 1969		CD: EMI CMS 763 9952

Strauss Lieder/continued

Wanderers Gemütsruhe (Uebers Niederträchtige niemand sich beklage)

Berlin June 1959	Engel	LP: DG LPM 18 590/SLPM 138 058
Berlin November 1969	Moore	LP: EMI SLS 792/1C 163 50043-50051 CD: EMI CMS 763 9952
Munich and Berlin October 1981- September 1983	Sawallisch	LP: DG 413 4551

Wasserrose (Kennst du die Blume, die märchenhafte?)

Berlin June 1968	Moore	LP: EMI SLS 792/1C 963 01939 LP: EMI 1C 163 50043-50051 CD: EMI CMS 763 9952

Weisser Jasmin (Bleiche Blüte, Blüte der Liebe)

Berlin June 1968	Moore	LP: EMI SLS 792/1C 065 01940 LP: EMI 1C 163 50043-50051 CD: EMI CMS 763 9952

Wenn (Und wärst du mein Weib)

Berlin June 1968	Moore	LP: EMI SLS 792/1C 065 01940 LP: EMI 1C 163 50043-50051 CD: EMI CMS 763 9952

Wer hat's getan? (Es steht mein Lied in Nacht und Frost)

Berlin May 1971	Reimann	LP: EMI 1C 065 02675/ 1C 161 02673-02677

Wer wird von der Welt verlangen?

Berlin June 1959	Engel	LP: DG LPM 18 590/SLPM 138 058
Berlin November 1969	Moore	LP: EMI SLS 792/1C 163 50043-50051 CD: EMI CMS 763 9952

Strauss Lieder/continued

Wie sollten wir geheim sie halten?

Berlin June 1968	Moore	LP: EMI SLS 792/1C 063 01939 LP: EMI 1C 163 50043-50051 CD: EMI CMS 763 9952
Munich and Berlin October 1981- September 1983	Sawallisch	LP: DG 413 4551

Winterliebe (Der Sonne entgegen in Liebesgluten)

Berlin July 1969	Moore	LP: EMI SLS 792/1C 163 50043-50051 CD: EMI CMS 763 9952

Winternacht (Mit Regen und Sturmgebrause)

Berlin September 1967	Moore	LP: EMI ASD 2399/SLS 792 LP: EMI 1C 063 00380 LP: EMI 1C 163 50043-50051 CD: EMI CMS 763 9952
Munich and Berlin October 1981- September 1983	Sawallisch	LP: DG 413 4551/415 4701 CD: DG 415 4702

Winterweihe (In diesen Wintertagen)

Berlin February and March 1964	Demus	LP: DG LPM 18 916/SLPM 138 916
Berlin July 1969	Moore	LP: EMI SLS 792/1C 163 50043-50051 CD: EMI CMS 763 9952

Wir beide wollen springen (Es ging ein Wind)

Berlin May 1970	Moore	LP: EMI SLS 792/1C 163 50043-50051 CD: EMI CMS 763 9952

Strauss Lieder/concluded

Wozu noch, Mädchen, soll es frommen?

Berlin December 1955	Moore	LP: HMV ALP 1487 LP: Electrola E 90007
Berlin June 1968	Moore	LP: EMI SLS 792 LP: EMI 1C 063 01939/1C 047 01247 LP: EMI 1C 163 50043-50051 CD: EMI CMS 763 9952
Munich and Berlin October 1981- September 1983	Sawallisch	LP: DG 413 4551

Xenion (Nichts vom Vergänglichen)

Berlin May 1970	Moore	LP: EMI SLS 792/1C 163 50043-500 51 CD: EMI CMS 763 9952

Die Zeitlose (Auf frischgemähtem Weideplatz)

Berlin September 1967	Moore	LP: EMI ASD 2399/SLS 792 LP: EMI 1C 063 00380 LP: EMI 1C 163 50043-50051 CD: EMI CMS 763 9952
Munich and Berlin October 1981- September 1983	Sawallisch	LP: DG 413 4551

Zueignung (Ja, du weisst es, teure Seele)

Berlin December 1955	Moore	LP: HMV ALP 1487 LP: Electrola E 90007
Berlin September 1967	Moore	LP: EMI ASD 2399/ASD 2549/SLS 792 LP: EMI 1C 063 00380 LP: EMI 1C 163 50043-50051 CD: EMI CMS 763 9952

Zugemess'ne Rhythmen reizen freilich

Berlin May 1970	Moore	LP: EMI SLS 792/1C 163 50043-500 51 CD: EMI CMS 763 9952

At the time of going to press DG announces the issue on CD of
Fischer-Dieskau's Strauss Lieder recordings with Sawallisch:
catalogue number 447 5122

STRAVINSKY

Abraham and Isaac

New York April 1967	Instrumental ensemble Craft	CBS unpublished
Stuttgart January 1982	SDR Orchestra members Bertini	LP: Orfeo S324 941A CD: Orfeo C324 941A

Babel, cantata for speaker, male chorus and orchestra

Stuttgart January 1982	SDR Orchestra and Chorus Bertini	LP: Orfeo S324 941A CD: Orfeo C324 941A

Elegy for John F. Kennedy

Stuttgart January '1982	SDR Orchestra and Chorus Bertini	LP: Orfeo S324 941A CD: Orfeo C324 941A

2 songs by Verlaine: Sagesse; La bonne chanson

Stuttgart January 1982	SDR Orchestra Bertini	LP: Orfeo S324 941A CD: Orfeo C324 941A

STREICHER

Ist dir ein getreues liebevolles Kind beschert

Berlin	Reimann	LP: EMI 1C 065 02674/
March 1971		1C 161 02673-02677

TCHAIKOVSKY

Eugene Onegin

Vienna	Role of Onegin	LP: Melodram MEL 046
January 1961	Jurinac, Cvejic,	
	Rössel-Majdan,	
	Dermota, Kreppel	
	Vienna Opera Chorus	
	VPO	
	Matacic	
	Sung in German	

Eugene Onegin, Querschnitt

Munich	Lear, Fassbaender,	LP: DG LPEM 19 430/SLPEM 136 430
June 1966	Wunderlich, Talvela	LP: DG 2535 232
	Bavarian State	CD: DG 447 8182
	Orchestra & Chorus	
	Gerdes	
	Sung in German	

Songs: My genius, my angel, my friend; I never talked to thee; A tear
quivers; Accept just once; As on hot ashes; Don't leave me; My naughty
girl; No sound, no word, no greeting; Don Juan's Serenade; Amid the noise
of the ball; Oh, if you could only; The love of one dead; Heroism;
I bless you, forests; On the golden fields; New Greek song; As they kept
on saying "Fool!"

Berlin	Reimann	LP: Philips 6514 116
January 1981		

Scottish Ballad

Berlin	De los Angeles	LP: HMV ALP 1891/ASD 459
December 1960	Moore	CD: EMI CMS 565 0612
	Sung in German	

TELEMANN

Erquicktes Herz sei voller Freuden, cantata

Berlin	Toyoda, viola	LP: EMI 1C 063 02258/1C 053 52288
August 1969	Donderer, cello	CD: EMI CZS 568 5092
	Nowak, double-bass	
	Picht-Axenfeld,	
	harpsichord	

Die Hoffnung ist mein Leben, cantata

Berlin	Heller, violin	LP: HMV ALP 2066/ASD 615
March 1957	Poppen, cello	LP: Electrola E 70488/STE 70488
	Picht-Axenfeld,	CD: EMI CZS 568 5092
	harpsichord	

Ihr Völker hört, cantata

London	Rampal, flute	LP: EMI ASD 2903/1C 063 02328
October 1971	Veyron-Lacroix,	CD: EMI CZS 568 5092
	harpsichord	

Trauermusik eines kunsterfahrenen Kanarienvogels, cantata

Berlin	Heller, violin	LP: HMV ALP 1985/ASD 534
March 1962	Kirchner, viola	LP: Electrola E 70488/STE 70488
	Poppen, cello	LP: EMI 1C 063 28160
	Koch, oboe	CD: EMI CZS 568 5092
	Picht-Axenfeld,	Excerpt
	harpsichord	LP: EMI EX 29 04353

Songs: Die Einsamkeit; Glück; Das Frauenzimmer; Seltenes Glück; Die vergessene Phillis; Falschheit; Lob des Weins

Berlin	Poppen, cello	45: Electrola E 50594/STE 50594
March 1962	Picht-Axenfeld,	LP: Electrola E 70488/STE 70488
	harpsichord	

TIESSEN

Vöglein Schwermut

| Berlin | Reimann | LP: EMI 1C 065 02675/ |
| May 1971 | | 1C 161 02673-02677 |

Un Ballo in maschera

Cologne February 1951	Role of Renato Wegner, Mödl, Fehenberger WDR Orchestra and Chorus Busch Sung in German	LP: Brüder-Busch-Gesellschaft 12PAL 4779-4784 CD: Gala GL 100.509 Also published on CD on the Eklipse label, where it is incorrectly described as a 1943 performance with different cast

Un Ballo in maschera, Querschnitt

Berlin November 1963	Borkh, Wagner, Lear, Thomas Deutsche Oper Orchestra & Chorus Patanè Sung in German	LP: DG LPEM 19 420/SLPEM 136 420 LP: DG 2535 396/2535 655 CD: DG 447 8152 Excerpt LP: DG LPEM 19 460/SLPEM 136 460

Un Ballo in maschera: Excerpt (Alla vita che t'arrida)

Berlin June 1959	BPO Erede	45: HMV 7ER 5225 LP: HMV ALP 1825/ASD 407 LP: EMI EX 29 04323

Un Ballo in maschera: Excerpt (Eri tu)

Berlin June 1959	BPO Erede	LP: HMV ALP 1825/ASD 407 LP: EMI EX 29 04323

Don Carlo

Berlin November 1948	Role of Posa Demuth, Blatter, Greverus, Greindl, J.Hermann Städtische Oper Orchestra & Chorus Fricsay Sung in German	Unpublished radio broadcast
London June and July 1965	Tebaldi, Bumbry, Bergonzi, Ghiaurov, Talvela Covent Garden Orchestra & Chorus Solti	LP: Decca MET 305-308/SET 305-308 CD: Decca 421 1142 Excerpts LP: Decca GRV 7 CD: Decca 440 4832

Don Carlo, Querschnitt

Berlin	Moser, Fassbaender,	LP: EMI 1C 063 28960
September 1973	Gedda, Moll	
	Berlin RO	
	Patanè	
	Sung in German	

Don Carlo: Excerpt (Per me giunto è il di supremo)

Berlin	BPO	LP: HMV ALP 1825/ASD 407
June 1959	Erede	LP: EMI EX 29 04323

Don Carlo: Excerpt (E lui! L'infante!)

Munich	Bergonzi	LP: Orfeo S028 821A
July 1982	Bavarian RO	CD: Orfeo C028 821A
	Lopez-Cobos	

Falstaff

Vienna	Role of Falstaff	LP: CBS BRG 72493-72495/
March 1966	Ligabue, Sciutti,	SBRG 72493-72495
	Rössel-Majdan,	LP: CBS 77392
	Resnik, Oncina,	CD: Sony M2K 42535
	Panerai	
	Vienna Opera Chorus	
	VPO	
	Bernstein	

Falstaff: Excerpts (Ehi! Paggio!; Mondo ladro!)

Berlin	BPO	LP: HMV ALP 1825/ASD 407
June 1959	Erede	LP: EMI EX 29 04323

Falstaff: Excerpt (Va, vecchio John!)

Berlin	Role of Ford	LP: DG LPEM 19 029
January 1951	Metternich	CD: Preiser 90125
	Berlin RO	
	Fricsay	
	Sung in German	

La Forza del destino, Querschnitt

Berlin	Role of Carlos	LP: DG LPEM 19 416/SLPEM 136 416
October 1962	Woytowicz, Ahlin,	LP: DG 2535 428
	Thomas, Stern	CD: DG 447 8132
	RIAS Choir	Excerpt
	Berlin RO	LP: DG LPEM 19 460/SLPEM 136 460
	Löwlein	LP: DG LPEM 19 456/2535 655
	Sung in German	

La Forza del destino: Excerpt (Morir, fremenda cosa urna fatale)

Berlin	Berlin RO	LP: DG LPM 18 700/SLPM 138 700
April 1961	Fricsay	LP: DG 2705 001
		CD: DG 447 6782

La Forza del destino: Excerpts (Solenne in quest' ora; Invano Alvaro)

Munich	Bergonzi	LP: Orfeo S028 821A
July 1982	Bavarian RO	CD: Orfeo C028 821A
	Lopez-Cobos	

Macbeth

Salzburg	Role of Macbeth	CD: Frequenz 011.036
August 1964	Bumbry, Lorenzi,	Excerpts
	Lagger	CD: Orfeo C335 931A
	Vienna Opera Chorus	
	VPO	
	Sawallisch	
London	Suliotis, Pavarotti,	LP: Decca SET 510-512
August 1970	Ghiaurov	CD: Decca 440 0482
	Ambrosian Chorus	Excerpts
	LPO	LP: Decca GRV 7
	Gardelli	CD: Decca 421 8892/440 4832

Otello

Walthamstow	Role of Iago	LP: EMI SLS 940/EX 29 01373
August and	Jones, McCracken	CD: EMI CMS 565 2962
October 1968	Ambrosian Chorus	Excerpt
	New Philharmonia	LP: EMI EX 29 04323
	Barbirolli	

Otello, Querschnitt

Munich	Stratas, Windgassen	LP: DG LPEM 19 434/SLPEM 136 434
June 1967	Bavarian State	LP: DG 2535 324/2537 017
	Orchestra & Chorus	CD: DG 447 8192
	Gerdes	Excerpt
	Sung in German	LP: DG 2535 655

Otello: Excerpt (Talor vedeste in mano)

Munich	Bergonzi	LP: Orfeo S028 821A
July 1982	Bavarian RO	CD: Orfeo C028 821A
	Lopez-Cobos	

Rigoletto

Milan	Role of Rigoletto	LP: DG LPM 18 931-18 933/
July 1964	Scotto, Cossotto,	SLPM 138 931-138 933
	Bergonzi, Vinco	LP: DG 2709 014/2740 197
	La Scala	CD: DG 437 7042
	Orchestra & Chorus	Excerpts
	Kubelik	LP: DG LPEM 19 280/SLPEM 136 280
		LP: DG 135 008/135 145
		LP: DG 2537 006/2705 001
		CD: DG 445 0492/447 6782

Rigoletto, Querschnitt

Berlin	Vivarelli, Rütgers,	LP: DG LPEM 19 412/SLPEM 136 412
April 1962	Kozub, Lauhöfer	LP: DG 2535 276
	Deutsche Oper Chorus	CD: DG 447 8172
	BPO	Excerpt
	Stein	LP: DG LPEM 19 460/SLPEM 136 460
	Sung in German	LP: DG 2535 655

Rigoletto: Excerpt (Pari siamo)

Berlin	BPO	LP: HMV ALP 1825/ASD 407
June 1959	Erede	LP: EMI EX 29 04323

Rigoletto: Excerpt (Cortigiani! Vil razza dannata!)

Berlin	BPO	45: HMV 7ER 5225
June 1959	Erede	LP: HMV ALP 1825/ASD 407
		LP: EMI EX 29 04323

La Traviata

Berlin	Role of Germont	LP: Decca SET 401-402
1968	Lorengar, Aragall	Excerpt
	Deutsche Oper	LP: Decca GRV 7
	Orchestra & Chorus	CD: Decca 440 4832
	Maazel	

La Traviata, Querschnitt

Munich	Güden, Wunderlich	LP: DG LPEM 19 431/SLPEM 136 431
June 1966	Bavarian Radio	LP: DG 2535 322
	Orchestra & Chorus	CD: DG 432 8732
	Bartoletti	Excerpt
	Sung in German	CD: DG 447 6782

La Traviata: Excerpt (Di provenza il mar)

Berlin	Berlin RO	LP: DG LPM 18 700/SLPM 138 700
April 1961	Fricsay	LP: DG 135 008

Il Trovatore: Excerpt (Il balen del suo soriso)

Berlin	BPO	LP: HMV ALP 1825/ASD 407
June 1959	Erede	LP: EMI EX 29 04323

I Vespri sicilani : Excerpt (In braccio alle dovizie)

Berlin	BPO	LP: HMV ALP 1825/ASD 407/ASD 2549
June 1959	Erede	LP: EMI EX 29 04323

I Vespri siciliani: Excerpt (Sogno, o son desto!)

Munich	Bergonzi	LP: Orfeo S028 821A
July 1982	Bavarian RO	CD: Orfeo C028 821A
	Lopez-Cobos	

WAGNER

Der fliegende Holländer

Berlin February 1960	Role of Holländer Schech, Wagner, Schock, Wunderlich, Frick Deutsche Staatsoper Chorus Staatskapelle Konwitschny	LP: HMV ALP 1806-1808/ASD 385-387 LP: EMI 1C 183 30206-30208 LP: EMI 1C 149 30206-30208 CD: Berlin Classics BC 20972 Excerpt LP: EMI EX 29 04323/SHZE 154

Der fliegende Holländer: Excerpt (Die Frist ist um)

Munich June 1977	Bavarian RO Kubelik	LP: EMI ASD 3499/1C 063 02969

Götterdämmerung

Vienna May, June, October and November 1964	Role of Gunther Nilsson, Watson, C.Ludwig, Windgasse, Frick, Neidlinger Vienna Opera Chorus VPO Solti	LP: Decca MET 292-297/SET 292-297 LP: Decca D100 D19/RING 1-22 LP: Decca 414 1001/414 1151 CD: DEcca 414 1002/414 1152 Excerpt LP: Decca GRV 7 CD: Decca 440 4832

Lohengrin

Bayreuth August 1954	Role of Heerrufer Nilsson, Varnay, Windgassen, Uhde, Adam Bayreuth Festival Orchestra & Chorus Jochum	LP: Cetra LO 77 LP: Melodram MEL 541 CD: Laudis LCD 44015
Vienna November and December 1962	Role of Telramund Grümmer, C.Ludwig, Thomas, Frick, Wiener Vienna Opera Chorus VPO Kempe	LP: EMI AN 121-125/SAN 121-125 LP: EMI SLS 5072/EX 29 09553 CD: EMI CDS 749 0178 Excerpts LP: EMI EX 29 04323/1C 063 00747

Die Meistersinger von Nürnberg

Berlin April 1976	Role of Sachs Ligendza, C.Ludwig, Domingo, Laubenthal, Lagger, R.Hermann Deutsche Oper Orchestra & Chorus Jochum	LP: DG 2713 011/2740 149 CD: DG 415 2782 Excerpts LP: DG 2536 383/2537 041 CD: DG 445 4702/447 6782

Parsifal

Bayreuth July 1956	Role of Amfortas Mödl, Vinay, Greindl, Hotter, Blankenheim Bayreuth Festival Orchestra & Chorus Knappertsbusch	LP: Cetra LO 79 LP: Melodram MEL 563 CD: Hunt CDLSMH 34035
Vienna December 1971 and March and June 1972	C.Ludwig, Kollo, Hotter, Frick, Kelemen Vienna Opera Chorus VPO Solti	LP: Decca SET 550-554 CD: Decca 417 1432 Excerpt LP: Decca GRV 7 CD: Decca 440 4832

Parsifal: Excerpt (Ja, wehe! Wehe!)

Munich June 1977	Bavarian Radio Orchestra & Chorus Kubelik	LP: EMI ASD 3499/1C 063 02969 LP: EMI EX 29 04323

Parsifal: Excerpt (Lass' ihn unenthüllt!)

Munich June 1977	Bavarian RO Kubelik	LP: EMI ASD 3499/1C 063 02969

Das Rheingold

Berlin December 1967- January 1968	Role of Wotan Veasey, Dominguez, Grobe, Stolze, Wohlfahrt, Kerns, Kelemen, Talvela, Ridderbusch BPO Karajan	LP: DG SKL 104 966-104 968 LP: DG 2709 023/2720 051 LP: DG 2740 145/2740 240 CD: DG 415 1412/435 2112 Excerpts LP: DG 135 118/136 437
Salzburg April 1968	Veasey, Dominguez, Grobe, Stolze, Wohlfahrt, Kerns, Kelemen, Talvela, Ridderbusch BPO Karajan	CD: Memories HR 4107-4121/ HR 4111-4113 CD: Hunt CDKAR 223

Tannhäuser

Berlin December 1949	Role of Wolfram Musial, Buchner, Suthaus, Greindl Städtische Oper Orchestra & Chorus L.Ludwig	LP: Melodram MEL 016
Bayreuth July 1954	Brouwenstijn, Wilfert, Vinay, Blankenheim Bayreuth Festival Orchestra & Chorus Keilberth	LP: Melodram MEL 544 CD: Melodram MEL 36105
Berlin October 1960	Grümmer, Schech, Hopf, Frick Deutsche Staatsoper Chorus Staatskapelle Konwitschny	LP: HMV ALP 1876-1879/ASD 445-448 LP: HMV HQM 1081-1084/HQS 1081-1084 CD: EMI CMS 763 2142 Excerpts LP: EMI ALP 2005/ASD 555/ASD 2549 LP: EMI EX 29 04323
Bayreuth July 1961	De los Angeles, Bumbry, Windgassen, Greindl, Crass Bayreuth Festival Orchestra & Chorus Sawallisch	LP: Ed Smith UORC 230 LP: Melodram MEL 614 CD: Myto MCD 93277 Also issued on LP by Teatro Dischi
Berlin December 1968 and February and May 1969	Nilsson, Windgassen, Laubenthal, Adam Deutsche Oper Orchestra & Chorus Gerdes	LP: DG 139 284-139 287 LP: DG 2711 008/2740 142 Excerpts LP: DG 2537 016/2705 001 CD: DG 447 6782

Tannhäuser: Excerpts (Als du im kühnem Sange; Blick' ich umher; Wie Todesahnung/O du mein holder Abendstern)

London March 1954	Philharmonia Schüchter	45: HMV 7ER 5033

Tristan und Isolde

London June 1952	Role of Kurwenal Flagstad, Thebom, Suthaus, Greindl Covent Garden Chorus Philharmonia Furtwängler	LP: HMV ALP 1030-1035 LP: Victor LM 6700 LP: Electrola E 90032-90037/ E 91170-91174 LP: EMI RLS 684/EX 29 06843 CD: EMI CDS 747 3228 Excerpt LP: EMI EX 29 04323
Dresden August 1980- April 1982	M.Price, Fassbaender, Kollo, Moll Leipzig Radio Chorus Dresden Staatskapelle C.Kleiber	LP: DG 2741 006 CD: DG 413 3152

Die Walküre: Excerpt (Leb' wohl, du kühnes herrliches Kind!)

Munich June 1977	Bavarian RO Kubelik	LP: EMI ASD 3499/1C 063 02969 LP: EMI EX 29 04323 CD: EMI CMS 565 2122

Branders Lied

Berlin September 1972	Demus, fortepiano	LP: DG 2533 149

Lied des Mephistopheles

Berlin September 1972	Demus, fortepiano	LP: DG 2533 149

Der Tannenbaum

Berlin March 1971	Reimann	LP: EMI 1C 065 02674/ 1C 161 02673-02677

WALTER, BRUNO

Der junge Ehemann (Hier unter dieser Linde)

| Berlin
May 1964 | Demus | LP: DG LPM 18 946/SLPM 138 946 |
| Salzburg
August 1975 | Sawallisch | CD: Orfeo C185 891A/C339 930T |

Musikantengruss

| Berlin
May 1964 | Demus | LP: DG LPM 18 946/SLPM 138 946 |

Der Soldat (Ist schmuck nicht mein Rösslein?)

| Berlin
May 1964 | Demus | LP: DG LPM 18 946/SLPM 138 946 |
| Salzburg
August 1975 | Sawallisch | CD: Orfeo C185 891A/C339 930T |

WEBER

Lieder: Meine Lieder, meine Sänge; Klage; Der kleine Fritz an seine jungen Freunde; Was zieht zu deinem Zauberkreise?; Ich sah ein Röschen am Wege steh'n; Er an sie; Meine Farben; Liebe-Glühen; Ueber die Berge mit Ungestüm; Es stürmt auf der Flur; Minnelied; Reigen; Sind es Schmerzen, sind es Freuden?; Mein Verlangen; Wenn ich ein Vöglein wär'; Mein Schatzerl is hübsch; Liebesgruss aus der Ferne; Herzchen, mein Schätzchen; Das Veilchen im Thale; Ich denke dein; Horch, leise horch Geliebte!; Sie war so hold

| Berlin
March and
September 1991 | Höll | CD: Claves CD 50 9118 |

Schottische Lieder und Volksweisen: Ein entmutigter Liebdender; Ein beglückter Liebender; Bewunderung; Glühende Liebe; Trinklied; Wein', weine nur nicht!

| Berlin
February 1961 | Heller, violin
Poppen, cello
Nicolet, flute
Engel | LP: DG LPM 18 706/SLPM 138 706 |

WEBERN

Am Ufer (Die Welt verstummt)

Berlin	Reimann	LP: DG 2530 107
October 1970		CD: DG 431 7442

An baches ranft

Berlin	Reimann	LP: DG 2530 107
October 1970		CD: DG 431 7442

Bild der Liebe (Vom Wald umgeben)

Berlin	Reimann	LP: DG 2530 107
October 1970		CD: DG 431 7442

Dies ist ein lied

Berlin	Reimann	LP: DG 2530 107
October 1970		CD: DG 431 7442

Erwachen aus dem tiefsten Traummesschosse

Berlin	Reimann	LP: EMI 1C 065 02677/
March 1974		1C 161 02673-02677

Gefunden (Nun wir uns lieben)

Berlin	Reimann	LP: DG 2530 107
October 1970		CD: DG 431 7442

Ihr tratet zu dem herde

Berlin	Reimann	LP: DG 2530 107
October 1970		CD: DG 431 7442

Kunfttag I (dem bist du kind dem freund)

Berlin	Reimann	LP: EMI 1C 065 02677/
March 1974		1C 161 02673-02677

Das lockere Staatsgebilde lechzet krank

Berlin	Reimann	LP: EMI 1C 065 02677/
March 1974		1C 161 02673-02677

Noch zwingt mich treue

Berlin   Reimann   LP: DG 2530 107
October 1970   CD: DG 431 7442

So ich traurig bin

Berlin   Reimann   LP: DG 2530 107
October 1970   CD: DG 431 7442

Trauer I (So wart', bis ich dies dir noch künde)

Berlin   Reimann   LP: EMI 1C 065 02677/
March 1974   1C 161 02673-02677
                                          LP: EMI EX 29 04293

Vorfrühling (Leise tritt auf)

Berlin   Reimann   LP: DG 2530 107
October 1970   CD: DG 431 7442

WEINGARTNER

Liebesfeier (An ihren bunten Liedern klettert)

Berlin   Reimann   LP: EMI 1C 065 02674/
March 1971   1C 161 02673-02677

WEISMANN

Der heilige Nikolaus; Schlaf' wohl, du Himmelsknabe

Berlin   Demus   LP: DG 2530 219
November 1970

WETZEL

An meine Mutter; Der Kehraus

Berlin   Reimann   LP: EMI 1C 065 02675/
May 1971   1C 161 02673-02677

Der Corregidor

Berlin 1985	Role of Tio Lucas Donath, Soffel, Hollweg, Moll RIAS Choir Berlin RO Albrecht	CD: Schwann 314 010 Also issued on LP

Abendbilder (Friedlicher Abend senkt sich aufs Gefilde)

Paris and Berlin January- November 1974	Barenboim	LP: DG 2709 066/2740 156 CD: DG (Japan) POCG 9013-9021

Abschied/Mörike-Lieder (Unangeklopft ein Herr tritt abends bei mir an)

Berlin September 1957	Moore	LP: HMV ALP 1617-1619 LP: Electrola E 90018-90020 LP: EMI 1C 181 01470-01476 CD: EMI CMS 763 5632
Salzburg August 1961	Moore	LP: Orfeo S140 855R CD: Orfeo C140 401A/C 339 930T
Berlin and Paris December 1972- June 1973	Barenboim	LP: DG 2709 053/2740 113 CD: DG 415 1922 CD: DG (Japan) POCG 9013-9021
Innsbruck October 1973	Richter	LP: DG 2530 584

Ach des Knaben Augen/Spanisches Liederbuch

Berlin May 1958	Moore	LP: HMV ALP 1750/ASD 378 LP: Electrola E 90922/E 200 000 LP: EMI 1C 181 01470-01476

Ach im Maien war's/Spanisches Liederbuch

Berlin May 1958	Moore	LP: HMV ALP 1750/ASD 378 LP: Electrola E 90922/E 200 000 LP: EMI 1C 181 01470-01476
Berlin December 1966- January 1967	Moore	LP: DG SLPM 139 329-139 330 LP: DG 2707 035/2726 071 CD: DG 421 9342 CD: DG (Japan) POCG 9013-9021

Ach wie lang die Seele schlummert/Spanisches Liederbuch

Berlin May 1958	Moore	LP: HMV ALP 1750/ASD 378 LP: Electrola E 90922/E 200 000 LP: EMI 1C 181 01470-01476
Berlin December 1966- January 1967	Moore	LP: DG SLPM 139 329-139 330 LP: DG 2707 035/2726 071 CD: DG 421 9342 CD: DG (Japan) POCG 9013-9021

Alle gingen, Herz, zur Ruh'/Spanisches Liederbuch

London 1953	Moore	LP: HMV ALP 1143 Also issued on LP by Electrola
Berlin May 1958	Moore	LP: HMV ALP 1750/ASD 378 LP: Electrola E 90922/E 200 000 LP: EMI 1C 181 01470-01476
Berlin December 1966- January 1967	Moore	LP: DG SLPM 139 329-139 330 LP: DG 2707 035/2726 071 CD: DG 421 9342 CD: DG (Japan) POCG 9013-9021

An den Schlaf/Mörike-Lieder (Schlaf, süsser Schlaf!)

Berlin September 1957	Moore	LP: HMV ALP 1617-1619 LP: Electrola E 90018-90020 LP: EMI 1C 181 01470-01476 CD: EMI CMS 763 5632
Salzburg August 1961	Moore	LP: Orfeo S140 855R CD: Orfeo C140 401A/C339 930T
Berlin and Paris December 1972- June 1973	Barenboim	LP: DG 2709 053/2740 113 CD: DG (Japan) POCG 9013-9021

An die Geliebte/Mörike-Lieder (Wenn ich, vor deinem Anschau'n tief gestillt)

Berlin September 1957	Moore	LP: HMV ALP 1617-1619/EX 29 04293 LP: Electrola E 90018-90020 LP: EMI 1C 181 01470-01476 CD: EMI CMS 763 5632
Salzburg August 1961	Moore	LP: Orfeo S140 855R CD: Orfeo C140 401A/C 339 930T
Berlin and Paris December 1972- June 1973	Barenboim	LP: DG 2709 053/2740 113 CD: DG 415 1922 CD: DG (Japan) POCG 9013-9021
Innsbruck October 1973	Richter	LP: DG 2530 584

An eine Aeolsharfe/Mörike-Lieder (Angelehnt an die Efeuwand)

Berlin and Paris December 1972– June 1973	Barenboim	LP: DG 2709 053/2740 113 CD: DG (Japan) POCG 9013-9021

Anakreons Grab/Goethe-Lieder (Wo die Rose hier blüht)

London 1953	Moore	LP: HMV ALP 1143 Also issued on LP by Electrola
Berlin April 1960	Moore	LP: HMV ALP 1852-1853/ASD 424-425 LP: Electrola E 91072-91073/ STE 91072-91073/E 200 000 LP: EMI 1C 181 01470-01476
Paris and Berlin January– November 1974	Barenboim	LP: DG 2709 066/2740 156 CD: DG 415 1922 CD: DG (Japan) POCG 9013-9021
Munich March and June 1990	Munich RO Soltesz	CD: Orfeo C219 911A Wolf's own orchestration

Andenken (Ich denke dein)

Paris and Berlin January 1974– November 1976	Barenboim	LP: DG 2709 067/2740 162 CD: DG (Japan) POCG 9013-9021

Auch kleine Dinge können uns entzücken/Italienisches Liederbuch

Berlin September 1965– February 1966	Moore	LP: EMI AN 210-211/SAN 210-211 LP: EMI 1C 165 01871-01872 LP: EMI EX 29 04293 CD: EMI CDM 763 7322

Auf dem grünen Balkon/Spanisches Liederbuch

Berlin May 1958	Moore	LP: HMV ALP 1750/ASD 378 LP: Electrola E 90922/E 200 000 LP: EMI 1C 181 01470-01476
Berlin December 1966– January 1967	Moore	LP: DG SLPM 139 329-139 330 LP: DG 2707 035/2726 071 CD: DG 421 9342 CD: DG (Japan) POCG 9013-9021

Wolf Lieder/continued

Auf der Wanderung (Ueber die Hügel und über die Berge hin)

Paris	Barenboim	LP: DG 2709 067/2740 162
and Berlin		CD: DG (Japan) POCG 9013-9021
January 1974–		
November 1976		

Auf ein altes Bild/Mörike-Lieder (In einer grünen Landschaft Sommerflor)

Berlin	Moore	LP: HMV ALP 1617-1619
September 1957		LP: Electrola E 90018-90020
		LP: EMI 1C 181 01470-01476
		CD: EMI CMS 763 5632
Berlin	Barenboim	LP: DG 2709 053/2740 113
and Paris		CD: DG 415 1922
December 1972–		CD: DG (Japan) POCG 9013-9021
June 1973		

Auf eine Christblume I & II/Mörike-Lieder (Tochter des Waldes; Im Winterboden schläft)

Berlin	Moore	LP: HMV ALP 1617-1619
September 1957		LP: Electrola E 90018-90020
		LP: EMI 1C 181 01470-01476
		CD: EMI CMS 763 5632
Berlin	Barenboim	LP: DG 2709 053/2740 113
and Paris		CD: DG (Japan) POCG 9013-9021
December 1972–		
June 1973		

Auf einer Wanderung/Mörike-Lieder (In ein freundliches Städtchen tret' ich ein

Berlin	Moore	LP: HMV ALP 1617-1619
September 1957		LP: Electrola E 90018-90020
		LP: EMI 1C 181 01470-01476
		CD: EMI CMS 763 5632
Salzburg	Moore	LP: Orfeo S140 855R
August 1961		CD: Orfeo C140 401A/C339 930T
Berlin	Barenboim	LP: DG 2709 053/2740 113
and Paris		CD: DG (Japan) POCG 9013-9021
December 1972–		
June 1973		
Innsbruck	Richter	LP: DG 2530 584
October 1973		

Wolf Lieder/continued

Auftrag/Mörike-Lieder (In poetischer Epistel)

Berlin September 1957	Moore	LP: HMV ALP 1617-1619 LP: Electrola E 90018-90020 LP: EMI 1C 181 01470-01476 CD: EMI CMS 763 5632
Berlin and Paris December 1972- June 1973	Barenboim	LP: DG 2709 053/2740 113 CD: DG (Japan) POCG 9013-9021

Aus meinen grossen Schmerzen

Feldkirch August 1986	Höll	CD: Claves CD 50 8706

Begegnung/Mörike-Lieder (Was doch heut' Nacht ein Sturm gewesen)

Berlin September 1957	Moore	LP: HMV ALP 1617-1619 LP: Electrola E 90018-90020 LP: EMI 1C 181 01470-01476 CD: EMI CMS 763 5632
Salzburg August 1961	Moore	LP: Orfeo S140 855R CD: Orfeo C140 401A/C339 930T
Berlin and Paris December 1972- June 1973	Barenboim	LP: DG 2709 053/2740 113 CD: DG 415 1922 CD: DG (Japan) POCG 9013-9021
Innsbruck October 1973	Richter	LP: DG 2530 584

Beherzigung I & II/Goethe-Lieder (Ach, was soll der Mensch verlangen?; Feiger Gedanken bängliches Schwanken)

Berlin April 1960	Moore	LP: HMV ALP 1852-1853/ASD 424-425 LP: Electrola E 91072-91073/ STE 91072-91073/E 200 000 LP: EMI 1C 181 01470-01476
Paris and Berlin January- November 1974	Barenboim	LP: DG 2709 066/2740 156 CD: DG (Japan) POCG 9013-9021

Bei einer Trauung/Mörike-Lieder (Vor lauter hochadligen Zeugen)

Berlin September 1957	Moore	LP: HMV ALP 1617-1619 LP: Electrola E 90018-90020 LP: EMI 1C 181 01470-01476 CD: EMI CMS 763 5632
Salzburg August 1961	Moore	LP: Orfeo S140 855R CD: Orfeo C140 401A/C339 930T
Berlin and Paris December 1972- June 1973	Barenboim	LP: DG 2709 053/2740 113 CD: DG 415 1922 CD: DG (Japan) POCG 9013-9021
Innsbruck October 1973	Richter	LP: DG 2530 584

Benedeit die sel'ge Mutter/Italienisches Liederbuch

Berlin 1949-1950	Klust	78: DG LM 68 458 LP: DG LPM 18 005
Salzburg August 1958	Werba	CD: Orfeo C220 901A/C339 930T
Berlin September- October 1958	Demus	LP: DG LPM 18 568-18 569/ SLPM 138 035-138 036 LP: DG 9108/109 108 CD: DG 435 7522
Berlin September 1965- February 1966	Moore	LP: EMI AN 210-211/SAN 210-211 LP: EMI 1C 165 01871-01872 LP: EMI EX 29 04293 CD: EMI CDM 763 7322
Berlin June 1975	Barenboim	LP: DG 2707 114 CD: DG 439 9752 CD: DG (Japan) POCG 9013-9021

Biterolf (Kampfmüd' und sonnenverbrannt)

Berlin May 1958	Moore	LP: HMV ALP 1783/ASD 362 LP: Electrola E 91002/STE 91002 LP: EMI 1C 181 01470-01476/E 200 000
Paris and Berlin January 1974- November 1976	Barenboim	LP: DG 2709 067/2740 162 CD: DG (Japan) POCG 9013-9021

Blindes Schauen, dunkle Leuchte/Spanisches Liederbuch

Berlin May 1958	Moore	LP: HMV ALP 1750/ASD 378 LP: Electrola E 90922/E 200 000 LP: EMI 1C 181 01470-01476
Berlin December 1966- January 1967	Moore	LP: DG SLPM 139 329-139 330 LP: DG 2707 035/2726 071 CD: DG 421 9342 CD: DG (Japan) POCG 9013-9021

Blumengruss/Goethe-Lieder (Den Strauss, den ich gepflückt)

Berlin April 1960	Moore	LP: HMV ALP 1852-1853/ASD 424-425 LP: Electrola E 91072-91073/ STE 91072-91073/E 200 000 LP: EMI 1C 181 01470-01476
Paris and Berlin January- November 1974	Barenboim	LP: DG 2709 066/2740 156 CD: DG (Japan) POCG 9013-9021

Cophtisches Lied I & II/Goethe-Lieder (Lasset Gelehrte sich zanken und streiten; Geh! Gehorche meinen Winken)

London 1953	Moore	LP: HMV ALP 1143 Also issued on LP by Electrola
Berlin April 1960	Moore	LP: HMV ALP 1852-1853/ASD 424-425 LP: Electrola E 91072-91073/ STE 91072-91073/E 200 000 LP: EMI 1C 181 01470-01476
Paris and Berlin January- November 1974	Barenboim	LP: DG 2709 066/2740 156 CD: DG 415 1922 CD: DG (Japan) POCG 9013-9021

Da nur Leid und Leidenschaft/Spanisches Liederbuch

Berlin May 1958	Moore	LP: HMV ALP 1750/ASD 378 LP: Electrola E 90922/E 200 000 LP: EMI 1C 181 01470-01476
Berlin December 1966- January 1967	Moore	LP: DG SLPM 139 329-139 330 LP: DG 2707 035/2726 071 CD: DG 421 9342 CD: DG (Japan) POCG 9013-9021

Wolf Lieder/continued

Dank des Paria/Goethe-Lieder (Grosser Brahma!)

Berlin April 1960	Moore	LP: HMV ALP 1852-1853/ASD 424-425 LP: Electrola E 91072-91073/ STE 91072-91073/E 200 000 LP: EMI 1C 181 01470-01476
Paris and Berlin January- November 1974	Barenboim	LP: DG 2709 066/2740 156 CD: DG (Japan) POCG 9013-9021

Das ist ein Brausen und Heulen

Feldkirch August 1986	Höll	CD: Claves CD 50 8706

Dass doch gemalt all' deine Reize wären/Italienisches Liederbuch

Salzburg August 1958	Werba	CD: Orfeo C220 901A/C339 930T
Berlin September- October 1958	Demus	LP: DG LPM 18 568-18 569/ SLPM 138 035-138 036 CD: DG 435 7522
Berlin September 1965- February 1966	Moore	LP: EMI AN 210-211/SAN 210-211 LP: EMI 1C 165 01871-01872 CD: EMI CDM 763 7322
Berlin June 1975	Barenboim	LP: DG 2707 114 CD: DG 439 9752 CD: DG (Japan) POCG 9013-9021

Deine Mutter, süsses Kind/Spanisches Liederbuch

Berlin May 1958	Moore	LP: HMV ALP 1750/ASD 378 LP: Electrola E 90922/E 200 000 LP: EMI 1C 181 01470-01476
Berlin December 1966- January 1967	Moore	LP: DG SLPM 139 329-139 330 LP: DG 2707 035/2726 071 CD: DG 421 9342 CD: DG (Japan) POCG 9013-9021

Wolf Lieder/continued

Denk' es, o Seele/Mörike-Lieder (Ein Tännlein grünet wo)

Berlin September 1957	Moore	LP: HMV ALP 1617-1619 LP: Electrola E 90018-90020 LP: EMI 1C 181 01470-01476 CD: EMI CMS 763 5632
Berlin and Paris December 1972- June 1973	Barenboim	LP: DG 2709 053/2740 113 CD: DG 415 1922 CD: DG (Japan) POCG 9013-9021
Munich March and June 1990	Munich RO Soltesz	CD: Orfeo C219 911A

Dereinst, dereinst, Gedanke mein/Spanisches Liederbuch

Berlin May 1958	Moore	LP: HMV ALP 1750/ASD 378 LP: Electrola E 90922/E 200 000 LP: EMI 1C 181 01470-01476
Berlin December 1966- January 1967	Moore	LP: DG SLPM 139 329-139 330 LP: DG 2707 035/2726 071 CD: DG 421 9342 CD: DG (Japan) POCG 9013-9021

Die du Gott gebarst, du Reine/Spanisches Liederbuch

Berlin May 1958	Moore	LP: HMV ALP 1750/ASD 378 LP: Electrola E 90922/E 200 000 LP: EMI 1C 181 01470-01476
Berlin December 1966- January 1967	Moore	LP: DG SLPM 139 329-139 330 LP: DG 2707 035/2726 071 CD: DG 421 9342 CD: DG (Japan) POCG 9013-9021

Dies zu deuten bin ich erbötig/Goethe-Lieder

Paris and Berlin January- November 1974	Barenboim	LP: DG 2709 066/2740 156 CD: DG (Japan) POCG 9013-9021

Du bist wie eine Blume

Paris and Berlin January- November 1974	Barenboim	LP: DG 2709 066/2740 156 CD: DG (Japan) POCG 9013-9021
Feldkirch August 1986	Höll	CD: Claves CD 50 8706

Wolf Lieder/continued

Epiphanias/Goethe-Lieder (Die heil'gen drei Könige)

| Berlin
April 1960 | Moore | LP: HMV ALP 1852-1853/ASD 424-425
LP: Electrola E 91072-91073/
     STE 91072-91073/E 200 000
LP: EMI 1C 181 01470-01476 |
| Paris
and Berlin
January-
November 1974 | Barenboim | LP: DG 2709 066/2740 156
CD: DG (Japan) POCG 9013-9021 |

Er ist's/Mörike-Lieder (Frühling lässt sein blaues Band)

| Berlin
and Paris
December 1972-
June 1973 | Barenboim | LP: DG 2709 053/2740 113
CD: DG 415 1922
CD: DG (Japan) POCG 9013-9021 |

Ernst ist der Frühling

| Feldkirch
August 1986 | Höll | CD: Claves CD 50 8706 |

Erschaffen und Beleben/Goethe-Lieder (Hans Adam war ein Erdenkloss)

London 1953	Moore	LP: HMV ALP 1143 Also issued on LP by Electrola
Berlin April 1960	Moore	LP: HMV ALP 1852-1853/ASD 424-425 LP: Electrola E 91072-91073/ STE 91072-91073/E 200 000 LP: EMI 1C 181 01470-01476
Paris and Berlin January- November 1974	Barenboim	LP: DG 2709 066/2740 156 CD: DG 415 1922 CD: DG (Japan) POCG 9013-9021

Erwartung/Eichendorff-Lieder (Grüss' euch aus Herzensgrund)

| Berlin
May 1958 | Moore | LP: HMV ALP 1778/ASD 356
LP: Electrola E 90989/STE 90989
LP: Electrola E 200 000
LP: EMI 1C 181 01470-01476 |
| Paris
and Berlin
January 1974-
November 1976 | Barenboim | LP: DG 2709 067/2740 162
CD: DG (Japan) POCG 9013-9021 |

Wolf Lieder/continued

Es blasen die blauen Husaren

Feldkirch	Höll	CD: Claves CD 50 8706
August 1986		

Es war ein alter König

Feldkirch	Höll	CD: Claves CD 50 8706
August 1986		

Der Feuerreiter/Mörike-Lieder (Sehet ihr am Fensterlein)

Berlin September 1957	Moore	45: HMV 7ER 5044 LP: HMV ALP 1617-1619 LP: Electrola E 90018-90020 LP: EMI 1C 181 01470-01476/SHZE 219 CD: EMI CMS 763 5632
Salzburg July 1961	Moore	LP: Orfeo S140 855R CD: Orfeo C140 401A/C339 930T
Berlin and Paris December 1972- June 1973	Barenboim	LP: DG 2709 053/2740 113 CD: DG 415 1922 CD: DG (Japan) POCG 9013-9021
Innsbruck October 1973	Richter	LP: DG 2530 584

Frage und Antwort/Mörike-Lieder (Fragst du mich, woher die bange Liebe)

Berlin and Paris December 1972- June 1973	Barenboim	LP: DG 2709 053/2740 113 CD: DG (Japan) POCG 9013-9021

Frage nicht (Wie sehr ich dein, soll ich dir sagen?)

Paris and Berlin January- November 1974	Barenboim	LP: DG 2709 066/2740 156 CD: DG (Japan) POCG 9013-9021

Frech und froh I & II/Goethe-Lieder (Mit Mädchen sich vertragen; Liebesqual verschmäht mein Herz)

Berlin April 1960	Moore	LP: HMV ALP 1852-1853/ASD 424-425 LP: Electrola E 91072-91073/ STE 91072-91073/E 200 000 LP: EMI 1C 181 01470-01476
Paris and Berlin January- November 1974	Barenboim	LP: DG 2709 066/2740 156 CD: DG 415 1922 CD: DG (Japan) POCG 9013-9021

Der Freund/Eichendorff Lieder (Wer auf den Wogen schliefe)

| Berlin
May 1958 | Moore | LP: HMV ALP 1778/ASD 356
LP: Electrola E 90989/STE 90989
LP: Electrola E 200 000
LP: EMI 1C 181 01470-01476 |

| Paris
and Berlin
January 1974-
November 1976 | Barenboim | LP: DG 2709 067/2740 162
CD: DG (Japan) POCG 9013-9021 |

| Munich
March and
June 1990 | Munich RO
Soltesz | CD: Orfeo C219 911A |

Frohe Botschaft (Hielt die allerschönste Herrin)

| Paris
and Berlin
January 1974-
November 1976 | Barenboim | LP: DG 2709 067/2740 162
CD: DG (Japan) POCG 9013-9021 |

Frühling übers Jahr/Goethe-Lieder (Das Beet schon lockert sich in die Höh')

| Berlin
April 1960 | Moore | LP: HMV ALP 1852-1853/ASD 424-425
LP: Electrola E 91072-91073/
STE 91072-91073/E 200 000
LP: EMI 1C 181 01470-01476
LP: EMI EX 29 04293 |

| Paris
and Berlin
January-
November 1974 | Barenboim | LP: DG 2709 066/2740 156
CD: DG (Japan) POCG 9013-9021 |

Frühlingsglocken (Schneeglöckchen tut läuten)

| Paris
and Berlin
January 1974-
November 1976 | Barenboim | LP: DG 2709 067/2740 162
CD: DG (Japan) POCG 9013-9021 |

Führ' mich, Kind, nach Bethlehem!/Spanisches Liederbuch

| Berlin
May 1958 | Moore | LP: HMV ALP 1750/ASD 378
LP: Electrola E 90922/E 200 000
LP: EMI 1C 181 01470-01476 |

| Berlin
December 1966-
January 1967 | Moore | LP: DG SLPM 139 329-139 330
LP: DG 2707 035/2726 071
CD: DG 421 9342
CD: DG (Japan) POCG 9013-9021 |

Wolf Lieder/continued

Fussreise/Mörike-Lieder (Am frischgeschnitt'nen Wanderstab)

London 1953	Moore	LP: HMV ALP 1143 Also issued on LP by Electrola
Berlin September 1957	Moore	LP: HMV ALP 1617-1619 LP: Electrola E 90018-90020 LP: EMI 1C 181 01470-01476 CD: EMI CMS 763 5632
Salzburg July 1961	Moore	LP: Orfeo S140 855R CD: Orfeo C140 401A/C339 930T
Berlin and Paris December 1972- June 1973	Barenboim ,	LP: DG 2709 053/2740 113 CD: DG 415 1922 CD: DG (Japan) POCG 9013-9021
Innsbruck October 1973	Richter	LP: DG 2530 584
Munich March and June 1990	Munich RO Soltesz	CD: Orfeo C219 911A

Ganymed/Goethe-Lieder (Wie im Morgenglanze du rings mich anglühst)

Berlin April 1960	Moore	LP: HMV ALP 1852-1853/ASD 424-425 LP: Electrola E 91072-91073/ STE 91072-91073/E 200 000 LP: EMI 1C 181 01470-01476 LP: EMI EX 29 04293
Paris and Berlin January- November 1974	Barenboim	LP: DG 2709 066/2740 156 CD: DG 415 1922 CD: DG (Japan) POCG 9013-9021

Der Gärtner/Mörike-Lieder (Auf ihrem Leibrösslein so weiss wie der Schnee)

Berlin September 1957	Moore	LP: HMV ALP 1617-1619 LP: Electrola E 90018-90020 LP: EMI 1C 181 01470-01476 CD: EMI CMS 763 5632
Berlin and Paris December 1972- June 1973	Barenboim	LP: DG 2709 053/2740 113 CD: DG 415 1922 CD: DG (Japan) POCG 9013-9021

Gebet/Mörike-Lieder (Herr, schicke was du willst)

Berlin September 1957	Moore	LP: HMV ALP 1617-1619 LP: Electrola E 90018-90020 LP: EMI 1C 181 01470-01476 CD: EMI CMS 763 5632
Berlin and Paris December 1972- June 1973	Barenboim	LP: DG 2709 053/2740 113 CD: DG (Japan) POCG 9013-9021
Munich March and June 1990	Munich RO Soltesz	CD: Orfeo C219 911A

Die Geister am Mummelsee/Mörike-Lieder (Vom Berge was kommt dort um Mitternacht spät)

Berlin September 1957	Moore	LP: HMV ALP 1617-1619 LP: Electrola E 90018-90020 LP: EMI 1C 181 01470-01476 CD: EMI CMS 763 5632
Berlin and Paris December 1972- June 1973	Barenboim	LP: DG 2709 053/2740 113 CD: DG (Japan) POCG 9013-9021

Der Genesene an die Hoffnung/Mörike-Lieder (Tödlich graute mir der Morgen)

Berlin September 1957	Moore	LP: HMV ALP 1617-1619 LP: Electrola E 90018-90020 LP: EMI 1C 181 01470-01476 CD: EMI CMS 763 5632
Salzburg July 1961	Moore	LP: Orfeo S140 855R CD: Orfeo C140 401A/C339 930T
Berlin and Paris December 1972- June 1973	Barenboim	LP: DG 2709 053/2740 113 CD: DG (Japan) POCG 9013-9021
Innsbruck October 1973	Richter	LP: DG 2530 584

Wolf Lieder/continued

Genialisch Treiben/Goethe-Lieder (So wälz' ich ohne Unterlass)

London 1953	Moore	LP: HMV ALP 1143 Also issued on LP by Electrola
Berlin April 1960	Moore	LP: HMV ALP 1852-1853/ASD 424-425 LP: Electrola E 91072-91073/ STE 91072-91073/E 200 000 LP: EMI 1C 181 01470-01476
Paris and Berlin January- November 1974	Barenboim	LP: DG 2709 066/2740 156 CD: DG (Japan) POCG 9013-9021

Gesang Weylas/Mörike-Lieder (Du bist Orplid, mein Land!)

Berlin September 1957	Moore	LP: HMV ALP 1617-1619 LP: Electrola E 90018-90020 LP: EMI 1C 181 01470-01476 CD: EMI CMS 763 5632
Berlin and Paris December 1972- June 1973	Barenboim	LP: DG 2709 053/2740 113 CD: DG (Japan) POCG 9013-9021
Munich August 1983	Klöcker, clarinet Wallendorf, horn Höll	LP: Orfeo S153 861A CD: Orfeo C153 861A
Munich March and June 1990	Munich RO Soltesz	CD: Orfeo C219 911A

Gesegnet sei, durch den die Welt entstund/Italienisches Liederbuch

Berlin 1949-1950	Klust	78: DG LM 68 455 LP: DG LPM 18 005
Salzburg August 1958	Werba	CD: Orfeo C220 901A/C339 930T
Berlin September- October 1958	Demus	LP: DG LPM 18 568-18 569/ SLPM 138 035-138 036 LP: DG 9108/109 108/135 026 CD: DG 435 7522
Berlin September 1965- February 1966	Moore	LP: EMI AN 210-211/SAN 210-211 LP: EMI 1C 165 01871-01872 CD: EMI CDM 763 7322
Berlin June 1975	Barenboim	LP: DG 2707 114 CD: DG 439 9752 CD: DG (Japan) POCG 9013-9021

Geselle, woll'n wir uns in Ketten hüllen/Italienisches Liederbuch

Berlin 1949-1950	Klust	78: DG LM 68 456 LP: DG LPM 18 005
Salzburg August 1958	Werba	CD: Orfeo C220 901A/C339 930T
Berlin September- October 1958	Demus	LP: DG LPM 18 568-18 569/ SLPM 138 035-138 036 CD: DG 435 7522
Berlin September 1965- February 1966	Moore	LP: EMI AN 210-211/SAN 210-211 LP: EMI 1C 165 01871-01872 CD: EMI CDM 763 7322
Berlin June 1975	Barenboim	LP: DG 2707 114 CD: DG 439 9752 CD: DG (Japan) POCG 9013-9021

Gesellenlied (Kein Meister fällt vom Himmel!)

Berlin May 1958	Moore	LP: HMV ALP 1783/ASD 362 LP: Electrola E 91002/STE 91002 LP: EMI 1C 181 01470-01476/E 200 000
Paris and Berlin January 1974- November 1976	Barenboim	LP: DG 2709 067/2740 162 CD: DG (Japan) POCG 9013-9021

Gleich und gleich/Goethe-Lieder (Ein Blumenglöckchen vom Boden hervor)

Berlin April 1960	Moore	LP: HMV ALP 1852-1853/ASD 424-425 LP: Electrola E 91072-91073/ STE 91072-91073/E 200 000 LP: EMI 1C 181 01470-01476
Paris and Berlin January- November 1974	Barenboim	LP: DG 2709 066/2740 156 CD: DG (Japan) POCG 9013-9021

Der Glücksritter/Eichendorff-Lieder (Wenn Fortuna spröde tut)

Berlin May 1958	Moore	LP: HMV ALP 1778/ASD 356 LP: Electrola E 90989/STE 90989 LP: Electrola E 200 000 LP: EMI 1C 181 01470-01476
Paris and Berlin January 1974- November 1976	Barenboim	LP: DG 2709 067/2740 162 CD: DG (Japan) POCG 9013-9021

Wolf Lieder/continued

Ein Grab (Wenn des Mondes bleiches Licht)

Paris and Berlin January 1974– November 1976	Barenboim	LP: DG 2709 067/2740 162 CD: DG (Japan) POCG 9013-9021

Grenzen der Menschheit/Goethe-Lieder (Wenn der uralte heilige Vater)

Berlin April 1960	Moore	LP: HMV ALP 1852-1853/ASD 424-425 LP: Electrola E 91072-91073/ STE 91072-91073/E 200 000 LP: EMI 1C 181 01470-01476
Paris and Berlin January– November 1974	Barenboim	LP: DG 2709 066/2740 156 CD: DG (Japan) POCG 9013-9021

Gutmann und Gutweib/Goethe-Lieder (Und morgen fällt Sankt Martins Fest)

Berlin April 1960	Moore	LP: HMV ALP 1852-1853/ASD 424-425 LP: Electrola E 91072-91073/ STE 91072-91073/E 200 000 LP: EMI 1C 181 01470-01476
Paris and Berlin January– November 1974	Barenboim	LP: DG 2709 066/2740 156 CD: DG (Japan) POCG 9013-9021

Harfenspieler-Lieder I, II & III/Goethe-Lieder (Wer sich der Einsamkeit ergibt; An die Türen will ich schleichen; Wer nie sein Brot mit Tränen ass)

London 1953	Moore	LP: HMV ALP 1143 Also issued on LP by Electrola
Berlin April 1960	Moore	LP: HMV ALP 1852-1853/ASD 424-425 LP: Electrola E 91072-91073/ STE 91072-91073/E 200 000 LP: EMI 1C 181 01470-01476
Paris and Berlin January– November 1974	Barenboim	LP: DG 2709 066/2740 156 CD: DG (Japan) POCG 9013-9021
Munich March and June 1990	Munich RO Soltesz	CD: Orfeo C219 911A Wolf's orchestrations

Wolf Lieder/continued

Hätt' ich irgendwohl Bedenken/Goethe-Lieder

| Paris
and Berlin
January-
November 1974 | Barenboim | LP: DG 2709 066/2740 156
CD: DG (Japan) POCG 9013-9021 |

Heb' auf dein blondes Haupt/Italienisches Liederbuch

| Berlin
1949-1950 | Klust | 78: DG LM 68 456
LP: DG LPM 18 005 |

| Salzburg
August 1958 | Werba | CD: Orfeo C220 901A/C339 930T |

| Berlin
September-
October 1958 | Demus | LP: DG LPM 18 568-18 569/
SLPM 138 035-138 036
CD: DG 435 7522 |

| Berlin
September 1965-
February 1966 | Moore | LP: EMI AN 210-211/SAN 210-211
LP: EMI 1C 165 01871-01872
CD: EMI CDM 763 7322 |

| Berlin
June 1975 | Barenboim | LP: DG 2707 114
CD: DG 439 9752
CD: DG (Japan) POCG 9013-9021 |

Heimweh/Eichendorff-Lieder (Wer in die Fremde will wandern)

| Berlin
May 1958 | Moore | LP: HMV ALP 1778/ASD 356
LP: Electrola E 90989/STE 90989/
E 70415/STE 70415
LP: Electrola E 200 000
LP: EMI 1C 181 01470-01476
CD: EMI CMS 763 5632 |

| Paris
and Berlin
January 1974-
November 1976 | Barenboim | LP: DG 2709 067/2740 162
CD: DG (Japan) POCG 9013-9021 |

Heimweh/Mörike-Lieder (Anders wird die Welt mit jedem Schritt)

| Berlin
September 1957 | Moore | LP: HMV ALP 1617-1619
LP: Electrola E 90018-90020
LP: EMI 1C 181 01470-01476
LP: EMI 1C 047 01247
CD: EMI CMS 763 5632 |

| Berlin
and Paris
December 1972-
June 1973 | Barenboim | LP: DG 2709 053/2740 113
CD: DG (Japan) POCG 9013-9021 |

Wolf Lieder/continued

Herbst (Nun ist es Herbst, die Blätter fallen)

Paris and Berlin January- November 1974	Barenboim	LP: DG 2709 066/2740 156 CD: DG (Japan) POCG 9013-9021

Herbstentschluss (Trübe Wolken, Herbstesluft)

Paris and Berlin January- November 1974	Barenboim	LP: DG 2709 066/2740 156 CD: DG (Japan) POCG 9013-9021

Herr, was trägt der Boden hier?/Spanisches Liederbuch

Berlin May 1958	Moore	LP: HMV ALP 1750/ASD 378/EX 29 04293 LP: Electrola E 90922/E 200 000 LP: EMI 1C 181 01470-01476
Berlin December 1966- January 1967	Moore	LP: DG SLPM 139 329-139 330 LP: DG 2707 035/2726 071 CD: DG 421 9342 CD: DG (Japan) POCG 9013-9021

Herz, verzage nicht geschwind/Spanisches Liederbuch

Berlin May 1958	Moore	LP: HMV ALP 1750/ASD 378 LP: Electrola E 90922/E 200 000 LP: EMI 1C 181 01470-01476
Berlin December 1966- January 1967	Moore	LP: DG SLPM 139 329-139 330 LP: DG 2707 035/2726 071 CD: DG 421 9342 CD: DG (Japan) POCG 9013-9021
Munich March and June 1990	Munich RO Soltesz	CD: Orfeo C219 911A

Heut' nacht erhob ich mich/Italienisches Liederbuch

Berlin 1949-1950	Klust	78: DG LM 68 458 LP: DG LPM 18 005
Berlin September 1965- February 1966	Moore	LP: EMI AN 210-211/SAN 210-211 LP: EMI 1C 165 01871-01872 CD: EMI CDM 763 7322
Berlin June 1975	Barenboim	LP: DG 2707 114 CD: DG 439 9752 CD: DG (Japan) POCG 9013-9021

Hoffärtig seid ihr, schönes Kind/Italienisches Liederbuch

Berlin 1949-1950	Klust	78: DG LM 68 456 LP: DG LPM 18 005
Salzburg August 1958	Werba	CD: Orfeo C220 901A/C339 930T
Berlin September- October 1958	Demus	LP: DG LPM 18 568-18 569/ SLPM 138 035-138 036 CD: DG 435 7522
Berlin September 1965- February 1966	Moore	LP: EMI AN 210-211/SAN 210-211 LP: EMI 1C 165 01871-01872 CD: EMI CDM 763 7322
Berlin June 1975	Barenboim	LP: DG 2707 114 CD: DG 439 9752 CD: DG (Japan) POCG 9013-9021

Ich esse nun mein Brot nicht trocken mehr/Italienisches Liederbuch

Berlin September 1965- February 1966	Moore	LP: EMI AN 210-211/SAN 210-211 LP: EMI 1C 165 01871-01872 CD: EMI CDM 763 7322

Ich fuhr über Meer/Spanisches Liederbuch

Berlin May 1958	Moore	LP: HMV ALP 1750/ASD 378 LP: Electrola E 90922/E 200 000 LP: EMI 1C 181 01470-01476
Berlin December 1966- January 1967	Moore	LP: DG SLPM 139 329-130 330 LP: DG 2707 035/2726 071 CD: DG 421 9342 CD: DG (Japan) POCG 9013-9021

Ich liess mir sagen/Italienisches Liederbuch

Salzburg August 1958	Werba	CD: Orfeo C220 901A/C339 930T
Berlin September- October 1958	Demus	LP: DG LPM 18 568-18 569/ SLPM 138 035-138 036 CD: DG 435 7522

Ich stand in dunklen Träumen

Feldkirch August 1986	Höll	CD: Claves CD 50 8706

Wolf Lieder/continued

Ihr seid die allerschönste weit und breit/Italienisches Liederbuch

Salzburg August 1958	Werba	CD: Orfeo C220 901A/C339 930T
Berlin September- October 1958	Demus	LP: DG LPM 18 568-18 569/ SLPM 138 035-138 036 CD: DG 435 7522
Berlin September 1965- February 1966	Moore	LP: EMI AN 210-211/SAN 210-211 LP: EMI 1C 165 01871-01872 CD: EMI CDM 763 7322
Berlin June 1975	Barenboim	LP: DG 2707 114 CD: DG 439 9752 CD: DG (Japan) POCG 9013-9021

Im Frühling/Mörike-Lieder (Hier lieg' ich auf dem Frühlingshügel)

Berlin September 1957	Moore	LP: HMV ALP 1617-1619 LP: Electrola E 90018-90020 LP: EMI 1C 181 01470-01476 CD: EMI CMS 763 5632
Salzburg July 1961	Moore	LP: Orfeo S140 855R CD: Orfeo C140 401A/C339 930T
Berlin and Paris	Barenboim	LP: DG 2709 053/2740 113 CD: DG (Japan) POCG 9013-9021
Innsbruck October 1973	Richter	LP: DG 2530 584
December 1972- June 1973		

In der Fremde I/Eichendorff-Lieder (Da fahr' ich still im Wagen)

Berlin May 1958	Moore	LP: HMV ALP 1778/ASD 356 LP: Electrola E 90989/STE 90989 LP: Electrola E 200 000 LP: EMI 1C 181 01470-01476
Paris and Berlin January 1974- November 1976	Barenboim	LP: DG 2709 067/2740 162 CD: DG 439 9752 CD: DG (Japan) POCG 9013-9021
Salzburg August 1975	Sawallisch	CD: Orfeo C185 891A/C339 930T
Feldkirch August 1986	Höll	CD: Claves CD 50 8706

Wolf Lieder/continued

In der Fremde II/Eichendorff-Lieder (Ich geh' durch die dunklen Gassen)

Paris and Berlin January 1974- November 1976	Barenboim	LP: DG 2709 067/2740 162 CD: DG 439 9732 CD: DG (Japan) POCG 9013-9021
Feldkirch August 1986	Höll	CD: Claves CD 50 8706

In der Fremde IV/Eichendorff-Lieder (Wolken, wälderwärts gegangen)

Paris and Berlin January 1974- November 1976	Barenboim	LP: DG 2709 067/2740 162 CD: DG 439 9732 CD: DG (Japan) POCG 9013-9021
Feldkirch August 1986	Höll	CD: Claves CD 50 8706

In der Frühe/Mörike-Lieder (Kein Schlaf noch kühlt das Auge mir)

	Moore	LP: HMV ALP 1143 Also issued on LP by Electrola
Berlin September 1957	Moore	LP: HMV ALP 1617-1619 LP: Electrola E 90018-90020 LP: EMI 1C 181 01470-01476 CD: EMI CMS 763 5632
Salzburg July 1961	Moore	LP: Orfeo S140 855R CD: Orfeo C140 401A/C339 930T
Berlin and Paris December 1972- June 1973	Barenboim	LP: DG 2709 053/2740 113 CD: DG 415 1922 CD: DG (Japan) POCG 9013-9021
Innsbruck October 1973	Richter	LP: DG 2530 584

Ja, die Schönst', ich sagt' es offen

Paris and Berlin January 1974- November 1976	Barenboim	LP: DG 2709 067/2740 162 CD: DG (Japan) POCG 9013-9021

Wolf Lieder/continued

Der Jäger/Mörike-Lieder (Drei Tage Regen fort und fort)

Berlin September 1957	Moore	LP: HMV ALP 1617-1619 LP: Electrola E 90018-90020 LP: EMI 1C 181 01470-01476 CD: EMI CMS 763 5632
Salzburg July 1961	Moore	LP: Orfeo S140 855R CD: Orfeo C140 401A/C339 930T
Berlin and Paris December 1972- June 1973	Barenboim	LP: DG 2709 053/2740 113 CD: DG (Japan) POCG 9013-9021
Innsbruck October 1973	Richter	LP: DG 2530 584

Jägerlied /Mörike-Lieder (Zierlich ist des Vogels Tritt im Schnee)

Berlin September 1957	Moore	LP: HMV ALP 1617-1619/EX 29 04293 LP: Electrola E 90018-90020 LP: EMI 1C 181 01470-01476 CD: EMI CMS 763 5632
Salzburg July 1961	Moore	LP: Orfeo S140 855R CD: Orfeo C140 401A/C339 930T
Berlin and Paris December 1972- June 1973	Barenboim	LP: DG 2709 053/2740 113 CD: DG 415 1922 CD: DG (Japan) POCG 9013-9021
Innsbruck October 1973	Richter	LP: DG 2530 584

Karwoche/Mörike-Lieder (O Woche, Zeugin heiliger Beschwerden!)

Berlin September 1957	Moore	LP: HMV ALP 1617-1619 LP: Electrola E 90018-90020 LP: EMI 1C 181 01470-01476 CD: EMI CMS 763 5632
Berlin and Paris December 1972- June 1973	Barenboim	LP: DG 2709 053/2740 113 CD: DG (Japan) POCG 9013-9021

Keine gleicht von allen Schönen

Berlin	Moore	LP: HMV ALP 1783/ASD 362
May 1958		LP: Electrola E 91002/STE 91002
		LP: EMI 1C 181 01470-01476/E 200 000

Paris	Barenboim	LP: DG 2709 067/2740 162
and Berlin		CD: DG (Japan) POCG 9013-9021
January 1974-		
November 1976		

Der Knabe und das Immlein/Mörike-Lieder (Im Weinberg auf der Höhe)

Berlin	Barenboim	LP: DG 2709 053/2740 113
and Paris		CD: DG (Japan) POCG 9013-9021
December 1972-		
June 1973		

Knabentod (Vom Berg der Knab', der zieht hinab)

Paris	Barenboim	LP: DG 2709 067/2740 162
and Berlin		CD: DG (Japan) POCG 9013-9021
January 1974-		
November 1976		

Komm' Liebchen komm', umwinde mir die Mütze!/Goethe-Lieder

Paris	Barenboim	LP: DG 2709 066/2740 156
and Berlin		CD: DG (Japan) POCG 9013-9021
January-		
November 1974		

Komm' o Tod, von Nacht umgeben/Spanisches Liederbuch

Berlin	Moore	LP: HMV ALP 1750/ASD 378
May 1958		LP: Electrola E 90922/E 200 000
		LP: EMI 1C 181 01470-01476

Berlin	Moore	LP: DG SLPM 139 329-139 330
December 1966-		LP: DG 2707 035/2726 071
January 1967		CD: DG 421 9342
		CD: DG (Japan) POCG 9013-9021

Der König bei der Krönung/Mörike-Lieder (Du angetraut am Altare)

Berlin	Moore	LP: HMV ALP 1783/ASD 362
April 1959		LP: Electrola E 91002/STE 91002
		LP: Electrola E 200 000
		LP: EMI 1C 181 01470-01476
		CD: EMI CMS 763 5632

Berlin	Barenboim	LP: DG 2709 053/2740 113
and Paris		CD: DG (Japan) POCG 9013-9021
December 1972-		
June 1973		

Königlich Gebet/Goethe-Lieder (Ha, ich bin der Herr der Welt!)

Berlin April 1960	Moore	LP: HMV ALP 1852-1853/ASD 424-425 LP: Electrola E 91072-91073/ STE 91072-91073/E 200 000 LP: EMI 1C 181 01470-01476
Paris and Berlin January- November 1974	Barenboim	LP: DG 2709 066/2740 156 CD: DG (Japan) POCG 9013-9021

Lass' sie nur geh'n, die so die Stolze spielt/Italienisches Liederbuch

Salzburg August 1958	Werba	CD: Orfeo C220 901A/C339 930T
Berlin September- October 1958	Demus	LP: DG LPM 18 568-18 569/ SLPM 138 035-138 036 CD: DG 435 7522
Berlin September 1965- February 1966	Moore	LP: EMI AN 210-211/SAN 210-211 LP: EMI 1C 165 01871-01872 CD: EMI CDM 763 7322
Berlin June 1975	Barenboim	LP: DG 2707 114 CD: DG 439 9752 CD: DG (Japan) POCG 9013-9021

Lebe wohl/Mörike-Lieder

London 1953	Moore	LP: HMV ALP 1143 Also issued on LP by Electrola
Berlin September 1957	Moore	LP: HMV ALP 1617-1619 LP: Electrola E 90018-90020 LP: EMI 1C 181 01470-01476 CD: EMI CMS 763 5632
Salzburg July 1961	Moore	LP: Orfeo S140 855R CD: Orfeo C140 401A/C339 930T
Berlin and Paris December 1972- June 1973	Barenboim	LP: DG 2709 053/2740 113 CD: DG (Japan) POCG 9013-9021
Innsbruck October 1973	Richter	LP: DG 2530 584

Liebchen, wo bist du? (Zaubrer bin ich, doch was frommt es?)

Paris and Berlin January 1974– November 1976	Barenboim	LP: DG 2709 067/2740 162 CD: DG (Japan) POCG 9013-9021

Lieber alles/Eichendorff-Lieder (Soldat sein ist gefährlich)

Berlin May 1958	Moore	LP: HMV ALP 1778/ASD 356 LP: Electrola E 90989/STE 90989 LP: Electrola E 200 000 LP: EMI 1C 181 01470-01476
Paris and Berlin January 1974– November 1976	Barenboim	LP: DG 2709 067/2740 162 CD: DG (Japan) POCG 9013-9021

Liebesbotschaft (Wolken, die ihr nach Osten eilt)

Paris and Berlin January 1974– November 1976	Barenboim	LP: DG 2709 067/2740 162 CD: DG (Japan) POCG 9013-9021

Liebesfrühling (Wie oft schon ward es Frühling wieder)

Paris and Berlin January 1974– November 1976	Barenboim	LP: DG 2709 067/2740 162 CD: DG (Japan) POCG 9013-9021

Liebesglück/Eichendorff-Lieder (Ich hab' ein Liebchen liebrecht von Herzen)

Berlin April 1960	Moore	LP: HMV ALP 1778/ASD 356/EX 29 04293 LP: Electrola E 90989/STE 90989 LP: Electrola E 200 000 LP: EMI 1C 181 01470-01476
Paris and Berlin January 1974– November 1976	Barenboim	LP: DG 2709 067/2740 162 CD: DG (Japan) POCG 9013-9021

Lied des transferierten Zettel (Die Schwalbe, die den Sommer bringt)

Berlin	Moore	LP: HMV ALP 1783/ASD 362
April 1959		LP: Electrola E 91002/STE 91002
		LP: Electrola E 200 000
		LP: EMI 1C 181 01470-01476

Paris	Barenboim	LP: DG 2709 067/2740 162
and Berlin		CD: DG (Japan) POCG 9013-9021
January 1974-		
November 1976		

Lied eines Verliebten/Mörike-Lieder (In aller Früh', ach, lang vor Tag)

Berlin	Moore	LP: HMV ALP 1617-1619
September 1957		LP: Electrola E 90018-90020
		LP: EMI 1C 181 01470-01476
		CD: EMI CMS 763 5632

Berlin	Barenboim	LP: DG 2709 053/2740 113
and Paris		CD: DG (Japan) POCG 9013-9021
December 1972-		
June 1973		

Lied vom Winde/Mörike-Lieder (sausewind! Brausewind!)

Berlin	Barenboim	LP: DG 2709 053/2740 113
and Paris		CD: DG (Japan) POCG 9013-9021
December 1972-		
June 1973		

Locken, haltet mich gefangen/Goethe-Lieder

Paris	Barenboim	LP: DG 2709 066/2740 156
and Berlin		CD: DG (Japan) POCG 9013-9021
January-		
November 1974		

Mädchen mit dem roten Mündchen

Paris	Barenboim	LP: DG 2709 066/2740 156
and Berlin		CD: DG (Japan) POCG 9013-9021
January-		
November 1974		

| Feldkirch | Höll | CD: Claves CD 50 8706 |
| August 1986 | | |

Mein Liebchen, wir sassen beisammen

| Feldkirch | Höll | CD: Claves CD 50 8706 |
| August 1986 | | |

Wolf Lieder/continued

Michelangelo-Lieder: Wohl denk' ich oft; Alles endet, was entsteht; Fühlt
meine Seele das ersehnte Licht

Berlin   Moore   LP: HMV ALP 1783/ASD 362
April 1959   LP: Electrola E 91002/STE 91002
                                           LP: Electrola E 200 000
                                           LP: EMI 1C 181 01470-01476
                                           CD: EMI CMS 763 5632

Paris   Barenboim   LP: DG 2709 067/2740 162
and Berlin   CD: DG 439 9752
January 1974-   CD: DG (Japan) POCG 9013-9021
November 1976

Munich   Munich RO   CD: Orfeo C219 911A
March and   Soltesz   Orchestration by Borg
June 1990

Mit schwarzen Segeln segelt mein Schiff

Paris   Barenboim   LP: DG 2709 066/2740 156
and Berlin   CD: DG (Japan) POCG 9013-9021
January-
November 1974

Feldkirch   Höll   CD: Claves CD 50 8706
August 1986

Mir träumte von einem Königskind

Feldkirch   Höll   CD: Claves CD 50 8706
August 1986

Der Mond hat eine schwere Klag' erhoben/Italienisches Liederbuch

Berlin   Klust   78: DG LM 68 455
1949-1950   LP: DG LPM 18 005

Salzburg   Werba   CD: Orfeo C220 901A/C339 930T
August 1958

Berlin   Demus   LP: DG LPM 18 568-18 569/
September-   SLPM 138 035-138 036
October 1958   LP: DG 9108/109 108
                                           CD: DG 435 7522

Berlin   Moore   LP: EMI AN 210-211/SAN 210-211
September 1965-   LP: EMI 1C 165 01871-01872
February 1966

Berlin   Barenboim   LP: DG 2707 114
June 1975   CD: DG 435 9752
                                           CD: DG (Japan) POCG 9013-9021

Morgenstimmung (Bald ist der Nacht ein End' gemacht)

Berlin April 1959	Moore	LP: HMV ALP 1783/ASD 362 LP: Electrola E 91002/STE 91002 LP: Electrola E 200 000 LP: EMI 1C 181 01470-01476
Paris and Berlin January 1974- November 1976	Barenboim	LP: DG 2709 067/2740 162 CD: DG (Japan) POCG 9013-9021

Der Musikant/Eichendorff-Lieder (Wandern lieb' ich für mein Leben)

Berlin April 1960	Moore	LP: HMV ALP 1778/ASD 356 LP: Electrola E 90989/STE 90989 LP: Electrola E 200 000/1C 047 01247 LP: EMI 1C 181 01470-01476
Paris and Berlin January 1974- November 1976	Barenboim	LP: DG 2709 067/2740 162 CD: DG (Japan) POCG 9013-9021
Salzburg August 1975	Sawallisch	CD: Orfeo C185 891A/C339 930T

Nach dem Abschiede (Dunkel sind nun alle Gassen)

Paris and Berlin January 1974- November 1976	Barenboim	LP: DG 2709 067/2740 162 CD: DG (Japan) POCG 9013-9021

Die Nacht/Eichendorff-Lieder (Nacht ist wie ein stilles Meer)

Berlin April 1960	Moore	LP: HMV ALP 1778/ASD 356 LP: Electrola E 90989/STE 90989 LP: Electrola E 200 000 LP: EMI 1C 181 01470-01476
Paris and Berlin January 1974- November 1976	Barenboim	LP: DG 2709 067/2740 162 CD: DG (Japan) POCG 9013-9021

Nachruf/Eichendorff-Lieder (Du liebe treue Laute)

Berlin April 1960	Moore	LP: HMV ALP 1778/ASD 356 LP: Electrola E 90989/STE 90989 LP: ELectrola E 200 000 LP: EMI 1C 181 01470-01476
Paris and Berlin January 1974– November 1976	Barenboim	LP: DG 2709 067/2740 162 CD: DG 439 9752 CD: DG (Japan) POCG 9013-9021
Salzburg August 1975	Sawallisch	CD: Orfeo C185 891A/C339 930T

Nachtgruss (In dem Himmel ruht die Erde)

Paris and Berlin January 1974– November 1976	Barenboim	LP: DG 2709 067/2740 162 CD: DG (Japan) POCG 9013-9021
Feldkirch August 1986	Höll	CD: Claves CD 50 8706

Nachtzauber/Eichendorff-Lieder (Hörst du nicht die Quellen rauschen?)

Berlin April 1960	Moore	LP: HMV ALP 1778/ASD 356 LP: Electrola E 90989/STE 90989 LP: Electrola E 200 000 LP: EMI 1C 181 01470-01476
Paris and Berlin January 1974– November 1976	Barenboim	LP: DG 2709 067/2740 162 CD: DG (Japan) POCG 9013-9021
Salzburg August 1975	Sawallisch	CD: Orfeo C185 891A/C339 930T

Der neue Amadis/Goethe-Lieder (Als ich noch ein Knabe war)

Berlin April 1960	Moore	LP: HMV ALP 1852-1853/ASD 424-425 LP: Electrola E 91072-91073/ STE 91072-91073/E 200 000 LP: EMI 1C 181 01470-01476
Paris and Berlin January– November 1974	Barenboim	LP: DG 2709 066/2740 156 CD: DG (Japan) POCG 9013-9021

Wolf Lieder/continued

Neue Liebe/Mörike-Lieder (Kann auch ein Mensch des andern auf der Erde)

Berlin September 1957	Moore	LP: HMV ALP 1617-1619 LP: Electrola E 90018-90020 LP: EMI 1C 181 01470-01476 CD: EMI CMS 763 5632
Salzburg July 1961	Moore	LP: Orfeo S140 855R CD: Orfeo C140 401A/C339 930T
Berlin and Paris December 1972- June 1973	Barenboim	LP: DG 2709 053/2740 113 CD: DG (Japan) POCG 9013-9021
Innsbruck October 1973	Richter	LP: DG 2530 584

Nicht Gelegenheit macht Diebe/Goethe-Lieder

Paris and Berlin January- November 1974	Barenboim	LP: DG 2709 066/2740 156 CD: DG (Japan) POCG 9013-9021

Nicht länger kann ich singen/Italienisches Liederbuch

Berlin 1949-1950	Klust	78: DG LM 68 458 LP: DG LPM 18 005
Salzburg August 1958	Werba	CD: Orfeo C220 901A/C339 930T
Berlin September- October 1958	Demus	LP: DG LPM 18 568-18 569/ SLPM 138 035-138 036 CD: DG 435 7522
Berlin September 1965- February 1966	Moore	LP: EMI AN 210-211/SAN 210-211 LP: EMI 1C 165 01871-01872 CD: EMI CDM 763 7322
Berlin June 1975	Barenboim	LP: DG 2707 114 CD: DG 439 9752 CD: DG (Japan) POCG 9013-9021

Nimmersatte Liebe/Mörike-Lieder (So ist die Lieb'!)

Berlin September 1957	Moore	LP: HMV ALP 1617-1619 LP: Electrola E 90018-90020 LP: EMI 1C 181 01470-01476 CD: EMI CMS 763 5632
Berlin and Paris December 1972- June 1973	Barenboim	LP: DG 2709 053/2740 113 CD: DG 415 1922 CD: DG (Japan) POCG 9013-9021

Nun bin ich dein, du aller Blumen Blume/Spanisches Liederbuch

Berlin May 1958	Moore	LP: HMV ALP 1750/ASD 378 LP: Electrola E 90922/E 200 000 LP: EMI 1C 181 01470-01476
Berlin December 1966- January 1967	Moore	LP: DG SLPM 139 329-139 330 LP: DG 2707 035/2726 071 CD: DG 421 9342 CD: DG (Japan) POCG 9013-9021

Nun lass' uns Frieden schliessen/Italienisches Liederbuch

Berlin 1949-1950	Klust	78: DG LM 68 455 LP: DG LPM 18 005
Salzburg August 1958	Werba	CD: Orfeo C220 901A/C339 930T
Berlin September- October 1958	Demus	LP: DG LPM 18 568-18 569/ SLPM 138 035-138 036 LP: DG 9108/109 108 CD: DG 435 7522
Berlin September 1965- February 1966	Moore	LP: EMI AN 210-211/SAN 210-211 LP: EMI 1C 165 01871-01872 CD: EMI CDM 763 7322
Berlin June 1975	Barenboim	LP: DG 2707 114 CD: DG 439 9752 CD: DG (Japan) POCG 9013-9021

Nun wandre, Maria/Spanisches Liederbuch

Berlin May 1958	Moore	LP: HMV ALP 1750/ASD 378/ASD 2549 LP: Electrola E 90922/E 200 000 LP: EMI 1C 181 01470-01476
Berlin December 1966- January 1967	Moore	LP: DG SLPM 139 329-139 330 LP: DG 2707 035/2726 071 CD: DG 421 9342 CD: DG (Japan) POCG 9013-9021

O wüsstest du, wieviel ich deinetwegen/Italienisches Liederbuch

Salzburg August 1958	Werba	CD: Orfeo C220 901A/C339 930T
Berlin September- October 1958	Demus	LP: DG LPM 18 568-18 569/ SLPM 138 035-138 036 CD: DG 435 7522
Berlin September 1965- February 1966	Moore	LP: EMI AN 210-211/SAN 210-211 LP: EMI 1C 165 01871-01872 CD: EMI CDM 763 7322
Berlin June 1975	Barenboim	LP: DG 2707 114 CD: DG 439 9752 CD: DG (Japan) POCG 9013-9021

Wolf Lieder/continued

Ob der Koran von Ewigkeit sei?/Goethe-Lieder

London 1953	Moore	LP: HMV ALP 1143 Also issued on LP by Electrola
Berlin April 1960	Moore	LP: HMV ALP 1852-1853/ASD 424-425 LP: Electrola E 91072-91073/ STE 91072-91073/E 200 000 LP: EMI 1C 181 01470-01476
Paris and Berlin January- November 1974	Barenboim	LP: DG 2709 066/2740 156 CD: DG 415 1922 CD: DG (Japan) POCG 9013-9021

Peregrina I & II/Mörike-Lieder (Der Spiegel dieser treuen braunen Augen);
Warum, Geliebte, denk' ich dein?)

Berlin September 1957	Moore	LP: HMV ALP 1617-1619 LP: Electrola E 90018-90020 LP: EMI 1C 181 01470-01476 CD: EMI CMS 763 5632
Salzburg July 1961	Moore	LP: Orfeo S140 855R CD: Orfeo C140 401A/C339 930T
Berlin and Paris December 1972- June 1973	Barenboim	LP: DG 2709 053/2740 113 CD: DG (Japan) POCG 9013-9021
Innsbruck October 1973	Richter	LP: DG 2530 584

Phänomen/Goethe-Lieder (Wenn zu der Regenwand Phöbus sich gattet)

London 1953	Moore	LP: HMV ALP 1143 Also issued on LP by Electrola
Berlin April 1960	Moore	LP: HMV ALP 1852-1853/ASD 424-425 LP: Electrola E 91072-91073/ STE 91072-91073/E 200 000 LP: EMI 1C 181 01470-01476
Paris and Berlin January- November 1974	Barenboim	LP: DG 2709 066/2740 156 CD: DG (Japan) POCG 9013-9021

Prometheus/Goethe-Lieder (Bedecke deinen Himmel, Zeus!)

Berlin April 1960	Moore	LP: HMV ALP 1852-1853/ASD 424-425 LP: Electrola E 91072-91073/ STE 91072-91073/E 200 000 LP: EMI 1C 181 01470-01476
Paris and Berlin January- November 1974	Barenboim	LP: DG 2709 066/2740 156 CD: DG (Japan) POCG 9013-9021
Munich March and June 1990	Munich RO Soltesz	CD: Orfeo C219 911A <u>Wolf's orchestration</u>

Der Rattenfänger/Goethe-Lieder (Ich bin der wohlbekannte Sänger)

Berlin April 1960	Moore	LP: HMV ALP 1852-1853/ASD 424-425 LP: Electrola E 91072-91073/ STE 91072-91073/E 200 000 LP: EMI 1C 181 01470-01476/SHZE 219
Paris and Berlin January- November 1974	Barenboim	LP: DG 2709 066/2740 156 CD: DG 415 1922 CD: DG (Japan) POCG 9013-9021

Ritter Kurts Brautfahrt/Goethe-Lieder (Mit des Bräutigams Behagen)

Berlin April 1960	Moore	LP: HMV ALP 1852-1853/ASD 424-425 LP: Electrola E 91072-91073/ STE 91072-91073/E 200 000 LP: EMI 1C 181 01470-01476
Paris and Berlin January- November 1974	Barenboim	LP: DG 2709 066/2740 156 CD: DG (Japan) POCG 9013-9021

Rückkehr/Eichendorff-Lieder (Mit meinem Saitenspiele)

Paris and Berlin January 1974- November 1976	Barenboim	LP: DG 2709 067/2740 162 CD: DG 439 9752 CD: DG (Japan) POCG 9013-9021
Feldkirch August 1986	Höll	CD: Claves CD 50 8706

Wolf Lieder/continued

Sankt Nepomuks Vorabend/Goethe-Lieder (Lichtlein schwimmen auf dem Strome)

Berlin April 1960	Moore	LP: HMV ALP 1852-1853/ASD 424-425 LP: Electrola E 91072-91073/ STE 91072-91073/E 200 000 LP: EMI 1C 181 01470-01476
Paris and Berlin January- November 1974	Barenboim	LP: DG 2709 066/2740 156 CD: DG (Japan) POCG 9013-9021

Der Sänger/Goethe-Lieder (Was hör' ich draussen vor dem Tor?)

Berlin April 1960	Moore	LP: HMV ALP 1852-1853/ASD 424-425 LP: Electrola E 91072-91073/ STE 91072-91073/E 200 000 LP: EMI 1C 181 01470-01476/SHZE 219
Paris and Berlin January- November 1974	Barenboim	LP: DG 2709 066/2740 156 CD: DG (Japan) POCG 9013-9021

Der Schäfer/Goethe-Lieder (Es war ein fauler Schäfer)

Berlin April 1960	Moore	LP: HMV ALP 1852-1853/ASD 424-425 LP: Electrola E 91072-91073/ STE 91072-91073/E 200 000 LP: EMI 1C 181 01470-01476
Paris and Berlin January- November 1974	Barenboim	LP: DG 2709 066/2740 156 CD: DG (Japan) POCG 9013-9021

Schlafendes Jesuskind/Mörike-Lieder (Sohn der Jungfrau, Himmelskind!)

Berlin September 1957	Moore	LP: HMV ALP 1617-1619 LP: Electrola E 90018-90020 LP: EMI 1C 181 01470-01476 LP: EMI EX 29 04293 CD: EMI CMS 763 5632
Berlin and Paris December 1972- June 1973	Barenboim	LP: DG 2709 053/2740 113 CD: DG (Japan) POCG 9013-9021

Der Scholar/Eichendorff-Lieder (Bei dem angenehmen Wetter)

Berlin May 1958	Moore	LP: HMV ALP 1778/ASD 356 LP: Electrola E 90989/STE 90989 LP: Electrola E 200 000 LP: EMI 1C 181 01470-01476
Paris and Berlin January 1974- November 1976	Barenboim	LP: DG 2709 067/2740 162 CD: DG (Japan) POCG 9013-9021

Schon streckt' ich aus im Bett die müden Glieder/Italienisches Liederbuch

Salzburg August 1958	Werba	CD: Orfeo C220 901A/C339 930T
Berlin September- October 1958	Demus	LP: DG LPM 18 568-18 569/ SLPM 138 035-138 036 CD: DG 435 7522
Berlin September 1965- February 1966	Moore	LP: EMI AN 210-211/SAN 210-211 LP: EMI 1C 165 01871-01872 CD: EMI CDM 763 7322
Berlin June 1975	Barenboim	LP: DG 2707 114 CD: DG 439 9752 CD: DG (Japan) POCG 9013-9021

Der Schreckenberger/Eichendorff-Lieder (Aufs Wohlsein meiner Dame)

Berlin May 1958	Moore	LP: HMV ALP 1778/ASD 356 LP: Electrola E 90989/STE 90989 LP: Electrola E 200 000 LP: EMI 1C 181 01470-01476
Paris and Berlin January 1974- November 1976	Barenboim	LP: DG 2709 067/2740 162 CD: DG (Japan) POCG 9013-9021

Der Schwalben Heimkehr (Wenn die Schwalben heimwärts zieh'n)

Paris and Berlin January 1974- November 1976	Barenboim	LP: DG 2709 067/2740 162 CD: DG (Japan) POCG 9013-9021

Seemanns Abschied/Eichendorff-Lieder (Ade, mein Schatz!)

Berlin May 1958	Moore	LP: HMV ALP 1778/ASD 356 LP: Electrola E 90989/STE 90989 LP: Electrola E 200 000 LP: EMI 1C 181 01470-01476
Paris and Berlin January 1974- November 1976	Barenboim	LP: DG 2709 067/2740 162 CD: DG (Japan) POCG 9013-9021
Salzburg August 1975	Sawallisch	CD: Orfeo C185 891A/C339 930T

Selbstgeständnis/Mörike-Lieder (Ich bin meiner Mutter einzig Kind)

Berlin September 1957	Moore	LP: HMV ALP 1617-1619 LP: Electrola E 90018-90020 LP: EMI 1C 181 01470-01476 CD: EMI CMS 763 5632
Berlin and Paris December 1972- June 1973	Barenboim	LP: DG 2709 053/2740 113 CD: DG 415 1922 CD: DG (Japan) POCG 9013-9021

Selig Ihr Blinden, die Ihr nicht zu schauen/Italienisches Liederbuch

Berlin 1949-1950	Klust	78: DG LM 68 455 LP: DG LPM 18 005
Salzburg August 1958	Werba	CD: Orfeo C220 901A/C339 930T
Berlin September- October 1958	Demus	LP: DG LPM 18 568-18 569/ SLPM 138 035-138 036 CD: DG 435 7522
Berlin September 1965- February 1966	Moore	LP: EMI AN 210-211/SAN 210-211 LP: EMI 1C 165 01871-01872 CD: EMI CDM 763 7322
Berlin June 1975	Barenboim	LP: DG 2707 114 CD: DG 439 9752 CD: DG (Japan) POCG 9013-9021

Seltsam ist Juanas Weise/Spanisches Liederbuch

Berlin May 1958	Moore	LP: HMV ALP 1750/ASD 378 LP: Electrola E 90922/E 200 000 LP: EMI 1C 181 01470-01476
Berlin December 1966- January 1967	Moore	LP: DG SLPM 139 329-139 330 LP: DG 2707 035/2726 071 CD: DG 421 9342 CD: DG (Japan) POCG 9013-9021

Seufzer/Mörike-Lieder (Dein Liebesfeuer, ach Herr, wie teuer)

Berlin September 1957	Moore	LP: HMV ALP 1617-1619 LP: Electrola E 90018-90020 LP: EMI 1C 181 01470-01476 CD: EMI CMS 763 5632
Berlin and Paris December 1972- June 1973	Barenboim	LP: DG 2709 053/2740 113 CD: DG (Japan) POCG 9013-9021
Munich March and June 1990	Munich RO Soltesz	CD: Orfeo C219 911A

Sie haben heut' abend Gesellschaft

Feldkirch August 1986	Höll	CD: Claves CD 50 8706

Sie haben wegen der Trunkenheit/Goethe-Lieder

Berlin April 1960	Moore	LP: HMV ALP 1852-1853/ASD 424-425 LP: Electrola E 91072-91073/ STE 91072-91073/E 200 000 LP: EMI 1C 181 01470-01476

Skolie (Reich' den Pokal mir schäumenden Weines voll)

Paris and Berlin January 1974- November 1976	Barenboim	LP: DG 2709 067/2740 162 CD: DG (Japan) POCG 9013-9021

Solang man nüchtern ist/Goethe-Lieder

Berlin April 1960	Moore	LP: HMV ALP 1852-1853/ASD 424-425 LP: Electrola E 91072-91073/ STE 91072-91073/E 200 000 LP: EMI 1C 181 01470-01476
Paris and Berlin January- November 1974	Barenboim	LP: DG 2709 066/2740 156 CD: DG (Japan) POCG 9013-9021

Wolf Lieder/continued

Der Soldat I & II/Eichendorff-Lieder (Ist auch schmuck nicht mein Rösslein;
Wagen musst du und flüchtig erbeuten)

Berlin	Moore	LP: HMV ALP 1778/ASD 356
May 1958		LP: Electrola E 90989/STE 90989
		LP: Electrola E 200 000
		LP: EMI 1C 181 01470-01476

Paris   Barenboim   LP: DG 2709 067/2740 162
and Berlin   CD: DG (Japan) POCG 9013-9021
January 1974-
November 1976

Sonne der Schlummerlosen

Berlin   Moore   LP: HMV ALP 1783/ASD 362
April 1959   LP: ELectrola E 91002/STE 91002
                                LP: Electrola E 200 000
                                LP: EMI 1C 181 01470-01476

Paris   Barenboim   LP: DG 2709 067/2740 162
and Berlin   CD: DG (Japan) POCG 9013-9021
January 1974-
November 1976

Spätherbstnebel, kalte Träume

Paris   Barenboim   LP: DG 2709 066/2740 156
and Berlin   CD: DG (Japan) POCG 9013-9021
January-
November 1974

Feldkirch   Höll   CD: Claves CD 50 8706
August 1986

Spottlied/Goethe-Lieder (Ich armer Teufel, Herr Baron)

Berlin   Moore   LP: HMV ALP 1852-1853/ASD 424-425
April 1960   LP: Electrola E 91072-91073/
                                    STE 91072-91073/E 200 000
                                LP: EMI 1C 181 01470-01476

Paris   Barenboim   LP: DG 2709 066/2740 156
and Berlin   CD: DG (Japan) POCG 9013-9021
January-
November 1974

Ständchen (Alles wiegt die stille Nacht)

Paris and Berlin January 1974- November 1976	Barenboim	LP: DG 2709 067/2740 162 CD: DG (Japan) POCG 9013-9021

Ständchen (Komm' in die stille Nacht)

Paris and Berlin January 1974- November 1976	Barenboim	LP: DG 2709 067/2740 162 CD: DG (Japan) POCG 9013-9021

Das Ständchen/Eichendorff-Lieder (Auf die Dächer zwischen blassen Wolken)

Berlin May 1958	Moore	LP: HMV ALP 1778/ASD 356 LP: Electrola E 90989/STE 90989 LP: Electrola E 200 000 LP: EMI 1C 181 01470-01476
Paris and Berlin January 1974- November 1976	Barenboim	LP: DG 2709 067/2740 162 CD: DG (Japan) POCG 9013-9021

Ein Ständchen euch zu bringen kam ich her/Italienisches Liederbuch

Berlin 1949-1950	Klust	78: DG LM 68 455 LP: DG LPM 18 005
Salzburg August 1958	Werba	CD: Orfeo C220 901A/C339 930T
Berlin September- October 1958	Demus	LP: DG LPM 18 568-18 569/ SLPM 138 035-138 036 CD: DG 435 7522
Berlin September 1965- February 1966	Moore	LP: EMI AN 210-211/SAN 210-211 LP: EMI 1C 165 01871-01872 CD: EMI CDM 763 7322
Berlin June 1975	Barenboim	LP: DG 2707 114 CD: DG 439 9752 CD: DG (Japan) POCG 9013-9021

Sterb' ich, so hüllt in Blumen meine Glieder/Italienisches Liederbuch

Berlin 1949-1950	Klust	78: DG LM 68 457 LP: DG LPM 18 005
Salzburg August 1958	Werba	CD: Orfeo C220 901A/C339 930T
Berlin September- October 1958	Demus	LP: DG LPM 18 568-18 569/ SLPM 138 035-138 036 CD: DG 435 7522
Berlin September 1965- February 1966	Moore	LP: EMI AN 210-211/SAN 210-211 LP: EMI 1C 165 01871-01872 CD: EMI CDM 763 7322
Berlin June 1975	Barenboim	LP: DG 2707 114 CD: DG 439 9752 CD: DG (Japan) POCG 9013-9021
Munich March and June 1990	Munich RO Soltesz	CD: Orfeo C219 911A Orchestration by Reger

Storchenbotschaft/Mörike-Lieder (Des Schäfers sein Haus und das steht auf zwei Rad)

Berlin September 1957	Moore	45: HMV 7ER 5044 LP: HMV ALP 1617-1619 LP: Electrola E 90018-90020 LP: EMI 1C 181 01470-01476 CD: EMI CMS 763 5632
Salzburg July 1961	Moore	LP: Orfeo S140 855R CD: Orfeo C140 401A/C339 930T
Berlin and Paris December 1972- June 1973	Barenboim	LP: DG 2709 053/2740 113 CD: DG 415 1922 CD: DG (Japan) POCG 9013-9021
Innsbruck October 1973	Richter	LP: DG 2530 584

Wolf Lieder/continued

Der Tambour/Mörike-Lieder (Wenn meine Mutter hexen könnt')

Berlin September 1957	Moore	45: HMV 7ER 5044 LP: HMV ALP 1617-1619 LP: Electrola E 90018-90020 LP: EMI 1C 181 01470-01476 CD: EMI CMS 763 5632
Berlin and Paris December 1972- June 1973	Barenboim	LP: DG 2709 053/2740 113 CD: DG 415 1922 CD: DG (Japan) POCG 9013-9021

Tief im Herzen trag' ich Pein/Spanisches Liederbuch

Berlin May 1958	Moore	LP: HMV ALP 1750/ASD 378 LP: Electrola E 90922/E 200 000 LP: EMI 1C 181 01470-01476
Berlin December 1966- January 1967	Moore	LP: DG SLPM 139 329-139 330 LP: DG 2707 035/2726 071 CD: DG 421 9342 CD: DG (Japan) POCG 9013-9021

Treibe nur mit Lieben Spott/Spanisches Liederbuch

Berlin May 1958	Moore	LP: HMV ALP 1750/ASD 378 LP: Electrola E 90922/E 200 000 LP: EMI 1C 181 01470-01476
Berlin December 1966- January 1967	Moore	LP: DG SLPM 139 329-139 330 LP: DG 2707 035/2726 071 CD: DG 421 9342 CD: DG (Japan) POCG 9013-9021

Trunken müssen wir alle sein/Goethe-Lieder

Berlin April 1960	Moore	LP: HMV ALP 1852-1853/ASD 424-425 LP: Electrola E 91072-91073/ STE 91072-91073/E 200 000 LP: EMI 1C 181 01470-01476
Paris and Berlin January- November 1974	Barenboim	LP: DG 2709 066/2740 156 CD: DG 415 1922 CD: DG (Japan) POCG 9013-9021

Ueber Nacht kommt still das Leid

Berlin April 1959	Moore	LP: HMV ALP 1783/ASD 362 LP: Electrola E 91002/STE 91002 LP: Electrola E 200 000 LP: EMI 1C 181 01470-01476
Paris and Berlin January 1974- November 1976	Barenboim	LP: DG 2709 067/2740 162 CD: DG (Japan) POCG 9013-9021

Um Mitternacht/Mörike-Lieder (Gelassen stieg die Nacht ans Land)

Berlin September 1957	Moore	LP: HMV ALP 1617-1619 LP: Electrola E 90018-90020 LP: EMI 1C 181 01470-01476 CD: EMI CMS 763 5632
Salzburg July 1961	Moore	LP: Orfeo S140 855R CD: Orfeo C140 401A/C339 930T
Berlin and Paris December 1972- June 1973	Barenboim	LP: DG 2709 053/2740 113 CD: DG (Japan) POCG 9013-9021

Und schläfst du, mein Mädchen/Spanisches Liederbuch

Berlin May 1958	Moore	LP: HMV ALP 1750/ASD 378 LP: Electrola E 90922/E 200 000 LP: EMI 1C 181 01470-01476
Berlin December 1966- January 1967	Moore	LP: DG SLPM 139 329-139 330 LP: DG 2707 035/2726 071 CD: DG 421 9342 CD: DG (Japan) POCG 9013-9021

Und steht ihr früh am Morgen auf vom Bette/Italienisches Liederbuch

Berlin 1949-1950	Klust	78: DG LM 68 457 LP: DG LPM 18 005
Salzburg August 1958	Werba	CD: Orfeo C220 901A/C339 930T
Berlin September- October 1958	Demus	LP: DG LPM 18 568-18 569/ SLPM 138 035-138 036 CD: DG 435 7522
Berlin September 1965- February 1966	Moore	LP: EMI AN 210-211/SAN 210-211 LP: EMI 1C 165 01871-01872 CD: EMI CDM 763 7322
Berlin June 1975	Barenboim	LP: DG 2707 114 CD: DG 439 9752 CD: DG (Japan) POCG 9013-9021

Und willst du deinen Liebsten sterben sehen/Italienisches Liederbuch

Berlin 1949-1950	Klust	78: DG LM 68 456 LP: DG LPM 18 005
Salzburg August 1958	Werba	CD: Orfeo C220 901A/C339 930T
Berlin September- October 1958	Demus	LP: DG LPM 18 568-18 569/ SLPM 138 035-138 036 LP: DG 9108/109 108/135 026 CD: DG 435 7522
Berlin September 1965- February 1966	Moore	LP: EMI AN 210-211/SAN 210-211 LP: EMI 1C 165 01871-01872 CD: EMI CDM 763 7322
Berlin June 1975	Barenboim	LP: DG 2707 114 CD: DG 439 9752 CD: DG (Japan) POCG 9013-9021
Munich March and June 1990	Munich RO Soltesz	CD: Orfeo C219 911A

Unfall/Eichendorff-Lieder (Ich ging bei Nacht einst über Land)

Berlin May 1958	Moore	LP: HMV ALP 1778/ASD 356 LP: Electrola E 90989/STE 90989 LP: Electrola E 200 000 LP: EMI 1C 181 01470-01476
Paris and Berlin January 1974- November 1976	Barenboim	LP: DG 2709 067/2740 162 CD: DG (Japan) POCG 9013-9021

Wolf Lieder/continued

Verborgenheit/Mörike-Lieder (Lass', o Welt, o lass' mich sein!)

Berlin September 1957	Moore	LP: HMV ALP 1617-1619 LP: Electrola E 90018-90020 LP: EMI 1C 181 01470-01476 CD: EMI CMS 763 5632
Berlin and Paris December 1972- June 1973	Barenboim	LP: DG 2709 053/2740 113 CD: DG 415 1922 CD: DG (Japan) POCG 9013-9021
Innsbruck October 1973	Richter	LP: DG 2530 584

Verschwiegene Liebe/Eichendorff-Lieder (Ueber Wipfel und Saaten)

London 1953	Moore	LP: HMV ALP 1143 Also issued on LP by Electrola
Berlin May 1958	Moore	LP: HMV ALP 1778/ASD 356 LP: Electrola E 90989/E 70415/ STE 90989/STE 70415/E 200 000 LP: EMI 1C 181 01470-01476
Paris and Berlin January 1974- November 1976	Barenboim	LP: DG 2709 067/2740 162 CD: DG (Japan) POCG 9013-9021
Salzburg August 1975	Sawallisch	CD: Orfeo C185 891A/C339 930T

Der verzweifelte Liebhaber/Eichendorff-Lieder (Studieren will nichts bringen)

Berlin May 1958	Moore	LP: HMV ALP 1778/ASD 356 LP: Electrola E 90989/STE 90989 LP: Electrola E 200 000 LP: EMI 1C 181 01470-01476
Paris and Berlin January 1974- November 1976	Barenboim	LP: DG 2709 067/2740 162 CD: DG (Japan) POCG 9013-9021
Salzburg August 1975	Sawallisch	CD: Orfeo C185 891A/C339 930T

Wolf Lieder/continued

Wächterlied auf der Wartburg (Schwingt euch auf, Posaunenchor!)

| Paris and Berlin January 1974– November 1976 | Barenboim | LP: DG 2709 067/2740 162 CD: DG (Japan) POCG 9013-9021 |

Wanderers Nachtlied (Der du von dem Himmel bist)

| Berlin April 1959 | Moore | LP: HMV ALP 1783/ASD 362 LP: Electrola E 91002/STE 91002 LP: Electrola E 200 000 LP: EMI 1C 181 01470-01476 |

| Paris and Berlin January– November 1974 | Barenboim | LP: DG 2709 066/2740 156 CD: DG (Japan) POCG 9013-9021 |

Was für ein Lied soll dir gesungen werden?/Italienisches Liederbuch

| Berlin 1949-1950 | Klust | 78: DG LM 68 457 LP: DG LPM 18 005 |

| Salzburg August 1958 | Werba | CD: Orfeo C220 901A/C339 930T |

| Berlin September– October 1958 | Demus | LP: DG LPM 18 568-18 569/ SLPM 138 035-138 036 CD: DG 435 7522 |

| Berlin September 1965– February 1966 | Moore | LP: EMI AN 210-211/SAN 210-211 LP: EMI 1C 165 01871-01872 CD: EMI CDM 763 7322 |

| Berlin June 1975 | Barenboim | LP: DG 2707 114 CD: DG 439 9752 CD: DG (Japan) POCG 9013-9021 |

Was in der Schenke waren heute/Goethe-Lieder

| Berlin April 1960 | Moore | LP: HMV ALP 1852-1853/ASD 424-425 LP: Electrola E 91072-91073/ STE 91072-91073/E 200 000 LP: EMI 1C 181 01470-01476 |

| Paris and Berlin January– November 1974 | Barenboim | LP: DG 2709 066/2740 156 CD: DG (Japan) POCG 9013-9021 |

Wenn du mich mit den Augen streifst/Italienisches Liederbuch

Salzburg August 1958	Werba	CD: Orfeo C220 901A/C339 930T
Berlin September- October 1958	Demus	LP: DG LPM 18 568-18 569/ SLPM 138 035-138 036 CD: DG 435 7522
Berlin September 1965- February 1966	Moore	LP: EMI AN 210-211/SAN 210-211 LP: EMI 1C 165 01871-01872 CD: EMI CDM 763 7322
Berlin June 1975	Barenboim	LP: DG 2707 114 CD: DG 439 9752 CD: DG (Japan) POCG 9013-9021

Wenn du zu den Blumen gehst/Spanisches Liederbuch

Berlin May 1958	Moore	LP: HMV ALP 1750/ASD 378 LP: Electrola E 90922/E 200 000 LP: EMI 1C 181 01470-01476
Berlin December 1966- January 1967	Moore	LP: DG SLPM 139 329-139 330 LP: DG 2707 035/2726 071 CD: DG 421 9342 CD: DG (Japan) POCG 9013-9021

Wenn ich dein gedenke/Goethe-Lieder

Paris and Berlin January- November 1974	Barenboim	LP: DG 2709 066/2740 156 CD: DG (Japan) POCG 9013-9021

Wenn ich in deine Augen sehe

Paris and Berlin Janauary- November 1974	Barenboim	LP: DG 2709 066/2740 156 CD: DG (Japan) POCG 9013-9021
Feldkirch August 1986	Höll	CD: Claves CD 50 8706

Wolf Lieder/continued

Wer sein holdes Lieb verloren/Spanisches Liederbuch

London 1953	Moore	LP: HMV ALP 1143 Also issued on LP by Electrola
Berlin May 1958	Moore	LP: HMV ALP 1750/ASD 378 LP: Electrola E 90922/E 200 000 LP: EMI 1C 181 01470-01476
Berlin December 1966- January 1967	Moore	LP: DG SLPM 139 329-139 330 LP: DG 2707 035/2726 071 CD: DG 421 9342 CD: DG (Japan) POCG 9013-9021

Wie des Mondes Abbild zittert

Paris and Berlin January- November 1974	Barenboim	LP: DG 2709 066/2740 156 CD: DG (Japan) POCG 9013-9021
Feldkirch August 1986	Höll	CD: Claves CD 50 8706

Wie soll ich fröhlich sein?/Italienisches Liederbuch

Salzburg August 1958	Werba	CD: Orfeo C220 901A/C339 930T
Berlin September- October 1958	Demus	LP: DG LPM 18 568-18 569/ SLPM 138 035-138 036 CD: DG 435 7522

Wie sollt' ich heiter bleiben?/Goethe-Lieder

Paris and Berlin January- November 1974	Barenboim	LP: DG 2709 066/2740 156 CD: DG (Japan) POCG 9013-9021

Wolf Lieder/continued

Wieviele Zeit verlor ich, dich zu lieben/Italienisches Liederbuch

Berlin 1949-1950	Klust	78: DG LM 68 458 LP: DG LPM 18 005
Salzburg August 1958	Werba	CD: Orfeo C220 901A/C339 930T
Berlin September-October 1958	Demus	LP: DG LPM 18 568-18 569/ SLPM 138 035-138 036 CD: DG 435 7522
Berlin September 1965-February 1966	Moore	LP: EMI AN 210-211/SAN 210-211 LP: EMI 1C 165 01871-01872 CD: EMI CDM 763 7322
Berlin June 1975	Barenboim	LP: DG 2707 114 CD: DG 439 9752 CD: DG (Japan) POCG 9013-9021

Wo find' ich Trost?/Mörike-Lieder (Eine Liebe kenn' ich, die ist treu)

Berlin September 1957	Moore	LP: HMV ALP 1617-1619 LP: Electrola E 90018-90020 LP: EMI 1C 181 01470-01476 CD: EMI CMS 763 5632
Berlin and Paris December 1972-June 1973	Barenboim	LP: DG 2709 053/2740 113 CD: DG (Japan) POCG 9013-9021

Wo ich bin, mich rings umdunkelt

Feldkirch August 1986	Höll	CD: Claves CD 50 8706

Wo wird einst des Wandermüden letzte Ruhestätte sein?

Berlin April 1959	Moore	LP: HMV ALP 1783/ASD 362 LP: Electrola E 91002/STE 91002 LP: Electrola E 200 000 LP: EMI 1C 181 01470-01476
Paris and Berlin January-November 1974	Barenboim	LP: DG 2709 066/2740 156 CD: DG (Japan) POCG 9013-9021

Wolf Lieder/concluded

Wohin mit der Freud'? (Ach, du klarblauer Himmel)

Paris   Barenboim   LP: DG 2709 067/2740 162
and Berlin   CD: DG (Japan) POCG 9013-9021
January 1974-
November 1976

Zitronenfalter im April/Mörike-Lieder (Grausame Frühlingssonne!)

Berlin   Moore   LP: HMV ALP 1617-1619
September 1957   LP: Electrola E 90018-90020
                                 LP: EMI 1C 181 01470-01476
                                 CD: EMI CMS 763 5632

Berlin   Barenboim   LP: DG 2709 053/2740 113
and Paris   CD: DG (Japan) POCG 9013-9021
December 1972-
June 1973

Zum neuen Jahr/Mörike-Lieder (Wie heimlicherweise ein Engelein leise)

Berlin   Barenboim   LP: DG 2709 053/2740 113
and Paris   CD: DG (Japan) POCG 9013-9021
December 1972-
June 1973

Zur Ruh', zur Ruh', ihr müden Glieder!

Berlin   Moore   LP: HMV ALP 1783/ASD 362
April 1959   LP: Electrola E 91002/STE 91002
                                 LP: Electrola E 200 000
                                 LP: EMI 1C 181 01470-01476

Paris   Barenboim   LP: DG 2709 067/2740 162
and Berlin   CD: DG (Japan) POCG 9013-9021
January 1974-
November 1976

Zur Warnung/Mörike-Lieder (Einmal nach einer lustigen Nacht)

Berlin   Moore   LP: HMV ALP 1617-1619
September 1957   LP: Electrola E 90018-90020
                                 LP: EMI 1C 181 01470-01476
                                 CD: EMI CMS 763 5632

Salzburg   Moore   LP: Orfeo S140 855R
July 1961   CD: Orfeo C140 401A/C339 930T

Berlin   Barenboim   LP: DG 2709 053/2740 113
and Paris   CD: DG (Japan) POCG 9013-9021
December 1972-
June 1973

At the time of going to press DG announces the issue on CD of
Fischer-Dieskau's Wolf Lieder recordings with Barenboim: catalogue
number 447 5152

ZELTER

Abschied

| Berlin | Reimann | LP: Orfeo SO97 841A |
| March 1983 | | CD: Orfeo CO97 841A |

An die Entfernte

| Berlin | Reimann | LP: Orfeo SO97 841A |
| March 1983 | | CD: Orfeo CO97 841A |

Berglied

| Berlin | Reimann | LP: Orfeo SO97 841A |
| March 1983 | | CD: Orfeo CO97 841A |

Beruhigung

| Berlin | Reimann | LP: Orfeo SO97 841A |
| March 1983 | | CD: Orfeo CO97 841A |

Erster Verlust

| Berlin | Reimann | LP: Orfeo SO97 841A |
| March 1983 | | CD: Orfeo CO97 841A |

Gesang und Kuss

| Berlin | Reimann | LP: Orfeo SO97 841A |
| March 1983 | | CD: Orfeo CO97 841A |

Gleich und gleich

| Berlin | Demus, fortepiano | LP: DG 2533 149 |
| September 1972 | | |

| Berlin | Reimann | LP: Orfeo SO97 841A |
| March 1983 | | CD: Orfeo CO97 841A |

4 Harfenspieler-Lieder: Einsamkeit; Harfenspieler II; Klage, 1st version; Klage, 2nd version

| Berlin | Reimann | LP: Orfeo SO97 841A |
| March 1983 | | CD: Orfeo CO97 841A |

Rastlose Liebe

Berlin September 1972	Demus, fortepiano	LP: DG 2533 149
Berlin March 1983	Reimann	LP: Orfeo S097 841A CD: Orfeo C097 841A

Ruhe

Berlin March 1983	Reimann	LP: Orfeo S097 841A CD: Orfeo C097 841A

Die Sänger der Vorwelt

Berlin March 1983	Reimann	LP: Orfeo S097 841A CD: Orfeo C097 841A

Selige Sehnsucht

Berlin March 1983	Reimann	LP: Orfeo S097 841A CD: Orfeo C097 841A

Ueber allen Gipfeln

Berlin March 1983	Reimann	LP: Orfeo S097 841A CD: Orfeo C097 841A

Um Mitternacht

Berlin September 1972	Demus, fortepiano	LP: DG 2533 149
Berlin March 1983	Reimann	LP: Orfeo S097 841A CD: Orfeo C097 841A

Wandrers Nachtlied

Berlin March 1983	Reimann	LP: Orfeo S097 841A CD: Orfeo C097 841A

Wo geht's, Liebchen?

Berlin September 1972	Demus, fortepiano	LP: DG 2533 149
Berlin March 1983	Reimann	LP: Orfeo S097 841A CD: Orfeo C097 841A

Wonne der Wehmut

Berlin March 1983	Reimann	LP: Orfeo S097 841A CD: Orfeo C097 841A

ZEMLINSKY

Lyrische Sinfonie

Berlin	Varady	LP: DG 2532 021
March 1981	BPO	CD: DG 419 2612
	Maazel	

Salzburg	Varady	Special LP issue by Austrian
August 1982	Austrian RO	Radio and Salzburg Festival
	Maazel	

MISCELLANEOUS

Erzähltes Leben

1961	Fischer-Dieskau	LP: DG LPM 18 727
	talks about his	
	career, with	
	illustrations from	
	DG recordings	

German TV documentaries on Dietrich Fischer-Dieskau were produced in 1985 and and 1995, to mark his 60th and 70th birthdays respectively; these show the singer performing or rehearsing the operas Falstaff, Il Tabarro, Don Carlo, Don Giovanni, Arabella, Götterdämmerung and Lear, also works by Bach, Brahms, Mahler, Schubert and Brahms

RAFAEL FRÜHBECK DE BURGOS

MENDELSSOHN

Elijah

Gwyneth Jones   Janet Baker

Nicolai Gedda   D. Fischer-Dieskau

Alfreda Hodgson   Simon Woolf

New Philharmonia Chorus
Chorus Master Wilhelm Pitz

New Philharmonia Orchestra
Leader Carlos Villa

ROYAL FESTIVAL HALL
General Manager John Denison CBE
Sunday 30 June 1968 at 7.30
Programme Two Shillings and Sixpence